DOCUMENTS OF

American Catholic History

DOCUMENTS OF
American Catholic History

Edited by JOHN TRACY ELLIS
PROFESSOR OF CHURCH HISTORY
IN
THE CATHOLIC UNIVERSITY OF AMERICA

THE BRUCE PUBLISHING COMPANY
MILWAUKEE

NIHIL OBSTAT:

JOHN K. CARTWRIGHT
Censor deputatus

IMPRIMATUR:

✠ PATRICK A. O'BOYLE
Archbishop of Washington
November 22, 1961

The *nihil obstat* and *imprimatur* are official declarations that a book or pamphlet is free of doctrinal or moral error. No implication is contained therein that those who have granted the *nihil obstat* and the *imprimatur* agree with the content, opinions, or statements expressed.

Library of Congress Catalog Card Number: 62–12432

MADE IN THE UNITED STATES OF AMERICA

(Second edition — 1962)

In Loving Memory of My Brother

NORBERT E. ELLIS

October 10, 1913–October 3, 1953

Preface

During the past generation an increasing amount of literature has been published on the history of the Catholic Church in the United States, a fact which indicates a growing interest in the part that the Church has played in American history. But nowhere in the literature on the American Church has any attempt been made to draw together in one volume a sampling from the original sources from which its history has been written. The need for such a book has long been felt by those who wished to integrate the story of Catholicism with courses and seminars in American history, and this has been especially true in recent years due to the constantly increasing emphasis on the study of the history of the United States directly from the sources. The lack of such a collection has likewise proved a handicap to the relatively few who offer courses in the history of the Church in this country in Catholic seminaries, colleges, and universities. It was with a view to supplying this need in part, as also to making some of the principal documents of American Catholicism readily available for interested readers outside the classroom, that the present work was undertaken.

In the choice of the contents of this volume the editor was guided by no precise rules of selection, except that the term "document" was broadly interpreted to include any written record that would illustrate an event from a contemporary point of view. Thus one will find here official documents, such as papal bulls and encyclicals and state laws and charters, as well as a wide variety of writings of a purely private and personal nature gathered from archival records, printed letters, newspaper editorials, biographies, memoirs, and even a few selections from the poetry and prose compositions of prominent Catholic literary figures. A conscious effort was made to have the principal churchmen and laymen of the American Catholic past represented, and to include sample material that would give some idea of the chief organizations and institutions of the Church. Yet in spite of the care that was taken in this regard, it was not possible to embrace all the persons, religious orders, institutions, and organizations that might, with some justice, be thought proper subjects for a collection of this kind. Doubtless some will look here in vain for a document on a favorite missionary, on a Catholic society at whose birth an ancestor stood sponsor, or for the mention of a local or sectional celebrity whose life reflected high credit upon the Church. With such readers the editor can only plead that he did not feel he should impose upon his publisher's generosity beyond the size which this volume has assumed. Moreover, he is of the conviction that the vast extent and complexity of the American Catholic body at the present time make it virtually impossible to represent within the covers of a single book all their manifold activities and historic backgrounds.

A word should be said about the method used in collecting and editing the documents. First, with the exception of those from the colonial period, the arrangement is chronological. Since the Catholic missions of the three European powers that sent out colonies from the sixteenth through the eighteenth centuries are usually treated as separate units, it seemed best to break the chronology in this earlier section and list the entries under the headings of Spain, France, and England. It was also thought preferable to put two or more items on a single person together under the date of the first document rather than to separate them. Most of the material was naturally taken from sources in English, but for that written in foreign languages standard translations were used whenever they were available. In a few cases, however, translations were made either by the editor himself or were supplied to him through the kindness of friends. In the main the documents are printed just as they appear in the original source, although in some instances minor changes have been made either to improve the translations from foreign sources or to insert punctuation in certain English documents in order to clarify the meaning. For each item a single source has been cited in the introductory note, although in some instances the same document may be found in several collections. The translations of papal bulls and encyclicals generally give the student a reference to the official collections of the Holy See where the original may be read in Latin. While reference has frequently been made in the introductory notes to pertinent books and periodicals, no effort has been made to add a formal bibliography with each document. Most of the better books in American Catholic history contain bibliographies, and for all the essential works published up to three years ago the editor's *A Guide to American Catholic History* (Milwaukee: 1959) will serve the purpose.

The editor is conscious of the fact that some readers may feel the need for more of a commentary than they will find in the introductory notes. An effort was made to supply the necessary background for a proper understanding of each document; nonetheless, a few over-all comments may help to clarify certain matters that recur in a number of the entries. This is especially true where the material touches on ecclesiastical points of a somewhat technical nature that are often not familiar to the lay reader. One of these points relates to the question of financial support for the clergy of the American Church in different areas and periods of its history. In the Europe of the sixteenth to eighteenth centuries, from which the missionaries came, the methods of support varied widely. In Spain and France where Church and State were united the clergy received a stipend or salary from the government, or lived off of the income from a benefice which had been assigned to them. This was also true of the missionaries in the areas of the future United States that were ruled by Spain and France during the whole of the colonial period. Their income was either direct, in the form of a yearly stipend that not infrequently was in arrears, or indirect such as the revenues from the Pious Fund (No. 116). In the English colonies, on the contrary, the missionaries were compelled to support themselves by taking up farm lands like any other colonist and living off their income. Needless to say, Protestant England furnished them no assistance at a time when the clergy in the mother country were reduced by the penal laws to living off the charity of the wealthy Catholic noble families. The subject of financial support thus frequently became the source of friction between the civil officials and the missionaries in the American dominions of Spain and France, and, at times, too, between the missionaries and the proprietary government of Maryland. One can easily imagine, for example, how the successful enterprises of a missionary like Father Kino (No. 12) might arouse the cupidity of greedy officials, and how the loss of all their temporal goods in Maryland (No. 33) and in Louisiana (No. 24) would seriously affect the Jesuit missions in those regions.

A second point involves the question of ecclesiastical jurisdiction. From the beginning of the colonial settlements down to 1790 the entire area of what later became the United States — whether it was ruled by Spain, France, or England — was regarded by the Holy See as missionary territory. In other words, America was then, in the familiar phrase, *in partibus infidelium.* The normal government of the Church, therefore, with its resident bishops and diocesan priests serving under them, was for the most part lacking, for one could scarcely regard the somewhat spasmodic efforts in behalf of the Catholic colonists by bishops in distant Havana, Durango, Quebec, or London as in any sense a regular form of episcopal rule. The missionaries got their faculties, or the authority to administer the sacraments, through various channels: the Spaniards from the crown which alone had the authority, given to it by the Holy See, to appoint the clergy to posts in the colonial empire; the French from the Congregation de Propaganda Fide, the superiors-general of their respective orders, or the Bishop of Quebec. In the English colonies the missionaries, practically all of whom were Jesuits, at first had their faculties from the Propaganda through their general or the English provincial, and at a later date from the Vicar Apostolic of the London District. But one can get some notion of how unsatisfactory this system was by the ignorance of American conditions revealed in the London vicar's report of 1756 (No. 37).

Because there were no resident bishops on the scene to implement normal ecclesiastical government and because of the awkward methods of jurisdiction employed, lengthy disputes over jurisdictional questions were not uncommon betweeen different religious orders, diocesan priests and religious, religious and distant bishops who claimed jurisdiction, and, of course, between missionaries and civil officials. It was small wonder, then, that neither the priests nor the people should have had any clear concept of the methods by which the Church was customarily ruled in old and settled places. Lack of experience of episcopal authority would in part explain the reluctance shown by the American priests when the Holy See raised the question of appointing a bishop (No. 38), and the abuses to which lay trusteeism gave rise in the rule of some Catholic congregations in the new Republic (Nos. 49, 52), to say nothing of the disorderly state of ecclesiastical affairs as pictured by the first resident bishop in Louisiana (No. 59).

There were real and deep differences among the clergy on these matters in colonial America, as well as differences of another kind in a later age. One encounters them, for example, in the conduct of certain unruly priests who threw in their lot with rebellious trustees (Nos. 67–68), in the school controversy which divided the hierarchy in the 1890's (No. 132), and in the agitation over Americanism at the turn of the century (No. 143). But these controversies were usually the outgrowth of factors like the loosely disciplined Church of the early national period (Nos. 38, 49), of conflicting national backgrounds and experience on the part of churchmen (No. 133), or of the natural division between prelates and priests of a conservative versus liberal turn of mind (Nos. 126–127). It would be easy to magnify these disputes out of their true context and to see in them grave violations of charity, or even doctrinal divergences. Actually more often than not they were but the legitimate differences of opinion of forceful and conscientious churchmen who availed themselves of the free American atmosphere to declare their minds. This is a phenomenon as old as the Church itself, for at the historic meeting between St. Peter and St. Paul in Antioch nineteen centuries ago they differed on the question of the Jews' relations to the Gentiles, and as St. Paul said, "I withstood him to his face, because he was deserving of blame."[1] When properly understood, therefore, the disputes of ecclesiastics need give no ground for scandal, for as Pope Leo XIII said in speaking of falsehoods circulated by the Church's enemies, "nothing is more proper, nothing more efficacious, than to bring them face to face with the truth itself as revealed in the irrefragable testimony of texts and documents."[2]

The idea for this edition of source materials on American Catholicism was first suggested to the editor six years ago by his former student and friend, the Reverend Colman J. Barry, O.S.B., assistant professor of history in St. John's University, Collegeville, Minnesota. Father Barry not only took a leading part in the work of the seminar which for two years was engaged in the task of collecting and editing, but after the completion of his graduate study he continued to follow the project with the closest interest and to furnish several lengthy documents which he had translated and edited from foreign sources. A special expression of gratitude is, therefore, owed to Father Barry. The editor wishes also to thank the following priests who were members of his seminar and who were most helpful in hunting out documents and editing them for the collection: the Reverends Francis T. Hueller, S.C.A., Vincent de Paul McMurray, S.S., Peter J. Rahill, David F. Sweeney, O.F.M., and R. Felix White, M.M. He is under obligation, too, to the students of the Catholic University of America who worked on various documents as a part of course assignments during the summer sessions of 1950–1952. For kindly supplying material from archives and manuscript collections, in several cases in their own translations, or for direction to the editor on questions of selection in the field of their specialization, he desires to thank the following: the Most Reverend Richard O. Gerow, the Right Reverend M. James Fox, O.C.S.O., the Right Reverend George G. Higgins, and the Reverends Patrick H. Ahern, Benjamin J. Blied, John J. Considine, M.M., Vincent F. Holden, C.S.P., Richard C. Madden, Paul Marx, O.S.B., Thomas T. McAvoy, C.S.C., Robert F. McNamara, William C. Repetti, S.J., and Antonine Tibesar, O.F.M. For similar assistance he is grateful to Professor Francis E. Litz, Mr. Ward Steimer, Mother Anselm McCann, S.B.S., Sisters Mary Virgina

[1] Gal. 2:11.

[2] E. Soutif, C.S.C., "Leo XIII and Historical Research — Recent Work in the Vatican Library," *American Catholic Quarterly Review,* XX (October, 1895), 756.

Geiger, S.S.N.D., Marie Carolyn Klinkhamer, O.P., and Isabel Toohey, D.C., Dr. Annabelle M. Melville, and Miss Betty Barbara Sipe.

It is a pleasant duty to record the numerous courtesies extended by the staff of the Library of Congress, and especially those of Mr. Raphael Brown. The editor is under the deepest obligation as well to Mr. Eugene P. Willging, director of the Mullen Library of the Catholic University of America, and to the staff whose patience he tried on more than one occasion, but who bore his incessant calls for assistance with real fortitude and met every demand with the most kindly and friendly treatment. To Miss Rosabelle A. Kelp he is likewise under obligation for her expert work in making the index. Finally a debt quite beyond the ordinary was incurred to two good friends who read through the entire work: the Right Reverend John K. Cartwright, rector of St. Matthew's Cathedral, Washington, whose sharp eye caught many a clumsy construction or doubtful translation, and the Reverend Henry J. Browne, former archivist of the Catholic University of America, who not only improved the manuscript by his critical reading, but also suggested items and handed over a number of documents to the editor's custody for inclusion in the collection.

JOHN TRACY ELLIS

Washington, D. C.
August 15, 1955

NOTE TO SECOND EDITION

In the second edition of this work a number of errors that appeared in the original edition have been corrected, and four documents have been added to illustrate new situations that have arisen for the American Catholic community in the years between 1955 and 1961.

JOHN TRACY ELLIS

November 15, 1961

Contents

THE SPANISH COLONIES

THE FRENCH COLONIES

THE ENGLISH COLONIES

THE NATIONAL PERIOD

DOCUMENTS OF

American Catholic History

THE SPANISH COLONIES

1. The Bull *Inter caetera* of Pope Alexander VI, May 4, 1493

WHEN the news of the success of Columbus' first voyage reached Europe it was rumored that the energetic King John II of Portugal was preparing to dispute the Spanish claims to the new territories. Ferdinand and Isabella, therefore, sent a hurried appeal to Pope Alexander VI (1492–1503), asking that he confirm their possession of the lands discovered by Columbus. As a consequence, the pontiff issued several documents in the year 1493, the best known being that which drew the imaginary "line of demarcation" which assigned to Spain all lands west of a meridian 100 leagues west of the Azores and Cape Verde Islands. Although the line was later changed to Portugal's advantage, the bull *Inter caetera* — known from the first words of the original Latin text — is included here to illustrate, among other things, the prestige which the Holy See enjoyed at the time for settling disputes between nations. Source: Frances Gardiner Davenport (Ed.), *European Treaties bearing on the History of the United States and Its Dependencies to 1648* (Washington: Carnegie Institution of Washington, 1917), I, 75–78.

Alexander, bishop, servant of the servants of God, to the illustrious sovereigns, our very dear son in Christ, Ferdinand, king, and our very dear daughter in Christ, Isabella, queen of Castile, health and benediction. We have indeed learned that you, who for a long time had intended to seek out and discover certain islands and mainlands remote and unknown and not hitherto discovered by others, to the end that you might bring to the worship of our Redeemer and the profession of the Catholic faith their residents and inhabitants, having been up to the present time greatly engaged in the siege and recovery of the kingdom itself of Granada were unable to accomplish this holy and praiseworthy purpose; but the said kingdom having at length been regained, as was pleasing to the Lord, with a wish to fulfill your desire, chose our beloved son, Christopher Columbus, a man assuredly worthy and of the highest recommendations and fitted for so great an undertaking, whom you furnished with ships and men equipped for like designs, not without the greatest hardships, dangers, and expenses, to make diligent quest for these remote and unknown mainlands and islands through the sea, where hitherto no one had sailed; and they at length with divine aid and with the utmost diligence sailing in the ocean sea, discovered certain very remote islands and even mainlands that hitherto had not been discovered by others; wherein dwell very many peoples living in peace, and, as reported, going unclothed, and not eating flesh. . . . wherefore, as becomes Catholic kings and princes . . . you have purposed . . . to bring under your sway the said mainlands and islands. . . . And, in order that you may enter upon so great an undertaking with greater readiness and heartiness endowed with the benefit of our apostolic favor, we, of our own accord, not at your instance nor the request of anyone else in your regard, but out of our own sole largess and certain knowledge and out of the fullness of our apostolic power, by the authority of Almighty God conferred upon us in blessed Peter and of the vicarship of Jesus Christ, which we hold on earth, do by tenor of these presents, should any of said islands have been found by your envoys and captains, give, grant, and assign to you and your heirs and successors, kings of Castile and León, forever, together with all their dominions, cities, camps, places, and villages, and all rights, jurisdictions, and appurtenances, all islands and mainlands found and to be found, discovered and to be discovered towards the west and the south, by drawing and establishing a line from the Arctic pole, namely the north, to the Antarctic pole, namely the south, no matter whether the said mainlands and islands are found and to be found in the direction of India or towards any other quarter, the said line to be distant one hundred leagues[1] towards the west and south from any of the islands commonly known as the Azores and Cape Verde. With this proviso, however, that none of the islands and mainlands, found and to be found, discovered and to be discovered, beyond that said line towards the west and south, be in the actual possession of any Christian king or prince up to the birthday of our Lord Jesus Christ just past from which the present year 1493 begins. . . . Furthermore, under penalty of excommunication *latae sententiae* to be incurred *ipso facto,* should anyone thus contravene, we strictly forbid all persons of whatsoever rank, even imperial and royal, or of whatsoever estate, degree, order, or condition, to dare without your special permit or that of your aforesaid heirs and successors, to go for the purpose of trade or any other reason to the islands or mainlands . . . apostolic constitutions and ordinances and other decrees whatsoever to the contrary notwithstanding. . . . Let

[1] The old Spanish *legua,* frequently mentioned in the documents that follow, was the equivalent of about 2.63 miles, although the Spaniards used another standard in California the exact equivalent of which was never determined.

no one therefore, infringe, or with rash boldness contravene, this our recommendation, exhortation, requisition, gift, grant, assignment, constitution, deputation, decree, mandate, prohibition, and will. Should anyone presume to attempt this, be it known to him that he will incur the wrath of Almighty God and of the blessed apostles Peter and Paul. Given at Rome, at St. Peter's, in the year of the incarnation of our Lord one thousand four hundred and ninety-three, the fourth of May, and the first year of our pontificate.

2. The Treaty of Tordesillas, June 7, 1494

THE provisions of the bull *Inter caetera* did not satisfy John II of Portugal, and the Spanish sovereigns agreed, therefore, to move the line of demarcation 370 leagues west from the Cape Verde Islands. The rectification was embodied in the document which follows and was approved by Alexander VI. Spain and Portugal have long since lost all their American possessions, but one of the enduring cultural effects of the alteration of the original division of the pope is the Portuguese language spoken in Brazil in contradistinction to the Spanish language which is spoken throughout the remainder of South and Central America and Mexico. Source: Frances Gardiner Davenport (Ed.), *European Treaties bearing on the History of the United States and Its Dependencies to 1648* (Washington: Carnegie Institution of Washington, 1917), I, 93–100.

. . . Whereas a certain controversy exists between the said lords, their constituents, as to what lands, of all those discovered in the ocean sea up to the present day, the date of this treaty, pertain to each one of the said parts respectively; therefore, for the sake of peace and concord, and for the preservation of the relationship and love of the said King of Portugal for the said King and Queen of Castile, Aragon, etc., it being the pleasure of their Highnesses, they . . . covenanted and agreed that a boundary or straight line be determined and drawn north and south, from pole to pole, on the said ocean sea, from the Arctic to the Antarctic pole. This boundary or line shall be drawn straight, as aforesaid, at a distant of three hundred and seventy leagues west of the Cape Verde Islands, being calculated by degrees. . . . And all lands both islands and mainlands, found and discovered already, or to be found and discovered hereafter, by the said King of Portugal and by his vessels on this side of the said line and bound determined as above, toward the east, in either north or south latitude, on the eastern side of the said bound, provided the said bound is not crossed, shall belong to and remain in the possession of, and pertain forever to, the said King of Portugal and his successors. And all other lands, both islands and mainlands, found or to be found hereafter . . . by the said King and Queen of Castile, Aragon, etc., and by their vessels, on the western side of the said bound, determined as above, after having passed the said bound toward the west, in either its north or south latitude, shall belong to . . . the said King and Queen of Castile, León, etc., and to their successors.

Item, the said representatives promise and affirm . . . that from this date no ships shall be dispatched — namely as follows: the said King and Queen of Castile, León, Aragon, etc., for this part of the bound . . . which pertains to the said King of Portugal . . . nor the said King of Portugal to the other side of the said bound which pertains to the said King and Queen of Castile, Aragon, etc. — for the purpose of discovering and seeking any mainlands or islands, or for the purpose of trade, barter, or conquest of any kind. But should it come to pass that the said ships of the said King and Queen of Castile . . . on sailing thus on this side of the said bound, should discover any mainlands or islands in the region pertaining, as abovesaid, to the said King of Portugal, such mainlands or islands shall belong forever to the said King of Portugal and his heirs, and their Highnesses shall order them to be surrendered to him immediately. And if the said ships of the said King of Portugal discover any islands or mainlands in the regions of the said King and Queen of Castile . . . all such lands shall belong to and remain forever in the possession of the said King and Queen of Castile . . . and their heirs, and the said King of Portugal shall cause such lands to be surrendered immediately. . . .

And by this present agreement, they . . . entreat our most Holy Father that his Holiness be pleased to confirm and approve this said agreement, according to what is set forth therein; and that he order his bulls in regard to it to be issued to the parties or to whichever of the parties may solicit them, with the tenor of this agreement incorporated therein, and that he lay his censures upon those who shall violate or oppose it at any time whatsoever. . . .

3. The Bull *Universalis ecclesiae* of Pope Julius II, July 28, 1508

BY THE bull *Universalis ecclesiae* of July 28, 1508, Pope Julius II (1503–1513) conceded to the Spanish crown universal patronage over all ecclesiastical benefices in its New World possessions. Whether or not this bull granted for the first time the *real patronato,* or whether it merely reconfirmed rights already bestowed by the Holy See, it continued to be regarded as the principal documentary evidence of the legal right of the Spanish sovereigns to exercise jurisdiction over the Catholic Church in the New World down to the nineteenth century. Source: J. Lloyd Mecham, *Church and State in Latin America* (Chapel Hill: University of North Carolina Press, 1934), pp. 18–20.

Julius, bishop, servant of the servants of God. We, presiding by divine choice, although unworthily, over the government of the Universal Church, do concede voluntarily to the Catholic kings principally those things that augment their honor and glory, and contribute effectively to the benefit and security of their dominions. Since our beloved son in Christ, Ferdinand, illustrious king of Aragon, and also of Sicily, and Isabella, of cherished memory, Queen of Castile and León, after having expelled the Moors from Spain, crossed the ocean and planted the Cross in unknown lands, and subjugated many islands and places, and among these being one very rich and extremely populous named New Spain, thereby fulfilling to the extent of their ability the saying *in omnem terram exivit sonus eorum* — Therefore, we, in order that it (New Spain) might be purged of false and pernicious rites, and the true religion be planted there, have acceded to the most urgent requests of the king and queen, and do hereby erect for the greater glory of the name of Christ, a metropolitan church in Ayguacen, and two cathedrals in Maguen and Bayunen,[1] and if the converts imbued by the new faith should attempt to found any church or pious place, they should do so in such a way as not to injure the new religion or the temporal dominions of the king.

In view of the fact that the said Ferdinand, who is also at present governor-general of the kingdoms of Castile and León, and our most cherished daughter in Christ, Juana, queen of the same kingdoms and daughter of the aforementioned Ferdinand, wish that no church, monastery, or pious place be erected or founded either in the islands and lands already possessed, or in those subsequently acquired, with-

---

[1] The Archdiocese of Ayguacen (Hyaguata) and the suffragan Sees of Maguen (Magua) and Bayunen (Bayuna) never existed except on paper. After the impracticality of their sites had become known, and after Ferdinand of Aragon had objected strenuously to assigning to the bishops a part of the tithes on gold, silver, and precious stones, Julius II issued a brief on August 8, 1511, that suppressed these jurisdictions and in their place erected three new dioceses at San Domingo and Conception de la Vega in Española (Haiti) and at San Juan in Puerto Rico, all made suffragans of the Archdiocese of Seville.

out their express consent and that of their successors; and considering that since it is convenient to those kings that the persons who preside over churches and monasteries be faithful and acceptable to them, they desire that they be conceded the right of patronage and of the cathedral churches already erected, or to be erected in the future, and for all the other ecclesiastical benefices inside of a year of their vacancy, and also for inferior benefices; and in case the ordinary should refuse without legitimate cause to grant the one presented with canonical institution inside of ten days, any other bishop, at the request of the king should grant it. We, appreciating that these privileges increase the honor, beauty and security of those islands, and also of the said kingdoms, whose kings are always devout and faithful to the Apostolic See, and heeding the reiterated demands made on us by King Ferdinand and Queen Juana, after mature deliberation with our brothers the cardinals of the Holy Roman Church, and with their advice, by these presents we concede with apostolic authority, other constitutions, ordinances, and laws to the contrary notwithstanding, to the said Ferdinand and Juana, and to the future kings of Castile and León, that nobody without their consent can construct or build in the above mentioned islands, now possessed or to be possessed, large churches; and we concede the right of patronage and of presenting qualified persons to cathedral churches, monasteries, *dignities,* collegiates, and other ecclesiastical benefices and pious places in this manner: respecting benefices that are instituted in the consistory, the presentation is to be made to Us, or Our successors, within one year after the vacancy occurs; and respecting the other benefices, presentation will be made to the respective ordinaries, and if these refuse without cause to give institution inside of ten days, any bishop in those lands, on the petition of King Ferdinand or of Queen Juana, or the king ruling at that time, can bestow, under those conditions, free and legal canonical institution on the person presented. Nobody should deign to infringe on or act contrary to this concession, and if any one attempts to do so, let him know that he will incur the indignation of God Almighty and of the blessed apostles Peter and Paul. Given in Rome, etc., July 28, 1508.

4. The Bull *Sublimis Deus* of Pope Paul III, June 2, 1537

TO COMBAT the charge that the Indians were not capable of receiving the Catholic faith, Paul III (1534–1549), following representations by the Dominicans, Bernardino de Minaya and Julian Garcés, Bishop of Tlaxcala in New Spain, issued on June 2, 1537, the bull *Sublimis Deus*. By this action the pope reaffirmed the traditional teaching of the Catholic Church concerning the spiritual equality and brotherhood of all men. This is a key document in the lengthy controversy over the intellectual capacities of the American Indians. Although it is impossible to say how many of the Spanish *conquistadores* really believed the Indians to be animals [*bruta animalia*], there is no doubt that some held this view. If it had prevailed without challenge it would have enabled the Spaniards to use the lives and properties of the defenseless natives unchecked by the protecting hand of the Church, and thus the task of the missionaries would have been rendered much more difficult than it actually was.

Emperor Charles V became so concerned over the effect of the *Sublimis Deus* in the Spanish dominions that he brought pressure to bear on Paul III to revoke it. As a consequence, the pope issued another bull on June 19, 1538, which revoked all previous papal briefs and bulls that might prejudice the power of Charles V in his colonial empire. In the latter document the pope did not take back what he had said in the *Sublimis Deus* concerning the Indians' capacity for conversion, but he did declare all ecclesiastical censures and penalties imposed by the missionaries on the *conquistadores* to be null and void. This action seriously hampered the missionaries' efforts to check the rapacity of the Spaniards, but as one scholar has stated, "the bull Sublimis Deus lived on as a force to be reckoned with in the endless disputes over the true nature of the American Indians because the nullification was not widely known." Lewis Hanke, "Pope Paul III and the American Indians," *Harvard Theological Review,* XXX (April, 1937), 97. Source: Francis Augustus MacNutt, *Bartholomew de Las Casas* (New York: G. P. Putnam's Sons, 1909), pp. 427–431.

Paul III Pope. To all faithful Christians to whom this writing may come, health in Christ our Lord and the apostolic benediction.

The sublime God so loved the human race that He created man in such wise that he might participate, not only in the good that other creatures enjoy, but endowed him with capacity to attain to the inaccessible and invisible Supreme Good and behold it face to face; and since man, according to the testimony of the sacred scriptures, has been created to enjoy eternal life and happiness, which none may obtain save through faith in our Lord Jesus Christ, it is necessary that he should possess the nature and faculties enabling him to receive that faith; and that whoever is thus endowed should be capable of receiving that same faith. Nor is it credible that any one should possess so little understanding as to desire the faith and yet be destitute of the most necessary faculty to enable him to receive it. Hence Christ, who is the Truth itself, that has never failed and can never fail, said to the preachers of the faith whom He chose for that office 'Go ye and teach all nations.' He said all, without exception, for all are capable of receiving the doctrines of the faith.

The enemy of the human race, who opposes all good deeds in order to bring men to destruction, beholding and envying this, invented a means never before heard of, by which he might hinder the preaching of God's word of Salvation to the people: he inspired his satellites who, to please him, have not hesitated to publish abroad that the Indians of the West and the South, and other people of whom We have recent knowledge should be treated as dumb brutes created for our service, pretending that they are incapable of receiving the Catholic Faith.

We, who, though unworthy, exercise on earth the power of our Lord and seek with all our might to bring those sheep of His flock who are outside into the fold committed to our charge, consider, however, that the Indians are truly men and that they are not only capable of understanding the Catholic Faith but, according to our information, they desire exceedingly to receive it. Desiring to provide ample remedy for these evils, We define and declare by these Our letters, or by any translation thereof signed by any notary public and sealed with the seal of any ecclesiastical dignitary, to which the same credit shall be given as to the originals, that, notwithstanding whatever may have been or may be said to the contrary, the said Indians and all other people who may later be discovered by Christians, are by no means to be deprived of their liberty or the possession of their property, even though they be outside the faith of Jesus Christ; and that they may and should, freely and legitimately, enjoy their liberty and the possession of their property; nor should they be in any way enslaved; should the contrary happen, it shall be null and of no effect.

By virtue of Our apostolic authority We define and declare by these present letters, or by any translation thereof signed by any notary public and sealed with the seal of any ecclesiastical dignitary, which shall thus command the same obedience as the originals, that the said Indians and other peoples should be converted to the faith of Jesus Christ by preaching the word of God and by the example of good and holy living.

5. Juan de Padilla, the Protomartyr of the United States, Is Murdered by the Plains Indians, c. 1542

IN THE three centuries between the entrance of the first priests into Florida in the early 1520's and the founding of the last of the California missions at San Francisco Solano in July, 1823, hundreds of Catholic missionaries labored in every section of what was to become the United States in an effort to convert the native Indians to Christianity. In the attempt many of these men met death at the hands of the savages. On the epochal exploring expedition of Coronado which started north from old Mexico in February, 1540, and during the next two years traversed so large a part of the American Southwest, there were three Franciscan friars, Fathers Juan de Padilla and Juan de la Cruz, and Brother Luís de Ubeda (DeEscalona). When Coronado turned back in disappointment in the spring of 1542 the friars remained behind in the hope of evangelizing the Indians. Soon thereafter Padilla was murdered by the red men and thus became the proto-martyr of the future United States; the other two were never heard from again. In the account which follows, written by one of Coronado's soldiers, Pedro de Castañeda, he described the little that is known about the fate of the friar. The exact date and location of Padilla's death are uncertain, although most authorities think it took place shortly after Coronado's departure southward and probably occurred somewhere in southern Kansas. Source: "The Narrative of the Expedition of Coronado by Castañeda," Frederick W. Hodge and Theodore H. Lewis (Eds.), *Spanish Explorers in the Southern United States, 1528–1543* (New York: Charles Scribner's Sons, 1907), pp. 372–374; now included in *Original Narratives of Early American History,* copyright Barnes & Noble, Inc., New York.

When the general, Francisco Vásquez,[1] saw that everything was now quiet, and that his schemes had gone as he wished, he ordered that everything should be ready to start on the return to New Spain by the beginning of the month of April, in the year 1543 [1542].

Seeing this, Friar Juan de Padilla, a regular brother of the lesser order, and another, Friar Luis [Descalona], a lay brother, told the general that they wanted to remain in that country — Friar Juan de Padilla in Quivira, because his teachings seemed to promise fruit there, and Friar Luis at Cicuye.[2] On this account, as it was Lent at the time, the father made this the subject of his sermon to the companies

[1] Francisco Vásquez Coronado (1510–1554) was Governor of Nueva Galicia and leader of the expedition.

[2] Cicuye was synonymous with Pecos in New Mexico.

one Sunday, establishing his proposition on the authority of the Holy Scriptures. He declared his zeal for the conversion of these peoples and his desire to draw them to the faith, and stated that he had received permission to do it, although this was not necessary. The general sent a company to escort them as far as Cicuye, where Friar Luis stopped, while Friar Juan went on back to Quivira with the guides who had conducted the general, taking with him the Portuguese, as we related, and the half-blood, and the Indians from New Spain. He was martyred a short time after he arrived there, as we related in the second part, Chapter 8.[3] Thus we may be sure that he died a martyr, because his zeal was holy and earnest.

Friar Luis remained at Cicuye. Nothing more has been heard about him since, but before the army left Tiguex[4] some men who went to take him a number of sheep that were left for him to keep, met him as he was on his way to visit some other villages, which were fifteen or twenty leagues from Cicuye, accompanied by some followers. He felt very hopeful that he was liked at the village and that his teaching would bear fruit, although he complained that the old men were falling away from him. I, for my part, believe that they finally killed him. He was a man of good and holy life, and may Our Lord protect him and grant that he may convert many of those peoples, and end his days in guiding them in the faith. We do not need to believe otherwise, for the people in those parts are pious and not at all cruel. They are friends, or rather, enemies of cruelty, and they remained faithful and loyal friends.

After the friars had gone, the general, fearing that they might be injured if people were carried away from that country to New Spain, ordered the soldiers to let any of the natives who were held as servants go free to their villages whenever they might wish. In my opinion, though I am not sure, it would have been better if they had been kept and taught among Christians. . . .

---

[3] At the point referred to Castañeda stated: "A friar named Juan de Padilla remained in this province, together with a Spanish-Portuguese and a negro and a half-blood and some Indians from the province of Capothan in New Spain. They killed the friar because he wanted to go to the province of the Guas [possibly the Kaw or Kansa Indians], who were their enemies. . . . The Indians from New Spain who accompanied the friar were allowed by the murderers to bury him . . ." (pp. 364–365).

[4] Tiguex was situated at the site of Bernalillo on the Rio Grande River in what is today New Mexico.

6. Assignment of the Florida Missions to the Dominicans; Don Luís de Velasco to King Philip II, September 30, 1558

ONCE the Spaniards had established themselves in Mexico they thought of settling the Florida coast which lay along the Atlantic route to the homeland, as well as on the route of the vessels coming northward from the mines of South America. A primary consideration of all colonization by the crown was the conversion of the native peoples to the Catholic faith. Hence it was not surprising that the Viceroy of New Spain should outline to Philip II his decision to entrust the mission of Florida to a single group of religious, in this instance to the Dominicans. Due to a series of disasters, however, the expedition failed and the Dominicans withdrew in 1561 with the Spanish military. Source: Herbert Ingram Priestley (Ed.), *The Luna Papers. Documents Relating to the Expedition of Don Tristán de Luna y Arellano for the Conquest of La Florida in 1559–1561* (Deland: Florida State Historical Society, 1928), II, 257–261.

The ships and people which are to colonize on the coast of the land of La Florida and the Punta de Santa Elena are being prepared; I think they will be ready to set sail sometime in May of 1559. Five hundred Spaniards will go; four hundred of them, soldiers, two hundred being mounted, and two hundred on foot armed with arquebuses and crossbows for the defense of the religious and ecclesiastics who are to go to preach our holy faith to the natives, and one hundred artisans to engage in building the towns and the fort which your Majesty commands to be built. Also the instructions are being drawn up which are to be given to the governor, religious, and officials of the royal treasury, and other persons who have positions of authority. . . .

I gathered together the provincials of the orders of St. Dominic, St. Francis, and St. Augustine, in the presence of this royal audiencia, and asked their opinion as to whether it would be fitting at the beginning for the religious of all three orders to go or only one, and if they agreed that only one should be represented, which it should be. They all were agreed that religious of but one order should go, and that they should be those of St. Dominic, as your Majesty will order herewith. Six religious have been named, men of chosen life, letters, doctrine, and of age to be able to work among the Indians and learn their languages. It seems that for the present these will suffice. They will have to be provided with ornaments, crosses, chalices, bells, and other things necessary for the service of the divine cult, with clothing and shoes for the religious, and these cost four times as much in this country as in Spain. . . .

In the meantime I am sending out three religious to the new mines of San Martín, which are between the mines of Los Zacatecas and Copala, thirty leagues from the mines [of Los Zacatecas] and as many more, according to what the Indians of that country say, from Copala. They are to assist a good cleric who has baptized a number of Indians between the country of San Martín and Copala, to attract the rest of the people of the district, and to make sure what the province of Copala is, so that when convenient it may be entered, pacified, and colonized. . .

. . . Mexico, the last day of September, 1558.
Your Catholic Royal Majesty's
faithful servant who kisses your Majesty's royal feet,
Don Luis de Velasco

7. Agreement Between Philip II and Pedro Menéndez de Avilés for the Conquest of Florida and the Assignment of Jesuit Missionaries, March 20, 1565

ON FIVE different occasions within a half century Spain had tried and failed to conquer and settle Florida. To the earlier insurmountable opposition of savage natives there was later added the armed hostility of European intruders. Among the first to foresee the dangers to the Spanish Empire and its commerce in the New World from a permanent loss of Florida was Pedro Menéndez. It was at his urgent appeal that the Velasco-Luna expedition was organized to construct defensive settlements on the Florida coast. Finally in 1565 Menéndez was authorized to organize another expedition, and while the *asiento,* or royal patent, granted to him and his heirs many titles and the revenues from the lands he should conquer, it likewise laid the expense and burden of the entire undertaking on the shoulders of the new Governor and Captain-General of La Florida. Source: Jeannette Thurber Connor (Ed.), *Pedro Menéndez de Avilés. . . . Memorial by Gonzalo Solís de Merás* (Deland: Florida State Historical Society, 1923), pp. 259–270.

The King: — Whereas we have given *asientos* at various times for the discovery and settlement of the provinces of Florida, and likewise charged Don Luís de Velasco, who was our Viceroy of New Spain, to send a certain number of people and religious to settle that country, and an *asiento* was last made concerning this with Lucas Vasquez de Ayllón; and efforts have been made by the persons to whom we gave the said *asientos,* as well as by the Viceroy aforesaid; never up to now has that land been colonized; nor has what we desired, which was the aforesaid settlement, been accomplished; nor the teaching and conversion of the natives of those provinces, and the bringing them into our Holy Catholic Faith; and as we have in mind the good and the salvation of those souls, we have decided to give the order to send religious persons to instruct the said Indians, and those other people who are good Christians and our subjects, so that they may live among and talk to the natives there may be in those lands and provinces of Florida, and that [the Indians] by intercourse and conversation with them may more easily be taught our Holy Catholic Faith and be brought to good usages and customs, and perfect polity. And to you, Pedro Menéndez de Avilés, Knight of the Order of Santiago, have I offered and do offer, because of the desire you have for the service of God Our Lord, and for the increase to the Royal Crown of these kingdoms, that during the coming month of May of this present year, you shall hold ready and prepared to sail, in San Lucar de Barrameda, in the port of Santa Maria or in the Bay of Cádiz, in order to depart with the first opportunity, six shallops of fifty *toneles* each, more or less; and four swift *zabras,* with their oars, arms and munitions, laden with supplies and fully prepared for war; and that you shall take five hundred men, one hundred of them farmers and one hundred sailors, and the rest of them naval and military men and officials, others professional stonecutters, carpenters, sawyers, smiths, barbers, locksmiths; all of them with their arms, arquebuses and crossbows, and helmets and bucklers, and other offensive and defensive weapons which you may see fit and which may be suitable for the said voyage; and two priests; and that you shall do other things declared above, all of this at your cost and under your commission, without Our being obligated, or the Kings who may come after Us, to pay or indemnify you anything thereof other than what may be conceded to you by this Agreement, as you have entreated me to make it with you and to grant you certain favors. . . .

Furthermore; You offer and pledge yourself that within the said time, and among the number of the said people whom you bind yourself to take, you will include at least ten or twelve religious, of the Order which may appear best to you: persons who are of a good life and example; likewise four others of the Society of Jesus, so that there may be religious instruction in the said land, and the Indians can be converted to our Holy Catholic Faith and to our obedience. . . .

Therefore by these presents, if you, the said Pedro Menéndez, do carry out the aforesaid at your cost, according to what is contained in the aforesaid, in the manner thereof; and if you fulfil all that is included in this agreement, in the instructions which shall be given you, and in those which shall be given you later on; likewise the provisions and ordinances We shall make, and order to be observed, for the said country and settlements, and for the good treatment and conversion to our Holy Catholic Faith of the natives there, and of the settlers who may go there; I say and promise, by my faith and my Royal word, that this Agreement shall be observed, in your favor, and everything therein contained, wholly and absolutely, according as it is therein contained, without your meeting any opposition thereto; but that if you should not so fulfil and accomplish that to which you obligate yourself, we shall not be compelled to keep with you and carry out the aforesaid [agreement], nor any part thereof; rather shall we order that you be punished, and we shall proceed against you as a person who does not observe and fulfil, but trespasses against, the commands of his King and natural Master.

And we order that these presents be given to that effect, signed by our hand, and by the members of our Council of the Indies, and countersigned by Francisco de Erasso, our Secretary.

I the King.
By order of his Majesty,
Francisco de Erasso.

Done in Madrid, on the
20th day of March, 1565.

8. St. Francis Borgia Withdraws the Jesuits From the Florida Missions, March 20, 1571

During the six years, 1566–1572, that the Jesuits spent in the missions of Florida they moved up the coast from St. Augustine into what are now the states of Georgia and South Carolina, with a brief and fatal effort in 1571 as far as Virginia. They met with little or no success and the deaths of a number of the missionaries at the hands of treacherous Indians convinced the Jesuit General that he could not retain so expensive a mission field in which there was so little prospect of permanent results, while the missions of New Spain were clamoring for more priests. In the following letter from Rome St. Francis Borgia (1510–1572), General of the Jesuits, explained to Pedro Menéndez the reasons for withdrawing his men from Florida. Source: Felix Zubillaga, S.J. (Ed.), *Monumenta antiquae Floridae*

(*1566–1572*) (Rome: Apud "Monumenta Historica Soc. Ieus," 1946), pp. 489–490.

. . . Since you know our Institute and the purpose of this small Company, it will be superfluous to speak of the desire which God, our Lord, gives to those who belong to the Company of going to help those people who are in greater need and in the danger of being lost, for this is our vocation; and according to this vocation may the infinite and divine goodness inspire us with such desires and the will to act in accord with them. This is the reason why the members of our Company so promptly go throughout the world, and why they went to Florida — the few that are there. They have worked and suffered in Florida with a constancy that has been manifest and yet they have seen little or no fruit of their labors, which is the greatest suffering of all for those who seek only the good of souls for the greater glory of God. Since, therefore, those pagans are so badly disposed that they are said to prefer the devil and to go to hell with him rather than to our God, and say that he who talks against their god, cannot be good; and since it is evident, in our long experience in Florida, that we could count, so to say, with the fingers of our hand those who during this long period have been converted, and even they have turned back to darkness, and since, moreover, there is in this Company, as I wrote to your Excellency, and it is truly so, such a small personnel for the many enterprises which the Company has assumed; it is evident that for a time until God our Lord, little by little, stirs those pagans in the capacity of their souls, that not only is it not fitting to keep the Company in that land, but it must not be done; for even if there were many missionaries, we are always obliged by the Christian religion and our own Institute to seek the greater glory of God and the greater good of our neighbor, for as our Lord says: 'If they do not receive the sacred Gospel in one place, we should go from that land to another, shaking the dust from our feet. . . .'

9. Alonso de Benavides' Description of the New Mexico Missions, February 12, 1634

DREAMS of the conquest and settlement of New Mexico had stirred up a great deal of enthusiasm in the sixteenth century and many competitors vied for the position of *adelantado* or Governor of New Mexico. In 1595 the contract for the conquest of New Mexico was awarded to Don Juan de

Oñate. Spiritual charge of the enterprise was assigned to the Franciscans and a custody of that order was established in 1616. In 1630 Fray Alonso de Benavides (d. 1636), commissary of the custody until 1629, returned to Spain to report to the king and to the Minister General of the Franciscan Order, Fray Bernardino de Siena, on the more notable happenings in the custody of New Mexico. In 1634 this same friar presented a revised report to Pope Urban VIII which was designed to promote missionary activity in New Mexico and to urge the establishment of a bishopric in that mission field. The following extract is indicative of the work of the friars for Church and State in colonial New Mexico. Source: Frederick Webb Hodge, George P. Hammond, and Agapito Rey (Eds.), *Fray Alonso de Benavides' Revised Memorial of 1634. . . .* (Albuquerque: University of New Mexico Press, 1945), pp. 100–103.

Since the land is very remote and isolated and the difficulties of the long journeys require more than a year of travel, the friars, although there are many who wish to dedicate themselves to those conversions, find themselves unable to do so because of their poverty. Hence only those go there who are sent by the Catholic king at his own expense, for the cost is so excessive that only his royal zeal can afford it. This is the reason that there are so few friars over there and that most of the convents have only one religious each, and he ministers to four, six, or more neighboring pueblos, in the midst of which he stands as a lighted torch to guide them in spiritual as well as temporal affairs. More than twenty Indians devoted to the service of the church, live with him in the convent. They take turns in relieving one another as porters, sextons, cooks, bell-ringers, gardeners, refectioners, and in other tasks. They perform their duties with as much circumspection and care as if they were friars. At eventide they say their prayers together, with much devotion in front of some image.

In every pueblo where a friar resides, he has schools for the teaching of praying, singing, playing musical instruments and other interesting things. Promptly at dawn, one of the Indian singers, whose turn it is that week, goes to ring the bell for Prime, at the sound of which those who go to school assemble and sweep the rooms thoroughly. The singers chant Prime in the choir. The friar must be present at all of this and takes notes of those who have failed to perform this duty, in order to reprimand them later. When everything is neat and clean, they again ring the bell and each one goes to learn his particular specialty; the friar oversees it all. . . . After they have been occupied in this manner for an hour and a half, the bell is rung for mass. All go into the church, and the friar says mass and administers the sacraments. . . . Mass over. . . . all kneel down by the church door and sing the *Salve* in their own tongue. . . .

At mealtime, the poor people in the pueblo who are not ill come to the porter's lodge, where the cooks of the convent have sufficient food ready which is served to them by the friar; food for the sick is sent to their homes. After mealtime, it always happens that the friar has to go to some neighboring pueblo to hear a confession or to see if they are careless in the boys' school, where they learn to pray and assist at mass, for this is the responsibility of the sextons and it is their duty always to have a dozen boys for the service of the sanctuary and to teach them how to help at mass and how to pray.

In the evening they toll the bell for vespers, which are chanted by the singers who are on duty for the week, and according to the importance of the feast they celebrate it with organ chants as they do for mass. . . .

One of the weekdays which is not so busy is devoted to baptism, and all those who are to be baptized come to the church on that day, unless some urgent matter should interfere; in that case, it is performed at any time. With great care, their names are inscribed in a book; in another, those who are married; and in another, the dead.

One of the greatest tasks of the friars is to adjust the disputes of the Indians among themselves, for, since they look upon him as a father, they come to him with all their troubles, and he has to take pains to harmonize them. If it is a question of land and property, he must go with them and mark their boundaries, and thus pacify them.

For the support of all the poor of the pueblo, the friar makes them sow some grain and raise some cattle, because if he left it to their discretion, they would not do anything. Therefore the friar requires them to do so and trains them so well, that, with the meat, he feeds all the poor and pays the various workmen who come to build the churches. With the wool he clothes all the poor, and the friar himself also gets his clothing and food from this source. All the wheels of this clock must be kept in good order by the friar, without neglecting any detail, otherwise all would be totally lost. . . .

This, Most Holy Father, is the state of that new and primitive church which the seraphic sons of Saint Francis, its only workers, have founded and watered with the blood and lives of ten of their brethren. . . .

10. Report of Bishop Calderón of Santiago to Queen Mother Marie Anne on the Florida Missions, August 14, 1674

WHEN Don Gabriel Diaz Vara Calderón (d. 1676) became Bishop of Santiago de Cuba in 1671, no bishop had visited Florida in more than sixty years, although it was a part of the Diocese of Santiago de Cuba. Having first made an episcopal visitation of the island of Cuba, Calderón set sail from Havana on August 18, 1674, convoyed by a fleet which entered the harbor of St. Augustine on August 23. While the record of his visitation of the missions in Florida is far from complete, there is sufficient evidence, as seen in his letter to the Queen Mother of Spain, to know that the episcopal visitation was no mere form. Source: Lucy L. Wenhold (Ed.), "A 17th Century Letter of Gabriel Diaz Vara Caldéron, Bishop of Cuba, Describing the Indians and Indian Missions of Florida," *Smithsonian Miscellaneous Collections* (Washington: Smithsonian Institution, 1936), Vol. 95, No. 16, pp. 2, 7–9, 12–14.

Señora:

Your Majesty is pleased to command me, in the two royal cédulas of the 4th of March of the year 73, to visit at this time the provinces of Florida and apply the proper remedy in the matter presented to Your Majesty by the Bishop of the city, Rodrigo, my predecessor here. No bishop has gone there [to Florida] in more than 60 years, and the presence of one is needed, not only to celebrate confirmations and correct the faults and abuses that have come in during so long a time in the case of [a] people so recently converted, and to investigate the state in which the priests of San Francisco have the work of converting the Indians and the instructions of the converts under their care, but also to lend encouragement to the converting of the Indians of the province of Apalachocoli who have for years been asking that missionaries be sent to teach and baptize them; a request never yet granted for lack [of missionaries]. In this field the Bishop believes the Dominican priests of this city would accomplish much.

Señora, this my predecessor said to me in the city of San Lucar where I was by order, awaiting the first opportunity of passage to this incumbency. I replied to him that I wished first to come to the city of Cuba, seat of this bishopric, visiting it, and to go then to the mission. Accordingly, as soon as I entered this city, obeying your Majesty I began to plan for the carrying out of that purpose. Having now completed the visitation of this entire island, I have it in such good condition that within 8 days under the favor of God I shall set forth.

And because [although I recognize the great zeal of the Dominican priests, who have offered themselves to me willingly], to take them now would be to introduce great discord with the Franciscans and jeopardize the conversion of those miserable heathen, it has seemed to me wiser to make use of the latter, both because they are well versed in that language and because they are in control of the entire province of Apalache which borders upon that of Apalachocoli. [I go] to investigate first the condition of that land, and then to enter upon the work of conversion for which I am taking chalices and all the necessary vestments of the Divine Cult. May it please Our Lord that the holy zeal of Your Majesty attain its end for the greater glory of the Divine One and the salvation of those souls.

May Our Lord keep the Catholic Royal Person of Your Majesty in His Holy grace with health and complete felicity to the greatest good of Your vassals.

Your Majesty's humble servant and chaplain,
Gabriel, Bishop of Cuba.

Havana,
August 14, 1674.

Florida and the Florida Missions

Señora:

What has been discovered, up to today, concerning the entire district of Florida, both along the seacoast and inland, is as follows:

On the coast of the northern border, 30 leagues from Cape Canaveral, [where] the canal of Bahama disembogues, is located, on the 30th parallel of latitude, the city of Saint Augustine which was founded about 1559 [1565] by the Adelantado Pedro Menéndes Avíles. It is the capital of the provinces of Florida and has more than 300 Spanish inhabitants, soldiers and married people. Its harbor is very secure by reason of a very dangerous sand bar which it has at its entrance, which shifts its position in storms and at high tide has 20 spans of water. The city is built lengthwise from north to south. It is almost cut off by an arm of the sea which surrounds it and buffets it, leaving it half submerged from hurricanes as it lies at sea level. Its climate is somewhat unhealthful, being very cold in winter, with freezes, and excessively hot in summer, both of which extremes are felt the more as there is no protection nor defense in the houses, they being of wood with board walls. The soil is sand and therefore unproductive;

no wheat grows, and corn only sparsely and at the cost of much labor. Thus the inhabitants are compelled regularly to depend for their sustenance upon the products of the province of Apalache. The section does not produce any sort of raw material which could attract trade, and has no resources other than the government allowance which it awaits each year from the city of Mexico, and by which the infantry is fed and clothed.

As regards its spiritual welfare, it has a parish church dedicated to Saint Augustine, served by a priest, a sacristan and acolytes, and a Franciscan convent, headquarters for the province, called Saint Helena, with three monks [*sic*], a superior, a preacher, a lay brother, and with authority by a royal decree of Your Majesty to have three curates for the three principal languages of these provinces, Guale, Timuqua and Apalache, for the teaching of Christian doctrine and the administering of the sacraments to the Indians who usually attend to the cultivating of the lands of the residents of the Post [Saint Augustine]. Of the four hermitages which formerly existed, only two remain: San Patricio and Our Lady of Solitude, and a hospital contiguous to the latter with six beds. For defense there is a fortress with 20 guns and a good garrison, a governor resident in the city, a sergeant-major, 2 captains, 300 enlisted men, and 2 royal officials.

Going out of the city, at half a league to the north there is a small village of scarcely more than 30 Indian inhabitants, called Nombre de Dios, the mission which is served by the convent. Following the road from east to west, within an extent of 98 leagues there are 24 settlements and missions of Christian Indians, 11 belonging to the province of Timuqua and 13 to that of Apalache. . . .

Nine leagues from Encarnación, on the northern frontier, is another [village] named San Nicolás, of about 30 inhabitants, and 3 leagues further on is another, San Carlos, of something like 100 inhabitants. Both these are of the Chacatos nation, which 14 years ago requested baptism and had not their desire fulfilled until the 21st of June of last year, 1674. In that section, living in encampments without any permanent dwellings, are more than 4,000 heathen called Chiscas, who sustain themselves with game, nuts and roots of trees. . . .

Characteristics of the Christianized Indians

In the four provinces of Guale, Timuqua, Apalache and Apalachocoli there are 13,152 Christianized Indians to whom I administered the holy sacrament of confirmation. They are fleshy, and rarely is there a small one, but they are weak and phlegmatic as regards work, though clever and quick to learn any art they see done, and great carpenters as is evidenced in the construction of their wooden churches which are large and painstakingly wrought. The arms they employ are bow and arrows and a hatchet they call *macâna.* They go naked, with only the skin [of some animal] from the waist down, and, if anything more, a coat of serge without a lining, or a blanket. The women wear only a sort of tunic that wraps them from the neck to the feet, and which they make of the pearl-colored foliage of trees, which they call *guano* and which costs them nothing except to gather it. Four thousand and eighty-one women, whom I found in the villages naked from the waist up and from the knees down, I caused to be clothed in this grass like the others.

Their ordinary diet consists of porridge which they make of corn with ashes, pumpkins, beans which they call *frijoles,* with game and fish from the rivers and lakes which the well-to-do ones can afford. Their only drink is water, and they do not touch wine or rum. Their greatest luxury is [a drink] which they make from a weed that grows on the seacoast, which they cook and drink hot and which they call *cazina.* It becomes very bitter and is worse than beer, although it does not intoxicate them and is beneficial. They sleep on the ground, and in their houses only on a frame made of reed bars, which they call *barbacôa,* with a bear skin laid upon it and without any cover, the fire they build in the center of the house serving in place of a blanket. They call the house *bujío.* It is a hut made in round form, of straw, without a window and with a door a *vara* high and half a *vara* wide. On one side is a granary supported by 12 beams, which they call a *garita,* where they store the wheat, corn and other things they harvest.

During January they burn the grass and weeds from the fields preparatory to cultivation, surrounding them all at one time with fire so that the deer, wild ducks and rabbits, fleeing from it fall into their hands. This sort of hunting they call *hurimelas.* Then they enter the forests in pursuit of bears, bison and lions which they kill with bows and arrows, and this they call *ojêo.* Whatever they secure in either way they bring to the principal cacique, in order that he shall divide it, he keeping the skins which fall to his share. Offering is made to the church of the best parts, and this serves for the support of the missionary priest, to whom they are in such subjection that they obey his orders without question.

In April they commence to sow, and as the man goes along opening the trench, the woman follows sowing. All in common cultivate and sow the lands of the caciques. As alms for the missionaries and the needy widows, they sow wheat in October and harvest it in June. This is a crop of excellent quality in the province of Apalache, and so abundant that it produces seventy *fanegas* [a *fanega* is about a bushel and a half], from one *fanega* sown.

Each village has a council house called the great *bujío,* constructed of wood and covered with straw, round, and with a very large opening in the top. Most of them can accommodate from 2,000 to 3,000 persons. They are furnished all around the interior with niches called *barbacôas,* which serve as beds and as seats for the caciques and chiefs, and as lodgings for soldiers and transients. Dances and festivals are held in them around a great fire in the center. The missionary priest attends these festivities in order to prevent indecent and lewd conduct, and they last until the bell strikes the hour of *las ánimas* [the *de profundis* bell].

These Indians do not covet riches, nor do they esteem silver or gold, coins of which do not circulate among them, and their only barter is the exchange of one commodity for another, which exchange they call *rescate.* The most common articles of trade are knives, scissors, axes, hoes, hatchets, large bronze rattles, glass beads, blankets, which they call *congas,* pieces of rough cloth, garments and other trifles.

As to their religion, they are not idolaters, and they embrace with devotion the mysteries of our holy faith. They attend mass with regularity at 11 o'clock on the holy days they observe, namely, Sunday, and the festivals of Christmas, the Circumcision, Epiphany, the Purification of Our Lady, and the days of Saint Peter, Saint Paul and All Saints Day, and before entering the church each one brings to the house of the priest as a contribution a log of wood. They do not talk in the church, and the women are separated from the men; the former on the side of the Epistle, the latter on the side of the Evangel [Gospel]. They are very devoted to the Virgin, and on Saturdays they attend when her mass is sung. On Sundays they attend the *Rosario* and the *Salve* in the afternoon. They celebrate with rejoicing and devotion the Birth of Our Lord, all attending the midnight mass with offerings of loaves, eggs and other food. They subject themselves to extraordinary penances during Holy Week, and during the 24 hours of Holy Thursday and Friday, while our Lord is in the Urn of the Monument, they attend standing, praying the rosary in complete silence, 24 men and 24 women and the same number of children of both sexes, with hourly changes. The children, both male and female, go to the church on work days, to a religious school where they are taught by a teacher whom they call *Athequi* of the church; [a person] whom the priests have for this service; as they have also a person deputized to report to them concerning all parishioners who live in evil.

Your Majesty's most humble servant and chaplain.
Gab'l Bishop of Cuba.

11. Fernando del Bosque's Account of the First High Mass in Texas, May 16, 1675

THE first authentic report of the celebration of Mass on the soil of Texas is found in the diary of Fernando del Bosque (d. c. 1700). Repeated requests for missionaries from the native tribes who lived beyond the Rio Grande and the insistence of Fray Juan Larios, O.F.M., were the incentives for a formal expedition. While the Bosque-Larios undertaking across the Rio Grande was not large in size, it was, nonetheless, important. It was the earliest well-authenticated expedition on record to cross that river from the south. On May 16, 1675, the party was at a place which they called San Ysidro and which must have been on one of the branches of the Nueces River. Concerning this episode Carlos E. Castañeda has said: "In the above statement about this being the first High Mass, the reason why it was not mentioned before, was, perhaps, the fact that they did not consider it extraordinary to hold regular low Mass. It is to be noted particularly in the description . . . concerning the administration of the Sacrament of Baptism, that contrary to the grossly inaccurate assertion that the missionaries, in their zeal and fervor, often baptized thousands of Indians without giving them adequate instruction to prepare them for the sacrament, Father Larios refused to baptize them 'until they knew their prayers.'" *Our Catholic Heritage in Texas, 1519–1936* (Austin, 1936), I, 240. Source: Herbert Eugene Bolton (Ed.), "Diary of Fernando del Bosque, 1675," *Spanish Exploration in the Southwest, 1542–1706* (New York: Charles Scribner's Sons, 1916), p. 301; now included in *Original Narratives of Early American History*, copyright Barnes & Noble, Inc., New York.

In said post and river of San Ysidro . . . on the 16th day of said month and year I, said lieutenant *alcalde mayor,* certify that this day there was erected in said post a portable altar, and that it was prepared to say mass; and at a signal made with a small bell the people came to hear it. It was chanted by the father commissary missionary, Fray Juan Larios, and was attended by all the people. After it was concluded they asked the said father to baptize them; and when they were given to understand by him through an interpreter that he could not baptize them until they knew their prayers, to console them he baptized fifty-five infants, the Spaniards acting as their godfathers.

They were instructed in the doctrine, and counted, and the people of the four chiefs [Xoman, Terrodan, Teaname, and Teimamar] were found to comprise four hundred and twenty-five warriors and seven hundred and forty-seven women, boys, and girls, of all ages, making in all eleven hundred and seventy-two persons.

In said post of San Ysidro, on said day, month, and year, I, said lieutenant *alcalde mayor,* put the father commissary, Fray Juan Larios, in possession of his office and of the administration in said post, in virtue of a royal provision and of licenses. . . . Of this legal record was made in his despatches, following the rest of the ecclesiastical despatches regarding this settlement.

12. Report of Eusebio Francisco Kino on the Missions of Pimería Alta (Arizona) in 1710

FATHER EUSEBIO KINO, S.J. (1644–1711), and his companions entered Pimería Alta in 1687. Pimería Alta, the home of the Upper Pimas, extended from the valley of the Alta River to that of the Gila and thus included that part of southern Arizona which was later contained in the Gadsden Purchase. In 1687 Kino established the mission of Nuestra Señora de los Dolores more than 100 miles south of Tucson. This mission became his headquarters for twenty-four years of exploration, missionary activity, and writing. Operating from this base, Kino crossed the line into Arizona and founded the Missions of San Xavier del Bac. Guévavi, and Tumacácori. The "Favores celestiales," a manuscript history by Kino of the work of himself and his associates in Pimería Alta, was discovered in 1915 by Bolton and edited by him. In the following selection from an account written in 1710, Kino summarized his efforts with a statement of possibilities for future development. Source: Herbert Eugene Bolton (Ed.), *Kino's Historical Memoir of Pimería Alta. A Contemporary Account of the Beginnings of California, Sonora, and Arizona by Father Eusebio Francisco Kino, S.J. . . . 1683–1711* (Cleveland: Arthur H. Clark Co., 1919), II, 234–253.

Beginnings and Progress of the New Conquests and New Conversions of the Heathendoms of This Extensive Pimería and the Other Neighboring New Nations

It is well known that during almost two whole centuries the royal Catholic crown of Spain has spent more than two millions and a half for new conquests and new conversions and for the extension of the Holy Evangel [Gospel], and for the eternal salvation of the souls of the Californias; but it appears that, thanks be to His Divine Majesty, the blessed time is now coming when not only the conquest and conversion of the Californias is being accomplished, but also at the same time that of these other neighboring extensive lands and nations of this North America, most of which has hitherto been unknown, and when the Lord is adding to the rather poor lands of the Californias the necessary succor of these very extensive and rich lands, abundant champaigns, and fertile rivers and valleys. . . .

As soon as I knew that the conversion of coveted California was suspended, I asked and obtained from my superiors and his Excellency permission to come meanwhile to these heathen coasts nearest to and most in sight of California, to the Guaimas and Seris; and I having arrived at the end of February, 1687, in this province of Sonora, and gone to Opossura to see the Father Visitor, Manuel Gonzales, his Reverence came with me to this post of heathen Pimas, as the father of Cucurpe, near by, Joseph de Aguilar, was asking of him a father for them. We named the place Nuestra Señora de los Dolores. It is in thirty-two degrees and a half of latitude. We entered March 12, 1687, accompanied by Father Joseph de Aguilar and his servants; and the father visitor returning the following day to observe Holy Week in his pueblos, I went inland two hours after his departure and with said Father Joseph de Aguilar and some guides, going ten leagues beyond Nuestra Señora de los Dolores, toward the west, to the good post and valley which we named de San Ygnacio, where we found even more people, although they were somewhat scattered. We returned by the north through the ranchería of Himeres, which we named San Joseph, and through that of Doagibubig, which we named Nuestra Señora de los Remedios, which rancherías immediately, thanks be to the Lord, we began reducing to new good pueblos, making a beginning of teaching them the Christian Doctrine and prayers, by means of a good interpreter and a good native helper, whom I procured from the old Pima mission of Los Ures, and of the building of the churches and houses, of crops, etc.

Afterward I made other missions, or expeditions, to the north and farther to the west, and despatched friendly messages inviting all the heathen of these environs to receive our holy Catholic faith for their eternal salvation, in imitation of these Pimas, their relatives and countrymen. Soon many came from various parts to see me for this purpose, and we arranged for the beginning of other new missions and pueblos. There came to see and to visit us, with great comfort on our part and his Father Manuel Gonzáles. He asked and obtained, through the Señor alcalde mayor, four additional alms from the royal chest, for four other new missions for this extensive Pimería; and four other missionary fathers came to it at the time when I dedicated this my first and capacious church of Nuestra Señora de los Dolores. . . .

In general, in these twenty-one years, up to the present time, I have made from the first pueblo of Nuestra Señora de los Dolores more than forty expeditions to the north, west, northwest, and southwest, of fifty, eighty, one hundred, two hundred, and more leagues, sometimes accompanied by other fathers, but most of the time with only my servants and with the governors, captains, and caciques of different rancherías or incipient pueblos from here and from the interior. . . .

With all these expeditions or missions which have been made to a distance of two hundred leagues in these new heathendoms in these twenty-one years, there have been brought to our friendship and to the desire of receiving our holy Catholic faith, between Pimas, Cocomaricopas, Yumas, Quiquimas, etc., more than thirty thousand souls, there being sixteen thousand of Pimas alone. I have solemnized more than four thousand baptisms, and I could have baptized ten or twelve thousand Indians more if the lack of father laborers had not rendered it impossible for us to catechise them and instruct them in advance. But if our Lord sends, by means of his royal Majesty and of the superiors, the necessary fathers for so great and so ripe a harvest of souls, it will not be difficult, God willing, to achieve the holy baptism of all these souls and of very many others, on the very populous Colorado River, as well as in California Alta, and at thirty-five degrees latitude and thereabouts, for this very great Colorado River has its origin at fifty-two degrees latitude.

And here I answer the question asked of me in the letter of the Father Rector Juan Hurtasum, as to whether some rivers run into the North Sea or all empty into the Sea of California, by saying that as this Colorado River, which is the Rio del Norte of the ancients, carries so much water, it must be that it comes from a high and remote land, as is the case with the other large volumed rivers of all the world and terraqueous globe; therefore the other rivers of the land of fifty-two degrees latitude probably have their slope toward the Sea of the North, where Husson wintered. Some more information can be drawn from the maps which I add to this report; and in order not to violate the brevity which I promised herein, I will add only that in regard to the fourteen journeys for two hundred leagues to the northwest, I have written a little treatise of about twenty-five sheets which is entitled "Cosmographical Proof that California is not an Island but a Peninsula," etc.; and that of these new discoveries and new conversions in general, by order of our Father-General, Thirso Gonzales, I am writing another and more extensive treatise, with maps, of which more than one hundred sheets are already written. By suggestion of his Reverence it is entitled "Celestial Favors of Jesus Our Lord, and of Mary Most Holy, and of the Most Glorious Apostle of the Indies, San Francisco Xavier, experienced in the New Conversions of these New Nations of these New Heathendoms of this North America."

13. Junípero Serra's Farewell to the Old World, August 20, 1749

ON THE eve of his departure for the new world Fray Junípero Serra (1713–1784) wrote a letter from Cádiz to his confrere though no relation in which he spoke his farewells to his parents, friends, and all his acquaintances. Leaving behind a promising career as a preacher and a professor of theology in his native island of Mallorca, Serra took literally the words of our Lord and lived them: "No man putting his hand to the plough, and looking back, is fit for the kingdom of God" (Lk. 9:62). The principal cities of California, founded as missions by Father Serra, stand today as monuments to his faith and zeal. Source: Antonine Tibesar, O.F.M. (Ed.), *The Writings of Junípero Serra* (Washington: Academy of American Franciscan History, 1955), I, 3–9.

Jesus, Mary, Joseph!

Very dear Friend in Jesus Christ, Father Francesch Serra:

I am writing this letter in farewell, while we are getting ready to leave the city of Cádiz and embark for Mexico. The day fixed upon is unknown to me, but the trunks containing our baggage are locked and strapped and they say that after two, three, or possibly four days, the ship called *Villasota,* in which we are to embark, will sail. We had thought it would be sooner, as I wrote; it was to be about Saint Bonaventure's day, but it has been put off till now.

Friend of my heart, on this occasion of my departure, words cannot express the feelings of affection that overwhelm me. I want to ask you again to do me the favor of consoling my parents who, I know, are going through a great sorrow.

I wish I could give them some of the happiness that is mine; and I feel that they would urge me to go ahead and never to turn back.

Tell them that the dignity of Apostolic Preacher, especially when united with the actual duty, is the highest vocation they could have wished me to follow.

After all, considering their old age, their life is far spent. Beyond any doubt, the remainder is short, and should they compare it with eternity, they will see that it is no more than an instant. If this be so, it is very important, and according to God's Will, that they lay no store by the little help I might be to them. And so they will merit from God, our Lord, that if we are no more to see each other in this world, we will be united forever in eternal glory.

Tell them how badly I feel at not being able to stay longer and make them happy as I used to do. Anyhow they know quite well that first things come first; and our first duty, undoubtedly, is to do the Will of God. Nothing else but the love of God has led me to leave them. And if I, for love of God and with the help of His grace, can muster courage to leave them, might I not suggest that they also, for the love of God, be content to forego the happiness of my presence?

Let them listen attentively to the advice they will receive on this matter from their Father Confessor; and they will see, in fact, that now God has truly entered their home. By practicing holy patience and resignation to the Divine Will, they will possess their souls, and attain eternal life.

They should hold nobody but Our Lord God alone responsible for the separation. They will find how sweet His yoke can be; that what they now consider and endure as a great sorrow will be turned into a lasting joy. Nothing in this life should cause us sadness. Our clear duty is to conform ourselves in all things to the Will of God, and to prepare to die well. That is what counts: nothing else matters. If this is secured, it matters little if we lose all the rest; without this all else is useless.

Happy they to have a son a priest — however bad and sinful — who, every day, in the holy Sacrifice of the Mass, prays for them, as best he can; and very often offers for them exclusively his Mass so that the Lord send them help, that they be not without the necessities of life; that He grant them the grace of patience in their trials, of resignation to His holy Will, peace and union with their neighbors, courage to resist the temptations of the devil, and finally, at the proper time, a happy death, in His holy grace.

If, by the help of God's grace from above, I succeed in being a good religious, these prayers of mine will be all the more powerful and my parents will be the first to profit from them. And the same is to be said as regards my younger sister in Christ, my Juana, and my brother-in-law Miquel; therefore they should remember me for the sole purpose of recommending me to God that I be a good priest, and a good minister of God. That is what counts, and in that they should all be interested.

I well remember that, while assisting my father (I was already a religious at the time) when he had taken so severely ill that Extreme Unction became advisable — convinced he was to die and the two of us being alone, he said to me:

"Son, what I am most anxious about is that you be a good religious of our Father Saint Francis."

Well, father, rest assured that I keep your words always before me, just as if I hear them from your mouth, at this very moment. But bear well in mind that it is to become a good religious that I have undertaken this voyage.

You must not feel bad, then, that I am doing your will, which is, at the same time, the Will of God. As regards my mother, I know well that she has never missed offering up her prayers for me to God for the same purpose — that I be a good religious. No wonder, then, my dear mother, that God, granting your prayers, directed me in this way. Rest satisfied then with the way in which God has disposed matters. In all your troubles say always: "Blessed be God, and His Holy Will be done!"

And Juana, my sister, knows that, a short time ago, she was at the door of death, and that the Lord, by the merits and the intercession of His most blessed Mother Mary, granted her a complete recovery of health. Had she died at that time, she would not now be worrying whether I be in Mallorca or not. Anyway, she should give thanks to the Lord for whatever He does. Now, whatever He wills is always for our good; and in all probability the Lord gave her complete recovery of health so that she might be a consolation for the old folk, against the time I had to leave them.

Let us bless God who loves and cares for us all. Of Miquel, my brother-in-law, and of Juana, my sister, I have a great favor to ask — they know what it is. May they ever continue to live together in perfect peace and love and, at the same time, by showing great reverence and patience, be the consolation of the old folk; and take good care of the education of their children. In a word, foster within yourselves a love of going to church, of receiving frequently the Sacraments of Confession and Communion, of making the Way of the Cross; in short, be zealous Christians.

I know quite well that just as they have always asked God's help for me — so they will continue to do the same in the future. Thus it will come about that by praying for one another — I for them, they for me — the selfsame Lord will protect us all, and grant all of us His holy grace in this life, and, at the end of it, eternal glory.

Good-by, my father! Good-by, my mother! Good-by, Juana, my sister; Good-by, brother Miquel! Take good care of Miquelet; may he be a good Christian and a good pupil at school; likewise the two little girls, may they be good Christians. And have confidence in God from now on their Senor uncle will be there to help them. Good-by, Good-by!

My very dear brother, Father Serra, good-by to you. My letters, from now on, will be less frequent. In fact, to cheer them up and encourage the old folk, my sister and her husband, I relied first of all on our good friendship existing also between them and you; and then Father Vicar, Father Guardian and Father Master also. You all must act in place of a letter from me. If the Father Vicar and Father Master could be present when this letter is read, my parents would be so happy. But don't let anybody else be present, only these four: I mean father, mother, sister, and brother-in-law.

But if one more is to be admitted to hear this letter, let it be Cousin Juana, our neighbor, and give her from me my kindest greetings. Also to Cousin Roig, her husband; to Aunt Apolonia; Boronada, Xurxa, and all my other relatives.

My greetings to each one of the members of the Community of Petra, without any exception whatever, especially to Fray Antonio Vivés.

My Greetings to Doctor Fiol and his Brother Señor Antonio, his father and his family.

My very special greetings to Amón Raphael Moragués Casta, and his wife. To Doctor Moragués, his brother and Señora Moragués, likewise the same to Doctor Serralta. To Señor Vicari Perello, Señor Alzamora, Señor Juan Nicoláu and to the Regidor Bartolomé, his brother and the whole family. In short: to all my friends.

Please tell Father Vicar that I think the book will be returned to Señor Negra, if it has not yet arrived from Madrid when I leave; I asked the Fornaris, when they return to Mallorca, to bring it with them. Ask him, too, to promote devotion to my Saint Francisco Solano.

I am enclosing also a letter from Medo Maxica, a neighbor of the monastery. It comes from her son, Sebastián, who came back from the Indies, and he seems to me to be in the best of health.

To conclude: May the Lord bring us all together in eternal glory, and, for the time being, keep Your Reverence for many more years: that is my prayer in this House of the Holy Mission, in the city of Cádiz, August 20, 1749.

Professor Palóu sends to Your Reverence many greetings; you will be so kind as to forward the same, from both of us, to Señor Guillerm Roca and to his family.

Your cordial friend in Christ,
Fray Junípero Serra,
a most unworthy priest.

14. Concordat Between the Franciscans and Dominicans Dividing the California Missions, April 7, 1772

ALTHOUGH Don José de Gálvez, the visitor general of the King of Spain, had contended that there was no need in California for the Dominican friars, the latter secured a decree from the king that missions should be assigned to their order without prejudice to the Franciscans of the College of San Fernando. In the concordat, the text of which follows, the Dominicans agreed to take charge of the missions of southern [Lower] California while the Franciscans were to retain those in the area of what is the present United States from San Diego to San Francisco and beyond. Source: Herbert Eugene Bolton (Ed.), *Historical Memoirs of New California by Fray Francisco Palóu, O.F.M. . . .* (Berkeley: University of California Press, 1926), I, 236–240.

Most Excellent Sir:

Fray Rafael Verger, present guardian of the College *de propaganda fide* of San Fernando in Mexico, and Fray Juan Pedro de Iriarte, minister of the Holy Order of Preachers and commissary of the mission which, by order of his Majesty (God save him) be conducted to this kingdom for the Peninsula of California, in obedience to the superior decree of your Excellency of the 1st of April of the present year of 1772, in which you order them to divide between themselves, and for their respective missionaries, the missions of the Peninsula of California, in accordance with the royal decree done at Madrid on April 8, 1770, desire to say: that they have come to the conclusion, after repeated conferences upon the subject, that it is the earnest will of our sovereign and Catholic monarch that the Dominican fathers shall enter the said Peninsula of California, with their commissary, the above-mentioned master Fray Juan Pedro de Iriarte, since he so commanded in his royal decree of November 4, 1768, and lately in the one mentioned of April 8, 1770, in which, after having ordered and commanded the division spoken of, he concludes by repeating the same order. This he does notwithstanding the adverse reports of His Excellency the Marquis de Croix, predecessor of your Excellency, and of the visitor-general, Don José de Gálvez, for he thinks it not best for his royal service that one Order, and much less one monastery or college, should occupy a peninsula so extensive as the one under discussion.

At the same time it is taken into consideration that this one college has to-day in its charge not only the entire Peninsula, but also all the country that has been discovered from the port of San Diego to that of San Francisco, making about two hundred leagues of *terra firma.* And it is also borne in mind that this division ought to be, according to the royal decree, with distinct frontiers for each Order, and with such separateness and difference of field that they shall not encroach upon each other, in order to avoid in this way dissensions that might arise from the opposite arrangement. It is likewise considered that the main body of the Peninsula, on account of the nature of its territory, does not permit a variety of fields, for, indeed, it has only one frontier, that of San Fernando Vellicatá, since the place called San Juan de Diós, which was thought to be suitable for another frontier, is not (according to Captain Don Fernando Rivera y Moncada, who has examined it all repeatedly) sufficient for even a ranch, in which several fathers of this College agree. We explain this to your Excellency with all humility, so that you may not uselessly spend time and the funds of the pious donations.

In view of all the aforesaid, and desiring to faithfully carry out the sovereign will of our Catholic monarch, we have agreed upon the following division: The Dominican fathers shall take in their charge the old missions which this College has in California and the above-mentioned frontier of San Fernando Vellicatá, extending their new conversions in this direction until they reach the confines of the mission of San Diego on the harbor of that name; and, placing their last mission on the arroyo of San Juan Bautista, this mission shall terminate five leagues farther on, at a point which projects from the Sierra Madre and ends before reaching the beach. Once arrived there, they can turn to the east, slightly to the northeast, and in this way they ought to come out at the head of the Gulf of California and the Colorado River, following afterwards the direction pointed out to them by your Excellency in the royal council. And if in the country between the Colorado and San Diego a suitable road to the north or northeast should appear, they can also take it without prejudice to the other Order. It is agreed that the fathers of the College of San Fernando shall retain the missions that they now have, from the port of San Diego, following the road which they have opened to Monterey, the port of San Francisco, and farther on.

In this way, most Excellent Sir, it will be arranged so that the long coast of Southern California and the *terra firma* that follows it shall not be in charge of one Order alone, which appears to be the principal purpose of our sovereign, and at the same time that the two Orders of Dominican and Franciscan fathers shall have in it their separate spheres. We do not hold it improper that the College of San Fernando shall resign these missions, for by no other way can the principal end of his Majesty be fulfilled. For this reason the father guardian gives them up, hoping that with the vigorous measures which your Excellency has taken, the new conversions from the port of San Diego to Monterey may succeed, and that you will also take care that a sufficient number of cattle and sheep for a start shall be sent to each of the new missions, as I [Father Verger] beg your Excellency in the memorial which I presented on October 26, 1771.

Since this conquest is of such great importance and consequence as his Majesty states in the royal decree cited, he will not lift his powerful hand without bringing it to a perfect conclusion, even in case (which God forbid) that some misfortune has happened in the port of San Diego, or in one of the other missions. For the reasons expressed they humbly beg your Excellency to give your approbation to the agreement, and that you will at the same time order that it be duly put into effect, giving to each one a certified copy, with the decision of your Excellency, by which they will be favored.

Mexico, April 7, 1772.

Fray Rafael Verger,
Guardian,
Fray Juan Pedro de Iriarte,
Vicar-General.

15. Junípero Serra Makes His Final Report on the Mission of San Carlos de Monterey, July 1, 1784

WE PREVIOUSLY met Junípero Serra as a young man of thirty-six on the eve of his departure for the New World in August, 1749 (No. 13). In the document that follows we find him signing his final missionary report. In the thirty-five years that had intervened this intrepid missionary had traveled thousands of miles on foot, founded nine of California's twenty-one missions, and brought hundreds of pagan Indians into the Catholic Church. This report on San Carlos de Monterey is one of the best factual surveys we possess of his efforts, illustrating as it does, the number of Indians who were made Christians with a description of the religious practices of the neophytes, the daily life as lived by the friars and Indians at the missions, and the hardships endured from the elements and from enemies. Eight weeks after the document was signed the great missionary, worn out by his unremitting and exhaustive labor in behalf of the Indians of Mexico and of Lower and Upper California, died on August 28, 1784, at his beloved San Carlos de Monterey where his remains lie buried beneath the sanctuary floor of the mission church. Source: Manuscript in the possession of the Academy of American Franciscan History.

Hail Jesus, Mary, Joseph!

On the most solemn feast of the Holy Spirit, Pentecost Sunday, June 3, 1770, this mission of San Carlos de Monterey was founded to the joy of the sea and land expeditions. In a short time the rejoicing was shared by the entire kingdom and eagerly celebrated in both Spains.

On that day, after imploring the assistance of the Holy Spirit, the sacred standard of the cross was blessed, raised, and adored by all. The ground was blessed, an altar set up, and a sort of chapel formed with naval flags. The holy sacrifice of the Mass was sung, a sermon was preached, and, at the end, the *Te Deum* was intoned. With these (ceremonies), possession was duly taken of Monterey for (our) holy Church and the crown of Spain. A legal document covering all was drawn up and will be found where it belongs. All this occurred on the beach at the landing place of the said port, the same spot on which one hundred sixty-seven years before, as it is written, the expedition of Don Sebastián Vizcaino had celebrated Mass.[1]

The following day, after choosing the most likely spot on that plain,

[1] Don Sebastián Vizcaino (1550?–1615) and his exploring party entered Monterey Bay on December 16, 1602.

the construction of the presidio was enthusiastically begun by the men of both sea and land forces. By the fourteenth of the same month, the most solemn feast of Corpus (Christi), a chapel had been built, as well as it could be, at the spot in the presidio which it still occupies, and a high Mass was sung with the Blessed Sacrament exposed in its monstrance. After the Mass there was a procession, in which His Sacramental Majesty passed over the ground that till then had been so heathen and miserable. It was a day of great consolation for all of us who were Christians.

So the presidio was begun but the troop was too small to be divided into two bodies. Thus we, the religious, were forced to establish ourselves in and remain incorporated with this presidio until further arrangements [could be made], even though we knew that there we could do no sowing or any other kind of work.

We remained like this for one year, spending the time putting in order our residence and the most necessary storerooms for our supplies and in making friends with the Indians who were coming to see us; and we tried to win some children. In fact, within a short time, we baptized three and when the boat returned at the end of the year [1771], we had already twenty new Christians at Monterey. As ten religious came on this vessel, we were then twelve. We all dressed in rich chasubles and had a most solemn procession for Corpus (Christi). We had here the vestments for future missions, the men from the ship, and those of the land force, etc. Thanks be to God!

In August, 1771, with the express consent of His Excellency, Marquis de Croix,[2] at that time viceroy of New Spain, and of the Illustrious Inspector General, Don José de Gálvez,[3] both of whom officially informed me about this, San Carlos Mission was begun at the site it now occupies on the banks of Carmel River and in view of the sea at the distance of about a cannon shot where it forms the little bay south of Point Pinos. [The mission is] a little more than a league from the royal presidio, which is to the north in latitude 36°44″. The next place to the south is San Antonio [Mission], about twenty-five leagues away. Santa Clara [Mission] is in the opposite direction and a little farther away.

On the twenty-fourth of the said month, the feast of St. Bartholomew, the apostle, the holy cross was set up at the site and the first

[2] Marquis Carlos Francisco de Croix served as Viceroy of New Spain during the years 1765–1771.

[3] Don José de Gálvez (1720–1787), an energetic explorer and administrator, was very helpful to Serra and the missionaries in his office of Inspector General of New Spain.

Mass celebrated under a temporary arbor. For four months only one father stayed here with the personnel doing the building. The other priest with the two missionaries destined for the future San Luis [Obispo] Mission remained at the presidio until Christmas Eve that same year. After previously transferring everything belonging to the mission, we left the presidio on foot and arrived here with an escort of eight men: four soldiers, one muleteer, and three servants [who had been] sailors. When we received our share of the stock, after the division, there were great and small eighteen head of cattle; namely, nine cows, one bull, two heifers, and six small calves. That is all the cattle of that which the mission has and all which the mission has spent. I will write further on about the rest.

The eight remaining days of the year were spent in fiestas and in putting things in order.

1772

This mission's baptisms numbered twenty-three. In the last half of the past year, we added only three and in the whole of this year only eight, because the scarcity of provisions which had been severe during the two preceding, this year became even more critical for no boat reached [Monterey]. Neither of the two which came were able to proceed here and ported at San Diego.

We passed the time erecting around [the buildings] a stockade of stout, closely set palings, with ravelins in the corners of the square. We also finished the buildings, added some [new ones], and started a garden to help with its vegetables. No sowing at all was done in this whole year.

Before definitely establishing [the mission] here, the first concern was to have men familiar with farming see and state whether it would be easy or difficult to take water from the river for irrigating these lands. All agreed that it would be [easy]. Now when we tried to carry it out, they all reversed themselves and declared it impossible. This was the chief, if not the only, reason why there was a delay about the sowing for which we longed. Finally, in the next year, and thereafter, we determined to dry farm, which was both wise and fruitful as shall be seen from the harvests of the following years.

This year we got news of the arrival of both vessels at San Diego, at a time when scarcity had brought the greatest distress to the presidio and the two missions, this one and San Antonio, which had been founded one year earlier. Father President Fray Junípero Serra decided to accompany Commander Don Pedro Fages[4] on the trip to San

[4] Don Pedro Fages, commandant at Monterey, was later Governor of California.

Diego in order to use his influence also in procuring aid for the religious and missions.

He left this mission for that trip on St. Bartholomew's day, August 24, the first anniversary of the first Mass at this site, as was stated above. On his way he founded, September 1, Mission San Luis Obispo, in the same place where it is today, under such circumstances of want of the necessary supplies that it should have been considered rashness had it not been justified by charity and trust in God, who in fact, did not abandon the agents of such a holy enterprise as He had promised everyone: "He who trusts in Him shall not be confounded."

When the commander and the father president arrived at San Diego, they sent by land what small aid the fewness of mules permitted and it was decided that one of the boats would return to San Blas, while the other would attempt to go on to Monterey. In fact, it reached there at the end of the same year.

The father president, considering that the state of things demanded better provision for the maintenance and advancement of these new establishments, sacrificed himself to the advice of the religious present, to go to Mexico to seek aid from His Excellency, the new viceroy.[5] He sent from there a religious, who would take his place here, and gave him strict orders to trust in the Lord and proceed with the work of God in things both spiritual and temporal, etc. The father [president] embarked in the middle of October and the other came up to take his place. The vessel arrived at the end of the year with the regular provisions.

1773

In this year, there were one hundred thirty-four baptisms, which with the thirty-one preceding total one hundred sixty-five. Twenty-six marriages of new Christians were celebrated. With the two that they had before, these made twenty-eight neophyte families belonging to this mission.

Towards the end of last year, three pecks and one quart of wheat had been sowed with great difficulty and on ground only half cultivated, because as yet there was no way to plow. Despite the entire absence of irrigation they harvested five bushels, four pecks, and three quarts of good wheat. From half a quart of barley, they gathered three pecks, and from two pecks of Indian corn, four and one-half bushels.[6]

---

[5] Don Antonio Maria Bucareli y Ursúa was Viceroy of New Spain from September, 1771, to his death in Mexico City on April 9, 1779.

[6] The original uses the Spanish terms: *fanega, almud,* and *quartillo,* for which there is no exact English equivalent. Each Spanish measure, however, was several times larger than the English measure given here.

Horse beans, chick peas, and beans, a little of each were also sowed, but all [this] was lost. Such was the first sowing and harvest of this mission.

In this whole year, no boat at all came, even though His Excellency, the viceroy, had ordered one to set out from San Blas with the usual provisions, while better arrangements were being made. This was not carried out and since the number of religious was increased by those who had come from Lower California after they had turned their missions over to the Reverend Dominican Fathers, the privations which they suffered were most severe. Even so, the ministers of this mission kept intact the above-mentioned harvest in order to sow it all the following year, which they did.

While in this and the rest of the missions they were suffering such want, in Mexico provisions were being ordered with the greatest enthusiasm and being sent to San Blas for the prosperity of these new establishments. By December, the Father President, Fray Junípero, was again in San Blas for his return trip in the new frigate, *Santiago,* which was loaded with every good thing as no other boat that ever came to this land before or since.

1774

The frigate, *Santiago,* sailed from San Blas, January 25, 1774, and, having favorable stern winds for several days, it arrived at the port of San Diego, March 13, or in less than a month and a half. These circumstances could have brought the boat to Monterey, but it was better this way, for this place was thus succored en route as was the expedition of Don Juan de Anza,[7] which had just arrived, hungry and in great need at San Gabriel Mission.

The father president disembarked and made the rest of the trip by land, so that he could see the missions and his religious brethren. The frigate and his reverence arrived at Monterey at almost the same time to the great consolation of the entire land, for then the famine, privations, and shortages were ended. In fact, they have not returned since.

It would not be out of place to specify the provisions which, out of pure charity and without charge, His Excellency, the viceroy, sent on this occasion for these missions: corn, beans, flour, hams, clothing for the Indians, beads, etc., but suffice it to say that [the missions] were abundantly supplied and equipped to begin and to continue their

---

[7] Don Juan Bautista de Anza (1735–1788), born in Sonora, led several expeditions from Mexico to California and was later Governor of New Mexico.

spiritual and temporal labors as they did with great success. Thanks be to God!

In this mission they had one hundred two baptisms, which added to the preceding made a total of two hundred sixty-seven. There were six marriages for a total of thirty-four. Work on the land consisted in sowing the above-mentioned wheat harvest. From it, without irrigation, one hundred twenty-five bushels were gathered this year. From three short pecks of barley, twenty bushels were reaped; from six pecks of beans, five bushels, seven pecks; from eight pecks of corn, one hundred fifty bushels, three pecks; and from one peck of horse beans, one bushel; total three hundred one bushels.

This year we began to profit by the help of the six servants granted to us by His Excellency, the viceroy. We got some capable farm hands from the boat, and oxen were broken; hence, more land was prepared for the year

1775

The baptisms this year were one hundred one, which added to the preceding made a total of three hundred sixty-eight. The marriages were thirty-five, which also added to the preceding made a total of sixty-nine families.

The grain harvest this year reached a total of seven hundred nine bushels, six and one-half pecks. From one bushel of barley, one hundred seven bushels, ten pecks, and one quart were gathered and measured; from one bushel of fine wheat, sixty-three bushels, twenty and one-half pecks; from six bushels of [ordinary] wheat, three hundred fifty-three bushels, four and one-half pecks; from ten pecks of corn, after very severe damage, one hundred fourteen bushels; and the rest was garden vegetables: beans, lentils, horse beans, chick peas, and a few peas. The entire harvest came without any irrigation.

During this whole year, like last, this mission maintained seven religious and quite a few [Lower] California Indians destined for future missions. Though the king had assigned a double ration for each religious, during a five year period, to date this mission has not received this ration for even one day, nor for any religious. Though I suppose the gentlemen who have administered the royal property will have notified their superiors of the merit of this saving in their accounts, nevertheless, it is but fair that we also speak up that their honors may be increased! They also have other merits in this line. Now that the missions are on their feet we can give thanks to the gentlemen!

At the end of this year the destruction of San Diego Mission took place, a tragedy in which we all shared.[8] Blessed be God!

1776

There were seventy-one baptisms during this year, which added to the preceding made four hundred thirty-nine Christians. The marriages were twenty-two and with the preceding they made ninety. In this way, Christianity was gradually progressing in proportion to the means available in the following years, 1777, 78, 79, and 80. At the end of this last [year] we reached six hundred thirty-eight baptisms and one hundred sixty-two marriages.

During all this time we failed to get water for irrigation, even though we took extreme steps. On this account, the harvests were diverse since they depended on the rain. There were two years in which we had scarcely harvested four hundred bushels of all grains, from which we had to take the seed which was to be sown in the following year. This left very little for so many people and in one year we had recourse to Mission San Luis [Obisp] to which this [mission] paid one hundred thirty pesos in cash.

In the other years the harvest was sufficient because even though the Indian corn was never abundant, since it was sowed too late for the rains, its place was taken by barley of which we regularly gathered from two hundred to four hundred and more bushels.

In the earlier years of this period, this mission had to transport and supply [grain] as best it could, for the fathers who founded the mission of our father, St. Francis, in the year 1776.

In the middle of this year, the father president embarked for the restoration of San Diego Mission and the reestablishment of San Juan Capistrano. Both were set up successfully because of the favorable provisions made by the Knight Commander, His Excellency Viceroy Bucareli may he be with God.

The following year, Mission Santa Clara was founded and its father ministers, too, quitted San Carlos where they had resided for more than two years. This mission did well while consuming the abundant supplies which the father president had brought for it from Mexico. But they served the purpose for which they came which was the propagation of our Catholic faith.

Meanwhile, noting the little security and the lack of protection afforded by the dwellings and other buildings no matter how much these were plastered with mud, we started to make buildings of adobes

---

[8] San Diego was destroyed by fire by the Indians in November, 1775.

and gradually those were erected which are now in use and which are listed at the end of this report.

In 1778, the father president made another voyage to San Diego to administer confirmation there and, on his return trip, at the rest of the missions. The apostolic faculty to confirm had come to him this year on the same boat.

He started the voyage on St. Bartholomew's day, August 24, and he returned by land, after he had accomplished his task, December 23, the same year. During this and other similar trips, this mission had always had at least two religious.

The year after the destruction of San Diego, this mission also was menaced with several rumors that a similar misfortune was being prepared for it by the pagans known as Sanjones, old and powerful enemies of the natives of this territory. On one occasion the indications appeared so certain that on his own initiative the sergeant, who commanded the presidio in the absence of the captain at San Diego, came with quite a force and begged us religious to sleep in one place so that we could be more easily protected. They locked the seven of us in the adobe blacksmith shop, the safest place, and there, packed together, we spent the night while the soldiers passed it in the saddle, patrolling the vicinity, but no enemy showed up, nor did any later evidence appear to prove that any such danger had existed. Those who were then painted to us as such enemies are almost all Christians today. So, we pass on to the year

1781

The supplies from the preceding harvest, that were used in the beginning of this year, were sufficient and the planting of barley, wheat, and some garden vegetables promised a harvest in accordance with the amount of water. Nevertheless, the hope [persisted] of bringing water with all the possibilities of irrigation, especially for the corn which for lack of water was valueless as a crop. Father Juan Crespí,[9] now deceased, decided to try to get water. He realized through his surveys that at least for irrigating the land so far cultivated, he could get water from a point closer than the one he had until then considered. The enterprise was started with such confidence of success that corn was sown where it was thought it could be irrigated.

When there were but a few days left [of Father Crespí's work], the famous steward of San Luis Obispo came to our house offering

[9] Juan Crespí, O.F.M. (1721–1782), had been a student of Serra's; he was a favorite of the founder of the missions and had acted as assistant to him at Monterey and Carmel.

to take the same job at this mission. He started May 1, at a salary of two hundred pesos in cash, etc. He saw and approved the work that the two fathers were doing toward extracting water and, after stating that within three days we would see the corn irrigated, he went out one morning and without saying anything to us, he took the people from the work and set them to digging another ditch a few yards further up the river, claiming that what had been done previously was valueless and, with that, the corn sown was lost and he spent seven months and used all the workmen in the new ditch.

Not a grain of corn was gathered and they got a little over four hundred bushels of barley. Because of the folly of this man, a great part of the wheat was lost in the fields. Less than four hundred bushels were obtained, when to be conservative we should have expected more than five hundred. But finally the water was extracted that same year in the month of December. From then on the mission has had irrigation. Thanks be to God!

This year there were only twenty-four baptisms and seventeen marriages. We sowed in a proper manner for the

Year 1782

Towards the end of the past year, thirty-one bushels of barley were sown and fifty-three of wheat. The barley was planted where the water could not reach it and as the drought was great, it was lost. This had never happened before in the case of this grain. We gathered only one hundred seven bushels.

The wheat which was irrigated did well but less was harvested than in the preceding year for the same reason and there were large stretches of sown land where [the major domo] did not attempt to gather a single head. There was a task that they were completing in less than an hour and, to make it shorter, they gathered only the tall ears and even so it took them a long time. A great many of the people got sick and the [steward] asked permission to betake himself to Mission San Luís Obispo, because they had sent to tell him that he was needed there. Leaving the wheat in the fields and the people down he departed and never returned.

The harvested wheat threshed out at four hundred fifty bushels. There were twenty-seven bushels of garden vegetables and one hundred sixty of Indian corn. These are the results of the first year of irrigation and such an intelligent steward.

In things spiritual it was better. We had one hundred and one baptisms and twenty-three marriages. The people gradually improved in health, even though some of them died, and without any steward, good or bad, we sowed for the

Year 1783

We can consider this the happiest year of the mission because the number of baptisms was one hundred seventy-five and of marriages thirty-six.

The sowing of all grains amounted to eighty-four bushels, eight pecks. This included one bushel and a half of wheat, half a bushel of corn, and two pecks of beans, which were sown for the [Lower] California Indians, who had moved here and were married in this mission.

And the harvest, less the amount of forty-seven bushels which belonged to these Indians and other concessions made to the people such as a portion of the barley which they might reap and some twenty bushels of wheat from the chaff of the threshing, which was stored in the mission granaries amounted to twenty-six hundred fourteen and a half bushels, that is, of measured barley six hundred seventy bushels, eight hundred thirty-five of wheat, only two hundred according to our estimate are kept in the ear. There were nine hundred seventy-one bushels of corn of both kinds according to our estimate, sixty-three bushels of peas, sixteen bushels of horse beans, four bushels of lentils, and fifty-three bushels of various kinds of beans.

Today the new Christians of this mission number six hundred fourteen living persons, even though some of them take a leave of absence from time to time. They have been maintained and are maintained without any scarcity and we supplied the quartermaster of the presidio of San Carlos with one hundred thirty bushels of Indian corn; because they did not ask for more, also with thirty bushels of beans. The escort of this mission, at the request of the ensign quartermaster, received rations in these two kinds of grain. There have not been other deliveries of consequence so that in our prudent judgment of the two chief commodities, wheat and corn, about half the amount harvested may still remain.

The value of the food supplied to the presidio has been paid already in cloth, which now covers the Indians who grew the crops, but at that we are still distressed at the sight of so much nudity among them.

We do not get clothing now from the soldiers, as we did formerly, not even from those who have debts to us no matter how small. The wool, which in some of the missions is enough to cover Indian nakedness, here has not been any help to us so far, because the thefts of sheep are so numerous that already for more than three years, we can not exceed two hundred head between goats and sheep, and from shearing the few that we have we get nothing worthwhile.

The condition, then, of the Mission in things spiritual is that up to this day in this Mission:

Baptisms	1,006
Confirmations	936
And since those of the other missions belong in some way to this it is noted in passing that their number is	5,307
Marriages in this mission	259
Burials	356

The number of Christian families living at the mission and eating jointly, as well as widowers, single men, and children of both sexes, is evident from the enclosed census lists and so is omitted here.

They pray twice daily with the priest in the church. More than one hundred twenty of them confess in Spanish and many who have died used to do it as well. The others confess as best they can. They work at all kinds of mission labor, such as farm hands, herdsmen, cowboys, shepherds, milkers, diggers, gardeners, carpenters, farmers, irrigators, reapers, blacksmiths, sacristans, and they do everything else that comes along for their corporal and spiritual welfare.

The work of clearing the fields once, sometimes twice, or even three times a year, is considerable because the land is very fertile. When we clear new land great hardship is required. Altogether there is sufficient land cleared for sowing more than one hundred bushels of wheat, and it is sowed in that grain, barley, vegetables, and corn. Every year we clear a little more.

To the seven months' work required to take water from the river for irrigation, as mentioned above, we must add the labor of bringing it to the lagoon near the mission residence. In some years, this lagoon used to be dry. Now it is always full, making it a great convenience and a delight to the mission. Some salmon have been placed in the pool and so we have it handy.

The timber palisade was inadequate to protect the seed grain because they steal the paling for firewood. So we dug a circular trench many thousands of varas[10] long. This was a two years' labor and withal nothing sufficed to prevent losses every year.

Some of the land which we cleared for farming was not only covered with long tough grasses and thickets but also with great trees, willows, alders, and so forth, and it has been hard work, as we have

---

[10] The Spanish *vara* was equivalent to about 2.8 feet.

already noted, but we hope that it will pay off at a profit. We also have a sizable walled garden [which produces] abundant vegetables and some fruit.

MISSION BUILDINGS

In the first few years we worked hard and well on the church and the rest of the buildings. [They were made] of paling with flat earthen roofs to minimize fire danger, but no matter what we did they always leaked like a sieve and between that and the humidity everything would rot. So we decided to build of adobe and thus today all buildings are [of that material] They are as follows:

An adobe church, forty by eight varas, with a thatched roof.

Likewise, the three-room residence of the three priests. One [room is] large, with an alcove for a bed. The floor is plain earth and the roof thatched.

Also, a granary about twenty varas long with several small compartments, a porch, and a thatched roof.

Likewise, another granary about thirty varas long with its porch and four wooden barred windows. The floor is plain earth and the roof thatched.

Also, another adobe house, thirty varas long, divided for the present into only three sections: one serves as a storeroom, another at the opposite end is used as a dormitory for the girls; the center section is a large room with two barred windows and doors. It is white-washed and clean and is used as a guest chamber for the ships' officers and for some other occasions. It is going to be divided into two rooms for which we already have the two doors with their hinges.

Likewise, another adobe building with an earthen roof and with its own shed and key. It houses the forge where the blacksmith works. It has a porch and window.

Also, next to this building is another which we call the carpenter shop. It has a room with a separate door and key for safeguarding the tools. It has two windows with bars and a door.

Likewise, another building next to the ones just mentioned where the women grind [grain], make cheese, and where different tools are kept.

Also, another building, larger than the preceding ones, where for the present the family of the Mexican blacksmith lives.

Likewise, four adobe buildings a little further on, which are [a place for] five carts, the wood shed, kitchen, and a hen house.

Also, there is a serviceable adobe corral with sections for sheep and goats and next to this a separate pen for pigs. The rest of the corrals for horses and cattle, with their corresponding stud and bull stalls, are all made of paling and from time to time give us quite a bit of repair trouble.

THE ANIMALS

number today:

Cattle, large and small	500
Sheep and goats, about the same number of each	220
Riding and draft mules	18
Tame and broken horses	20
Four herds of mares with their colts . . .	90
Also with them, two young mules from the time we had a jack	
One old ass that may be with foal	1
Pigs	25

ACCOUNTS

Regarding the remainder of the status of the mission, [we note] that when the vessels arrive from Mexico with the supplies we know whether we have credits or debits from our stipends. This year the [boats] have not yet reached here, so we do not have this information.

We know of no local debts but there may be some hidden or unexpected debt like those we have had in the past.

The mission paid Lieutenant Ortega[11] eighteen pesos for a tent from the King's stores, which was given the father president for use when he was at San Buenaventura Mission, and while he assisted at the foundation of the new presidio of Santa Barbara. He did not think such a debt existed until they came to collect it.

Not long ago this mission paid fifteen pesos as a donation for the war, more than a year after the conflict ended,[12] as a result of misinformation given the commandancy general to the effect that the father president had excluded from the count some Indians who had run away from the mission after the lists had been completed. This was not true, for when we made the lists everyone of them had been apostates for at least two years and some for more than three. He mentioned them only as an incentive so that they might return them [to the mission] for me.

---

[11] José Francisco Ortega (d. 1798) was a Mexican-born soldier who rose to the rank of brevet captain in the Spanish colonial forces.

[12] The preliminary articles of peace between Great Britain and Spain were signed on January 20, 1783.

We did not even think about mentioning those who ran away, nor those who died, after the lists were made, nor did we discount them, but just the same we paid the fifteen pesos and the [entire] donation amounted to over one hundred pesos, the sum they finally asked for. At the beginning of the year when the governor showed me these [directions for] reports, inventories, and census lists, of the missions [that were] to be sent to the commandancy general, I told him that I would care for it gladly, since the reverend father guardian of my holy college[13] had given me the same order.

But, that it had to be on condition, that the papers and letters for those documents would be post free, for I had received a letter from the commander general of much less bulk than any of these reports and it bore the notation: eleven reales. What would so many papers cost?

He answered me that yes [they were post free] and, in fact, the ensign always urged me to accept [such] letters saying, even in writing, that the figures in question had reference to other accounts and that I would not have to pay it.

With that assurance, I went ahead certain that the envelope which came from San Gabriel entitled: "Reports, Inventories, and Census List of San Gabriel Mission" [was free even though] there was a notation, twenty reales, which I have kept by accident. Despite this, a few days ago we received a bill from the quartermaster for twenty-five pesos, two reales for [postage on] letters sent to the mission. They were the creditors and they collected. All we need now is some other arbitrary debt unknown to us.

What we get in the annual distributions purchased in Mexico with our stipends is known already. After using enough for our clothing, chocolate, wine, and candles for Mass, and some minor objects for the church, the rest goes for the Indians, especially for clothing to cover them. So far as we can see, nothing more need be said on this point.

If anything else should be made known about the administration and state of the mission, it can be asked of us specifically and with assurance that we will hide nothing, for thanks to the goodness of God we do not fear the light, and, since what has been said so far is true, we the ministers of the mission sign it, July 1, 1784.

Fray Junípero Serra — Fray Mathías Antonio de Santa Cathalina Noriega [rubrica].

[13] The College of San Fernando in Mexico City had been formally established in 1733.

16. "Instructions for the Fathers of Our Society Who Shall be Sent to the Hurons," by Jean de Brébeuf, S.J., 1637

ONE of the most resplendent periods in the history of French Catholicism occurred in the seventeenth century, and no finer pages in that history have been written than those which describe the heroic sacrifices made by the French Récollets, Jesuits, and other missionary priests in their efforts to win the Indians of France's North American colonies to the Catholic faith. That effort began in what is today Canada, but as time went on it was extended to areas south and west that embraced large sections of the present United States. Among the leaders of the Jesuits was an intrepid Norman, Jean de Brébeuf (1593–1649), who entered upon his extraordinary missionary career in 1625 at the age of thirty-two, and who persisted amid almost incredible suffering and privation until he was captured, tortured, and put to death in 1649 by a roving band of Iroquois in a raid on St. Ignatius and St. Louis Missions near Georgian Bay. Brébeuf had worked with the Huron Indians for several years and he could thus enlighten his confreres as to how they should conduct themselves among the savages. The following account was written in 1637 and foreshadowed the life of self-denial that awaited the missionaries. It was incorporated into the relation for 1637 by Paul le Jeune, S.J. St. Jean de Brébeuf was canonized by Pope Pius XI in 1930, along with seven of his fellow Jesuit martyrs of North America, of whom three met their deaths within the area of the present Diocese of Albany, New York. Source: Reuben Gold Thwaites (Ed.), *The Jesuit Relations and Allied Documents* (Cleveland: Burrows Brothers Co., 1898), XII, 117–123.

The Fathers and Brethren whom God shall call to the Holy Mission of the Hurons ought to exercise careful foresight in regard to all the hardships, annoyances, and perils that must be encountered in making this journey, in order to be prepared betimes for all emergencies that may arise.

You must have sincere affection for the Savages, — looking upon them as ransomed by the blood of the son of God, and as our brethren with whom we are to pass the rest of our lives.

To conciliate the Savages, you must be careful never to make them wait for you in embarking.

You must provide yourself with a tinder box or with a burning mirror, or with both, to furnish them fire in the daytime to light their pipes, and in the evening when they have to encamp; these little services win their hearts.

You should try to eat their sagamité or salmagundi in the way they prepare it, although it may be dirty, half-cooked, and very tasteless. As to the other numerous things which may be unpleasant, they must be endured for the love of God, without saying anything or appearing to notice them.

It is well at first to take everything they offer, although you may not be able to eat it all; for, when one becomes somewhat accustomed to it, there is not too much.

You must try and eat at daybreak unless you can take your meal with you in the canoe; for the day is very long, if you have to pass it without eating. The Barbarians eat only at Sunrise and Sunset, when they are on their journeys.

You must be prompt in embarking and disembarking; and tuck up your gowns so that they will not get wet, and so that you will not carry either water or sand into the canoe. To be properly dressed, you must have your feet and legs bare; while crossing the rapids, you can wear your shoes, and, in the long portages, even your leggings.

You must so conduct yourself as not to be at all troublesome to even one of these Barbarians.

It is not well to ask many questions, nor should you yield to your desire to learn the language and to make observations on the way; this may be carried too far. You must relieve those in your canoe of this annoyance, especially as you cannot profit much by it during the work. Silence is a good equipment at such a time.

You must bear with their imperfections without saying a word, yes, even without seeming to notice them. Even if it be necessary to criticise anything, it must be done modestly, and with words and signs which evince love and not aversion. In short, you must try to be, and to appear, always cheerful.

Each one should be provided with half a gross of awls, two or three dozen little knives, called jambettes (pocket-knives), a hundred fishhooks, with some beads of plain and colored glass, with which to buy fish or other articles when the tribes meet each other, so as to feast the Savages; and it would be well to say to them in the beginning, "Here is something with which to buy fish." Each one will try, at the portages, to carry some little thing, according to his strength; however little one carries, it greatly pleases the Savages, if it be only a kettle.

You must not be ceremonious with the Savages, but accept the comforts they offer you, such as a good place in the cabin. The greatest conveniences are attended with very great inconvenience, and these ceremonies offend them.

Be careful not to annoy anyone in the canoe with your hat; it would be better to take your nightcap. There is no impropriety among the Savages.

Do not undertake anything unless you desire to continue it; for example, do not begin to paddle unless you are inclined to continue paddling. Take from the start the place in the canoe that you wish to keep; do not lend them your garments, unless you are willing to surrender them during the whole journey. It is easier to refuse at first than to ask them back, to change, or to desist afterwards.

Finally, understand that the Savages will retain the same opinion of you in their own country that they will have formed on the way; and one who has passed for an irritable and troublesome person will have considerable difficulty afterwards in removing this opinion. You have to do not only with those of your own canoe, but also (if it must be so stated) with all those of the country; you meet some to-day and others to-morrow, who do not fail to inquire, from those who brought you, what sort of man you are. It is almost incredible, how they observe and remember even the slightest fault. When you meet the Savages on the way, as you cannot yet greet them with kind words, at least show them a cheerful face, and thus prove that you endure gayly the fatigues of the voyage. You will thus have put to good use the hardships of the way, and already advanced considerably in gaining the affection of the Savages.

This is a lesson which is easy enough to learn, but very difficult to put into practice; for, leaving a highly civilized community, you fall into the hands of barbarous people who care little for your Philosophy or your Theology. All the fine qualities which might make you loved and respected in France are like pearls trampled under the feet of swine, or rather of mules, which utterly despise you when they see that you are not as good pack animals as they are. If you go naked, and carry the load of a horse upon your back, as they do, then you would be wise according to their doctrine, and would be recognized as a great man, otherwise not. Jesus Christ is our true greatness; it is He alone and His cross that should be sought in running after these people, for, if you strive for anything else, you will find naught but bodily and spiritual affliction. But having found Jesus Christ in His Cross, you have found the roses in the thorns, sweetness in bitterness, all in nothing.

17. "How Father Jogues was Taken by the Hiroquois, and What He Suffered on his First Entrance into Their Country," by Jerome Lalemant, S.J., 1647

AMONG the most famous of the Jesuit missionaries in colonial times was St. Isaac Jogues (1607–1646). In his search for Indian converts Jogues became one of the first white men to penetrate inland as far as Sault Ste. Marie on Lake Superior where in October, 1641, he and Charles Raymbault, S.J., preached to the savages. Upon his return to the west after a visit to Quebec, Jogues was captured by the Mohawks in August, 1642, and for over a year he was forced to endure almost superhuman tortures at their village of Ossernenon near the present Auriesville, New York. Through the intervention of the Dutch he was finally released and taken to New Amsterdam and thus became the first Catholic priest to visit the future New York City. After some months in his native France the missionary returned to the New World in the spring of 1644. In spite of warnings about the dangers due to the restive state of the western tribes, he undertook another missionary journey westward in the autumn of 1646. He was captured by the Iroquois and once more taken to Ossernenon where after further cruelties he was put to death on October 18, 1646. One of his confreres, Jerome Lalemant, incorporated the following vivid description of Jogues' sufferings and martyrdom in the account which he forwarded to the Jesuit superior in 1647. Source: Reuben Gold Thwaites (Ed.), *The Jesuit Relations and Allied Document* (Cleveland: Burrows Brothers Co., 1898), XXXI, 17–119.

Father Isaac Jogues had sprung from a worthy family of the City of Orleans. After having given some evidences of his virtue in our Society, he was sent to New France, in the year 1636. In the same year, he went up to the Hurons, where he sojourned until the thirteenth of June in the year 1642, when he was sent to Kebec [Quebec] upon the affairs of that important and arduous Mission.

From that time until his death, there occurred many very remarkable things, — of which one cannot, without guilt, deprive the public. . . .

The Reverend Father Miersome L'alemant [*sic*], at that time Superior of the Mission among the Hurons . . . sent for him, and proposed to him the journey to Kebec, — a frightful one, on account of the difficulty of the roads, and very dangerous because of the ambuscades of the Hiroquois, who massacred, every year, a considerable number of the Savages allied to the French. Let us hear him speak upon this subject and upon the result of his journey. "Authority having made me a simple proposition, and not a command, to go down to Kebec, I offered myself with all my heart. . . . So there we were, on the way and in the dangers all at once. We were obliged to disembark forty times, and forty times to carry our boats and all our baggage amid the currents and waterfalls that one encounters on this journey of about three hundred leagues. . . . At last, thirty-five days after our departure from the Hurons, we arrived, much fatigued, at Three Rivers; thence we went down to Kebec. . . . Our affairs being finished in fifteen days, we solemnly observed the feast of St. Ignace; and the next day, the first of August in the same year 1642, we left Three Rivers, in order to go up again to the country whence we came. The first day was favorable to us; the second caused us to fall into the hands of the Hiroquois. We were forty persons, distributed in several canoes; the one which kept the vanguard, having discovered on the banks of the great river some tracks of men, recently imprinted on the sand and clay, gave us warning. A landing was made; some say that these are footprints of the enemy, others are sure that they are those of Algonquins, our allies. In this dispute, Eustache Ahatsistari . . . exclaimed: 'Be they friends or enemies, it matters not; I notice by their tracks that they are not in greater number than we; let us advance and fear nothing.' We had not yet made a half-league,[1] when the enemy, concealed among the grass and brushwood, rises with a great outcry, discharging at our canoes a volley of balls. The noise of their arquebuses so greatly frightened a part of our Hurons that they abandoned their canoes and weapons in order to escape by flight into the depth of the woods. . . . We were four French, — one of whom, being in the rear, escaped with the Hurons, who abandoned him before approaching the enemy. Eight or ten, both Christians and Catechumens, joined us . . . they oppose a courageous front to the enemy. . . . But, having perceived that another band — of forty Hiroquois, who were in ambush on the other side of the river — was coming to attack them, they lost courage; insomuch that those who were least entangled fled. . . . A Frenchman named René Goupil, whose death is precious before God . . . was surrounded and captured, along with some of the most courageous Hurons. I was watching this disaster," says the Father, "from a place very favorable for concealing me from the sight of the enemy . . . but this thought could never enter my mind. 'Could I, indeed,' I said to myself, 'abandon our French and leave those good Neophytes and those poor Catechumens, without giving them the help which the Church of my God has entrusted to me?' Flight seemed horrible to me. 'It must be,' I said in my heart, 'that my body suffer

---

[1] The old French *lieue,* mentioned many times in these French documents, was the equivalent of about 2.76 miles.

the fire of earth, in order to deliver these poor souls from the flames of Hell; it must die a transient death, in order to procure for them an eternal life.' My conclusion being reached without great opposition from my feelings, I call the one of the Hiroquois who had remained to guard the prisoners. . . . He advances and, having seized me, puts me in the number of those whom the world calls miserable. . . . Finally, they brought that worthy Christian Captain named Eustache, who, having perceived me, exclaimed, 'Ah, my Father, I had sworn and protested to you that I would live or die with you.' The sight of him piercing my heart, I do not remember the words that I said to him. Another Frenchman, named Guillaume Couture, seeing that the Hurons were giving way, escaped like them into the great forests; and, as he was agile, he was soon out of the enemy's grasp. But, remorse having seized him because he had forsaken his Father and his comrade, he stops quite short, deliberating aside with himself whether he should go on or retrace his steps. The dread of being regarded as perfidious makes him face about; he encounters five stout Hiroquois. One of these aims at him, but, his arquebus having missed fire, the Frenchman did not miss him, — he laid him, stone-dead, on the spot; his shot being fired, the other four Hiroquois fell upon him with a rage of Lions, or rather of Demons. Having stripped him bare as the hand, they bruised him with heavy blows of clubs. . . . In short, they pierced one of his hands with a javelin, and led him, tied and bound in this sad plight, to the place where they were. Having recognized him, I escaped from my guards and fall upon his neck. . . . The Hiroquois, seeing us in these endearments, at first remained quite bewildered, looking at us without saying a word; then, all at once, — imagining, perhaps, that I was applauding that young man because he had killed one of their Captains, — they fell upon me with a mad fury, they belabored me with thrusts and with blows from sticks and war-clubs, flinging me to the ground, half dead. When I began to breathe again, those who had not struck me, approaching, violently tore out my finger-nails; and then biting, one after another, the ends of my two forefingers, destitute of their nails, caused me the sharpest pain — grinding and crushing them as if between two stones, even to the extent of causing splinters or little bones to protrude. They treated the good René Goupil in the same way, without doing, at that time, any harm to the Hurons. . . .

"As I saw them engrossed in examining and distributing our spoils, I sought also for my share. I visit all the captives; I baptize those who were not yet baptized; I encourage those poor wretches to suffer with constancy, assuring them that their reward would far exceed the severity of their torments. I ascertained on this round of visits, that we were twenty-two captives, without counting three Hurons killed on the spot. . . . So there we were, on the way to be led into a country truly foreign. Our Lord favored us with his Cross. It is true that, during the thirteen days that we spent on that journey, I suffered in the body torments almost unendurable, and, in the soul, mortal anguish; hunger, the fiercely burning heat, the threats and hatred of those Leopards, the pain of our wounds, — which, for not being dressed, became putrid even to the extent of breeding worms, — caused us, in truth, much distress. But all these things seemed light to me in comparison with an inward sadness which I felt at the sight of our earliest and most ardent Christians of the Hurons. I had thought that they were to be the pillars of that rising Church, and I saw them become the victims of death. The ways closed for a long time to the salvation of so many peoples, who perish every day for want of being succored, made me die every hour, in the depth of my soul. . . .

"Eight days after our departure from the shores of the great river of the saint Lawrence, we met two hundred Hiroquois, who were coming in pursuit of the French, and of the Savages, our allies. At this encounter we were obliged to sustain a new shock. It is a belief among those Barbarians that those who go to war are the more fortunate in proportion as they are cruel toward their enemies; I assure you that they made us thoroughly feel the force of that wretched belief.

"Accordingly, having perceived us, they first thanked the Sun for having caused us to fall into the hands of their Fellow-countrymen. . . . That done, they set up a stage on a hill; then, entering the woods, they seek sticks or thorns, according to their fancy. Being thus armed, they form in line, — a hundred on one side, and a hundred on the other, — and make us pass, all naked, along that way of fury and anguish. . . . I had not accomplished the half of this course when I fell to the earth under the weight of that hail and of those redoubled blows. . . . Seeing, then, that I had not fallen by accident, and that I did not rise again for being too near death, they entered upon a cruel compassion; their rage was not yet glutted, and they wished to conduct me alive into their country. . . . I would be too tedious if I were to set down in writing all the rigor of my sufferings. . . .

"I had always thought, indeed, that the day on which the whole Church rejoices in the glory of the blessed Virgin — her glorious and triumphant Assumption — would be for us a day of pain. . . . We arrived on the eve of that sacred day at a little river, distant from the first village of the Hiroquois about a quarter of a league. We found on its banks, on both sides, many men and youth, armed with sticks which they let loose upon us with their accustomed rage. . . .

"After they had glutted their cruelty, they led us in triumph into that first village; all the youth were outside the gates, arranged in a line, — armed with sticks and some with iron rods, which they easily secure, on account of their vicinity to the Dutch. . . . We were following one another at an equal distance; and, that our executioners might have more leisure to beat us at their ease, some Hiroquois thrust themselves into our ranks in order to prevent us from running and from avoiding any blows. . . . Such was our entrance into Babylon. . . .

"Evening having come, they made us descend, in order to be taken into the cabins as the sport of the children. They gave us for food a very little Indian corn, simply boiled in water; then they made us lie down on pieces of bark, binding us by the arms and the feet to four stakes fastened in the ground in the shape of St. Andrew's Cross. . . . Oh, my God, what nights! To remain always in an extremely constrained position; to be unable to stir or to turn, under the attack of countless vermin which assailed us on all sides; to be burdened with wounds, some recent and others all putrid; not to have sustenance for the half of one's life; in truth, these torments are great, but God is infinite. At Sunrise they led us back upon our scaffold, where we spent three days and three nights in the sufferings that I have just described.

"The three days having expired, they paraded us into two other villages, where we make our entrance as into the first . . . these villages are several leagues distant from one another. . . . The sentence decreed in the Council is intimated to me; the following night is to be (as they say) the end of my torments and of my life. My soul is well pleased with these words, but not yet was my God, — he willed to prolong my martyrdom. Those Barbarians reconsidered the matter, exclaiming that life ought to be spared to the Frenchmen, or rather, their death postponed. They thought to find more moderation in our forts, on account of us. . . ."

When these poor captives had recovered a little of their strength, the principal men of the country talked of conducting them back to Three Rivers, in order to restore them to the French. . . . But, as their captors could not agree, the Father and his companions endured, more than ever, the pangs of death. Those Barbarians are accustomed to give prisoners, whom they do not choose to put to death, to the families who have lost some of their relatives in war. These prisoners take the place of the deceased, and are incorporated into that family, which alone has the right to kill them or let them live . . . but when they retain some public prisoner, like the Father, without giving him to any individual, this poor man is every day within two fingerlengths of death. . . .

The young Frenchman who was the Father's companion was accustomed to caress the little children, and to teach them to make the sign of the Cross. An old man, having seen him make this sacred sign upon the forehead of his grandson . . . said to a nephew of his: "Go and kill that dog . . . that act will cause some harm to my grandson." Father Jogues . . . wished to forewarn and strengthen his poor companion. He leads him to a grove near the village, and explains to him the dangers in which they stood. . . . While they were returning . . . the nephew of that old man, and another Savage, armed with hatchets and watching for an opportunity, go to meet them. Having approached them, one of these men says to the Father, "March forward," and at the same time he breaks the head of poor René Goupil, who, on falling and expiring, pronounced the Holy Name of Jesus. . . . "Give me a moment's time," the Father said to them, supposing that they would accord him the same favor as to his companion. . . . "Get up," they reply; "thou wilt not die this time. . . ."

That young man, or that blessed martyr, being thus slain, the Father returns to his cabin; his people apply their hands to his breast, in order to feel whether fear did not agitate his heart. Having found it steady, they said to him: "Do not again leave the village, unless thou art accompanied by some one of us; they intend to beat thee to death; look out for thyself. . . ."

They gave their poor Father to some families, to serve them as a menial in their hunts; he follows them at the approach of Winter and makes thirty leagues with them, serving them through two months, as a slave. All his clothes sheltered him no more than would a shirt and sorry pair of drawers; his stockings and his shoes made like tennis slippers, and of a leather just as thin, without any soles, — in a word, he was all in rags. . . . As they did not account him fit for hunting, they gave him a woman's occupation, — that is, to cut and bring the wood to keep up the cabin fire. The chase beginning to furnish supplies, he could to some extent repair his strength, — meat not being stinted to him; but when he saw that they were offering to the Demon of the chase all that they took, he told them plainly that he would never eat of flesh sacrificed to the devil. He therefore contented himself with a little very thin sagamité, that is to say with a little indian meal boiled in water; and even then he had it but seldom, because, gorged with meat, they despised their dry cornmeal. . . .

From the month of August to the end of March, the Father was every day in the pains and terrors of death. A lesser courage had died a hundred times, from apprehension. It is easier to die all at once than to die a hundred times. Toward the end of April, a Savage Captain from the country of the Sokokuois appeared in the land of the Hiroquois, laden with presents, which he came to offer for the ransom and deliverance of a Frenchman named Ondesson,—thus the Hurons and the Hiroquois named Father Jogues. . . . This embassy gave some credit to the Father, and caused him to be regarded for a short time with more compassionate eyes; but those Barbarians, having accepted the gifts, nevertheless did not set him at liberty,—violating the law of nations, and the law accepted among all these tribes. . . .

About that time,—some Hiroquois Captains going to visit some small nations which are, as it were, tributary to them, in order to get some presents,—that man who had the Father in custody, being of the party, led him in his train; his design was to display the triumphs of the Hiroquois over even the nations which are in Europe. . . . The Father's fatigues in that journey of more than eighty leagues were fully soothed and rewarded by the salvation of his Benefactor. . . .

Upon the return from this journey, they command the Father to go and accompany some fishermen, who conducted him 7 or 8 leagues below a Dutch settlement. While he was engaged in that exercise, he learned from the lips of some Hiroquois who came to that quarter that they were awaiting him in the village to burn him. This news was the occasion of his deliverance. . . . The Dutch having given him the opportunity to enter a ship, the Hiroquois complained of it;—he was withdrawn thence and conducted to the house of the Captain, who gave him in custody to an old man, until they should have appeased those Barbarians. . . . Now, while they were awaiting the opportunity to send him back to Europe, he remained six weeks under the guard of that old man, who was very miserly, and lodged him in an old garret. . . . [Here follows a description of Jogues's journey to and stay at New Amsterdam.]

Finally, the Governor of the country, sending a bark of one hundred tons to Holland, sent the Father back at the beginning of the month of November . . . [and] on the fifth of Janaury in the year 1644, in the morning, he was knocking at the door of our College at Rennes. . . . He made no long sojourn in France; the Spring of the year 1644, having come, he betook himself to la Rochelle in order to cross back to the country of his martyrdom, — where, having arrived, he was sent to Montreal. . . . Peace being made with the Hiroquois . . . the Father was taken from Montreal, to go and lay the foundations of a Mission in their country, which was named "The Mission of the martyrs." . . . On the sixteenth of May, 1646, this good Father left three rivers in company with Sieur Bourdon, the engineer of Monsieur the Governor. . . . Sieur Bourdon has told me that this good Father was indefatigable; that they suffered extremely on that road of iron. In short, they arrived at three rivers, — having accomplished their embassy, — on the day of Saint Peter and Saint Paul, the 29th of the month of June. . .

Hardly had the poor Father been refreshed among us two or three months, when he recommenced his expeditions; on the twenty-fourth of September in the same year, 1646, he embarks with a young Frenchman, in a canoe conducted by some Hurons, in order to return to the land of his crosses. He had strong premonitions of his death. . . . We have learned that he was slain directly upon his entrance into that country full of murder and blood: here follows a letter announcing this, from the Governor of the Dutch to Monsieur the Chevalier de Mont-Magny. . . .

"For the rest, I have not much to tell you, except how the French arrived, on the 17th of this present month of October, 1647, at the fort of the Maquois. . . . The very day of their coming, they began to threaten them, — and that immediately, with heavy blows of fists and clubs, saying: 'You will die tomorrow: be not astonished. But we will not burn you; have courage; we will strike you with the hatchet and will set your heads on the palings,' (that is to say, on the fence above their village) 'so that when we shall capture your brothers they may still see you.' You must know that it was only the nation of the bear which put them to death; the nations of the wolf and the turtle did all that they could to save their lives, and said to the nation of the bear: 'Kill us first.' But, alas! they are not in life for all that. Know, then, that on the 18th, in the evening, when they came to call Isaac to supper, he got up and went away with that Barbarian to the lodge of the bear. There was a traitor with his hatchet behind the door, who, on entering, split open his head; then immediately he cut it off, and set it on the palings. The next day, very early, he did the same to the other man, and their bodies were thrown into the river. Monsieur, I have not been able to know or to learn from any Savage why they have killed them. . . ."

Such is, word for word, what the Dutch have written concerning the death of Father Isaac Jogues. . . .

18. France's Representatives Take Formal Possession of the Western Country, June 4, 1671

IN THE late seventeenth century the colonial rivalry of the European powers had grown more pronounced in North America as it had elsewhere. As a consequence France decided to tighten its hold upon the western reaches of its empire, and in June, 1671, an elaborate ceremony was held at Sault Ste. Marie which signalized the new policy of the French government. The ceremony was likewise intended to impress the native peoples with the power and majesty of King Louis XIV. Claude Dablon, S.J. (1618–1697), the superior of the Jesuit missions, was, of course, aware of the significance of all this, and in the report which he submitted for that year he gave a description of the share which the famous missionary, Claude Allouez, S.J. (1620–1689), had in the Sault Ste. Marie ceremony with extracts from his confrere's speech to the Indians on that occasion. It affords an interesting example, among other things, of the united action of Church and State in the French colonies of the seventeenth century. Source: Reuben Gold Thwaites (Ed.), *The Jesuit Relations and Allied Documents* (Cleveland: Burrows Brothers Co., 1899), LV, 105–115.

It is not our present purpose to describe this ceremony in detail, but merely to touch on matters relating to Christianity and the welfare of our Missions, which are going to be more flourishing than ever after what occurred to their advantage on this occasion.

When Monsieur Talon, our Intendant, returned from Portugal, and after his shipwreck, he was commanded by the King to return to this country; and at the same time received his Majesty's orders to exert himself strenuously for the establishment of Christianity here, by aiding our Missions, and to cause the name and the sovereignty of our invincible Monarch to be acknowledged by even the least known and the most remote Nations. These commands, reinforced by the designs of the Minister, — who is ever equally alert to extend God's glory, and to promote that of his King in every land, — were obeyed as speedily as possible. Monsieur Talon had no sooner landed that he considered means for insuring the success of these plans, — choosing to that end sieur de Saint Lusson, whom he commissioned to take possession, in his place and in his Majesty's name, of the territories lying between the East and the West, from Montreal as far as the South sea, covering the utmost extent and range possible.

For this purpose, after wintering on the Lake of the Hurons, Monsieur de saint Lusson repaired to sainte Marie du Sault early in May of this year, sixteen hundred and seventy one. First, he summoned the surrounding tribes living within a radius of a hundred leagues, and even more; and they responded through their Ambassadors, to the number of fourteen Nations. After making all necessary preparations for the successful issue of the whole undertaking to the honor of France, he began, on June fourth of the same year, with the most solemn ceremony ever observed in these regions.

For, when all had assembled in a great public council, and a height had been chosen well adapted to his purpose, — overlooking, as it did, the Village of the people of the Sault, — he caused the Cross to be planted there, and then the King's standard to be raised, with all the pomp that he could devise.

The Cross was publicly blessed, with all the ceremonies of the Church, by the Superior of these Missions; and then, when it had been raised from the ground for the purpose of planting it, the *Vexilla* was sung. Many Frenchmen there present at the time joined in this hymn, to the wonder and delight of the assembled Savages; while the whole company was filled with a common joy at the sight of this glorious standard of JESUS CHRIST which seemed to have been raised so high only to rule over the hearts of all these poor peoples.

Then the French Escutcheon, fixed to a Cedar pole, was also erected, above the Cross, while the *Exaudiat* was sung, and prayer for his Majesty's Sacred person was offered in that far-away corner of the world. After this, Monsieur de saint Lusson, observing all the forms customary on such occasions, took possession of those regions, while the air resounded with repeated shouts of "Long live the King!" and with the discharge of musketry, — to the delight and astonishment of all those peoples, who had never seen anything of the kind.

After this confused uproar of voices and muskets had ceased, perfect silence was imposed upon the whole assemblage; and Father Claude Allouez began to Eulogize the King, in order to make all those Nations understand what sort of a man he was whose standard they beheld, and to whose sovereignty they were that day submitting. Being well versed in their tongue and in their ways, he was so successful in adapting himself to their comprehension as to give them such an opinion of our incomparable Monarch's greatness that they have no words with which to express their thoughts upon the subject.

"Here is an excellent matter brought to your attention, my brothers," said he to them, — "a great and important matter, which is the cause of this council. Cast your eyes upon the Cross raised so high above your heads; there it was that JESUS CHRIST, the Son of God, making himself man for the love of men, was pleased to be fastened and to die, in atonement to his Eternal Father for our sins. He is the master of our lives, of Heaven, of Earth, and of Hell. Of him I have always spoken to you, and his name and word I have borne into all these countries. But look likewise at that other post, to which are affixed the armorial bearings of the great Captain of France whom we call King. He lives beyond the sea; he is the Captain of the greatest Captains, and has not his equal in the world. All the Captains you have ever seen, or of whom you have ever heard, are mere children compared with him. He is like a great tree, and they, only like little plants that we tread under foot in walking. You know about Onnontio, that famous Captain of Quebec. You know and feel that he is the terror of the Iroquois, and that his very name makes them tremble, now that he has laid waste their country and set fire to their Villages. Beyond the sea there are ten thousand Onnontios like him, who are only the Soldiers of that Great Captain, our Great King, of whom I am speaking. When he says, 'I am going to war,' all obey him; and those ten thousand Captains raise Companies of a hundred soldiers each, both on sea and on land. Some embark in ships, one or two hundred in number, like those you have seen at Quebec. Your Canoes hold only four or five men — or, at the very most, ten or twelve. Our ships in France hold four or five hundred, and even as many as a thousand. Other men make war by land, but in such vast numbers that, if drawn up in double file, they would extend farther than from here to Missis-saquenk, although the distance exceeds twenty leagues. When he attacks, he is more terrible than the thunder; the earth trembles, the air and the sea are set on fire by the discharge of his Cannon; while he has been seen amid his squadrons, all covered with the blood of his foes, of whom he has slain so many with his sword that he does not count their scalps, but the rivers of blood which he sets flowing. So many prisoners of war does he lead away that he makes no account of them, letting them go about whither they will, to show that he does not fear them. No one now dares make war upon him, all nations beyond the sea having most submissively sued for peace. From all parts of the world people go to listen to his words and to admire him, and he alone decides all the affairs of the world. What shall I say of his wealth? You count yourselves rich when you have ten or twelve sacks of corn, some hatchets, glass beads, kettles, or other things of that sort. He has towns of his own, more in number than you have people in all these countries, five hundred leagues around; while in each town there are warehouses containing enough hatchets to cut down all your forests, kettles to cook all your moose, and glass beads to fill all your cabins. His house is longer than from here to the head of the Sault," — that is, more than half a league, — "and higher than the tallest of your trees; and it contains more families than the largest of your villages can hold."

The Father added much more of this sort, which was received with wonder by those people, who were all astonished to hear that there was any man on earth so great, rich, and powerful.

Following this speech, Monsieur de Saint Lusson took the word, and stated to them in martial and eloquent language the reasons for which he had summoned them, — and especially that he was sent to take possession of that region, receive them under the protection of the great King whose Panegyric they had just heard; and to form thenceforth but one land of their territories and ours. The whole ceremony was closed with a fine bonfire, which was lighted toward evening, and around which the *Te Deum* was sung to thank God, on behalf of those poor peoples, that they were now the subjects of so great and powerful a Monarch.

19. The Conversion and Holy Death of Catharine Tegahkouita, 1676–1680

THE strenuous efforts put forth by the missionaries to win the Indians to Christianity more frequently than not met with failure. Occasionally, however, they encountered souls of rare virtue, and of none was this more true than Catharine Tegahkouita (1656–1680), the Mohawk maiden, who was received into the Church by Jacques de Lamberville, S.J. (1641–1710), in 1676, at the Mohawk village near present-day Fonda, New York. Catharine spent her last years at La Prairie de la Madeleine, a Christian Indian village in Canada, and died a holy death there in 1680. Her cause has been introduced at Rome for beatification. The following biographical sketch of Catharine was written by a French Jesuit whose work was first published in 1744. He gathered the facts from accounts left by some of his confreres, Jacques de Lamberville. Claude Chauchetière, and Pierre Cholenec, who either knew her personally or were contemporaries. Source: John Gilmary Shea (Ed.), Pierre François Xavier Charlevoix, S.J., *History and General Description of New France* (New York: John Gilmary Shea, 1870), IV, 283–296.

New France has had her apostles and her martyrs, and has given the church saints in all conditions, and I do not hesitate to say that they would have done honor to the primitive ages of Christianity.

Several I have made known so far as the course of this history permitted me. The lives of some have been published; but God, who exalted his glory during their life-time by the great things which he effected through them; by the lustre which their sanctity has diffused over this vast continent; by the courage with which he inspired them to found with untold toil a new Christiandom amid the most fearful barbarism, and to cement it with their blood, chose none of these to display on their tombs, all the riches of his power and mercy; but conferred this honor on a young neophyte, almost unknown to the whole country during her life. For more than sixty years she has been regarded as the Protectress of Canada, and it has been impossible to oppose a kind of *cultus* publicly rendered to her.

This holy virgin, so celebrated under the name of Catharine Tegahkouita, was born in 1656, at Gandahouhagué [Fonda, New York], a town in the Mohawk canton, of a heathen Iroquois father and a Christian Algonquin mother. She lost her mother at the age of four, and was still quite young when her father died, leaving her to the care of one of her aunts, and under the control of an uncle who had the chief authority in his village. The smallpox which she had in her infancy having weakened her sight, she was long compelled as it were to remain in the corner of a cabin, her eyes being unable to stand the light, and this retirement was the first source of her happiness. What she did at first from necessity, she continued to do from choice, thereby avoiding whatever could cause her to lose that moral purity so hard to preserve amid idolatrous and then very dissolute youth.

As soon as she saw herself of age to act, she took on herself all the toil of the household; and this shielded her from two dangers, fatal to most Indian girls; I mean, private conversations and idleness. Her relatives however wished her to use the decorations common to young persons of her sex, and although she yielded from simple compliance with their wishes, and with all possible repugnance, it was a matter of much scruple to her, when, favored by the light of faith, she learned how dangerous it is to seek to please men.

The first knowledge that she acquired of Christianity, was imparted by some missionaries sent to the Iroquois after M. de Tracy's expedition.[1] On their way they passed through the town where she lived and were received at her cabin. She was appointed to take care of

---

[1] The French Commander, Alexandre de Prouville, Marquis de Tracy (1603–1670), had cleared the way for the missionaries by a western military expedition against the hostile Iroquois in 1666.

them, and waited on them in a manner that surprised them. She had herself, on beholding them, been moved by an impulse that excited sentiments in her heart, regarded subsequently by her as the first sparks of the heavenly fire, by which she was in the sequel so completely inflamed. The fervor and recollection of those religious in their devotions, inspired her with the desire of praying with them, and she informed them of it. They understood much more than she expressed; they instructed her in the Christian truth, as far as the short stay which they made in that town permitted them, and left her with a regret that on her side was heartily reciprocated. Some time after, a marriage was proposed to her; as she showed strong opposition, her relatives did not press it; but they soon returned to the charge, and to save themselves the trouble of overcoming her resistance, they, without mentioning it to her, betrothed her to a young man, who at once went to her cabin and sat down beside her. To ratify the marriage, it only required that she should remain near the husband selected for her, such being the way of these tribes; but she abruptly left the cabin, and protested that she would not return till he withdrew. This conduct drew on her much ill treatment, which she endured with unalterable patience. She was more sensible to the reproach made that she had no affection for her kindred, that she hated her tribe, and gave all her attachment to that to which her mother belonged. Nothing however could overcome her repugnance for the state of life in which they sought to involve her.

Meanwhile Father James de Lamberville arrived at Gandahouhagué, with orders to found a mission there. Tegahkouita then felt her former desires to become a Christian revive; but she was still for some time without mentioning it, either from respect to her uncle, who did not relish our religion, or from simple timidity. At last an opportunity came for avowing her conviction, and she was not wanting. A wound in the foot which she had received, kept her in the cabin, while all the other women were busy harvesting the Indian corn. Father de Lamberville, compelled to suspend his public instructions, which no one would attend, took this time to visit the cabins, and instruct those whom age or infirmity detained there. One day he entered that where Tegahkouita was.

Unable to dissemble the joy which this visit caused her, she did not hesitate to open her mind to the missionary in the presence of two or three women, who were in company with her, on her design of embracing Christianity. She added that she would have great obstacles to overcome, but that nothing appalled her. The energy with which she spoke, the courage she displayed, a certain modest yet resolute air, that lighted up her countenance, at once told the missionary that his new proselyte would not be an ordinary Christian. He accordingly carefully taught her many things, which he did not explain to all preparing for baptism. God doubtless infuses into hearts, of which he has especially reserved possession, a sort of purely spiritual sympathy, forming even in this life the sacred bond which will unite them hereafter in the abode of glory. Father de Lamberville, whom I knew well, was one of the most holy missionaries of New France, where he died, at Sault Saint Louis, spent with toil and austerity, and, if I may use the expression, in the arms of Charity. He often declared that in his first interview with Tegahkouita, he thought he could discern that God had great designs as to that virgin; yet he would not exercise any haste in conferring baptism on her, and he adopted in her case all the precautions that experience has counselled as necessary, to make sure of the Indians, before administering the sacrament of regeneration.

The whole winter was spent in these trials, and on her side the young catechumen employed this precious time in rendering herself worthy of a grace, whose importance she fully comprehended. Before granting it to adults, the missionaries took great pains to inquire privately into their conduct and morality. Father de Lamberville asked all who knew Tegahkouita, and was greatly surprised to find that there was not one, even among those who had given her most to suffer, but sounded her praises. This was all the more glorious for her, as Indians are much given to slander, and naturally inclined to put an evil interpretation on the most innocent actions. The missionary accordingly no longer hesitated to grant her what she solicited with such earnestness. She was baptized on Easter Sunday, 1676, and received the name of Catharine.

The grace of the sacrament received into a heart which her uprightness and innocence had so well prepared, produced wondrous effects. Whatever idea the missionary had already conceived of the young Iroquois maiden, he was astonished to find in her, immediately after baptism, not a neophyte needing to be confirmed in the faith, but a soul filled with the most precious gifts of heaven, and whom he too would have to guide in the most sublime spiritual ways. In the outset her virtue excited the admiration of those even who were least inclined to imitate her, and those on whom she depended, left her free to follow every impulse of her zeal, but this did not last long. The innocence of her life, the precautions which she took to avoid all that could in the least affect it, and especially her extreme reserve as to whatever could in the slightest degree offend purity, appeared to the young men of her village as a reproach on the dissolute life they led, and many laid snares with the sole view of dimming a virtue which dazzled them.

On the other hand, although she had relaxed nothing in her domestic occupations, and was ever found ready to give her services to all, her relatives were displeased to see her give to prayer all the time left her, and to prevent her suspending on Sundays and holidays the work which the church forbids on those days consecrated to the Lord, they made her pass them without food. Seeing, however, that they gained nothing by this course, they had recourse to still more violent means; they often ill-treated her in a most unbecoming manner; when she went to the chapel, they sent young men to pursue her with hooting and pelt her with stones; men either really drunk or pretendedly drunk rushed upon her, as though they designed to take her life; but, undismayed by these artifices and acts of violence, she continued her devotions as though she enjoyed the most perfect liberty.

One day when she was in her cabin, a young man entered abruptly, with flashing eyes, brandishing his hatchet as if intending to tomahawk her. At this sight she displayed no emotion, and bowed down her head to receive the blow; but the madman, seized at the instant by a panic fear, fled as precipitately as though pursued by a war-party. These first storms were succeeded by a still more dangerous persecution. Catharine's aunt was a woman of morose disposition, who was displeased with all that her niece did to satisfy her, for the simple reason that she could find nothing to reprove. One day the virtuous neophyte happened to call the husband of this woman by his own name, instead of calling him Father, as usual; her aunt imagined, or pretended to believe, that this familiar mode of speaking showed an improper connection between the uncle and the niece, and she hastened on the spot to Father de Lamberville to assert that she had surprised Catharine soliciting her husband to sin. The missionary promised to examine the case, and when he learned on what this atrocious accusation rested, he gave the slanderer a rebuke that covered her with confusion; but which ultimately increased the annoyance of the innocent girl.

Had all this involved merely suffering, than which nothing was more to her taste, she would never have thought of changing her position; but she feared that she could not always hold firm against the seduction of bad example, or escape being overcome gradually by human respect, so powerful in the Indian mind. She accordingly began to look for an asylum, where her innocence and religion would be shielded from danger. La Prairie de la Magdeleine, where several Iroquois Christians began to settle, seemed to her well adapted, and she felt an ardent desire to remove thither; but this was not easily done.

Her uncle beheld with great displeasure the depopulation of his canton, and he declared himself the avowed enemy of all who contributed to it. It was therefore apparently impossible to obtain his consent, and it was not easy for Catharine to leave him without it. But God, who had destined her to be the example and ornament of this transplanted Christian colony, facilitated what had at first seemed impossible. She had an adopted sister, a neophyte like herself, married to a Christian very zealous for the conversion of his countrymen. This man had already taken up his abode at La Prairie de la Magdeleine, and he was one of those who under various pretexts, traversed the Iroquois towns in order to make proselytes. He knew that the greatest favor he could do to Catharine would be to take her to his home: he spoke of the matter to his wife, who confirmed him in his design, and earnestly exhorted him to give her sister this consolation.

He resolved on the project, and to effect it more surely, he pretended to go hunting with one of his friends in the direction of New York, and set out, after warning Tegahkouita to hold herself in readiness at a fixed time. Fortunately for her her uncle was away, though not far distant, and he was almost at once informed of his niece's departure. Without losing a moment he set out in pursuit bent on bringing her back dead or alive, and on tomahawking the first who resisted him. He soon overtook the two hunters, but not finding his niece with them, because, whenever they halted, they took the precaution to conceal her in the woods, he thought that he had been misinformed; accordingly, without avowing his purpose, he conversed for a time on different topics and left them, convinced that Catharine had taken some other route and followed other guides.

The holy virgin, rescued from this peril, gaily pursued her journey, and at last reached the bourne which had been the object of her prayers. This was in the month of October, 1677. Her sister had not yet a cabin to herself, and dwelt with her husband in that of a fervent Christian woman named Anastasia, whose sole employment it was to prepare persons of her own sex for baptism. A hostess of this character and such exercises were greatly to the taste of Catharine. She was, moreover, charmed with all that she beheld done in the village, nor could she sufficiently admire the omnipotence of grace, which could transform wolves into lambs, nor chant the mercies of the Lord, to see men now dwelling in the purity of gospel morality, whose debauchery had more than once paralyzed her with horror.

Animated by new fervor at this sight, she gave herself unreservedly to God, renouncing in future the least thought of self, and began to run with great steps in the career of sanctity. Prayers, toil, spiritual conversation, was henceforth her sole occupation; and after the example of Saint Anthony, she made it a duty to imitate every edifying trait that she perceived in those who composed this new church. She spent at the foot of the altar all her spare time; she lived solely by her own labor, and busied as she might be exteriorly, her heart was ever in constant communion with God.

She had not yet made her first communion when she arrived in the colony, and it is not usual in these missions to grant this favor to neophytes till after long trials. Catharine was fearful that she would be subjected to this rule, but her virtue, far more than her repeated entreaties, soon induced her director to make an exception in her favor; nor had he any reason to repent. The frequent communions, which she was permitted to receive, did not diminish in the least her fervor in preparing for them. It was enough to see her in her most ordinary actions to be roused to devotion; but when she partook of the divine mysteries, it was impossible to be near her, and not be filled with the most tender love for God.

When she was obliged to go with a hunting party, the distraction inseparable from that time deranged in nothing her interior life; she built an oratory within her heart which she never quitted. She avoided company as much as she could, and when she could not, she imparted her recollectedness to others much more than she took part in their amusements. Yet there was nothing constrained in her manners, and her devotion was neither forbidding nor troublesome. She was ever wonderfully dexterous in concealing her private practices of piety, and her austerities, which were great. One of her most common was to mingle earth with all she ate, and very few perceived it. . . .

She was seen to advance visibly in virtue. Already naught was spoken of in the country except her eminent sanctity. The people were never weary of admiring the secret spring of Divine Goodness, which, from amid a nation the most hostile to the establishment of Christianity, had drawn forth a young virgin, to make her a perfect model of all Christian virtues.

There then reigned in the mission of Sault Saint Louis a spirit of mortification which went to great length. These neophytes had just been declared, by all the Iroquois cantons, enemies of their country, and they confidently expected that after this outburst, all who fell into the hands of their idolatrous brethren, would be given over without mercy to the most fearful tortures. Hence they thought only of preparing for martyrdom by all the means that austerity can suggest for chastising the flesh. Men, women, and even children, in this manner proceeded to excesses which the missionaries would never have permitted had they been fully informed in regard to them.

Catharine more fully possessed the interior spirit than all the others, was too the most unsparing to herself of all. She consulted naught but her fervor, and believed herself in no wise bound to depend in this on her director as formerly, believing that this general concert of the whole village could not be unknown to him, and that his silence in regard to it was a consent. She was accordingly soon reduced to a state of languor and suffering from which she never recovered. Some time after she paid a visit to Montreal, where the sight of the Hospital Nuns, whom she had never even heard mentioned, increased her desire to consecrate herself to God by the vow of chastity; she renewed her entreaties to her confessor, who judged it his duty no longer to withhold his consent. She accordingly took the long desired vow, with a joy that seemed to revive all her strength, and she was the first of her tribe who took upon herself such an engagement with heaven.

The heavenly spouse of chaste souls was not slow in giving her manifest proofs that he had accepted her sacrifice, and in treating her as His well-beloved spouse. She, on her side, exerted herself to correspond to His caresses and the internal communications with which He favored her, by perfect fidelity and unreserved love. But her strength could not long sustain its ardor, and the flesh soon gave way beneath the efforts of the spirit. She fell into a dangerous disease, which left her only a lingering existence subject to constant pain. In this state she united herself more and more to Jesus Christ by meditating on His death and sufferings, and the frequent reception of the sacraments. She could no longer endure human conversation; Anastasia and Teresa were the only two persons with whom she retained any kind of intimacy, because they spoke to her only of God.

She felt well only at the foot of the altar, buried in profound contemplation, and shedding torrents of tears, whose inexhaustible fountain was His love and the wound it had inflicted on her heart, she often so forgot the wants of her body, as not even to feel the cold, with which her whole frame was benumbed. She always came from this contemplation with renewed love of suffering, and it is unconceivable [*sic*] how ingenious her mind was in inventing means to crucify her flesh. Sometimes she walked barefooted on the ice and snow, till she lost all feeling. Sometimes she strewed her couch with thorns. She rolled for three days in succession on branches of thorns, which pierced deeply into her flesh, causing inexplicable pain. Another time she burned her feet, as is done to prisoners, wishing thus to give herself the stamp and mark of a slave of Christ; but what attests far better the solidity of her virtue, is the unalterable gentleness, patience, joy even, manifested by her in the sufferings which she experienced toward the close of life. . . .

She was at last attacked by a malady, which was at once deemed mortal; and that at a time when the labors in the field so engaged all, that she could scarcely expect care from any one. She remained alone whole days with a platter of Indian corn, and a little water beside her bed. Delighted to behold herself thus forsaken of men, she communed constantly with her God, and found the days only too short. On Tuesday in Holy Week, 1678 [1680], she grew worse and received Holy Viaticum. The missionary wished also to administer Extreme Unction at once, but she assured him that it could be deferred till next day. She spent all the ensuing night in a loving colloquy with her divine Saviour, and with His Holy Mother, whom she had always singularly honored, regarding herself as a spouse of Christ, and as attached to the retinue of the Queen of Virgins.

On Wednesday morning she received the sacred anointing, and about three o'clock in the afternoon she expired after a gentle agony of half an hour, retaining her complete consciousness and sound judgment till her last sigh. . . . Her countenance, extremely attenuated by austerity and by her last illness, suddenly changed as soon as she ceased to live. It was seen assuming a rosy tint that she had never had; nor were her features the same. Nothing could be more beautiful, but with that beauty which love of virtue inspires. The people were never weary gazing on her, and each retired, his heart full of the desire to become a saint. As a distinction her body was placed in a coffin, and her tomb soon became celebrated by the concourse of the faithful, who flocked from all parts of Canada, and by the miracles wrought there. . . .

20. The French Récollets in the Illinois Country, 1680

EVERY religious order that engaged in missionary activities in colonial North America had its toll of martyrs. From the time when Juan de Padilla, O.F.M., the protomartyr of the United States, was murdered c. 1542 by the Plains Indians of the Southwest, the sons of St. Francis continued to give their lives in pursuit of their high ideal of converting the savages. As friends of the remarkable explorer, René-Robert Cavelier, Sieur de La Salle (1643–1687), the French Franciscans, or Récollets, played a prominent role in his far-flung expeditions in the Mississippi Valley. Thus we find two of these friars, Zénobe Membré (1645–1689) and Gabriel de la Ribourde (d. 1680), carrying on their missionary labors in 1680 at Fort Crêvecoeur near present-day Peoria, Illinois. An outbreak of war between the Iroquois and the Illinois compelled the French to abandon the area, and the description which Membré wrote of their experiences combined an explanation of why the missionaries had made so few converts with a touching account of the murder of his confrere which took place in September, 1680, at a point along the Illinois River some distance west of the present town of Seneca, Illinois. Membré himself met a violent death in January, 1689, along with his fellow religious, Maxim Le Clercq, when they were murdered by Karankawa Indians at Fort St. Louis near Matagorda Bay, Texas, where they had accompanied La Salle on his fatal expedition of 1684. Source: John Gilmary Shea (Ed.), *Discovery and Exploration of the Mississippi Valley* (New York: J. S. Redfield, 1852), pp. 152–153, 157–159.

Meanwhile, from the flight and desertion of our men about the middle of March to the month of September, Father Gabriel and I devoted ourselves constantly to the mission. An Illinois named Asapista, with whom the sieur de la Salle had contracted friendship, adopted Father Gabriel as his son, so that that good father found in his cabin a subsistence in the Indian fashion. As wine failed us for the celebration of the divine mysteries, we found means, toward the close of August, to get wild grapes which began to ripen, and we made very good wine which served us to say mass till the second disaster, which happened a few days after. The cluster of these grapes are of prodigious size, a very agreeable taste, and have seeds larger than those of Europe.

With regard to conversions, I can not rely on any. During the whole time Father Gabriel unraveled their language a little, and I can say that I spoke so as to make myself understood by the Indians on all that I wished; but there is in these savages such an alienation from the faith, so brutal and narrow a mind, such corrupt and anti-christian morals, that great time would be needed to hope for any fruit. It is, however, true that I found many of quite docile character. We baptized some dying children, and two or three dying persons who manifested proper dispositions. As these people are entirely material in their ideas, they would have submitted to baptism, had we liked, but without any knowledge of the sacrament. We found two who had joined us, and promised to follow us everywhere; we believed that they would keep their word, and that by this means we would insure their baptisms; but I afterward felt great scruples when I learned that an Indian named Chassagonaché, who had been baptized, had died in the hands of the medicine-men, abandoned to their superstitions, and consequently doubly a child of hell.

During the summer, we followed our Indians in their camps, and to the chase. I also made a voyage to the Myamis to learn something of their dispositions; thence I went to visit other villages of the Illinois all, however, with no great success, finding only cause for chagrin at the deplorable state and blindness of these nations. It is such that I can not express it fully. . . . [Shortly thereafter war broke between the Iroquois and the Ilinois and the French had to flee]. The reverend father Gabriel, the sieur de Tonty,[1] the few French who were with us, and myself, began our march on the 18th of September, without provisions, food, or anything, in a wretched bark canoe, which breaking the next day, compelled us to land about noon to repair it. Father Gabriel seeing the place of our landing fit for walking in the prairies and hills with little groves, as if planted by hand, retired there to say his breviary while we were working at the canoe all the rest of the day. We were full eight leagues from the village ascending the river. Toward evening I went to look for the father seeing that he did not return; all our party did the same; we fired repeatedly, to direct him, but in vain; and as we had reason to fear the Iroquois during the night, we crossed to the other side of the river and lit up fires which were also useless. The next morning at daybreak, we returned to the same side where we were the day before, and remained till noon, making all possible search. We entered the wood, where we found several fresh trails, as well as in the prairie on the bank of the river. We followed them one by one without discovering anything, except that M. de Tonty had ground to believe and fear that some hostile parties were in ambush to cut us all off, for seeing us take flight, the

[1] Henri de Tonty (1650–1704), French explorer, established Arkansas Post at the mouth of the Arkansas River in 1686, the earliest French settlement in the lower Mississippi Valley.

savages had imagined that we declared for the Ilinois. I insisted on staying to wait for positive tidings; but the sieur de Tonty forced me to embark at three o'clock, maintaining that the father had been killed by the enemy, or else had walked on along the bank, so that following it constantly, we should at last infallibly meet him. We got, however, no tidings of him, and the more we advanced, the more this affliction unmanned us, and we supported this remnant of a languishing life by the potatoes and garlick, and other roots, that we found by scraping the ground with our fingers.

We afterward learned that we should have expected him uselessly, as he had been killed soon after landing. The Kikapous, a little nation you may observe on the west, quite near the Winnebagoes, had sent some of their youth in war-parties against the Iroquois, but learning that the latter were attacking the Ilinois, the war-party came after them. Three braves who formed a kind of advanced guard having met the good father alone, although they knew that he was not an Iroquois, killed him for all that, cast his body into a hole, and carried off even his breviary, and diurnal, which soon after came to the hands of a Jesuit father. They carried off the scalp of this holy man, and vaunted of it in their village as an Iroquois scalp. Thus died this man of God by the hands of some mad youths. We can say of his body what the Scripture remarks of those whom the sanguinary Herod immolated to his fury, "Non erat qui sepeliret." Surely he deserved a better fate, if, indeed, we can desire a happier one before God, than to die in the exercise of the apostolic functions, by the hands of nations to whom we are sent by God. He had not been merely a religious of common and ordinary virtue; it is well known that he had in Canada, from 1670, maintained the same sanctity of life which he had shown in France as superior, inferior, and master of novices. He had for a long time in transports of fervor acknowledged to me the profound grief which he felt at the utter blindness of these people, and that he longed to be an anathema for their salvation. His death, I doubt not, has been precious before God, and will one day have its effect in the vocation of these people to the faith, when it shall please the Almighty to use his great mercy. . . .

21. Louis Hennepin's Description of the Difficulties Encountered in Trying to Convert the Indians, 1697

THE French Récollets inaugurated their labors in North America in 1615. Among the most colorful — and controversial — of these friars was Louis Hennepin (c. 1640–c. 1701), a native of the Low Countries. Hennepin was one of the most widely traveled of all the colonial missionaries and he later wrote extensively — although not always accurately — of his experiences. He was with La Salle on the famous voyage of the *Griffon* westward through the Great Lakes in 1679, and in 1680 it was Hennepin who discovered and named St. Anthony Falls at the present site of Minneapolis. The following account describes the intellectual difficulties encountered in trying to win the Indians to the Catholic faith, and the chief obstacles mentioned by Hennepin, *mutatis mutandis,* were found among practically all the native tribes. Source: Reuben Gold Thwaites (Ed.), *Louis Hennepin, A New Discovery of a Vast Country in America* (Chicago: A. C. McClurg & Co., 1903), II, 457–474.

CHAP. XII

What Method is most proper to convert the Savages; what Manner of Persons they are that ought not to be baptized.

Our ancient Missionary Recollects of *Canada,* and those that succeeded them in that work, have always given it for their opinion, and I now own 'tis mine, that the way to succeed in converting the Barbarians, is to endeavour to make them men before we go about to make them Christians. Now in order to civilize them, 'tis necessary that the *Europeans* should mix with them, and that they should dwell together, which can never be done for certain till the Colonies are augmented: but it must be acknowledged, that the Company of *Canada* Merchants, have made great Obstacles to the increasing of the Colonies; for out of greediness to keep all the Trade in their own hands, these Gentlemen would never permit any particular Society to settle themselves in the Country, nor suffer the Missionaries to perswade [*sic*] the Barbarians to dwell constantly in a place. Yet before this be done, there's no way to convert these Unbelievers. Thus the covetousness of those who are for getting a great deal in a short time, has mightly retarded the establishment of the Gospel among the Savages.

Hence 'tis manifest, that the office of a Missionary is very troublesome and laborious amongst these numerous Nations, and it must be granted that 'tis necessary to spend many Years, and undergo a great deal of pains to civilize People so extremely stupid and barbarous.

And therefore, one would not venture without much caution, to administer the Sacraments to adult Persons, who pretend themselves Converts; for we see that after so many Years of Mission, there has been but little progress made, though no pains have been wanting on the Missionary's hands.

So that Christianity is not like to gain much ground among the Savages, till the Colonies are strengthened by a great Number of Inhabitants, Artisans and Workmen, and then the Treaty betwixt the Barbarians and us should be freer, and extended to all *Europeans:* But chiefly it should be endeavour'd to fix the Barbarians to a certain dwelling Place, and introduce our Customs and Laws amongst them, further'd by the Assistance of zealous People in *Europe,* Colleges might be founded to breed up the young Savages in the Christian Faith, which might in time contribute very much to the Conversion of their Country-men. This is a very proper Method without doubt, to strengthen the Temporal and Spiritual Interests of the Colonies; but the generality of Mankind are bent upon Gain and Traffick, and are little concern'd to procure God's Blessing upon them, and endeavour the advancement of his Glory.

God is often pleas'd to prove his Children, and amongst 'em those that employ themselves in saving Souls, by those means that most afflict them, but Dangers, Labors, Sufferings, and even Death it self would be welcome to them, provided in sacrificing themselves for the Salvation of their Brethren, God would afford them the Consolation to see their Undertakings Crown'd with success to his Glory, and the Conversion of Infidels.

It is impossible for us to look upon so great a Number of People as this relation mentions, and consider the little progress Religion has made among the Savages of these vast Countries, but we must needs admire the inscrutable Decrees of God, and cry out with the Apostle, *O the Depth of the Riches of the Wisdom and Knowledge of God!* a great Number of learned secular Priests, and zealous Religious men of our Order, have carried the Light of the Gospel into all Parts of the Earth, and labour'd hard in the Lord's Vineyard. But God would have us know, that the Conversion of Souls is the Work of his Grace, the blessed Moments of which are not yet come. . . .

These miserable dark Creatures listen to all we say concerning our Mysteries, just as if 'twere a Song; they are naturally very vitious, and addicted to some Superstitions that signifie nothing; there Customs are savage, brutal and barbarous; they will suffer themselves to be baptized ten times a Day for a Glass of Brandy, or a Pipe of Tobacco, and offer their Children to be baptiz'd, but without any Religious Motive. Those that one takes the pains to instruct, for a Winter together, as I my self taught some of them while I dwelt at Fort *Frontenac,* give no better sign of Edification, than others in our Articles of Faith: so wrapt up are they in Insensibility, to what concerns Religion, which occasion'd terrible Checks of Conscience in our Religious, in the beginning of their Mission among the People of *Canada;* they saw that the few Persons of years of Discretion that they had instructed, and afterwards admitted to Baptism, soon fell again into their ordinary indifference for Salvation, and that the Children follow'd the unhappy Example of their Parents, insomuch that 'twas no better than a plain of profanation of Baptism to administer it to them. . . .

CHAP. XIII

The Barbarians of North-America *don't acknowledg any God. Of the pretended Souls of terrestrial Animals.*

Our antient Missionaries Recollects were acquainted with several different Nations within the compass of 600 leagues in *North-America;* and I have been among many more, because I went farther than any of them, having made a Voyage all along the River of St. *Lawrence,* and *Meschasipi.* I observed, as my Predecessors, that the Savages don't want good Sense in which concerns the general and particular Interest of their Nation. They pursue their Point, and take right Methods to come to the end of their designs; but 'tis what I am astonished at, that whilst they are so clear sighted in their common Affairs, they should have such extravagant notions of the concerns of Religion, the Manners, Laws, and Maxims of Life.

We must all of us own, that almost all the Savages in general have no Belief of a Deity, and that they are incapable of the common and ordinary Arguments and Reasonings that the rest of Mankind are led by upon this Subject; so dark and stupid are their Understandings. At the same time we may acknowledg, that now and then in some of them we discover some glimmerings of a confus'd Notion of God. Some will confess, but very cloudily, that the Sun is God: Others say, 'tis a Genius that rules in the Air: Some again look upon the Heavens as a kind of Divinity. But these only make a shew of believing something that we can hardly guess at: we can't fix them to any settled

Principle. The Nations Southward seem to believe an Universal Spirit that governs all: they imagine after a fashion, that there's a Spirit in every thing, even in those that are inanimate; and they address themselves to it sometimes, and beg something of it; as we took notice of one Barbarian, who made a kind of Sacrifice upon an Oak, at the Cascade of St. *Anthony* of *Padua,* upon the River *Meschasipi.*

All these Nations don't profess their Belief of a Deity out of any respect to Religion: They talk of it ordinarily, as a thing they were prepossessed with; or frolicksomly, not regarding any thing they say themselves, any otherwise than as a kind of a Fable. They have no outward Ceremony to signify that they worship any Deity: There's no Sacrifice, Priest, Temple, nor any other Token of Religion amongst them.

Their Dreams are to them instead of Prophecy, Inspiration, Laws, Commandments, and Rules, in all their Enterprizes, in War, Peace, Commerce, and Hunting: They regard them as Oracles. The Opinion they have of their Dreams draws them into a kind of necessity to be ruled by them; for they think 'tis an Universal Spirit, that inspires them by Dreams, and adviseth them what to do: And they carry this so far, that if their Dream orders them to kill a Person, or commit any other wicked Action, they presently execute it, and make satisfaction for it afterwards, as we shall show anon. The Parents dream for their Children, the Captains for their Village. There are some among them, that take upon them to interpret Dreams, and explain them after their own fancy or inclination; and if their Interpretations don't prove true, they are not lookt upon as Cheats ere the more for that.

Some have taken notice, that when they meet with any Cascade or Fall or Waters, which is difficult to cross, and apprehend any danger, they throw a Bever's [*sic*] skin, Tobacco, Porcelain, or some such matter into it by way of Sacrifice, to gain the Favor of the Spirit that presides there.

There's no Nation but what have their Jugglers, which some count Sorcerers: but 'tis not likely that they are under any Covenant, or hold communication with the Devil. At the same time, one may venture to say, that the evil Spirit has a hand in the Tricks of these Jugglers, and makes use of them to amuse these poor People, and render them more incapable of receiving the Knowledge of the true God. They are very fond of these Jugglers, tho they cozen them perpetually.

These Impostors would be counted Prophets, who fortel things to come: they would be look'd upon as having almost an infinite Power: they boast that they make Rain or fair Weather, Calms and Storms, Fruitfulness or Barrenness of the Ground, Hunting lucky or unlucky. They serve for Physicians too, and frequently apply such Remedies, as have no manner of virtue to cure the Distemper.

Nothing can be imagined more horrible than the Cries and Yellings, and the strange Contortions of these Rascals, when they fall to juggling or conjuring; at the same time they do it very cleverly. They never cure any one, nor predict any thing that falls out, but purely by chance: mean time they have a thousand Fetches to bubble (*i.e.* cheat) the poor people, when the accident does not answer their Predictions and Remedies; for, as I said, they are both Prophets and Quacks. They do nothing without Presents or Reward. 'Tis true, if these Impostors are not very dexterous at recommending themselves, and bringing themselves off, when any person dies under their hands, or Enterprizes do not succeed as they promis'd, they are sometimes murdered upon the place, without any more Formality.

These blind Wretches are wedded to many other Superstitions, which the Devil makes use of to delude them: They believe that several kinds of Animals have a reasonable Soul: They have an unaccountable Veneration for certain Bones of Elks, Bevers, and other Beasts; they never throw these to their Dogs, which are the only Domestick Animals they keep, because they serve for Hunting: So they preserve these precious Bones, and are very unwilling to cast them into the River. They pretend, that the Souls of these Animals come back into the World to see how they treat their Bodies, and give notice accordingly to the rest of the Beasts both dead and living: and that if they should find they are ill us'd, the Beasts of that kind would never let themselves be taken, neither in this World nor the next.

One may say, that the Corruption of Sin has spread a strange Darkness in the Souls of these unhappy people, and a perfect Insensibility to all Religion; insomuch that they are not to be match'd in any History. 'Tis true, they are obstinately superstitious in some things; and yet at the same time, they are not mov'd by any principle of Religion. 'Tis nothing but strong Prejudice and Imagination. When we dispute with them, and put them to a nonplus, they hold their tongues; their Minds are stupid, their Faculties are besotted. If we propose our Mysteries to them, they heed them as indifferently as their own nonsensical Whimsies. I have met with some of them, who seem to acknowledge that there is one first Principle that made all things; but this makes but a slight Impression upon their Mind, which returns again to its ordinary Deadness, and former Insensibility.

CHAP. XIV

Of the great difficulty in converting the Savages. Of the Prayers they get by rote; and of Martyrdom.

The great Insensibility of these Barbarians is caused principally by their Carelessness and neglect to be thoroughly instructed. They come to us, and attend to what we say, purely out of Idleness, and natural Curiosity to converse with us, as we with them; or rather they are tempted to follow us, by the Kindness and Flatteries we express towards them, or because of the Benefit their Sick receive from us, or out of hope to gain by trafficking with us; or lastly, because we are Europeans, and they think us stouter than themselves, and hope we will defend them from their Enemies.

We teach them Prayers; but they repeat them like Songs, without any distinction by Faith. Those we have catechized a long time, are very wavering, except some few: They renounce all, return into their Woods, and take up their old Superstitions upon the least Crotchet that comes into their Heads.

I don't know whether their Predecessors had any Knowledge of a God; but 'tis certain their Language, which is very natural and expressive in every thing else, is so barren on this Subject, that we can't find any expression in it to signify the Deity, or any one of our mysteries, not even the most common: this gives us great perplexity when we would convert them.

Another great Obstacle to their Conversion is this: Most of them have several Wives; and in the Northern parts they change them as often as they please: They can't conceive how people can tie themselves indissolubly to one person in Marriage. See how silly you are, cry they, when we argue with them about it. My Wife is uneasy to me, I am so to her; she'll agree very well with such a one, who is at odds with his Wife: now why should we four lead a miserable Life all our days?

Another hinderance lies in a Custom of theirs, not to contradict any Man; they think every one ought to be left to his own Opinion, without being thwarted: they believe, or make as if they believed all you say to them; but 'tis their Insensibility, and Indifference for every thing, especially Matters of Religion, which they never trouble themselves about.

America is no place to go out of a desire to suffer Martyrdom, taking the Word in a Theological Sense: The Savages never put any Christian to death upon the score of his Religion; they leave every body at liberty in Belief: They like the outward Ceremonies of our Church, but no more. These Barbarians never make War, but for the Interest of their Nation; they don't kill people, but in particular Quarrels, or when they are brutish, or drunk, or in revenge, or infatuated with a Dream, or some extravagant Vision: they are incapable of taking away any Person's Life out of hatred to his Religion.

They are brutish in all their Inclinations; they are naturally Gluttons, and know no other Happiness in this Life, but the pleasure of eating and drinking: This is remarkable in their very eyes, and their Diversions, which are always begun and ended with feasting.

The Passion of Revenge which they are possessed with, is another great Obstacle to Christianity: They are very tender and affectionate to their own Nation, but cruel and revengeful beyond imagination towards their Enemies: They are naturally Inconstant, Revilers, Scoffers, and Lascivious. In short, among all the Vices they are addicted to, we can perceive no Principle of Religion or Morality: and to be sure this must needs render their Conversion extremely difficult.

To persuade them to any thing, and dispose them to the Faith, 'tis requisite to make them familiar with us, and contract a good acquaintance with them; but this is not to be done presently, because first of all the Colonies ought to be multiplied, and planted every where. When they have passed away a few Weeks with the Europeans, they are obliged to go to War, Hunting, or Fishing, for their Subsistence, and this depraves 'em extremely. They should be fix'd, inticed to clear the Ground, and cultivate it, and work at several Trades, as the Europeans do; and then we should see 'em reform their barbarous Customs, and become more civiliz'd, as well towards one another as us. . . .

22. The Quebec Seminary Priests in the Mississippi Valley, 1700, and the Installation of the First Pastor at Mobile, September 28, 1704

WHEN the Holy See erected the Vicariate Apostolic of New France into the Diocese of Quebec in 1674 it was made to embrace all the territories of North America then claimed by the French crown. Canonically speaking, therefore, the Church in the Mississippi Valley was under the jurisdiction of the Bishop of Quebec and remained so until after the American Revolution. In 1665 François de Montmorency de Laval (1623–1708), first Bishop of Quebec, had affiliated his infant seminary to the Seminary of Foreign Missions at Paris, and the missionary spirit was strong among the graduates of the Quebec institution. In time they sought to enter the western mission field and in May, 1698, they received authorization to do so, with the result that at mission stations among the Tamarois, Cahokias, and other tribes along the Mississippi friction developed between them and the Jesuits who had previously been on the scene. Apart, however, from the differences between the two groups over the missions to the Indians — wherein both did notable work — the secular priest performed valuable service by ministering to the French inhabitants of the scattered western settlements. To them was entrusted the first canonically erected parish in the western country when, on July 20, 1703, Bishop Jean Baptiste de la Croix de Saint Vallier (1653–1727) performed that action for the Church of the Immaculate Conception at Fort Louis, the forerunner of the present city of Mobile, Alabama. The first two documents that follow are excerpts from letters which Father Jean Bergier (d. 1707), a seminary priest, addressed to the Bishop of Quebec from the Tamarois post, the first in late February, 1700, the second dated June 14, 1700. The third document describes the formal installation of the first pastor by Father Antoine Davion with the civil officials in attendance and attesting the act. Sources: Edward Joseph Fortier, "The Establishment of the Tamarois Mission," *Transactions of the Illinois State Historical Society,* No. 13 (1909), 236–237; John Gilmary Shea, *History of the Catholic Church in the United States* (New York: John G. Shea, 1886), I, 547–548.

At the Tamarois, February, 1700.

I related to your highness our trip to the Illinois, from which place I wrote you all I had found out about the condition of the missions and that which concerns the government of your church. There remains but to inform you of the condition of the latter.

I arrived there the 7th of this month with young Mr. de St. Cosme. I have counted there a hundred cabins in all, or thereabouts, of which nearly half are vacant because the greater part of the Cahokias are still in winter quarters twenty or twenty-five leagues from here up the Mississippi.

The village is composed of Tamarois, Cahokias, some Michigans and Peorias. There are also some Missouri cabins, and shortly, there are to come about thirty-five cabins of this last named nation who are winterquartering, some ten or fifteen leagues from here below the village, on the river. We must not, however, count this nation as forming part of the village and of the Tamarois mission, because it remains there only a few months to make its Indian wheat, while awaiting a day to return to its village, which is more than a hundred leagues away, upon the shores of the Missouri river. This it has not dared to undertake for the last few years for fear of being surprised and defeated on the way by some other hostile nation.

The Tamarois and the Cahokias are the only ones that really form part of this mission. The Tamarois have about thirty cabins and the Cahokias have nearly twice that number. Although the Tamarois are at present less numerous than the Cahokias, the village is still called Tamaroa, gallicized "Des Tamarois," because the Tamarois have been the first and are still the oldest inhabitants and have first lit a fire there, to use the Indian expression. . . .

At the Tamarois, June 14, 1700.

We have frequent alarms here and we have several times been obliged to receive within our walls nearly all the women and children of the village. Pentecost Sunday there was one [alarm] which was not without consequence. Four Sioux on the edge of the woods of the Tamarois, in plain sight of the village, cut off the neck of a slave belonging to a Frenchman; stabbed two women to death and scalped them; wounded a girl with a knife and crushed another under foot. They were all picking strawberries. We were about to finish singing compline when the chief ran to our door to warn us that the Sioux were killing them. He threw himself into Mr. de St. Cosme's canoe, with some Indians and Frenchmen to reconnoitre, partly by water and then by land. Great excitement prevailed. Finally the Sioux were discovered and three were captured, killed, burned and eaten. . . . The last of these three Sioux, who was burned only the next day was baptized by F. Pinet who made use of the "Lorrain" as an interpreter. . . .

One may say that we are "inter lupos, in medio nationis pravae et perversae." Their greatest and most universal passion is to destroy, scalp and eat men, that, is all their ambition, their glory; an essential drawback to Christianity, as long as it will last. But the mercy of Jesus Christ is all powerful. Beseech him that he diffuse it very abundantly over this mission and over the missionaries and that he make them 'Prudentes ut serpentes, simplices ut comumbat [*sic*] — Amen.'

I, undersigned, Priest and Missionary Apostolic, attest to all whom it may concern that in the year of our salvation 1704, on the 28th of the month of September, by virtue of letters of provision and collation granted and sealed on the 20th of July of last year, by which Monseigneur the most Illustrious and most Reverend Bishop of Quebec erects a parish church in the place called Fort Louis de la Louisiane, and the cure and care of which he gives to Mr. Henry Roulleux de la Vente, Missionary Apostolic of the diocese of Bayeux, I have placed the said priest in actual and corporal possession of said parish church and of all the rights thereto belonging, after observing the accustomed and requisite ceremonies, namely, the entry into the church, the sprinkling of holy water, the kissing of the high altar, the touching of the missal, the visit to the Blessed Sacrament of the altar, the ringing of the bells, which taking of possession I attest that no one opposed.

Given in the parish church of Fort Louis, the day of the month and year aforesaid, in presence of John Baptiste de Bienville, Lieutenant of the King, and Commander of the said fort; of Peter du Quay de Boisbriant, major; Nicolas de la Salle, scribe and acting commissary of the Marine.

Davion, Bienville, Boisbriant, de la Salle.

23. The Government's Provision for Capuchin Missionaries in French Louisiana, May 16, 1722

FRANCE staked its claim to possession of the Mississippi Valley on the Jolliet-Marquette expedition of 1673. In the late seventeenth century the rivalry between Spain, France, and England for the western country grew keener, and after the efforts of a number of individual Frenchmen to settle the area had failed the French government determined upon turning over responsibility for the task to a commercial company. As a consequence, the Company of the West (later called the Company of the Indies) was formed in August, 1717. The company was anxious to have the participation of the Church in its undertaking and, therefore, the council of the company — with the consent of the Bishop of Quebec — divided the Province of Louisiana into three ecclesiastical districts which were assigned to the Carmelites, the Jesuits, and the Capuchins. The question of ecclesiastical jurisdiction caused a great deal of friction and after a brief time the Carmelites withdrew. But the Capuchins remained on in Louisiana from their advent in 1722 down to and beyond the purchase of the colony by the United States in 1803. From the outset these friars were entirely dependent upon the government as is evident in the provisions made for them by the council of the company in the document which follows. It provides a further example of the close union of Church and State which obtained in Louisiana all through the colonial era. Source: Claude L. Vogel, O.F.M.Cap., *The Capuchins in French Louisiana (1722–1766)* (Washington: The Catholic University of America Press, 1928), pp. 25–26.

His Majesty, having granted Letters Patent of August 1717, the colony of Louisiana to the Company of the West, now Company of the Indies, on condition that the said Company build churches at its own expense in the places where it forms settlements and maintain there the necessary number of ecclesiastics to work for the salvation of the inhabitants, French, Indian and Negro, and having accorded to the Company the right of patronage and the faculty to name the pastors and other ecclesiastics as shall be suitable to establish within the colony, We are informed that hitherto the Company has not taken the proper measures to fulfill that which in this matter is the intention of His Majesty; and it being necessary to make provisions to this end, We have believed that, to establish religion solidly in the colony and to work there successfully for the glory of God, We cannot make a better choice than the Capuchin Fathers of the Province of Champagne, who have shown so much zeal for that mission that We cannot doubt that they will acquit themselves most worthily and will furnish the necessary number of religious. Wherefore, We have agreed upon and have accepted Father Bruno of Langres, Father Christopher of Chaumont, Father Philibert of Viander and Brother Eusebius of Chaumont, to establish under the authority of the Bishop of Quebec a convent of their order at New Orleans, situated on the St. Louis River [Mississippi] in the land of Louisiana, to perform through the superior of the convent the pastoral functions in the town; to send to all the Company's settlements, extending from the mouth of the river unto and comprising the bank of the Wabash [Ohio], religious who shall be demanded from him by the Council of the colony; to conduct there the divine service and to administer the sacraments in the capacity of pastors and according to the faculties given him by the Bishop of Quebec; to have jurisdiction over the other ecclesiastics who shall be in the parts established along the river or its affluents and, in general, to do through the superior of the convent all that he shall judge necessary for the good and advancement of the Roman, Catholic and Apostolic Religion, and for the salvation of souls. We order the commanders and the directors of the colony to install the Capuchin Fathers as explained above, to aid and protect them with all their power in the exercise of their functions both as regards their rule and their Apostolic and parochial ministry. We order, therefore, that there be constructed in New Orleans at the expense of the Company a parish church of convenient size, with an adjoining house for four religious, in order to put the Capuchins in possession there; that they be given in the same place sufficient ground for a garden and poultry yard, and that in whatever place of the colony they may be established, the Company shall furnish them lodging and all that shall be necessary for divine service.

We also order that for their maintenance, they be provided by the Company with the necessary clothing according to their Rule, and for their sustenance, namely, for each religious, one cask of Bordeaux wine, two quarts of flour, one half quart of bacon, one half quart of beef, one half quart (ancre) of brandy, twenty-five pounds of large beans, or like quantity of peas and kidney beans, eight pounds of Holland or *Gruyere* cheese, twenty-four pounds of candles, one half pound of pepper, twenty pots of vinegar, twenty-five pounds of salt and twelve pounds of olive oil.

We also expect that they be provided from the magazines of the Company with household utensils and with whatever tools may be necessary for their houses, on condition that all they shall receive in this way from the Company shall be held only for use, and that they shall not cultivate more land than is required for the needs of their houses in the colony. We finally enjoin the Directors of the colony to keep and send annually to the Company a particular account of that which shall be furnished the Capuchin Fathers, in which account shall be noted the value of the furniture in money at the rate of its worth in the market of the country.

Given at Paris, May 16, 1722, *Signed:* Jagon de Mauhault, Ougran, Fontaineu.

24. The Banishment of the Jesuits From Louisiana and the Illinois Country According to François Philibert Watrin, S.J., September 3, 1764

THE current of opinion in the countries of Europe was often felt with real force in their distant American colonies. By the mid-eighteenth century the Society of Jesus had attained great strength and influence in France, but it had also acquired many powerful enemies among the disciples of the Enlightenment, the nobility, and even so highly placed a figure as Jeanne Poisson, Marquise de Pompadour, the mistress of Louis XV. This enmity finally triumphed over the Jesuits and their supporters and in 1762 there began the systematic suppression of their society. The French Jesuits had been evangelizing the Illinois Country ever since Jacques Marquette, S.J., had introduced Christianity to the Mississippi Valley at the Mission of the Immaculate Conception which he established among the Kaskaskia Indians at one of their villages on the Illinois River in the spring of 1675. Moreover, they had been steadily at work in Louisiana since the founding of their first mission in that colony in 1725. But the action taken in France against the Jesuits soon found a counterpart in the colonies and on July 9, 1763, the superior council of Louisiana decreed the suppression of the society in that colony and the Illinois Country. It need hardly be emphasized what a blow this proved to the Church's missions in those vast areas. François Philibert Watrin, S.J. (1697–1771), was superior of the Illinois mission at the time, a man who had spent thirty years in Louisiana. After his banishment to Europe he wrote an account of the Jesuits' last days in the colony and gave details of the brutal manner in which the missionaries' work was brought to an abrupt close. Source: Reuben Gold Thwaites (Ed.), *The Jesuit Relations and Allied Documents* (Cleveland: Burrows Brothers Co., 1900), LXX, 212–301.

. . . In the month of June, 1763, the Jesuits of New Orleans, the capital of Louisiana, were still between hope and fear as to their future fate. As early as the preceding year, they had seen their enemies distribute with a triumphant air, manuscript copies of the decree given by the Parliament of Paris, August 6, 1761. But people worthy of respect had calmed their fears. They were expecting a great deal from the information given in their favor, and above all, from the petition addressed to the King by the bishops of France. They finally learned what they were to expect, at the arrival of the ship, which brought, with the news of peace, orders for their destruction. . . .

Proceedings were begun. It was decreed that the Institute of the Jesuits should be brought to the council, to be examined. It was a great undertaking for this tribunal. All the judges who composed it ought at least to have studied theology, and civil and ecclesiastical law. But, above all, they ought to have understood the language in which the institute is written. Now, this is not the kind of knowledge that is required from judges of colonies. In selecting them, search is not made for pupils of universities, but those among the inhabitants who show some capacity for business are chosen. Accordingly, one finds in these councils elderly shopkeepers, physicians, and officers of troops. . . .

For these reasons we are justified in saying that it was a great undertaking for the council of New Orleans to pronounce upon the Institute of the Jesuits. . . .

The decree was declared on the 9th of July. It was said that the Institute of the Jesuits was hostile to the royal authority, the rights of the bishops, and the public peace and safety; and that the vows uttered according to this institute were null. It was prohibited to these Jesuits, hitherto thus styled, to take that name hereafter, or to wear their customary garb, orders being given them to assume that of secular ecclesiastics. Excepting their books and some wearing apparel which was allowed to them, all their property, real and personal, was to be seized and sold at auction. It was ordained that the chapel ornaments and the sacred vessels of New Orleans should be delivered up to the Reverend Capuchin Fathers; that the chapel ornaments and sacred vessels of the Jesuits living in the country of the Illinois should be delivered up to the Royal Procurator for that country, and that the chapels should then be demolished; and that, finally, the aforesaid Jesuits, so-called, should return to France, embarking upon the first ships ready to depart, — prohibiting them, meanwhile, from remaining together. A sum of six hundred livres was assigned to pay each one's passage, and another, of 1,500 francs, for their sustenance and support for six months. They were enjoined to present themselves, after that term, to Monsieur the duke de Choiseul, secretary of State in the department of marine, to ask him for the pensions which would be assigned from the proceeds of the sale of their property. . . .

. . . It is time to speak of the execution of the decree; it was to be carried out first at New Orleans, and afterward in the Illinois country, at a distance of four or five hundred leagues. There was in that country, as has been said above, a mission of the Jesuits, established at four different posts. They were not forgotten, and a courier was sent to carry the decree of destruction. Meanwhile, it was executed promptly against those of New Orleans. Their establishment was quite near this town, and proportioned to the needs of twelve missionaries; there was quite a large gang of slaves for cultivating the land, and for plying other trades, as is the custom in the colonies; there were also various buildings, with herds of cattle and suitable works. Everything was seized, inventoried, and sold at auction, and this execution lasted a long time; those who were employed therein took their meals in the house. These were the higher officers of justice, with the lesser agents; it is right to suppose that the former kept themselves within the decent behavior that beseemed them, but the others did not consider themselves obliged to assume any disguise. They found themselves well feasted and they were sure that their employment was a lucrative one; so they did not dissemble their feelings. The superior of the Jesuits was obliged to be present at the great feasts which were given at his house during the depredation, and he saw the joy that was shown there. After the sale of the real and personal property, there remained the chapel, with its ornaments and sacred vessels: it was stated in the decree that these effects should be taken to the Reverend Capuchin Fathers; this was done, and it was the least objectionable use that could be made of them. After that, the chapel was razed to the ground; and the sepulcher of the bodies buried for thirty years in this place, and in the neighboring cemetery, remained exposed to profanation. The Jesuits who came back from Louisiana to France have often been asked the reason for this proceeding; they have been told what astonishment and horror was felt at this event; it has been said to them that this was only to be expected from open enemies of the Catholic religion; the Jesuits could only answer these sayings by silence.

The execution of the decree lacked nothing, save to send back the condemned to France; those who were at New Orleans did not wait to be notified of the order to depart. Father Carette embarked to cross over to San Domingo; Father Roy took refuge at Pensacola, at the very time when the English entered this port to take possession of it, and the Spaniards evacuated it by virtue of the treaty of peace; he entered the ship which was to bear the Governor of that place to Vera Cruz. The Father was welcomed there, by the Spanish Fathers of the college, with the greatest kindness; a little while afterward he was made an associate in the province that the Jesuits have in Mexico, by Father François Zéballos, superior of that province. His letter written upon this subject expressed most generous and most Christian sentiments, and all the Jesuits banished from the lands under French domination were invited thither to the same refuge.

Father Le Prédour was among the Alibamons, at a distance of about two hundred leagues, and much time was necessary for transmitting a copy of the decree to him. Then, after he had received it, he was obliged to await an opportunity to reach the fort of Mobile, and from that place, New Orleans; we have recently learned that he has returned to France. There were no more to send away, then, but Father Baudoin, superior of all missions; but he was seventy-two years old, and infirm, — as one may expect of a man who had passed thirty-five years in Louisiana, and of those thirty-five years about twenty in the midst of the forests, with the Chactas; he had no relatives in France, nor was he accustomed to this country; as he was born in Canada, he was permitted to remain. He was assigned a pension of nine hundred livres, which would be equivalent in France to the sum of three or four hundred francs. Monsieur Boré, an old resident of the country, offered him an asylum with himself, upon his estate, and thus proved the sincerity of the friendship which he had always shown toward the Jesuits.

Meanwhile the courier despatched to Illinois to bear the decree arrived on the night of September 23, at fort Chartres, distant six leagues from the residence of the Jesuits. He delivered to the procurator of the king the commission which charged him to execute the decree; and on the next day, about eight or nine o'clock in the morning, that officer of justice repaired to the house of the Jesuits, accompanied by the registrar and the baliff of that jurisdiction. Some days afterward, he tried to turn to account the moderation that he used in not arriving during the night, "as his orders directed," said he; with that exception, they ought to have been satisfied with his exactness. He read to Father Watrin, the superior, the decree of condemnation, and, having given him a copy of it, he made him at once leave his room to put the seal upon it; the same thing was done with the other missionaries who happened to be in the house. There remained one hall where they could remain together, although with great inconvenience; but this favor was refused them, because the guards placed in custody of the property seized opposed this; they were unwilling that the Jesuits should be able to watch their conduct so closely. The procurator of the King feared to displease these guardians, and would not permit the Jesuits even to remain at the house of one of their confrères, — who, being curé of the place, had his private lodging near the parish church; they did not put the seal thereon, because they knew there was nothing to seize. The missionaries, driven from their own house, found quarters as best they could. The superior, sixty-seven years old, departed on foot to find a lodging, a long league away, with a confrère of his, a missionary to the savages; and the French who met him on this journey groaned to see persecution begin with him.

As soon as the savages learned that he had arrived among them, they came to show to him and to Father Meurin, his associate, the share which they took in the distress of their Fathers; the news of their condemnation had already caused many tears to be shed in the village. They were asked why they were thus treated, especially in a country where so many disorders had been so long allowed. The old missionary, after several repeated interrogations, finally replied: *Arechi Kiécouègane tchichi ki canta manghi,* — *It is because we sternly condemn their follies.* They comprehended the meaning of this answer, — indeed they knew that the Jesuits, in whatever place they may be established, consider themselves bound by their profession to combat vice; and that, in fighting it, they make enemies for themselves.

The Christian savages proposed to send their chief men to Monsieur Neyon, commandant, and to Monsieur Bobé, subdeputy-commissary of the country, to ask that at least Father Meurin, their missionary, be kept in this mission. The two Jesuits told them plainly to do nothing of the kind, because this proceeding would be scoffed at and ineffectual, as having been suggested. They wished, then, to ask that at least the chapel and the house of the missionary be preserved, in order that the best instructed person among them might assemble the children and repeat prayers to them; and that every Sunday and feast-day he might summon those who prayed, that is to say, the Christians, — by the ringing of the bell, to fulfill as well as possible the duties of religion. They did, in fact, make such a request, and obtained what they asked.

Meanwhile, the Procurator of the King relaxed a little in his severity. About the same time he received in a single day four letters from Monsieur Bobé, the commissary, who begged him to moderate his zeal, and allowed the Jesuits to live together with their brethren, the curés of the French. They were closely crowded there, in a house that was built for only one man. Their rooms had been opened, in order that each might be able to take out his mattress and blankets, which they spread upon the floor in the house of the curé. This way of taking their rest, which lasted nearly a month, prepared them for the voyage which they were soon to make upon the Mississippi, for upon the banks of that river one encamps in hardly other fashion. The Jesuits were also permitted to take their clothes and their books, which the decree had left to them. At last, the support of these Fathers was provided for until the time when they should embark to go down to New Orleans. The greater part of the food that was found in their house, was given up to them, and this provision was, in fact, sufficient for the rest of the time that they passed in Illinois.

Finally, it came to making the inventory; time was necessary to collect and put in order the furniture of a large house, the chattels of an important estate, and the cattle scattered in the fields and woods. Besides, there was reason for not hurrying too much; the longer the delays the better they paid those who were employed in that task. . . .

Meanwhile, the auction was finished; the house, the furniture, the cattle, the land had been sold; the slaves were to be taken to New

Orleans, to be sold there for the benefit of the king; and the chapel was to be razed by the man to whom the house had been adjudged. The Jesuits were then permitted to reenter their former home, the use of which was, by a clause inserted in the bill of sale, reserved to them until their embarkation. They found it well cleared; nothing was left except the bedsteads and the straw mattresses; and, in order to lodge there they were obliged to borrow from their friends each a chair and a little table. They found their chapel in a still more melancholy condition; after the sacred vessels and the pictures had been taken away, the shelves of the altar had been thrown down; the linings of the ornaments had been given to negresses decried for their evil lives; and a large crucifix, which had stood above the altar, and the chandeliers, were found placed above a cupboard in a house whose reputation was not good. To see the marks of spoliation in the chapel, one might have thought that it was the enemies of the Catholic religion who had caused it. . . .

Finally the day set for the embarkation came; it was the 24th of November. The baggage of the Jesuits did not embarrass the vessel in which they had taken their passage; they had only their beds and their clothes in small quantities, with some provisions which they had saved for the voyage; this food served not only for them, but for forty-eight negroes embarked with them. These slaves no longer belonged to the Jesuits, having been confiscated for the benefit of the King. But their former masters always preserved the same care in regard to them, and shared quite willingly with these wretches the provisions which they had saved. . . .

The voyage, which might have been very long, lasted only twenty-seven days, because the weather was not so bad as it usually is at that season. The Jesuits found means to say mass every Sunday and every feast-day. . . . Finally, at seven or eight leagues from New Orleans, they reached the estate of Monsieur de Maccarty, former lieutenant of the King in that city, who by his kind attentions recalled . . . the benevolence he had always shown at Illinois. . . . But on departing from that estate, they found themselves in great perplexity. They saw that they were about to enter New Orleans, and they did not know where they could lodge; they were unable to enter their old house, knowing well that it was sold and occupied by other masters. . . . Meanwhile the Reverend Capuchin Fathers, hearing of the arrival of the Jesuits, had come . . . to the landing-place to manifest to them their intention of rendering them all the kind offices that they could . . . and during the six weeks which elapsed before they embarked, there were no marks of friendship which they did not receive from these Reverend Fathers. . . .

However, the Jesuits perceived that their departure was desired. The season was disagreeable, it being still the month of January, the time of rough seas. But an entirely new and well-built ship presented itself; it was the *La Minerve,* of Bayonne, commanded by Monsieur Balanquet, a famous shipowner in the last war, and very much esteemed for his integrity. These reasons determined the Jesuits to embark upon this ship. There were two, however, out of this band of six, who parted from them. Father de la Morinie, remembering that he had suffered upon the sea every evil that can be felt there, almost to death itself, postponed his departure until spring . . . and Father Meurin asked the Gentlemen of the Council for permission to return to the Illinois. This was a brave resolution, after the sale of all the property of the Jesuits: he could not count upon any fund for his subsistence, the French were under no obligation to him, and the savages have more need of receiving than means for giving. . . . His request was granted, and a promise was given to him that a pension of six hundred livres would be asked for him at the court. . . .

THE ENGLISH COLONIES

25. The Charter of Maryland, June 20, 1632

SIR GEORGE CALVERT (c. 1580–1632), one of the chief secretaries and favorites of King James I of England, belonged to that rather rare breed of men who do not hesitate to forfeit a promising political career when it conflicts with their religious convictions. After his conversion to Catholicism in 1625, Calvert resigned his royal secretaryship, although he continued to employ the favor which he retained at court to secure a haven of religious peace in the English colonies for his harassed coreligionists. Attempts to establish a settlement in Newfoundland and Virginia having failed, the first Baron of Baltimore died before he could fulfill his dream. But in June, 1632, Charles I redeemed his father's promises by issuing a generous charter to Baltimore's son, Cecilius Calvert. In view of the anti-Catholic laws of the mother country, and the hostility and suspicion that permeated the government of Charles I in all that related to Catholicism, it is not suprising to find the charter encouraging the erection of churches in the colony which were to be "dedicated and consecrated according to the Ecclesiastical Laws of our Kingdom of England. . . ." In actual fact, however, religious toleration for all Christians was preserved by Calvert, and by reason of the tact and common sense of the proprietor and his Catholic representatives in the colony that policy endured until it was abolished in 1654 by the Puritans who had overthrown Baltimore's government. Source: Francis Newton Thorpe (Ed.), *The Federal and State Constitutions* (Washington: Government Printing Office, 1909), III, 1677–1686.

. . . II. Whereas our well beloved and right trusty Subject Caecilius Calvert, Baron of Baltimore, in our Kingdom of Ireland . . . being animated with a laudable, and pious Zeal for extending the Christian Religion, and also the Territories of our Empire, hath humbly besought Leave of Us, that he may transport, by his own Industry, and Expense, a numerous Colony of the English Nation to a certain Region, herein after described, in a Country hitherto uncultivated, in the Parts of America, and partly occupied by Savages, having no Knowledge of the Divine Being, and that all that Region, with some certain Privileges, and Jurisdiction, appertaining unto the wholesome Government, and State of his Colony and Region aforesaid, may by our Royal Highness be given, granted, and confirmed unto him, and his Heirs.

III. Know Ye, therefore, that We . . . by this our present Charter

. . . do Give, Grant, and Confirm, unto the aforesaid Caecilius, now Baron of Baltimore, his Heirs, and Assigns, all that Part of the Peninsula, or Cherosonese, lying in the Parts of America, between the Ocean on the East, and the Bay of Chesapeake on the West . . .

IV. Also We do Grant . . . unto the said Baron of Baltimore . . . all Islands and Islets within the Limits aforesaid, all and singular Islands and Islets, from the Eastern Shore of the aforesaid Region, towards the East, which have been, or shall be formed in the Sea, situate within Ten marine Leagues from the said Shore . . . And furthermore the Patronages, and Advowsons of all Churches which (with the increasing Worship and Religion of Christ) within the said region . . . hereafter shall happen to be built, together with Licence, and Faculty of erecting and founding Churches, Chapels, and Places of Worship, in convenient and suitable places, within the Premises, and of causing the same to be dedicated and consecrated according to the Ecclesiastical Laws of our Kingdom of England, with all, and singular such, and as ample Rights, Jurisdictions, Privileges, Prerogatives, Royalties, Liberties, Immunities, and royal Rights, and temporal Franchises whatsoever, as well by Sea as by Land, within the Region . . . aforesaid, to be had, exercised, used, and enjoyed, as any Bishop of Durham, within the Bishoprick or County Palatine of Durham, in our Kingdom of England, ever heretofore, hath had, held, used, or enjoyed or of Right could, or ought to have, hold, use, or enjoy.

V. And we do by these Presents . . . Make, Create, and Constitute Him, the now Baron of Baltimore, and his Heirs, the true and absolute Lords and Proprietaries of the Region aforesaid, and of all other the Premises (except the before excepted) saving always the Faith and Allegiance and Sovereign Dominion due to Us . . . To Hold of Us . . . as of our Castle of Windsor, in our County of Berks, in free and common Soccage, by Fealty only for all Services, and not in Capite, nor by Knight's Service, Yielding therefore unto Us . . . Two Indian Arrows of these Parts, to be delivered at the said Castle of Windsor, every Year, on Tuesday in Easter Week: And also the fifth Part of all Gold and Silver Ore, which shall happen from Time to Time, to be found within the aforesaid Limits.

VI. Now, That the aforesaid Region . . . may be eminently distinguished above all other Regions of that Territory . . . Know Ye, that . . . We do . . . Erect and Incorporate the same into a Province, and nominate the same Maryland, by which Name We will that it shall from henceforth be called.

VII. And . . . We . . . do grant unto the said now Baron . . . and to his Heirs, for the good and happy Government of the said Province, free, full, and absolute Power, by the tenor of these Presents, to Ordain, Make, and Enact Laws, of what kind soever, according to their sound Discretions, whether relating to the Public State of the said Province, or the private Utility of Individuals, of and with the Advice, Assent, and Approbation of the Free-Men of the same Province, or of the greater Part of them, or of their Delegates or Deputies, whom We will shall be called together for the framing of Laws, when and as often as Need shall require, by the aforesaid now Baron of Baltimore . . . and in the Form which shall seem best to him . . . and duly to execute the same upon all Persons, for the Time being, within the aforesaid Province, and the Limits thereof, or under his or their Government and Power . . . by the Imposition of Fines, Imprisonment, and other Punishment whatsoever; even if it be necessary, and the Quality of the Offence require it, by Privation of Member, or Life . . . So, nevertheless, that the Laws aforesaid be consonant to Reason and be not repugnant or contrary, but (so far as conveniently may be) agreeable to the Laws, Statutes, Customs and Rights of this Our Kingdom of England.

XVII. Moreover, We will, appoint, and ordain, and by these Presents, for Us, our Heirs and Successors, do grant unto the aforesaid now Baron of Baltimore, his Heirs and Assigns, from Time to Time, forever, shall have, and enjoy the Taxes and Subsidies payable, or arising within the Ports, Harbors, and other Creeks and Places aforesaid, for Wares bought and sold, and Things there to be laden, or unladen, to be reasonably assessed by them, and the People there as aforesaid, on emergent Occasion; to whom We grant Power by these Presents, for Us, our Heirs and Successors, to assess and impose the said Taxes and Subsidies there, upon just Cause and in due Proportion.

XVIII. And Furthermore . . . We . . . do give . . . unto the aforesaid now Baron of Baltimore . . . full and absolute Licence, Power, and Authority . . . that he assign, alien, grant, demise, or enfeoff so many, such, and proportionate Parts and Parcels of the Premises, to any Person or Persons willing to purchase the same, as they shall think convenient, to have and to hold . . . in Feesimple, or Fee-tail, or for Term of Life, Lives, of Years; to hold of the aforesaid now Baron of Baltimore . . . by . . . such . . . Services, Customs and Rents of This Kind, as to the same now Baron of Baltimore . . . shall seem fit and agreeable, and not immediately of Us. . . .

XIX. We . . . also . . . do . . . grant Licence to the same Baron of Baltimore . . . to erect any Parcels of Land within the Province aforesaid, into Manors, and in every of those Manors, to have and to hold a Court-Baron, and all Things which to a Court-Baron do belong . . .

26. Baron Baltimore's Instructions to His Colonists, November 13, 1633

THE second Baron Baltimore, Cecilius Calvert (1606–1675), was conciliatory by nature and a man of great astuteness and tact. Only twenty-seven when he launched his colony, he was mature enough to realize that the entire project might quickly be wrecked if his colonists fell to quarrelling over religion. He, therefore, counseled his deputies in a set of instructions written a few days before the party sailed to see to it that the Catholics practiced prudence and forebearance toward their Protestant associates — a numerical majority — on the subject of religion. The same spirit lay behind his instruction to have only Church of England men sent as ambassadors of peace to the Governor of Virginia and to William Claiborne, the man who was so soon to bring grief upon the colony of Maryland. It is evident, too, in Baltimore's way of stating that his first intention in founding the colony was to convert the Indians "to Christianity," and that "a church or a chapel" should immediately be built, thus avoiding any mention of a particular denomination. The proprietor's realism and political sense can likewise be seen in his demand that the colonists at once take an oath of allegiance to Charles I. Source: Clayton Colman Hall (Ed.), *Narratives of Early Maryland, 1633–1684* (New York: Charles Scribner's Sons, 1910), pp. 16, 18–21; now included in *Original Narratives of Early American History*, copyright Barnes & Noble, Inc., New York.

---

1. Inpri: His Lo^{pp} requires his said Governor and Commissioners th^{t} in their voyage to Mary Land they be very carefull to preserve unity and peace amongst all the passengers on Shipp-board, and that they suffer no scandal nor offence to be given to any of the Protestants, whereby any just complaint may heereafter be made, by them, in Virginea or in England, and that for that end, they cause all Acts of Romane Catholique Religion to be done as privately as may be, and that they instruct all the Romane Catholiques to be silent upon all occasions of discourse concerning matters of Religion; and that the said Governor and Commissioners treate the Protestants wth as much mildness and favor as Justice will permit. And this to be observed at Land as well as at Sea. . . .

4. That by the first oportunity after theyr arrivall in Mary Land

they cause a messenger to be dispatcht away to James Town such a one as is conformable to the Church of England, and as they may according to the best of their judgments trust; and he to carry his maties letter to Sr John Harvie the Governor and to the rest of the Councell there, as likewise his Lopps letter to Sr Jo: Harvie, and to give him notice of their arrivall: And to have in charge, upon the delivery of the said letters to behave himself wth much respect unto the Governor, and to tell him tht his Lopp had an intention to have come himself in person this yeare into those parts, as he may perceive by his maties letter to him but finding that the setling of that business of his Plantation and some other occasions, required his presence in England for some time longer than he expected, he hath deferred his owne coming till the next years, when he will not faile by the grace of god to be there. . . .

5. That they write a letter to Cap: Clayborne as soon as conveniently other more necessary occasions will give them leave after their arrivall in the Countrey; to give him notice of their arrivall and of the Authority and charge committed to them by his Lopp and to send the said letter together wth his Lopps to him by some trusty messenger that is likewise conformable unto the Church of England, wth a message also from them to him if it be not inserted in their letter wch is better, to invite him kindly to come unto them, and to signify that they have some business of importance to speake wth him about from his Lopp wch concernes his good very much; And if he come unto them then that they use him courteously and well, and tell him, that his Lopp understanding that he hath settled a plantacion there wthin the precincts of his Lopps Pattent, wished them to lett him know that his Lopp is willing to give him all the encouragement he cann to proceede. . . .

6. That when they have made choice of the place where they intend to settle themselves and that they have brought their men ashoare wth all their provisions, they do assemble all the people together in a fitt and decent manner and then cause his maties letters pattents to be publickely read by his Lopps Secretary John Bolles, and afterwards his Lopps Commission to them, and that either the Governor or one of the Commissioners presently after make some short declaration to the people of His Lopps intentions wch he means to pursue in this his intended plantation, wch are first the honor of god by endeavoring the conversion of the savages to Christianity, secondly the augmentation of his maties Empire and Dominions in those parts of the world by reducing them under the subjection of his Crowne,

and thirdly by the good of such of his Countreymen as are willing to adventure their fortunes and themselves in it, by endeavoring all he cann, to assist them, that they may reape the fruites of their charges and labors according to the hopefulness of the thing, wth as much freedome comfort and incouragement as they cann desire. . . . And that at this time they take occasion to minister an oath of Allegeance to his ma^{tie} unto all and every one upon the place, after having first publikely in the presence of the people taken it themselves; letting them know that his Lo^{pp} gave particular directions to have it one of the first things that were done, to testify to the world that none should enjoy the benefitt of his ma^{ties} gratious Grant unto his L^{opp} of that place, but such as should give a publique assurance of their fidelity and allegeance to his ma^{tie}. . . .

9. That where they intended to settle the Plantacion they first make choice of a fitt place, and a competent quantity of ground for a fort wthin wch or neere unto it a convenient house, and a church or a chappel adjacent may be built, for the seate of his L^{opp} or his Governor or other Commissioners for the time being in his absence, both wch his L^{opp} would have them take care should in the first place be erected, in some proportion at least, as much as is necessary for the present use though not so complete in every part as in fine afterwards they may be and to send his L^{opp} a Platt of it and of the scituation, by the next oportunity, if it be done by that time, if not or but part of it nevertheless to send a Platt of what they intend to do in it. That they likewise make choice of a fitt place neere unto it to seate a towne. . . .

27. The English Jesuits Establish the Mission of Maryland, March–April, 1634

IN MANY ways the most significant Catholic mission in colonial America was that inaugurated by three English Jesuits in southern Maryland in March, 1634. These men, Fathers Andrew White (1579–1656) and John Altham (1589–1640) and Brother Thomas Gervase (1590–1637), were the pioneers of a religious enterprise that was to endure — often under severe persecution — beyond the American Revolution. From their original headquarters at St. Mary's City there sprang an unbroken succession of priests from whose number the first bishop of the United States was ultimately chosen. The English Jesuits began their American undertaking under conditions very different from those of their Spanish and French confreres. From the very outset they were entirely devoid of any temporal assistance from the government and were compelled to earn their livelihood from the land in the same manner as the lay gentlemen adventurers; they represented a Church which had been heavily persecuted in the mother country and which within twenty years would feel the whip of penal legislation in the colony; and they were part of a colony which was composed of men of mixed religious beliefs. They had to walk circumspectly, therefore, lest their missionary zeal be the cause of creating difficulties for the lord proprietor with the Protestant government in England. The following document was written by Andrew White, S.J., from St. Mary's City late in April, 1634, to Mutius Vitelleschi, General of the Jesuits, and described the voyage and the first month in Maryland. Source: E. A. Dalrymple (Ed.), *Narrative of a Voyage to Maryland by Father Andrew White, S.J. An Account of the Colony of the Lord Baron of Baltimore. Extracts from Different Letters of Missionaries, from the Year 1635 to the Year 1677* (Baltimore: Maryland Historical Society, 1874), pp. 10–43.

On the 22nd of the month of November, in the year 1633, being St. Cecilia's day, we set sail from Cowes, in the Isle of Wight, with a gentle east wind blowing. And, after committing the principal parts of the ship to the protection of God especially, and of His most Holy Mother, and St. Ignatius, and all the guardian angels of Maryland, we sailed on a little way between the two shores, and the wind failing us, we stopped opposite Yarmouth Castle, which is near the southern end of the same Island, (Isle of Wight). Here we were received with a cheerful salute of artillery. Yet we were not without apprehension; for the sailors were murmuring among themselves, saying that they were expecting a messenger with letters from London, and from this it seemed that they were contriving to delay us. But God brought their plans to confusion. For that very night, a favorable but strong wind, arose; and a French cutter, which had put into the same harbor with us, being forced to set sail, came near running into our pinnace. The latter, therefore, to avoid being run down, having cut away and lost an anchor, set sail without delay; and since it was dangerous to drift about in that place, made haste to get farther out to sea. And so that we might not lose sight of our pinnace, we determined to follow. Thus the designs of the sailors, who were plotting against us, were frustrated. This happened on the 23d of November, St. Clement's day, who, because he had been tied to an anchor and thrown into the sea, obtained the crown of martyrdom. "And showed the inhabitants of the earth, how to declare the wonderful things of God. . . ."

Now on Sunday the 24th, and Monday the 25th of November, we had fair sailing all the time until evening. But presently, the wind getting round to the north, such a terrible storm arose, that the merchant ship I spoke of from London, being driven back on her course, returned to England, and reached a harbor much resorted to, among the Paumonians. Those on board our pinnace also, since she was a vessel of only 40 tons, began to lose confidence in her strength, and sailing near, they warned us, that if they apprehended shipwreck, they would notify us by hanging out lights from the mast-head. We meanwhile sailed on in our strong ship of four hundred tons — a better could not be built of wood and iron. We had a very skilful captain, and so he was given his choice, whether he would return to England, or keep on struggling with the winds: if he yielded to these, the Irish shore close by awaited us, which is noted for its hidden rocks and frequent shipwrecks. Nevertheless his bold spirit, and his desire to test the strength of the new ship, which he then managed for the first time, prevailed with the captain. He resolved to try the sea, although he confessed that it was the more dangerous, on account of being so narrow.

And the danger was near at hand; for the winds increasing, and the sea growing more boisterous, we could see the pinnace in the distance, showing two lights at her masthead. Then indeed we thought it was all over with her, and that she had been swallowed up in the deep whirlpools; for in a moment she had passed out of sight, and no news of her reached us for six months afterwards. Accordingly we were all of us certain the pinnace had been lost; yet God had better things in store for us, for the fact was, that finding herself no match for the violence of the waves, she had avoided the Virginian ocean, with which we were already contending, by returning to England, to the Scilly Isles. And making a fresh start from thence . . . she overtook us . . . at a large harbor in the Antilles. And thus God, who oversees the smallest things, guided, protected, and took care of the little vessel. . . .

So Tuesday, Wednesday, and Thursday passed with variable winds, and we made small progress. On Friday, a southeast wind prevailing, and driving before it thick and dark clouds, so fierce a tempest broke forth towards evening, that it seemed every minute as if we must be swallowed up by the waves. Nor was the weather more promising on the next day, which was the festival of Andrew the Apostle. . . .

At this juncture the minds of the bravest among us, both passengers and sailors, were struck with terror; for they acknowledged that they had seen other ships wrecked in a less severe storm; but now, this hurricane called forth the prayers and vows of the Catholics in honor of the Blessed Virgin Mary and Her Immaculate Conception, of Saint Ignatius, the Patron Saint of Maryland, Saint Michael, and all the guardian angels of the same country. And each one hastened to purge his soul by the Sacrament of penance. For all control over the rudder being lost, the ship now drifted about like a dish in the water, at the mercy of the winds and the waves, until God showed us a way of safety. At first, I confess, I had been engrossed with the apprehension of the ship's being lost, and of losing my own life; but after I had spent some time, in praying more fervently than was my usual custom, and had set forth to Christ the Lord, to the Blessed Virgin, St. Ignatius, and the angels of Maryland, that the purpose of this journey was to glorify the Blood of Our Redeemer in the salvation of the barbarians, and also to raise up a kingdom for the Saviour (if he would condescend to prosper our poor efforts), to consecrate another gift to the Immaculate Virgin, His Mother, and many things to the same effect; great comfort shone in upon my soul, and at the same time so firm a conviction that we should be delivered, not only from this storm, but from every other during that voyage, that with me there could be no room left for doubt. I had betaken myself to prayer, when the sea was raging its worst, and (may this be to the glory of God,) I had scarcely finished, when they observed that the storm was abating. That indeed brought me to a new frame of mind, and filled me at the same time with great joy and admiration, since I understood much more clearly the greatness of God's love towards the people of Maryland, to whom your Reverence has sent us. Eternal praises to the most sweet graciousness of the Redeemer!!

When the sea had thus immediately abated, we had delightful weather for three months, so that the captain and his men declared they had never seen it calmer or pleasanter; for we suffered no inconvenience, not even for a single hour. However, when I speak of three months, I do not mean to say we were that long at sea, but I include the whole voyage, and also the time we stopped at the Antilles. For the actual voyage occupied only seven weeks and two days: and that is considered a quick passage. . . .

. . . if you except the usual sea-sickness, no one was attacked by any disease, until the Festival of the Nativity of our Lord. In order that that day might be better kept, wine was given out; and those who drank of it too freely, were seized the next day with a fever; and of these, not long afterwards, about twelve died, among whom two were Catholics. The loss of Nicholas Fairfax and James Barefote was deeply felt among us.

[Stops were made at Barbodos and Virginia.] After being kindly treated for eight of nine days, we set sail on the third of March, and entering the Chesapeak Bay, we turned our course to the north to reach the Potomeack River. The Chesopeacke Bay, ten leagues (30 Italian miles) wide, . . . is four, five, and six fathoms deep, and abounds in fish when the season is favorable; you will scarcely find a more beautiful body of water. Yet it yields the palm to the Potomeack River, which we named after St. Gregory.

Having now arrived at the wished-for country, we allotted names according to circumstances. And indeed the Promontory, which is toward the south, we consecrated with the name St. Gregory (now Smith Point), naming the northern one (now Point Lookout) St. Michael's, in honor of all the angels. Never have I beheld a larger or more beautiful river. . . . Just at the mouth of the river, we observed the natives in arms. That night, fires blazed through the whole country, and since they had never seen such a large ship, messengers were sent in all directions, who reported that a *Canoe,* like an island had come with as many men as there were trees in the woods. We went on, however, to Herons' Islands, so called from the immense number of these birds. The first island we came to, [we called] St. Clement's Island, and as it has a sloping shore, there is no way of getting to it except by wading. Here the women, who had left the ship, to do the washing, upset the boat and came near being drowned, losing also a large part of my linen clothes, no small loss in these parts. . . .

On the day of the *Annunciation of the Most Holy Virgin* Mary in the year 1634, we celebrated the mass for the first time, on this island. This had never been done before in this part of the world. After we had completed the sacrifice, we took upon our shoulders a great cross, which we had hewn out of a tree, and advancing in order to the appointed place, with the assistance of the Governor and his associates and the other Catholics, we erected a trophy to Christ the Saviour, humbly reciting, on our bended knees, the Litanies of the Sacred Cross, with great emotion.

Now when the Governor had understood that many Princes were subject to the Emperor of the Pascatawaye, he determined to visit him, in order that, after explaining the reason of our voyage, and gaining his good will, he might secure an easier access to the others. . . . And when he had learned that the Savages had fled inland, he went on to a city which takes its name from the river, being also called Potomeack. Here the young King's uncle named *Archihu* was his guardian, and took his place in the kingdom; a sober and discreet man. He willingly listened to Father (John) Altham, (Altam, that is

Oliver) who had been selected to accompany the Governor, (for he (the Governor) kept me still with the ship's cargo.) And when the Father explained, as far as he could through the interpreter, Henry Fleet . . . the errors of the heathen, he would every little while, acknowledge his own: and when he was informed that we had come thither, not to make war, but out of good will towards them, in order to impart civilized instruction to his ignorant race, and show them the way to heaven, and at the same time with the intention of communicating to them the advantages of distant countries, he gave us to understand that he was pleased with our coming. The interpreter was one of the Protestants of Virginia. And so, as the Father could not stop for further discourse at the time, he promised that he would return before very long. "That is just what I wish," said Archihu, "we will eat at the same table; my followers too shall go to hunt for you, and we will have all things in common.". . .

Going about nine leagues (that is about 27 miles) from St. Clement, we sailed into the mouth of a river, on the north side of the Potomac, which we named after St. George. This river, (or rather, arm of the sea,) like the Thames, runs from south to north about twenty miles before you come to fresh water. At its mouth are two harbors, capable of containing three hundred ships of the largest size. We consecrated one of these to St. George: the other, which is more inland, to the Blessed Virgin Mary.

The left side of the river was the abode of King *Yaocomico* (Yaocomico.) We landed on the right-side, and going in about a mile from the shore, we laid out the plan of a city, naming it after St. Mary. And, in order to avoid every appearance of injustice, and afford no opportunity for hostility, we bought from the King thirty miles of that land, delivering in exchange, axes, hatchets, rakes, and several yards of cloth. This district is already named *Augusta Carolina*. The *Susquehanoes,* a tribe inured to war, the bitterest enemies of King *Yaocomico,* making repeated inroads, ravage his whole territory, and have driven the inhabitants, from their apprehension of danger, to seek homes elsewhere. This is the reason why we so easily secured a part of his kingdom: God by this means opening a way for His own Everlasting Law and Light. They move away every day, first one party and then another, and leave us their houses, lands and cultivated fields. Surely this is like a miracle, that barbarous men, a few days before arrayed in arms against us, should so willingly surrender themselves to us like lambs, and deliver up to us themselves and their property. The finger of God is in this, and He purposes some great benefit to this nation. Some few, however, are allowed to dwell among us until next year. But then the land is to be left entirely to us. . . .

They live in houses built in an oblong, oval shape. . . . Their kings . . . and chief men have private apartments, as it were, of their own, and beds, made by driving four posts into the ground, and arranging poles above them horizontally. One of these cabins has fallen to me and my associates, in which we are accommodated well enough for the time, until larger dwellings are provided. You would call this the first chapel of Maryland, though it is fitted up much more decently than when the Indians lived in it. At the next voyage, if God favors our undertaking, our house shall not be destitute of those things, which are found useful in others.

The race are of a frank and cheerful disposition, and understand any matter correctly when it is stated to them: they have a keen sense of taste and smell, and in sight too, they surpass the Europeans. They live, for the most part, on a kind of paste, which they call *Pone,* and *Omini,* both of which are made of Indian corn; and sometimes they add fish, or what they have procured by hunting and fowling. They are especially careful to refrain from wine and warm drinks, and are not easily persuaded to taste them, except some whom the English have corrupted with their own vices. With respect to chastity, I confess that I have not yet observed, in man or woman, any act which even savored of levity, yet they are daily with us and among us, and take pleasure in our society. They run to us of their own accord, with a cheerful expression on their faces, and offer us what they have taken in hunting or fishing sometimes also they bring us food, and oysters boiled or roasted . . . and this they do, when invited in a few words of their own language, which we have hitherto contrived to learn by means of signs. They marry several wives, yet they keep inviolate their conjugal faith. The women present a sober and modest appearance.

They cherish generous feelings towards all, and make a return for whatever kindness you may have shown them. They resolve upon nothing rashly, or while influenced by a sudden impulse of the mind, but they act deliberately, therefore, when anything of importance is proposed at any time, they think it over for a while in silence; then they speak briefly for or against it: they are very tenacious of their purpose. Surely these men, if they are once imbued with Christian precepts, (and there seems to be nothing to oppose this, except our ignorance of the language spoken in these parts,) will become eminent observers of virtue and humanity. They are possessed with a wonderful longing for civilized intercourse with us, and for European garments. And they would long ago have worn clothing, if they had not been prevented by the avarice of the merchants, who do not exchange their cloth for anything but beavers. But everyone cannot get a beaver by hunting. God forbid that we should imitate the avarice of these men!

On account of our ignorance of their language, it does not yet appear what ideas they have besides, about Religion. We do not put much confidence in the Protestant interpreters: we have (only) hastily learned these few things. They acknowledge one God of Heaven, yet they pay him no outward worship. But they strive in every way to appease a certain imaginary spirit, which they call *Ochre,* that he may not hurt them. They worship corn and fire, as I hear, as Gods that are very bountiful to the human race. Some of our party report that they saw the following ceremony in the temple at (of?) *Barchuxem.* On an appointed day, all the men and women of every age, from several districts, gathered together round a large fire; the younger ones stood nearest the fire, behind these stood those who were older. Then they threw deer's fat on the fire, and lifting their hands to heaven, and raising their voices, they cried out *Yaho! Yaho!* Then making room, someone brings forward quite a large bag: in the bag is a pipe and a powder which they call *Potu.* The pipe is such a one as is used among us for smoking tobacco, but much larger; then the bag is carried round the fire, and the boys and girls follow it, singing alternately with tolerably pleasant voices, *Yaho, yaho.* Having completed the circuit, the pipe is taken out of the bag, and the powder called *Potu* is distributed to each one, as they stand near; this is lighted in the pipe, and each one, drawing smoke from the pipe, blows it over the several members of his body, and consecrates them. They were not allowed to learn anything more, except that they seem to have had some knowledge of the Flood, by which the world was destroyed, on account of the wickedness of mankind.

We have been here only one month, and so the remaining particulars must be kept for the next voyage, but this I do say that the soil seems remarkably fertile: in passing through the very thick woods, at every step we tread on strawberries, vines, sassafras, acorns, and walnuts. The soil is dark and not hard, to the depth of a foot, and overlays a rich, red clay. There are lofty trees everywhere, except where the land has been cultivated by a few persons. Numerous springs furnish a supply of water. No animals are seen except deer, beavers and squirrels, which are as large as the hares of Europe.

There is an infinite number of birds of various colors, such as eagles, cranes, swans, geese, partridges and ducks. From these facts, it is inferred that the country is not without such things, as contribute to the prosperity or pleasure of those, who inhabit it.

28. The State of Catholicism in Maryland, 1638

IN THE first years of their mission in the colony of Maryland the Jesuits were hampered from carrying out their desire to convert the Indians by the hostile acts of neighboring tribes and of the Puritans from Virginia, the reluctance of the colonial officials to run the risk of losing their priests, and the necessity of establishing themselves on the land as their sole source of income. But their religious ministrations to the colonists bore fruitful results as can be seen from the following account embodied in the *Annual Letter* for 1638 which reveals a healthy state of religion among the Maryland Catholics, progress in converting some Protestants, and comfort afforded to a number of Catholics among the indentured servants of Virginia. At the time the letter was written there were three Jesuit priests in Maryland: Andrew White, John Altham, and Thomas Copley. If the original letter carried the name of the author it was eliminated by the Jesuit editor in England before it was sent on to the Jesuit headquarters in Rome. Source: E. A. Dalrymple (Ed.), *Narrative of a Voyage to Maryland by Father Andrew White, S.J. An Account of the Colony of the Lord Baron of Baltimore. Extracts from Different Letters of Missionaries, from the Year 1635 to the Year 1677* (Baltimore: Maryland Historical Society, 1874), pp. 54–62.

Four Fathers gave their attention to this Mission, with one assistant in temporal affairs; and he, indeed, after enduring severe toils for the space of five years, with the greatest patience, humility, and ardent love, chanced to be seized by the disease prevailing at the time, and happily exchanged this wretched life for an immortal one.[1]

He was also shortly followed by one of the Fathers,[2] who was young indeed, but on account of his remarkable qualities of mind, evidently of great promise. He had scarcely spent two months in this mission, when, to the great grief of all of us, he was carried off by the common sickness prevailing in the Colony, from which no one of the three remaining priests has escaped unharmed; yet we have not ceased to labor, to the best of our ability among the neighboring people.

[1] Brother Thomas Gervase (1590–1637), who had come out with the original colonists.

[2] John Knowles (1607–1637).

And though the rulers of the Colony have not yet allowed us to dwell among the savages, both on account of the prevailing sickness, and also, because of the hostile disposition which the barbarians evince towards the English, they having slain a man from this Colony, who was staying among them for the sake of trading, and having also entered into a conspiracy against our whole nation; yet we hope that one of us will shortly secure a station among the barbarians. Meanwhile, we devote ourselves more zealously to the English; and since there are Protestants as well as Catholics in the Colony, we have labored for both, and God has blessed our labors.

For, among the Protestants, nearly all who have come from England, in this year 1638, and many others, have been converted to the faith, together with four servants, whom we purchased in Virginia, (another Colony of our Kingdom), for necessary services, and five mechanics, whom we hired for a month, and have in the meantime won to God. Not long afterwards, one of these, after being duly prepared for death, by receiving the sacraments, departed this life. And among these persons hardly anything else worth mentioning has occurred. . . .

Besides these, one of us, going out of the Colony, found two Frenchmen, one of whom had been without the sacraments of the Catholic Church for three entire years; the other, who was already near death, having spent fifteen whole years among Heretics, had lived just as they do. The Father aided the former with the sacraments and confirmed him in the Catholic faith as much as he could. The latter he restored to the Catholic Church, and, administering all the sacraments, prepared him for dying happily.

As for the Catholics, the attendance on the sacraments here is so large, that it is not greater among the Europeans, in proportion to the number of Catholics. The more ignorant have been catechised, and Catechetical Lectures have been delivered for the more advanced every Sunday; but, on Feast days sermons have been rarely neglected. The sick and the dying, who have been very numerous this year, and who dwelt far apart, we have assisted in every way, so that not even a single one has died without the sacraments. We have buried very many, and baptized various persons. And, although there are not wanting frequent occasions of dissension, yet none of any importance has arisen here in the last nine months, which we have not immediately allayed. By the blessing of God, we have this consolation, that no vices spring up among the new Catholics, although settlements of this kind are not usually supplied from the best class of men.

We bought off in Virginia, two Catholics, who had sold themselves into bondage, nor was the money ill-spent, for both showed themselves good Christians: one, indeed, surpasses the ordinary standard. Some others have performed the same duty of Charity, buying thence Catholic servants, who are very numerous in that country. For every year, very many sell themselves thither into bondage, and living among men of the worst example, and, being destitute of all spiritual aid, they generally make shipwreck of their souls.

In the case of one, we adore the remarkable providence and mercy of God, which brought a man encompassed in the world with very many difficulties, and now at length living in Virginia, almost continually without any aid to his soul, to undertake these exercises, not long before his death. This design a severe sickness prevented, which he bore with the greatest patience, with a mind generally fixed on God; and at length having properly received all the sacraments in the most peaceful manner, beyond what is usual, renders back to the Creator the breath of the life that remained, which had been so full of troubles and disquietudes. . . .

29. Virginia's Act Against Catholics and Priests, March, 1642

FROM the foundation of Virginia as a colony a strong hostility toward Catholics had been evident. When the first Baron of Baltimore visited there in October, 1629, with a view to finding a place for his coreligionists to settle, he was at once confronted by a demand that he take the oath of supremacy recognizing the king as head of the Church. By 1640 matters had become critical again for the Catholics in England and in the years 1641–1642 eleven priests were put to death. This situation was reflected in Virginia with attacks upon the neighboring colony of Maryland, and the passage of an act by the Virginia assembly in March, 1642, which sought to seal off the colony from affording refuge to those who might secretly be Catholics by exacting the oath of supremacy, as well as from giving any stay or comfort to refugee priests. Source: William Waller Hening (Ed.), *The Statutes at Large; Being a Collection of all the Laws of Virginia* (Richmond: Samuel Pleasants, Jr., 1809), I, 268–269.

Whereas it was enacted at an Assembly in January 1641, that according to a statute made in the third year of the reigne of our sovereign Lord King James of blessed memory, that no popish recusants should at any time hereafter exercize the place or places of secret councellors, register, comiss: surveyors or sheriffe, or any other publique place, but he utterly disabled for the same, And further it was enacted that none should be admitted into any of the aforesaid offices or places before he or they had taken the oath of allegiance and supremacy, And if any person or persons whatsoever should by sinister or corrupt meanes assume to himselfe any of the aforesaid places of any other publique office whatsoever and refuse to take the aforesaid oaths, he or they so convicted before an Assembly should be dismissed of his said office, And for his offence therein forfeit one thousand pounds of tobacco to be disposed of at the next Assembly after conviction, And it is further enacted by the authoritie aforesaid that the Statute in force against the popish recusants be duely executed in this government, And that it should not be lawfull under the penaltie aforesaid for any popish priest that shall hereafter arrive to remaine above five days after warning given for his departure by the Governour or commander of the place, where he or they shall bee, if wind and weather hinder not his departure, And that the said act should be in force ten days after the publication thereof, at James City, this present Grand Assembly to all intents and purposes doth hereby confirm the same.

30. Massachusetts Bay Passes an Anti-Priest Law, May 26, 1647

IT DID not need the example of Virginia in 1642, the religious bitterness of the Thirty Years' War in Europe, and the proximity of the French Catholics with their missionaries in present-day Maine and Nova Scotia to alarm the Puritans of Massachusetts Bay over the prospects of what might happen if a Catholic priest were to settle in their midst. Actually some of the Puritans believed that were were disguised priests at work in the colony. These circumstances served, therefore, as an occasion for the passage of a law in May, 1647, that would bar the presence of priests in the future. Source: Nathaniel B. Shurtleff (Ed.), *Records of the Governor and Company of the Massachusetts Bay in New England* (Boston: William White, 1854), III, 112.

This Court, taking into consideration the great warrs & combustions which are this day in Europe, & that the same are obserued to be cheifly raysed & fomented by the secrit practises of those of the Jesuiticall order, for the prevention of like euills amongst o^r^selues, its ordred, by the authorities of this Court, that no Jesuit or ecclesiasticall pson ordayned by ye authoritie of the pope shall henceforth come w[th]in o[r] jurisdiction; & if any pson shall give any cause of suspision that he is one of such societie, he shalbe brought before some of the magists, & if he cannot free himselfe of such suspitiō, he shalbe comitted or bound on to the next Court of Assistants, to be tried & proceeded with by banish[nt] or otherwise, as the Court shall see cause, & if any such pson so banished shalbe taken the 2d time w[th]in this jurisdiction, he shall vppon lawfull triall & conviction, be put to death; pvided this law shall not extend to any such Jesuit as shalbe cast vppon o[r] shores by shippwrack or other accydent, so as he contynew no longer then he may haue opptunitie of passage for his departure, nor to any such as shall come in company w[th] any messenger sent hither vppon publick occasions, or any marchant or master of any shipp belonging to any place not in enmitie w[th] the state of England or o[r]selves, so as they depart agayne w[th] the same messenger, marchant, or m[r], & behaue themselues inoffenciuely duringe their abode here.

31. Maryland's Act of Religious Toleration, April 21, 1649

AMONG the famous documents of American religious liberty Maryland's bill of April, 1649, entitled "An Act Concerning Religion," deserves a prime place, even though it was not included among the documents carried on the Freedom Train in 1947. From the very beginning of the colony Cecilius Calvert, the second Baron of Baltimore (1606–1675), and his lieutenants had maintained religious freedom for all the inhabitants; thus the assembly's action of 1649 in no way constituted a new policy for Maryland. But with the current running strongly in favor of Cromwell in England, the Puritans who had found a refuge in Maryland from oppression in Virginia and elsewhere grew bolder in attacks upon their Catholic neighbors. Baltimore sought, therefore, to insure religious peace by a specific enactment. The fact that he acted from motives of expediency, as well as from personal conviction, should not be permitted to deprive the lord proprietor and his assembly of credit for a remarkably broad grant of religious toleration for the mid-seventeenth century; nor should it be forgotten that the Protestants in the assembly joined with their Catholic colleagues to pass the measure. Source: William Hand Browne (Ed.), *Archives of Maryland. Proceedings and Acts of the General Assembly of Maryland, January 1637/38–September 1664* (Baltimore: Maryland Historical Society, 1883), I, 244–247.

---

fforasmuch as in a well governed and Xpian Cōmon Weath matters concerning Religion and the honor or God ought in the first place to bee taken into serious consideratōn and endeavoured to bee settled. Be it therefore ordered and enacted . . . That whatsoever pson or psons within this Province . . . shall from henceforth blaspheme God . . . or deny our Saviour Jesus Christ to bee the sonne of God, or shall deny the holy Trinity the ffather sonne and holy Ghost, or the Godhead of any of the said Three psons of the Trinity or the Unity of the Godhead . . . shalbe punished with death and confiscatōn or forfeiture of all his or her lands and goods to the Lord Proprietary and his heires. . . . And bee it also Enacted by the Authority and with the advise and assent aforesaid. That whatosever pson or psons shall from henceforth use or utter any reproachfull words or Speeches concerning the blessed Virgin Mary the Mother of our Saviour or the holy Apostles or Evangelists or any of them shall in such case for the first offence forfeit to the Lord Proprietary and his heires . . . the sume of ffive pound Sterling or the value thereof to be Leveyed on the goods and chattells of every such pson soe offending. . . . And be it also further Enacted by the same authority. . . . that whatsoever pson or psons shall from henceforth uppon any occasion of Offence or otherwise in a reproachful manner or Way declare call or denonimate any pson or psons whatsoever inhabiting . . . . within this Province . . . an heritick, Scismatick, Idolator, puritan, Independant, Prespiterian popish prest, Jesuite, Jesuited papist, Lutheran, Calvenist, Anabaptist, Brownist, Antinomian, Barrowist, Roundhead, Sepatist, or any other name or terme in a reproachfull manner relating to matter of Religion shall for every such Offence forfeit and loose some or tenne shillings sterling or the value thereof to bee leveyed on the goods and chattels of every such Offender. . . . And whereas the inforceing of the conscience in matters of Religion hath frequently fallen out to be of dangerous Consequence in those commonwealthes where it hath been practised, And for the more quiett and peaceable government of this Province, and the better to pserve mutuall Love and amity amongst the Inhabitants thereof. Be it Therefore . . . enacted (except as in this psent Act is before Declared and sett forth) that noe person or psons whatsoever within this Province, or the Islands, Ports, Harbors, Creekes, or havens thereunto belonging professing to beleive in Jesus Christ, shall from henceforth bee any waies troubled, Molested or discountenanced for or in respect of his or her religion nor in the free exercise thereof within this Province or the Islands thereunto belonging nor any way compelled to the beleife or exercise of any other Religion against his or her consent, soe as they be not unfaithfull to the Lord Proprietary, or molest or conspire against the civill Governemt established or to bee established in this Province under him or his heires. And that all & every pson or psons that shall presume Contrary to this Act and the true intent and meaning thereof directly or indirectly either in person or estate willfully to wrong disturbe trouble or molest any person whatsoever within this Province professing to beleive in Jesus Christ for or in respect of his or her religion or the free exercise thereof within this Province other than is provided for in this Act that such pson or psons soe offending, shalbe compelled to pay trebble damages to the party soe wronged or molested, and for every such offence shall also forfeit 20s sterling in money or the value therof. . . . Or if the ptie soe offending as aforesaid shall refuse or bee unable to recompense the party so wronged, or to satisfy such ffyne or forfeiture, then such Offender shalbe severly punished by publick whipping & imprisonmt during the pleasure of the Lord Proprietary, or his Lieuetenāt or cheife Governor of this Province for the tyme being without baile or maineprise. . . .

32. Disfranchisement of Catholics in Maryland, October 20, 1654

FOR years William Claiborne (c. 1587–c. 1677), a leader of the Puritan element in Virginia, has been feuding with the Calvert regime in Maryland over the possession of Kent Island and other matters. The victory of Cromwell, therefore, gave Claiborne and his followers a pretext for an all-out assault in which they succeeded in overthrowing the government of Governor William Stone (c. 1603–c. 1660) and imposing their own rule upon Maryland. Claiborne was, of course, bitterly anti-Catholic and one of the first things which he did was to put through the assembly an act disfranchising Catholics. Thus the toleration practiced since 1634, and made the subject of special legislation in 1649, was abolished. Source: William Hand Browne (Ed.), *Archives of Maryland. Proceedings and Acts of the General Assembly of Maryland, January 1637/38–September 1664* (Baltimore: Maryland Historical Society, 1883), I, 340–341.

It is Enacted and Declared in the Name of his Highness the Lord Protector with the Consent and by the Authority of the present Generall Assembly That none who profess and Exercise the Popish Religion Commonly known by the Name of the Roman Catholick Religion can be protected in this Province by the Lawes of England formerly Established and yet unrepealed . . . but are to be restrained from the

Exercise thereof, Therefore all and Every person or persons Concerned in the Law aforesaid are required to take notice

Such as profess faith in God by Jesus Christ (though Differing in Judgment from the Doctrine worship & Discipline publickly held forth shall not be restrained from but shall be protected in the profession of the faith) & Exercise of their Religion so as they abuse not this Liberty to the injury of others The Disturbance of the publique peace on their part, Provided that this Liberty be not Extended to popery or prelacy nor to such as under the profession of Christ hold forth and practice Licentiousness

33. Persecution of the Maryland Catholics, 1656

OLIVER CROMWELL'S triumph over the Stuart monarchy in England was seized upon by the Puritans in Virginia — abetted by Puritans from that colony who had been afforded a refuge in Maryland — to overthrow Baron Baltimore's government and to impose upon the colony a regime that quickly reversed the policy of religious toleration and disfranchised the Catholics. With the exception of the interval of the Stuart restoration, the Catholics experienced from 1654 on to the American Revolution almost as harsh a penal code as that imposed on their coreligionists in England. The Jesuits, needless to say, were among the first to feel the hatred of Maryland's new masters, and the *Annual Letter* for 1656 which follows relates the story of their hardships during the previous year, a theme which found frequent repetition in their annual reports to the superiors in the years ahead. Source: E. A. Dalrymple (Ed.), *Narrative of a Voyage to Maryland by Father Andrew White, S.J. An Account of the Colony of the Lord Baron of Baltimore. Extracts from Different Letters of Missionaries from the Year 1635 to the Year 1677* (Baltimore: Maryland Historical Society, 1874), pp. 91–93.

In Maryland, during the year last past, our people have escaped grievous dangers, and have had to contend with great difficulties and straits, and have suffered many unpleasant things as well from enemies as from our own people. The English who inhabit Virginia had made an attack on the colonists, themselves Englishmen too; and safety being guarantied on certain conditions, received indeed the governor of Maryland, with many others in surrender; but the conditions being treacherously violated, four of the captives, and three of them catholics, were pierced with leaden balls. Rushing into our houses, they demanded for death the impostors, as they called them, intending inevitable slaughter to those who should be caught. But the fathers, by the protection of God, unknown to them, were carried from before their faces: their books, furniture, and whatever was in the house, fell a prey to the robbers. With almost the entire loss of their property, private and domestic, together with great peril of life, they were secretly carried into Virginia; and in the greatest want of necessaries, scarcely, and with difficulty, do they sustain life. They live in a mean hut, low and depressed, not much unlike a cistern, or even a tomb, in which that great defender of the faith, St. Athanasius, lay concealed for many years. To their other miseries this inconvenience was added, that whatever comfort or aid this year, under name of stipend, from pious men in England, was destined for them, had been lost, the ship being intercepted in which it was carried. But nothing affects them more than that there is not a supply of wine, which is sufficient to perform the sacred mysteries of the altar. They have no servant, either for domestic use, or for directing their way through unknown and suspected places, or even to row and steer the boat, if at any time there is need. Often, over spacious and vast rivers, one of them, alone and unaccompanied, passes and repasses long distances, with no other pilot directing his course than Divine Providence. By and by the enemy may be gone and they may return to Maryland; the things which they have already suffered from their people, and the disadvantages which still threaten are not much more tolerable.

34. New York's Grant of Religious Toleration, October 31, 1683

ON TWO occasions in American colonial history Catholics held the office of governor of a colony. In both instances religious toleration was granted to all Christians. We have already seen how the early Calverts made provision for such toleration in Maryland. The second case was in New York under Colonel Thomas Dongan (1634–1715), appointed governor in 1682 by the Duke of York, the future James II, himself a Catholic. The new governor summoned the first representative assembly in the history of the colony in October, 1683, and sponsored the passage by that body of the Charter of Liberties and Privileges. Dongan's broad grant of religious freedom endured in New York until 1688 when James II lost his throne, the governor was recalled, and Jacob Leisler's usurping government disfranchised the Catholics. Source: Hugh Hastings (Supervisor), *Ecclesiastical Records of the State of New York* (Albany: James B. Lyon, 1901), II, 864–865.

. . . that no person or persons, which profess faith in God by Jesus Christ, shall at any time, be any ways molested, punished, disquieted, or called in question for any difference in opinion or matter of religious concernment, who do not actually disturb the civill peace of the Province, but that all and every such person or persons may, from time to time, and at all times freely have and fully enjoy his or their judgements or consciences in matters of religion throughout all the Province, they behaving themselves peaceably and quietly and not using this liberty to Licentiousnesse nor to the civill injury or outward disturbance of others

Provided always, that this liberty, or anything conteyned therein to the contrary, shall never be construed or improved to make void the settlement of any public Minister on Long Island, whether such settlement be by two thirds of the voices in any Towne thereon, which shall always include the minor part; or by subscriptions of perticuler inhabitants in said townes; Provided, they are the two thirds thereof: Butt thatt all such agreements, covenants and subscriptions thatt are there already made and had, or thatt hereafter shall bee in this manner consented to, agreed and subscribed shall att all time and times hereafter, bee firm and stable:

And in confirmation hereof, it is enacted by the Governor Councell, and Representatives: That all such sums of money so agreed on, consented to, or subscribed as aforesaid, for maintenance of said public ministers, by the two thirds of any towne on Long Island, shall always include the minor part, who shall bee regulated thereby: and also such subscriptions and agreements as are beforemenconed, are and shall be always ratifyed, performed and payed, and if any towne of said Island, in their public capacity of agreement with any such minister or any perticuler persons, by their private subscriptions aforesaid, shall make default, deny, or withdraw from such payments so covenanted to, agreed upon, and subscribed thatt in such case, upon complaint of any Collector appointed and chosen by two thirds of such towne upon Long Island, unto any Justice of that County, upon his hearing the same, he is hereby authorized, empowered, and required to issue out his warrant unto the constable or his deputy or any other person appointed for the collection of said rates or agreement, to levy upon the goods and chattells of the said delinquent or defaulter, all such sums of money so covenanted and agreed to be paid, by distresse, with costs and charges, without any further suit in law, any lawe, custom or usage to the contrary in any wise notwithstanding; provided always, the said sum or sumes be under forty shillings, otherwise to be recovered as the law directs.

And whereas all the respective Christian Churches now in practice within the City of New York, and the other places of this Province, do appear to be privileged [*sic*] Churches, and have been soe established and confirmed by the former authority of this Government; Bee it hereby enacted by this present Generall Assembly, and by the Authority thereof, That all the said respective Christian Churches be hereby confirmed therein, and thatt they and every of them shall from henceforth, forever, be held and reputed as privileged Churches, and enjoy all their former freedoms of their religion in Divine Worship and Church Discipline; and thatt all former contracts made and agreed on for the maintenances of the several ministers of the said Churches, shall stand and continue in full force and vertue, and thatt all Contracts for the future to be made, shall be of the same power; and all persons that are unwilling to perform their part of the said contract shall be constrained thereunto by a warrant from any Justice of the Peace; Provided it be under forty shillings, or otherwise, as the law directs; Provided also That all other Christian Churches that shall hereafter come and settle within this Province, shall have the same privileges.

35. An Act Against Jesuits and Popish Priests in Massachusetts, June 17, 1700

THE Treaty of Ryswick in September, 1697, brought no settlement of the rival claims of England and France in North America, and in the interval which led up to England's renewal of war against France in May, 1702, the border warfare between the two powers took an increasing toll in lives and property. In 1697 Richard Coote, the Earl of Bellomont (1636–1701), a son of the notorious Richard Coote who had committed so many outrages against the Catholic population of Ireland under Cromwell, was appointed Governor of New York, Massachusetts, and New Hampshire. Bellomont was himself fiercely anti-Catholic, and the widespread belief that Catholic missionaries were stirring up the Indians to attack the English made it an easy matter for him to put through anti-priest laws in both Massachusetts and New York within a few months' time. The Massachusetts law of 1700 was broader in application than that of 1647 and its terms were more severe. Source: *The Acts and Resolves, Public and Private, of the Province of the Massachusetts Bay* (Boston: Wright & Potter, 1869), I, 423–424.

Whereas divers Jesuits, priests and popish missionaries have of late come, and for some time have had their residences in the remote parts of this province, and other his majesty's territories near adjacent, who by their subtile insinuations industriously labour to debauch, seduce and withdraw the Indians from their due obedience unto his majesty, and to excite and stir them up, to sedition, rebellion and open hostility against his Majestie's government; for prevention whereof, —

Be it enacted by His Excellency the Governour, Council, and Representatives in General Court assembled, and it is enacted by the authority of the same

[Sect. 1] That all and every Jesuit, seminary priest, missionary, or other spiritual or ecclesiastical person made or ordained by any authority, power or jurisdiction derived, challenged or pretended from the pope or see of Rome, now residing within this province or any part thereof, shall depart from and out of the same at or before the tenth day of September next, in this present year one thousand and seven hundred.

And be it further enacted by the authority aforesaid,

[Sect. 2] That all and every Jesuit, seminary priest, missionary or other spiritual or ecclesiastical person made or ordained by any authority, power or jurisdiction, derived, challenged or pretended, from the pope or see of Rome, or that shall profess himselfe or otherwise appear to be such by practising and teaching of others to say any popish prayers, by celebrating masses, granting of absolutions, or using any other of the Romish ceremonies and rites of worship, by or of what name, title or degree soever such person shall be called or known, who shall continue, abide, remain or come into this province, or any part thereof, after the tenth day of September aforesaid, shall be deemed and accounted an incendiary and disturber of the publick peace and safety, and an enemy to the true Christian religion, and shall be adjudged to suffer perpetual imprisonment; and if any person, being so sentenced and actually imprisoned, shall break prison and make his escape, and be afterwards re-taken, he shall be punished with death.

And further it is enacted

[Sect. 3] That every person which shall wittingly and willingly receive, relieve, harbour, conceal, aid or succour any Jesuit, priest, missionary or other ecclesiastical person of the Romish clergy, knowing him to be such, shall be fined two hundred pounds, one moiety therof to be unto his majesty for and towards the support of the government of this province, and the other moiety to the informer; and such person shall be further punished by being set in the pillory on three several days, and also be bound to the good behaviour at the discretion of the court. . . .

And further be it enacted by the authority aforesaid,

[Sect. 5] That it shall and may be lawful to and for every justice of the peace to cause any person or persons suspected of being a Jesuit, seminary priest, or of the Romish clergy, to be apprehended and convented before himself or some other or his majestie's justices; and if such person do not give satisfactory account of himselfe, he shall be committed to prison in order to a tryal. Also it shall and may be lawful to and for any person or persons to apprehend without a warrant any Jesuit, seminary priest, or other of the Romish clergy as aforesaid, and to convent him before the governour or any two of the council, to be examined and imprisoned in order to a tryal, unless he give a satisfactory accompt of himselfe. And as it will be esteemed and accepted as a good service done for the king by the person who shall seize and apprehend any Jesuit, priest, missionary, or Romish ecclesiastic as aforesaid, so the governour, with the advice and consent of the council, may suitably reward him as they shall think fit; *provided,* this act shall not extend or be construed to extend to any of the Romish clergy which shall happen to be shipwrackt, or through other adversity shall be cast on shore, or driven into this province, so as he continue or abide no longer within the same than until he may have opportunity of passage for his departure; so also as such person immediately upon his arrival shall forthwith attend the governour, if near to the place of his residence, or otherwise on one or more of the council or next justices of the peace, and acquaint them with his circumstances, and observe the directions which they shall give him, during his stay in the province.

36. The Coming of the Acadians to Massachusetts, November, 1755–August, 1756

THE largest number of Catholics to come to colonial America were the conservatively estimated 6000 Acadians who were exiled by the British to the thirteen colonies in 1755–1756. These simple people were caught in the war between France and England for the mastery of North America, and they were bewildered by the contrary advice of their priests concerning the oath of allegiance demanded of them by their British conquerors. Their circumstances were extremely pitiful, and it is small wonder that some of them responded to the spirit of resistance encouraged by the Abbé Jean Louis Le Loutre at Beauséjour and the Abbé Henri Daudin at Annapolis Royal and Piziquid. Yet the author of a recent scholarly and sympathetic account of their exile has stated: "Indeed, one may say with confidence that had the Acadians determinedly followed the example and wise counsel of such worthy and venerable priests among them as Father Desenclaves

(Deseuclaves) and Chauvreux, rather than the exhortations to desperate measures of Le Loutre and his pupil Daudin, misfortunes would never have been heaped upon them" (Lawrence Henry Gibson, *The Great War for the Empire. The Years of Defeat, 1754–1757* [New York, 1946], p. 285). As a consequence of their refusal to renounce their loyalty to France, they were seized, transported, and landed along the American coasts where, by reason of their religion, political sympathies, and the trouble they occasioned, they received a generally hostile reception. Between November, 1755, and August, 1756, over 3000 Acadians were landed in Massachusetts. Many of these, it is true, were later sent south, but as late as 1763 there were still over 1000 of the exiles in that colony. Their best friend in Massachusetts was Thomas Hutchinson (1711–1780), a member of the provincial council and later governor. It was Hutchinson who wrote the first general history of the colony, and in the final volume, finished in 1778, he included the following vivid picture of the Acadians' fate in Massachusetts. Source: Thomas Hutchinson, *The History of the Colony and Province of Massachusetts-Bay,* edited by Lawrence Shaw Mayo (Cambridge: Harvard University Press, 1936), III, 28–31.

The French forts at Beau Sejour, Bay Vert, and the river St. John, in Nova Scotia, had been recovered. The state of that province was, notwithstanding, deemed very insecure; many thousand French inhabitants still continued in it. They had been admitted by lieutenant-governor Armstrong, after that province was reduced in the reign of Q. Ann, to such a sort of oath, as to consider themselves rather in a neutral state between England and France, than in subjection to either, and from thence they took the name of French neutrals. Being all Roman catholicks and great bigots, and retaining the French language, they were better affected to the French than to the English. In civil matters, they had been more indulged by the English than they would have been by the French, being in a manner free from taxes; and a great part of them were so sensible of it, that they wished to avoid taking part on one side or the other. But the Indians, who were engaged on the part of the French, had constant intercourse with them, their houses being scattered, and where there were any number together to form a village, open to both French and Indians from Canada, without any sort of defence. And it was the general opinion, that, if an attempt should be made by the French to recover the province of Nova Scotia, the whole body of the Acadians, some from inclination, others from compulsion, would join in the attempt.

The commander-in-chief of his majesty's ships, then at Halifax, as well as the governor of the province, supposed that the principle of self-preservation would justify the removal of these Acadians; and it was determined to take them by surprise, and transport them all, men, women, and children, to the English colonies. A few days before the determination was executed, notice was given to the governors of the several colonies to prepare for their reception. The greatest part by far were accordingly seized by the king's troops, which had remained in the province, and hurried on board small vessels prepared to receive them, with such part of their household goods as there was room for; the remainder, with their stock of cattle, the contents of their barns, their farm utensils, and all other moveables, being left behind, and never recovered, nor any satisfaction made for them.

In several instances, the husbands who happened to be at a distance from home, were put on board vessels bound to one of the English colonies, and their wives and children on board other vessels, bound to other colonies remote from the first. One of the most sensible of them, describing his case, said, "it was the hardest which had happened since our Saviour was upon earth."

About a thousand of them arrived in Boston, just in the beginning of winter, crowded almost to death. No provision was made, in case government should refuse to take them under its care. As it happened, the assembly was sitting when they arrived; but several days were spent without any determination, and some aged and infirm persons, in danger of perishing, were received on shore in houses provided for them by private individuals. At length, the assembly passed a resolve, that they should all be permitted to land, and that they should be sent to such towns as a committee appointed for that purpose should think fit; and a law of the province was passed, to authorize justices of the peace, overseers of the poor, &c., to employ them in labour, bind them out to service, and, in general, provide for their support, in like manner as if they had been indigent inhabitants of the province.

Favour was shewn to many elderly people among them, and to others who had been in circumstances superior to the rest, and they were allowed support without being held to labour. Many of them went through great hardships, but in general they were treated with humanity. They fared the better, because the towns where they were sent, were to be reimbursed out of the province treasury, and the assembly was made to believe the province would be reimbursed by the crown; but this expectation failed. It was proposed to them to settle upon some of the unappropriate lands of the province, and to become British subjects, but they refused. They had a strong persuasion, that the French king would never make peace with England, unless they were restored to their estates. A gentleman who was much affected with their sufferings,[1] prepared a representation proper for

[1] **This was Hutchinson himself.**

them to make to the British government, to be signed by the chief of them in behalf of the rest, praying that they might either have leave to return to their estates, or might receive a compensation; and he offered to put it into the hands of a proper person in England to solicit their cause. They received the proposal thankfully, took the representation to consider of, and, after some days, returned it without having signed it. They were afraid of losing the favour of France, if they should receive or solicit for compensation from England. Despair of the free exercise of their religion was another bar to every proposal tending to an establishment.

The people of New England had more just notions of toleration than their ancestors, and no exception was taken to their prayers in their families, in their own way, which, I believe, they practised in general, and sometimes they assembled several families together; but the people would upon no terms have consented to the publick exercise of religious worship by Roman catholick priests. A law remained unrepealed, though it is to be hoped it would never have been executed, which made it a capital offence in such persons to come within the province.[2] It was suspected that some such were among them in disguise; but it is not probable that any ventured. One of the most noted families, when they were dissuaded from removing to Quebec, lest they should suffer more hardship from the French there, than they had done from the English, acknowledged they expected it; but they had it not in their power since they left their country, to confess and to be absolved of their sins, and the hazard of dying in such a state distressed them more than the fear of temporal sufferings.*

* When these unhappy persons despaired of being restored to their own estates, they began to think of a removal to places where they might find priests of their own religion, and other inhabitants of their own language. Many hundreds went from the New England colonies to Hispaniola, where, in less than a year, by far the greatest part died. Others went to Canada, where they were considered as an inferior race of Frenchmen, and they were so neglected, that some of them wrote to a gentleman in Boston who had patronized them, they then wished to return. In 1763, Monsieur Bougainville[3] carried several families of them, who had found their way to France, to the Malouines, or Falkland's Islands, where they remained but a short time, being turned off by Mr. Byron.[4] Bougainville says, "they are a laborious intelligent set of men, who ought to be dear to France, on account of the inviolate attachment they have shewn as honest but unfortunate

[2] Hutchinson was referring here to the anti-priest law of May, 1647 (No. 30).

[3] Louis Antoine de Bougainville (1729–1811) was an aide-de-camp of Montcalm at Quebec who later was given command of a fleet to found a French colony in the Falkland Islands.

[4] John Byron (1723–1786) was a British naval officer.

citizens." Thus they were dispersed through the world, until they were in a manner extinct, the few which remained being mixed with other subjects in different parts of the French dominions.

37. Bishop Challoner on Ecclesiastical Jurisdiction in the British Colonies, September 14, 1756

FROM 1631 to 1685 there was no Catholic bishop in England. Faculties for the first missionaries who came to Maryland were secured, therefore, from the Jesuit General by a special privilege granted by Gregory XIII in 1579. In the very year that the Holy See appointed four vicars apostolic to rule over the English Catholics, 1688, James II lost his throne and a systematic persecution of the Church began which lasted for almost a century. In these circumstances — aggravated by intermittent wars, infrequent communication over immense distances, and the constant feuds between the secular and regular clergy in England — it is small wonder that the question of ecclesiastical jurisdiction over the colonial Catholics should at times have become confused. After 1688 the Vicar Apostolic of the London District was the official to whom application for faculties was normally made, although the system seems never to have become regularized in a satisfactory way. One of those who tried repeatedly to have a bishop appointed for the colonies, or to have the Bishop of Quebec administer confirmation to them, was Richard Challoner (1691–1781), who served as coadjutor to old Bishop Benjamin Petre in London from 1741 to 1758, and as vicar apostolic from the latter date to his death in 1781. But nothing came of Challoner's efforts, and his death some months before the Battle of Yorktown prompted his biographer to say that "his jurisdiction over his American priests and people remained the only remnant of authority in the hands of an Englishman that was still recognised in America" (p. 148). In the following letter of September 14, 1756, to Dr. Christopher Stonor, agent of the English clergy at Rome, Challoner revealed the lack of clarity about ecclesiastical jurisdiction, mentioned the need for a bishop in America, and reflected something of the secular clergy's bias against the Jesuits in the American missions. Source: Edwin H. Burton, *The Life and Times of Bishop Challoner (1691–1781)* (New York: Longmans, Green and Co., 1909), II, 125–127.

As to the state of religion in our American settlements; the best account I can give is: —

1. There are no missioners in any of our colonies upon the continent, excepting Mariland and Pensilvania; in which the exercise of the Catholic religion is in some measure tolerated. . . . [Then follows a paragraph on the missions in the West Indies.]

3. All our settlements in America have been deemed subject in spirituals to the ecclesiastical Superiors here, and this has been time

out of mind, even, I believe, from the time of the Archpriests. I know not the origin of this, nor have ever met with the original grant. I suppose they were looked upon as appurtenances or appendixes of the English Mission. And, after the division of this kingdom into four districts, the jurisdiction over the Catholicks in those settlements has followed the London district (as they are all reputed by the English as part of the London diocese); I suppose because London is the capital of the British Empire; and from hence are the most frequent opportunities of a proper correspondence with all those settlements. Whether the Holy See has ordered anything in this regard, I cannot learn. But all the missioners in those settlements do now, and have, time out of mind, applied to the Vicar Apostolic here for their faculties, which is true of the *padri* also [the Jesuits] in Mariland and Pennsilvania; at least from the time of the Breve of Innocent XII. in 1696, only that they used rather to ask for approbation, but now also for faculties.

4. Some have wished, considering the number of the faithful, especially in those two provinces, destitute of the sacrament of confirmation, and lying at so great a distance from us, that a bishop or vicar apostolic should be appointed for them. But how far this may be judged practicable by our superiors I know not: especially as perhaps it may not be relished, by those who have engrossed that best part of the mission to themselves, and who may, not without show of probability, object that a novelty of this kind might give offence to the governing part there; who have been a little hard upon them of late years. . . .

38. The Missionaries' Reasons for Not Wanting a Bishop, April 22, 1773

ENGLAND'S victory over France in the Seven Years' War brought more American possessions under the British flag and thus caused renewed emphasis on the need for a bishop. The Congregation of Propaganda Fide was aware of the situation, but knowing the hostility of the British government toward the Church, the Roman officials were uncertain how to proceed. When requested by Propaganda for his views, Bishop Challoner had replied on August 2, 1763, as follows:

> "It is to be desired that provision should be made for so many thousand Catholics as are found in Maryland and Pennsylvania, that they may receive the Sacrament of Confirmation, of the benefit of which they are utterly deprived. Now that Canada and Florida are brought under the

> English sway, the Holy Apostolic See could easily effect this, a Bishop or a Vicar Apostolic being established at Quebec or elsewhere, with the consent of our Court, by delegating jurisdiction to him throughout all the other English colonies and islands of America. This would be far from displeasing to us, and would redound greatly to the advantage of those colonies" (*American Catholic Historical Researches,* XII [January, 1895], 44–45).

But Challoner's letter got lost, further delays ensued, and in 1771 Propaganda suggested to Joseph-Olivier Briand (1715–1794), Bishop of Quebec, that he undertake the responsibility. Briand, in turn, asked Bernard Well, a Jesuit missionary in Canada, to inquire of his confreres about the prospects for a bishop in the American colonies. In the absence of John Baptist Diderich, S.J., then on the Pennsylvania missions, Well's letter was answered by Ferdinand Farmer, S.J. (1720–1786), who summarized conditions among the Catholics and gave reasons why he thought it would be unwise to send a bishop. It was a view which the Jesuits continued to hold until the late 1780's when their suspicions of opposition from the American government, and of what a bishop might mean to their property interests, were finally dissipated. Source: *American Catholic Historical Researches,* XXI (July, 1904), 118–120.

Philadelphia, 22nd April, 1773.

Reverend Father in Christ,

P.C. (Pax Christi)

Your Reverence's most welcome letter, dated February 15, was delivered to me on the 17th of April. In the absence of Rev. Father Diderick I opened it, according to directions given in the address. The above mentioned Father had been in one of the Pennsylvania Missions, a hundred or more miles distant from Philadelphia; having, in a private discussion with a non-Catholic man, made use of some rather harsh and insulting words, he came nigh being killed, a musket having been twice discharged by night on his dwelling or chapel. Wherefore he was obliged to remove to the Missions in the Province of Maryland. I shall, in due time, send him your Reverence's letter. Your Reverence desires to know the state of our Missions. I shall describe them briefly. In only two of the several English Provinces or Colonies is the Catholic Religion tolerated, namely in Maryland and Pennsylvania; in the latter in virtue of a Royal Charter given to the founder of the Colony; in the former, more from ancient possession than owing to any right. In Pennsylvania, by virtue of a Royal deed, all religions are tolerated, not that each one is free to publicly perform the rites of his religion, but in this sense that he may accomplish them in private, and that he may be in no wise compelled by anyone to share in any exercise whatsoever of another Religion than his own.

As, however, the oath must be exacted of all such as desire to be numbered among the born subjects of the Kingdom, or who hold divers offices in the Commonwealth, contains a renunciation of the Catholic religion, none of our faith can obtain the like favors. In Pennsylvania there are presently five Missionaries, one Englishman and four Germans, who attend with no mean labor to small congregations of men nearly all poor and widely scattered throughout the Province. In Philadelphia, however, where reside two missionaries, there is a greater number of souls comprising men of different nationalities. In Maryland, there are both more missionaries and a greater and better number of faithful, but, as I already mentioned, they enjoy less liberty than that which we here enjoy. All of these Missionaries are of our Society; the Superior resides in Maryland. I shall have to consult him regarding the matter treated in your Reverence's letter. But as a prompt answer is requested, until the Reverend Father Superior can examine the question and advise thereon, I beg to express my own sentiment.

From the foregoing it is easy to see that the Catholic Religion is practised with far greater authority and freedom in Canada than in our own country. Wherefore it is most certain that the advent in our midst of the Right Reverend and Illustrious [Bishop of Quebec] would create great disturbances, with the danger of depriving us of the paltry privileges we are now enjoying, especially in Maryland, where, as already mentioned, the exercise, even in private, of our Religion rests upon no authority. For the same reason, when several years ago, the Vicar Apostolic of London intended to send some one hither for the purpose either of visiting or of giving Confirmation, the gentlemen of Maryland placed under our care, by a letter to the Right Reverend Vicar, informed him of the danger to which they were exposed; wherefore the aforesaid Vicar, under whom are all these colonies, gave up his intention.

I do not wish you to understand by this that we are not greatly desirous of having Confirmation administered to those of our flock born in this country, but that it is plain to our eyes, being given especially the character of Americans, that such rite could not safely be conferred by a person established in dignity. For it is incredible how hateful to non-Catholics in all parts of America is the very name of Bishop, even to such as should be members of the Church which is called Anglican. Whence many considered it a most unworthy measure that a Bishop be granted to the Canadians; and, as for several years past the question is being agitated in England of establishing in these Provinces a Protestant Bishop of the Anglican Communion, so many obstacles were found, due especially to the character of the Americans (of whom most of the early colonists were dissidents from the Anglicans, not to mention such as left our own faith) that nothing has as yet been effected. Hardly I can persuade myself that the Right Reverend (Bishop) might succeed in obtaining from the Governor of Canada or from the King, the faculty of exercising his power beyond the limits of the Provinces belonging formerly to the Canadian government, and lately ceded by treaty to the English.

From Europe we have received no letters for several months past, so that we are ignorant as to what may be the state of our society. However, from what we learned last year from Ours, and also from what the newspapers announce, we justly infer that our interests in Rome are not succeeding favourably, though that doth succeed favourably whichsoever it pleaseth Divine Providence to ordain.

Your Reverence will excuse me for not having written this more neatly, as in this city, especially at the present time, we are very busy with the various labors of our ministry. I urgently recommend myself in all holy intentions.

Of Your Reverence,
The most humble servant in Christ,
FERDINAND FARMER, S.J.

P.S. — My Reverend colleague, Father Robert Mollineux [*sic*], most cordially greets your Reverence. Should it please ye to send me other letters, they may be addressed as follows:

To Mr. Ferdinand Farmer,
Walnut Street,
Philadelphia.

39. Charles Carroll's Defense of His Religious Beliefs, 1773

IN THE struggle for American independence the Catholics joined with their fellow countrymen without reserve. Among their number no one played a more prominent and honorable role than Charles Carroll of Carrollton (1737–1832), signer of the Declaration of Independence, who from the time he entered politics in 1773 until his retirement in 1800 filled a number of important state and federal offices. The occasion which brought him to public notice was the appearance on February 4, 1773, of the first of a series of letters when he published in the *Maryland Gazette* over the pen name of "First Citizen." Carroll had been roused by Daniel Dulany's ("Antillon") attempt to defend the arbitrary action of Governor Robert Eden in proroguing the Maryland assembly and reaffirming by proclamation officers' fees and stipends for the clergy of the established church. With the development of the debate the argument broadened and in the end Carroll's effective polemics not only vanquished Dulany but helped to swing the Maryland election of May, 1773, in favor of the patriot party who had opposed the royal governor. In the course of the exchange Dulany sought to discredit Carroll by an attack on his religion. This appeal to prejudice angered the Catholic statesman and he struck back in defense of his political and religious beliefs. The excerpts from his letters of May 16 and July 1, 1773, which follow illustrate Carroll's method of meeting the insinuations against his religious faith. Source: Kate Mason Rowland, *The Life of Charles Carroll of Carrollton, 1737–1832, With His Correspondence and Public Papers* (New York: G. P. Putnam's Sons, 1898), I, 284–285, 316, 359.

Maryland Gazette, May 6, 1773.

In vindication of his conduct, Antillon has not endeavoured to convince the minds of his readers by the force of reason, but *"in the favourite method of illiberal calumny, virulent abuse and shameless asseveration to affect their passions"* has attempted to render his antagonist ridiculous, contemptible and odious; he has descended to the lowest jests on the person of the Citizen, has expressed the utmost contempt of his understanding, and a strong suspicion of his *political and religious principles.* What connection, Antillon, have the latter with the Proclamation? Attempts to rouse popular prejudices, and to turn the laugh against an adversary, discover the weakness of a cause, or the inabilities of the advocate, who employs ridicule, instead of argument. *"The Citizen's patriotism is entirely feigned";* his reasons must not be considered, or listened to, because his *religious principles* are not to be trusted. Yet if we are to credit Antillon, the Citizen is so little attached to these principles, *"That he is most devoutly wishing for the event,"* which is to free him from their shackles. What my speculative notions on religion may be, this is neither the place nor time to declare; my political principles ought only to be questioned on the present occasion; surely they are constitutional, and have met, I hope, with the approbation of my countrymen; if so Antillon's aspersions will give me no uneasiness. He asks, who is this Citizen? A man, Antillon, of an independent fortune, one deeply interested in the prosperity of his country: a friend to liberty, a settled enemy to lawless prerogative. . . .

. . . I comprehend fully, Antillon, your threats thrown out against certain religionists; to shew the *greatness of your soul,* and your utter detestation of malice, I shall give the public a translation of your

Latin sentence; the sentiment is truly noble, and reflects the highest lustre on its author or adopter; *Eos tamen laedere non exoptemus, qui nos laedere non exoptant,* we would not wish to hurt those who do not wish to hurt us; — in other words, "I cannot wreak my resentment on the Citizen, without involving all of his religion in one common ruin with him; they have not offended me, it is true, but it is better that ninety-nine just should suffer, than one guilty man escape — a thorough paced politician never sticks at the means of accomplishing his ends; why should I, who have so just a claim to the character?" These, Antillon, are the sentiments and threats, couched under your Latin phrase, which *you even* were ashamed to avow in plain English. . . .

Ibid., July 1, 1773.

. . . The Citizen did not deliver his sentiment only but likewise the sentiment of others. We Catholics, who think we were hardly treated on occasion, *we* still remember the treatment though our resentment hath entirely subsided. It is not in the least surprising that a man incapable of forming an exalted sentiment, should not readily comprehend the force and beauty of one. . . . To what purpose was the threat thrown out of enforcing the penal statutes by proclamation? Why am I told that my conduct is very inconsistent with the situation of one, who "owes even the *toleration* he enjoys to the favour of government"? If by instilling prejudices into the Governor, and by every mean and wicked artifice you can rouse the popular resentment against certain religionists, and thus bring on a persecution of them, it will then be known whether the toleration I enjoy, be due to the favour of government or not. . . .

40. The Quebec Act Grants Religious Freedom to the Catholics of Canada, June 22, 1774

BY THE spring of 1774 the angry temper of the American colonists made it evident to the government in London that something should be done to insure the loyalty of its Canadian subjects to the crown. The result was the Quebec Act by which French law was restored in the colony, its boundaries were given a broad extension to the west and north, and the Catholic Church was guaranteed its freedom. All these features of the bill were resented by the Canadian's southern neighbors, and none to a great degree than the privileged status accorded to the Catholic religion. The act's provision for the French Catholics to take a simple oath of allegiance to the king put no strain upon their religious beliefs as the exaction of the oath of supremacy would have done. In the crisis of the Revolution the Catholics of Canada remained steadfast in their loyalty to Britain despite the blandishments — and force — used by the Americans to win them to their side. Source: Adam Shortt and Arthur G. Doughty (Eds.), *Documents Relating to the Constitutional History of Canada, 1759–1791,* 2 rev. ed. (Ottawa: Historical Documents Publication Board, 1918), Pt. I, 570–576.

And whereas the Provisions, made by the said Proclamation, in respect to the Civil Government of the said Province of *Quebec* and the Powers and Authorities given to the Governor and other Civil Officers of the said Province, by the Grants and Commissions issued in consequence thereof, have been found, upon Experience, to be inapplicable to the State and Circumstances of the said Province, the Inhabitants whereof amounted, at the Conquest, to above Sixty-five thousand Persons professing the Religion of the Church of *Rome*. . . .

And for the more perfect Security and Ease of the Minds of the Inhabitants of the said Province, it is hereby declared, That His Majesty's Subjects, professing the Religion of the Church of *Rome* of and in the said Province of *Quebec,* may have, hold, and enjoy, the free Exercise of the Religion of the Church of *Rome,* subject to the King's Supremacy, declared and established by an Act, made in the First Year of the Reign of Queen *Elizabeth,* over all the Dominions and Countries which then did, or thereafter should, belong to the Imperial Crown of this Realm; and that the Clergy of the said Church may hold, receive, and enjoy their accustomed Dues and Rights, with respect to such Persons only as shall profess the said Religion.

Provided nevertheless, That it shall be lawful for His Majesty, His Heirs or Successors, to make such Provisions out of the rest of the said accustomed Dues and Rights, for the Encouragement of the Protestant Religion, and for the Maintenance and Support of a Protestant Clergy within the said Province, as he or they shall, from Time to Time, think necessary or expedient.

Provided always, and be it enacted, That no Person professing the Religion of the Church of *Rome,* and residing in the said Province, shall be obliged to take the *Oath* required by the said Statute passed in the First Year of the Reign of Queen *Elisabeth,* or any other Oaths substituted by any other Act in the Place thereof; but that every such Person who, by the said Statute is required to take the Oath therein mentioned, shall be obliged, and is hereby required, to take and subscribe the following Oath before the Governor, or such other Persons in such Court of Record as His Majesty shall appoint, who are hereby authorized to administer the same; *videlicet.* [Then follows the form of an oath of simple allegiance to the king with a promise to report all treasonable conspiracies to the authorities.]

And be it further enacted by the Authority aforesaid, That all His Majesty's *Canadian* Subjects, within the Province of *Quebec,* the religious Orders and Communities only excepted, may also hold and enjoy their Property and Possessions, together with all Customs and Usages relative thereto, and all their other Civil Rights. . . .

Provided also, That no Ordinance touching Religion, or by which any Punishment may be inflicted greater than Fine or Imprisonment for Three Months, shall be of any Force or Effect, until the same shall have received His Majesty's Approbation. . . .

41. John Adams' Impressions of a Catholic Service, October 9, 1774

MOST of the founding fathers of the Republic had been nourished on a deep prejudice against the Catholic Church, and whatever tolerance some of them later displayed sprang from a belief in the necessity of religious toleration as a public policy for all rather than from any softening of their attitude toward Catholicism. During the sessions of the Continental Congress John Adams (1735–1826), a delegate from Massachusetts, at times found his official duties very dull. He enlivened one day, therefore, by visiting some of Philadelphia's churches with George Washington. The letter which he wrote to his wife Abigail on October 9, 1774, contained a vivid impression of his reactions after a visit to St. Mary's Church during an afternoon service. Source: Charles Francis Adams (Ed.), *Familiar Letters of John Adams and His Wife Abigail, During the Revolution* (New York: Hurd and Houghton, 1876), pp. 45–46.

I am wearied to death with the life I lead. The business of the Congress is tedious beyond expression. . . .

This day I went to Dr. Allison's meeting in the forenoon, and heard the Dr.; a good discourse upon the Lord's supper. . . . This is a Presbyterian meeting. I confess I am not fond of Presbyterian meetings in this town. . . . And I must confess that the Episcopal Church is quite as agreeable to my taste as the Presbyterian. They are both slaves to the domination of the priesthood. I like the Congregational way best, next to that Independent.

This afternoon, led by curiosity and good company, I strolled away to mother church, or rather grandmother church. I mean the Romish chapel. I heard a good, short moral essay upon the duty of parents to their children, founded in justice and charity, to take care of their interests, temporal and spiritual. This afternoon's entertainment was to me most awful and affecting; the poor wretches fingering their beads, chanting Latin, not a word of which they understood; their pater nosters and ave Marias; their holy water; their crossing themselves perpetually; their bowing to the name of Jesus, whenever they hear it; their bowings, kneelings and genuflections before the altar. The dress of the priest was rich white lace. His pulpit was velvet and gold. The altar-piece was very rich, little images and crucifixes about; wax candles lighted up. But how shall I describe the picture of our Saviour in a frame of marble over the altar, at full length, upon the cross in the agonies, and the blood dropping and streaming from his wounds! The music, consisting of an organ and a choir of singers, went all the afternoon except sermon time, and the assembly chanted most sweetly and exquisitely.

Here is everything which can lay hold of the eye, ear, and imagination — everything which can charm and bewitch the simple and ignorant. I wonder how Luther ever broke the spell. Adieu.

42. Reactions of the Continental Congress to the Quebec Act, September 17–October 26, 1774

AS THE break of the American colonies from Great Britain grew closer the delegates to the Continental Congress determined upon more energetic measures. On September 9, 1774, a convention in Suffolk County, Massachusetts, had adopted a set of resolutions which summarized the principal colonial grievances against the mother country. These so-called Suffolk Resolves were immediately sent to Philadelphia and on September 17 the more radical delegates in the Continental Congress succeeded in having them adopted by that body. On October 21 the congress issued an address to the British people which was followed five days later by an address to the French Canadians and a petition to King George III. All these documents — except that to the Canadians — reflected the resentment felt at Britain's grant of freedom to the Catholic Church in Canada by the Quebec Act which had become law on the previous June 22. In fact, that measure was judged one of the chief sources of grievance against the British crown. It should hardly have surprised the Continental Congress to find that their appeal to the Canadians for assistance had fallen on deaf ears, for the French Catholic leaders knew the true opinions of most Americans about their religious faith, even if they were not aware at the time of the striking contradiction in sentiment between the address sent to them on October 26 and that directed to the British people five days before. The following excerpts from the documents relate to the Catholic Church. Source: Worthington Chauncey Ford (Ed.), *Journals of the Continental Congress, 1774–1789* (Washington: Government Printing Office, 1904).

Suffolk County Resolutions Adopted by the Continental Congress, September 17, 1774:

10. That the late act of parliament for establishing the Roman Catholic religion and the French laws in that extensive country, now called Canada, is dangerous in an extreme degree to the Protestant religion and to the civil rights and liberties of all America; and, therefore, as men and Protestant Christians, we are indispensably obliged to take all proper measures for our security. (*Ibid.,* I, 34–35).

Address to the People of Great Britain, October 21, 1774:

Know then, That we consider ourselves, and do insist, that we are and ought to be, as free as our fellow-subjects in Britain, and that no power on earth has a right to take our property from us without our consent. . . .

That we think the Legislature of Great-Britain is not authorized by the constitution to establish a religion, fraught with sanguinary and impious tenets, or, to erect an arbitrary form of government, in any quarter of the globe. . . .

And by another Act the dominion of Canada is to be so extended, modelled, and governed, as that by being disunited from us, detached from our interests, by civil as well as religious prejudices, that by their numbers daily swelling with Catholic emigrants from Europe, and by their devotion to Administration, so friendly to their religion, they might become formidable to us, and on occasion, be fit instruments in the hands of power, to reduce the ancient free Protestant Colonies to the same state of slavery with themselves. This was evidently the object of the Act: — And in this view, being extremely dangerous to our liberty and quiet, we cannot forbear complaining of it, as hostile to British America. . . . Nor can we suppress our astonishment, that a British Parliament should ever consent to establish in that country a religion that has deluged your island in blood, and dispersed impiety, bigotry, persecution, murder and rebellion through every part of the world. (*Ibid.,* I, 82–83; 88.)

Address to the Inhabitants of the Province of Quebec, October 26, 1774:

We, the Delegates of the Colonies . . . having accordingly assembled and taken into consideration the state of public affairs on this continent, have thought proper to address your province, as a member therein deeply interested. [Then follows a summary of the rights for which they are fighting.]

. . . These are rights *you* are entitled to and ought at this moment in perfection, to exercise. And what is offered to you by the late Act of Parliament in their place? Liberty of conscience in your religion? No. God gave it to you; and the temporal powers with which you have been and are connected, firmly stipulated for your enjoyment of it. If laws, divine and human, could secure it against the despotic caprices of wicked men, it was secured before. . . .

We are too well acquainted with the liberality of sentiment distinguishing your nation, to imagine, that difference of religion will prejudice you against a hearty amity with us. You know, that the transcendent nature of freedom elevates those, who unite in her cause, above all such low-minded infirmities. The Swiss Cantons furnish a memorable proof of this truth. Their union is composed of Roman Catholic and Protestant States, living in the utmost concord and peace with one another, and thereby enabled, ever since they bravely vindicated their freedom, to defy and defeat every tyrant that has invaded them. . . .

We do not ask you, by this address, to commence acts of hostility against the government of our common Sovereign. We only invite you to consult your own glory and welfare. . . .

That Almighty God may incline your minds to approve our equitable and necessary measures, to add yourselves to us . . . and may grant to our joint exertions an event as happy as our cause is just, is the fervent prayer of us, your sincere and affectionate friends and fellow-subjects. (*Ibid.,* I, 105–106, 108, 112–113.)

Petition to the King, October 26, 1774:

We your majesty's faithful subjects of the colonies . . . by this our humble petition, beg leave to lay our grievances before the throne. . . .

In the last sessions of parliament, an act was passed for blocking up the harbour of Boston; another, empowering the governor of the Massachusetts-bay to send persons indicted for murder in that province to another colony or even to Great Britain for trial whereby such offenders may escape legal punishment; a third, for altering the chartered constitution of government in that province; and a fourth for extending the limits of Quebec, abolishing the English and restoring the French laws, whereby great numbers of British freemen are subjected to the latter, and establishing an absolute government and the Roman Catholick religion throughout those vast regions, that border on the westerly and northerly boundaries of the free protestant English settlements; and the fifth for the better providing suitable quarters for officers and soldiers in his majesty's service in North America. . . . (*Ibid.,* I, 115–117.)

43. George Washington Bans Guy Fawkes Day in the Army, November 5, 1775

THE American Revolution served to dissipate to some extent the prejudices which had operated so strongly against Catholics all through the colonial period. Among the many indignities which they had had to suffer was to witness in most of the principal towns on November 5 of each year a commemoration of the fateful attempt of Guy Fawkes to blow up the houses of parliament at London in 1605. At these colonial celebrations one of the principal attractions was the burning of the pope in effigy. Washington's sense of decency put a stop to this practice among the troops under his command at the siege of Boston. His general orders were written while the Commander in Chief was still seemingly confident that the effort to bring the French Catholics of Canada in on the side of the revolting colonies would succeed, and he used that as his main motive for issuing the order. Source: John C. Fitzpatrick (Ed.), *The Writings of George Washington* (Washington: United States Government Printing Office, 1931), IV, 64–65.

GENERAL ORDERS

Head Quarters, Cambridge, November 5, 1775.

As the Commander in Chief has been apprized of a design form'd for the observance of that ridiculous and childish custom of burning the Effigy of the pope — He cannot help expressing his surprise that there should be Officers and Soldiers in this army so void of common sense, as not to see the impropriety of such a step at this Juncture; at a Time when we are solliciting, and have really obtain'd, the friendship and alliance of the people of Canada, whom we ought to consider as Brethren embarked in the same Cause. The defence of the general Liberty of America: At such a juncture, and in such Circumstances, to be insulting their Religion, is so monstrous, as not to be suffered or excused; indeed instead of offering the most remote insult, it is our duty to address public thanks to these our Brethren, as to them we are so much indebted for every late happy Success over the common Enemy in Canada.

44. The Dawn of Religious Freedom for American Catholics, 1776–1791

THE approach of American independence brought to the Catholics in a number of the new states quick relief from the laws that had penalized them through most of the colonial period. But the action of the individual states differed very widely in this respect, and in some cases the legal disabilities lasted well into the nineteenth century. Virginia led the way by its adoption of a bill of rights on June 12, 1776, which embodied the principle of religious freedom, and Pennsylvania and Maryland followed suit before the end of that year. In the constitutions of New York and Massachusetts, however, the old prejudices against Catholics lingered in certain clauses. Meanwhile the general government had agreed to the Articles of Confederation on November 15, 1777, and they went into force on March 1, 1781. Once the Constitution was adopted on September 17, 1787, and its first ten amendments were put into effect on December 15, 1791, it pointed the way for similar action in those states which had hitherto withheld full religious liberty from all their citizens. The following excerpts from the state constitutions were chosen to illustrate the varied action taken by several of the more important states where Catholics were either most numerous or were destined to become so. These are followed by those articles in the two federal instruments of government which pertained in any way to religion. Source: Francis Newton Thorpe (Ed.), *The Federal and State Constitutions* (Washington: Government Printing Office, 1909).

PENNSYLVANIA: Declaration of Rights adopted September 28, 1776.

II. That all men have a natural and unalienable right to worship Almighty God according to the dictates of their own consciences and understanding: And that no man ought or of right can be compelled to attend any religious worship, or erect or support any place of worship, or maintain any ministry, contrary to, or against, his own free will and consent: Nor can any man, who acknowledges the being of a God, be justly deprived or abridged of any civil rights as a citizen, on account of his religious sentiments or peculiar mode of religious worship: And that no authority can or ought to be vested in, or assumed by any power whatever, that shall in any case interfere with, or in any manner controul, the right of conscience in the free exercise of religious worship. (*Ibid.,* V, 3082.)

MARYLAND: Declaration of Rights adopted November 11, 1776.

XXXIII. That, as it is the duty of every man to worship God in such manner as he thinks most acceptable to him; all persons, professing the Christian religion, are equally entitled to protection in their religious liberty; wherefore no person ought by any law to be molested in his person or estate on account of his religious persuasion or profession, or for his religious practice; unless, under colour of religion, any man shall disturb the good order, peace or safety of the State, or shall infringe the laws of morality, or injure others, in their natural, civil, or religious rights; nor ought any person to be compelled to frequent or maintain, or contribute, unless on contract, to maintain any particular place of worship, or any particular ministry; yet the Legislature may, in their discretion, lay a general and equal tax, for the support of the Christian religion; leaving to each individual the power of appointing the payment over of the money, collected from him, to the support of any particular place of worship or minister, or for the benefit of the poor of his own denomination, or of the poor in general of any particular county: but the churches, chapels, glebes, and all other property now belonging to the church of England, ought to remain to the church of England forever. And all acts of Assembly, lately passed, for collecting monies for building or repairing particular churches or chapels of ease, shall continue in force, and be executed, unless the Legislature shall, by act, supersede or repeal the same: but no county court shall assess any quantity of tobacco, or sum of money, hereafter, on the application of any vestrymen or churchwardens; and every encumbent of the church of England, who hath remained in his parish, and performed his duty, shall be entitled to receive the provision and support established by the act, entitled "An act for the support of the clergy of the church of England, in this Province," till the November court of this present year, to be held for the county in which his parish shall lie, or partly lie, or for such time as he hath remained in his parish, and performed his duty. (*Ibid.,* III, 1689–1690.)

NEW YORK: Constitution adopted April 20, 1777.

XXXVIII. And whereas we are required, by the benevolent principles of rational liberty, not only to expel civil tyranny, but also to guard against that spiritual oppression and intolerance wherewith the bigotry and ambition of weak and wicked priests and princes have scourged mankind, this convention doth further, in the name and by the authority of the good people of this State, ordain, determine, and declare, that the free exercise and enjoyment of religious profession and worship, without discrimination or preference, shall forever hereafter be allowed, within this State, to all mankind: *Provided,* That the liberty of conscience, hereby granted, shall not be so construed as to excuse acts of licentiousness, or justify practices inconsistent with the peace or safety of this State.

XXXIX. And whereas the ministers of the gospel are, by their profession, dedicated to the service of God and the care of souls, and ought not to be diverted from the great duties of their functions; therefore, no minister of the gospel, or priest of any denomination whatsoever, shall, at any time hereafter, under any pretence or description whatever, be eligible to, or capable of holding, any civil or military office or place within this State.

XLII. And this convention doth further, in the name and by the authority of the good people of this State, ordain, determine, and declare that it shall be in the discretion of the legislature to naturalize all such persons, and in such manner, as they shall think proper: *Provided,* All such of the persons so to be by them naturalized, as being born in parts beyond the sea, and out of the United States of America, shall come to settle in and become subjects of this State, shall take an oath of allegiance to this State, and abjure and renounce all allegiance and subjection to all and every foreign king, prince, potentate, and State in all matters, ecclesiastical as well as civil. (*Ibid.,* V, 2636–2638.)

MASSACHUSETTS: Constitution ratified by popular vote June 7, 1780.

II. It is the right as well as the duty of all men in society, publicly, and at stated seasons, to worship the SUPREME BEING, the great Creator and Preserver of the universe. And no subject shall be hurt, molested, or restrained in his person, liberty, or estate, for worshipping God in the manner and season most agreeable to the dictates of his own conscience; or for his religious profession of sentiment; provided he doth not disturb the public peace, or obstruct others in their religious worship.

III. As the happiness of a people, and the good order and preservation of civil government, essentially depend upon piety, religion and morality; and as these cannot be generally diffused through a community but by the institution of the public worship of God, and of public instructions in piety, religion and morality; Therefore, to promote their happiness, and to secure the good order and preservation of their government, the people of this commonwealth have a right to invest their legislature with power to authorize and require the several towns, parishes, precincts and other bodies politic, or religious societies, to make suitable provision, at their own expense, for the institution of the public worship of GOD, and for the support and maintenance of public Protestant teachers of piety, religion, and morality, in all cases where such provision shall not be made voluntarily.

And the people of this commonwealth have also a right to, and do, invest their legislature with authority to enjoin upon all the subjects an attendance upon the instructions of the public teachers aforesaid, at stated times and seasons, if there be any on whose instructions they can conscientiously and conveniently attend. . . .

And all moneys paid by the subject to the support of public worship, and of the public teachers aforesaid, shall, if he require it, be uniformly applied to the support of the public teacher or teachers of his own religious sect or denomination, provided there be any on whose instructions he attends; otherwise it may be paid towards the support of the teacher or teachers of the parish or precinct in which the said moneys are raised. (*Ibid.,* III, 1889–1890.)

ARTICLES OF CONFEDERATION: Agreed to by Congress November 15, 1777; ratified and in force March 1, 1781.

III. The said States hereby severally enter into a firm league of friendship, with each other, for their common defence, the security of their liberties, and their mutual and general welfare, binding themselves to assist each other, against all force offered to, or attack made upon them, or any of them, on account of religion, sovereignty, trade, or any other pretence whatever (*Ibid.,* I, 10).

CONSTITUTION: Adopted September 17, 1787; government inaugurated April 30, 1789; first ten amendments in effect December 15, 1791.

VI. No religious Test shall ever be required as a Qualification to any Office of public Trust under the United States (*Ibid.,* I, 27).

I. (Amendments) Congress shall make no law respecting an establishment of religion, or prohibiting the free exercise thereof. (*Ibid.,* I, 29.)

45. Father Gibault Lends Assistance to the American Cause, 1778–1780

ONE of the last of the seminary priests of Quebec to serve in the Illinois Country was Pierre Gibault (1737–1804) who began his missionary career there in 1768. After the outbreak of the American Revolution a group of Virginia militia led by George Rogers Clark (1752–1818) determined upon capturing the British forts in the area. They surprised and took Kaskaskia on July 4, 1778, where Father Gibault was then stationed. Won by Clark's friendly treatment of the French Catholic settlers, the priest volunteered to help when he learned the Americans intended to advance on Vincennes. The leader of the little party was Jean Baptiste Laffont, the village doctor at Kaskaskia, since it was Gibault's wish to keep in the background. The effort was entirely successful and Vincennes and the neighboring Indian tribes declared for the Americans. For this action Gibault won the praise of Governor Patrick Henry of Virginia and a resolution of thanks from the legislature in 1780. But to his superior, Bishop Briand of Quebec, who was intent upon keeping his flock loyal to the British following their generous treatment of the Church in the Quebec Act, Gibault's action was anything but pleasing, and the British authorities themselves regarded him as a traitor. Sensing their reactions from the outset, Gibault kept his hand as hidden as possible and he later denied that he had done more at Vincennes than to counsel peace. The first of the two letters that follow gives Laffont's account of the episode, while the second shows Gibault's warmth toward the American cause as well as revealing something of the confused situation of the Church on the Illinois frontier during the war. Source: Clarence Walworth Alvord (Ed.), *Kaskaskia Records, 1778–1790* (Springfield: Illinois State Historical Library, 1909), pp. 50–51, 518–519.

To Colonel George Roger Clark, present.

I cannot but approve that which M. Gibault said in the contents of his journal. [Even] if he did omit some historical truths which might have been worthy of narration, that which he said is the pure truth. All that he has begged me to add and which he will tell to you, and has asked me to be present (and which he forgot) is that in all the civil affairs, not only with the French but with the savages, he meddled with nothing, because he was not ordered to do so and it was opposed to his vocation; and that I alone had the direction of the affair, he himself having confined himself towards both French and Indians solely to exhortation tending towards peace and union and to the prevention of bloodshed; and so, sir, for the temporal affairs with which I am wholly entrusted, I hope to have all the satisfaction possible, for I acted in all things with an irreproachable integrity.

My zeal and my sincerity persuade me that you will have, sir, the kindness to accept the good wishes which I have the honor to make to you, and to believe me, with a most respectful regard,

Your very humble and very obedient servant,
Laffont.

Kaskaskia, August 7th. 1778

Mr. G. R. Clark,
Sir,

We have been greatly disappointed in not having the pleasure of seeing you in our village. The joy was general when we knew that you were so near us. The kindness and benefits you showed us during your stay here gave us the promise of the same when you should return. I was not one of those who desired you with the least ardor. You know my heart; and, if the public affairs of my ministry did not demand my presence, I should have given myself the pleasure and honor of making you a visit in your new establishment; but I hope that it is only a postponement and that another opportunity will find me less occupied. We are very poor and destitute of all things. We are impatiently expecting the village boats. We fear the savages and the evilly disposed people who are urging them to kill us. In a word we are truly in a sad situation. In spite of this we are of good courage and are so good Americans that we are ready to defend ourselves to the death against any who attack us. I pray you to accept my respects and to employ me in any way in my power for your service. I always have true pleasure in being useful to you and in calling myself with all possible consideration

Your very humble and obedient servant,
P. Gibault, Priest.

Kaskaskia, May 10, 1780.

49. John Carroll Is Appointed Superior of the American Missions, June 9, 1784

THE recognition of American independence by Great Britain in the provisional treaty of November 30, 1782, confronted the Holy See with a difficult and unprecedented situation. Obviously the jurisdiction of the Vicar Apostolic of the London District over American Catholics could no longer be exercised and some substitute would have to be found. But an overseas republic with a strong tradition of hostility toward the Church, wherein the priests themselves were known to oppose the appointment of a bishop, did not offer a promising prospect for direct negotiations. In his perplexity, therefore, Lorenzo Cardinal Antonelli (1730–1811), Prefect of Propaganda, turned to France, the new republic's ally, for guidance. He first raised the question with the nuncio at Paris on January 15, 1783, and for the next year and a half the correspondence continued and ultimately involved a number of officials, including Benjamin Franklin, the American Minister to France. Finally Propaganda reached a decision by naming John Carroll (1735–1815) as superior of the American missions with very limited faculties. Thus did there come about the first step toward giving a form and government to the Church in the United States. The following letter of Antonelli to Carroll informed him of his appointment, acknowledged that it was only a temporary arrangement, and asked for more information on the state of Catholicism in the new country. Source: Latin text in Donald C. Shearer, O.F.M.Cap. (Ed.), *Pontificia Americana. A Documentary History of the Catholic Church in the United States, 1784–1884* (Washington: The Catholic University of America Press, 1933), pp. 58–59; English translation by John Gilmary Shea, *History of the Catholic Church in the United States* (New York: John G. Shea, 1888), II, 243–245.

Rome, June 9, 1784.

Very Rev. Sir:

In order to preserve and defend Catholicity in the Thirteen United States of North America, the Supreme Pontiff of the Church Pius VI., and this sacred Congregation, have thought it extremely proper to designate a pastor who should, permanently and independently of any ecclesiastical power, except the same Sacred Congregation, attend to the spiritual necessities of the Catholic flock. In the appointment of such a pastor, the Sacred Congregation would have readily have cast its eyes on the Rev. John Lewis if his advanced age and the labors he has already undergone in the vineyard of the Lord, had not deterred it from imposing on him, a new and very heavy burden; for he seems to require repose rather than arduous labor. As then, Rev. Sir, you have given conspicuous proofs of piety and zeal, and it is known that your appointment will please and gratify many members of that republic, and especially Mr. Franklin, the eminent individual who represents the same republic at the court of the Most Christian King, the Sacred Congregation, with the approbation of his Holiness, has appointed you Superior of the Mission in the thirteen United States of North America, and has communicated to you the faculties, which are necessary to the discharge of that office; faculties which are also communicated to the other priests of the same States, except the administration of confirmation, which is reserved for you alone, as the enclosed documents will show.

These arrangements are meant to be only temporary. For it is the intention of his Holiness soon to charge a Vicar-Apostolic, invested with the title and character of bishop, with the care of those states, that he may attend to ordination and other episcopal functions. But, to accomplish this design, it is of great importance that we should be made acquainted with the state of the orthodox religion in those thirteen states. Therefore we request you to forward to us, as soon as possible, a correct report, stating carefully the number of Catholics in each state; what is their condition, their piety and what abuses exist; also how many missionary priests labor now in this vineyard of the Lord; what are their qualifications, their zeal, their mode of support. For though the Sacred Congregation wish not to meddle with temporal things, it is important for the establishment of laborers, that we should know what are the ecclesiastical revenues, if any there are, and it is believed there are some. In the meantime for fear the want of missionaries should deprive the Catholics of spiritual assistance, is has been resolved to invite hither two youths from the states of Maryland and Pennsylvania, to educate them at the expense of the Sacred Congregation in the Urban College; they will afterwards, on returning to their country, be substitutes in the mission. We leave to your solicitude the care of selecting and sending them. You will make choice of those who have more promising talents and a good constitution, who are not less than twelve, nor more than fifteen years of age; who by their proficiency in the sanctuary may give great hopes of themselves. You may address them to the excellent archbishop of Seleucia, Apostolic Nuncio at Paris, who is informed of their coming. If the young men selected are unable to defray the expenses of the voyage, the Sacred Congregation will provide for them: we even wish to be informed by you frankly and accurately of the necessary traveling expenses, to serve as a rule for the future. Such are the things I had to signify to you; and whilst I am confident you will discharge the office committed to you with all zeal, solicitude and fidelity, and more than answer the high opinion we have formed of you, I pray God that he may grant you all peace and happiness.

L. Card. Antonelli,
Prefect.

Stephen Borgia,
Secretary.

47. Carroll Answers an Attack Upon the Catholic Faith, 1784

ONE of the most unpleasant duties which John Carroll, first superior of the American Catholics, had to perform in the year of his appointment was to answer an attack made upon the Catholic faith by an apostate priest. Charles H. Wharton (1748–1833) was a Maryland-born ex-Jesuit like Carroll himself who had served for some years as chaplain to the Catholics in Worcester, England. After his return to the United States he had published at Philadelphia in the early summer of 1784 *A Letter to the Roman Catholics of the City of Worcester*. The following excerpts from Carroll's reply indicate something of his method as well as the method used by Wharton in his efforts to justify his action. Carroll was a warm admirer of the religious toleration which was then becoming a reality in the United States and he was pained at the prospect of disrupting the present harmony between Americans of different religious beliefs by engaging in religious controversy. The priests of that day were accustomed to charges against the Church, but by reason of the nature and source of Wharton's publication they felt it could not be ignored, and they were agreed that Carroll was the man to answer it. Source: *An Address to the Roman Catholics of the United States of America*. By a Catholic Clergyman [John Carroll] (Annapolis: Frederick Green, 1784), pp. 59–60, 113–115.

I will not deny, that I was surprised when I read the first passage cited by the Chaplain; it appeared so opposite to the principles which St. Chrysostom had laid down in several parts of his works. It was a mortifying circumstance, that I could not conveniently have recourse to that holy doctor's writings, nor minutely examine the passage objected, together with its context. I procured a friend to examine the edition of Chrysostom's works, belonging to the public library at Annapolis; he has carefully and repeatedly read the 49th homily on St. Matthew; and not one syllable of the Chaplain's citation is to be found in it. After receiving this notice, I was for some time doubtful, whether it might not be owing to a difference in the editions. I could not persuade myself, that he, who so solemnly calls heaven to witness for the impartiality and integrity of his inquiry, would publicly expose himself to a well-grounded imputation of unpardonable negligence, in a matter of such serious concern. But I have now the fullest evidence, that the passage, for which Chrysostom on Matthew, hom. 49, is quoted, is not taken from that father. It is extracted from a work of no credit, supposed to be written in the 6th century, entitled, *The unfinished work on Matthew*. But had it ever been fairly quoted from him, the Chaplain would not have had so much cause for triumph as he imagines. For the passage, he adduces, carries with it equal condemnation of the protestant and catholic rule of faith. . . .

I have now gone through a task, painful in every point of view, in which I could consider it. To write for the public eye, on any occasion whatever, is neither agreeable to my feelings, my leisure, or opportunities; that it is likewise disproportioned to my abilities, my readers, I doubt [not], will soon discover. But if reduced to the necessity of publishing, I would wish that my duty led me to any species of composition, rather than that of religious controversy. Mankind have conceived such a contempt for it, that an author cannot entertain a hope of enjoying those gratifications, which in treating other subjects may support his spirits and enliven his imagination. Much less could I have a prospect of these incitements in the prosecution of my present undertaking. I could not forget, in the beginning, progress, and conclusion of it, that the habits of thinking, the prejudices, perhaps even the passions of many of my readers, would be set against all the arguments, I could offer; and that the weaknesses, the errors, the absurdities of the writer would be imputed to the errors and absurdity of his religion. But of all considerations the most painful was, that I had to combat him, with whom I had been connected in an intercourse of friendship and mutual good offices; and in connection with whom I hoped to have consummated my course of our common ministry in the service of virtue and religion. But when I found these expectations disappointed; when I found that he not only had abandoned our faith and communion, but had imputed to us doctrines foreign to our belief, and having a natural tendency to embitter against us the minds of our fellow-citizens, I felt an anguish too keen for description; and perhaps the Chaplain will experience a similar sentiment, when he comes coolly to reflect on this instance of his conduct. It did not become the friend of toleration to misinform, and to sow in minds so misinformed, the seeds of religious animosity.

Under all these distressful feelings, one consideration alone relieved me in writing; and that was, the hope of vindicating your religion to your own selves at least, and preserving the steadfastness of your faith. But even this prospect should not have induced me to engage in the controversy, if I could fear that it would disturb the harmony now subsisting amongst all christians in this country, so blessed with civil and religious liberty; which if we have the wisdom and temper to preserve, America may come to exhibit a proof to the world, that general and equal toleration, by giving a free circulation to fair argument, is the most effectual method to bring all denominations of christians to a unity of faith.

The motives, which led the Chaplain to the step he has taken, are known best to God and himself. For the vindication of his conduct, he appeals to the dictates of conscience with a seriousness and solemnity, which must add greatly to his guilt, if he be not sincere. He is anxious to impress on his readers a firm conviction, that neither views of preferment or sensuality, had any influence on his determination. He appears to be jealous, that suspicions will arise unfavourable to the purity of his intentions. He shall have no cause to impute to me the spreading of these suspicions. But I must entreat him with an earnestness suggested by the most perfect good will and zealous regard for his welfare, to consider the sanctity of the solemn and deliberate engagement, which at an age of perfect maturity he contracted with Almighty God. . . .

48. The First American Report to Propaganda on Catholicism in the United States, March 1, 1785

FATHER JOHN CARROLL did not find his appointment as superior of the American Catholic missions to his liking, but from the time he received word of it in late November, 1784, he set about to fulfill the duties of the office as efficiently as he possibly could. One of his most pressing tasks was to furnish Propaganda with the data they had requested concerning the condition of the Church in the United States. For that purpose Carroll turned to the twenty-four priests then in the country and asked them to supply him with the facts on their missions. From the reports submitted to him, and from his own knowledge, he composed the document which follows. It has interest as being the most authentic account of the state of the Church at that time, as well as being the first of a lengthy series of reports on American Catholicism which found their way into Propaganda's archives from 1784 until 1908 when the American Church was removed from the jurisdiction of that congregation. Source: The original Latin was published from a photostat of the document in the archives of the Congregation de Propaganda Fide by Peter Guilday, *The Life and Times of John Carroll, Archbishop of Baltimore, 1735–1815* (New York: Encyclopedia Press, 1922), I, 223–225; the translation is taken from John Gilmary Shea, *History of the Catholic Church in the United States* (New York: John G. Shea, 1888), II, 257–261.

Report for the Eminent Cardinal Antonelli

Concerning the State of Religion in the United States of America.

1. On the Number of Catholics in the United States.

There are in Maryland about 15,800 Catholics; of these there are about 9,000 freemen, adults or over twelve years of age; children under that age, about 3,000; and above that number of slaves of all ages of African origin, called negroes. There are in Pennsylvania about 7,000, very few of whom are negroes, and the Catholics are less scattered and live nearer to each other. There are not more than 200 in Virginia who are visited four or five times a year by a priest. Many other Catholics are said to be scattered in that and other States, who are utterly deprived of all religious ministry. In the State of New York I hear that there are at least 1,500. (Would that some spiritual succor could be afforded them!) They have recently, at their own expense, sent for a Franciscan Father from Ireland, and he is said to have the best testimonials as to his learning and life; he had arrived a little before I received the letters in which faculties were transmitted to me, communicable to my fellow-priests. I was for a time in doubt whether I could properly approve this priest for the administration of the sacraments. I have now, however, decided, especially as the feast of Easter is so near, to consider him as one of my fellow-priests, and to grant him faculties, and I trust that my decision will meet your approbation. As to the Catholics who are in the territory bordering on the river called Mississippi and in all that region which following that river extends to the Atlantic Ocean, and from it extends to the limits of Carolina, Virginia and Pennsylvania, — this tract of country contains, I hear, many Catholics, formerly Canadians, who speak French, and I fear that they are destitute of priests. Before I received your Eminence's letters there went to them a priest, German by birth, but who came last from France; he professes to belong to the Carmelite order: he was furnished with no sufficient testimonials that he was sent by his lawful superior. What he is doing and what is the condition of the Church in those parts, I expect soon to learn. The jurisdiction of the Bishop of Quebec formerly extended to some part of that region; but I do not know whether he wishes to exercise any authority there now, that all these parts are subjects to the United States.

2. On the Condition, Piety, and Defects, etc., of Catholics.

In Maryland a few of the leading more wealthy families still profess the Catholic faith introduced at the very foundation of the province by their ancestors. The greater part of them are planters and in Pennsylvania almost all are farmers, except the merchants and mechanics living in Philadelphia. As for piety, they are for the most part sufficiently assiduous in the exercises of religion and in frequenting the sacraments, but they lack that fervor, which frequent appeals to the sentiment of piety usually produce, as many congregations hear the word of God only once a month, and sometimes only once in two months. We are reduced to this by want of priests, by the distance of congregations from each other and by difficulty of travelling. This refers to Catholics born here, for the condition of the Catholics who in great numbers are flowing in here from different countries of Europe, is very different. For while there are few of our native Catholics who do not approach the sacraments of Penance and the Holy Eucharist, at least once a year, especially in Easter time, you can scarcely find any among the newcomers who discharge this duty of religion, and there is reason to fear that the example will be very pernicious especially in commercial towns. The abuses that have grown among Catholics are chiefly those, which result with unavoidable intercourse with non-Catholics, and the examples thense derived: namely more free intercourse between young people of opposite sexes than is compatible with chastity in mind and body; too great fondness for dances and similar amusements; and an incredible eagerness, especially in girls, for reading love stories which are brought over in great quantities from Europe. Then among other things, a general lack of care in instructing their children and especially the negro slaves in their religion, as these people are kept constantly at work, so that they rarely hear any instructions from the priest, unless they can spend a short time with one; and most of them are consequently very dull in faith and depraved in morals. It can scarcely be believed how much trouble and care they give the pastors of souls.

3. On the number of priests, their qualifications, character and means of support.

There are nineteen priests in Maryland and five in Pennsylvania. Of these two are more than seventy years old, and three others very near that age: and they are consequently almost entirely unfit to undergo the hardships, without which this Vineyard of the Lord cannot be cultivated. Of the remaining priests some are in very bad health, and there is one recently approved by me for a few months only, that in the extreme want of priests I may give him a trial: for some things were reported of him, which made me averse to employing him. I will watch him carefully, and if anything occurs unworthy priestly gravity I will recall the faculties granted, whatever inconvenience this may bring to many Catholics: for I am convinced that the Catholic faith will suffer less harm, if for a short time there is no priest at a place, than if living as we do among fellow-citizens of another religion, we admit to the discharge of the sacred ministry, I do not say bad priests, but incautious and imprudent priests. All the other clergymen lead a life full of labour, as each one attends congregations far apart, and has to be riding constantly and with great fatigue, especially to sick calls. Priests are maintained chiefly from the proceeds of the estates; elsewhere by the liberality of the Catholics. There is properly no ecclesiastical property here: for the property by which the priests are supported, is held in the names of individuals and transferred by will to devisees. This course was rendered necessary when the Catholic religion was cramped here by laws, and no remedy has yet been found for this difficulty, although we made an earnest effort last year.

There is a college in Philadelphia, and it is proposed to establish two in Maryland, in which Catholics can be admitted, as well as others, as presidents, professors and pupils. We hope that some educated there will embrace the ecclesiastical state. We think accordingly of establishing a Seminary, in which they can be trained to the life and learning suited to that state.

John Carroll.

March 1, 1785.

49. Lay Trusteeism in New York, January 25, 1786

THE most serious trouble that confronted the Catholic Church in the United States after the Revolution arose from the abuse of lay trusteeism. The root causes of the difficulty were: an imperfect knowledge, on the part of both clergy and laity, of the canon law pertaining to the holding and administration of church property; small groups of laymen imbued with the heady wine of their newly won religious freedom, and the example of their Protestant neighbors who had the dominant voice in ruling their congregations; wayward priests who for selfish reasons abetted the laymen's ambitions to govern the congregations; and a mounting antagonism among Catholics of varying national backgrounds. All the principal elements were present at St. Peter's Church, New York City, in the 1780's, plus the frustration suffered by John Carroll as ecclesiastical superior due to his limited faculties to deal with situations of this kind. St. Peter's got its start with an Irish-born Capuchin, Charles Whelan, who arrived in 1784, but with the appearance of another Irish Capuchin, Andrew Nugent, in 1785, quarrels arose and the congregation was soon divided between warring factions with the trustees finally casting Whelan out and going over to Nugent as the better preacher. Carroll was appealed to and in his reply to the trustees he cogently set forth the chief issues involved. The ugly affair eventually resulted in schism and it was only with the coming of Father

William V. O'Brien, O.P. (1740–1816), in October, 1787, that peace was restored. Carroll's letter is included here to illustrate the nature of an evil that would plague the American Church in one form or another until near the middle of the nineteenth century. Source: *American Catholic Historical Researches,* XVII (January, 1900), 1–4.

R.C. [Rock Creek] near Georgetown, Jan. 25, 1786.

Gentlemen:

I was honored yesterday at the same time with your letters of Dec. 22, 1785, and January 11, 1786. You did me justice in supposing that the former was delayed on its way or had miscarried; for certainly I should not have failed in my duty of immediately answering so respectable a part of the congregation. You will however readily conceive, that this is not an easy nor, allow me to say, a very agreeable office in the present instance. One circumstance indeed gives me comfort; you profess to have no other views than for the service and credit of religion; and as I make it my endeavor to be influenced solely by the same motive, I trust that proposing to ourselves the same end we shall likewise agree in the means of obtaining it.

The first advices of any disturbances among you, were transmitted to me in letters from Messrs. Whelan and Nugent which I answered on the 17th and 18th inst. Both these gentlemen represented the steps taken as extreme and improper. I spoke of them therefore in the same manner in my answers, and the more freely as neither of them mentioned the name of one single person concerned. Having now received a communication of your sentiments, I shall likewise deliver mine with the respect due to your representations, and with the freedom and plainness becoming the responsible and burdensome office, of which I feel myself every day more unworthy, in proportion as the duties and the weight of it grow upon me.

But I must first state to you the previous information I had received: 1st, that the trustees denied having agreed to the articles, of which I left a copy with Mr. Whelan; and which to my best apprehension had been adopted at the meeting I had the honor of having with those gentlemen. 2d, that an opinion was formed and propagated of the congregation having a right not only to choose such parish priest as is agreeable to them, but discharging him at pleasure, and that after such election, the bishop or other ecclesiastical superior cannot hinder him from exercising the usual functions. 3dly, that two of the congregation (by whose orders I am not informed) on Sunday, December 18th, after Divine Service and in the face of all present in the chapel, seized in a tumultuary manner and kept possession of the collection then made. The first part of this intelligence shocked me very much both because it reflected on my veracity which in this instance I will steadily assert and because I considered the matters then agreed on as right in point of justice as the renewal of confidence and foundation of future union. The next point of intelligence was still more important. If ever the principles then laid down should become predominant, the unity and catholicity of our Church would be at an end; and it would be formed into distinct and independent societies, nearly in the same manner as the congregational Presbyterians of our neighboring New England States. A zealous clergyman performing his duty courageously and without respect of persons would be always liable to be the victim of his earnest endeavors to stop the progress of vice and evil example, and others more complying with the passions of some principal persons of the congregation would be substituted in his room; and if the ecclesiastical superior has no control in these instances, I will refer to your own judgment what the consequences may be. The great source of misconception in this matter is that an idea appears to be taken both by you and Mr. Whelan that the officiating clergyman at New York is a parish priest, whereas there is yet no such office in the United States. The hierarchy of our American Church not being yet constituted, no parishes are formed, and the clergy coming to the assistance of the faithful, are but voluntary laborers in the vineyard of Christ, not vested with ordinary jurisdiction annexed to their office, but receiving it as delegated and extra hierarchical commission. Wherever parishes are established no doubt, a proper regard (and such as is suitable (?) to our governments) will be had to rights of the congregation in the mode of election and representation; and even now I shall ever pay to their wishes every deference consistent with the general welfare of religion: of which I hope to give you proof in the sequel of this letter. The third article of my information was particularly mortifying; for I could not but fear, that a step so violent, at such a time and place, and probably in the presence of other religionists would breed disunion among yourselves and make a very disadvantageous impression, to the prejudice of the Catholic cause, so soon after the first introduction of public worship into your city.

I now return to the contents of your letters, and observe that after stating some censurable instances of Mr. Whelan's conduct, you desire me to remove him, and imply a desire that Mr. Nugent, as being very acceptable, may succeed to his office. I can assure you, Gentlemen, that I have a very advantageous opinion of Mr. Nugent's abilities, and he shewed me very good testimonials of his zeal and virtue. I repeatedly told him, as I did to many of yourselves, that nothing but my own want of sufficient authority prevented me from giving him every power requisite for the exercise of his ministry. I hoped before this to have that restriction of my authority removed, but as it is not, it remains still out of my power to employ him agreeably to your and my desires. If I am ever able to do it, I will certainly remember my assurances to him. But in the mean time what can I do? Can I revoke Mr. Whelan's faculties and leave so great a congregation without assistance? Can I deprive him, when neither his morals, his orthodoxy, or his assiduity have been impeached? especially while I am uncertain whether his removal be desired by a majority of the congregation? For I have received assurances very much to the contrary. But even if a considerable part are still attached to him, would the great object of unanimity be obtained by his removal? Would not his adherents consider Mr. Nugent as coming in upon the ruins of his predecessor and consequently would they not keep alive the spirit of discord? Upon these considerations I have taken a resolution which will, I hope, meet your wishes, as well as of every part of the congregation. As soon as I am at liberty to grant them, Mr. Nugent shall have powers from me [to] act as your joint-chaplain; for the idea of parish-priest is not admissible. He has repeatedly assured me he never will accept of an appointment to the exclusion of his brother: in his letter he says a sufficient maintenance of both may be obtained. In the mean time he has full authority to announce the word of God, and I promise myself he will do it with effect, especially by including the great duty of charity and unanimity. He and Mr. Whelan will concur in recommending this characteristic virtue of christianity, by their examples as well as advice. Educated in the same school of religion, and connected by special ties to the same order, they will assist each other in the work of the ministry and every part of the congregation will have it in their power to apply to him of the two, in which they have the greatest confidence. I must not omit taking notice of Mr. Whelan's address to the congregation inclosed in your last. I greatly disapprove it, and shall so inform him. When I wrote the letter to which he refers, I had heard nothing from New York concerning your uneasiness. I lamented that my hands being still tied, I was prevented from giving full employment to Mr. Nugent's zeal; and I must add, for Mr. La Valinère's[1] credit, that when I declined granting him leave to administer the Sacraments to the Canadian refugees, it was for the same reason, because I had no power to do it. Otherwise I have such a conviction of his many qualities, that I should gladly have indulged the wishes of those good people who solicited [this power] and of this I beg to inform him.

[At the close?] of your last letter you make some mention of eventually having recourse to legal means to rid yourselves of Mr. Whelan. The insinuation makes me very unhappy. I cannot tell what assistance the laws might give you; but allow me to say that you can take no step so fatal to that respectability, in which as a religious Society you wish to stand, or more prejudicial to the Catholic cause. I must therefore entreat you to decline a design so pernicious to all your prospects; and protesting against measures so extreme, I explicitly declare, that no clergyman, be he who he may, shall receive any spiritual powers from me who shall advise or countenance so unnecessary . . . [the copy breaks off at this point].

50. Thomas FitzSimons Urges Pennsylvania's Early Ratification of the Constitution, September 29, 1787

IN THE convention that drafted the federal Constitution at Philadelphia in May-September, 1787, there were two Catholic delegates: Thomas FitzSimons of Pennsylvania and Daniel Carroll of Maryland. FitzSimons (1741–1811) had early won prominence as a member of both the Pennsylvania legislature and the congress established under the Articles of Confederation, and from 1789–1795 he served as a member of the national House of Representatives. He was active in the debates of the constitutional convention in behalf of a strong national government and, therefore, when the Constitution was laid before the legislature and a threat of delay developed, FitzSimons vigorously contended that neither the old congress nor the state legislatures had any right to make the decision; that right, said FitzSimons, rested with the people in an election for delegates to a ratifying convention. FitzSimons belonged to the Federalist group of delegates from Philadelphia and the commercial towns who were intent upon quick ratifica-

[1] Pierre Huet de la Valinière (1732–1806), a French-born Sulpician, who had incurred the displeasure of both Bishop Briand and the British authorities in Canada during the Revolution because of his flirtations with the Americans. He was a rather erratic fellow whose many wanderings seemed to bring him little peace of mind.

tion lest the anti-Federalist forces of the German farmers and Scotch-Irish frontiersmen be given time to crystallize. His speech in the legislature on September 29, 1787, helped to hasten action and in the squel Pennsylvania was the second state to ratify the Constitution on December 12, 1787. FitzSimons was one of Philadelphia's most outstanding citizens, filling for many years such posts as president of the Chamber of Commerce, trustee of the University of Pennsylvania, trustee of the Bank of North America, and founder and director of the Insurance Company of North America. He was always a devout Catholic and was the largest single contributor to St. Augustine's Church in Philadelphia. Source: *Proceedings and Debates of the General Assembly of Pennsylvania* (Philadelphia: Daniel Humphreys, 1787), I, 131–132.

I think too highly of the good sense of this House, to suppose it necessary to say anything to prove to them, that their *agreement* to calling a convention is *not unfederal,* as every member must have fully considered the point before this time; now I do not think a single gentleman supposes, that it would be unfederal. Though the member from Westmoreland has taken some pains to persuade us, that Pennsylvania has been hitherto a federal state, and that we are about to depart from that conduct, and to run before even prosperity itself — I think it greatly to the honor of Pennsylvania that she deserves the gentleman's commendation, by having always stood foremost in support of federal measures, and I think it will redound still more to her honor, to enter foremost into this new system of confederation, seeing the old is so dissolved or rotten as to be incapable of answering any good purpose whatsoever. Has the gentleman ever looked at the new constitution? If he has, he will see it is not an alteration of an article in the old, but that it departs in every principle from the other. It presupposes, Sir, that no confederation exists; or if it does exist, it exists to no purpose, as it can answer no useful purpose; it cannot provide for the common defense, nor promote the general welfare — Therefore, arguments that are intended to reconcile one with the other, or make the latter an appendage to the former, are but a mere waste of words. Does the gentleman suppose that the convention thought themselves acting under any provision made in the confederation for altering its articles? No, Sir, they had no such idea. They were obliged, in the first instance, to begin with the destruction of its greatest principle, *equal representation.* They found the confederation without vigor, and so decayed, that it was impossible to graft a useful article upon it; nor was the *mode,* Sir, prescribed by that confederation, which requires alterations to originate with Congress. They found at an early period, that no good purpose could be effected by making such alterations, as were provided by the first articles of union. They also saw, that what alterations were necessary could not be ratified by the legislatures, as they were incompetent to ordaining a form of government. They knew this belonged to the people only, and that the people only would be adequate to carry it into effect. What have Congress and the legislature to do with the proposed constitution? Nothing, Sir — they are but the mere vehicles to convey the information to the people. The convention, Sir, never supposed it was necessary to report to Congress, much less to abide their determination: they thought it decent to make the compliment to them of sending the result of their deliberations — concluding the knowledge of that would be more extensively spread through their means — not that I would infer there is the least doubt of the most hearty concurrence of that body. But, should they decline, and the State of Pennsylvania neglect calling a convention, as I said before, the authority is with the people, and they will do it themselves: but there is a propriety in the legislatures, providing the mode by which it may be conducted in a decent and orderly manner.

The member from Westmoreland agrees that a convention ought to take place. He goes further, and declares that it must and will take place, but assigns no reason why it should not early take place. He must know that any time after the election will be proper, because at that time the people, being collected together, have full opportunity to learn each other's sentiments on this subject. Taking measures for calling a convention is a very different thing from deciding on the plan of government. The sentiments of the people, so far as they have been collected, have been unanimously favorable to its adoption, and its early adoption, if their representatives think it a good one; if we set the example now, there is a great prospect of its being generally come into; but if we delay, ill consequences may arise. And I should suppose, if no better arguments are offered for the delay than what has been advanced by the gentleman on the other side of the house, that we will not agree to it. As to the time for election, that has been all along conceded, and gentlemen will propose such time as they think proper.

51. Daniel Carroll Argues for Marylanders to Ratify the Constitution, October 16, 1787

DANIEL CARROLL (1730–1796), brother of the first Archbishop of Baltimore, served the nation in a number of important offices, viz., as delegate to both the Continental Congress and the Constitutional Convention, United States Senator from Maryland, and as one of the three commissioners appointed by President Washington to survey the federal district. Like his fellow Catholic in the convention that drafted the Constitution, FitzSimons of Pennsylvania, Carroll was intent that the new government should be a strong one. When Samuel Chase, writing over the pen name of "Caution," counseled his fellow Marylanders to delay action, Carroll as "A Friend to the Constitution" came forward with a persuasive appeal urging a speedy ratification. Source: *Maryland Journal,* October 16, 1787.

To the Inhabitants of Baltimore Town:

You have been addressed in the last Friday's Paper, by a writer under the signature of Caution, who would persuade you that you ought to withhold your approbation at the time, from the Federal Constitution recommended by the Convention.

This writer may have the best intention in the world toward the PUBLIC WELFARE, and the PROSPERITY of Baltimore; but every one must perceive that he is an enemy to the proposed Constitution, and wishes to prevent you from expressing yourselves in its favor, not only AT THIS TIME, but at any future time.

Mr. C—— is said to be the author of this admonition; but that this is a malicious insinuation, aimed at his sincerity, will appear by considering his recent promise on this subject, signed and published by himself, in reference with the resolution of the Convention, upon which that promise is founded. I shall date both the resolution and promise, that you may judge for yourselves.

The resolve of the Convention declares, that the Constitution should be submitted to a Convention of Delegates, chosen in each State by the people, under the recommendation of its legislature, for their assent and ratification.

Mr. C—— being called upon, before his election, to declare himself on this point, promised to the people, "that he will use his endeavors, if elected to call a Convention."

I would just observe on this resolve and promise: — First, that the resolve make it an absolute condition that the legislature recommend a Convention TO ASSENT TO AND RATIFY THE CONSTITU-

TION. Secondly — that the promise made by Mr. C—— is obligating upon him to use his endeavors to procure a Convention FOR THIS PURPOSE.

Another remark which occurs on this occasion, is that Mr. C—— could not mean that a Convention ought to be called FOR ANY OTHER PURPOSE than to assent and ratify the Constitution; for it is absurd to suppose he meant the Convention should be authorized by the legislature TO PROPOSE AMENDMENTS OR ALTERATIONS, that being CONTRARY to the declared intention of the resolution, and the Sense which his friends entertained of his engagement at the time he entered into it: Mr. C—— therefore (without presuming him capable of doing the greatest violence to his promise) strenuously, though indirectly, against adopting the Constitution.

From the brief view of the nature and intention of the resolve, I think it is evident that the people ought WITHOUT DELAY, to signify their approbation of the Constitution by a PETITION TO THE LEGISLATURE, to this end that the legislature, which is called upon by the Convention, and Congress to recommend to the people to choose Delegates to ratify it, may have the authority of this largest and most promising commercial and manufacturing Town in the State to countenance so important a recommendation. But Caution thinks a petition improper and unnecessary because says he "Your Delegates will move for and exert themselves to procure the calling a Convention." Admitting your Delegates to move to have a Convention called, does it follow that they will add to the motion these essential words, to confirm and ratify the Constitution. Does it not rather appear, from the tenor of this writer's remarks that your Delegates ought to leave these words out of their motion? But the propriety and necessity of a petition does not depend on what your Delegates may or may not do. It is PROPER at this time because the Constitution meets your approbation. It is NECESSARY at this time, because wanted as an inducement to the legislature to call upon the people to appoint a Convention to carry into effect the object of the resolution. In other words, as the recommendation for a Convention involve the legislature in a complete approbation of the Constitution, there is the greatest propriety and necessity for your telling the legislature that it meets your approbation.

I am sorry to find, by Caution's publication and insinuations, which I am told are circulated with great industry, that an opposition is opened against the Constitution. I did not, I confess, expect to see it adopted without some opposition, but I could not bring myself to believe, that this opposition could have originated in Baltimore, which is so peculiarly interested in its speedy adoption. But what I intended to say on this point, is so well expressed in a late speech of Mr. Wilson,[1] to the people of Philadelphia, previous to their election for representation, that I shall take the liberty of closing with it.

"After all, my fellow-citizens (says this excellent politician) it is neither extraordinary nor unexpected that the Constitution offered to your consideration should meet with opposition. It is the nature of man to pursue his own interest in preference to the PUBLIC GOOD; and I do not mean to make any personal reflection when I add, that it is the interest of a very numerous, powerful and respectable body to counteract and destroy the excellent work produced by the late convention. All the offices of government, and all the appointments for the administration of justice, and the collection of the public revenue, which are transferred from the individual to the aggregate sovereignty of the States, will necessarily turn the stream of influence and emolument into a new channel. EVERY PERSON, therefore, who either enjoys, or expects to enjoy, a place of profit under the present establishment, will object to this proposed innovation, not in truth because it is injurious to the liberties of his country; but because it effects his schemes of wealth and consequences. I will confess, indeed, that I am not a blind admirer of this plan of government, and that there are some parts of it, which if my wish had prevailed, would certainly have been altered. But, when I reflect how widely men differ in their opinions, and that every man (and the observation applies likewise to every state) has an equal pretension to assert his own, I am satisfied that anything nearer to perfection could not have been accomplished. If there are errors, it should be remembered, that the seeds of reformation are sown in the work itself, and the concurrence of two thirds of the Congress may, at any time, introduce alterations and amendments. Regarding it then, in every point of view, with a candid and disinterested mind, I am bold to assert, that it is the best form of government which has ever been offered to the world."

A FRIEND TO THE CONSTITUTION.

---

[1] James Wilson (1742–1798) of Pennsylvania, one of the best informed and most influential members of the convention that drafted the Constitution.

52. The Foreshadowing of Trusteeism in the First National Parish of the United States, 1787

THE most important group of Catholics in the thirteen original colonies—aside from those of English and Irish extraction—were the Germans who had begun immigrating in the early eighteenth century to Philadelphia and the rural settlements west of the city where in time they had developed relatively flourishing congregations. In 1741 two German Jesuits, Theodore Schneider and William Wappeler, came from Europe to minister to these families, and when Robert Harding, S.J., reported a census of the Catholics in Pennsylvania in April, 1757, he gave the total as 1365 of whom 949 were Germans. Motivated by the recent grant of religious liberty and by their nationalist sentiments, in 1787 a group of German laymen in Philadelphia decided to erect a church for those of their own nationality. In spite of the opposition of Fathers Robert Molyneux and Francis Beeston, who were in charge of St. Mary's Church, they persisted and asked John Carroll for permission to proceed. Carroll gave a somewhat reluctant consent; the laymen secured legal incorporation in October, 1788; elected as their own pastor John Charles Helbron, a German Capuchin; and on November 22, 1789, Holy Trinity Church was opened for services. This first national parish in the United States contained all the elements of the later widespread abuse of trusteeism: laymen acting in church affairs on their own initiative, abetted by vagrant priests who had no regard for ecclesiastical authority, appeals to the civil law, etc. In fact, Holy Trinity Church ultimately went into schism in September, 1796, and the trustees did not finally yield to Carroll's authority until January, 1802. The documents which follow are the laymen's original request to Carroll (undated, late in 1787) and his letter of November 24, 1787, in which he refused to concede their right to choose Helbron in place of Father Laurence Graessl whom he had designated to be their priest. Source: Martin I. J. Griffin, "The Church of the Holy Trinity, Philadelphia," *Records of the American Catholic Historical Society of Philadelphia,* XXI (1910), 9–11.

[late in 1787]

To the Right Reverend Father in God, John Carroll.

Right Reverend Sir: We the subscribers duly appointed by a respectable German Catholic Congregation in and about Philadelphia to wait on your Right Reverence with a memorial, humbly set forth:

Whereas by the late glorious revolution in this part of the globe Heaven has blessed with liberty and free and uninterrupted exercise of our most holy Religion, and is the more fully confirmed by the new Federal Constitution, and whereas the German Catholic congregation in and about Philadelphia has largely increased and is dayly more and more increasing, that the new chappel in Fourth Street is, as it is well known, too small to accommodate conveniently and hold such great number of people of all nations at the time of divine service.

Therefore your humble memorialists, warm wishers to keep up their respective nation and Language, have the honor to inform your Right Reverence that they have concluded and by the divine assistance of Allmighty God and your Right Reverence's gracious approbation are fully determined to build and erect another new place of divine worship for the better convenience and accommodation of Catholics of all nations, particularly the Germans under whose direction the aforesaid new building is to be constructed, they have already bought and deeded a fine and commodious piece of ground situated on the corner of Spruce and Sixth streets.

Your humble memorialists would rather preferred a lot more up town, but it could not be had at so moderate a price as the aforesaid lot bought, the difference of price is near two thousand pounds. They have the pleasure further to acquaint your Right Reverence that they already opened a subscription and with good success, they find great incouragement by all denominations. The inclosure is the preamble of the subscription handed about, which to meet with your Right Reverence's kind approbation is their ardent wish and sanguine hope. Your humble memorialists have made several applications to the Rev. Mr. Molyneux for his concurrence but his kind answer and injunction was, to apply, pray for, and obtain your Right Reverence's liberal approbation which would suffice and compleat the whole.

Therefore your humble and dutifull memorialists earnestly beg your Right Reverence as to deign their undertaking with your most kind and gracious approbation and concurrence, which will give Life and Sanction to their true minded endeavor, for such great favor they will ever pray and with the greater acknowledgment and submission they have the honor to call themselves

Right Reverend Father in God,

Your most humble and most dutiful Children,

Jacob Cline,

George Lechler, Sen.,

Adam Premir *et al*

[November 24, 1787]

Carroll to Joseph Cauffman:

Sir: I have received a petition or remonstrance last night signed by yourself, Mess[rs]Oellers and Premir, and as requested direct my answer to you. As the Congregation of this place never before had the nomination of the Clergymen appointed to serve I now see no reason why I should depart from a right which has been always exercised by my predecessors. I am governed by important and weighty considerations of justice, prudence and gratitude so that I cannot make my determination agreeable to the wishes of the petitioners & of the Gentlemen who wrote the remonstrance of last night. This congregation has ever flourished & drawn on itself the admiration of all, who have visited Phil[a] and I trust in God it ever will unless it be disturbed by an interference, that has never been exercised before. In my way to New York I was requested to procure a German Clergyman. This I promised to do as soon as in my power, & informed the Gentlemen, who did me the honour of calling on me, that I expected Mr. Cresler [Graessl] to come expressly for Philad[a] with which they were much satisfied. I now see no sufficient reason for changing his destination.

With great respect I have the honour to be, sir,

Y[r] most obed[t] Ser[t],

J. Carroll.

Be pleased to communicate this to Messrs. Premir & Oellers.

THE NATIONAL PERIOD

53. The Brief *Ex hac apostolicae* of Pope Pius VI Erecting the Diocese of Baltimore and Appointing John Carroll as the First Bishop, November 6, 1789

WHEN the subject of a Catholic bishop for the new United States was first raised the clergy had opposed the idea out of fear of incurring the displeasure of the civil authorities, as well as from an uneasiness lest the coming of a bishop affect adversely the property interests of the suppressed Society of Jesus. Such was the unanimous opinion of the priests at their general meeting at Whitemarsh, Maryland, in October, 1784, and for the next few years they continued to hold that view. But in time the clergy changed their minds. The change was due chiefly to the rise of serious problems among the American Catholics which Carroll found himself unable to handle with his limited faculties as superior of the missions, to the growing experience of religious freedom which became more general and real, and to the action of the Protestant Episcopalians who in November, 1784, had a bishop consecrated for their church with no untoward results from the government. The priests met again in March, 1788, and this time they drew up a petition to Pope Pius VI (1775–1799) in which they stated the need for a bishop with full status of an ordinary, and they asked for permission to be allowed, at least for the first time, to choose him themselves. The Holy See acted favorably on their request and after learning of the priests' choice of Baltimore for the site of the new see and the virtually unanimous election of John Carroll, the formal bull erecting the Diocese of Baltimore and appointing Carroll as its first bishop was issued. Source: Latin text in Donald C. Shearer, O.F.M.Cap. (Ed.), *Pontificia Americana. A Documentary History of the Catholic Church in the United States, 1784–1884* (Washington: The Catholic University of America Press, 1933), pp. 81–84; English translation by John Gilmary Shea, *History of the Catholic Church in the United States* (New York: John G. Shea, 1888), II, 337–343.

When from the eminence of our apostolical station, we bend our attention to the different regions of the earth, in order to fulfill, to the utmost extent of our power, the duty which our Lord has imposed upon our unworthiness of ruling and feeding his flock; our care and solicitude are particularly engaged that the faithful of Christ, who, dispersed through various provinces, are united with us by Catholic communion, may be governed by their proper pastors, and diligently instructed by them in the discipline of evangelical life and doctrine. For it is our principle that they who, relying on the divine assistance, have regulated their lives and manners agreeably to the precepts of Christian wisdom, ought so to command their own passions as to promote by the pursuit of justice their own and their neighbor's spiritual advantage; and that they who have received from their bishops, and by checking the intemperance of self-wisdom, have steadily adhered to the heavenly doctrine delivered by Christ to the Catholic Church, should not be carried away by every wind of doctrine, but, grounded on the authority of divine revelation, should reject the new and varying doctrines of men which endanger the tranquillity of government, and rest in the unchangeable faith of the Catholic Church. For in the present degeneracy of corrupt manners into which human nature, ever resisting the sweet yoke of Christ, is hurried, and in the pride of talents and knowledge which disdains to submit the opinions and dreams of men to the evangelical truth delivered by Jesus Christ, support must be given by that heavenly authority which is entrusted to the Catholic Church, as to a steady pillar and solid foundation which shall never fail; that from her voice and instructions mankind may learn the objects of their faith and the rules of their conduct, not only for the obtaining of eternal salvation, but also for the regulation of this life and the maintaining of concord in the society of this earthly city. Now, this charge of teaching and ruling first given to the apostles, and especially to St. Peter, the Prince of the Apostles, on whom alone the Church is built, and to whom our Lord and Redeemer entrusted the feeding of his lambs and of his sheep, has been derived in due order of succession to Bishops, and especially to the Roman Pontiffs, successors of St. Peter and heirs of his power and dignity, that thereby it might be made evident that the gates of hell can never prevail against the Church, and that the divine founder of it will ever assist it to the consummation of ages; so that neither in the depravity of morals nor in the fluctuation of novel opinions, the episcopal succession shall ever fail or the bark of Peter be sunk. Wherefore, it having reached our ears that in the flourishing commonwealth of the Thirteen American States many faithful Christians united in communion with the chair of Peter, in which the centre of Catholic unity is fixed, and governed in their spiritual concerns by their own priests having care of souls, earnestly desire that a Bishop may be appointed over them to exercise the functions of episcopal order; to feed them more largely with the food of salutary doctrine, and to guard more carefully that portion of the Catholic flock.

We willingly embraced this opportunity which the grace of Almighty God has afforded us to provide those distant regions with the comfort and ministry of a Catholic Bishop. And that this be effected more successfully, and according to the rules of the sacred canons, We commissioned our venerable Brethren the Cardinals of the holy Roman Church, directors of the Congregation 'de propaganda fide,' to manage this business with the greatest care, and to make a report to us. It was therefore appointed by their decree, approved by us, and published the twelfth day of July of the last year, that the priests who lawfully exercise the sacred ministry and have care of souls in the United States of America, should be empowered to advise together and to determine, first, in what town the episcopal see ought to be erected, and next, who of the aforesaid priests appeared the most worthy and proper to be promoted to this important charge, whom We, for the first time only, and by special grace permitted the said priests to elect and to present to this apostolic See. In obedience to this decree the aforesaid priests exercising the care of souls in the United States of America, unanimously agreed that a bishop with ordinary jurisdiction, ought to be established in the town of Baltimore, because this town situate in Maryland, which province the greater part of the priests and of the faithful inhabit, appeared the most conveniently placed for intercourse with the other States, and because from this province Catholic religion and faith had been propagated into the others. And at the time appointed for the election, they being assembled together, the sacrifice of holy Mass, being celebrated, and the grace and assistance of the Holy Ghost being implored, the votes of all present were taken, and of twenty-six priests who were assembled twenty-four gave their votes for our beloved Son, John Carroll, whom they judged the most proper to support the burden of episcopacy, and sent an authentic instrument of the whole transaction to the aforesaid Congregation of Cardinals. Now all things being materially weighed and considered in this Congregation, it was easily agreed that the interests and increase of Catholic religion would be greatly promoted if an episcopal see were erected at Baltimore, and the said John Carroll were appointed the Bishop of it. We, therefore, to whom this opinion has been reported by our beloved son, Cardinal Antonelli, Prefect of the said Congregation, having nothing more at heart than to ensure success to whatever tends to the propagation of true religion, and to the honor and increase of the Catholic Church, by the plenitude of our apostolical power, and by the tenor of these presents, do establish and erect the aforesaid town of Baltimore into an episcopal see forever, for one Bishop to be chosen by us in all future vacancies; and We, therefore, by the apostolical authority aforesaid, do allow, grant and permit to the Bishop of the said city and to his successors in all future times, to exercise episcopal power and jurisdiction, and every other episcopal function which Bishops constituted in other places are empowered to hold and enjoy in their respective churches, cities and dioceses, by right, custom, or by other means, by general privileges, graces, indults and apostolical dispensations, together with all pre-eminences, honors, immunities, graces and favors, which other Cathedral Churches, by right or custom, or any other sort, have, hold and enjoy. We moreover decree and declare the said Episcopal see thus erected to be subject or suffragan to no Metropolitan right or jurisdiction, but to be forever subject, immediately to us and to our successors the Roman Pontiffs, and to this Apostolical See. And till another opportunity shall be presented to us of establishing other Catholic Bishops in the United States of America, and till other dispositions shall be made by this apostolical See, We declare, by our apostolical authority, all the faithful of Christ, living in Catholic communion, as well ecclesiastics as seculars, and all the clergy and people dwelling of the aforesaid United States of America, though hitherto they may have been subject to other Bishops of other dioceses, to be henceforward subject to the Bishop of Baltimore in all future times; And whereas by special grant, and for this first time only, we have allowed the priests exercising the care of souls in the United States of America, to elect a person to be appointed Bishop by us, and almost all their votes have been given to our beloved Son, John Carroll, Priest; We being otherwise certified of his faith, prudence, piety, and zeal, forasmuch as by our mandate he hath during the late years directed the spiritual government of souls, do therefore by the plenitude of our authority, declare, create, appoint and constitute the said John Carroll, Bishop and Pastor of the said Church of Baltimore, granting to him the faculty of receiving the rite of consecration from any Catholic bishop holding communion with the apostolical see, assisted by two ecclesiastics, vested with some dignity, in case that two bishops cannot be had, first having taken the usual oath according to the Roman Pontifical.

And we commission the said Bishop elect to erect a church in the said city of Baltimore, in form of a Cathedral Church, inasmuch as the times and circumstances may allow, to institute a body of clergy deputed to divine worship, and to the service of said church, and moreover to establish an episcopal seminary, either in the same city or elsewhere, as he shall judge most expedient, to administer ecclesiastical incomes, and to execute all other things which he shall think in the Lord to be expedient for the increase of Catholic faith and the augmentation of the worship and splendor of the new erected church. We moreover enjoin the said Bishop to obey the injunctions of our venerable brethren, the Cardinals Directors of the Sacred Congregation 'de propaganda fide,' to transmit to them at proper times a relation of his visitation of his church, and to inform them of all things which he shall judge to be useful to the spiritual good and salvation of the flock trusted to his charge. We therefore decree that these our letters are ever and ever shall be firm, valid and efficacious, and shall obtain their full and entire, effect; and be observed inviolable by all persons whom it now doth or hereafter may concern; and that all judges ordinary and delegated, even auditors of causes of the sacred apostolical palace, and Cardinals of the holy Roman Church, must thus judge and define, depriving all and each of them of all power and authority to judge or interpret in any other manner, and declaring all to be null and void, if any one, by any authority should presume, either knowingly or unknowingly, to attempt anything contrary thereunto. Notwithstanding all apostolical, general or special constitutions and ordinations, published in universal, provincial and synodical councils, and all things contrary whatsoever.

Given at Rome at St. Mary Major, under the Fisherman's Ring, the 6th day of November, 1789, and in the fifteenth year of our Pontificate.

54. The Beginnings of the First Catholic College in the United States, 1789

BY REASON of the penal legislation against Catholics in colonial America it had never been possible to have a Catholic school. The brief existence of the furtive little academy at Bohemiá Manor was but the exception that proved the rule. But with the coming of religious liberty the Catholics were free to have a school of their own, and John Carroll took the lead among the clergy in urging its establishment. At a meeting of the priests on May 15, 1789, it was agreed to issue a prospectus which would explain the nature of the school they had in mind and to solicit subscriptions. The following document was printed later that year and the work got under way. After some delays caused by lack of funds Georgetown Academy opened in September, 1791, with William Gaston of North Carolina, future associate justice of the state's supreme court, as the first student. As will be noted, the academy welcomed students of all religious faiths. Thus was begun the institution from which there developed the first Catholic college in the United States. Source: John Gilmary Shea, *Memorial of the First Centenary of Georgetown College, D.C., Comprising a History of Georgetown University* (New York: P. F. Collier, 1891), pp. 12–13.

PROPOSALS TO ESTABLISH AN ACADEMY AT GEORGE TOWN, PATOWMACK RIVER, MARYLAND.

The object of the proposed Institution is to unite the means of communicating Science with an effectual provision for guarding and preserving the Morals of Youth. With this View, the Seminary will be superintended by those who, having had Experience in similar Institutions, know that an undivided Attention may be given to the Cultivation of Virtue and literary Improvement, and that a System of Discipline may be introduced and preserved incompatible with Indolence and Inattention in the Professor, or with incorrigible habits of Immorality in the Student.

The Benefit of this Establishment should be as general as the Attainment of its Object is desirable. It will therefore receive Pupils as soon as they have learned the first Elements of Letters, and will conduct them through the several Branches of Classical Learning to that Stage of Education from which they may proceed with Advantage to the Study of higher Sciences in the University of this or those of the neighboring States. Thus it will be calculated for every Class of Citizens; — as Reading, Writing, Arithmetic, the earlier Branches of the Mathematics, and the Grammar of our native Tongue, will be attended to no less than the learned Languages.

Agreeably to the liberal Principal of our Constitution, the Seminary will be open to Students of every religious profession. They, who, in this Respect differ from the Superintendent of the Academy, will be at Liberty to frequent the places of Worship and Instruction appointed by their Parents; but with Respect to their moral Conduct, all must be subject to general and uniform Discipline.

In the choice of Situation, Salubrity of Air, Convenience of Communication and Cheapness of Living have been principally consulted, and George Town offers these united Advantages.

The Price of Tuition will be moderate; in the Course of a few

Years it will be reduced still lower, if the System formed for this Seminary be effectually carried into execution.

Such a plan of Education solicits, and, it is not presumption to add, deserves public Encouragement. The following gentlemen, and others that may be named hereafter will receive subscriptions and inform the subscribers to whom and in what proportion payments are to be made. In Maryland, the Hon. Charles Carroll of Carrollton; Henry Rozer, Notley Young, Robert Darnall, George Digges, Edmond Plowden, Esq'rs, Mr. Joseph Millard, Captain John Lancaster, Mr. Baker Brooke, Chandler Brent, Esq., Mr. Bernard O'Neill and Mr. Marsham Waring, merchants; John Darnall and Ignatius Wheeler, Esq., on the western shore; and on the eastern, Rev. Mr. Joseph Mosley, John Blake, Francis Hall, Charles Blake, William Matthews and John Tuitte, Esq'rs. In Pennsylvania, George Mead and Thomas Fitzsimmons, Esq'rs, Mr. Joseph Cauffman, Mr. Mark Wilcox and Mr. Thomas Lilly. In Virginia, Colonel Fitzgerald and George Brent, Esq'rs, and at New York, Dominick Lynch, Esq.

Subscriptions will also be received and every necessary Information given by the following Gentlemen, Directors of the Undertaking: The Rev. Messrs. John Carroll, James Pellentz, Robert Molyneux, John Ashton and Leonard Neale.

55. The Catholics' Congratulations to President Washington, 1789, and His Reply, March 12, 1790

EARLY in his first administration President Washington received congratulatory messages from a number of American religious groups. Late in 1789 the Catholics sent such a message signed by John Carroll for the clergy and by four prominent laymen in the name of the laity. The Catholics alluded to the participation of their coreligionists in the struggle that had won national independence and the full rights of citizenship which it had won them in some states, to which they added their expectation of the same rights from those states that still withheld them from Catholics. Washington, who had abolished the army's commemoration of Guy Fawke's Day out of consideration for Catholic sensibilities, had known at firsthand the patriotic role that had been played by Catholics like Stephen Moylan (1737–1881), mustermaster general of the forces, and others. In his reply, therefore, he expressed the belief that as mankind became more liberal all worthy citizens would be admitted to equal treatment by civil governments, and he presumed that non-Catholic Americans would not forget the patriotic part which Catholics had played in the Revolution and in the establishment of the government, as well as the assistance which the revolutionary cause had received from Catholic France. Source: Washington Papers, 334, Division of Manuscripts, Library of Congress.

[undated, late in 1789]

To George Washington
President of the United States of America.
Sir,

We have been long impatient to testify our joy and unbounded confidence in your being called, by an unanimous vote, to the first station of a country, in which that unanimity could not have been obtained without the previous merit of unexampled services, of eminent wisdom, and unblemished virtue. Our congratulations have not reached you sooner, because our scattered situation prevented the communication, and the collection of those sentiments, which warmed every breast. But the delay has furnished us with the opportunity, not merely of presaging the happiness to be expected under your administration, but of bearing testimony to that which we experience already. It is your peculiar talent, in war and in peace, to afford security to those, who commit their protection into your hands. In war, you shield them from the ravages of armed hostility: in peace you establish public tranquillity by the justice and moderation, not less than by the vigour, of your government. By example as well as by vigilance, you extend the influence of laws on the manners of our fellow-citizens. You encourage respect for religion, and inculcate, by words and actions, that principle, on which the welfare of nations so much depends, that a superintending providence governs the events of the world, and watches over the conduct of men. Your exalted maxims and unwearied attention to the moral and physical improvement of our country have produced already the happiest effects. Under your administration, America is animated with zeal for the attainment and encouragement of useful literature. She improves her agriculture, extends her commerce, and acquires with foreign nations a dignity, unknown to her before. From these happy events, in which none can feel a warmer interest than ourselves, we derive additional pleasure by recollection, that you, Sir, have been the principal instrument to effect so rapid a change in our political situation. This prospect of national prosperity is peculiarly pleasing to us on another account; because whilst our country preserves her freedom and independence, we shall have a well founded title to claim from her justice equal rights of citizenship, as the price of our blood spilt under your eyes, and of our common exertions for her defence, under your auspicious conduct, rights rendered more dear to us by the remembrance of former hardships. When we pray for the preservation of them, where they have been granted; and expect the full extension of them from the justice of those States, which still restrict them; when we solicit the protection of Heaven over our common country: we neither omit nor can omit recommending your preservation to the singular care of divine providence; because we conceive that no human means are so available to promote the welfare of the United States, as the prolongation of your health and life, in which are included the energy of your example, the wisdom of your counsels, and the persuasive eloquence of your virtues.

J. Carroll, in behalf of the Roman Catholic Clergy
Charles Carroll of Carrollton, Daniel Carroll,
Thos. FitzSimons, Domk. Lynch.[1] — in behalf
of the Roman Catholic Laity.

To the Roman Catholics in the United States of America.

Gentlemen, — While I now receive with much satisfaction your congratulations on my being called, by an unanimous vote, to the first station in my country; I cannot but duly notice your politeness in offering an apology for the unavoidable delay. As that delay has given you an opportunity of realizing, instead of anticipating, the benefits of the general government; you will do me the justice to believe that your testimony of the increase of the public prosperity enhances the pleasure which I should otherwise have experienced from your affectionate Address.

I feel that my conduct in war and in peace has met with more general approbation than could reasonably have been expected: and I find myself disposed to consider that fortunate circumstance, in a great degree, resulting from the able support and extraordinary candor of my fellow-citizens of all denominations.

The prospect of national prosperity now before us is truly animating, and ought to excite the exertions of all good men to establish and secure the happiness of their Country, in the permanent duration of its freedom and independence. America, under the smiles of a Divine Providence — the protection of a good government — the cultivation of manners, morals and piety, can hardly fail of attaining an uncom-

---

[1] The Irish-born Dominik Lynch (1754–1825) was the leading Catholic layman of New York at the time. The other laymen have been identified in previous notes.

mon degree of eminence in literature, commerce, agriculture, improvements at home, and respectability abroad.

As mankind become more liberal, they will be more apt to allow, that all those who conduct themselves as worthy members of the community are equally entitled to the protection of civil government. I hope ever to see America among the foremost nations in examples of justice and liberality. And I presume that your fellow-citizens will not forget the patriotic part which you took in the accomplishment of their Revolution, and the establishment of their government; or the important assistance which they received from a nation in which the Roman Catholic religion is professed.

I thank you, Gentlemen, for your kind concern for me. While my life and my health shall continue, in whatever situation I may be, it shall be my constant endeavor to justify the favorable sentiments you are pleased to express of my conduct. And may the members of your Society in America, animated alone by the pure spirit of christianity, and still conducting themselves as the faithful subjects of our free government, enjoy every temporal and spiritual felicity.

(March 12, 1790) G. Washington.

56. Bishop Carroll's Sermon on Taking Possession of His See, St. Peter's Pro-Cathedral, Baltimore, December 12, 1790

THE consecration of John Carroll took place at Lulworth Castle, England, on August 15, 1790, and was performed by Bishop Charles Walmesley, O.S.B. (1722–1797), Vicar Apostolic of the Western District. Upon the new bishop's return to the United States in early December the task that awaited him was truly frightening, for, as he said, everything had to be raised from its foundations in a diocese which comprised the entire country. How well he conceived the immensity of his task, how clearly he envisioned from the outset the need for a school, a seminary, native priests, spiritual aid for the Catholics in distant and scattered settlements, and the danger to his tiny flock from doctrinal errors — all these were before Carroll's mind in his first sermon as an American bishop. His manly piety directed him to put his confidence in God, and how splendidly he fulfilled his difficult mission the history of the next quarter century would tell. Source: Peter Guilday, *The Life and Times of John Carroll, Archbishop of Baltimore, 1735–1815* (New York: Encyclopedia Press, 1922), I, 384–385.

In this, my new station, if my life be not one continued instruction and example of virtue to the people committed to my charge, it will become, in the sight of God, a life not only useless, but even pernicious. It is no longer enough for me to be inoffensive in my conduct and regular in my manners. God now imposes a severer duty upon me. I shall incur the guilt of violating my pastoral office, if all my endeavours be not directed to bring your lives and all your actions to a conformity with the laws of God; to exhort, to conjure, to reprove, to enter into all your sentiments; to feel all your infirmities; to be all things to all, that I may gain all to Christ; to be superior to human respect; to have nothing in view but God and your salvation; to sacrifice to these health, peace, reputation, and even life itself; to hate sin, and yet love the sinner; to repress the turbulent; to encourage the timid; to watch over the conduct of even the ministers of religion; to be patient and meek; to embrace all kinds of persons; these are now my duties — extensive, pressing, and indispensable duties; these are the duties of all my brethren in the episcopacy, and surely important enough to fill us with terror. But there are others still more burdensome to be borne by me, in this particular portion of Christ's church which is committed to my charge, and where everything is to be raised, as it were, from its foundation; to establish ecclesiastical discipline; to devise means for the religious education of Catholic youth — that precious portion of pastoral solicitude; to provide an establishment for training up ministers for the sanctuary and the services of religion, that we may no longer depend on foreign and uncertain coadjutors; not to leave unassisted any of the faithful who are scattered through this immense continent; to preserve their faith untainted amidst the contagion of error surrounding them on all sides; to preserve in their hearts a warm charity and forebearance toward every other denomination of Christians, and at the same time to preserve them from that fatal and prevailing indifference which views all religions as equally acceptable to God and salutary to men. Ah! when I consider these additional duties, my heart sinks almost under the impression of terror which comes upon it. In God alone can I find any consolation. He knows by what steps I have been conducted to this important station, and how much I have always dreaded it. He will not abandon me unless I first draw upon His malediction by my unfaithfulness to my charge. Pray, dear brethren, pray incessantly, that I may not incur so dreadful a punishment. Alas! the punishment would fall on you as well as on myself; my unfaithfulness would rebound on you and deprive you of some of the means of salvation. . . .

57. John Carroll's Prayer for the Civil Authorities, November 10, 1791

LESS than a year after returning from his consecration Bishop Carroll assembled the clergy at his residence in Baltimore on November 7–10, 1791, for the holding of the first diocesan synod of the American Church. During those days the bishop and his twenty-two priests framed twenty-four decrees to regulate and render uniform such matters as the administration of the sacraments, divine services, the conduct of the clergy, and the support of the churches. Among the regulations for divine services it was stated that after the gospel in Masses on Sundays and feast days there should be read the prayer prescribed "for all the ranks of society and for the welfare of the Republic." In this session of November 10 the synod adopted the beautiful prayer which Carroll had composed for the civil authorities and which revealed the combination of piety and patriotism which was so characteristic of him, as well as showing his charity for the welfare of all his fellow citizens, regardless of their religious faith. The prayer is still used in Catholic churches in the United States on occasions of a national character. Source: Peter Guilday, *The Life and Times of John Carroll, Archbishop of Baltimore, 1735–1815* (New York: Encyclopedia Press, 1922), II, 432.

We pray Thee, O almighty and eternal God! Who through Jesus Christ hast revealed Thy glory to all nations, to preserve the works of Thy Mercy, that Thy Church, being spread through the whole world, may continue with unchanging faith in the confession of Thy name.

We pray Thee, Who alone art good and holy, to endow with heavenly knowledge, sincere zeal, and sanctity of life, our chief bishop, N.N., the vicar of Our Lord Jesus Christ, in the government of His Church; our own bishop, N.N. (or archbishop); all other bishops, prelates, and pastors of the Church; and especially those who are appointed to exercise amongst us the functions of the holy ministry, and conduct Thy people into the ways of salvation.

We pray Thee, O God of might, wisdom, and justice! through Whom authority is rightly administered, laws are enacted, and judgment decreed, assist with Thy holy spirit of counsel and fortitude the President of the United States, that his administration may be conducted in righteousness, and be eminently useful to Thy people over whom he presides; by encouraging due respect for virtue and religion; by a faithful execution of the laws in justice and mercy; and by restraining vice and immorality. Let the light of Thy divine wisdom direct the deliberations of Congress, and shine forth in all the proceedings and laws framed for our rule and government, so that they may tend to the preservation of peace, the promotion of national happiness, the increase of industry, sobriety, and useful knowledge; and may perpetuate to us the blessing of equal liberty.

We pray for his excellency, the Governor of this State, for the members of the Assembly, for all judges, magistrates, and other officers who are appointed to guard our political welfare, that they may be enabled, by Thy powerful protection, to discharge the duties of their respective stations with honesty and ability.

We recommend likewise, to Thy unbounded mercy, all our brethren and fellow citizens throughout the United States, that they may be blessed in the knowledge and sanctified in the observance of Thy most holy law; that they may be preserved in union, and in that peace which the world can not give; and after enjoying the blessings of this life, be admitted to those which are eternal.

Finally, we pray to Thee, O Lord of mercy, to remember the souls of Thy servants departed who are gone before us with the sign of faith, and repose in the sleep of peace; the souls of our parents, relatives, and friends; of those who, when living, were members of this congregation, and particularly of such as are lately deceased; of all benefactors who, by their donations or legacies to this church, witnessed their zeal for the decency of divine worship and proved their claim to our grateful and charitable remembrance. To these, O Lord, and to all that rest in Christ, grant, we beseech Thee, a place of refreshment, light, and everlasting peace, through the same Jesus Christ, our Lord and Saviour. Amen.

58. The French Sulpicians and St. Mary's Seminary, Baltimore, April 23, 1792

THE arrival in Baltimore on July 10, 1791, of four French Sulpicians and five seminarians for the purpose of inaugurating a seminary for the training of priests for the United States proved to be a singular blessing to the American Church. For 150 years the Sulpicians had been among the most prominent and successful trainers of the priests of France. The establishment of their first American seminary — financed entirely by themselves — was, needless to say, a tremendous boon to the infant Diocese of Baltimore. These priests not only provided a faculty for St. Mary's Seminary which began classes in October, 1791, in a building called the One Mile Tavern, but they likewise accepted assignment to take charge of missions in Maryland

and in places as far distant as Illinois and Michigan. The first years of the new seminary were exceedingly trying ones and for a time there was serious discussion of its abandonment. But the seven students of 1791 had increased by 1810 to twenty-four, and by the time Archbishop Carroll died in 1815 thirty priests had been ordained from this mother seminary. In the following letter Carroll expressed to Cardinal Antonelli, Prefect of Propaganda, what the coming of the Sulpicians meant to him and to his impoverished diocese. Source: Peter Guilday, *The Life and Times of John Carroll, Archbishop of Baltimore, 1735–1815* (New York: Encyclopedia Press, 1922), II, 470–471.

It is already known to the Sacred Congregation how singular a blessing has come to us from the disorders that threaten religion in France, since on account of the same has arisen the opportunity of sending thither some priests from the Seminary of St. Sulpice, at Paris. While I was in London, this matter was seriously considered as I have already made known to the Sacred Congregation; after my return to my diocese, the plan was fully decided upon, and in July of last year four priests with five clerics, students of philosophy and theology, reached this port, led by the Venerable Nagot,[1] formerly Superior of the Seminary of St. Sulpice. . . . The establishment of a seminary is certainly a new and extraordinary spectacle for the people of this country; the remarkable piety of these priests is admirable, and their example is a stimulant and spur to all who feel themselves called to work in the vineyard of the Lord. Such are the great and remarkable effects of God's bounty. But what is still more important is that, owing to the establishment of this seminary, the clergy will be brought up in the purity of faith and in holiness of conduct. All our hopes are founded on the Seminary of Baltimore. Since the arrival of the priests of St. Sulpice, the celebration of the offices of the Church and the dignity of divine worship have made a great impression, so that, though the church of Baltimore is hardly worthy of the name of cathedral, if we consider its style and its size, it may be looked upon as an episcopal church in view of the number of its clergy.

[1] François Charles Nagot (1734–1816), the first superior of the Sulpicians in the United States, had been one of the most prominent members of the society in France, being vice superior of the Seminary of St. Sulpice in Paris and a member of the superior-general's council at the time of his appointment to Baltimore.

59. Religious Conditions in Louisiana, November 1, 1795

THE first Bishop of Louisiana and the Two Floridas, a diocese which had been erected on April 25, 1793, was a Cuban-born priest, Luís Ignacio Maria de Peñalver y Cardenas (1749–1810). Upon Peñalver's arrival in New Orleans in July, 1795, he found religious conditions at a very low ebb. On November 1, 1795, the bishop made a report to the Spanish government which described not only the spiritual abuses among the populace but which also reflected the nationalist feeling between the French and Spanish colonists. Peñalver did all he could to revive religious life during his six years of residence in Louisiana, but when he left in November, 1801, to become Archbishop of Guatemala he could point to only qualified success for his efforts. Source: Charles Gayarré, *History of Louisiana. The Spanish Domination* (New York: Redfield, 1854), pp. 376–379.

Since my arrival in this town, on the 17th of July, I have been studying with the keenest attention the character of its inhabitants, in order to regulate by ecclesiastical government in accordance with the information which I may obtain on this important subject.

On the 2d of August, I began the discharge of my pastoral functions. I took possession without any difficulty of all the buildings appertaining to the church, and examined all the books, accounts, and other matters thereto relating. But as to re-establishing the purity of religion, and reforming the manners of the people, which are the chief objects El Tridentino[1] has in view, I have encountered many obstacles.

The inhabitants do not listen to, or if they do, they disregard, all exhortations to maintain in its orthodoxy the Catholic faith, and to preserve the innocence of life. But without ceasing to pray the Father of all mercies to send his light into the darkness which surrounds these people, I am putting into operation human means to remedy these evils, and I will submit to your Excellency those which I deem conducive to the interests of religion and of the state.

Because his Majesty tolerates here the Protestants, for sound reasons of state, the bad Christians, who are in large numbers in this colony, think that they are authorized to live without any religion at all. Many adults die without having received the sacrament of communion. Out of the eleven thousand souls composing this parish, hardly three to four hundred comply with the precept of partaking at least once a year of the Lord's supper. Of the regiment of Louisiana,

[1] The bishop was referring to the reform legislation of the Council of Trent.

there are not above thirty, including officers and soldiers, who have discharged this sacred duty for the last three years. No more than about the fourth part of the population of the town ever attends mass, and on Sundays only, and on those great holydays which require it imperiously. To do so on the other holydays they consider as a superfluous act of devotion to which they are not bound. Most of the married and unmarried men live in a state of concubinage, and there are fathers who procure courtezans for the use of their sons, whom they thus intentionally prevent from getting lawful wives. The marriage contract is one which, from a universal custom, admitting only a few accidental exceptions, is never entered into among the slaves. Fasting on Fridays, in Lent, and during *vigilas y temporas* [vigils of feasts and ember days], is a thing unknown; and there are other mal-practices which denote the little of religion existing here among the inhabitants, and which demonstrate that there remains in their bosoms but a slight spark of the faith instilled into them at the baptismal font.

I presume that a large portion of these people are vassals of the king, because they live in his domain, and accept his favors. But I must speak the truth. His Majesty possesses their bodies and not their souls. Rebellion is in their hearts, and their minds are imbued with the maxims of democracy; and had they not for their chief so active and energetic a man as the present governor,[2] there would long since have been an eruption of the pent-up volcano; and should another less sagacious chief ever forget the fermenting elements which are at work under ground, there can be no doubt but that there would be an explosion.

Their houses are full of books written against religion and the state. They are permitted to read them with impunity, and, at the dinner table, they make use of the most shameful, lascivious, and sacrilegious songs.

This melancholy sketch of the religious and moral customs and condition of the flock which has fallen to my lot, will make you understand the cause of whatever act of scandal may suddenly break out, which, however, I shall strive to prevent; and the better to do so, I have used and am still using some means, which I intend as remedies, and which I am going to communicate to your Excellency.

The Spanish school, which has been established here at the expense of the crown, is kept as it ought to be; but as there are others which

[2] Francisco Luís Hector, Baron de Carondelet, was Governor of Louisiana from 1791 to 1797.

are French, and of which one alone is opened by authority and with the regular license, and as I was ignorant of the faith professed by the teachers and of their morality, I have prescribed for them such regulations as are in conformity with the provisions of our legislation.

Excellent results are obtained from the Convent of the Ursulines,[3] in which a good many girls are educated; but their inclinations are so decidedly French, that they have even refused to admit among them Spanish women who wished to become Nuns, so long as these applicants should remain ignorant of the French idiom, and they have shed many tears on account of their being obliged to read in Spanish books their spiritual exercises, and to comply with the other duties of their community in the manner prescribed to them.

This is the nursery of those future matrons who will inculcate on their children the principles which they here imbibe. The education which they receive in this institution is the cause of their being less vicious than the other sex. As to what the boys are taught in the Spanish school, it is soon forgotten. Should their education be continued in a college, they would be confirmed in their religious principles, in the good habits given to them, and in their loyalty as faithful vassals to the crown. But they leave the school when still very young, and return to the houses of their parents mostly situated in the country, where they hear neither the name of God nor of King, but daily witness the corrupt morals of their parents. . . .

60. Father Badin's Description of the Church on the Kentucky Frontier, April 11, 1796

KENTUCKY entered the union in 1792 as the first state of the new West. A large immigration from the eastern states had poured into the area during the 1780's to swell the population to almost 75,000 by 1790, and among those who had made the long journey over the mountains and down the Ohio River were many Catholic families from Maryland. The first two priests sent to minister to these scattered frontier settlements proved to be rather unhappy choices, and it was only with the arrival in November, 1793, of Stephen Theodore Badin (1768–1853) that the Kentucky missions received continuous and proper attention. Badin was the first priest to be ordained in the United States on May 25, 1793. This remarkable man was to serve the Catholics of Kentucky and other western states as an itinerant missionary off and on for nearly sixty years. He was a wonderfully zealous priest to whom many souls in the West owed, under God, their salvation,

[3] Cf. No. 61.

but he was of a somewhat exacting and contentious disposition with the result that his lengthy career was marked by many stormy episodes. In the letter which follows Badin gave Bishop Carroll a vivid description of the state of the Church in this distant part of his diocese after the missionary had been on the scene for about two years and a half. Source: Edward I. Devitt, S.J. (Ed.), "Letters from the Baltimore Archives," *Records of the American Catholic Historical Society of Philadelphia,* XIX (1908), 258–264.

Priestland, Harden's Creek, Washington County,
April 11th, 1796.

My Lord

I wrote to you last month, and a few days afterwards Mr. Sanders brought me the letters which you sent by him. Last fall and winter I wrote you several letters which you have not answered, doubtless for the reason that they were lost or intercepted during the journey, which frequently happens. In them I proposed some cases of conscience and asked for several dispensations; I therein exposed to you the needs of my congregations and especially my own; would that you could know them, Monseigneur, as I know them — although even I know them imperfectly; — you would be deeply afflicted, your charity for the people and priests of whom you are the pastor would rend your fatherly heart, because there is no pasturage in Kentucky for the souls that, as you assured me when I was leaving Baltimore, you tenderly love. Probably there is not in all your diocese as large congregations as are those of Kentucky, and they are increasing from day to day; there is not a Catholic here that does not bitterly lament at finding himself deprived of those means of salvation that were to be had in Maryland &c. I can assure you, Monseigneur, and you will be touched to hear it, that some among them are so afflicted as to lose their mind. Faith yet sustains me, thanks be to God, but I am as worried as any among them, since I share the troubles of each; but no one can share mine, or at least the only person in Kentucky who could share them makes himself incapable of doing so.[1] I shall keep silence until I am better informed.

You speak to me of French priests: I entreat you, my Lord, to send me at least one whose virtue is known to you. I would willingly decide to send him my horse were it not imprudent to deprive myself of it for I have no other of my own in Kentucky, and I often need it

---

[1] Badin was apparently referring here to Father William de Rohan, a somewhat erratic priest who had come to Kentucky c. 1790, and who was responsible for the state's first Catholic church, that of Holy Cross at Pottinger's Creek, built in 1792.

in order to visit the sick, by day and by night. In my present abandonment I am utterly incapable, my lord, of fulfiling the heavy charge of the ministry. I have neither the virtue nor the bodily strength necessary: If I had at least one priest to consult with me, to advise and encourage me! If I walked with a firmer footstep myself, I might, with God's grace, guide those whom I ought to direct in the path of salvation. I once more beseech you, my lord, to look with an eye of pity on the poor priests of Kentucky, and on the other faithful, of whom you are the father, and who depend, after God, upon your charity in order to obtain a favorable entrance to the mansions of eternity. . . .

The faithful Scot [*sic*] county are forsaken and disheartened: last year there was some difference of opinion between them about the land which was bought for the support of their priests. It is situated about four miles from the chapel, and is today in the midst of Catholic plantations which have extended since peace was concluded with the Indians. All the Fenwick families, who incontestably are the most prominent, were united for the success of this business. The heads of only two rich families sought to place obstacles to it, because they considered it too far away, under present circumstances, from the resident of the priest: another motive may have influenced their opposition, — the rich are not always the most disposed to make sacrifices. The poorer families were now of one opinion now of another, according as they listened to the arguments of the prejudiced and considered the distance at which they lived from the chapel or from the priest's land. It seems to me that this congregation has not always followed the natural law of prudence; when they resolved to build a chapel, before my coming to Kentucky, land was very cheap; they could have and should have purchased enough of it to make a good plantation which would have in a few years brought more than the cost of the purchase and would have enabled them to cover the expense of a chapel &c. They did quite the contrary; and moreover the priest will have the trouble of travelling to the chapel which at present is located almost at the extreme end of their plantations. The congregations at Nelson and Washington bought the land for the priest in Washington when they built their chapel at a distance of two miles and a half, near the frontier of Nelson [County]. During the four months that Mr. Barriere[2] stayed in Kentucky he changed his mag-

---

[2] Father Michel Bernard Barrière, a French-born priest, had come to Kentucky with Badin in 1793, but had left in the spring of 1794 for Spanish Louisiana.

nificent plans several times, and finally adopted one which causes us some embarrassment at present: he gave power of attorney to Mr. J. Lancaster[3] which to me seems about as valid as the powers of the vicar general with which he claimed to have invested me; Mr. Lancaster could act independently of the priests who were serving Kentucky, and consequently a rectory was begun; the purchase and the payment for the ground and for several negroes, the salary of Mr. Roan [*sic*], some other expenditures by Mr. Barriere, building and furnishing the chapel &c. have made it impossible for us now even to put under roof this immense presbtery. *Quis volens turrim aedificare non p. ejus computat.* . . . About six months after the departure of Mr. Barriere I engaged a score of men to build a cabin, which although but a cabin, is one of the best residences to be found among the congregation. During my absence, the work was interrupted and the laborers were discouraged because they were not working for Mr. Barriere's orders: I took the inertness of Mr. R [B.?] for humility: but, after all, when I settled here last year, I took half of a little house that I had not had built for myself. The bad management of affairs and my occupations caused a lack of any harvest for me, so I am reduced this year to beggary; and the country seems to have suffered a genuine famine this summer. Divine Providence had perhaps allowed this as a punishment of their indolence.

After what I said, my lord, you can judge of what was told you also by Mr. D. McCarthy. Mr. Joseph Fenwick is now on the way to the Illinois, where he thinks of establishing himself with his family, in order to procure for them the advantages of religion. Another Catholic from Nelson undertook a like journey last Christmas, but without any success, because there was no land to buy, and the Indians of the Spanish side of the Mississippi kill and rob Americans although they leave the French unmolested.

I informed you last winter, my lord, in one of my letters that Mr. Dubois[4] wished to come to Kentucky and had commissioned several of his friends to buy him some land. They tell me that Mr. Thomas Yates procured for him some of his on Cartwright's creek, near the chapel which is being built there, about eight miles from here. I am sure that Mr. George Hamilton will devote to a rectory two or

---

[3] John Lancaster (d. 1838) was a leader of the group of Maryland Catholics who came to Kentucky in 1788. He became one of the most prominent Catholics in Kentucky and served for several terms in the legislature. He was the grandfather of John Lancaster Spalding (1840–1916), first Bishop of Peoria.

[4] Jean Dubois (1764–1842), the future third Bishop of New York, was a missionary in Maryland at the time.

three hundred acres of land, about 80 miles from here on the Green river. His plan is to help a Catholic settlement and to sell them a portion of the land that he bought there. Those [Catholics] in Scot can never be as numerous as in the other counties for the reason that land there sells for six, eight or even ten times higher; they are also much richer, and more favored as to commerce, manufactures, education &c. But I will add also that luxury and vice are more general there — I can not be everywhere at once; they are nearly all discontented; and where I am I do very little good and undoubtedly much harm; the people do not always like my principles, or rather the principles of my ritual *videat autem diligenter Sacerdos* &c. You were right, my lord, when you complained in your letter to me some four months ago that the rules of theology are not always followed. I am in charge of all general confessions, and I do not suffice: I have so little courage, my lord! Can't you send us Mr. Thayer[5] or Mr. F. Neale?[6] I would even venture to ask you for both of them and others beside; would that you might listen to me! At least I shall ask God for a good French priest who may save one soul and most likely many another. He will have an opportunity to learn English quickly in Kentucky, and at all events it is not essential to know English in order to celebrate the divine Mysteries, to edify the people, to baptize, to absolve the dying, to direct me &c. Please, I beg of you, have compassion on me.

I am told that Mr. Henry Jarber [Jarboe?] of St. Inigoes, left in his will a sum of money for the Church in Kentucky. If you can get it, my lord, it might be of some service to the priest you intend for here. I mentioned in one of my letters that my faculties expire the third of September. I suppose I should repeat this fact, because my letter might not have reached you: I have so often acknowledged to you my difficulties and incapacity that you will readily conclude that I have no pretentions to new powers. I trust in the goodness of the Lord that before that time there will be worthy laborers to cultivate the soil that at present lies almost fallow because of my cowardice.

I asked you some time ago to have sixty Masses said; I must now ask you to attend to more than thirty intentions. . . .

. . . I hope that my anxieties will not be of long duration, and that good priests who may be favorably inclined to serve in your

---

[5] John Thayer (1758–1815), a Boston-born convert priest, came to Kentucky in 1799 but left after four years of rather unsatisfactory service.

[6] Francis Neale (1755–1837) was on the Maryland missions at the time; he was later prominent in the restored Society of Jesus and served as president of Georgetown College, 1810–1812.

diocese will hasten to follow your wishes and those of the people of Kentucky. Mr. Wm. Hamilton who carries my letters can tell you in person how much they suffer.

I am very grateful for the trouble you take to keep me informed about the general conditions in France. They tell me that the city in which I was born has been consigned to the flames by a philanthropic decree of the legislators. I have reason to believe that my relations [or parents] were included in the decree for I have received no letters from them for several years.

Let me observe in regard to the coming of priests to Kentucky that they will not have to face the dangers to which they would have been exposed in preceding years, as peace has been concluded with the Indians.

I have the honor to be &c &c &c.

Etienne Theodore Badin

P.S. — The holy oils that I brought with me to Kentucky need to be renewed. The ritual asserts that clerics should carry them wherever there is need; I hope that you will give them to one or more priests. Mr. Hamilton should return here next July; he would be a very suitable companion for them [the priests] if they have not already started before that time.

61. President Jefferson Reassures the Louisiana Ursulines About Their Future Under the American Government, May 15, 1804

IN AUGUST, 1727, a little band of eleven Ursuline nuns arrived in Louisiana from France to open the first convent of religious women in what was later to be the United States. All through the eighteenth century they persisted — often under the greatest handicaps — with their teaching the young, nursing the sick, and other works of charity. The sisters witnessed the colony change hands several times, and in 1803 they found themselves citizens of the United States. The anxiety which they felt about their property rights and status under the American regime were conveyed by their superior to both Bishop Carroll and President Jefferson. In his reply Jefferson set their fears at rest about the future and assured them of the appreciation which Americans of all religious faiths felt for the charitable labors which they had carried on in Louisiana for so many years. Source: Henry C. Semple, S.J. (Ed.), *The Ursulines in New Orleans and Our Lady of Prompt Succor. A Record of Two Centuries, 1727–1925* (New York: P. J. Kenedy & Sons, 1925), facsimile facing p. 60.

Washington May the 15, 1804

To the Soeur Therese de St. Xavier Farjon, Superior; and the Nuns of the Order of St. Ursula at New Orleans.

I have received, holy sisters, the letter which you have written me, wherein you express anxiety for the property vested in your institution by the former government of Louisiana. The principles of the Constitution and government of the United States are a sure guarantee to you that it will be preserved to you sacred and inviolate, and that your institution will be permitted to govern itself according to it's own voluntary rules, without interference from the civil authority, whatever diversity of shade may appear in the religious opinions of our fellow citizens, the charitable objects of your institution cannot be indifferent to any; and it's furtherance of the wholesome purposes of society, by training up it's younger members in the way they should go, cannot fail to ensure it the patronage of the government it is under. Be assured that it will meet with all the protection which my office can give it.

I salute you, holy sisters, with friendship and respect,

Th. Jefferson

62. The United States Government Declines to Commit Itself on a Bishop for Louisiana, November 17–20, 1806

AT THE time that Louisiana was transferred by France to the United States in December, 1803, the Church in that colony was riddled by dissension. The *marguilliers* or trustees of St. Louis Cathedral in New Orleans supported Antonio de Sedella (1748–1829), a refractory Spanish Capuchin, against the authority of Fathers Thomas Hassett and Patrick Walsh whom Bishop Peñalver had left as administrators of the see when he departed in 1801. A schism in the cathedral congregation finally resulted and an intrigue was set on foot to have Sedella named bishop through the intervention of Emperor Napoleon. News of the trouble reached the Holy See and on September 20, 1805, Bishop Carroll was named administrator of the Diocese of Louisiana and the Two Floridas. Carroll fully realized the practical impossibility of his being able to settle the difficulties satisfactorily at so great a distance. Moreover, his awareness of the resentment of many of the French and Spanish inhabitants at the cession of their colony to the Americans gave him additional worry. In his perplexity Carroll turned to James Madison (1751–1836), Secretary of State in Jefferson's cabinet, to inquire if there would be any objection to his recommending a French priest to be the bishop of Louisiana. The following exhange of letters reveals, first, Carroll's patriotic feeling and his reluctance to make any recommendation that might jeopardize American interests in Louisiana and, second, Jefferson's and Madison's scrupulous care to keep the government clear of the charge of meddling in religious matters, as well as their high personal confidence and esteem for Carroll. Sources: John Gilmary Shea, *History of the Catholic Church in the United States* (New York: John G. Shea, 1888), II, 591–592; *Records of the American Catholic Historical Society of Philadelphia,* XX (1909), 63–64.

November 17, 1806.

. . . I was not so satisfied with the accounts of Louisiana, of the clergymen living there, as would justify a recommendation of any of them for the important trust, which requires not only a virtuous but very prudent conduct, great learning, especially in matters of a religious nature, and sufficient resolution to remove gradually the disorders which have grown up during the relaxed state of civil and ecclesiastical authority. I therefore directed my views to two others, who, tho' Frenchmen, have been long resident in this country and steady in their attachment to it. But the removal of either of them to Louisiana was rendered impracticable, and circumstances have since occurred which perhaps makes it unadviseable in the opinion of this government, to nominate for the bishop of that country any native of France or Louisiana. I therefore declined hitherto taking any concern in this business, tho' the situation of the church there has long required, and requires now more particularly a prompt interference, not only for the interests of religion, but likewise for quieting and composing the minds of the inhabitants. You will observe that my first commission to take a provisional charge of the diocese of N. Orleans was received long before the intermeddling of the Emperor Napoleon. This has been procured, as I am credibly informed from N.O. by a mission to Paris from a Mr. Castillon,[1] who is at the head of the municipality, and an artful Spanish friar, Antonio de Sedilla [*sic*], the intimate friend of the Marquis of Caso [*sic*] Calvo.[2] This mission was entrusted to a certain Castanedo,[3] who was furnished with $4,000 to obtain a recommendation from the Emperor Napoleon for the immediate nomination of de Sedilla to the bishopric: but the attempt was completely miscarried, as you will see by the duplicate copy of the commission sent to me, &c. To this commission allow me to join

[1] Jean-Baptiste-Victor Castillon was president of the *marguilliers* of St. Louis Cathedral in New Orleans.

[2] Sebastián de la Puerta y O'Farril, Marquis de Casa Calvo, had been acting Governor of Spanish Louisiana for some months in 1799.

[3] Jean Castanedo was a member of the board of the cathedral *marguilliers.*

an extract from a letter of Card. Pietro, prefect of the Congreg. de Prop. fide at Rome, which I received at the same time. He says, &c. . . . From which it appears, that the acquiescence of our government is necessary with respect to the measures to be adopted for settling the ecclesiastical state of Louisiana. Something, as has been mentioned, is immediately necessary, before I proceed to determine on the choice of a subject fit to be recommended for the future bishop. If a native of this country, or one who is not a Frenchman, tho' well acquainted with the language, cannot be procured, would it be satisfactory to the Executive of the U.S. to recommend a native of France who has long resided amongst us, and is desirous of continuing under this government? In the meantime, as the only clergyman in Louisiana, in any degree qualified to act with vigor and intelligence in restoring order in the Cath. church, is a French emigrant priest, far from any attachment to the present system of his country, may be appointed to act as my vicar, without the disapprobation of our Executive? I have many reasons for believing that this person rejoices sincerely in the cession of that country to the United States.

Department of State
November 20th 1806.

Right Reverend Sir,

I have had the honor to receive and lay before the President your letter of the 17th inst, inclosing a duplicate of the commission which places under your care the Roman Catholic Church at New Orleans, and requesting the sentiments of the Executive on certain discretionary points affecting the selection of the functionaries to be named by you.

The delicacy towards the public authority and the laudable object which led to the enquiry you are pleased to make, are appreciated by the President, in the manner which they so justly merit. But as the case is entirely ecclesiastical it is deemed most congenial with the scrupulous policy of the Constitution in guarding against a political interference with religious affairs, to decline the explanations which you have thought might enable you to accommodate the better, the execution of your trust, to the public advantage. I have the pleasure, Sir, to add, that if that consideration had less influence, the President would find a motive to the same determination, in his perfect confidence in the purity of your views, and in the patriotism which will guide you, in the selection of ecclesiastical individuals, to such as combine with their professional merits, a due attachment to the independence, the Constitution and the prosperity of the United States.

I enclose the document which you requested might be returned, and pray you to accept assurances of the perfect respect and esteem with which,[1]

I remain,
Your most obt Servt
James Madison.

[1] In a private letter of the same date Madison told Carroll that he shared his views on Sedella, that he wished Carroll would be placed in permanent control of the Church in Louisiana, and that the "foreign interposition" of the New Orleans trustees to further the candidacy of Sedella for the bishopric was known by the government and regarded as "manifestly reprehensible." *Ibid.*, XX (1909), 64–65.

63. Mother Seton's Plans for Her Religious Community, February 9, 1809

THE founder of the first American religious congregation of women, the Sisters of Charity of St. Joseph, was Elizabeth Ann Seton (1774–1821). This convert widow of a distinguished Protestant Episcopalian family of New York laid the foundations of her community at Baltimore in 1808 under the auspices of Archbishop Carroll and the Sulpicians. In the summer of 1809 she moved to Emmitsburg, Maryland, where the mother house was permanently established and where the school for small children which had been begun in Baltimore was continued. Mother Seton's sisters increased in number and within six months after her death they had schools in Philadelphia, New York, and Baltimore. In the following letter to Filippo Filicchi she described the plans of herself and her advisers for the future of the infant community. Mother Seton's cause for beatification is now being studied by the Congregation of Rites. Source: Annabelle M. Melville, *Elizabeth Bayley Seton, 1774–1821* (New York: Charles Scribner's Sons, 1951), pp. 145–146.

My dear Filicchi,[1] you will think, I fear, that the poor little woman's brain is turned who writes you so often on the same subject, but it is not a matter of choice on my part, as it is my indispensable duty to let you know every particular of a circumstance which has occurred since I wrote you last week relative to the suggestions so strongly indicated in the letters I have written both yourself and your Antonio[2] since my arrival in Baltimore. Some time ago I mentioned to you the

[1] Filippo Filicchi, a well-to-do merchant of Leghorn, Italy, had long been a friend of the Seton family. He had assisted and encouraged Mrs. Seton in becoming a Catholic.

[2] Antonio was the brother of Filippo Filicchi.

conversion of a man of family and fortune in Philadelphia.[3] This conversion is as solid as it was extraordinary, and as *the person* is soon to recieve [*sic*] the Tonsure in our seminary, in making the disposition of his fortune he had consulted our Rd. Mr. Dubourg,[4] the Prest. of the College on the plan of establishing an institution for the advancement of Catholick female children in habits of religion and giving them an education suited to the purpose. He also desires extremely to extend the plan to the reception of the aged and also uneducated persons who may be employed in spinning, knitting, etc., etc., so as to found a Manufactory on a small scale which may be very beneficial to the poor. You see I am bound to let you know the disposition of Providence that you may yourself judge how far you may concur with it. Dr. Matignon[5] of Boston to whom Mr. Cheverus[6] the Bishop elect and Antonio referred me on every Occasion, [*sic*] had suggested this plan for me before the gentleman in question ever thought of it. I have invariably kept in the background and avoided even reflecting voluntarily on anything of the kind, knowing that Almighty God alone could effect it if indeed it will be realized. Father Mr. Dubourg has always said the same, be quiet; God will in his own time discover His intentions, nor will I allow one word of intreaty [*sic*] from my pen. His blessed will be done.

In my former letter I asked you if you could not secure your own property and build something for this purpose on the lot (which is an extensive one) given by Mr. Dubourg. If you will furnish the necessary expenditures for setting us off, and supporting those persons or children who at first will not be able to support themselves. Dr. Matignon will appoint a Director for the establishment which if you knew how many good and excellent souls are sighing for would soon obtain an interest in your breast, so ardently desiring the glory of God. But all is in his hands. If I had a choice and my will would decide in a moment, I would remain silent in his hands. Oh how sweet it is there to rest in perfect confidence, yet in every daily Mass and at communion I beg him to dispose of me and mine in any way which may please him. YOU are Our Father in him, thro your hands

---

[3] Samuel Sutherland Cooper (1769–1843), a convert of means who became a priest, gave financial aid to Mother Seton's community in its early years.

[4] Louis W. V. Dubourg, S.S. (1766–1833), was at the time president of St. Mary's College, Baltimore. He died as Archbishop of Besançon.

[5] François A. Matignon (1753–1818) was a French-born priest who was pastor of what was soon to become the Cathedral of the Holy Cross in Boston.

[6] Jean Cheverus (1768–1836) was the first Bishop of Boston who died as Cardinal Archbishop of Bordeaux.

we received that new and precious being which is indeed true life. And may you in your turn be rewarded with the fullness of the divine benediction. Amen a thousand times.

MEA Seton

64. Robert Walsh's Prospectus for His *American Review of History and Politics,* January 1, 1811

THE American Catholic minority had no more articulate representative in the ranks of the intellectuals of the early national period than Robert Walsh (1784–1859), even if his ideas were often at variance with many of his coreligionists. Educated at Georgetown and St. Mary's College, Baltimore, he later read law with Robert Goodloe Harper (1765–1825), son-in-law of Charles Carroll of Carrollton and a haughty Federalist of aristocratic bearing. Possessed of means, a penetrating mind, a deep love for literature and the arts, and the benefit of years of leisurely travel and study in Europe, Walsh's literary talents found an outlet in a variety of enterprises such as editing the *American Register,* contributing to the *Port Folio,* and establishing at Philadelphia the first formal quarterly review in the United States, the *American Review of History and Politics.* Due to Walsh's tenacious Federalist views in the midst of the War of 1812, the last venture lasted only two years. But he went on to become a founder of the *National Gazette and Literary Register* in 1820 and in 1827 launched the *American Quarterly Review* which for a decade held its place as one of the country's leading journals. Walsh was a striking contrast to his fellow townsman and fellow Catholic, Mathew Carey, in his execration of the Madison administration, his advocacy of Adam Smith's *laissez-faire* doctrines, his suspicion of the embryonic labor movement, and his opposition to the movement for public schools for the masses. Yet this conservative aristocrat, whose Philadelphia salon drew the city's elite, was personally a kindly and charitable man, a devoted husband to Anna Maria Moylan, niece of Stephen Moylan (1737–1811) of Revolutionary War fame, and a fond father to their twelve children. In August, 1844, Walsh was named American consul at Paris by President Tyler, a post he held until 1851. His remaining years were spent mostly in the French capital where he was on familiar and easy terms with the political and literary great. At the time that he launched the *Review* in January, 1811, his detestation of Napoleon Bonaparte was matched only by his grave misgivings over the way the Jeffersonian Republicans were running the government of the United States. These ideas, together with his reflections on the current literary trends in England and this country, were well summarized in the prospectus he wrote for the first issue of the new magazine and which is printed in the document which follows. Walsh's death took place in Paris on February 7, 1859, his last words being, "I die in the faith of my ancestors — in the faith of the Holy Catholic Church" (Sister M. Frederick Lochemes, *Robert Walsh: His Story* [New York, 1941], p. 221). Source: *American Review of History and Politics,* I (January, 1811), i–x.

This work will be conducted under adequate management, and modelled upon a plan calculated to render it extensively and permanently useful. It will embrace a review of the public occurrences of Europe, and of our own relations with that quarter of the globe, — an examination of the parliamentary history and domestic policy of this country, — an inquiry into the merits of foreign and native productions — particularly of such as profess to delineate our own condition and character; — original essays, and selections in every department of literature; — an application of the principles of political economy to the peculiar circumstances of the United States, — and a collection of state papers, in the form of an appendix — fitted to illustrate and to confirm the facts and opinions advanced in the historical and political articles.

The chief ends of this miscellany, to which the most indefatigable attention will be given, and for which ample resources will be provided, — are the propagation of sound political doctrines, and the direction and improvement of the literary taste of the American people. It has been thought advisable to adopt a plan of a nature so comprehensive as to exclude nothing which may conduce to the attainment of these ends. The preference given to a quarterly over a monthly or annual publication is founded upon the idea, that it will combine the advantages, while it obviates the inconveniences, peculiar to both, — by affording an interval of time, not so great as to divest the historical and political disquisitions of the interest of novelty, and yet sufficient for the exercise of care and discrimination in the composition, the selection, and the arrangement of materials.

Whatever maxims of wisdom applicable to our institutions the best writers either ancient or modern can afford on the science of government, will be industriously sought and quoted, as well as such cases in the history of the past, as may serve to enlighten the public opinion both with regard to our own situation and to the transactions of European powers. It will be made a principal object to furnish the readers of this miscellany with correct views of the true condition and policy of the two great belligerents by whose distant struggles our domestic peace is shaken, and in whose dispositions and projects our highest interests are deeply involved. Every document, therefore, calculated to throw light on this topic, and which an extensive correspondence and the best opportunities can yield, will be minutely examined, and rendered subservient to a purpose, on the importance of which it would be superfluous to dwell. The proceedings of congress will be vigilantly watched, and temperately discussed, — but not, however, without that degree of zeal which an ardent love of country naturally excites, and which, so far from proving an obstruction, is, in fact, auxiliary to the surest operations of the judgment. Genuine sentiment and sound policy can never be dissociated, — and it is, therefore, that full scope will be given to the natural, elevated, warm feelings, and to the vehement, unsuborned, virtuous passions, of the heart, whenever the subject of discussion shall be those schemes of profligate ambition which now menace the liberties of all mankind, and those acts of portentous corruption, — the crimes of unexampled depravity, — which assail the moral and political order of Europe — and which awaken terror while they kindle indignation in the mind of every reflecting and honest individual of every country.

The utility of the present undertaking must be too obvious to require a particular exposition, and should it be well executed — it is hoped that no necessity will arise for an elaborate appeal to the public on the score of patronage. A work of the nature now contemplated has been long desired by the most enlightened men of this country, and claims the cooperation as well as the protection of those who unite the ability with the desire of promoting the interests of freedom and of letters.

There is something in the melancholy character of the times, — in the signal and extraordinary dangers with which the United States, together with the rest of the civilized world, are threatened, — that calls loudly for the utmost activity in the defence of those institutions and that system of knowledge, which constitute our best riches, and which ennoble and decorate human nature. At a moment when the whole continent of Europe is sinking under the ascendant of a military despotism, and the same dark cloud of ignorance and tyranny is settling upon it, which a few centuries ago was dispelled by the genius of commerce, it is incumbent upon the American public to encourage the development and the application of whatever resources may be found in the faculties of individuals, in order to secure from the same fatal influence, the inestimable blessings and the pure lights which this country drew from the very fountain that is now partly, and which may be hereafter, totally choked up and polluted. . . .

Independently of such considerations as these which affect our highest interests and appeal to the nobler feelings of the breast, there are others of secondary importance, which operate as a recommendation to an undertaking like the present and are not to be overlooked. The critical examination of European works particularly of those which come to us from England, will be made to enter, as has been before stated, into the structure of this journal. Whatever may be the ability with which the English reviews are conducted, it is certain that truth in them is often distorted or wholly suppressed,—that their decisions are materially influenced by the spirit of party—the suggestions of private friendship, or the authority of popular names; and not infrequently, by the prejudices of literary patriotism and the intolerance of national pride. The formation therefore, of a domestic tribunal exempt from the operation of feelings which vitiate the taste, and mislead the judgment, and whose province it shall be both to vindicate our own merits when injuriously attacked, and to exhibit faithfully those of foreign writers when erroneously reported, cannot but be productive of the most beneficial consequences, not merely in relation to the purity of our relish for elegant literature, but also to the accuracy of our opinions on questions connected with the domestic politics of another country, of the utmost importance to our own national welfare.

Another topic which it is deemed expedient to urge in favour of a journal on the plan mentioned above, is, the apparent necessity for some such enterprize with a view to the promotion of the literary fame of this country. The period has arrived when a platform at least, should be laid, and it is in this mode only—under the peculiar circumstances of our condition—that the object can be accomplished. If the foundation were once settled, there remains no doubt but that with the scaffolding of English literature, a fabric of literary reputation might be ere long erected, of materials which both for their variety and excellence would delight and surprise the nations of Europe. It is certain that our means are not duly appreciated abroad;—that we ourselves have not done justice to our resources, either of genius or of learning. Whatever may be said by the prejudiced or the uninformed critics of Europe, there is, nevertheless, among us an ample portion of the "ethereal spirit," and an abundant store of erudition, competent to extend the limits of human knowledge and to shed lustre on the national character,—as there is, also, a solid fund of legislative wisdom and public virtue fitted to raise us to a proper standard of estimation in the eyes of the world, and to fashion and fortify this republic into a "deeplaid indissoluble state."

But through the agency of a combination of unavoidable circumstances in the one case, and of a train of unfortunate contingencies and lamentable errors in the other, all these advantages lie inert and obscure, and mankind judging only from external indications and practical results, have come to this fallacious but natural conclusion, that we are no less miserably deficient in the treasures of learning and in the powers of genius, than ridiculously weak in our public councils, and improvidently backward in the organization of our physical strength. From the actual composition of our deliberative assemblies, and the measures of our cabinet, they infer that we are altogether without that gallantry of spirit, that generous and lofty enthusiasm, the liberal studies, and enlarged "courageous wisdom" which, if they had uniformly presided over our affairs, might have given an irresistible momentum and a most imposing attitude to a nation so singularly favoured by nature and fortune. They make the rarity and insignificance of our productions in literature, the criterion of our ability to produce, and imagine that a mercenary, groveling, narrow-minded system of policy is accompanied by a correspondent poverty of conception and scantiness of knowledge.

It shall be one of the ends of this journal to refute these imputations, and it is one of its chief advantages that it may itself become a practical illustration of their falsehood. The sound doctrines and the elevated sentiments of which it may be made the receptacle, and which, together with habits of profound investigation and a rich fund of political science, belong to so many individuals in this country, may serve to convince the world that it is to causes merely accidental that we owe the coarse texture of our legislative bodies, and the abject spirit of our administration. It may be asserted without presumption that this country has not shone in periodical literature rather on account of the absence of proper excitements and of suitable repositories for the productions of taste and learning, than for any want either of capacity or leisure. The analysis of important works and the literary disquisitions which fall within the scope of the present publication, will afford an ample field for the display of ingenuity and of erudition, and should the materials of this description which may form a part of the first numbers, be wrought with skill and elegance, a spirit of emulation, the natural effect of classical models, — may be excited, so as to lead to efforts of the highest and happiest order.

In Europe, profound statesmen, eminent authors, brilliant scholars, cooperate ambitiously in journals of this nature, — and communicate to the world, through such channels, their most elaborate researches, and their most finished productions. They know that in so doing, they derogate nothing from their own dignity, while they contribute infinitely to the advantage of the public. Sound doctrines are, in this way, more widely disseminated, a more habitual and certain influence is given to the principles of taste, and a more prompt and diffusive fame secured to the labours of learning and of genius. The delicacy and solidity of the tissue which they weave, the rich and lasting colours which they employ, counteract the perishable nature of the frame in which they exhibit their productions; and it may, therefore, be asserted with confidence, that such disquisitions as those of the Edinburgh Review and the Mercure de France, will be no less durable, as they are no less elegant and instructive, than the most formal or ambitious treatises, however profound or original. The enlightened and the patriotic of every country will always zealously advance the progress of letters — and will not disdain to become, as it were, militant themselves, in a cause which is inseparable from that of pure morals, of national glory, of refined humanity, of generous and elevated sentiment, of true policy, and heroic conduct.

The illustrous example just quoted should be here imitated by those whose proper stations in our political world have been usurped by the most incapable and contemptible men that ever presumed to be ambitious; by men who are no less devoid of the accomplishments of liberal and useful science than of all the distinguishing qualifications of real statesmen; — who are not the guides but the instruments of the people; — who are at once the shame and the scourge of their country. This example may be held up to our ingenuous youth as pointing to the only mode in which they can, at this moment when the principles of natural subordination are overthrown among us, and the just correspondence and symmetry of our political system completely deranged, — gratify that avidity to serve the commonwealth — which is the passion of noble minds — and restore to liberal studies and to vigorous talents that due and wholesome preponderance of which — by the most mischievous of all kinds of oppression, — in defiance of the dispensations of divine wisdom, and in violation of the laws of true political equality as well as of the prerogatives of nature, — they are here systematically and almost universally deprived. If those who are our brightest ornaments, — our legitimate instructors — and our natural rulers, — who have from nature authentic evidence of delegation to the functions of government, who, in the possession of superior capacity, wisdom and learning, carry with them "the passport of Heaven to human place and honour," are excluded from the management of public affairs, they are not, however, absolved from the obligation of struggling for the regeneration of the state in another course of exertion which, although less direct and sure than the exercise of official authority, may nevertheless, produce the most salutary results. They still lie under engagements of interest and duty which they violate in resigning themselves to total inaction, when by the concentration of their desultory and scattered efforts in one focus, — by the speculations of the closet widely circulated, — by the admonitions of wisdom constantly reproduced, and by specimens of sound literature and chaste composition, they may finally succeed in touching the mastersprings and the nobler passions of our nature, — in refining and enlarging our habits of thought — in extending the range of our literary and scientific inquiries, and in correcting that low and degenerate fashion of argument which would sacrifice national honour to pecuniary interests, and which mistakes the suggestions of a sordid and improvident parsimony for those of genuine state economy — a principle both magnificent and prospective, and often opposed to all arithmetical calculation. . . .

This country is hideously metamorphised since the days of Washington, — but we are far from despairing of the public fortunes. It is not credulity to imagine that much of that spirit still remains which then seemed to pervade the great majority of this nation, and that to be made to reappear it needs only to be "ritually invoked." Although the repetition of enormous crimes since the commencement of the French revolution, is calculated to render the present generation callous to any excesses of profligate power, we are not without a numerous body composing the best and most efficient class of citizens, who are justly shocked at the horrible depravity of the conduct and views of the Imperial government of France, particularly as they are exemplified in the cases of Spain and Holland. Although the grossest delusions and the most pernicious errors prevail generally on the subject of France, a large proportion of the intelligent proprietaries of this country are alive to most of the dangers which impend over us from that quarter, and look with a fearful and watchful eye on the tremendous growth of her power. It shall be one of the leading objects of this journal to unfold the whole extend of those dangers, and to administer in every form and at every recurrence of opportunity, the strongest antidotes to that blind security, which we consider as the capital evil, and the most serious distemper of the state. Should this journal become what by suitable exertions it may be rendered — "a bank of deposit and a bank of circulation" for correct representations of facts, for the fundamental truths of state-policy, and for the lessons of experience, much more may be accomplished than can be now distinctly foreseen or even readily imagined. It is a remark of Bolingbroke that truth and reason when vigourously and pertinaciously maintained will often bear down all prejudices and surmount all obstacles. "Their progress," he adds, "is generally sure although "sometimes not observable by every eye. — Contrary prejudices may "seem to maintain themselves in vigour, and these prejudices may be "long kept up by passion and artifice. But when sound principles and "natural sentiments continue to be urged, a little sooner, or a little "later, and often when the revolution is least expected, the prejudices "vanish at once and give place to the dominion of wisdom and of "truth." Such should be the expectation of the enlightened and virtuous portion of our community, and upon this rational ground of hope should they persevere in combating abuses and in resisting delusions, that menace our very existence, and have already entailed upon the infancy of this republic all the marks of weakness and folly which usually accompany the dotage of governments.

65. The First Bishop of the Middle West Arrives in His See, June, 1811

ON APRIL 8, 1808, Pope Pius VII divided the original Diocese of Baltimore and erected four new sees, the only one west of the Alleghenies being the Diocese of Bardstown, Kentucky. The man appointed to rule this see in the wilderness was a French-born Sulpician, Benedict Joseph Flaget (1763–1850), who had come to the United States in 1792. After an unsuccessful attempt to escape the episcopacy Flaget was consecrated by Archbishop Carroll on November 4, 1810, but he was so poor at the time that he did not have enough money to cover his traveling expenses. It was not until May, 1811, that he was able to set out with a small party of three priests, three seminarians, and three servants. The data for the following description of their journey westward and their first days in Kentucky were gathered from various sources by Bishop Martin J. Spalding, Flaget's coadjutor, and published two years after the latter's death. Source: M. J. Spalding, *Sketches of the Life, Times, and Character of the Rt. Rev. Benedict Joseph Flaget, First Bishop of Louisville* (Louisville: Webb & Levering, 1852), pp. 68–72.

To give you a clear idea of the bishoprics of the United States, I propose to lay before you a brief statement of the condition in which I found myself, after the Holy See, on the representation of Bishop Carroll, had nominated me to the bishopric of Bardstown. I was compelled to accept the appointment, whether I would or not; I had not a cent at my disposal; the Pope and the Cardinals, who were dispersed by the revolution, were not able to make me the slightest present; and Archbishop Carroll, though he had been Bishop for more than sixteen (*twenty*) years, was still poorer than myself; for he had debts, and I owed nothing. Nevertheless, my consecration took place on the 4th of November, 1810; but for want of money to defray the expenses of the journey, I could not undertake it. It was only six months afterwards, that, through a subscription made by my friends in Baltimore, I was enabled to reach Bardstown, my episcopal see.

At length, on the 11th of May, 1811, the Bishop and his suite left Baltimore for the West. They traveled over the mountains to Pittsburg; whence they embarked on the 22d in a flat-boat, chartered especially for the purpose. They were thirteen days in descending the Ohio river to Louisville, where they arrived on the 4th of June. . . .

The boat on which we descended the Ohio became the cradle of our seminary, and of the church of Kentucky. Our cabin was, at the same time, chapel, dormitory, study room and refectory. An altar was erected on the boxes, and ornamented so far as circumstances would allow. The Bishop prescribed a regulation which fixed all the exercises, and in which each had its proper time. On Sunday, after prayer, every one went to confession; then the priests said Mass, and the others went to communion. After an agreeable navigation of thirteen days, we arrived at Louisville, next at Bardstown, and finally at the residence of the Vicar General.[1]

While we were there (in Louisville), the faithful of my episcopal city put themselves in motion to receive me in a manner conformable to my dignity. They despatched for my use a fine equipage drawn by two horses; and a son of one among the principal inhabitants considered himself honored in being the driver. Horses were furnished to all those who accompanied me, and four wagons transported our baggage.

It was then, for the first time, that I saw the bright side of the episcopacy, and that I began to feel its dangers. Nevertheless, God be thanked, if some movements of vanity glided into my heart, they had not a long time to fix their abode therein. The roads were so detestable, that, in spite of my beautiful chargers and my excellent driver, I was obliged to perform part of the journey on foot; and I should have traveled the entire way, had not one of my young seminarians dismounted and presented me his horse. . . .

The next day, the sun was not risen when we were already on our journey. The roads were much better; I entered the carriage with two of my suite. I was not the more exalted (*fier*) for all this; the

[1] Father Badin was vicar general of the new diocese.

idea that I was henceforward to speak, to write, and to act as Bishop, cast me into a profound sadness. How many sighs did I not breathe forth while traversing the four or five remaining leagues of our journey!

At the distance of a half league (a mile and a half) from town, an ecclesiastic of my Diocese, accompanied by the principal inhabitants, came out to meet me. So soon as they had perceived us, they dismounted to receive my benediction. I gave it to them, but with how trembling a hand, and with what heaviness of heart! Mutual compliments were now exchanged, and then we all together proceeded towards the town. This *cortege,* though simple and modest in itself, is something very new and extraordinary in this country. It was the first time a Bishop was ever seen in these parts (*deserts*); and it was I, the very last of the last tribe, who was to have this honor!

In entering the town, I devoted myself to all the guardian angels who reside therein, and I prayed to God, with all my heart, to make me die a thousand times, should I not become an instrument of His glory in this new Diocese. O, my dear brother, have compassion on me, overloaded with so heavy a burden, and pray fervently to God that he would vouchsafe to lighten it.

The Bishop entered Bardstown,—where there was as yet no church,—on the 9th of June; and he reached St. Stephen's, the residence of M. Badin, on the 11th. Here he was met by the clergy of his Diocese, and was greeted by a large concourse of his people, anxious to see their Bishop. The ceremony of his installation is thus described by M. Badin:

The Bishop there found the faithful kneeling on the grass, and singing canticles in English; the country women were nearly all dressed in white, and many of them were still fasting, though it was then four o'clock in the evening; they having entertained a hope to be able on that day to assist at his Mass, and to receive the holy communion from his hands. An altar had been prepared at the entrance of the first court, under a bower composed of four small trees which overshadowed it with their foliage. Here the Bishop put on his pontifical robes. After the aspersion of the holy water, he was conducted to the chapel in procession, with the singing of the Litany of the Blessed Virgin; and the whole function closed with the prayers and ceremonies prescribed for the occasion in the Roman Pontifical.

Under circumstances so simple, yet so touching, did the first Bishop of the West enter into formal possession of his see.

66. A Detroit Visitor Records His Impressions of Gabriel Richard, S.S., June, 1816

ONE of the principal gains made by the American Church among the priests who were forced into exile by the French Revolution was the Sulpician, Gabriel Richard (1767–1832). After some years on the Illinois missions Richard arrived in Detroit in June, 1798, and for the next thirty-four years his life was identified with practically every important event in Michigan. He served as missionary to the Indians, built Detroit's first schools, and introduced the first printing press whereon were printed the first books and the first newspaper in Michigan, the *Michigan Essay or Impartial Observer* (August 31, 1809). When the British took Detroit during the War of 1812 he refused to silence his American sympathies and was deported to Windsor and placed under house arrest. Richard not only carried out all his priestly duties but found time to serve as vice president of the incipient University of Michigan and to win the distinction of being the only priest ever to hold a seat in Congress as delegate of Michigan Territory. While attending the cholera victims he contracted the disease and died on September 13, 1832. During the visitation tour of Upper Canada in June, 1816, Joseph-Octave Plessis (1763–1822), Bishop of Quebec, visited Detroit and the impressions of Richard which he recorded in his journal give a good idea of the multiplicity of the priest's occupations and the place he held in the life of the community. Source: Henri Têtu (Ed.), *Journal des visites pastorales de 1815 et 1816 par Monseigneur Joseph-Octave Plessis, Evêque de Québec* (Québec, 1903); translation by Lionel Lindsay, *American Catholic Historical Researches,* XXII (July, 1905), 224–226, 228–230.

June 19 . . . .

This ecclesiastic is, moreover, thoroughly estimable on account of his regularity, of the variety of his knowledge, and especially of an activity of which it is difficult to form an idea. He has the talent of doing, almost simultaneously, ten entirely different things. Provided with newspapers (*gazettes*) well informed on all political questions, ever ready to argue on religion when the occasion presents itself, and thoroughly learned in theology, he reaps his hay, gathers the fruit of his garden, manages a fishery fronting his lot, teaches mathematics to one young man, reading to another, devotes times to mental prayer, establishes a printing-press, confesses all his people, imports carding and spinning wheels and looms, to teach the women of his parish how to work, leaves not a single act of his parochial register unwritten, invents an electric machine, goes on sick calls at a very great distance, writes letters to and receives others from all parts, preaches on every Sunday and holy-day both lengthily and learnedly, enriches his library, spends whole nights without sleep, walks for whole days, loves to converse, receives company, teaches catechism to his young parishioners, supports a girls' school, under the management of a few female teachers of his own choosing, whom he directs like a religious community whilst he gives lessons in plain-song to young boys assembled in a school he has founded, leads a most frugal life, and is in good health, as fresh and able, at the age of fifty, as one usually is at thirty. Such is the abridged portrait of this more than ordinary man; extremely appreciated by the Bishop of Quebec and his traveling companions, but having against him the great majority of his parishioners; entirely set against him, and several of whom, in their self-conceit and folly, would prefer remaining without a priest, to having that one. . . .[1]

June 24. M. Richard having paid a visit to the Bishop of Quebec on Thursday evening [June 20], it was agreed that he would introduce the latter to the American commanders, civil and military, of Detroit, whom he intended visiting on the following Monday. . . . They began by visiting the Governor,[2] who lived in a small house quite at the east or northeast extremity of the city. . . .

It would be folly on the part of the ecclesiastics to count on military honors. They should have no pretension thereto, but consent through politeness to accept them, when they are offered with good grace. It happened thus at the quarters of Major General McComb,[3] Military Commander of Detroit. He lives at the other extremity of the city, that is to say at the east or southeast. . . .

The visitors thought they had done with ceremony, at least for the remainder of that day, and hoped to dine leisurely and fraternally at M. Richard's house where they were expected. On the contrary. While they were going there by water, the Governor and the General arrived by land. . . .

The Abbé Richard, who had summoned all these guests without the participation of the Bishop of Quebec, placed him simply between the Governor and the General, and served them, on a rather badly disposed table, a dinner too abundant in meat, too scant in vegetables, in too small an apartment, whose windows he had had the precaution of removing to give more air to his company. A shower of rain

---

[1] The situation to which Bishop Plessis alluded had arisen over the refusal of certain parishioners to accept Richard's arrangements with the civil authorities for the location of a new church. Ultimately seven of the ringleaders were excommunicated and the breach was healed only by the personal visit of Bishop Flaget of Bardstown to Detroit in June, 1818.

[2] Lewis Cass (1782–1866) was Governor of Michigan Territory at the time.

[3] General Alexander Macomb was military commander at Detroit.

driven by the southerly wind, which occurred during the repast, sprinkled the chief guests. They would have desired to have the windows closed; but there were none to close, so they had to give it up.

However, the conversation was quite lively, and each one seemed to rejoice in the reunion of a company whose members, French, Canadians, Americans, English, civil, military, ecclesiastics, laymen, Catholics, Protestants, were strangers to each other.

The hour for departing had come. General McComb's band, which had followed the company, was ready to play in the adjoining room. Toasts or healths had to be drunk: the Americans attach great importance to this. The first was in the Bishop's honor. He proposed one to the President of the United States, expecting that it would be returned by another to the King of England. Not at all. Governor Cass proposed his to our Holy Father the Pope, and the General to the prosperity of the Catholic clergy. It must be remarked that these two dignitaries had quite recently received from M. Richard an honor that the Catholic clergy do not ordinarily grant to Protestants, which was that at the solemn procession of Corpus Christi, the 13th of the same month, he had invited them to hold the ribbons of the *dais* or canopy under which was the Blessed Sacrament, and had had the procession accompanied by an American regiment under arms. The parishioners had not been, in general, edified by such a mixture, and had justly complained of this novelty. The Abbé Richard justifies his conduct by what the Bishop of Baltimore had given as a principle to his clergy: to do towards the Protestants all that might draw them to the Catholic church: an excellent principle, so long as it does not violate the rules in essential points.

67. Archbishop Maréchal's Report to Propaganda, October 16, 1818

THREE years after the death of Archbishop Carroll his second successor in the See of Baltimore, the French-born Sulpician, Ambrose Maréchal (1764–1828), made a detailed report on the state of religion in the archdiocese to Lorenzo Cardinal Litta, Prefect of the Congregation de Propaganda Fide. It is an important source for the history of American Catholicism in the early nineteenth century since it covered practically all phases of the Church's activities in the large area from Maryland south to Florida and west to the Mississippi River. Maréchal not only gave an account of the priests, parishes, seminaries, religious congregations of men and women, with side lights on the religious life of the laity, but he also included some interesting reflections on topics such as American social customs, the trustee problem in the South, and the nationalist feeling that was causing an increasing amount of friction in various Catholic congregations. Source: A Latin text was published in the *Catholic Historical Review,* I (January, 1916), 439–453, from which the translation which follows was made by the Reverend Urban J. Stang of the College of Mount Saint Joseph on-the-Ohio.

Baltimore, October 16, 1818.

Your Eminence:

Having returned to Baltimore after a visit to most of the missions in my diocese, I have undertaken to commit to writing the present status of the Catholic Church in these regions, to the extent that it is known to me, and to transmit this account to the Sacred Congregation, until the time that I may be able to submit a more accurate record.

1. In the United States of North America the Sees of Boston, New York, Pennsylvania and Bardstown have also been erected. The Diocese of Baltimore however includes the following provinces, namely, Maryland, Virginia, North and South Carolina, Georgia and that vast territory which is contained in the limits of Georgia, the Floridas, Tennessee and the Mississippi River. Before the American Revolution there were at most 10,000 Catholics in the aforesaid provinces. At present there are at least 100,000 in these same regions,[1] the greatest part of them residing in Maryland. This multitude of the faithful, favored by divine Providence, is increasing marvelously by the natural progress of generation, by the conversion of Protestants, and especially by the immense number of Europeans who immigrate to our Republic every year. In my diocese there are 52 priests exercising the sacred ministry. They have come from various nations, namely, Italians 1, Germans 3, English 4, Belgians 7, Americans 12, Irish 11, and French 14. Each of these missionaries has a church in which he celebrates the most holy sacrifice of the Mass; many of them also have two or three missions some distance removed, which they visit at least once a month. Some of these churches are built of wood, others of brick, others of polished stone; but scarcely any of them is sufficiently large to accommodate the increasing number of Catholics. And so during the coming year ten new churches will be built in the various parts of my diocese.

2. There are four churches in the city of Baltimore, namely, the

---

[1] Maréchal's figures on the Catholic population were not accurate. For a correction cf. Gerald Shaughnessy, S.M., *Has The Immigrant Kept The Faith?* (New York, 1925), pp. 69–73.

church of St. Patrick in the Eastern part of the city; the church of St. John in the central portion; the church of the Seminary to the West; there is also the old metropolitan church, dedicated to St. Peter, towards the Northern part. The latter was the only church in the city of Baltimore, when, having come over from France, I entered it in 1792. But with the growth of the city the number of the faithful increased and the church of St. Patrick was erected. It was spacious and in the beginning was large enough but now it is too small for the congregation. Later the church of St. John was built. It is frequented principally by those of German descent. The Directors of the Seminary also built a large and very beautiful chapel at their own expense. A devout multitude of the faithful flock to it on Feastdays and Sundays, allured by the majestic Gregorian chant, the splendor of the divine worship, and the ceremonies performed with the help of the seminarians. Within the past year at least 10,000 communions were distributed to the faithful in this chapel. With regard to the old metropolitan church of St. Peter, it is so small in comparison to the multitude of parishioners that it can scarcely hold one-tenth part of them; and unless many masses be celebrated successively in it on Sundays, an immense number of the faithful could not be present at the most holy Sacrifice. Weighing carefully this most grave inconvenience, my predecessor, the Most Illustrious Bishop Carroll, undertook the building of a Cathedral Church of such dimensions that the Catholics of Baltimore might easily be admitted to it. But he had scarcely finished the foundation when the work was left unfinished because of a lack of funds. However during the past year, collections and alms having been taken up here and there, it was decided, at my suggestion, to complete the work which had been begun; and such was the industry and activity of the workers that I now have a well founded hope that after about eighteen months I will be able to perform the solemn ceremony of the consecration of this Basilica. Without a doubt its size and grandeur will far surpass that of any temple built up to this time in the United States of America, whether by the Protestants or by the Catholics. Even the Protestants of Baltimore take pride in it. It is, indeed, the greatest ornament of their city. But it grieves me very much that its interior is almost completely lacking in decoration. Would that the Sacred Congregation or some noble Roman would give to us as a gift some pious statues such as may be found around Rome. Four or six would suffice and they could be sent to us easily by way of Leghorn. Such a gift would elicit the supreme gratitude of all the Catholics of the United States towards the munificent donor. In vain did I wish to buy two statues, namely one of Our Lord and Saviour and one of the Blessed Virgin to whom the Metropolitan Church will be consecrated; none whatsoever could be found in these regions and there were no workers who could make them. In the year 1792 scarcely 800 Catholics could be found in the city of Baltimore; now there are about 10,000.

3. In my diocese there are two Seminaries under the direction of the priests of St. Sulpice. These are the major Seminary of Baltimore and the minor, located near the village of Emmitsburg, which is about 15 leagues from Baltimore. In the major seminary the junior clergy apply themselves to the study of philosophy and theology, and they are educated in all the sciences and virtues which are necessary for missionaries. A spacious college is connected with this seminary. In it the sons of wealthy or noble Catholic families pursue their studies of the humanities and of letters. All the youths living within the walls of this college are industriously taught by their kind directors and are educated in the principles of the Catholic religion. Many others, and among them many Protestants, daily frequent the schools outside of the city. The legislature of Maryland has conferred upon this college the dignity of a university. The minor seminary at Emmitsburg was founded especially according to the mind of the Council of Trent, that youths might be received in it, who wished to consecrate themselves to the service of God and the church. There are about 80 young men in this seminary. Of these fifteen have already received clerical tonsure and there are also the others whose ecclesiastical vocation is not yet sufficiently manifest. These two seminaries are most precious to the Catholic religion. Upon their prosperity depends to a great extent the prosperity of our holy faith in North America. They were erected at the expense of the Society of St. Sulpice. Since their income is exceedingly meager, it has caused me to wonder just how they have been able to sustain them. May it please God to inspire American citizens, who have wealth and means at their command, to sustain from time to time, by means of pious and liberal gifts, these two venerable institutions; then there would soon be at our command a sufficient number of missionaries both for fostering and propagating our holy faith, on all sides, in the immense republic of America.

Besides these two seminaries, whose principal end is the education of the secular clergy, there is also Georgetown. It is a magnificent college, near the capital city Washington, and is directed by the Fathers of the Society of Jesus. It consists of two principal buildings.

The former is occupied by secular youths who study the humanities and letters; the latter contains the novices and scholastics of the Society. Of these there are thirty-three. It is very much to be regreted that the college is deeply in debt. However, since the Society recently recovered all their belongings and the other properties, which they possessed before the destruction of the Society, without a doubt they will soon be wealthy enough. All wonder why their superiors at Rome do not send to Georgetown six or eight religious men, outstanding for their knowledge and piety, to foster this rising institution in our regions. For there is no part of the Catholic world in which the Society of Jesus could exist more securely, spread more widely and produce more abundant fruits.

4. There are three monasteries of nuns in the diocese of Baltimore. The first is that of the Carmelites. It is not far distant from a village called Port Tobacco, high up on the bank of the Potomac River which separates Maryland from Virginia. Twenty-three nuns live there. They have a sufficiently large income. These virgins of St. Teresa live so holily, that I scarcely believe that any other house of this order exists anywhere in the Catholic world in which piety and monastic discipline flourish to the same extent. They strictly observe the cloister. The second house is that of the Visitation of Georgetown situated near Washington. It contains nearly fifty nuns. Their resources are limited but they live partly on their income and partly by the labor of their own hands. This house is certainly most pious and most holy. In it the virtues of Francis de Sales shine very brightly; never do these nuns go beyond the limits of their monastery. Near the monastery is a building in which Catholic girls reside and are educated. Some of the nuns undertake the work of giving them a pious and liberal education. Besides these there are also many younger girls, Catholic and Protestant, who come for classes at appointed hours. Every year there goes forth from this religious home a number of young ladies, who diffuse far and wide in the world the lessons of piety taught them in this school. The third house is that of the Daughters of St. Vincent de Paul.[2] Their house is not far distant from the village of Emmitsburg. They have thirty-two sisters, who live holy lives according to the rules of their Holy Founder, with the exception of the modifications demanded by American customs and dispositions. They do not take care of hospitals, nor could they since the administrators of these hospitals are Protestant. Their

[2] The Sisters of Charity of St. Joseph at Emmitsburg, founded in 1808, were not affiliated to the Daughters of Charity of St. Vincent de Paul until 1850.

principal work is the pious education of Catholic girls, those of the poor as well as those of the rich. There are about eighty young girls in the house at Emmitsburg as well as some who are destitute of parents or means. This pious institute has produced most abundant fruits of religion. So if at some time in the future, with God's favor, I may be able to collect a large enough sum of money, I intend to erect another house, besides that of Emmitsburg, and this house for girls I intend to erect at Baltimore. These three monasteries, which I have visited very recently, reflect wonderfully the greatest piety, fervor of spirit, strict discipline, and indeed all virtues. Certainly I cannot thank God enough for all this. The Protestants themselves treat them with a certain veneration. Assuredly the sisters and their work are like so many overflowing fonts of grace to water abundantly my flock. Besides these religious communities, there are, in nearly all the churches of my diocese, confraternities, whether of the scapular, or the rosary, or of the Most Blessed Sacrament, or of the Sacred Heart of Jesus. Especially noteworthy is the association in the city of Baltimore for the good that it has accomplished. It is made up of outstanding Catholic men who strive to serve God. Once every month the members of the confraternity gather together in the lower chapel of the Seminary, where they attend Mass and listen to a sermon on the dogmas of the faith and the principal moral precepts of the gospel. The purpose of this pious association is that its members should show by example the virtues of the gospel to their fellow citizens, Catholic and Protestant. Among the regulations by which they are bound, one is of the greatest importance, namely, that on four of the more solemn feast days they as a group publicly receive Holy Communion in the metropolitan church. This wonderful example of their brethren has a marvelous effect upon those who see them and drives from them that mundane fear under which many in these regions labor and which caused them to refrain from receiving the sacraments.

I will conclude this article by announcing to the Sacred Congregation that by next winter I shall have established in Baltimore free schools. The poor youths of either sex, whether Catholic or Protestant, may attend these schools free of charge, if the parents consent that they be educated in the principles of our most holy religion.

5. In the United States of America all the Protestant sects have their followers, ministers and churches. They care little about the dogmas which Luther, Calvin and Henry VIII formerly preached. There is a manifest and general tendency of all towards Socinianism. The Anglican church, which was predominant before the American

Revolution and was protected by the rule of Great Britain, has tottered and fallen to pieces everywhere, for like all other religions it is only tolerated. The Catholic Church has vindicated for herself general veneration and the Protestants turn their eyes towards her. The prejudices, with which formerly the young were imbued, have disappeared to such an extent that pseudoministers no longer dare to suggest them in their preaching; and if one of them does do so he is branded a calumniator by his hearers.[3] Many Protestants now come to our churches on Sundays and of these not a few have embraced our holy faith. I refer to this fact for it gives me the greatest consolation and proves how quickly the Catholic faith can be propagated in these regions. In the visitation of my diocese, which I undertook this year, I administered confirmation in a certain village called *Taneytown*. The pastor of this mission is a Roman priest, the Rev. D. Zocchy [*sic*].[4] At least a third part of those who received this sacrament were Protestants who had recently become converts to the Catholic religion. Americans are endowed with keen minds and the best of natural dispositions. They possess naturally the art of reasoning, even the workmen. Nearly all the citizens are engaged in commerce, agriculture, or in the mechanical arts. They strive after riches with the greatest industry of mind and body. The civil arts and delicacies of life, in which Europeans indulge, are found amongst us in abundance. But no one among them can be said to be outstanding for his knowledge. Yet it can be said truthfully that the mass of people, taken in general, far surpass the European people in education, in the politeness of their customs, and a certain cultivation of the intellect. It is almost with divine worship that they adore the liberty which they enjoy; and since there are within the limits of this Republic vast forests, which are sold at a very cheap price, it is almost impossible to believe what large number of Europeans come to this country. It is estimated that during the present year about two hundred immigrants per day came to our shores from Europe. Among these there were very many Catholics.

Among the principal vices of the Americans are the desire for unlimited riches, which seems to have seized the minds of all, and the vice of drunkenness among laborers and the lower classes. And so

[3] In view of the Nativist uprisings against Catholics in the 1830's Maréchal's remarks concerning the disappearance of Protestant prejudice were altogether too optimistic.

[4] Nicholas Zocchi (1773–1845), a member of the Fathers of the Faith, a society made up principally of ex-Jesuits, had come to the United States from Canada in 1803.

it is exceedingly difficult to provide for the sustenance of missionaries, even though the people are wealthy in earthly possessions. Whenever a church is to be built or some charitable or pious institution to be erected, each will contribute a few coins to the common fund, but seldom are their gifts exceptionally large. The men live chastely enough, especially after they are once married. Those living in the cities go to the sacraments quite frequently, much oftener in fact than those living in rural areas. The eagerness with which they listen to the divine word is almost unbelievable. Any priest of even mediocre eloquence is certain to attract to himself a multitude of eager listeners in our churches. With regard to the women of my diocese, the purity of the customs of the whites is beyond question. Adultery or fornication are crimes that are seldom, if ever committed in my diocese. Most of them frequently receive Holy Communion. They take great care in adorning themselves and making themselves appear beautiful, although with few exceptions they cultivate Christian modesty. Their clothes are so luxurious that it is difficult to distinguish the daughter of a cobbler from European ladies of rank. Those who are not dutiful eagerly read books of romance and frequent theaters and dances. However they never do so on Sundays. The civil laws forbid it and it is considered the greatest of scandals. Among the women of African descent many indeed serve God faithfully; but there are also many, even among those who are Catholic, who are ignorant of religion and live and die addicted to vice and especially that of impurity.

In the United States of America, there are, besides the Colleges and Universities, many schools of lower rank in which the pupils are taught to read and write, and there is scarcely any American who is not versed in this art. All the books, which are printed in England or France, are publicly sold here in the bookstores. Among these there are innumerable books which teach doctrines that are harmful to faith and good morals. Nor are the civil laws a remedy for this evil. Americans strenuously defend the freedom of the press. Perhaps more gazettes are published daily by the press in the state of Maryland alone, than in Italy and France taken together.

6. In the early and subsequent ages of the Church, nations were converted to Christ by the sweat and labors of missionaries from without. In like manner, the Catholic faith has been introduced into our American Union by the work and zeal of priests from Europe, and they still continue to serve and propagate the faith here. Therefore it is not surprising that the American clergy is made up chiefly of missionaries, who were born in various parts of Europe. For my

part, I will certanly leave nothing undone that will help me build up an entirely native clergy. And yet, no matter to what extent the seminaries at Baltimore and Emmitsburg may flourish now or in the future, or how great the number of novices for the Society of Jesus, which is well established at Georgetown, I can never hope that they will supply me with a sufficiently large number of missionaries, which would be necessary to preserve and extend the faith in this growing country. Placed in these circumstances, we cannot be thankful enough to God, Who has inspired many European priests to cross the ocean, to cultivate the vineyard of the Lord in these regions. American priests, who are acquainted with the customs and characteristics of their fellow citizens, are, however, of all, the most dear to them. They are acquainted with only the necessary ecclesiastical sciences. The reason for this is the fact that before their ordination they can spend only a few years in studying the humanities, letters, and theology, and afterwards they are impeded from further study because of the ever pressing need of their ministry. So they find it difficult to talk on more erudite topics. However those who have a sufficient knowledge of moral and dogmatic theology, combined with true and solid piety, produce most abundant fruits. According to the Americans, English priests are more pleasing to the citizens in these regions, and prove themselves more useful to religion. There are only four English priests in my diocese; of these three came at my suggestion last year. One of these was formerly my pupil in theology in the Seminary of Lyons.[5] When he had heard that I had been promoted to the episcopal dignity, he said farewell to his fatherland that he might live with me, and he also brought with him two friends. One exercises the sacred ministry at Baltimore; another at Richmond, which is the capital city of Virginia; the third is at Alexandria, which is also a town of Virginia; and the fourth is in the missions of Zacchia.[6] Would that I could obtain many more like them, but such is the poverty of the priests in this country, that I have no hopes of being able to bring others into my diocese. From this brief exposition it is easy to conclude, that the Sacred Congregation, in urging me to place English at the head of missions, exhorts me to do that which is altogether impossible. For besides the four aforesaid priests, I have no other, nor can I obtain others. The Belgian, French and

[5] This was James Whitfield (1770–1834) who was to succeed Maréchal in 1828 as fourth Archbishop of Baltimore.

[6] The missions of what was then called Upper and Lower Zacchia embraced the area of the present parishes of Waldorf and Bryantown, Maryland.

German priests have shown themselves to be the best of missionaries. They are to be highly commended for their zeal for souls, purity of customs, learning and love of ecclesiastical discipline. Some indeed do not pronounce English perfectly; but they do announce the word of God in a manner that is not displeasing to Americans, notwithstanding the calumnies that have been uttered against them by Doctor Gallagher[7] and his impious faction. Besides it is to be very much regretted that the Sacred Congregation so readily gave ear to the accusations of these enemies of the church of Christ. If there exists any piety, love of religion and especially veneration towards the Holy See in the diocese of Baltimore, it must be referred especially to the example and untiring labors of these missionaries. The Americans love and venerate them. The Irish, who are moved by the spirit of God and imbued with truly ecclesiastical habits, serve religion fruitfully. For they are prompt in their work, speakers of no mean ability, and outstanding in their zeal for souls. Indeed, it gives me great joy that many of this race are in my diocese; I would certainly gladly receive many more like them with open arms. But alas, so many priests who have come hither from Ireland, are addicted to the vice of drunkenness, and I cannot place them in charge of souls until after a mature and thorough examination. For when they have once obtained faculties from us, it is hard to say what harm they would bring down upon the Church of God, if they should fall back into the vice of drunkenness. Nor would there be much of a remedy left to us by which we could put an end to their scandals. For if we should take away their faculties or attempt to do so, they would shake off the yoke completely and trouble the American Church with unbelievable seditions. They can do nothing among the faithful who are Americans, English, or belong to any of the European nationalities. These indeed flee from them. But it is truly surprising how much authority these drunkard priests exercise among the lowest classes of their own race. For since these consider drunkenness only a slight imperfection, they strenuously defend their profligate pastors, associate with them, and enter into and remain with them in schism. That lamentable fact is proved clearly in the history of all the dissensions that have occurred in the Church in North America, since it was established here. It was not the Americans, nor the English, nor

---

[7] Simon Felix Gallagher had come to the United States from Ireland in 1793 and had been assigned to St. Mary's Church, Charleston, South Carolina, where he became a key figure in the trustee war which ultimately led to a schism in the congregation.

the immigrants who came from other countries in Europe who disturbed or are disturbing the peace at Charleston, Norfolk, Philadelphia, etc., etc.; but it was those priests from Ireland who were given over to drunkenness or ambition, together with their accomplices, whom they win over to their side by means of innumerable artifices. Most recently they tried by means of various writings to persuade these ignorant people that the Bishops of Boston, Bardstown, and myself intended secretly to establish a French hierarchy in these provinces and to expel the Irish priests. They did not hesitate to broadcast this absurd calumny at Rome by means of letters and messengers. But indeed 1. Ten Irish priests received faculties from me and are exercising the sacred ministry in the missions of my diocese. 2. The greatest part of the clergy who are now studying theology in the Seminary in Baltimore, are Irish. Moreover of the fourteen French priests whom I now have here, eight exercise no functions in the missions, but live within the walls of the Seminaries of Baltimore and Emmitsburg. With the exception of the priests of the Society of Jesus, who possess many and very rich estates, all the rest of the missionaries have no other source of income but the pious and voluntary offerings of the faithful and the money which each one of the faithful pays every year for the seat he occupies in the church. Hence they live in the greatest of poverty in the country districts; in the cities, however, their sustenance is much better taken care of. They wear black clothes and in the sacrifice of the Mass they use the cassock, which comes to the ankles; but outside of the church, the vestments they wear are shorter but nevertheless modest. Nor is this surprising, since they live among Protestants and they have to ride on horseback very frequently. All administer the sacraments; every Sunday they preach the divine word. In places where it is possible for the children to gather together, they catechize them thoroughly. As far as I am concerned, I am most poor. Up till now my income has scarcely been sufficient to pay the expenses of the letters, which are sent to me from all sides (postage). I indeed have a right to receive yearly one thousand dollars Mexican; but for certain reasons, which perchance I shall at some time explain to the Sacred Congregation, it is doubtful whether this will ever be paid to me. I do not even have a secretary; and although I am weighed down by the administration of an immense diocese, I hear many confessions, administer the other sacraments, and also preach the divine word. I live in the same house with two priests who have the pastoral care of the metropolitan church and am happily destitute of all the comforts of this world.

7. There is no region in the world, where the Catholic religion can be propagated more quickly or widely and where it exists more securely than in the United States of America. Here there is no danger whatsoever that converts to the faith will suffer persecution or that their churches will be destroyed by the arbitrary command of some tyrant, as often occurs in the Chinese Empire and in the other missions of the Indes. All religious, which recognize Christ as the Saviour of the world, are tolerated here, and the laws of the Republic protect them all and most severely punish those who attempt to disturb the divine worship of any sect. And since religious liberty is the fundamental principle of the American Republic, there is no magistrate from the President to the least official, who can with impunity molest Catholics even in the slightest way. The only danger that blocks the path of our most holy religion, consists in the internal dissensions which divide the faithful against each other. The magistrates do not care about these dissensions. Only offenses which affect public peace and the liberty of the citizens are punished by the civil law. The nations which border our republic profess the Catholic religion. These are Canada, Florida and Mexico. Besides there is a very large number of Catholics in our United States. The Protestants, who constitute the greatest part of the citizens, have almost completely rejected the prejudices under which they formerly labored, and they look upon the Catholic religion with a certain amount of veneration. There is also an immense number of Europeans, who come hither daily, and among them there are many Catholics. It seems that this immigration will not be lessened for a number of years. Since the American republic possesses such an extensive territory, it might easily sustain, by the millions, those who migrate to it, and it is evident that the multitudes, who come to America from Europe, will not be quickly diminished. If the Sacred Congregation ponders over these facts it will perceive clearly that there is no region which offers a wider or more fertile field for apostolic zeal.

However, we do have many difficulties here that must be overcome:

1. *Insufficient number of missionaries.* Young American ladies, who formerly could scarcely refrain from laughing aloud when they heard Europeans telling of nuns living uninterruptedly in monasteries, now embrace the religious life so willingly, that I must needs exercise vigilance lest more than can be cared for be admitted to the monas-

teries which exist in my diocese. But it is an altogether different story with regard to youths embracing the clerical state. Some are deterred by celibacy; others are frightened away by the labors of acquiring a knowledge of the ecclesiastical sciences, for this takes a long time and must be undertaken before ordination; but most of all they are afraid of the poverty which is suffered by missionaries, who exercise the sacred ministry in the country districts. For with a little industry on their part, they can hope to live in comfort, nay even in abundance, if they engage in commerce or agriculture.

2. *Among those who otherwise wish to consecrate themselves to the service of the church, there are many who do not have the necessary funds to pay for the expenses of their own education.* The directors of the Seminaries of Baltimore and Emmitsburg have very limited incomes, and as a result they can receive only a limited number of seminarians free of charge. So until the time that divine Providence supplies me with the means with which to provide for the education of poor clerics, the number of missionaries, necessary to propagate our most holy religion, will not be sufficient.

3. *The schisms which occur very frequently in these regions.* It is of the greatest concern that the Sacred Congregation know accurately their principal cause. It should therefore be noted: — 1. that the American people pursue with a most ardent love the civil liberty which they enjoy. For the principle of civil liberty is paramount with them, so that absolutely all the magistrates, from the highest to the lowest, are elected by popular vote at determined times in the year. Likewise all the Protestant sects, who constitute the greater part of the people, are governed by these same principles, and as a result they elect and dismiss their pastors at will. Catholics in turn, living in their midst, are evidently exposed to the danger of admitting the same principles of ecclesiastical government. Clever and impious priests, who flatter them and appeal to their pride, easily lead them to believe that they also possess the right of choosing their pastors and dismissing them as they please. 2. When the Catholics in some part of my diocese become numerous enough to think that they can build a church, first of all each contributes a few coins to the common fund; and since the amount is seldom sufficient, then they select two or three men, whom they depute as their representatives to solicit contributions in the cities and villages from their fellow citizens, both Catholics and Protestants. When they have once collected enough money, then they buy a large enough tract of land upon which to build a church and priest house and to have a cemetery. However,

when they have once decided to buy this tract, sometimes they hand over to the bishop the title of possession, so that he is the true possessor of this ecclesiastical property and is considered as such by the civil tribunals. But it often happens that the legislators of the province approach and obtain from them the title of possession, upon the condition that they transmit it to four or five Caholic men, who are elected annually by the congregation. In this case, these men are not only the temporal administrators of the temporalities of the church (*marguilliers*) as they are in Europe, but they have possession and are considered the true possessors of all the temporal goods of the church in the eyes of the civil tribunals and they can with impunity exercise over them the same authority as they do over their own homes and lands. However, a schism has never taken place in those churches, of which the bishop holds the civil title; in fact, it is impossible for it to happen there. For if the priest, who is constituted the pastor of this church, is addicted to drunkenness or impurity or other scandalous vices, and will not correct his life, then the bishop, by reason of the title he possesses, can at once remove him, just as any citizen has the right of expelling those who presume to occupy his home against his will. For he could easily obtain an order of eviction from the magistrates. But if the title of possession is in the hands of the temporal administrators (*marguilliers*), then they can easily raise the flag of rebellion against the bishop. If indeed the greater part of them do not fear God and conceive a hatred for their pastor, they will continually remove him from the church, no matter how great the sanctity of his life and customs; besides they deprive the entire Catholic congregation of the use of the church. This is the state of affairs at Norfolk, where the impious Doctor Oliver Fernandez and two Irish drunkards, destitute of all religion, removed from their church a most holy man, the pastor, Mr. Lucas,[8] and all his Catholic fellow citizens. Likewise when a priest is leading a scandalous life and, instead of nourishing, is rather devastating the flock of the Lord by his bad example, if the bishop takes measures against him, or also threatens to punish him, it often happens that the temporal administrators come to his defense with cunning and impious theories, whether by maintaining that the bishop is proceeding unjustly against him, or by declaring that he has appealed to Rome, or by arguing that they, and they alone, have the natural right of selecting and removing their pastors. And if he has once been able to convince them of these

[8] James Lucas, a French-born priest, had been appointed in December, 1815, to serve the congregation at Norfolk, Virginia, by Archbishop Leonard Neale.

wicked principles, then the impious priest, protected by the temporal administrators, publicly withstands the authority of his bishop, calumniates him, sacrilegiously performs his sacred ministry, and lays waste the flock of Christ. Nor do the civil laws of the American republic offer any remedy for this great evil. Over and above, if such a priest is even more brazen and skilled in deceit, he gathers false testimony everywhere from the offscourings of the people. Then he busies himself in strengthening this testimony, by obtaining upon it the seal of Protestant magistrates, who secretly rejoice in the dissensions of this kind among Catholics. After this, having collected money here and there, he sends to Rome a messenger, who knows well how to assume a semblance of piety and to speak in a reverential manner. This was the method of procedure used by Doctor Gallaher and Mr. Browne[9] at Charleston.

In the beginning of organization here, the most illustrious Bishop Carroll, the first bishop of Baltimore, thought that the propagation of the Catholic religion would be furthered if the temporal administrators not only had charge of the administration of church property but also had the title of possession. For a number of years he defended this system.[10] However so many dissensions and schisms resulted from it, that shortly before he died he regretted very much that he had ever permitted it. Bishop Neale, his venerable successor, who was inflamed with the deepest love of God and the Church, after mature deliberation upon the evils resulting from the aforesaid system, fought it with all his strength and constantly opposed it. As far as I am concerned, it seems to me that it could be allowed without danger if the temporal administrators were restricted by means of certain clauses, either in the title of possession itself or in a contract, which they would be obliged to sign at the time of their election, so that they could not abuse the civil right entrusted to them; for example, that a pastor in his sacred functions be altogether independent of them; that if he be guilty or accused of some fault, the case be taken to the bishop and that he be considered innocent as long as the bishop has not condemned him; that they might never remove him from the church on their own private authority, that they might never permit a priest, who had been deprived of jurisdiction, to celebrate

---

[9] Robert Browne was an Irish-born Augustinian who was the source of considerable difficulty in the trustee troubles of congregations in Georgia and South Carolina in these years.

[10] It would be more accurate to say that Archbishop Carroll had rather tolerated and tried to work along with the lay trustee control of church properties than to say that he had defended it.

mass in a church under their care, nor retain there, against the will of the bishop a priest publicly bound by censures, etc., etc., etc.

8. In my previous letter to the Sacred Congregation, I made the observation that it would give me great joy if the provinces of the two Carolinas, Georgia, and the territory which is called Mississippi, were separated from my diocese. And since it seemed to me, as well as to other prudent and learned men, that under the present circumstances of times and conditions it would not be for the good of religion to erect immediately an episcopal see at Charleston, I humbly begged that a Vicariate Apostolic be established there for a number of years; telling them that I would help them as much as possible in this matter, I besought the Sacred Congregation to please send me the instrument, which when once handed over to a priest, chosen from among those who labor more worthily in the United States of America, he would thereby be constituted the Vicar Apostolic of the above mentioned regions. Most certainly I have never dreamed (as is gratuitously insinuated in a letter which I recently received from the Sacred Congregation) to have or wish to exercise the power of establishing a Vicariate Apostolic. I suggested this means only because it was the very one previously used by the Sacred Congregation with regard to Louisiana when the see of New Orleans was vacant. For it sent such an instrument to my predecessor, Bishop Carroll, who presented it to Bishop DuBourg and in this way he was appointed the Vicar Apostolic of Louisiana.[11] Be that as it may, an event of greatest importance, of which I wrote to the Sacred Congregation, has taken place and it demands that the episcopal see of Charleston be erected without delay. For very recently the American government began to sell at public auction the immense territory which is now called Mississippi. Besides, since the land is exceptionally fertile and most productive, innumerable Americans and Europeans, who come hither daily, are buying these lands and are going thither to cultivate them. Among them there is quite a number of Catholics. Hence the good of religion demands that there be appointed as soon as possible for these southern provinces a bishop, who can sow, foster and cultivate the seed of the Catholic faith in this territory, before the Protestant ministers can disseminate their errors there. Therefore I most humbly and eagerly beseech the Sacred Congregation to obtain from the Holy Father the erection of the episcopal see of Charleston, in South Carolina, and that as soon as possible. I regret

[11] Louis W. V. Dubourg had been appointed apostolic administrator of the Diocese of Louisiana and the Two Floridas in 1812 by Carroll.

that I know of no priest in the United States of America whom I can spontaneously recommend to occupy that see. But it seems certain to me that an English priest would be better suited for fulfilling this important office; nor is there a lack of priests in Great Britain who are outstanding for their piety, zeal, and learning. One of them would be far more acceptable to the people than a Frenchman or an Irishman or one of another nationality. Yet it would be desirable that he know how to speak French, for many inhabitants of the Mississippi territory speak French. He would prove far more useful if he were about forty years of age, since an old man cannot sustain the labors of the missions.

9. Although the most pious Mr. Clorivière[12] would be exceedingly useful to those in Charleston who are sincerely attached to the Catholic religion, and though he has gained for himself the love and veneration of all of these, yet he has been deprived of real power by the numerous calumnies and persecutions arising from the impiety of Mr. Gallaher [*sic*] and some of the Irish seduced by Mr. Gallaher, so that I finally recalled him from that city. Then I sent two outstanding priests of the Society of Jesus, one an American, the other an Irishman. I obtained them from the superior Provincial only after many negotiations. It is impossible for me to say whether these new pastors can bring back peace and some sense of religion to those wicked men. It is true that they retain the name of Catholics but they are most certainly exceedingly dangerous enemies of our holy religion. They possess the same customs, principles, and turbulent passions which imbued those impious men who tried to overthrow the altars of Christ in the abominable French Revolution (*Jacobins*). Even though they send messengers to Rome, they despise the authority of the Sacred Congregation and even of the Supreme Pontiff just as much as mine. To make this clear to the Most Eminent Fathers of the Sacred Congregation I am sending to them a little book, which these men very recently published. It is hard to say whether the impudence of the calumnies referred to are greater than the brazenness of their impiety. Nor can I here pass over the fact that these enemies of the church of Christ, led on by a fanatical spirit, have sent messengers into all the provinces of the American Union to induce all the Irish, whom they know to be given over to impiety and vice, to enter with them into a society, whose purpose is to compell the Holy

[12] Joseph Pierre Picot de Limoëlan de Clorivière (1768–1826), a French-born priest, had been sent to Charleston in 1812 by Carroll to try to heal the schism in St. Mary's Church.

See to enter into an agreement with them, in which they will be granted the right of choosing their bishops and pastors by popular vote. Perhaps it may seem strange to the Sacred Congregation that I have written to them so often about these dangers. But here we are dealing with a matter of the utmost importance. For if these impious men should again deceive the Sacred Congregation whether by threats or by means of false promises, or if it were to give them the least bit of protection, it would do more harm to religion in these regions than the labor of a thousand missionaries could accomplish for it. The vast multitude of faithful American Catholics is horrified at this impious faction, and is surprised that its messengers going to Rome from our shores have any hope of again deceiving the Sacred Congregation of the Propagation of the Faith.

With a few words I will now conclude this very long letter.

During four months I have visited all the missions of Maryland and the principal ones of Virginia, and I administered the sacrament of Confirmation in all the congregations, also taking care of other episcopal duties. It gave me great joy to see our holy religion flourishing everywhere as well as being propagated in a wonderful manner. Since the time of my consecration I have conferred on many the sacrament of Orders, namely:

first tonsure, to eight young men
minor orders 2
subdiaconate 6
diaconate 4
priesthood 4

Just a few days ago I received all the faculties which the Holy Father has kindly granted to me and which the Sacred Congregation has deigned to transmit to me; except, however, the faculty for a few cases of validating the marriage *in radice,* when the consent of both parties could not be renewed without most grave consequences. With regard to the admonition which is found at the bottom of the Baltimore calendar, it was inserted at the order of the most illustrious Bishop of St. Louis. I cannot say upon what authority he based his concession of a dispensation from the laws of fast and abstinence in his diocese at certain times of the year. However, I suspect that those derogations from the law were introduced in the Louisiana diocese because the province has been subject to Spanish rule. The entire matter will be explained better to the Sacred Congregation by the most illustrious Bishop DuBourg himself to whom I wrote very recently.

The Diocese of Philadelphia remains in the same state of widowhood. Last year it was announced that the bulls would be sent without delay, but they were never transmitted here.

This is the account of the status of the Catholic religion in the diocese of Baltimore, which, although very imperfect, I have undertaken to submit to the judgment of the Sacred Congregation. I hope that at some time I may be able to give testimony of my greatest veneration, filial love, and obedience to Their Eminences, for these are the sentiments with which I am imbued towards them all. I again most humbly commend to their kindness and good will my difficulties in the dangers which beset me. In the meanwhile prayers and sacrifices shall not be lacking, that the Pastor of Pastors, Our Lord Jesus Christ, keep you safe for many years to come.

I am, Most Eminent Cardinal,

Your most humble and devoted servant,
✠ Ambrose, Archbishop of Baltimore

68. The Abuse of Lay Trusteeism at Norfolk, Virginia, June–September, 1819

ONE of the most notorious cases of the abuse of lay trusteeism in the early nineteenth century occurred in Norfolk, Virginia, where a group of laymen gained financial control of the church in 1808. For over a decade they dominated the congregation against the pastors appointed by the Archbishop of Baltimore to the point of actual schism and an attempt to set up an independent national church, free from the "French" influence of Baltimore. Not only did the Norfolk trustees repudiate the rightful jurisdiction of the ordinary, but they appealed over his head to Pope Pius VII, the Congregation of Propaganda, the state officials of Virginia, and even to President Jefferson and the Congress. On June 14, 1819, the trustees sent a letter (given first below) to Archbishop Maréchal which affords a sample of the sort of thing with which bishops had to contend during this period. On September 28 of the same year Maréchal signed a pastoral letter to the Norfolk congregation which ran to sixty-three printed pages in which he outlined in detail the history and teaching of the Church on the question of ecclesiastical jurisdiction, and he struck especially at the trustee's pretension to the *jus patronatus* or the right of patronage. Maréchal's pastoral (in the second place below) was termed by Guilday "the historical turning-point in the schismatic movement in America of these years" (p. 123). Sources: Peter Guilday, *The Catholic Church in Virginia, 1815–1822* (New York: United States Catholic Historical Society, 1924), pp. 108–110; *Pastoral Letter of the Archbishop of Baltimore to the Roman Catholicks of Norfolk, Virginia* (Baltimore: J. Robinson, 1819), pp. 1–3, 5, 28–29, 34–38, 40–42, 44.

At a joint meeting of the Trustees of the Roman Catholic Congregation of Norfolk and Portsmouth, convened on the 14th day of June, 1819, to take into consideration a letter directed by the Rev. Archbishop of the Catholic Church of Baltimore, to the Norfolk Pastor, the Reverend Dr. Thomas Carbry,[1] dated on the 8th instant, by which the Reverend Archbishop summons the Right Reverend Pastor to appear before or to send to him the authentic Title, in virtue of which the Right Reverend Dr. Carbry is exercising the functions of Pastor in Norfolk and Portsmouth which said Reverend Archbishop calls his Diocese.

After mature consideration of the contents of the letter aforesaid, the Trustees of the Norfolk and Portsmouth congregations immediately resolved:

First that the Priest James Lucas[2] and the Reverend Archbishop Maréchal, after the resolutions passed by the Trustees of the Roman Catholic Congregation aforesaid on the 4th of Jan., 1817, and 16th of March of last year; being neither their Prelate and Pastor which resolutions were rendered public through the press; and distributed amongst the members of both Congregations, a protest shall be legally intimated to the Reverend Archbishop of the Catholic Church of Baltimore, that himself not being a lawful Prelate of this state, and still less of these congregations he has no right at all to interfere with these congregations or any of their religious matters, whatever. And likewise, with the Right Reverend Pastor thereof duly elected by the Congregation, approved of by His Holiness and communicated to us by his Eminence Cardinal Litta.[3]

Resolved that besides the right inherent in them as Christians and patrons of their churches acknowledged by the Holy See, the impertinence of the demand of the Right Reverend Archbishop of the Catholic Church of Baltimore, being a most glaring violation of their civil right and religious liberties and in direct opposition to the state

[1] Thomas Carbry, an Irish-born Dominican, went to Norfolk from New York in June, 1819, at the invitation of the trustees and assumed charge of the congregation without any authorization from the Archbishop of Baltimore.

[2] James Lucas, a French-born priest, had been appointed to Norfolk in December, 1815, by Archbishop Leonard Neale.

[3] Lorenzo Cardinal Litta, Prefect of Propaganda, with only a meager knowledge of the facts, had made the mistake of receiving one of the trustees at Rome in the summer of 1817 and of writing a letter to Fernandez on September 20, 1817, which gave them hope of attaining their objective of a separate bishopric in Virginia. When he later realized the true nature of the case Litta assured Maréchal on April 1, 1818, that nothing would be done by the Holy See without "the light of your counsel and after mature consideration" (Guilday, *op. cit.*, p. 79).

laws of Virginia, an extract of the same laws, shall be forwarded to him by which he may see, that he has no authority to meddle with the choice of our Pastors or to interfere with the exercise of his sacred functions, resolved that the Reverend Archbishop of the Catholic Church of Baltimore, be reminded of the proceedings in former times, viz:

At Rome in the African church (St. Cyprian, Lib. 2. Ep. 2)
(St. Cyprian, Lib. 1. Ep. 4)
(Conc. Carth; 4th Can. 1)

At Alex., etc., etc. [*sic*].

Likewise of the proceedings, etc., of the Archbishop of Goa towards the Catholics of Bombatin [*sic*] on the coast of Malabar and its results by Lord Minto's decision, the whole published by the House of Commons of July 13th, 1814, as well as of the sentiments of the present Pope, Pius VII, in his Bull to the Archbishop and Bishops of Ireland of the first of February, 1816, acknowledging the right of the people in the election of their Prelates, alledging [*sic*] the authority of his predecessor St. Leo the Great, viz., that no more be ordained Bishops without the consent and postulation of the flock lest an unwelcome intruder incur its contempt and hatred,[4] as it has been unfortunately the case with the Reverend Amb. Maréchall [*sic*] in this and other cities of the different states of the union.

Resolved that should said Reverend Archbishop of the Catholic Church of Baltimore, proceed (which God forbid) to any public act or calumnious deed against either the Reverend Dr. Thomas Carbry or any of the members of the congregation, all his illegal, absurd and impious proceedings, as well as the causes leading to them shall be rendered public through the press and himself held responsible to the laws of the state of Virginia.

Resolved that a copy of these resolutions signed by the President and Secretary of this board, be forwarded to the Reverend Archbishop of the Catholic Church of Baltimore.

---

[4] In neither Goa nor Ireland had there been a real parallel with the Norfolk situation. The British had declined to recognize the ancient Portuguese right of patronage over Catholic churches in India, and in 1720 the Portuguese clergy had been expelled from the Malabar coast as anti-British. The Portuguese, in turn, refused to relinquish their claim and thus there ensued a long period of strife involving a defiance of the British by the Archbishop of Goa and a double jurisdiction that led to endless confusion. Pius VII's letter of February, 1816, to the hierarchy of Ireland had been concerned with the proposed veto of the British government over the selection of Irish bishops and again had no true relevance in the Norfolk case.

Norfolk, June 14, 1819 and 43d year of the independence of the United States.

Thomas Reilly, President
John F. Oliveira Fernandez,
acting as secretary of the Board of the Roman Catholic Church and Congregation of Norfolk.

Beloved Brethren,

After having enjoyed the consolation of spending several days with you last year, we thought it our duty, as your first Pastor, before we left your city, to address a few words to you from the Altar, on the danger to which some of you might eventually be exposed, of being seduced from the pale of the Holy Church, in which, through the infinite mercy of God, you have been baptized and educated.

It is true, the few individuals who have brought so many calamities on your Congregation, could not hope, by their affected zeal for the cause of religion, to make any considerable impression on the minds of the great majority of you, and much less to induce you to join them in the execution of their desperate scheme. . . . We still recollect, Beloved Brethren, with feelings of admiration and gratitude, the virtuous grief you manifested, when you were informed, that relying on the impossibility of your ever recovering by legal process, the sacred property they have wrested from your hands, they rejected with stern pride, every offer of peace which was tendered to them; and particularly your consternation and tears, at hearing the impious language they employed against the Episcopal Dignity, which their religion commands them to respect, and which the laws of common decency protect from insult in every country of the civilized world. Our Protestant Brethren themselves, whom we had the pleasure of visiting in Norfolk, prompted by the spirit of benevolence and the delicacy of manners which distinguish them, were justly shocked at such excesses.

But although these pretended Catholicks, by their scandalous conduct and virulent language, must naturally have deterred you from adopting their principles and joining their party, yet we could not help apprehending, lest, by the concurrence of many unfortunate causes, some of you might be insensibly drawn over to the schismatical plan they were then meditating, and which they have since put into execution. . . . But in order to guard you, my Beloved Brethren, against their seducing language, it will be sufficient for us to recall to your minds, some of the fundamental principles of your Religion; and with these before you, to fix your attention to undeniable facts which invincibly prove the absolute vanity of their reasonings and prentensions. [Then follows an explanation of Christ's authority to His apostles based on the New Testament, the teaching of the Council of Trent, the distinction between the power of the citizens in a republican government to elect their magistrates and the lack of such power in the Church, the canon law on the right of patronage in the Middle Ages, etc.]

From this slight sketch of Canon law, you readily discover, Dealy [*sic*] Beloved Brethren, how vainly those characters, who have involved your Congregation in confusion and misery, pretend to the right of patronage, and flatter you with it. This right does not exist, and probably never will exist in the United States of America. Because it is contrary to the spirit at least of the constitution and of the laws of the land. For the government of the United States stretches indeed the shield of its protection, over every denomination of christians; but without giving the least preference to any: and surely it would be ridiculous to suppose, that following the example of Catholick powers on the other side of the Atlantic, the United States will ever shew a partiality to us, by any considerable donation to our Church. And as this alone is the groundwork of all the *concordates* between Catholick Powers and the Holy See, and of the consequent right of patronage in the nominations of Bishops, it is manifest that such a Politico-religious treaty can never take place in this country. We are grateful for the protection, which we enjoy under the equal laws of the U. States, in common with the rest of our fellow christians; but we neither wish nor expect any particular favours. . . .

Some sectarians, Dear Brethren, consider their ministers as clerical characters, not by virtue of any spiritual mission derived from the Redeemer of mankind through his Church; but in virtue only of the temporary civil contract entered upon, between them and their respective congregations. Consistently with this principle, it is evident that those who appointed them Pastors, justly dismiss them, whenever their services cease to be acceptable. But the case is very different with the clergy of the Catholick church. When a Bishop appoints a Priest Pastor of a congregation, he presents himself to all its members, under a point of view highly respectable. By the act of his institution, the faithful who are committed to his charge, become immediately and in reality his flock; and he is invested with spiritual powers in their regard, which all the world can neither give nor take away. It becomes his duty to govern, and sanctify by his instructions and example, the faithful entrusted to his pastoral solicitude . . . . Enlightened and virtuous

Catholicks do not consider this Clergyman as a hireling, whom they may retain or expel at pleasure, but as an ambassador from Heaven, a minister of the altar, and an Apostle. If the Bishop be bound to impress deeply on his mind, the great obligations and responsibility, which are laid upon him, and the sublime and awful functions he has to perform, surely he is obliged likewise to admonish the Faithful, to respect, love, and obey him. And as he is prevented by his orders from any lucrative secular employment, and bound to devote himself exclusively to God, and to the good of souls, so is it the imperative duty of his flock to provide for his temporal necessities. Is this Apostolic language, Dearly Beloved, a transgression of the laws of Virginia?

In 1786, the General Assembly of that state, in order to establish religious freedom on a broad and permament basis, enacted, that *no man shall be compelled to frequent or support any religious worship, place, or ministry, whatsoever; nor shall be enforced, restrained, molested, or burthened in his body or goods, nor shall he suffer on account of his religious opinions or belief*. Such is one of the fundamental laws of Virginia. Has any Catholick clergyman ever transgressed it? Who is the man, who can say, that his Pastor has compelled him, or attempted to compel him by legal means, to frequent his Church, or support him: Not one. It is true, there is no obligation whatever, imposed upon the citizens, to support any ministers of religion, not even their own Pastors. But because there is no legal obligation of doing it, is there not a moral and religious one? Has a Christian and a Catholick no other duties to fulfil, besides those composed by the law of the land? And is it in a Pastor, a transgression of this law, to exhort his people to a performance of them? If this were a violation of the laws of Virginia, then indeed not only Catholick, but all Protestant ministers are guilty of it; for the habitual and principal subjects of their instructions and labours are to inculcate on the minds of the christian people, the moral and religious duties, proclaimed in the Gospel, on which the civil law is perfectly silent.

After having proceeded so far, and proved that neither the Catholick congregations nor their representatives, have power to elect, institute or dismiss their Pastors, it may naturally be asked whether the right, at least of election, would not prove advantageous to religion in our days?

Relying on the authority of the Catholick Church, Dear Brethren, we may without any fear of error, answer negatively to this question. For the Christians of the present age, are certainly no better than their ancestors who lived a thousand years ago; and if the Church thought it necessary, on account of the perpetual confusion and scandals which took place at these elections, to withdraw the privilege she had granted to the Faithful: can we imagine that the exercise of it would not now be attended with the same bad consequences? However let us suppose this privilege were conceded to the present generation. Who would be the electors? Would every man, who bears the name of Catholick be admitted to give in his vote, whatever may be his impiety and the immorality of his life? Or would the privilege be restrained to those only whose conduct is pious and edifying? Shall the drunkard, the impure, the professed libertine, and he who hardly knows the elements of his religion, and lives in an open transgression of her laws, be allowed to choose the ministers of Jesus Christ, together with the sober, the chaste, the enlightened and regular Catholick who punctually fulfills all the commandments of God and the Church? It is evident that in a matter of a nature so sacred, a discrimination ought to be made; and would not this first and necessary step be obnoxious to insuperable difficulties? Upon whom would the choice most probably fall? Would it fall on the modest and pious clergyman, who spends his days in instructing the poor and the ignorant; in carrying the last consolations of religion to dying christians; in reconciling repenting sinners to the offended Majesty of God in the tribunal of Penance, — who every day in his private oratory and at the altar, raises his pure hands to God, to draw down the blessing of Heaven on his flock — who mounts the pulpit, not to please his auditory and glean from the world the pitiful reward of praise; but to instruct, exhort and move — who consecrates his intervals of leisure, not to idle visits and frivolous conversation; but to meditation and studies suitable to his state of life? The merits of such a clergyman being generally unknown or not sufficiently felt, he would very likely not be elected: and yet *him has the Lord chosen*. The gay and sprightly companion — he who at home spends his time in idleness or frivolous occupations — who, in the societies of worldlings which he habitually frequents, can command their attention by some light accomplishment — who can preach a fashionable discourse, or pronounce a vapid declamation which he probably had not even the slender merit of composing, this man will unite the votes of the multitude. In vain might a few pious and sensible Catholicks raise their voices against his election; they would be drowned in the general clamour. Under such a pastor what would become of the unfortunate congregation? Instead of exhibiting the endearing spectacle of sincere religion and piety, it would soon present disgusting scenes, of irreligion and immorality. . . .

From the principles which we have laid down, Dearly Beloved Brethren, it is evident, that Rev. Thomas Carbry has no jurisdiction whatever among you, in virtue of the choice which the above mentioned writer,[1] and some other laymen have made of him for their Pastor. To cover this defect, and to compose the fear of conscientious Catholicks, it has been industriously circulated, that he has received a *secret* appointment from the Holy See, to the place which he now holds. And as this report is calculated to lead some of you astray, it is important that we should shew you, that it is absolutely unfounded and false. . . .

69. The Inauguration of the *United States Catholic Miscellany* of Charleston, June 5, 1822

THE birth of American Catholic journalism may be dated from the founding of the *United States Catholic Miscellany* by John England (1786–1842), first Bishop of Charleston. Before that there had been the brief issue of the *Michigan Essay or Impartial Observer* in August, 1809, by Gabriel Richard, S.S., in Detroit and a number of Irish papers which were edited by Catholics and contained a considerable amount of Catholic news. But the *Miscellany* was the first American Catholic newspaper properly so called. England had gained valuable experience in journalism during his time on the staff of the Cork *Mercantile Chronicle,* 1812–1817, and as a result his paper not only served admirably in answering the attacks of the nativists, but through its discussions of current problems affecting the Church in all aspects of its life the *Miscellany* was one of the leading agencies of the 1820's and 1830's in making for an informed Catholic opinion. The support England received for his paper was always meager and twice, throughout the year 1823 and again from January-July, 1826, he was compelled to suspend it. But after July, 1826, the *Miscellany* carried on unbrokenly until the disastrous Charleston fire of December, 1861, which destroyed the cathedral, bishop's house, diocesan library, and the office of the paper, put an end to it forever. Source: *United States Catholic Miscellany,* June 5, 1822.

PROSPECTUS

The object of this publication is to supply an apparent want in the United States of North America.

In these states perfect freedom of conscience exists; hence, men of various religions have fled hither as to an asylum from the per-

[1] Maréchal was referring to Dr. John F. Oliveiria Fernandez, secretary of the Board of Trustees of the Norfolk congregation, who had written several pamphlets against the archbishop's authority.

secutions of the dominant sects in other countries. Almost every division of Christians here has its peculiar publication, for the expositions of its doctrines, the communication of facts, and if necessary, the vindication of its tenets. The Roman Catholics of these states form a considerable portion of the citizens; it is natural they should be desirous of having a similar publication for like purposes.

To supply this want, the Miscellany is intended. By its means the thousands of Roman Catholics spread through these states, from Maine to Florida, and from Arkansas to the Atlantic, may hold constant communication; by its means they may also learn the state of their brethren in communion with them in the other quarters of the globe: by its means those persons who have been misled into erroneous opinions of the principles of their neighbors, will be enabled to judge correctly of their tenets, and to form rational opinions of their practices.

The principles of the publication will be candour, moderation, fidelity, charity, and diligence. Not that its conductors presume to attain the perfection of all or any of those qualities; but they will constantly keep them in view.

The topics which it will embrace are,

I. The simple explanation and temperate maintenance of the doctrines of the Roman Catholic Church; in exhibiting which, its conductors are led to hope, that many sensible persons will be astonished at finding they have imputed to Catholics doctrines which the Catholic Church has formally condemned, and imagined they were contradicting Catholics, when they held Catholic doctrine themselves.

II. The examination of history for the purpose of investigating the truth of many assertions which have been, perhaps, too lightly hazarded, and which have obtained too ready and general credence; and which have excited unfounded prejudices in the minds of many well-disposed individuals.

III. The correct statement of occurrences regarding the Catholic religion: for the purpose of better discharging which duty, communications and periodical publications from Rome, Paris, London, Dublin, Canada, South-America, the various parts of the United States, and other portions of the world will be obtained, and are solicited.

IV. Memoirs and anecdotes of the several eminent persons who have distinguished themselves in the Church, or against it, in ancient or modern times.

V. A summary of political events and domestic occurrences.

VI. Occasional reviews of religious publications.

Advertisements wll be received at the usual rates.

THE MISCELLANY will be published in the city of Charleston, S. C. weekly, on a fine sheet of paper, quarto size; containing eight pages of three columns each, so that the numbers may be bound at the end of each year.

All communications to be *post paid* and directed *"To the Editor of The Catholic Miscellany, Charleston, S. C."*

Any person wishing to receive the Paper will please to enclose his subscription, and send it *post paid,* directed as above; and give also the name of the Post Office to which his Paper may be sent.

70. Bishop England's Account of His Address Before Congress, January 29, 1826

IN THE generation after Archbishop Carroll's death the most striking public figure in the American hierarchy was John England (1786–1842), first Bishop of Charleston. This Irish-born prelate engaged actively in newspaper controversies, debates, and public addresses, but his most famous address was the speech which he delivered before Congress on Sunday, January 8, 1826, in which he discoursed for two hours on the principal doctrines of the Catholic faith. On the previous Christmas day he had preached at St. Patrick's Church, Washington, where he took occasion to answer certain charges against the Church which had been made by John Quincy Adams in 1821 when he was Secretary of State. Within a few days England was a dinner guest at the White House where he and President Adams got on in a friendly fashion and when the bishop made his appearance before Congress, Adams was there to hear him. Three weeks after the speech England wrote his impressions of the affair to William Gaston (1778–1844), the most prominent Catholic layman of North Carolina, who in 1833 was appointed associate justice of the state's supreme court where he served with distinction until his death. Source: *Records of the American Catholic Historical Society of Philadelphia,* XIX (1908), 104–106.

Fayetteville (N.C.), Jan'y 29, 1826.

My Dear Friend:

I posted a letter for you, directed to Newbern, to inform you that I was not at present sufficiently master of my own movements to delay in this State longer than until next Monday morning, when I intend leaving this place for Georgetown & Charleston, — a variety of pressing business calls me to headquarters as soon as possible. I hope to return speedily & to see you in Newbern.

I directed the publisher of the sketch of what I preached at the

Capitol to send to you & to my friend Judge Taylor[1] copies from me. You will find only what you have often heard from myself, but I thought you would like to see in print what would bear better to be heard than to be read. Perhaps I might have been the humble instrument of removing some prejudices. If so, I am more than repaid.

Without seeking for the occasion, or feeling myself upon the topics until I had gone too far to recede, & then, & only then, my eyes rested upon Mr. Adams, I on Christmas day met foot to foot the 4th of July oration in which he so unkindly assailed us four years since. I then as cooly & as firmly as I could did my utmost, & I am told by many, with sufficient success. The next Wednesday I was at his levee, where I was received in a very flattering manner, & upon my arrival at home found a card for dinner on the succeeding Saturday. We had much conversation upon several topics, & a little about yourself, in which he appeared to think it news that you were a Popish churchwarden.

On the day I filled the Speaker's chair I was indeed a show, & all Washington must have thought so, for the throng was so great that the President found it very difficult to get in, & when in, much more so to get a seat. Upon my arrival, nearly half an hour after, I found vast numbers returning without a hope of getting upstairs, so as even to see in, — & for once I must own I felt ashamed at hearing my own name proclaimed by my friends Haynes[2] & Hamilton[3] of S.C. who formed my bodyguard, whilst in all the pomp of Prelacy I struggled through and heard the proclamation renewed still to make way for me to enter. If I could blush, I am convinced I then did, because I had some unusual sensation of heart and some unwonted glow *in* my cheek & *in* my forehead. When I was done I certainly felt a very extraordinary gratification at the intense attention with which I was heard, & that every face seemed to say "go on." But I thought two hours enough for them & for me, — I made the sign of the cross, & my gratification was indeed increased by the vast & respectable portion of the assembly that exhibited its faith. You will, perhaps, smile at my saying that even elevated as I was, I could not forget that I once was an

[1] John L. Taylor (1769–1829), Chief Justice of the Supreme Court of North Carolina, was married to Gaston's sister, Jane.

[2] Charles Eaton Haynes (1784–1841) was a representative in Congress from Georgia, 1825–1831; 1835–1839.

[3] James Hamilton (1786–1857) was a representative in Congress from South Carolina and later governor of the state.

insignificant being, & I vouchsafed to come down from my seat to recognize the President of the U.S. & converse a little with him.

Do not think me vain or childish in this; I know you would wish to learn, even if you did not care for the individual, what was the first appearance of a Catholic clergyman before the legislature of the union, & I would not write thus to another.

I love your countrymen more as I know them better. They are a well-disposed, religiously-inclined people; there is but one true Church, & that is the Roman Catholic; but how can they believe without evidence? — they have never received it. They must be instructed, not abused. They must be expostulated with, not quarrelled with. They are not obstinate heretics — they are an enquiring, thinking, reasoning, well-disposed, I will add, a pious people, — & God will bless them & bring them to truth. I every day see abundant evidence to support me in this position, & to some of your apparently accidental remarks I owe much of the reflection which has led me to know how to appreciate their character & to aid in removing their prejudices. I hope long to profit by many more of them & for many years of more frequent intercourse.

My sister joins with me in affectionate respects to your sister, to the Judge & all the family.

Yours sincerely,

✠ John, Bishop of Charleston.

71. The Cholera Epidemic in the Diocese of Mobile, November 10, 1832

ONE of the greatest scourges in the history of American medicine struck the United States in 1832 in the form of Asiatic cholera. The losses suffered by the Catholic Church were exceedingly heavy, and among the many deaths of priests, religious, and laity which occurred during those terrible months were two notable churchmen of the Middle West who died within a few days of each other, Gabriel Richard, the heroic Sulpician missionary of the Detroit area, who succumbed on September 13, and Edward D. Fenwick, O.P. (1768–1832), first Bishop of Cincinnati, who died on September 26 at Wooster, Ohio, in the course of a diocesan visitation. All parts of the country felt the consequences of the epidemic, and in the South the effects were especially grievous. At the time the French-born priest, Mathias Loras (1792–1858), was vicar-general of the Diocese of Mobile, and in a letter to his mother in France he described the conditions in southern Alabama. Source: *Acta et Dicta,* V (July, 1917), 113–114.

College of Spring Hill, November 10, 1832.

My dear Mother:

Your dear letter, the second which you kindly sent me, came to me happily on October 28th; that of Madame Tallon of July 19th arrived on September 18th; that of Emile of May 31st, which enclosed another from Marie Richard and a "P.S." from dear Fleury, just about two months later, are also in my hands. All these writers may be sure that they have given me great pleasure and if I do not answer directly this time it is according to the words of Jesus Christ, "Do you not know that I must concern myself directly with the glory of my Father?" Will you therefore act as intermediary between me and them?

You have written about the cholera in Paris and in the Provinces. It is a small matter, compared to the terrible ravages which this disease is working in New Orleans. Here it is combined with yellow fever, small-pox and so forth. The disease broke out in New Orleans on October 24th and has brought to the grave daily nearly 200 persons. The terror is at its height; the dead are buried clothed as they are and pell-mell; it is hard to find negroes who are willing to do this work. The people of Mobile are in a state of consternation.

This plague will certainly visit us also. Our pupils are likewise filled with fear. Some of them have left the college. We who are here place ourselves in the kind hands of Divine Providence. As for me, my dear mother, I am perfectly calm; my greatest trouble is to see that this great warning which Heaven sends to us all does not make more impression upon sinners and heretics. This shows that faith is dead in their hearts, if indeed it was ever there. Nevertheless we redouble our efforts and our prayers that this fatal veil of blindness may at last be lifted. I should be only too happy to die in aiding these unfortunate people. I shall write to M. Miolland[1] after some time; he will be able to tell you what the state of affairs is here. . . .

We are seriously considering the foundation here of a community of Sisters of the Visitation for the education of girls.[2] This is one of the things which I beg to see before I die. The first is the college,

---

[1] Jean Marie Miolland was superior of the diocesan missionary band of Lyons when Loras joined it in 1827; he was Bishop of Amiens, 1838–1849, and Archbishop of Toulouse until his death in 1859.

[2] A small group of nuns from the Visitation Convent at Georgetown, D. C., arrived in Mobile in late December, 1832, to open Georgetown's first daughter house.

which exists and is flourishing;[3] the second is the establishment of several parishes in this diocese; the fourth will be to see you once more, my good, dear mother; then I shall say my "Nunc dimittis."

Excuse my brevity; you yourself suggested to me that I might be brief; and believe that nothing will ever be able to change the sentiments of most filial attachment of

Your most devoted son,
M. Loras.

P.S. We are perfectly well. Give my sincerest regards, I pray you, to all my dear brothers and sisters and my respects to my dear cousin, etc.

[3] Loras had been the founder and first president of Spring Hill College near Mobile which had its formal opening in July, 1830, with fifty students and a faculty of six professors.

72. De Tocqueville on American Catholics in Relation to Democracy, 1835

A RECENT writer has declared Alexis de Tocqueville (1805–1859) to have been "the best friend democracy ever has had, and democracy's most candid and judicious critic" (Russell Kirk, *The Conservative Mind* [Chicago, 1953], p. 179). In May, 1831, De Tocqueville arrived in the United States for a tour of investigation of the prison system. He remained in the country until February, 1832, and when the first volume of his celebrated work, *De la démocratie en Amérique,* appeared in 1835 it became obvious at once what a thorough study he had made of the American political system as well as of social institutions and customs. His observations concerning the religious beliefs of Catholics and their relation to democracy as a form of government were far different from those of most contemporary American Protestants, but the century that has passed since their publication has produced nothing that would destroy their general validity. Source: Alexis de Tocqueville, *Democracy in America,* edited by Phillips Bradley (New York: Alfred A. Knopf, Inc., 1945), I, 300–302; II, 26–30; paper-back edition by Vintage Books, Inc.

About fifty years ago Ireland began to pour a Catholic population into the United States; and on their part, the Catholics of America made proselytes, so that, at the present moment more than a million Christians professing the truths of the Church of Rome are to found in the Union.[1] These Catholics are faithful to the observances of their religion; they are fervent and zealous in the belief of their doctrines. Yet they constitute the most republican and the most democratic class

[1] De Tocqueville was in error on the number of Catholics in the United States in 1831; the best estimate for the year 1830 was 318,000.

in the United States. This fact may surprise the observer at first, but the cause of it may easily be discovered upon reflection.

I think that the Catholic religion has erroneously been regarded as the natural enemy of democracy. Among the various sects of Christians, Catholicism seems to me, on the contrary, to be one of the most favorable to equality of condition among men. In the Catholic Church the religious community is composed of only two elements; the priest and the people. The priest alone rises above the rank of his flock, and all below him are equal.

On doctrinal points the Catholic faith places all human capacities upon the same level; it subjects the wise and ignorant, the man of genius and the vulgar crowd, to the details of the same creed; it imposes the same observances upon the rich and the needy, it inflicts the same austerities upon the strong and the weak; it listens to no compromise with mortal man, but, reducing all the human race to the same standard, it confounds all the distinctions of society at the foot of the same altar, even as they are confounded in the sight of God. If Catholicism predisposes the faithful to obedience, it certainly does not prepare them for inequality; but the contrary may be said of Protestantism, which generally tends to make men independent more than to render them equal. Catholicism is like an absolute monarchy; if the sovereign be removed, all the other classes of society are more equal than in republics.

It has not infrequently occurred that the Catholic priest has left the service of the altar to mix with the governing powers of society and to take his place among the civil ranks of men. This religious influence has sometimes been used to secure the duration of that political state of things to which he belonged. Thus we have seen Catholics taking the side of aristocracy from a religious motive. But no sooner is the priesthood entirely separated from the government, as is the case in the United States, than it is found that no class of men is more naturally disposed than the Catholics to transfer the doctrine of the equality of condition into the political world.

If, then, the Catholic citizens of the United States are not forcibly led by the nature of their tenets to adopt democratic and republican principles, at least they are not necessarily opposed to them; and their social position, as well as their limited number, obliges them to adopt these opinions. Most of the Catholics are poor, and they have no chance of taking a part in the government unless it is open to all the citizens. They constitute a minority, and all rights must be respected in order to ensure to them the free exercise of their own privileges. These two causes induce them, even unconsciously, to adopt political doctrines which they would perhaps support with less zeal if they were rich and preponderant.

The Catholic clergy of the United States have never attempted to oppose this political tendency; but they seek rather to justify it. The Catholic priests in America have divided the intellectual world into two parts: in the one they place the doctrines of revealed religion, which they assent to without discussion; in the other they leave those political truths which they believe the Deity has left open to free inquiry. Thus the Catholics of the United States are at the same time the most submissive believers and the most independent citizens. . . .

I showed in the first Part of this work how the American clergy stand aloof from secular affairs. This is the most obvious but not the only example of their self-restraint. In America religion is a distinct sphere, in which the priest is sovereign, but out of which he takes care never to go. Within its limits he is master of the mind; beyond them he leaves men to themselves and surrenders them to the independence and instability that belong to their nature and their age. I have seen no country in which Christianity is clothed with fewer forms, figures, and observances than in the United States, or where it presents more distinct, simple, and general notions to the mind. Although the Christians of America are divided into a multitude of sects, they all look upon their religion in the same light. This applies to Roman Catholicism as well as to other forms of belief. There are no Roman Catholic priests who show less taste for the minute individual observances, for extraordinary or peculiar means of salvation, or who cling more to the spirit and less to the letter of the law than the Roman Catholic priests of the United States. Nowhere is that doctrine of the church which prohibits the worship reserved to God alone from being offered to the saints more clearly inculcated or more generally followed. Yet the Roman Catholics of America are very submissive and very sincere. . . .

America is the most democratic country in the world, and it is at the same time (according to reports worthy of belief) the country in which the Roman Catholic religion makes most progress. At first sight this is surprising.

Two things must here be accurately distinguished: equality makes men want to form their own opinions; but, on the other hand, it imbues them with the taste and the idea of unity, simplicity, and impartiality in the power that governs society. Men living in democratic times are therefore very prone to shake off all religious authority; but if they consent to subject themselves to any authority of this kind, they choose at least that it should be single and uniform. Religious powers not radiating from a common center are naturally repugnant to their minds; and they almost as readily conceive that there should be no religion as that there should be several.

At the present time, more than in any preceding age, Roman Catholics are seen to lapse into infidelity, and Protestants to be converted to Roman Catholicism. If you consider Catholicism within its own organization, it seems to be losing; if you consider it from outside, it seems to be gaining. Nor is this difficult to explain. The men of our days are naturally little disposed to believe; but as soon as they have any religion, they immediately find in themselves a latent instinct that urges them unconsciously towards Catholicism. Many of the doctrines and practices of the Roman Catholic Church astonish them, but they feel a secret admiration for its discipline, and its great unity attracts them. If Catholicism could at length withdraw itself from the political animosities to which it has given rise, I have hardly any doubt but that the same spirit of the age which appears to be so opposed to it would become so favorable as to admit of its great and sudden advancement.

One of the most ordinary weaknesses of the human intellect is to seek to reconcile contrary principles and to purchase peace at the expense of logic. Thus there have ever been and will ever be men who, after having submitted some portion of their religious belief to the principle of authority, will seek to exempt several other parts of their faith from it and to keep their minds floating at random between liberty and obedience. But I am inclined to believe that the number of these thinkers will be less in democratic than in other ages, and that our posterity will tend more and more to a division into only two parts, some relinquishing Christianity entirely and others returning to the Church of Rome.

73. Mathew Carey Explains How He Came to Write the *Olive Branch,* March 13, 1835

THE administrations of Jefferson and Madison marked one of the most exciting and vituperative periods in American political history. Americans were not only sharply divided between Jefferson's Republicans and the Federalists of Hamiltonian persuasion, but they likewise took violent sides between Britain and France whose renewal of war in May, 1803, ushered in over a decade of international conflict that had disastrous results for American commerce and finally led to the declaration of war on England in June, 1812. In all of this no citizen took a more lively interest than the Irish-born Mathew Carey (1760–1839) of Philadelphia who had fled Ireland in September, 1784, disguised as a woman to escape arrest for the attacks he had written in his *Volunteer's Journal* of Dublin against the government of William Pitt. Carey was a versatile fellow whose activities included a publishing business that made him the leading publisher of the nation in the first years of the nineteenth century, the founder of the Hibernian Society for relief of Irish immigrants, a director of the United States Bank, and a charter member of the Philadelphia Society for the Promotion of National Industry, for which he wrote a series of addresses that economists recognize as the classic American argument in behalf of the protective system. Moreover, Carey was a devout Catholic and the father of nine children, the oldest of whom, Henry C. Carey (1793–1879), became by the mid-century the acknowledged leader of the only American group that can lay claim to being a distinct school of political economy. The elder Carey went astray for a brief time in the lay-trustee troubles of St. Mary's Church, Philadelphia, but he soon righted his course and became a stanch defender of episcopal authority and a forthright contender for Catholic civil liberties as well. One of his most famous works was the *Olive Branch,* published in 1814, with a view to bringing peace between the embittered Federalists and Republicans. When Andrew Jackson had read the gift copy sent to him by Carey he told the latter that the book, "by unveiling the eyes of many who have been long hoodwinked by the misrepresentations of folly and falsehood, must have a most salutary effect in allaying that factious spirit which threatens so much evil to our happy government" (Jackson to Carey, Nashville, August 28, 1815, "Selections from the Correspondence of Mathew Carey," *Records of the American Catholic Historical Society of Philadelphia,* XI [1900], 347). The editor of the *New England Magazine* induced Carey to write his autobiography which was published in a series of letters in that journal (V–VII [July, 1833–December, 1834]). He explained that his aim in writing was to show an example of how a man who for years had been on the brink of bankruptcy had escaped through unflinching perseverance and industry, and of how such a man is offered an abundance of aid from others when success seems assured, although the same persons had withheld it when it was really needed. To Carey's main objectives in writing, he confessed he should add, "perhaps, a spice of vanity, from which no human being is wholly exempt" (p. 115). In the letter that follows Carey described how he came to write the *Olive Branch* and the success with which it was greeted. Source: *Mathew Carey. Autobiography* (reprint) (Brooklyn: Eugene L. Schwabb, 1942), pp. 118–122.

The publication of the Olive Branch was one of the most important incidents of my life. I proceed to state the circumstances that led to it, and the extraordinary success that attended the work.

The lawless and outrageous depredations on our commerce, by the belligerents, most of which, under pretexts the most fallacious, violated every principle of honor, honesty, justice and international law, had divided the people of the United States into two hostile parties, by which, as is the case in times of faction in all countries, the solid interests of the nation were often in some degree lost sight of.

It was on the one side asserted that Mr. Jefferson, and the administration generally, were in the interests and in the pay of the French Government — and this was as firmly believed by the mass of the party whose leaders had promulgated the idea, as if it had been judicially proved.

On the other side it was confidently asserted, and as implicitly believed, that the opposition was so blindly devoted to the interests of Great Britain, that they were ready to sacrifice those of their own country in her favour.

It is not my intention to enter into any discussion of the causes that led to the formation of those opinions, nor to the pleas on which they were grounded or defended — that would be, *renovare infandum dolorem*. It is sufficient for my purpose simply to state the facts — and that a most formidable and menacing excitement existed among our citizens.

I had watched for years the progress of this excitement in New England with the most intense anxiety. It foreboded, in my estimation, civil war and all its horrors. That we were on the verge of it can scarcely at this moment be doubted by those who have a perfect recollection of the perturbed state of the public mind at that period. I had written to Mr. Madison, between the time of his inauguration and November, 1814, at least a dozen letters, expatiating at length on the deplorable circumstances of the country, and urging him to adopt some measures to allay the popular ferment. Among the means I suggested, one was, to establish a Washington Union Society. A constitution, prepared for the purpose, is to be seen at the commencement of some editions of the Olive Branch. He objected to have any agency in the affair, on the ground that it would be improper for him, the first executive officer in the nation, to interfere in such a scheme. In the force of his reasoning I could never agree.

In the month of September, 1814, in a moment of ardent zeal and enthusiasm, I was seized with a desire of making an effort, by a candid publication of the numerous errors and follies on both sides, (to call them by no stronger names,) to allay the public effervescence and calm the embittered feelings of the parties. The idea was truly Quixotic, which nothing but the excited state of my feelings could have suggested.

I accordingly commenced about the 8th of September, and made some progress. A part of the plan was a proposition, that, for the sake of peace, and to concentrate the energies of the country, some leading federalists should be brought into the administration, or even that a total change should be made. This was in a moment of deep despondency. I thought it better to submit to such a bitter pill, than have the country torn in pieces, as appeared probable, or to lie at the mercy of a foreign enemy. I wrote twelve or fourteen pages of this tenor. To judge of this extraordinary proposition, it is necessary to reflect on the appalling state of affairs at that period, when, at home or abroad, nothing was to be discerned but the most awful prospects. It was after the shameful defeat at Bladensburg, and the Vandalic conflagration at Washington.[1] The stoutest hearts felt qualms, and were lost in suspense as to the fearful result of such an awful state of things. Those were really "times that tried men's souls." I attempt neither to palliate or justify my daring proposition. I simply state facts. But great as was my despondency, I felt dissatisfied with what I had written — tore the pages — and, for some days, relinquished the idea of pursuing the subject.

Meanwhile three events occurred, admirably calculated to raise the spirits of our citizens generally, viz; the victory of Commodore McDonough [*sic*] the defeat of Prevost at Plattsburg,[2] and that of Ross in his attempt on Baltimore.[3] These exhilarating circumstances dispelled the gloom of the public mind; removed the despondence by which I had been borne down; and, on the 18th of September I commenced anew, on a different plan, abandoning the presumptuous and inadmissible idea of suggesting any change in the administration; in a word, on the plan pursued in the Olive Branch as it now stands.

But it does not require much study of human nature to know, that zeal is a quality remarkably subject to ebbs and flows; and that the higher the flow, the lower the ebb. This, at all events, I experienced.

---

[1] The defeat of the Americans at Bladensburg, Maryland, occurred on August 24, 1814, and Washington was occupied by the British immediately thereafter.

[2] Captain Thomas Macdonough's victory on Lake Champlain took place on September 11, 1814, and compelled Sir George Prevost's army to retreat from Plattsburg back to Canada.

[3] The unsuccessful attack on Baltimore led by General Robert Ross took place on September 12–14, 1814.

When the work was about two-thirds printed, my ardor began to ebb, and I was struck with dismay at the presumption of supposing, that a man in private life, wholly without influence, unsupported by party or by family connexions, could calm the raging waves of faction which threatened shipwreck to the vessel of state. At this moment, although the work, as I have said, was two-thirds printed, I felt half resolved to suppress it, and make waste paper of what was done.

This ague fit continued a few days, but was succeeded by a feverish excitement, which continued long enough to enable me to finish the work. It was begun, as I have stated, on the 18th of September; finished at press about the 6th of November; and published on the 8th; that is to say, it occupied the leisure time of six or seven weeks.

This rapid movement will appear marvellous to the reader. But the wonder will be dispelled when I state the facts of the case. The work is printed in 12mo., large type, (except public documents and other quotations) containing only 252 rather small pages, of which about 80 are public documents, which one of my daughters copied for me: so that my share of the work was only 172 pages. Moreover, as for years I had my mind engrossed by the subject, it was almost as familiar to me as the *ut re mi* of the gamut is to a practised musician. In truth, with the advantages I possessed, I might have completed it in one week, had I applied as closely to it as I have done on other occasions. It cost little more time than the mere transcription would have done.

The edition consisted of 500 copies. The reason why I published so small a number were, partly because political books or pamphlets have generally a very limited circulation, rarely ever defraying cost — and partly because, presuming that it must be imperfect, from the rapidity of its execution. I was desirous of having an opportunity of correcting it in a future edition, should one be required.

The edition was sold out in a few weeks. I sent to Washington to ascertain the success of some that had been sent there, and to order those unsold to be returned. It appeared that only *thirty-seven* copies had been sold! There were there, at that time, about 200 legislators — a number of foreign ministers — and probably two or three hundred visiters [*sic*]. That among such a number of persons, so few should have been sold, a book on such absorbing subjects, whatever might be its demerits, displays a degree of apathy not often exceeded. It was not because the work was unknown; as I had sent a few copies by the mail to members, and others, some of whom particularly Elbridge Gerry[4] and the Secretary of the Treasury, Richard Rush,[5] had written me respecting it, in encomiastic terms.

I was preparing for a new edition, when the thrice-welcome news of peace arrived — which, I thought, would render a new edition unnecessary. I was much mistaken. The demand increased daily, and I need not say that I had every motive to induce me to supply it. I used such diligence, that the second edition, of 1000 copies, was published on the 4th of January 1815, in less than two months from the appearance of the first.

This edition was greatly enlarged. . . . The demand increased, instead of diminishing. I went on adding to the quantity of matter, and published another edition of 1000 copies. This edition was in two volumes, containing 516 pages. It was published on the 10th of April 1815, in a little more than two months from the appearance of the second, and about four from that of the first.

Having reason to believe that the book was doing much good, in allaying the spirit of party, the object for which it was written — desirous to extend that beneficent result as far as possible — and being utterly regardless of pecuniary interests, so far as this work was concerned, I offered the privilege of the republication to at least eight or ten printers and booksellers. . . . *I did not require nor receive a cent for copyright.* May I not ask, is not this a case of rare occurrence? The book was at that time in high favor with a large portion of the community — in demand with both sides of the question — and bid fair to be lucrative to every man who republished it. Of course I might with propriety, according to the general practice of writers, have required payment for the privilege of reprinting it. But had I adopted this course it would have limited the circulation of the work, and so far defeated the great object I had in view. . . .

The sixth edition was published September 6, 1815; the seventh, December 20, same year; the eighth in the same month of 1816; the ninth July 9th, 1817, and the tenth, June 1818.

Thus in three years and a half it went through ten editions. The whole number sold was about 10,000 copies, a greater sale probably than any *book* ever had in this country, except some religious ones.

Various attempts were made to depreciate the work. It was asserted

[4] Elbridge Gerry (1744–1814) of Massachusetts was Vice-President of the United States at the time.

[5] Richard Rush (1780–1859) of Pennsylvania was Attorney General, not Secretary of the Treasury, in Madison's cabinet. He was later Secretary of State under Monroe.

by an influential federal printer, in New York, that he had positive proof that I had not written a line of it — that it was the production of an elevated character, who was understood to be Oliver Wolcott[6] — others asserted that there were false titles printed — that I had them prepared to suit my purpose. . . . One person, a New York bookseller, said that he supposed I kept a set of title pages to insert at pleasure; that it reminded him of a soldier who had but two shirts, and numbered them No. 19 and 20.

As this ridiculous assertion was calculated to throw doubt on my character for candor, I deemed it of sufficient importance to submit the ten editions to four respectable citizens, the Rev. James Abercrombie, D.D., Messrs. Thomas Dobson, W. W. Woodward, and A. Small, who, after due examination, testified that there was

> "Such a total difference in the arrangement of the matter, the size of the pages and types, and more particularly in the number of pages contained in them, as *to convince the most superficial observer that they were bona fide different editions.*"

This difference arose from the fact that I had not allowed any edition to go to press after the first, without making additions, alterations and improvements; as I was determined to spare neither pains nor expense to have the work as complete as was compatible with human imperfection.

M. Carey.

Philadelphia, March 13, 1835.

74. William Gaston Pleads for Complete Religious Freedom in North Carolina, June 30, 1835

ONE of the most distinguished Catholic statesmen of the early nineteenth century was William Gaston (1778–1844). He was the first student to enroll in Georgetown College when it opened in September, 1791, and in 1796 he graduated from the College of New Jersey (Princeton) with the highest honors in his class. Gaston was a Federalist in politics and he served in both the state legislature and in Congress for two terms, 1813–1817. When a vacancy occurred on the Supreme Court of North Carolina in 1832 at a time when that bench was in very low repute, Gaston was named, in spite of an article in the state constitution which forbade any person to

[6] Oliver Wolcott, Jr. (1760–1833), of Connecticut had been Secretary of the Treasury in Washington's cabinet and was president of the Bank of America in New York up to April, 1814, when he was dismissed in what he regarded as a political plot. The incident turned Wolcott from a loyal Federalist into a man of "war hawk" mentality.

be appointed to a civil office who denied the truth of the Protestant religion. Eminent lawyers, both within and without the state, including John Marshall (1755–1835), gave it as their judgment that the article in question did not bar Gaston and he was, therefore, elected by the general assembly in 1833. One of his most notable services was performed in the constitutional convention of 1835 where he made an impassioned plea to have the article on religious qualifications for office holding deleted entirely. Gaston failed of his objective but he scored, nonetheless, a real triumph in having the final draft of the controverted article substitute the word "Christian" in place of "Protestant" in the revised constitution of North Carolina. Following are excerpts from the lengthy speech which Gaston made in the convention. Source: *Proceeding and Debates of the Convention of North-Carolina, Called to Amend the Constitution of the State, Which Assembled at Raleigh, June 4, 1835* (Raleigh: Joseph Gales and Son, 1836), pp. 264–265, 283–285, 292.

Mr. Chairman — The peculiar situation in which I am known to stand with respect to the question now under consideration, and the character of the debate which has already taken place upon it, may be thought to render it indelicate in me to interfere at all in the discussion. But no considerations of delicacy ought to deter me from the full and faithful performance of my duties as a Delegate of the People of this Convention. Besides, silence is likely to subject me to much greater misconstruction than the most frank and fearless exposition of my opinions. At all events, the latter is the course to which I am prompted by inclination as well as by a sense of propriety, and therefore is it, that I must ask the patient and kind attention of this Committee. . . . I am not, indeed, aware that any one decent citizen of the State has called in question the purity of my motives or questioned the propriety of my conduct, or has expressed dissatisfaction at my course. But this is an age of detraction. Calumnies are the ordinary weapons of warfare with religious as well as political factions; and if I have not yet been assailed by slander on this subject, it is not unlikely that I soon shall be. This explanation is therefore due, not only to my character, but to the character of the State, whose honor is always involved in the fair fame of her sons. [Gaston then entered upon a detailed explanation of how he came to accept appointment to the Supreme Court of North Carolina in 1833 in view of the controverted article thirty-two of the state constitution barring those who denied the truth of the Protestant religion.]

Prejudice and cupidity are formidable foes, and will no doubt oppose an obstinate resistance to every effort which may be made to dislodge them from their hold. But we should be false to this people, if we distrusted their ability to decide correctly on this question. Lay it *fairly* before them, and no man need doubt the issue. The question is, ought there to be any Religious test in the Constitution? Shall any man be debarred from office, merely because of his *opinions* on matters of Religion? To me it seems, if there can be any certainty in moral or political science, the answer must be in the negative. It is an invasion of the right of the people to select those whom they deem worthy of confidence, and a violation of the right of the citizen to acquire the confidence of his fellow men, and to enjoy the rewards which they wish to bestow on his intelligence, industry, patriotism and virtue. In those governments which undertake to prescribe a religious faith to their subjects, and command its profession as a part of civil duty, there is at least a congruity in visiting disobedience by appropriate penalties. Incapacitation for office is *there* a punishment for disloyalty — and if it be supposed not adequate to its end, it is followed up by imprisonment, fine, confiscation, exile, torture and death. The *principle* is the same in all these grades of punishment. It is a visitation of the vengeance of the State upon those who offend against its institutions. But where a State is avowedly based on Religious Freedom, where it proclaims that every man has from nature a right, which he cannot surrender, and which none may take away — a "natural and unalienable right" to worship Almighty God according to the dictates of *his own conscience* — a right, of the correct exercise of which, his conscience is the sole judge — how can that State, without a violation of first principles, punish him by degradation because of the exercise of that very right? To this question, an answer is attempted to be given; and if the indefensible character of the cause did not forbid all wonder at any sophism that might be pressed into its defence, I should find it difficult either to restrain, or fitly to express my surprise at the nature of the pretended answer. It is very gravely said, that no man has any natural right to office, and therefore, the refusal of an office to him cannot be a punishment. . . .

Sir, I am opposed, out and out, to any interference of the State with the *opinions* of its citizens, and more especially with their opinion on Religious subjects. The good order of society requires that *actions* and *practices* injurious to the public peace and public morality, should be restrained, and but a moderate portion of practical good sense is required to enable the proper authorities to decide what conduct is really thus injurious. But to decide on the truth or error, on the salutary or pernicious consequences of *opinions,* requires a skill in dialectics, a keenness of discernment, a forecast and comprehension of mind, and above all, an exemption from bias, which do not ordinarily belong to human tribunals. The preconceived opinions of him, who is appointed to try, become the standard by which the opinions of others are measured, and as these correspond with, or differ from his own, they are pronounced true or false, salutary or pernicious. . . . Law is the proper judge of *action,* and reward or punishment its proper sanction. Reason is the proper umpire of *opinion,* and argument and discussion its only fit advocates. To denounce opinions by law is as silly, and unfortunately much more tyrannical, as it would be, to punish crime by logic. Laws [*sic*] calls out the force of the community to compel obedience to its mandates. To operate an opinion by law, is to enslave the intellect and oppress the soul — to reverse the order of nature, and make reason subservient to force. But of all the attempts to arrogate unjust dominion, none is so pernicious as the efforts of tyrannical men to rule over the human conscience. Religion is exclusively an affair between man and his God. If there be any subject upon which the interference of human power is more forbidden, than on all others, it is on Religion. Born of Faith — nurtured by Hope — invigorated by Charity — looking for its rewards in a world beyond the grave — it is of Heaven, heavenly. The evidence upon which it is founded, and the sanctions by which it is upheld, are addressed solely to the understanding and the purified affections. Even He, from whom cometh every pure and perfect gift, and to whom Religion is directed as its author, its end, and its exceedingly great reward, imposes no coercion on his children. They believe, or doubt, or reject, according to the impression which the testimony of revealed truth makes upon their minds. He causes His Sun to shine, alike on the believer and the unbeliever, and His dews to fertilize equally the soil of the orthodox and the heretic. . . . [Gaston here described the services of George Calvert, Roger Williams, and William Penn to religious freedom in colonial America, and how that principle had won out in most of the United States.] But finally, in every other of the twenty-four States of this Union, *perfect Religious Freedom,* perfect equality of sects, an entire exemption from religious tests, are now solemnly declared to be the basis on which rest all their Institutions. This salutary principle has spread across the Atlantic, and triumphed over the misrule and inveterate usages of the ancient Governments there. With scarcely an exception, it now prevails throughout *all* Europe, and Religious opinions are no longer there a qualification for, or an incapacity for Civil employment. And can it be, that *we* shall prove recreant in this noble strife for securing the sanctity of conscience and purity of religion?

Shall *we* afford to the bigots, the fanatics, and the friends of arbitrary power abroad, an apology for claiming this State as an ally in the cause of Intolerance? — I hope not. I trust that we shall act *up* to the axiom proclaimed in our Bill of Rights, and permit no man to suffer inconvenience or to incur incapacity, because of religion, whether he be Jew or Gentile, Christian or Infidel, Heretic or Orthodox. Pollute not the ark of God with unholy touch. Divine Truth *needs* not the support of human power, either to convince the understanding or to regulate the heart. Dare not to define divine truth, for it belongs not to your functions, and you may set up falsehood and error in its stead. Prohibit, restrain and punish, as offences against human society, all practices insulting to the faith, the institutions, and the worship of your people, but offer no bribes to lure men to profess a faith which they do not believe, inflict no penalties to deter them from embracing what their understandings approve, and make no distinction of ranks and orders in the community because of religious opinions. . . .

75. The Aid of the Society for the Propagation of the Faith to the Archdiocese of Baltimore, January 31, 1838

ONE of the greatest sources of financial support to the American Church throughout the nineteenth century was the Society for the Propagation of the Faith which had been organized by two priests and ten zealous laymen at Lyons, France, in May, 1822. The year after its establishment the society began its benefactions to the Archdiocese of Baltimore which were continued to 1865 when it had contributed $56,757. Equally generous sums were distributed to other American dioceses and by 1922, the centennial year of the society, a total of $6,375,218 had been sent from France to the United States. By that time American Catholics were relatively well off and had become mission-minded with the result that they had given back $10,983,452 to the society's headquarters in France to be distributed to more needy mission lands. In the following letter Samuel Eccleston, S.S. (1801–1851), fifth Archbishop of Baltimore, not only recorded his gratitude for the assistance sent to him, but he gave insights as well on the nativist movement, the problem of the slaves, and the need for more priests. Eccleston's letter is typical, not only of dozens of such reports received from bishops and religious superiors in the United States and published all through the nineteenth century in the society's annual volumes, but as well of hundreds of unpublished reports. Source: *Annales de la Propagation de la Foi,* X (1837), 494–500.

Baltimore, January 31, 1838.

Gentlemen,

I have already written to you to acknowledge the money which the Propagation of the Faith has been good enough to grant me. Today, according to your request, I am going to give you some details on the state of my diocese. There is certainly very much to say on this subject, but my many duties will not permit me to enter into all the necessary explanations. Allow me, above all, Gentlemen, to repeat my thanks in my name and in the name of my confrères in the episcopate: Oh! how I wish I could adequately express all the sentiments of gratitude and admiration which rise in my heart, when I consider the noble and truly Catholic zeal of your pious Association. A few months ago I was surrounded by the venerable Prelates of this province assembled for the last council,[1] and I had then the consolation to learn from their own lips the immense good that is being done by your means. If new churches are rising in the midst of our forests and deserts; if the Savages, who are more and more being driven back beyond our frontiers by the progress of civilization, carry with them at least the torch of the Faith; if, in a country where learning and talents are perhaps more than elsewhere exposed to the seduction of ambition and avarice, the small number of those who are called to the ecclesiastical life, find a safe shelter where they are formed to the virtues and the knowledge which the holy ministry demands; if — in a word — the Catholic religion is every day better known and as a consequence more respected from one end to the other of these vast regions, to whom do we owe it? It pleases me to say, that it is to you, Gentlemen; it is to your prayers and donations that we are for the most part indebted for these inestimable advantages. Yet, what title have we to your benefactions? Humanly speaking, and under the triple relation of country, of language, and of customs we are only strangers to you. But enlightened by the light of the Faith, you have recognized in us members of the Catholic unity, you have seen in us, brothers; you have treated us like brothers. And we also, Gentlemen, look upon you as brothers, and we cherish you like brothers. It must, however, be said, and, moreover, without it something would be lacking to your merit: your Association, excellent as it is, encounters opposition here as it undoubtedly does elsewhere. It is not that the most intelligent portion of my fellow citizens are not well disposed, or at least without animosity toward the Catholic religion; but there is among us a numerous and well organized association of religious fanatics who

[1] The Third Provincial Council of Baltimore had met April 16–22, 1837.

watch our progress with only a mortal envy: these people are your calumniators and ours.[2] While on the one hand they try to disparage our doctrines, on the other, they accuse us of lacking loyalty to our country, of distorting or exaggerating the nature and extent of the help which we receive from our brothers in the Faith; and while they waste millions to hire their emissaries and to spread their slanders under all forms, they pretend to see treason and a flagrant conspiracy in the pious liaison which we maintain with you. But their fury is the surest sign of the progress which our holy Religion is making, and therefore it should tend on one hand to stimulate your charity, and on the other to make us redouble our zeal.

My diocese comprises Maryland and the district of Columbia. I am also charged with the administration of the diocese of Richmond in the state of Virginia. Maryland contains 13,950 square miles and 450,000 inhabitants of whom 102,294 are slaves. The Catholics number 70,000.

The district of Columbia contains 100 square miles and 40,000 inhabitants of whom 10,000 are Catholics. Virginia has about 70,000 square miles and 1,220,000 inhabitants of whom 470,000 are slaves: the number of Catholics is 9,000. There are in my two dioceses 61 churches or chapels, eight of which belong to the diocese of Richmond. The churches in general are small and of a very simple construction, a few of them not even of wood. About twelve congregations or parishes have no churches and are visited only now and then by a Priest who happens to be near.

My clergy is composed of 74 Priests employed either in the missions or in the Catholic establishments: among them there are some whose parishes are 20 to 150 miles in extent; about twenty of them work in our principal towns. I do not speak of the Ecclesiastics who belong to religious communities and who also render us very great service.

Although many of the Catholic families are emigrating toward the south and west, the Faith is making solid progress in this diocese, the first one where the missionaries who came from Europe exercised in the past their apostolic zeal. As I have already mentioned, our success has roused against us the fanaticism of several sects; but it is among the Presbyterians especially that there arises the greatest

[2] Speaking of the American nativist reaction to the foreign missionary societies, the historian of the movement has said: "Annual reports of the Leopold Association and the Association for the Propagation of the Faith were widely published in the religious press, with warnings of the fate awaiting America if these activities were continued" (Ray Allen Billington, *The Protestant Crusade* [New York, 1938], p. 127).

animosity.[3] There is in Baltimore a class of men who are always disposed to receive avidly the most atrocious calumnies against the Catholics, and who more than once have tried to inflame the passions of the people by inflammatory pamphlets in order to destroy some of our religious establishments. Happily, the vulgar impostures which they are using are beginning to be appreciated at their face value by those who are more reasonable among our separated brethren; one may even say that this blind rage becomes for some an occasion of salvation by inspiring in them the desire to see and investigate for themselves. Not long ago a Jew from one of our southern states came to see me to ask some questions relating to the doctrines which are the object of our Faith; he told me that he had never read a Catholic book, but that the violent tone and the malignity which appeared in the Protestant treatises and pamphlets which he received every day had in the end made him suspect a cause which had recourse to such odious means of defense. He therefore decided that a religion which was attacked with such persistent hatred must be sustained by proofs that its adversaries had a thousand reasons to keep secret. I procured for him the necessary books to help him understand the basis of Catholic doctrine, and he promised that he would read them carefully: may the sincerity of his heart be rewarded by the knowledge of truth and by the sweet consolations which it alone can bring to man! Thus it is that the efforts of our adversaries by an admirable disposition of Providence turn to their own disadvantage.

It is true that round about us there are souls who will, perhaps, never be better disposed to receive favorable impressions of the true Religion. What I have had occasion to observe during the visitation of the vast territory under my jurisdiction has more and more confirmed me in this opinion; everywhere a laudable curiosity to know the doctrines of the Catholic Religion; everywhere a good number of upright men who would very probably renounce their prejudices if we had a sufficient number of Priests to attend to their conversion. But before thinking of these poor souls, there is a still more urgent duty to fulfill, and that is to procure for the Catholic population religious in-

[3] In Eccleston's see city of Baltimore two Presbyterian ministers, the Reverends Robert J. Breckinridge and Andrew B. Cross, had launched in 1835 the *Literary and Religious Magazine,* a fiery anti-Catholic journal. A few years later when the controversy between Bishop Hughes and the school authorities broke in New York the Presbyterians were again in the lead. "Nearly all of the Protestant denominations in the United States responded to this appeal but none with more enthusiasm than the Presbyterians whose heritage of antagonism toward Rome fitted them to take full advantage of the excitement over the New York controversy (Billington, *op. cit.,* p. 173).

struction and the facilities for them to receive the sacraments. They are now numerous and whole congregations who cry out to me for the bread of life and I have no one to distribute it to them. The consequences of this situation are deplorable; because, lacking the means to practice their religious duties, these Catholics end by succumbing to indifference, and their children who grow up among Protestant companions, unfortunately soon no longer distinguish between the true Church from the ephemeral sects which surrounded them.

The slaves of these states also present a vast harvest for the apostolic workers. Their souls, redeemed by the same Savior, and destined to the same blessed immortality, are not, in the eyes of God, less precious than the souls of their masters; and often in their very simplicity, they are better prepared to receive divine grace and make it bear fruit. I have done some special research on this subject, and I have constantly found that every time a Priest had given careful attention to these poor people, his zeal has soon been richly rewarded by their happy change of life, and by their edifying regularity in frequenting the sacraments. In our towns, many of the Protestant families prefer Catholic servants; in the country many of the Protestant planters who, have in their neighborhood some pious Catholic congregations, seeing how our Religion has influenced the slaves, have more than once sought to have them instructed in our salutary beliefs. I do not think that there is in this country, without excepting the Savages, any class of men among whom it would be possible to work more fruitfully. But, I repeat, far from being able to do what I should like to do for the salvation of unfortunate Negroes, I find myself unable to satisfy the thousands of whites who equally deprived of the help of Religion, feel more keenly their spiritual abandonment.

It was the opinion of my venerable predecessor, and it is also mine, that the only way to obtain a clergy sufficient for our needs, and suitable for the missions of these regions, is to found an establishment solely consecrated to the education of those who are destined for the priesthood; because our colleges, able to maintain themselves only by the number of students, are forced to receive all the youths who present themselves, Catholic or Protestant. The result is that when there are found among them several who have some inclination toward the ecclesiastical state, their contact and their necessary relations with the young men who have opposite views to theirs necessarily exposes their vocation. In order to obviate these disadvantages, there was begun a few years ago the building of a minor seminary a few miles from Baltimore.[4] The roof is covered, and the first floor is almost finished. We have done all that was in our power to finish this purely ecclesiastical college and to get it started; but the lack of funds has forced us to suspend the work, and to wait until Providence would come to our assistance. Certainly it is not for lack of effort on my part that the work remains incomplete: considering this nursery of students as the hope of my diocese, I have several times assembled the faithful in order to excite their charity; I have even gone from door to door to solicit help. Unfortunately, I have no resources of my own. Will not my cathedral furnish me with it? But it is burdened with a considerable debt, and besides it is not even finished; the walls still lack decoration and the suitable embellishments befitting such an edifice.

As to myself, thank God, I have need of little and that little I do not lack: my worries, my prayers, are for my flock. I look only for the honor of the sanctuary; I seek only to save souls redeemed by the blood of J.C., of whom one day he will ask an accounting of me.

This is, Gentlemen, the state of my dioceses, of which there has been fashioned, perhaps, in France a little different idea; however that be, I am extremely grateful for everything that you have done either for my predecessors or for myself; once more please accept my thanks. I pray the good God, Gentlemen, that he send you his most abundant graces, on all the charitable members of the Association and that he may reward you a hundredfold in this life and in the next.

Samuel Eccleston, Archbishop of Baltimore.

76. The Papacy's Relation to Temporal Affairs Explained by Bishop Kenrick, 1838

THE outstanding American Catholic theologian of the nineteenth century was Francis Patrick Kenrick (1796–1863). During the nativist agitation of the 1830's the Church was often challenged in regard to the institution of the papacy and its claims to primacy. Making a bid for unity among the Christian churches, the Protestant Episcopal Bishop of Vermont, John Henry Hopkins, published a work called *The Church of Rome in her Primitive Purity compared to the Church of Rome at the Present Day* (New York, 1835). To this Kenrick, then Coadjutor Bishop of Philadelphia, prepared

[4] St. Charles College, Ellicott City, opened with five students on November 1, 1848, under the presidency of Oliver L. Jenkins, S.S.

an answer which is generally regarded as the best of his numerous writings on theological and apologetic subjects. It first appeared in the spring of 1838, passed through numerous editions, and was translated into German in 1853. In the excerpt below Kenrick sought to explain the historical background for the papacy's exercise of jurisdiction in temporal concerns and to show the changes that had taken place in regard to that practice since the Middle Ages. He not only had in mind a reply to Hopkins but the hope of dispelling the prejudices which so many Americans entertained concerning the papacy. Source: Francis Patrick Kenrick, *The Primacy of the Apostolic See, and the Authority of General Councils, Vindicated,* 7 rev. ed. (Baltimore: John Murphy Co., 1875), p. 282.

. . . The divine law, doubtless, embraces all classes of men, princes and people, and all varieties of human actions, political as well as personal. The chief Pastor of the Church is placed on his high eminence, to proclaim the command of God, and in His name to instruct in justice those that judge the earth. As expounder of the moral law, he speaks to all with power and authority, condemning all that God has forbidden, and inculcating the observance of each divine commandment. He can cast forth from the Church every one, prince or subject, who is notoriously guilty of flagrant immorality, if he will not yield to paternal admonition. But secular concerns are not, of themselves, subject to his cognizance: and the complicated social relations which arise from the free acts of individuals, or from public law, or from the action of the civil authorities, are not the matter of his judgment, unless where they involve a violation of the great principles of Christian morality. In the Middle Ages, kings and nations implored his judgment, and consequently brought within the sphere of his authority those secular transactions and controversies, of which otherwise he might have said, in the words of our Redeemer, to those who called for his interference: "Who hath appointed me judge over you?" Whencesoever the conviction of his right to take cognizance of them may be supposed to have arisen, it was universally admitted, and it was consequently a part of the public and common law of nations. Guizot[1] testifies that it was generally believed, in the middle of the ninth century, that he was above temporal governments, even in temporal affairs, when connected with religion: he might have qualified it by adding, in their moral aspect, since he observes that it was by developing the principles of morality ecclesiastics exercised power over governments.

The key to the whole history of the Middle Ages appears to us

---

[1] François Guizot (1787–1874), a Protestant, was Premier of France in the last month of the reign of King Louis Philippe.

to be the sentiment then prevailing, that Christian principle should regulate all the departments of government and all the relations of life. We do not think that the authority of the Popes over sovereigns is to be accounted for, merely by reason of the relations in which they actually stood to them, or of the concessions which had been made by former princes. On the contrary, we trace those concessions and relations to the persuasion which was universal, that the head of the Christian Church was the fittest arbiter of the respective obligations of princes and their subjects, and the natural judge of all, in what regarded the application of the Christian maxims to society.

77. The Church in the Republic of Texas, April 11, 1841

EVER since the time when the Spanish Franciscans had begun their labors in Texas in 1690 that vast area had proved a difficult terrain for the Church's missionaries. In 1836 Texas broke from Mexico and declared its independence with the result that a new arrangement had to be made for spiritual care of the widely scattered Catholics. On October 24, 1839, the Holy See erected the Prefecture Apostolic of Texas and its care was entrusted to the Vincentian Fathers with John Timon (1797–1867) as first prefect. By reason of Timon's many preoccupations elsewhere the practical establishment of the Texas mission was delegated to Jean-Marie Odin (1800–1870) who was later first Vicar Apostolic of Texas, 1841–1847; first Bishop of Galveston, 1847–1861; and second Archbishop of New Orleans, 1861–1870. The following letter of Odin was written to Jean-Baptiste Etienne who was Superior-General of the Vincentians from 1843–1874. Besides the description of religious conditions, it demonstrates how primitive life was in large sections of Texas four years before it entered the American Union. Source: *Annales de la Propagation de la Foi,* XIV (1842), 453–460.

Galveston, Texas, 11 April 1841

My dear Brother,

Last year the Holy See having conferred on our Congregation the spiritual direction of the Catholics of Texas, I left the seminary of the Barrens,[1] on May 2, 1840, in order to explore this new Mission in my capacity of vice-prefect apostolic. It was not without regret that I left Missouri; to separate myself from a people who had become very dear to me, and from flourishing establishments that I had seen born, was like expatriating myself a second time.

[1] St. Mary's Seminary, Perryville, Missouri (the Barrens), had been established by the Vincentians in 1818 at the little village about eighty miles south of St. Louis.

Texas, situated between the 26th and the 35th degrees of latitude and extending from the 93rd to the 102nd of longitude, possesses vast prairies, and more abundant pasturage than any other region of America. Woods are rare here, especially in the west. Several rivers irrigate the country, but they are not large or deep enough for navigation. Although the exact figure of the population of Texas is not known, it is rather generally agreed not to exceed thirty thousand souls.

When the first Spaniards settled in Texas more than a century and a half ago, some Franciscans came and founded several Missions in order to convert and civilize the savage tribes. The most celebrated of these were: *San Antonio, de la Conception de San Jose, del Refugio,* and *San Sabas* and *Nacogdoches;* they became very flourishing and soon counted a great number of fervent neophytes. Each year the Reverend Fathers plunged into the forests, earning by their gifts and their very affable manners the confidence of the Indians, and conducting them to the stations where they fashioned them little by little to piety and work. In 1812 these precious establishments were suppressed; today they are only heaps of ruins. For the poor savages, deprived of their Fathers, were dispersed: some returned to Mexico; several succumbed under the blows of the uncivilized tribes, and others returned to their primitive state. The fervor which I have found in the small number of those who still inhabit the country clearly indicates that they had been formed to virtue by capable hands. Two churches, the only ones that have resisted the assaults of time and of the recent wars, are of a beauty which does honor to the taste and zeal of the old Missionaries. . . .

From Liunville, a small seaport where we debarked, we proceeded to Victoria. I left in that post M. l'abbé Estany,[2] and I took the route to San Antonio with M. Calvo[3] and a coadjutor brother. The distance which separates the two towns is only fifty leagues, but the numerous bands of savage *Comanches* and *Tonakanies* who roam the country without ceasing make the trip extremely perilous: it is even pretty nearly certain that one will be massacred, if one does not travel in sufficient numbers to intimidate the Indians. We therefore joined a convoy of twenty-two wagons which were transporting some merchandise. All of our companions were very well armed; but, if on the one hand the force of the caravan reassured us against the attacks of the Indians, on the other, what miseries to endure! What slowness

---

[2] Eudald Estany was a Spanish Vincentian who had accompanied Odin to Texas.

[3] Michael Calvo was another Spanish Vincentian who had come to Texas in May, 1840.

in our advance! The heat was excessive, and scarcely a bush offered itself in the shade of which we might enjoy a moment of repose. Toward sunset we moved forward; but often at first step one of our vehicles got out of order and it was necessary to pass a part of the night in repairing it. These accidents sometimes happened far from any springs or rivers; we then had to scour the wastes, very happy when after a lot of searching we found in a mudhole some drops of muddy and distasteful water. Moreover, we were very poorly provisioned, and yet we hastened to partake as brothers with our traveling companions, worse provided for than ourselves; it was even necessary to have recourse to hunting at the risk of attracting the savages by the noise of the guns.

To scarcity there was also joined the fever; I had several attacks, like the others; but some medicines which I had provided myself proved opportune, and they restored us little by little to health. The relief that I obtained for our poor sufferers gave me a reputation by which I was later often embarrassed; because some of our good wagoners recognized me under the name of the *"Father who knows how to heal,"* all the sick came to ask me for consultations and remedies. Several times along the way, the cry of *Los Indios* spread alarm in our midst: this was, I believe, only a mistake of our scouts, because we arrived at San Antonio without striking a blow.

That city, founded in 1678 by the Spaniards from the Canary Islands,[4] includes a population of two thousand souls: one notices there some houses of stone; the other houses are only miserable huts covered with rushes. It is irrigated on the east by the San Antonio river, on the west by a very small stream; in the center one finds a canal from which the abundant water fertilizes all the gardens; it was built by the Indians under the direction of the Missionaries. There is nothing more beautiful than the valley of San Antonio: agreeable climate, pure and healthful air, rich and fertile soil, all contribute to make it a delightful place, without the continual hostility of the savages, who up to the present have not permitted its immense resources to be exploited. There is not a family who does not mourn the death of a father, of a son, of a brother, or of a spouse pitilessly slaughtered by the *Comanches.* To the massacre of the colonists, these brigands add the devastation of the land and the kidnapping of the herds: thus poverty is extreme in the country, and if ever it would have been consoling to have some aid to distribute, it would un-

[4] Odin was wrong here. San Antonio had been founded in 1718 and the Canary Islanders did not arrive until 1730.

doubtedly have been at the sight of so many needy and unfortunate.

A few days after our arrival at San Antonio, there took place a ceremony which filled us with consolation in proving to us how much of the faith still lived among the Mexicans. A sick person, in danger of death, needed to receive holy viaticum; we judged it opportune to carry it to him publicly and with pomp. At the sound of the bell, the people hastened to the holy place in order to accompany Our Lord through the streets; many tears fell from the eyes of the old people who for forty years had not been witnesses of this homage rendered to our Religion. Some among them cried out that they did not fear death any longer now that heaven had sent them Fathers to assist them in their last moment.

After three months in San Antonio, seeing that, thanks to God, all went as we desired, I directed myself toward Seguin, Gonzales, and Victoria. My visit in these towns was very brief because I was not able to separate myself from my traveling companions without exposing myself to be killed by the Indians. Later I reascended alone the Lavaca river, which offers less danger, and I found on its banks seventy Catholics, formerly my parishioners at the Barrens. It was very consoling to me to see them again, and especially to convince myself that they had lost nothing of their faith and their early piety, because since their arrival in Texas they had been deprived of the aid of Religion. All of them went to confession and had the good fortune to receive holy communion.

I was able to remain with them only one week. From Lavaca I went to Austin, a powerful little town, recently designated to be the seat of the Texas government. The congress was then in session; I solicited from some of the legislators a decision which would confirm to the Catholic Church all the churches constructed by the Spaniards in former times. It is true that, with the exception of *Conception* and *San Jose,* these edifices are almost all in ruins; nevertheless they can be repaired, and considering the poverty and small number of the faithful, they can be turned to account while awaiting happier times that will give us the chance of constructing new ones. Thanks to the generous intervention of M. de Saligny,[5] chargé d'affaires of France, my request has been well received.

There still remains the eastern part of Texas to visit. What difficulties and obstacles present themselves on that long route! Sometimes it is a river there which it will be necessary to cross by swimming, some-

[5] Alphonse Dubois de Saligny was *chargé d'affaires* in Texas for the government of King Louis Philippe of France.

times a vast and desolate swamp where we will run the risk of losing our horses; here the famine and nothing to alleviate it; elsewhere torrents of rain and no shelter. Thus we proceeded from Montgomery to Huntsville, from Cincinnati to Crok and to Douglas, from Nacogdoches to San Augustine. It is true that we were well compensated for our fatigue by the eagerness to hear our instructions which was manifested by the inhabitants of these diverse localities; rarely have I seen the word of God heard with more joy and recollection. This visit, although short, has contributed not a little to dissipate the prejudice of the Protestants, and to awaken pious sentiments in the heart of the faithful.

Outside of the Catholic population of Texas, estimated to be about ten thousand souls, there are some savage tribes to which it will be urgent to apply ourselves: these are the *Comanches* to the number of 20,000; the *Tonakanies,* the *Lipans,* the *Tankanago,* the *Bidaïs,* the *Karankanags,* the *Nacoës,* etc. Most of these Indians like to eat human flesh; the feet and hands are their favorite parts. I have already made several approaches to the *Karankanags,* in order to unite them in a mission: M. Estany has also visited them, and they have expressed to him the desire to have a priest. The *Comanches* will be the most difficult to win over. From time immemorial this tribe has been constantly at war with the civilized inhabitants and the neighboring tribes. Clever horsemen, skillful thieves, they handle the spear and the lance with great dexterity; one sees them in bands of ten, twenty, thirty, or fifty, running about the country without ceasing. From the heights where they lie in wait for their prey, when they discover a convoy too feeble to resist them, they pounce on the travelers with the rapidity of lightning and they gorge themselves without pity. It would be impossible to say how many unfortunates have succumbed under their blows, how many women and children have been taken captive.

A short time after my arrival in Texas one party of five or six hundred *Comanches* penetrated almost to Liunville. The inhabitants, who were not expecting this visit, were obliged to hide themselves in the middle of the Labaca [*sic*] bay in order to protect themselves from their spears: there were eight victims; a young woman married only ten days became their prisoner after having seen her husband fall pierced in his sides. When the savages had plundered the stores and had made a minute search of all that might enrich them, they delivered the town to the flames. From Liunville they went to Victoria. The first house they attacked was the one where our confrère M. Estany lived: he had the good fortune to pass through a hail of spears without receiving any wound; but all that he possessed was taken: linens, ornaments, books, nothing was spared. There were again some murders; several women and children were carried off. Soon the alarm was spread, and they rushed forth in pursuit of the brigands and caught up with them near the *Plombereek* and *St. Marc* rivers. The battle was bloody; eighty-four *Comanches* lost their lives, without mentioning those who a short time after succumbed to wounds they had received. These unfortunates, at the approach of the Texans, sought to kill all the prisoners whom they had carried off. One poor mother who fell into their hands with her little infant, scarcely ten months old, had the anguish of seeing this innocent creature crushed under her eyes, and was herself finally pierced by several blows of the lance! I have counted, in the space of ten months, almost two hundred slaughtered by that tribe alone.

In spite of the devastation to which this country is prey, heaven has already begun to bless our feeble work. From August 1, 1840, to March 1, 1841 we have heard 911 confessions and administered 281 baptisms; there have been 478 communions. . . . The good of Religion will demand that there be erected immediately at least six chapels at the most important places of the republic; but where to find the funds? We are without resources, and the population is poor. In my travels, I pass part of the night in the woods in the open air; I cook my own food, nevertheless my traveling expenses are always considerable. Thus lately in order to have two armed men accompany me during three days of traveling, I was obliged to pay them twenty-four piasters. Schools are also necessary at San Antonio and Galveston: who will cover the first expenses? We are without lodgings, obliged to beg hospitality among the Catholics, often even with the Protestants. . . . Here one learns, indeed, how to lead the life of a Missionary: I thought that I had already made a long apprenticeship; but since my arrival in Texas I have discovered that I was not yet initiated.

Your devoted servant,
J.-M. Odin.

78. Father De Smet's Promotion of the Indian Missions of the Far West, May 1, 1841

WHEN Charles Van Quickenborne, S.J., left Whitemarsh in Maryland on April 11, 1823, as the superior of a small group to reopen Jesuit activities in the Middle West for the first time since their forcible expulsion in 1763, there was among the seven novices a Belgian-born youth, Pierre-Jean De Smet (1801–1873), who was destined to become one of the most famous promoters of Catholic missions among the American Indians. The Flathead Indians of Montana had made four different attempts at St. Louis to secure a Catholic priest, the last in the summer of 1839. De Smet's zeal was fired by this striking manifestation of faith, and after securing the permission of his superiors he set out in March, 1840, for the first of his journeys to the Rocky Mountain country. Not only did he make several trips to the Far West, but he traveled widely in both the United States and Europe — in all about 180,000 miles — begging for the Indian missions and advertising them as only he could do. If De Smet's imagination sometimes outran his practical sense, he had no peer as a propagandist of the mission cause, or as a man in whom the Indians felt complete confidence. That was witnessed by the help he gave to the peace commissioners in negotiating the peace treaty with the Sioux in July, 1868. Some months after his return to St. Louis from his first trip to the Rockies he wrote the following letter to a friend in which he showed how he was making good on his promises to the Indians of the Far West. Source: Hiram Martin Chittenden and Alfred Talbot Richardson (Eds.), *Life, Letters and Travels of Father Pierre-Jean De Smet, S.J., 1801–1873* (New York: Francis P. Harper, 1905), I, 272–274.

To the Editor of the *Catholic Herald*
Steamboat *Oceana,* Mo. River,
May 1, 1841

. . . On my arrival at St. Louis, I gave an account to my superior of my journey and of the flattering prospects which the mission beyond the Rocky Mountains held out. You will easily believe me when I tell you that my heart sank within me on learning from him that the funds at his disposal for missionary purposes would not enable him to afford me scarcely the half of what would be necessary for the outfit and other expenses of an expedition. The thought that the undertaking would have been given up, that I would not be able to redeem my promise to the poor Indians, pierced my very heart and filled me with the deepest sorrow. I would have desponded had I not already experienced the visible protection of the Almighty in the prosecution of this great work. My confidence in him was unabated. Whilst in this state of mind one of my friends encouraged me to appeal to the zealous and learned coadjutor of Philadelphia [Francis Patrick Kenrick] and to his indefatigable clergy. I immediately acted upon the thought. I did appeal and with what success the Catholic public already know. To the Bishop who gave his sanction to the plan of a general and simultaneous collection throughout his diocese; to the clergy of the different churches of the city who so kindly interested themselves in this good work and proposed it to their congregations; to the generous people of Philadelphia who so liberally responded to the call of their pastors, I return my sincere thanks and will daily beg the father of mercies to reward them with his choicest blessings.

I must not omit to make mention of other generous contributors. After having written to Philadelphia I was advised to visit New Orleans and recommend the cause of the Indians to the good Bishop [Antoine Blanc] of that city and to his clergy and people. I did so. The Bishop received me with great kindness; gave his approbation to a collection, and placed his name first on the list. His clergy followed his example. As I had only a few days at my disposal, I thought it best to solicit subscriptions through several generous ladies who offered themselves for this purpose. In the space of three or four days, they collected nearly $1,000. You have no idea with what spirit the pious portion of the people entered into the affair. Almost every moment of my stay persons came to offer me something for the Indian mission. Several ladies gave me various trinkets, such as ear-rings, bracelets, and ornaments of every description; others brought implements and articles, which will be of great use in the Indian country. In a word, Reverend Sir, I left New Orleans with $1,100 in cash and six boxes full of various and most useful articles. From the Reverend Mr. Durbin[1] of Kentucky I received $300, and the Reverend Jno. O'Reilly[2] remitted $140, the amount collected in St. Paul's Church, Pittsburg. St. Louis supplied the balance of what was necessary for the outfit, the expenses of the journey and the commencement of the establishment in the Indian country. To the Bishops and to the zealous clergy and laity of Philadelphia and New Orleans; to the clergy and laity of other places who aided the good cause; in a word, to all the benefactors of the mission beyond the Rocky Mountains, I again return my sincere thanks. . . .

---

[1] E. J. Durbin was stationed at Sacred Heart Church, Union County, Kentucky, at this time.

[2] John O'Reilly was pastor of St. Paul's Church, Pittsburgh.

79. Canon Salzbacher's Observations on American Catholic Colleges for Men, 1842

AMONG the principal foreign benefactors of American Catholicism in the nineteenth century was the Leopoldinen-Stiftung of Vienna which was founded in April, 1829, and which between 1830 and 1913 sent over $700,000 to the assistance of German Catholic immigrants in this country. Early in the 1840's complaints began to reach Vienna of the neglect of the German immigrants by the American bishops, and the society decided, therefore, to send the editor of its annual *Berichte,* Canon Josef Salzbacher (1790–1867) of St. Stephen's Cathedral, to investigate conditions in the United States. Salzbacher landed at New York from the *Great Western* on April 17, 1842, and during the next three months he covered about 10,000 miles and visited German Catholic immigrant groups in eleven dioceses spread over seventeen states. By the time he departed for home on July 27 he had accumulated a large body of data from which he later wrote a book. His volume was one of the most careful factual accounts ever published by a foreign visitor on the Church in the United States. Toward the end of the work the author included some general observations. The passage which follows covered the Catholic colleges for men as he saw them in 1842. Source: Josef Salzbacher, *Meine Reise nach Nord-Amerika in Jahre 1842 mit statistischen Bemerkungen über die Züstande der katholischen Kirche bis auf neuste Zeit* (Vienna: Wimmer, Schmidt & Leo, 1845), pp. 354–357.

Besides the elementary, Sunday and free-schools and orphanages the Catholic Church in America has institutions of higher learning as colleges, academies and universities which are devoted to the so-called classical studies which in America as elsewhere are the mark of the people of higher rank. The classical course, philosophy, mathematics, and sciences are about the same as in Europe and ordinarily require for their completion four years. One can assert that the instructors in many of these institutions are fully competent to teach the subjects entrusted to them. Since many Catholic youth want to obtain a higher education to become physicians, attorneys, or priests, it has long been the ambition of the bishops to erect such higher institutions of learning and to supervise them in order that these young men, who otherwise would attend the public state schools, might not go astray. Realizing that religious orders can accomplish more than individuals, the bishops have called upon the Sulpicians, Jesuits, Lazarists, etc., to conduct these institutions of higher learning. It is hardly necessary to say that the bishops and the faithful are obliged to assume the entire burden of financing these institutions. How well they have succeeded is shown by the long list of educational institutions which we have catalogued under the heading of the various dioceses. Outstanding are the Jesuit colleges at Georgetown, St. Louis, Cincinnati, and the Sulpician college, St. Mary's at Baltimore. The state governments liberally concede the privileges of universities to these schools so that they can grant their distinguished students doctor's and master's diplomas, notwithstanding the fact that these colleges are under the control of the bishops and the religious orders and the secular authorities have not the slightest authority over them. Usually, as is the case in Europe, these colleges are conducted as boarding schools. The number of the externes so-called is usually small.

Not all the students in Catholic colleges and schools are Catholics. . . . Such Protestant students are accepted by Catholic colleges because of the insufficient number of Catholic students available and because the income derived from Protestant students makes it possible for the college to provide better facilities for the students, more teachers and better equipment. Moreover, these non-Catholic students by constant association with priests and Catholic teachers lay aside their prejudices against the Catholic Church which from youth have been impressed upon them; many become Catholics; if not permitted to take this step because of the opposition of parents or relatives, they later, as men of influence, become defenders of the Church and will more readily allow their people to enter the Church.

Experience also teaches that Protestant parents place great confidence in the methods of instruction and in the competency of the Catholic instructors and, convinced of the excellence of Catholic schools, they send their children preferably to these institutions. True it is that the Protestant preachers do their utmost to prevent the attendance of Protestants at Catholic schools, and in their public addresses and sermons they inveigh bitterly against Catholic educational institutions, but their calumnies have often produced results opposite to those they intended. Many Protestants began to visit the Catholic schools, and seeing the beauty and order of such institutions, they concluded that the preachers had indulged in slanderous assertions and determined to send their children to Catholic colleges. The good order and discipline of the colleges is in no manner impaired by the presence of the non-Catholic students. Every father and mother who place their son in the college are at once made acquainted with the rules of the institution and, if they are unwilling to submit their son to such discipline, the student in question is not accepted. Non-Catholic students are not obliged to attend instruction on Catholic doctrine. Every appearance of proselytism is carefully avoided but the non-Catholic students are required to respect the Catholic exercises of religion and they are obliged to attend morning and evening devotions, to be present for the prayers before and after meals, and to participate with the Catholics in the prayers before and after each class. Attendance at divine worship is not insisted upon, however, in the case of non-Catholics. Attached to every college is a church or chapel of sufficient capacity to accommodate all the students and on all the Sundays and holy days services are held as in parish churches. All the Catholic students must attend these.

In 1844 there were twenty-four Catholic colleges for young men in the United States. Of these six are conducted by the Jesuits, three are in charge of the Lazarists, two belong to the Sulpicians, one is directed by the Eudists and one is in the hands of the Redemptorists. The others are taught by secular priests. About 3,000 young men receive instruction in these colleges. Nearly every college possesses a select library, equipment for the teaching of the sciences and a scientific laboratory. Public examinations are held each year and prizes are awarded to the best students. Without exaggeration one may say that these institutions, distinguished by the strict morality and ability of their professors, contribute much to the respect which the Catholic religion enjoys in the United States.

80. The Launching of the American Protestant Association Against the Catholic Church, November 22, 1842

AFTER 1820 the numerical strength of the Catholic Church in the United States rose rapidly by reason of immigration, and by 1840 there were estimated to be 663,000 Catholics out of a total population of 14,195,805 white Americans. This increase alarmed many American Protestants who disliked the Church and who feared, too, lest native Americans be supplanted in their jobs by the cheaper labor of Irish and German immigrants, so many of whom were Catholics. The result was an organized effort against Catholics under the banner of American nativism. The nativists needed only a very slender excuse to go into action and when Francis P. Kenrick (1796–1863), Bishop of Philadelphia, on November 14, 1842, respectfully petitioned the board of the city's public schools for redress against Catholic children having to use the King James Bible and to be present at Protestant religious exercises in the schools, an excuse was at hand. A group of the city's Protestant leaders met and on November 22 ninety-four ministers, representing twelve denominations, signed the constitution of what they called the American Protestant Association. The association was responsible for arousing antagonism between Protestants and Catholics and its agents were in good measure to blame for the public riots in May and July, 1844, in which thirteen citizens were killed, over fifty wounded, and two of Philadelphia's Catholic churches burned. The constitution of this association which follows was typical of the numerous organizations of this kind which were actively at work against the Church throughout the country up to the Civil War. Source: Ray Allen Billington, *The Protestant Crusade, 1800–1860: A Study of the Origins of American Nativism* (New York: The Macmillan Co., 1938), pp. 438–439; reissued in 1952 by Rinehart & Co., New York.

Whereas, we believe the system of Popery to be, in its principles and tendency, subversive of civil and religious liberty, and destructive to the spiritual welfare of men, we unite for the purpose of defending our Protestant interests against the great exertions now making to propagate that system in the United States; and adopt the following constitution: —

Article I. This Society shall be called the American Protestant Association.

Article II. The objects of its formation, and for the attainment of which its efforts shall be directed, are —

1. The union and encouragement of Protestant ministers of the gospel, to give to their several congregations instruction on the differences between Protestantism and Popery.

2. To call attention to the necessity of a more extensive distribution, and thorough study of the Holy Scriptures.

3. The circulation of books and tracts adapted to give information on the various errors of Popery in their history, tendency, and design.

4. To awaken the attention of the community to the dangers which threaten the liberties, and the public and domestic institutions, of these United States from the assaults of Romanism.

Article III. This Association shall be composed of all such persons as agree in adopting the purposes and principles of this constitution and contribute to the funds by which it is supported.

Article IV. The officers of the Association shall be a President, three Vice-Presidents, a treasurer, a corresponding secretary, a recording secretary, and two lay directors from each denomination represented in the Association, to be elected annually; together with all the ministers belonging to it; who shall form a Board for the transaction of business of whom any seven, at a meeting duly convened, shall be a quorum. The stated meetings of the Board to be quarterly.

Article V. The Board of managers shall, at the first meeting after their election, appoint an executive committee, consisting of a minister and layman from each of the denominations represented in the association, of which the secretaries and treasurer shall be ex-officio members. This committee to meet as often as they may find necessary for the transaction of the business committed to them, and to report quarterly to the Board of managers.

Article VI. The duties of the Board shall be, to carry out, in every way most expedient in their view, the ends and purposes for which this Association is organized; and to aid and encourage the formation of similar associations in the various parts of the United States; and to render an annual report of their proceedings to the Association, at their annual meeting on the second Tuesday in November.

Article VII. The Board of managers shall have power to enact such by-laws as may not be inconsistent with this constitution, and to fill all vacancies that may occur between the annual meetings.

Article VIII. This constitution shall be subject to amendments only at the annual meetings of the Association, by a vote of two thirds of the members present at such meeting.

81. A Rural Colonization Project for German Catholic Immigrants, October 12, 1843

BY 1840 Catholic immigrants were finding life increasingly unpleasant in the eastern cities by reason of the bitter campaigns waged by the nativists against their religion and foreign birth. As a consequence a number of Philadelphia and Baltimore families banded together to form the German Catholic Brotherhood with the idea of establishing a new home at some remote spot where they would be free from religious and racial prejudice. Their leaders purchased large tracts of land in what is today Elk County, Pennsylvania, and the arrival of the wives and children of the pioneers on December 8, 1842, prompted them to call the settlement St. Mary's. They had originally consulted with Father Alexander Czvitkovicz, C.SS.R., (1806–1883), Hungarian-born superior of the Redemptorists in the United States, who after a visit to the colony recommended that the Redemptorists invest $10,000 in the project. This was done and schools for both boys and girls were provided, but the Redemptorists lost so heavily in the undertaking that they felt compelled to withdraw in November, 1849. They were succeeded by the German Benedictines from St. Vincent's Priory in Westmoreland County who were more experienced farmers and who in time brought the mission to a flourishing state. The following letter of Czvitkovicz to the Society for the Propagation of the Faith outlined the objectives of the colonizers and vividly described the perils of life in the forests of northwestern Pennsylvania at the time. St. Mary's was typical of many rural colonization projects of the German Catholic immigrants before the Civil War, a period noted for some rather bizarre backwoods communitarian experiments as well. Source: *Annales de la Propagation de la Foi,* XVI (1844), 401–406.

Baltimore, October 12, 1843.

Dear Mr. President,

. . . After having given a mission in Detroit, I returned directly to Baltimore where there awaited me duties apparently less apostolic.

A great number of our German brothers of Baltimore and Philadelphia, seeing all the different sects with which our cities are populated, and the great danger for them and for their children of losing faith, proposed to form an exclusively Catholic community; and to that end they purchased last year at a very moderate price, a piece of waste land in the neighborhood of thirty-six thousand acres. Some of the faithful, before entering into the association, consulted me on the project, which forced me to examine the laws; and as I soon perceived that it would remain without result and that it would soon break up, I straight-forwardly said so to those who spoke to me about it, explaining to them the reasons which prompted my advice. Nevertheless, before my departure for Europe the colony seemed to make some progress; many families eagerly joined it: but soon this false appearance of success disappeared, and on my return to America, the enterprise was at the point of death. Around thirty-eight families had already quit the community; its principal members and the twenty-six families who were still there, seeing the impossibility of restoring it to life and fearing to lose all the capital they had already expended in the first tillage which would have ruined a hundred families, remembering my prediction, sent some delegates to me in order that I might aid them with my counsel and my credit.

I pitied their condition, especially since the honor of Religion was at stake, for already the heretics and the infidels triumphing at the dissolution, mocked the colonists in their newspapers. Some concluded that Catholicism was powerless to found lasting establishments, others have so little union and fraternity with our coreligionists that there is rarely found among them men with enough charity to interest themselves in the fate of their unfortunate brothers. I therefore went to the colony where I was received by the twenty-six families who had been vegetating there for a year with as much lively joy as if my presence alone was capable of changing this land of malediction into a terrestrial paradise. The next day, accompanied by all the colonists to the number of twenty-six, armed with the proper instruments for measuring the land, and with guns to procure ourselves some game and protect ourselves against the ferocious beasts, such as the wolves and bears, of which there are still great numbers in these regions, I began with the compass and map in hand, to seek out the limits of the land that had been bought. What was my surprise in soon learning that these poor people had watered with their daily sweat an unknown land that they had taken for their own! After having surveyed the ground well, I made a general demarcation; after that I divided it into portions of twenty-five, fifty, seventy-five and a hundred acres, marking out the limits by the trees. I determined the place where the village ought to be constructed; I made the plan, counseling them to group the houses instead of spreading them as they had done up to now, at two, three, four or five miles from one another.

It is impossible to give an idea of the fatigue caused by these excursions; those who have seen and inhabited these immense American forests, whose origin dates from the beginning of the world, without ever the hand of man having touched this chaos, can alone understand: one meets at almost every step thick brushwood, roots intertwined with the branches which bend to the ground, entire trees uprooted by age and the winds, heaped up here and there like impassable ramparts; moreover, since the sun is not able to penetrate beneath these vaults of foliage it is very humid, the ground is so slippery that one is never sure of his footing and has almost as many falls as steps.

The property purchased extends for nine miles. We covered scarcely the space of three miles in a day and in order to manage that we were forced to pass the night in the middle of these forests. Then at night we lighted a big fire because it was the end of October, and we were already very cold; seated around the fire we took our supper which ordinarily left the stomach pretty empty. After evening prayer, which we said in common, each made his own bed as he wished, and slept if he were able. One may well imagine that being exposed to the cold, the snow, and the rain, that we slept very little; nevertheless, I passed these nights very agreeably, occupied during my long hours of insomnia in calculating the advantages that Religion would one day derive from this civilizing work, accomplished in solitude under the eyes of God alone. It was then that I called to mind the fruitless pains that others before me, and I myself for three years, had taken to find some young Americans destined to become Missionaries of their own land; I believe that I can see in the new establishment the future refuge where this infant Christianity sheltered from the corruption of the world and perversion of heresy, will increase in knowledge without losing virtue and will furnish generous vocations among which God will be pleased to choose Apostles for America. It seems to me that thousands of Catholics will yet rally around the cross as around the religious symbol of true liberty. I already foresee a nascent congregation, a humble daughter of the universal Church, flowering in the desert beneath the divine benediction; I assist in spirit in the holy ceremonies of its solemn mysteries. There is the place, I think, that henceforth we will point out to the German Catholics who arrive on these distant shores and who remain in the cities of this country only long enough to obtain the necessary money to acquire a piece of land; it is there that they will be able to earn their living and at the same time preserve their faith and save their souls. Finally I also see there a peaceful retreat for our own Missionaries who, having spent their strength in apostolic works, will be able to settle down to the exercises of their state and the practice of their rule.

Such were my preoccupations at night, and in the morning I found myself happier than if I had enjoyed a long and comfortable sleep. With the dawn we began again as on the previous day our laborious work with the same courage, for as the days passed we felt more exhausted from the hunger and fatigue; we likewise often thought that we would faint entirely, especially when we were violently assailed by the snow, rain, and gales, then it was not only strength which failed; but what to do when the humidity and the cold seized the body and penetrated to the marrow of the bone, when the winds uprooted even the greatest trees *en masse* and the workmen had to risk being crushed in their fall.

For six weeks I lived this truly Indian life, pretty nearly like the Missionaries who live among the savages.

Before my departure from the colony I traced out once more the public roads, as they are marked by the government, so that at present those who oftentimes chance along are able to penetrate into these wastes without danger of getting lost. More than once some Catholics have already strayed for several days under the terrible dread of not being able to get out, and a Protestant minister who went hunting there disappeared forever. One still finds these remarkable forests in great numbers, even in the most civilized regions of the New World; those who wish to found new settlements ought not to plunge into these distant regions since there the prime necessities of life are naturally rarer and the dangers greater.

The land of which I speak is in Pennsylvania, the diocese of Pitsburg [*sic*]; it is fertile, it abounds in streams and springs of which the water is pure and good; the climate, so much like that of Germany, furnishes all that is necessary for a comfortable life; it is therefore a place very well chosen for a colony.

On returning to Baltimore, I found my confrères in the greatest consternation; as I had not been able to write to them during my long absence, they had made a thousand conjectures about my death; they believed it to be certain that having lost myself in the depth of the forests, I had died there of hunger, or had been eaten by the bears; so that I was received by them as one risen from the dead who was even yet only half alive. Believing myself to be in good health, I laughed at their taking me for a walking skeleton; but I soon found out that the fatigues of this trip had so exhausted me that my days of active labor seemed passed. God did not judge that this was yet enough sacrifice; after an illness of three weeks, he so restored my strength as to enable me to exercise again my missionary functions. Please Heaven that I may be able to establish similar colonies at this price! I will gladly consent to lose for each of them not only my health but even life itself.

I have the honor to be, etc.,

Alexandre Czwitkowietz [*sic*], *General Superior of the Redemptorists Missionaries in America.*

82. Bishop Spalding's Impressions of Protestant Revivalism on the Frontier, 1844

NOT long after the first Maryland Catholic families had immigrated to Kentucky in the 1780's that area was overrun by a series of Protestant revivalist meetings that created tumult on the Kentucky frontier for almost a generation. The prime motive for these unusual gatherings has been stated by one historian as follows: "When the godlessness of the backwoodsmen began to be a matter of concern to the missionaries and the circuit riders, drastic measures were used to bring conviction of sin, repentance, and conversion" (Alice Felt Tyler, *Freedom's Ferment* [Minneapolis, 1944], p. 35). The Kentucky Catholics were amazed at what they witnessed among some of their Protestant neighbors, and one of them, Martin J. Spalding (1810–1872) who died as Archbishop of Baltimore, devoted a chapter of one of his early books to a description of the strange phenomenon. Spalding had had a great deal of experience with Protestants as a religious debater and as editor of the *Catholic Advocate,* a weekly paper which he founded in February, 1835. At the time he wrote the book from which the following passage is taken he was vicar-general of the Diocese of Louisville and four years removed from his consecration as Coadjutor Bishop of Louisville. Source: M. J. Spalding, *Sketches of the Early Catholic Missions of Kentucky* (Louisville: B. J. Webb & Brother, 1844), pp. 82–83, 101, 104–106.

Before we proceed farther in our rapid sketch of the early history of the Catholic missions in Kentucky, it may be well to pause a little, in order to survey the contemporary history of the principal Protestant sects. These often came into collision, not only with each other, but with the Catholic church. Differing in almost all else, they united in the principle of hatred of the Catholic religion. And we cannot fully understand the early history of the latter, in our State, without examining the corresponding phases in the history of the former.

Our sketch, confined, as it necessarily must be, to one chapter, will be very brief and summary, embracing only some of the principal facts and features in the history of the most conspicuous among the early sects of Kentucky. We shall state nothing which is not undoubted, and little that cannot be satisfactorily proved from respectable Protestant authority. To show that we mean to be impartial, we will farther remark, that our chief authority will be a work of some antiquity, and of considerable weight among the sects themselves.[1] . . . [Spalding then treats the religious revivals among the Kentucky Protestants in the early years of the nineteenth century.]

This same great revival was truly an "astonishing and precious work" — the most astonishing perhaps, if not the most precious, that ever was witnessed in this world! It marked an era in the Protestant church history of Kentucky. It was on the whole so very singular, that we will be pardoned for dwelling on it in some detail. . . . [He then quotes from the work of the Protestant writer, William Stone,[2] who wrote critically of religious deceptions in *Matthias and His Impostures* (New York, 1835).]

To understand more fully how very "precious and astonishing" this great revival was, we must farther reflect: 1st. That it produced, not

---

[1] The book in question was *An Outline of the History of the Church in the State of Kentucky,* edited by Robert H. Bishop (Lexington, 1824), which contained the memoirs of the Reverend David Rice, a Presbyterian minister, born in Virginia, in 1733, migrated to Kentucky in 1783, and died there is 1816. Spalding's chapter quoted generously from Rice's memoirs.

[2] William L. Stone (1792–1844), journalist and historian, editor of the New York *Commercial Advertiser,* later exposed the frauds of Maria Monk in his volume, *Maria Monk and the Nunnery of the Hôtel Dieu* (New York, 1836).

a mere momentary excitement, but one that lasted for several successive years: 2ndly. That it was not confined to one particular denomination, but, to a greater or less extent, pervaded all: 3rdly. That men of sense and of good judgment in other matters, were often carried away by the same fanaticism which swayed the mob: 4thly. That this fanaticism was as wide-spread, as it was permanent — not being confined to Kentucky, but pervading most of the adjoining States and territories: and 5thly. That though some were found who had good sense enough to detect the imposture, yet they were comparatively few in number, and wholly unable to stay the rushing torrent of fanaticism, even if they had had the moral courage to attempt it.

Such are some of the leading features of a movement in religion, (!) which is perhaps one of the most extraordinary recorded in history, and to which we know of but few parallels, except in some of the fanatical doings of the Anabaptists in Germany, during the first years of their history. The whole matter furnishes one more conclusive evidence of the weakness of the human mind, when left to itself; and one more sad commentary on the Protestant rule of faith. Here we see whole masses of population, spread over a vast territory, boasting too of their enlightenment and Bible-learning, swayed for years by a fanaticism, as absurd as it was blasphemous; and yet believing all this to be the work of the Holy Spirit!! Let Protestants after this talk about Catholic ignorance and superstition! Had Catholics ever played the "fantastic tricks," which were played off by Protestants during these years, we would perhaps never hear the end of it.

The picture drawn above by Col. Stone is not only not exaggerated, but it even falls short of the original, in many of its features. Besides the "exercises" which he mentions, there was also the *jumping* exercise. Spasmodic convulsions, which lasted sometimes for hours, were the usual sequel to the *falling* exercise. Then there were the "exercises" of *screaming,* and *shouting,* and *crying*. A Camp-meeting during that day exhibited the strangest bodily feats, accompanied with the most Babel-like sounds. An eye-witness of undoubted veracity, stated to us that in passing one of the camp-grounds, he noticed a man in the "*barking* exercise," clasping a tree with his arms, and dashing his head against it until it was all besmeared with blood, shouting all the time that he had "treed his Saviour"!! Another eye-witness stated, that in casually passing by a camp in the night, while the exercises were at the highest, he witnessed scenes of too revolting a character even to be alluded to here.

One of the most remarkable features, perhaps, of these "exercises" is, the apparently well authenticated fact, that many fell into them, by a kind of sympathy, almost in spite of themselves, and some even positively against their own will! Some who visited the meetings to laugh at the proceedings, sometimes caught the contagion themselves. There seems to have then existed in Kentucky a kind of mental and moral epidemic — a short of contagious frenzy — which spread rapidly from one to another.

Yet the charm was not so strong that it could not be broken, as the following incident, related to us by a highly intelligent Protestant gentleman, clearly proves. Some young ladies of his acquaintance came from one of these meetings to pass the night at his father's house. They were laboring under great nervous excitement, and, in the course of the evening, began to *jerk* most violently. The father, one of the most intelligent men in Kentucky, severely rebuked them, and told them bluntly, that he would "have no such behavior as this in his house." The reproof was effectual, and the *jerking* spirit was exorcised! . . .

83. Samuel Mazzuchelli, O.P., on the Catholic Temperance Societies, 1844

ALTHOUGH the evangelical trends in American Protestantism of the early nineteenth century had little in common with American Catholicism, except, perhaps, during the preaching of the parish mission, they shared an interest in the eradication of the evils of intemperance. Beginning in the late 1830's Catholic temperance societies spread rapidly. The American tour (June, 1849–November, 1851) of the famous Irish Capuchin temperance crusader, Theobald Mathew (1790–1856), gave them fresh impetus, and when a national union of these groups was formed at Baltimore in February, 1872, the meeting drew delegates from over 200 societies. One of those who had great admiration for the work of the temperance societies was the remarkable missionary, Samuel Charles Mazzuchelli (1806–1864). This Italian-born Dominican came to the United States in 1828 and for nearly forty years labored tirelessly in behalf of the Indians of the Middle West, in establishing parishes for the new settlers in Iowa, Illinois, and Wisconsin, in founding a teaching sisterhood of Dominican nuns, to say nothing of building the bishop's residence in Dubuque, designing the first capitol at Iowa City, and serving as chaplain to the first territorial legislature of Wisconsin. In 1843 he made his only visit home to Milan, the city of his birth, and there in the following year he published a volume of memoirs of his American experiences with a view to acquainting Italians with the progress of the Church in the United States and of preserving certain documentary materials for its history. Mazzuchelli's appreciation of the American Catholic temperance societies was deep and sincere, even if it was too optimistic about the permanency of the results obtained. Source: *Memoirs Historical and Edifying of a Missionary Apostolic of the Order of Saint Dominic among Various Indian Tribes and among the Catholics and Protestants in the United States of America,* translated by Sister Mary Benedicta Kennedy, O.S.D. (Chicago: W. F. Hall Printing Co., 1915), pp. 282–284; copyright The Dominican Sisters of Sinsinawa, Wisconsin.

Very few persons in the United States cultivate the vine or make wine to any extent, so this beverage forms one of the objects of commerce with France, Spain and Italy, while the distance, imposition of duties, etc., render it not only costly, but also very scarce. But to supply the lack of the vine in America, extensive use is made of strong spirits extracted from Indian corn, which grows there in prodigious quantities and can be had at a very low price. Many of the people are addicted to the abuse of this strong liquor to such a degree as to fall unhappy victims of intoxication.

A great number of the emigrants from Ireland, notwithstanding the Faith, the generosity, the honesty, the industry and all the other virtues that so eminently distinguish the race, were often too weak upon this one point, giving themselves up in bondage to the vice of intemperance. The more zealous among the Protestants, especially the Presbyterians, took occasion from this to hurl bitterest reproaches and invectives against the Catholic Church, which they accused of being far from the Evangelical sanctity she professed, while she held within her own bosom so many leading scandalous lives. But God who often makes use of His very enemies as instruments to carry out the inscrutable designs of His grace, raised up our far-famed Father Matthew [*sic*] in Ireland to banish the demon of drunkenness from that island, and to enroll millions of his compatriots in the Temperance Societies by virtue of which they pledged themselves to taste no beverage that could intoxicate.

The Irish who comprise more than half of the Catholics of the United States, followed the example of their brethren in Europe, and Temperance Societies were founded in every city and village of the land. It could be asserted now that these children of that Saint Patrick to whom Ireland owes her conversion to the Faith are now with very few exceptions models of temperance. The Catholic Clergy exerted themselves to the utmost in America, to bring about a change so marvelous and so necessary to the advancement of the Faith; the Faith that had retrograded among many Catholics through the vice of intemperance. A number of the Bishops and nearly all of the Priests are zealous members of this Society. . . .

If the tree is to be judged by its fruits, there is no doubt as to the Religious influence exerted by the Temperance Society, — in truth we must ascribe thereto these wonderful effects, the conversion of a great number of sinners hardened in vice for years, who approached the tribunal of penance only after they had promised to give up entirely the use of intoxicating liquors. From the year 1839 when the Societies had become established in the various Missions recorded in these Memoirs, piety actually made visible progress from day to day, in proportion as the virtue of Temperance won its blessed victories among the people; peace and plenty reigned in the families, Catholicity won the respect and reverence of its very enemies, and the Faith spread among the more sincere of those outside the Church. Many of the Catholic Irish abandoned entirely the dangerous traffic in intoxicating drink and sought more honorable means of subsistence. . . .

84. A Report to the Ludwig-Missionsverein on Catholicism in Wisconsin, April 23, 1845

AMONG the most important agencies for financial assistance to the American Church was the Ludwig-Missionsverein, founded at Munich in December, 1838, under the patronage of King Louis I of Bavaria, from whom it derived its name. The special objects of this missionary society's benefactions in the United States were the German Catholic immigrants. No center of German Catholic activity was more prominent than the Diocese of Milwaukee which had been erected on November 28, 1843, and which included the entire state of Wisconsin with its 54,715 square miles. When John Martin Henni (1805–1881), the first Bishop of Milwaukee, arrived in his see city in May, 1844, he found only four priests to care for the 15,000 Catholics scattered throughout the state. The fact that by 1850 there were over 60,000 Catholics in Wisconsin with forty-three priests will give some idea of the rapidity of growth of the See of Milwaukee. Between 1838 and 1921 the Ludwig-Missionsverein gave nearly a million dollars to the American missions and the Diocese of Milwaukee was among its principal beneficiaries. Less than a year after his arrival Henni sent a report on religious conditions to the Reverend Joseph Mueller, general manager of the Munich society, in which he included some interesting observations on the secular scene, even to anticipating the St. Lawrence Waterway. Source: *Salesianum,* XXXVII (April, 1942), 82–85, translated by Augustine C. Breig and edited by Peter Leo Johnson.

Milwaukee, April 23rd, 1845.

I received your letter of February 17th. You may imagine how anxiously I was waiting for it for some time. I am very grateful to you for having released at least to a certain extent the suspense I was in and still partly am in on account of some intervening "difficulties" as you remark. In the meanwhile you bid me to be of good cheer. In fact I am, especially since your esteemed letter assures me of your good will towards me and also of the sincere efforts of you and of the rest of the friends in Munich in behalf of my cause, in which no one can be indifferent who has the welfare of the church in this part of America at heart. This holds good especially as far as I am concerned, for I more than others must realize the importance of this cause. I shall therefore very anxiously wait for further developments. In the meanwhile I shall leave the matter entirely to God and to the efforts and prudence of my friends in Munich.

Complying with your advice I have sent a petition directly to the board of directors, as enclosure shows. But since I presumed that the lengthy report on my diocese and my mission journeys, especially among the Indians, which I have sent at the same time to Vienna and Einsiedeln[1] and also to the Catholics of Bavaria, would become known, I have purposely avoided all repetitions and mentioned only the most pressing needs. However I did not dare to ask for a definite sum fearing that such a request might be misinterpreted by some at least. I would prefer that one or the other of my benefactors would suggest this to the board of directors.

With regard to the German-English seminary I have nothing else to add than that the proposed plan appeals to me more day by day. The establishment of such an institute in Bavaria itself should certainly not be undertaken in order to spare the young men the slur of being emissaries because it is this slur the sly bigots yell continuously into our ears. They do not write any more so strongly against the truths of our religion because here they have overcome the strongest prejudices perhaps more than in Germany. But now these people accuse us as being anti-republicans, dangerous to the state. Nothing more than this lie arouses the American, who is generally broad minded, to follow without hesitation justice and truth wherever he finds them. Just this political lie especially invites the American of all

[1] The Leopoldinen-Stiftung of Vienna, founded in April, 1829, was the Austrian counterpart to the Ludwig-Missionsverein. The Abbey of Our Lady of the Hermits at Einsiedeln, Switzerland, was generous in its help to German Catholic missions abroad; it was from Einsiedeln that several Benedictine monks founded the future St. Meinrad's Archabbey in southern Indiana in March, 1854.

classes to investigate our teachings and principles; they are the first ones who follow their conviction. For this reason, to be honest, I like them better than all other Protestants. Lately I received Dr. Hunt an excellent physician into the church. Several others are taking instructions. A good Catholic priest is certainly more respected than the numerous preachers. In spite of my poverty as bishop every one of our outstanding state officials wished to get acquainted with me.

At present I am about to arrange an old frame building for a temporary seminary. I have three seminarists, a German, an Irishman and an Italian, the latter of whom has studied for some time in America, and upon whom I will soon confer major orders. Three other clerics I expect towards the end of August from the Jesuit college in Cincinnati and a fourth one from Montreal, Canada.

Good Father Boeswald[2] is still waiting for a "German bishop" to carry out his grand plan as he lately wrote to Father Heiss.[3] Father Heiss whom I did not keep in the dark about my plans regarding the seminary made him acquainted with it. In the meanwhile I endeavor to get the Rev. Boeswald here if our plan should become a reality. I believe that he would come if he should realize that Covington has not more Germans than Milwaukee. South of the Ohio (river) among the Negroes Germans will never settle. Their main settlements in fact are in the northwestern states. Yes, the majority of the domiciled Germans are there; there only the poor farmer from Europe can acquire the desired land at a low price. It is also easier for him to come to Milwaukee from New York than to Cincinnati. Besides only two or three years may elapse till the English-shipping Well and canal will connect Quebec with Lake Erie. Then ships from Liverpool (and from the Rhein and Trieste, if you wish) shall enter the harbor of Milwaukee. Do not smile dear friend. The time when this shall happen is not far off.

However I do not wish that your box packed with the different church utensils should wait till then. Unfortunately I am not acquainted with anybody on one of the seaports to whom you could send the goods intended for me. For the present I have to ask to inquire [*sic*] of the Liguorians [Redemptorists] who certainly have shipping agents everywhere, how and to what place to send the goods. Even in New

---

[2] Charles Boeswald was pastor of Immaculate Conception Church in Louisville.

[3] The Bavarian-born Michael Heiss (1818–1890) was pastor of St. Mary's Church, Covington, Kentucky, when he volunteered to accompany Henni to Milwaukee in 1844. He later became the first rector of St. Francis Seminary, Milwaukee, 1856–1868; first Bishop of La Crosse, 1868–1880; and Henni's successor in the See of Milwaukee.

York their society might be the surest agent also for me. I shall inform the Rev. Rumpler of this.[4] But I kindly ask you not to send my goods with any belonging to them.

With joy we are looking for the arrival of the Rev. Schraudenbach.[5] Should you be able to find one or the other priest or theological student, I would be very well pleased. I need also two priests who speak French very well, for this reason I shall write to the bishop of Strassburg. Last fall I received at last from Lyons 15,000 francs. What help this was you may imagine. Perhaps you would do well to order for several 100 florins some vestments from the factory you spoke of. Should they be cheap and come up to our expectations some more could be ordered. Could you perhaps get a suitable mitre for me? For all this I authorize you to handle in my name the money granted by the board of directors.

We are informed that Europe had a very severe winter. We had hardly any snow. In fact I have never lived through a more pleasant winter. No doubt the climate here is the healthiest in the United States especially for Europeans. People who come sickly from southern regions grow here healthy and strong. I have also to confess that the spiritual life here is a comfort to me. Since the enlargement of my frame cathedral and a better arrangement of the divine services an excellent spirit manifests itself around me, even among the Protestants.

I have been informed that Miss Linder of Basle was received into the church and that she is living in Munich. Should this be the case kindly give her my best regards and tell her that that I still gratefully remember her kindness towards me. She gave me a beautiful painting representing Christ. Unfortunately I had to leave it at Cincinnati where it adorns a side altar in Holy Trinity church. If Miss Linder still devotes her time to painting I would like to ask her for a picture of St. Francis de Sales. Dear friend in doing so use your own good judgment.

May God bestow his blessing on us and grant that our friends in Munich, you yourself and canon Speth, may work for a long time for the distant missions.

---

[4] The Redemptorists first came to the United States in June, 1832, from Austria and all through the nineteenth century they continued to be one of the leading religious congregations to devote its labors to the German immigrants. Gabriel Rumpler, C.SS.R., was pastor of St. Alphonsus Church in Baltimore at this time.

[5] Charles Schraudenbach was pastor of St. Ignatius Church, Racine, Wisconsin.

85. Consecration of the Cathedral of St. Peter in Chains, Cincinnati, November 2, 1845

ONE of the evidences of the marked growth of American Catholicism in the Middle West in the mid-nineteenth century was the improved quality in both design and materials of the church buildings erected for divine services. Among the fastest growing of the western sees was Cincinnati where by 1845 there were an estimated 65,000 Catholics in a diocese served by sixty-six priests. In 1840 Bishop John B. Purcell (1800–1883) began construction of the new Cathedral of St. Peter in Chains, an edifice which was described a century later as "one of the handsomest and most monumental of Greek Revival churches" (Talbot Hamlin, *Greek Revival Architecture in America* [New York, 1944], p. 285). Hamlin stated that the architect was probably Henry Walters. The cathedral was consecrated on Sunday, November 2, 1845, by Samuel Eccleston, S.S., fifth Archbishop of Baltimore, in the presence of eight bishops and a large gathering of clergy and laity. The unusual ceremony for those days was described in Cincinnati's Catholic weekly newspaper, of which Father Edward Purcell, brother of the bishop, was editor, in an editorial entitled "Consecration of St. Peter's Cathedral." Source: *Catholic Telegraph,* November 6, 1845.

This long expected and gratifying ceremony took place on last Sunday. The clergy of the diocese had been in retreat for eight days previous, under the spiritual direction of V. Rev. Dr. Spalding[1] of Kentucky, and with very few exceptions, all the English Catholics of Cincinnati received the Holy Communion in the old Cathedral, to prepare their souls for celebrating with proper dispositions, their joyous entrance into their new and magnificent Church. The day was chilly and damp, but the crowds in attendance were very great, and the utmost decorum was observed by all, both outside as well as in the interior of the building. The most Rev. Dr. Eccleston, Arch-Bishop of Baltimore was the consecrating Prelate; when the procession entered the Church bearing the relics, the following Bishops attended their metropolitan, The Rt. Rev. Dr. Flaget, Bishop of Louisville; Rt. Rev. Dr. Portier, Bishop of Mobile; Rt. Rev. Dr. Chabrat, Co-adjutor Bishop of Louisville; Rt. Rev. Dr. Henni, Bishop of Milwaukie [*sic*]; Rt. Rev. Dr. Hailandiere, Bishop of Vincennes; Rt. Rev. Dr. Miles, Bishop of Nashville; Rt. Rev. Dr. McClosky [*sic*], Coadjutor Bishop of New York and Rt. Rev. Dr. Purcell of Cincinnati — being altogether nine Bishops, eight of whom had left their distant homes, moved by

---

[1] Martin J. Spalding (1810–1872) succeeded Flaget as Bishop of Louisville in 1850 and died as seventh Archbishop of Baltimore.

the Spirit of charity and kindness, to assist at the consecration. Sixty five clergymen, mostly from Ohio and Kentucky, took part in the services of the day, also the Seminarians of the diocese and Scholastics of the Society of Jesus; all of whom found room in the ample Sanctuary. Amongst them were the Provincials of the Dominican and Jesuit Orders in the West. The services of the Consecration were concluded about noon, having lasted nearly four hours, when the High Mass was celebrated by the Bishop of Mobile. The sermon was an appropriate and polished discourse, delivered with grace and emphasis by Bishop McClosky.[2] His text was from the eighty-third Psalm. "How lovely are thy tabernacles, O Lord of Hosts! my soul longeth and fainteth for the courts of the Lord. . . . For the sparrow hath found herself a house, and the turtle a nest for herself where she may lay her young ones: Thy altars O Lord of Hosts, my King and my God." In the evening the Rev. Mr. Hayden[3] addressed the audience in a very sound and beautiful discourse on Faith. During the ensuing day discourses were delivered by Rev. Mr. McGill[4] and Dr. Spalding of Kentucky, the reputation of both attracting large crowds who were pleased and instructed. Thus, after more than five years labor, the Catholics of Cincinnati have crowned their hopes by the erection and consecration of a Cathedral, which no one can behold without expressing their admiration of its beauty, proportions and durability.

86. Boniface Wimmer Outlines the Future of the Benedictine Order in the United States, November 8, 1845

THE origin of the work of the monks of St. Benedict in the United States was owed to Boniface Wimmer (1809–1887), one of the first five novices to be received at the Abbey of Metten after its restoration in 1830. This Bavarian-born religious began dreaming about an American foundation for the spiritual care of German immigrants as early as 1843. In 1845 Wimmer discussed the American situation with a fellow countryman, Peter Henry Lemcke (1796–1882), then pastor of a congregation at Carrolltown in western Pennsylvania, on the latter's visit to Munich. He likewise spoke with Canon Josef Salzbacher (1790–1867) of Vienna who had been in the United States three years before, and with the Vienna-born Frederick de

[2] John McCloskey (1810–1885) became second Archbishop of New York in 1864 and in 1875 the first cardinal of the United States.

[3] This priest was probably Thomas Heyden (1798–1870) who for years was pastor at Bedford, Pennsylvania, and a friend of Bishop Purcell.

[4] John McGill (1809–1872) became the third bishop of Richmond in 1850.

Held (1799–1881), provincial of the Belgian province, to which the Redemptorists' American missions were subject. It was a period when there was a great deal of criticism in German and Austrian Catholic circles about the money they gave through the Ludwig-Missionsverein and Leopoldinen Stiftung for their compatriots in the United States, being channeled off to non-German projects by Irish-American bishops. In answer to reports brought back by men like Salzbacher and de Held, Wimmer composed the document that follows and had it published anonymously. Fired by his zeal for the missions in the New World, and having secured the permission of his superiors, Wimmer set out in July, 1846, with four ecclesiastical students and fourteen young laymen who desired to embrace the Benedictine life in the United States. Accepting the offer of Michael O'Connor (1810–1872), first Bishop of Pittsburgh, to have his little community settle on some church lands in Westmoreland County, he invested his eighteen companions with the religious habit on October 24, 1846, and thus inaugurated his great work. Wimmer opened a college and a seminary in 1848 at St. Vincent's Priory and in August, 1855, Pope Pius IX granted his petition and raised his foundation to the rank of an abbey and at the same time made Wimmer president of the newly founded American congregation of Benedictines. During his forty years of unceasing labors he sent out missionaries from St. Vincent's who founded six future abbeys: St. John's in Minnesota (1856), St. Benedict's in Kansas (1857), Belmont in North Carolina (1876), St. Bernard's in Alabama (1876), St. Procopius in Illinois (1885), and Holy Cross in Colorado (1886), besides numerous smaller missions in parishes in twenty-five states which by 1885 were ministering to over 100,000 souls, especially among German, Irish, and Italian immigrants. By the time he died Wimmer had more than fulfilled the dream about which he had written over forty years before, in a document which is in many ways the charter of the American Benedictines since the aims and methods it embodied were consistently and successfully developed in the United States. Source: Augsburg *Postzeitung,* November 8, 1845. This document was printed as an appendix in Colman J. Barry, O.S.B., *Worship and Work. St. John's Abbey and University, 1856–1956* (Collegeville, 1956), pp. 345–351.

Every Catholic who cherishes his faith must take a deep interest in missionary labors; but religion as well as patriotism demands that every German Catholic should take a special interest in the missions of America. To us it cannot be a matter of indifference how our countrymen are situated in America. I, for my part, have not been able to read the various and generally sad reports on the desolate condition of Germans beyond the ocean without deep compassion and a desire to do something to alleviate their pitiable condition. Thus, I have given much thought to the question of how they might be practically assisted. It is not difficult to understand what should be done — more German-speaking priests should be found laboring for the spiritual welfare of our countrymen in America. The only question is how to get priests and what kind of priests will do the work most successfully. The answer to the second question will also give the solution for the first. I do not wish to offend anyone, but my opinion is that secular priests are not the best adapted for missionary labors. History shows that the Church has not availed herself of their services to any great extent in missionary undertakings. I do not mean to say that a secular priest cannot labor effectually within a limited territory in America, for there are many who labor successfully even at the present day. But they cannot satisfy themselves. They are in great danger of becoming careless and worldly-minded. I cannot agree with Dr. Salzbacher when he says that the spiritual needs of our countrymen can be provided by perambulating missionaries, who go about like the Wandering Jew from forest to forest, from hut to hut; for unless such a missionary be a *Saint* not much of the spiritual man would remain in him, and even then by such transient visits not much lasting good could be accomplished. The missionary, more than any other priest, stands in need of spiritual renewal from time to time, consolation and advice in trials and difficulties. He must, therefore, have some place where he can find such assistance: this may be given by his bishop but he will find it more securely in a religious community — in the midst of his confrères.

He should also have a home to receive him in his old age or when he is otherwise incapacitated for missionary labors; he should have no worldly cares, otherwise he might neglect or even forget his own and others' spiritual welfare. All this can be had only in a religious community. For this reason, therefore, religious are better adapted to missionary work than secular priests. In a community the experiences of the individual become common property; all have a common interest, stand together and have the same object in view. A vacancy caused by death or otherwise can be filled more readily and having fewer temporal cares, they can devote themselves more exclusively to the spiritual interests of themselves and others. Thus, all other things being equal, a religious priest in a community should be able to work more effectively on the missions than the secular priest who stands alone.

The next question is: What religious Order is most adapted for the American missions, not to convert the native Indians but to provide for the spiritual necessities of German immigrants?

As far as I know the only Religious in the strict sense of the word now found in America are the Jesuits and Redemptorists. The missionaries of the Middle Ages, the Benedictines, Dominicans and Franciscans are not yet represented in the New World, except by a few individuals who do not live in monasteries.[1] The Jesuits devote their energies principally to teaching in colleges; their students are mostly from the higher classes of society and many of them belong to Protestant families. Many Jesuits are also doing excellent work among the Indians, and others have charge of congregations in cities near their colleges. But while they accomplish so much in their sphere of labors, they can do little for Germans, because few of them speak their language. The Redemptorists are doing noble work for our countrymen in the States: in cities and thickly settled country districts they have large congregations, and also do what they can for others as travelling missionaries. Some secular priests likewise go about among the scattered Catholics doing good, but they naturally and necessarily concentrate in cities where there is a large Catholic population.

We see, therefore, that much is being done in America; very much, indeed, when we consider the small band of priests and the difficulties under which they labor. But as yet nothing has been done for the stability of the work, no provision has been made for an increase of German-speaking priests, to meet the growing demand for missionary laborers. It is not difficult to see that secular priests, whose labors extend over a district larger than a diocese, can do nothing to secure reinforcements to their own number. But why have the Redemptorists and Jesuits not accomplished more in this line? By his vows neither the Jesuit nor the Redemptorist is bound to any particular place, but he must always be prepared to leave his present position at the command of his superiors, and may also request, if not demand, his removal for weighty reasons. This has many advantages, but for America it seems to me also to have disadvantages. For the successor of the one who has been removed will require a long time to become acquainted with all the circumstances with which his predecessor was familiar, and even the uncertainty as to how long he will remain at any particular place will be an obstacle in his way. Moreover, the fact that Jesuits generally receive only the children of richer families, many of whom are Protestants, into their institutions, because they depend upon them for their sustenance, and that the Redemptorists are by their statutes required to devote themselves to missionary work, and can, therefore, not be expected to take charge of seminaries, gives us no reason to hope that the spiritual wants of Americans, particularly of German-

[1] Wimmer was unaware that Edward D. Fenwick, O.P. (1768–1832), first Bishop of Cincinnati, had opened St. Rose Priory near Springfield, Kentucky, as the first Dominican convent in the United States as early as December, 1806.

Americans will be provided for by native German-speaking priests. And in case the mission societies of Europe should unexpectedly be rendered incapable of supplying money or reinforcements in priests, the situation would become even more serious. But even supposing that everything remains as it is, we cannot hope to have an efficient supply of priests as long as we have no means of securing a native clergy for the United States of America. For the number of those who are educated at Alt-Oetting[2] or elsewhere in Germany is not in proportion to the continually increasing emigration to America, not to speak of the natural increase of Germans in America itself. Jesuits and Redemptorists are, therefore, doing noble work in America and their number should be increased as much as possible; but they will scarcely be able to remove the chief cause of the deficiency of German-speaking priests. We need not speak of the Dominicans and Franciscans; there are very few German Dominicans, and the present social condition of America seems not to call for Mendicant Friars.

We now come to the Benedictines, who are not as yet represented in the United States. In my opinion they are the most competent to relieve the great want of priests in America. In support of my opinion I will adduce some facts: but I must again state that I have not the remotest intention of belittling the efforts and successes of other religious Orders; on the contrary, I am desirous of seeing them labor in the same field, side by side with the Benedictines.

History abundantly proves:

1. That we owe the conversion of England, Germany, Denmark, Sweden, Norway, Hungary, and Poland almost exclusively to the Benedictines, and that in the remaining parts of Europe Christendom is deeply indebted to them.
2. That the conversion of these countries was not transient but lasting and permanent.
3. That this feature must be ascribed to the fact that the Benedictines are men of stability; they are not wandering monks; they acquire lands and bring them under cultivation and become thoroughly affiliated to the country and people to which they belong, and receive their recruits from the district in which they have established themselves.
4. That the Benedictine Order by its Rule is so constituted that

[2] Wimmer was doubtless referring here to the seminary for candidates to the diocesan priesthood at Altötting, permission for which he had received from King Ludwig I of Bavaria. Altötting was the site of a popular shrine to our Lady where Wimmer had served as an assistant priest for a short time.

> it can very readily adapt itself to all times and circumstances. The contemplative and practical are harmoniously blended; agriculture, manual labor, literature, missionary work, education, were drawn into the circle of activity which St. Benedict placed before his disciples. Hence they soon felt at home in all parts of Europe and the same could be done in America.

When we consider North America as it is today, we can see at a glance that there is no other country in the world which offers greater opportunities for the establishment and spread of the Benedictine Order, no country that is so much like our old Europe was. There are found immense forests, large uncultivated tracts of land in the interior, most fertile lands which command but a nominal price; often for miles and miles no village is to be seen, not to speak of cities. In country districts no schools, no churches are to be found. The German colonists are scattered, uncultured, ignorant, hundreds of miles away from the nearest German-speaking priest, for, practically, they can make their homes where they please. There are no good books, no Catholic papers, no holy pictures. The destitute and unfortunate have no one to offer them a hospitable roof, the orphans naturally become the victims of vice and irreligion — in a word, the conditions in America today are like those of Europe 1000 years ago, when the Benedictine Order attained its fullest development and effectiveness by its wonderful adaptability and stability.

Of course, the Benedictine Order would be required to adapt itself again to circumstances and begin anew. To acquire a considerable tract of land in the interior of the country, upon which to found a monastery, would not be very difficult; to bring under cultivation at least a portion of the land and to erect the most necessary buildings would give employment for a few years to the first Benedictine colony, which should consist of at least two or three priests and ten to fifteen brothers skilled in the most necessary trades.

Once the colony is self-supporting, which could be expected in about two years, it should begin to expand so that the increased number of laboring hands might also increase the products and revenues to be derived from the estate. A printing and lithographing establishment would also be very desirable.

Since the Holy Rule prescribes for all, not only manual labor and the chanting of the Divine Office, but also that the monks should devote several hours a day to study, this time could be used by the Fathers to instruct the Brothers thoroughly in arithmetic, German grammar, etc., thereby fitting them to teach school, to give catechetical instruction and in general to assist in teaching children as well as grown persons.

Such a monastery would from the very start be of great advantage to German settlers, at least to those who would live near it. They would have a place where they could depend upon hearing Mass on Sundays and hear a sermon in their own language; they would also have a place where they could always be sure to find a priest at home to hear their confessions, to bless their marriages, to baptize their children and to administer the last sacraments to the sick if called in time.

Occasionally the Superior might send out even the Brothers two by two to hunt up fallen-away Catholics, to instruct children for their first Communion etc. All subsequent monasteries that might be established from the mother house would naturally exercise the same influence.

So far, the services rendered by the Benedictines would not be extraordinary; any other priests or religious could do the same, except that they would not likely be able to support themselves without assistance from Europe; whereas a community of Benedictines, when once firmly established would soon become self-sustaining.

But such a monastery if judiciously located would not long remain isolated; all reports from America inform us that the German immigrants are concentrating themselves in places where churches have been erected or where a German-speaking priest has taken up his residence. This would also be found, and to a greater extent, if there were a monastery somewhere with a good school. In a short time a large German population would be found near the monastery, just as in the Middle Ages, villages, towns and cities sprang up near Benedictine abbeys. Then the monks could expect a large number of children for their school, and in the course of time, as the number of priests increases, a college with a good Latin course could be opened. They would not be dependent upon the tuition fee of the students for their support, which they could draw from the farm and the missions (though these would not be a source of much income in the beginning). Thus they could devote their energies to the education of the poorer classes of boys who could pay little or nothing, and since these boys would daily come in contact with the priests and other monks, it could scarcely be otherwise but that many of them would develop a desire of becoming priests or even religious. I am well aware that to many readers these hopes and expectations will appear too sanguine, since all efforts at securing a native American clergy have hitherto failed so signally. But we must remember that the annals of the missions as well as the oral reports of priests who have labored in America, inform us that these efforts were more theoretical than practical, that there was a desire of making such efforts, but they they were not really made, and that those which were really made were more or less restricted to the English-speaking clergy, and that in general there were neither sufficient means nor sufficient teachers to train a native German-speaking clergy. It is said that the young American is not inclined to devote himself to the sacred ministry because it is so easy for him to secure a wife and home; that the American has nothing in view but to heap up the riches of this world; that fathers need their sons on the farms or in the workshops and, therefore, do not care to see them study. But, let me ask, is it not the same here in Europe? Are the rich always pleased when their sons study for the priesthood? Are all Germans in America well-to-do or rich? Are they not as a rule the very poorest and to a certain extent the menials of the rest? Moreover, is the first thought of a boy directed to matrimony? Is it any wonder that he should show no inclination for the priesthood when he sees a priest scarcely once a year; when divine services are held in churches which resemble hovels rather than churches, without pomp and ceremony, when the priest has to divest himself of his priestly dignity, often travels on horse-back, in disguise, looking more like a drummer than a priest, when the boy sees nothing in the life of a priest but sacrifice, labor and fatigue?

But all this would become quite different if boys could come in daily contact with priests, if they received instructions from them, if the priest could appear to advantage, better dressed and better housed than the ordinary settler, if young men could learn from observation to realize and appreciate the advantages of a community life, if they could learn to understand that while the life of a priest requires self-denial and sacrifice, his hopes of a great reward are also well grounded. Yes, I do not doubt but that hundreds, especially of the lower classes, would prefer to spend their lives in well regulated monasteries in suitable and reasonable occupations, than to gain a meager livelihood by incessant hard labor in forest regions. Let us remember that here in Bavaria from the year 740 to the year 788 not less than 40 Benedictine monasteries were founded and the communities were composed almost entirely of natives from the free classes, who had enjoyed the advantages of freedom in the world and could have chosen the married state without any difficulty or hindrance. Why should we not reasonably expect the same results in the United States where the conditions are so similar?

But such a monastery in North America would not draw its recruits exclusively from the surrounding country, but also from the great number of boys, who either during the voyage or soon after their arrival in America lose their parents and thereby become helpless and forsaken. An institution, in which such unfortunate children could find a home, would undoubtedly be a great blessing for that country. And where could this be done more easily than in Benedictine monasteries as described above, in which young boys could not only attend school, but also do light work on the farm or in the workshops and according to their talents and vocation become priests or at least educated Christians and good citizens. Surely, many of these would gladly join the community as brothers or priests, and thus repay the monastery for the trouble of educating them.

In this way a numerous religious clergy could soon be secured, and then some of the Fathers might be sent out to visit those Catholics who scarcely ever see a priest; occasionally at least they might preach the word of God and bring the consolations of religion even to those who live at a great distance from the monastery; small congregations could be established, and the seminary could soon furnish a goodly number of the secular clergy.

But where could the Benedictines be found to establish such a monastery in North America, and where are the necessary means for such an undertaking? The writer is informed that there are several Fathers in the Benedictine Order here in Bavaria who would gladly go upon such a mission, and with regard to Brothers there would be no difficulty whatever; within a few years not less than 200 good men have applied for admission into one of our monasteries. It is a well known fact that of those who are studying for the priesthood many are joining the Redemptorist Order simply because it offers them the hope of becoming missionaries in America.

The necessary funds could easily be supplied by the Louis Mission Society.[3] Bavaria annually pays 100,000 florins into the treasury of this Society. Would it be unfair to devote one tenth of this sum to the establishment of monasteries in America, especially since just now hundreds of our own nationality are seeking homes in the United States, and consequently the money contributed would be used to

[3] The Ludwig-Missionsverein was founded in Munich in December, 1838, to assist German Catholic emigrants. Between 1842 and 1922 the society contributed $886,504.52 to the Catholic missions in the United States.

further the interests of Germans in general and our countrymen in particular? Could a better use of such contributions be made or could anything appeal more loudly to our national patriotism? Is it right that we should continually look after the interests of strangers and forget our own countrymen? Moreover, whatever would be done for the Germans would advance the well-being of the entire Church in America. We must not stifle our feelings of patriotism. The Germans, we hear it often enough, lose their national character in the second or third generation, they also lose their language, because like a little rivulet they disappear in the mighty stream of the Anglo-American population in the States. Is this not humiliating for us Germans? Would this sad condition of affairs continue if here and there a German center were established, to which the stream of emigration from our country could be systematically directed, if German instruction and sermons were given by priests going forth from these centers, if German books, papers and periodicals were distributed among the people, if German boys could receive a German education and training, which would make themselves felt in wider circles?

Let us, therefore, no longer build air castles for our countrymen in America. Let us provide for their religious interests, then their domestic affairs will take care of themselves. Benedictine monasteries of the old style are the best means of checking the downward tendencies of our countrymen in social, political and religious matters. Let Jesuits and Redemptorists labor side by side with the Benedictines; there is room enough for all and plenty of work. If every Religious Order develops a healthy activity within its sphere, the result will be doubly sure and great. North America will no longer depend upon Europe for its spiritual welfare, and the day may come when America will repay us just as England, converted by the Benedictines, repaid the continent of Europe.

87. The Inauguration of the First Conference of the Society of St. Vincent de Paul in the United States, November 20, 1845

ONE of the most important agencies of private charity in the United States is the Society of St. Vincent de Paul. Founded in Paris in 1833 by Frédéric Ozanam (1813–1853), a young professor of literature in the Sorbonne, it had an immediate appeal and rapidly spread throughout the Catholic world.

Through John Timon, C.M. (1797–1867), first Bishop of Buffalo, who witnessed its beneficent results on a visit to France, the idea was brought to St. Louis while Timon was still working in Missouri. Father Ambrose J. Heim (1807–1854), a French-born assistant pastor in the old cathedral parish, took it up and won the immediate support of a small group of zealous laymen who held their first meeting in the schoolroom of the old cathedral on November 20, 1845. A week later on November 27 a second meeting — the minutes of which are given below — worked out the details as to the procedure they would employ in relieving the city's Catholic poor. From these humble beginnings the society fanned out across the country until today it is a recognized feature of numerous parishes and embraces thousands of Catholic laymen in its membership. Source: Minute Book, St. Louis Old Cathedral Conference, St. Vincent de Paul Society, p. 26, quoted in Daniel T. McColgan, *A Century of Charity. The First One Hundred Years of the Society of St. Vincent de Paul in the United States* (Milwaukee: The Bruce Publishing Co., 1951), I, 79–80.

At a second meeting of the St. Vincent de Paul Society held at the Cathedral School Room on the Thursday evening of the 27th ultimo, the minutes of the preceding meeting were read by the Secretary and approved.

Dr. Linton[1] on the part of the committee appointed to wait upon the right Reverend Bishop[2] to apprize him of the organization and purposes of the Society read a letter received by the committee from him fully approving of the organization and objects of it, being designed to relieve and alleviate the suffering and wants of those in a poor and destitute condition during the inclement season of the year.

The Visitors selected at the previous meeting to ascertain the particular cases in the neighborhood of their respective Parishes requiring immediate attention and assistance on the part of the Society, made their reports, in which several cases of suffering and destitution were portrayed that appealed thoroughly to the liberal and charitable feelings of the meeting.

On motion it was resolved and carried that a collection be immediately taken up in furtherance of the objects had in view in the formation of the society, in order to place funds in the hands of the visitors whereby individual suffering for want of means may be relieved to the extent at least of the means placed by the Society at the disposal of the visiting committee.

The collection amounted to the sum of twenty dollars forty seven

[1] Moses L. Linton (1808–1872), first president of the society, was a convert to Catholicism and a professor of medicine in St. Louis University.

[2] Peter Richard Kenrick (1806–1896) was the second bishop and first Archbishop of St. Louis.

and a half cents which added to the sum collected at the previous meeting, made the total sum of thirty seven dollars seventeen and a half cents was placed in the hands of the Treasurer.

On motion it was resolved and carried unanimously that half the funds collected should be equally divided among the different Parishes, giving to each an equal proportion: and that one-fourth be applied to the immediate relief of the cases just mentioned to the meeting, and the remaining fourth be kept on hand for contingency.

A motion was made and carried that a committee of three be appointed to draft a letter of communication to the parent Society in Paris, whereupon the President appointed the following gentlemen as that Committee — Judge Mullanphy,[3] Judge Manning, Revd. Mr. Heim.

A motion was made and carried that the fourth of the funds for present distribution be numerically divided among the visitors present who were acquainted with the locality where the distress was to be found whereupon the President appointed the following gentlemen as distributors of this fund:

Mr. Everhart
Mr. O'Neil
Mr. O'Keefe
Mr. Ridener (Reidener?)

A motion was then put and carried that the several visitors appointed should severally report themselves to the Priests and distribute the funds entrusted to their care according to their sense of propriety, taking into consideration those most in need of their assistance, whereupon the President appointed as the Visiting Committee (one Visitor for each of the following) —

1) For the Parish of St. Vincent de Paul
2) For the Cathedral
3) For the Parish of Saint Francis Xavier
4) For the Parish of Saint Patrick

[3] Byran Mullanphy (1809–1851) was a judge of the Circuit Court who in 1847 became Mayor of St. Louis. He was the only son of the wealthy merchant and philanthropist, John Mullanphy (1758–1833), whose generosity brought about the first Catholic hospital in the United States at St. Louis in November, 1828, besides generous gifts to the Jesuits, the Religious of the Sacred Heart, and the Sisters of Loretto. Speaking of the elder Mullanphy's death in August, 1833, John E. Rothensteiner stated, "With him died the noblest Catholic layman St. Louis has ever known. . . ." (*History of the Archdiocese of St. Louis* [St. Louis, 1928], I, 450). At his death in 1851 the younger Mullanphy left one third of his estate, valued at about $200,000, as a trust fund to furnish relief to poor immigrants passing through St. Louis to settle in the West.

88. A Broadside on the Infant University of Notre Dame, January 1, 1847

AMONG American Catholic institutions of higher learning none has found a more secure place in the hearts of all Americans, and none has had a brighter record of achievement in education for Christian manhood, than the University of Notre Dame. Like most universities, its origins were humble and obscure. A generous gift of land from Father Stephen Badin to the Bishop of Vincennes, the latter's determination to have a college for boys, but above all the zeal and resourcefulness of Edward Sorin (1814–1893), American founder of the Congregation of Holy Cross, were the principal factors that brought it into being. Sorin came to Notre Dame in November, 1842, and the following year he and his little community of Holy Cross priests and brothers began classes with two students on a site hallowed by the missionary labors of priests like Badin and Louis Deseille. In January, 1844, the school received a university charter from the legislature of Indiana. Less than a week after his arrival at Notre Dame the founder had outlined the prospect he entertained for its future to Basile-Antoine Moreau, Superior-General of Holy Cross, and in his letter of December 5, 1842, he predicted, "This college will be one of the most powerful means of doing good in this country. . . ." (*Circular Letters of the Very Reverend Edward Sorin* [Notre Dame, 1885], I, 261). The ensuing century fully justified the prediction for the university that today enrolls some 5,500 students taught by a faculty of nearly 600 teachers. The following broadside — a way of attracting students used by all schools of the period — was printed when the college was three years old; it gives a picture of the conditions and rules of student life in the days of its infancy. Source: Archives of the University of Notre Dame.

UNIVERSITY OF NOTRE-DAME-DU-LAC,
St. Joseph County, Indiana.

UNDER THE DIRECTION OF THE PRIESTS OF THE HOLY CROSS.

This Institution commenced under the auspices of the Rt. Rev'd Bishop of Vincennes who presented to the priests of the Holy cross, the beautiful and elegant site upon which the buildings are erected, is now in full operation.

Notre-Dame-du-Lac is at a distance of 1 mile from South Bend, the County seat; 80 miles from Chicago, Illinois; 180 from Detroit, Mich. with which there is direct communication by railroad, and 80 from Fort Wayne, Ia.

The edifice is of brick, four and half story [*sic*] high and not inferior in point of style or structure to any of the colleges of the

United States, and is situated upon a commanding eminence on the verge of two picturesque and commodious Lakes, which, with the river St. Joseph and the surrounding country, present a most magnificent prospect. The rooms are spacious, well ventilated and furnished, with every thing conducive to regularity and comfort.

The Infirmary is intrusted to Sisters similar in their Institute to the Sisters of Charity; their well known kindness and skill are a sufficient guarantee, that the invalids will be attended to with all the diligence and care, which devotion and affection can suggest.

The disciplinary government is mild, yet sufficiently energetic, to preserve that good order, so essential to the well-being of the Institution. The morals and general deportment of the pupils are watched over with the greatest assiduity and solicitude; their personal comfort receives the most paternal attention, and no pains are spared to prepare them for fulfilling their respective duties in society. In their daily recreations, they are always accompanied by a member of the Institution; all books in their possession are subject to the inspection of the Prefect of Studies; and none are allowed circulation without his approval. Corporal punishments will never be inflicted, but more conciliatory and effective means of correction are judiciously used; should a pupil prove refractory, and incorrigible, he will be dismissed.

The faculty is formed of the priests of the Holy Cross: a member is annually sent to Europe to complete whatever contingent circumstances may require. In the reception of pupils no distinction of creed is made, and the parents of those, not professing the Catholic faith, may rest assured that there will be no interference with their religious tenets; they are required only to attend to the religious exercises with decorum, this being in conformity with the rules of all the catholic colleges in the United States.

TERMS,

Board, washing and medical attendance, with the English Course, embracing all the branches of a practical education;

Orthography, Reading, Writing, Arithmetic, Grammar and Composition, to which particular attention is paid; Geography, Ancient and Modern History; the most approved methods of Book-keeping, Surveying, Mensuration, Mathematics, Astronomy, the use of the Globes, Rhetoric, Vocal Music, &c. Free admittance to the Museum, lessons of natation and

Equestrian exercises &c. . . . . $100 per ann.

Half Boarders, ... 40 " "

Day scholars in the above course	20 " "
The same in the preparatory School, ...	16 " "
The classical course of Latin, and Greek an additional sum of	20 " "
The French, German languages are taught at an extra charge of	12 " "
Instrumental Music and Drawing	20 " "
Piano	40 " "

Class books, Stationary [*sic*], and Medicines furnished at the usual rates.

The payments must be made semi-annually in advance; from this rule there can be no deviation whatever, as the charges are based upon the lowest estimate, the object of the Institution being to increase the facilities of instruction, without any view to pecuniary reward.

The distribution of Premiums takes place on the 1st Tuesday of August, and the commencement of the scholastic year is irrevocably fixed on the 1st Friday of October.

The Institution being in possession of all the powers and privileges of a University: degrees will be conferred after the public examination.

No boarder will be received for a shorter term than half a year, and no deduction made for absence, except in case of sickness or dismission.

Examinations take place at the end of each Quarter, and reports are forwarded semi-annually to parents, informing them of the progress, health, &c., of their children. Public examinations, before the distribution of premiums, will take place in the last week of July in every year.

DIRECTIONS FOR PARENTS.

Each pupil must be provided with bed and bedding, (if furnished by the Institution, they form an extra charge,) six shirts, six pair of stockings, six pocket handkerchiefs, six towels (all of which must be marked,) a knife and fork, a table and tea spoon, a hat and cap, two suits of clothes, an over-coat, a pair of shoes and a pair of boots for winter; three suits of clothing and two pair of shoes for summer. No advances will be made by the Institution for clothing or other expenses.

The pupils will not be allowed to have money in their possession; their pocket money must be deposited in the Treasurer's hands, in order to guard against abuses, and to enable the Institution to apply the money as an incentive to virtue and industry. When parents wish to have their children sent home, they must give timely notice, settle all accounts, and supply means to defray their traveling expenses.

Visitors cannot be permitted to interrupt the pupils during the hours of study. The mid-day recreation commences at half past 12 and ends at half past one o'clock. This is the most appropriate time for the visits of parents and friends.

☞ All letters to pupils or members of the Institution must be post paid.

Rev. E. SORIN, President

Notre Dame du Lac, St. Joseph)
County, Indiana, January 1st, 1847.)
References to the Rt. Rev. Bishop of Vincennes and to the Rt. Rev. Bishop of Detroit Rev. Mr. Benoit, Fort-Wayne, Ia. [*sic*].

89. The Act of Foundation for the First Permanent Trappist Monastery in the United States, October 23, 1848

ONE of the most extraordinary developments in recent Catholicism has been the growth of the contemplative religious life among American men. As far back as 1802 a party of Trappists, hunted out of France by the anticlerical laws of the revolution and Napoleon I, had come to the United States under the leadership of Urban Guillet (1766–1817). But repeated attempts to establish a permanent foundation in various parts of the country — including the years 1805–1809 near the present site of the American mother abbey in Kentucky — ended in failure and in 1814 the monks returned to France. Thirty-four years later the superior of the Abbey of Our Lady of Melleray near Nantes, finding his house overcrowded and worried about the effects of the revolution of February, 1848, decided upon an American foundation. A party of forty-some monks arrived in Kentucky in December, 1848, and took up residence on a farm located about fifteen miles southeast of Bardstown, giving to their house the name of Our Lady of Gethsemani. Of its early years Thomas Merton has said, "The devil does not like monasteries, especially contemplative ones. He has spent a hundred years trying to interfere with Gethsemani — and in the early days the battle was not altogether to his disadvantage" (*The Waters of Siloe* [New York, 1949], p. 108). Gethsemani, however, endured and before the end of the century two other Trappist houses — founded from Ireland and Canada — had been established near Dubuque, Iowa, and Providence, Rhode Island. But it is our own day that has seen the amazing development of the contemplative life with the American Church now having eleven Trappist monasteries, eight of which have been founded since 1944, with a total of over 1,000 monks. Moreover, in 1951 the first house of Carthusians, the strictest order in the Church, was established at Sky Farm near Whitingham, Vermont. In the following document the Abbot of Melleray issued authorization for the new foundation in Kentucky and addressed his farewell words to the monks on the eve of their departure for the New World. Source: Archives of the Abbey of Our Lady of Gethsemani.

We, Brother Maxime,[1] Abbot of Our Lady of La Trappe of Melleray, of the Order of Citeaux, in the Diocese of Nantes, near Chateaubriand (Lower Loire), penetrated with the most lively gratitude toward God for the grace He has vouched to Us in calling Us to the religious state, and fully appreciating the wonderful merit there is in embracing a state of life wherein so many have so highly sanctified themselves; after having had recourse to God in prayer, and after having interceded long with Mary, the Most Blessed Virgin, and with St. Joseph, We have resolved for the greater glory of Our Lord, to make a foundation in Kentucky, in the neighborhood of Louisville, in the Diocese of Mgr. Flaget,[2] in a place called Gethsemani, which now, according to the custom of our Fathers of Citeaux, shall be called Our Lady of La Trappe of Gethsemani. For the establishment of this foundation We have sent out forty-four members under the jurisdiction of the Reverend Father Eutropius,[3] whom We have appointed Prior. Their names are FF. MM. Eutropius, Prior, Paulinus, Euthymius, Benezet, Robert, John Chrysostom, Emmanuel, Jerome, Timothy, Dorotheus, Edward, Ephrem, Michael and Adrian; to these choir religious we add the novices: Philemon, Augustine and Benedict. We send twenty-three lay brothers: i.e., Leo, Medard, James, Charles, Hilarion, Amedeus, Thomas, Augustine, Theodoret, David, Saturninus, Matthew, Isaac, Philibert, Antoninus, Julius, Eugene, Elias and Jerome, the novice Orsis, the oblate Lazarus, the postulants Ferdinand and Isidore; and finally three family-brothers: Julian, Bedoue, and Father Huig.

After furnishing them with all We judged necessary for the starting of such an enterprise. We have placed them in the hands of the good Providence, praying that He may cause this holy undertaking

---

[1] Maxim Maulouin (1801–1852) was elected abbot of the Abbey of Our Lady of Melleray in February, 1839.

[2] Benedict J. Flaget, S.S. (1763–1850), was the first Bishop of Bardstown. The see was transferred to Louisville in February, 1841.

[3] Eutropius Proust, O.C.S.O. (1809–1874), was made the first abbot of Our Lady of Gethsemani when the foundation was raised to the rank of an abbey on July 21, 1850.

to prosper and increase in numbers, that they may themselves one day be able to establish other houses, thereby facilitating the salvation of many souls.

Our dear Brethren will secure happy results if they persevere in the spirit of their holy vocation which will lead them to make a special study of the virtues of Charity, Obedience, Purity, Poverty, Mortification and Patience. Let Our Brethren never cease devoting themselves to the spirit of prayer; for then they shall be happily surprised to see the progress that they will make in virtue, provided only that they persevere in this holy exercise. Let perfect union reign in their midst. The world and the devil will be unable to achieve anything against them so long as they remain united. Let them remember: "every house divided against itself shall fall;" let them love their Superior reverently and with warm hearts. Let them console him in his solicitudes by union and obedience. Let them on no account adopt an attitude that might compel the Superior to tone down his orders to suit them. Considering their own misery, let them be humble of mind and heart. Do this, my dearly beloved Brethren, and you shall live. Amen. Amen.

Given at Our Abbey of Melleray, under Our seal and that of Our Secretary on this 23rd day of the month of October, in the year 1848 — the eve of their departure.

Fr. Maxime O.C. Abbot
Fr. Serapion, Secretary.

90. The Catholic Missions in the Far Northwest, January 12, 1849

WHILE missionaries in the Southwest were struggling against floods and rattlesnakes their counterparts in the far Northwest were contending with the bitterly cold winters as one of their chief handicaps. But in every section the Indian medicine men, epidemics, and general deprivation were their lot. Among the earliest Catholic missionaries in the Northwest were the Oblates of Mary Immaculate who arrived in September, 1847, with Bishop Magloire Blanchet when he came to take possession of his new Diocese of Walla Walla, erected on July 24, 1846, only a month after the treaty between the United States and Great Britain had settled the Oregon boundary dispute. In the party which had Pascal Richard, O.M.I., as superior were Eugene Casimir Chirouse and Jean F. Pandosy who were ordained on January 2, 1848, the first priests to be ordained in what would become Washington Territory in 1853. A year after his ordination Chirouse wrote a letter to Richard in which he described the hardships of his life in the Northwest, but rigorous as it was he remained there until the Oblate missions were closed in 1878. The Archdiocese of Oregon City had been established in July, 1846, with Walla Walla as a suffragan see and in the tremendous area of both sees there were in 1850 only 10,000 Catholics who were served by about twenty priests. Source: *Annales de la Propagation de la Foi,* XXIII (1851), 75–80.

Holy Cross of Simkoné [*sic*], January 12, 1849.

My Reverend Father,

A few days after my return from Nesqually, I went to the camp of Kamayarken where I have built a small cabin with the aid of good Brother Verney and some savages. Saint Joseph is the patron whom the Bishop[1] wished to give to this poor, little house, and that great saint protected me until the winter. The cold commencing to make itself felt, the chief and all his Indians prepared to leave for their snow encampment on the Yakima River — a day's journey from St. Rose.[2] They begged me to go and spend the severe season with them. I acceded to their request only on condition that they build me a second cabin where I could be sheltered from the winds and snows. In less than a month the house was built from trunks of poplar trees. My new dwelling, thirty feet long by fifteen wide, gave me enough space to have two rooms — one for myself, and one for the assembly of the Indians for prayer. It is there, Reverend Father, that the troubles, the sorrows, and the crosses of everyone fall on me like hail upon a young plant which is commencing to bud. That is why I call my new residence by the name of the Holy Cross, a sweet name which always inspires me with the proper conduct in the trials of this life.

At this moment savages from nearly all the neighboring nations are assembled at Holy Cross. I count sixty cabins in my village, around one hundred families. There I have *Yellow-Serpent* [chief of the Yakima tribe] with his following as an opponent. He himself presides at all the abominations which are spoken or committed in his infernal den. An old trickster does his best to help him to embarrass me: irritated because my instructions are contrary to his maxims and diabolical acts, he has invented this strange calumny in order that I might be put to death: "The Blackrobe," he says, "catches rattle-snakes, and makes them vomit a black poison with which he poisons

---

[1] Augustin Magloire Blanchet (1797–1887) was first Bishop of Walla Walla.

[2] St. Rose, later called St. Rose of Simcoe, was located on the Yakima River about where it meets the Columbia.

the tobacco with the intention of killing everyone." That is the reason I no longer give tobacco to anyone. The result of that resolution has been a very happy one: I thus conserve my small supply of tobacco for myself, and all the men are furious against the old calumniator. I am afraid of only one thing, and that is that they will hang him at the first opportunity.

In spite of all the shafts of the enemy, I have only thanks to render to the Lord and to congratulate myself on the numerous blessings which he has bestowed on my feeble efforts. In the space of a month or two I have been able to baptize over thirty children and seven adults, well enough instructed in the principles of our holy Religion. Most of our new Christians of St. Rose have come to spend the winter at Holy Cross where they have edified more by their good example than I have by my preaching.

Up to the present I have been able to visit without fear the savages of my village and to instruct them publicly. Most of them now have the fever or the grippe. In each cabin there are some dead or dying. In less than fifteen days more than thirty people have died from this plague. Furthermore, the cold is so intense that several of our hunters have been frozen in the saddle; the animals succumb to these rigors united to the scarcity, because famine has added evils to such a degree that they overwhelm my poor neophytes. One has a treat when he has a horse, a dog, or a wolf to eat. The public calamity does not spare me, R. Father, and I consider myself very fortunate to still have in reserve a dog and two wolves for food. I hope that will last me until the end of the carnival and that at that time the good God, moved with compassion for us, will send us some venison or bears.

In the midst of this desolation I have rest neither day nor night. During the day I run from one cabin to another to baptize the children, to instruct the adults who wish to hear me, and to bury the new Christians whom death has taken from us. At night I baptize again, then I say my office if the first rays of the sun do not surprise me at the bedside of someone in agony. At this moment I have near me a little angel who sleeps the sleep of the just; I say a little angel because he is yet only six months old. Yesterday I purified him with baptismal water, and this morning at daybreak his beautiful soul went to heaven. This evening I shall accompany him to the cemetery. Five of my newly-baptized have refused the diabolical ministry of the deceiver; according to my advice, which they took eagerly, they have perspired and they now enjoy perfect health. The deceiver, furious because he is not able to cure any of the sick, in spite of his infernal contortions, does not cease to vomit forth against me a thousand maledictions. "You see," he has said in pointing out my cabin, "look at that wooden house, surmounted with a white cross; it is there whence comes our misery; it is there that death gets loose; it is the blackrobe who kills us by his prayer, by his words, and by his medicine water (baptism). Burn his cabin and cut off his head, after that I will heal all of you." The reprobates believe the speeches of the deceiver, and some have evil intentions against me. I do not deceive myself that I am not in danger; but what does it matter! I shall die with joy for the cause of Jesus Christ. With his grace I shall not cease to bring help to the unfortunate. No, I shall not allow all these poor children who expire every day to die without baptism. The good God will not abandon me.

According to the news that I receive, it seems that death has also extended itself among the neighboring tribes, especially near the mountains: among the *Nez-perces, the Cayuse,* and the *Flat-Heads* there are already over fifty victims. The horses and cattle are perishing, buried in the snow. I am told that there are seven to eight feet at *Conception.* Poor Father Pandosy and Brother Verney[3] can no longer leave, and are obliged to shiver night and day under a roof of a thousand windows. Fortunately, they have killed two oxen they had for a short time. I have sent them a pig of 190 pounds, four sacks of wheat and two sacks of potatoes; that is why I am reduced to eating a dog and a wolf. They will suffer, then, from cold, but not from hunger.

You ask me, R. Father, to tell you the most secure route by which to send the necessary supplies. It would be best for us to seek these articles at The Dalles, and from there we could take them to Vancouver. We are no longer able to cross the dangerous passes of the Nesqually Mountains where one is in danger of splitting his head open at each moment or of dying of hunger before he again sees the plains. As you urge me to mention my temporal needs, I will tell you that I no longer suffer from hunger since I have a dog and two wolves in my larder; but in the matter of utensils and vestments I am not so well supplied. Having only one tattered soutane, which does not protect me from the north wind, I have made one out of a rough, white wool blanket which I threw in some blueing-water; it turned violet and I thought I was a bishop: but the rains having come, my soutane returned to its original white, and all of a sudden I found myself the pope, but a pope so poor that having lost my only

[3] Jean F. Pandosy and Celestine Verney were among the first Oblate missionaries in the Northwest.

needle, I have not been able to find another in my Quirinal palace. Meanwhile it being necessary to sew up the holes in my old black soutane, what was I to do? I took off the head of a pin and made a needle out of it. This invention succeeded: the needle is coarse, but solid; it bends but never breaks. I had in all about a dozen nails for the construction of my house of the Holy Cross, and they have been stolen from me. Send me some trinkets which please the savages, I will use them to gain them to our holy religion. By the enticement of reward they assemble for work, and one profits by these gatherings to instruct them. Thanks to God, I make myself understood well enough, and the greater part of the adults are very attentive when I speak to them. There is really much to do at Saint Joseph of Simkoné; but poor little Chirouse will never be able to clear this field alone; at least two Fathers and two Brothers are needed here. I have been alone here for over four months; I am not able to speak familiarly with anyone except my cat and my dog; with the savages there is great reserve; familiarity would spoil everything. The great chief comes often to visit me; but what a pleasure to entertain oneself with naked princes who only know how to ask for a smoke or for food! ! ! . . . Think then of me, R. Father, and send me R. Father Sempfrit and Brother Sareau;[4] we will do wonders here.

I earnestly recommend myself to your fervent prayers and to those of all our Brothers and Fathers of Nesqually, and beg you to accept the homage of my respect.

C. Chirouse, O.M.I.

61. Conditions in the Diocese of Chicago, December 13, 1849

DURING the 1840's approximately 700,000 Catholic immigrants entered the United States. Although many of them settled in the eastern states, other thousands made the trek across the mountains into the rapidly developing states of the Middle West where they found work on the canals and railroads, in the rising towns, and on the rich farm lands. It proved practically impossible for the bishops to provide priests, churches, and schools fast enough to accommodate the increase, and since most of the immigrants were very poor the financial aid of the European missionary societies was all the more welcome. The See of Chicago had been erected on November 28, 1843, and embraced the entire state of Illinois (55,947 square miles). James O. Van de Velde, S.J. (1795–1855), the second Bishop of Chicago, was con-

[4] No identification of Father Sempfrit and Brother Sareau was found.

secrated on February 11, 1849, and ten months later he wrote the following letter to the Society for the Propagation of the Faith after he had completed his first visitation tour. At the time there were 80,000 Catholics in the diocese served by fifty-seven priests. It is difficult to imagine now that the Archdiocese of Chicago with its nearly two million Catholics was so impoverished as it was a little over a century ago. Yet the condition described was typical of most of the dioceses of the Middle West at the mid-century. Source: *Annales de la Propagation de la Foi,* XXII (1850), 313–314.

Since my consecration, I have visited almost a third of my new diocese. This episcopal journey, which corresponds to twelve hundred French leagues, has revealed to me all the misery of the flock entrusted to my care. You will judge it, Sirs, by this simple picture, whose distressing exactness I have verified with my eyes.

In general, the emigrants who arrive in this country, and who form almost all the Catholic population, are beyond the state of taking care of their particular needs. Poverty is so extensive that there is not one parish, even among the oldest, which has provided the most necessary things for the celebration of the holy liturgy. One priest sometimes has eight churches to take care of, and since for these different stations he possesses only one chalice, one missal, one chasuble, one alb, one altar-stone, he must carry all these things with him wherever he goes, no matter how tiring or how long the journey may be. As for ostensoria and ciboria, these types of articles are almost unknown in this diocese. Until the present time I have seen only three ostensoria and five ciboria in all the parishes which I have visited, over a space of 3,700 English miles. In lieu of these sacred vessels, the Most Holy Sacrament is kept either in a corporal, or in a tin box, or in a porcelein [*sic*] cup, etc., etc.

After these details, I believe it superfluous to give you a description of my episcopal residence. It is in harmony with the rest. I do not know if it is the most humble in the world, but at least it is certainly not the poorest in America.

92. The Advent of Bishop Lamy to the Southwest, June 29, 1851

ONE of the most attractive missionary bishops of the nineteenth century was John Baptist Lamy (1814–1888). He had come originally from France in 1839 to the Diocese of Cincinnati where his success recommended him to his superiors and on November 24, 1850, he was consecrated as first Vicar

Apostolic of New Mexico. It was Lamy's colorful career in the Southwest that inspired Willa Cather's charming novel, *Death Comes for the Archbishop* (New York, 1926). Following his consecration he left for New Mexico by way of New Orleans and Texas, and after being laid up some months in San Antonio as the result of an accident, he reached Santa Fe in the summer of 1851. New Mexico had formerly been part of the Diocese of Durango in Mexico and some of the Mexican clergy were not disposed to bow to Lamy's authority. He decided to settle the question of jurisdiction by a personal visit to Bishop José A. Laureano de Zubiria at Durango, traveling the more than 1,000 miles each way by mule pack. In the letter that follows Lamy described for Antoine Blanc, Archbishop of New Orleans, his experiences on his first trip to the Southwest. Source: *American Catholic Historical Researches,* XV (April, 1898), 136–137.

El Passo del Norte, Mexico, June 29, 1851.

Monseigneur:

After a journey of six weeks on the plains we arrived here. The country we saw has nothing very interesting — barren plains, barren mountains — with the exception of a few places. The last week there was a great scarcity of water and grass. Then we generally travelled at night. We had beautiful weather, some days rather too warm, but the nights were delightful; we generally preferred to sleep out than in our tent. We did not use it much except for Mass. We had the consolation to offer the Divine Sacrifice, at least one of us, almost every day. The first week I felt rather stiff from lying on a mere blanket, but I soon got use [*sic*] to it, and I never enjoyed my rest better.

There are three fine villages near El Passo on the Texas side. When the people heard of my arrival, they came several miles to meet us. In one place particularly, called Succoro, I had a grand reception with music, national guards, arks of triumph, etc. Circumstances obliged me the next morning to make *mon premier debut* in public *en la langua de Dios* to a crowded congregation. We are now at the house of the cura d'El Passon, who kindly offered us hospitality. This village of El Passo is truly a beautiful spot. They have here all kinds of fruits; they make good wine. It rains very seldom; it has not rained to any consequence these two years, but irrigation supplies the want of rain water. This is a place very much scattered. It contains at least eight thousand inhabitants. The people seem to be good and docile. Their houses are mud; they call it, I think, adobe, but very clean inside; it is so warm that many go half naked. The few churches that I have seen are of the same materials as the houses, but they might be kept in better order with very little trouble.

I have yet four hundred miles to go; but after I have traveled one-third of it. I will get in the pueblos of New Mexico, and see at least the half of my district before I reach Santa Fé. From what I have heard, and the little I have seen here, no doubt I may expect to meet with serious difficulties and obstacles, but my hope is in the God of power. Please, Monseigneur, to remember me in your prayers, and also to recommend me to the prayers of the Ursuline Sisters who have been so kind to me. I hope my little niece is well and doing well. I received news from her parents; they are all well. I expect to start this week for Santa Fé.

Your most obedient serv't and devoted friend,

✠ JOHN LAMY, Vic. Ap. of N. Mexico.

93. A Missionary Bishop on the Edge of the Great Plains, August 6, 1852

JOHN BAPTIST LAMY, who served the Church with distinction in the Southwest from 1851 to his death in 1888, was named first Archbishop of Santa Fe in February, 1875. He was one of only three American bishops to have been in attendance at all three of the plenary councils of Baltimore. He used his presence in the East and the Middle West for the council of May, 1852, to good advantage in recruiting personnel and supplies for the missions of New Mexico. But upon his return journey to his vicariate that summer he encountered more than the ordinary number of vicissitudes, and in the following letter to Archbishop Blanc of New Orleans he told of the losses he had sustained, indicating as well the hazards of travel in the trans-Mississippi West. Source: *American Catholic Historical Researches,* V (April, 1898), 137.

Blue River Camp [Mission], August 6, 1852.

Monseigneur:

I am writing to you from under a tree twenty miles west from Independence. The first time I went to New Mexico I met with some *contretemps;* but it seems that the Divine Providence has been pleased to send me this time more severe trials, disappointments and troubles than at my first start. A good priest from the diocese of Cleveland was coming with me to share the labor of our mission in New Mexico, but he died of the cholera at St. Louis on the 11th of July. His name was Rev. Mr. Pendesprat [*sic*].[1] From St. Louis to Independence the

[1] Father Peter Pandeprat had been a professor at St. Mary's Seminary, Cleveland.

Mother Superior of the Sisters of Loreto died also of the cholera, on board the steamboat *Kansas,* the 16th of July; the same day another Sister was taken sick and is yet very low. I have been obliged to leave for Independence to my great regret. Two more Sisters were also attacked by the same dreadful epidemic, but thank God, they got over it. My Mexican priest has been very sick, and now he is just able to travel in a carriage; besides, I have lost nine of my best animals. You know that we have to travel through the plains with caravans, and that everything has to be brought by wagons. Besides some animals I had here, I bought a few more, but I have lost a great number of them. I have been very much fatigued myself, but still God has given me the grace to bear all with patience, and my strong constitution has stood the labor and the care I had on my mind. I hope to take a fair start tomorrow for the plains; we are only two or three miles from the boundaries between the State of Missouri and the Indian Territory. I have twenty-five persons in my company, ten wagons or other conveyances. My expenses are very great; but still, with God's help, I hope to meet all in one or two years. Recommending myself to your prayers, I have the honor to be,

Your most grateful friend and ob't serv't.
✠ JOHN LAMY, Vic. Ap. of N. Mexico.

64. The Church in San Francisco in the Days of the Gold Rush, June 15, 1853

AT NO time in the nineteenth century were there enough native-born priests in the United States to care for the rapidly increasing Catholic population. No foreign country was more generous in supplying priests for the American Church than Ireland, and no institution of that land sent so many to the American missions as All Hallows College, Dublin, which had been established as a missionary seminary in 1842. Among the best known of the All Hallows men in the United States was Eugene O'Connell (1815–1891). He had come out to California for the first time in 1851 to collect funds but was induced by Bishop Alemany to remain and assist him with his infant seminary. O'Connell returned to the faculty of All Hallows in 1854 and remained there until 1861 when he was appointed the first Vicar Apostolic of Marysville, California. In 1868 he was made first Bishop of Grass Valley, a see that was the predecessor to the present Diocese of Sacramento. The following letter to Father David Moriarty, president of All Hallows, contains some picturesque details on the type of surroundings in which the Church operated in San Francisco in the years immediately after the gold rush. Source: *All Hallows Annual, 1953–1954* (Dublin: Browne and Nolan, Ltd., 1954), pp. 152–153.

San Francisco.
June 15th [1853].

My dear Father Moriarty, — Your welcome letter, after an unsuccessful search about the solitude of Santa Ynez,[1] reached me a few days ago in this noisy city. How then can I express to you my gratitude for your kind invitation to All Hallows after my wanderings in the Far West? I only await the arrival of one of the six missionaries whom Dr. Alemany[2] expects from All Hallows previous to my departure. You would really pity the poor Bishop were you to see the fluctuating soldiers he has to fight his battle; like Dr. Whelan[3] of Virginia, he was obliged to make the two seminarians he has swear to remain with him. Therefore, under these circumstances, I presume on your leave to remain. . . .

You must, I'm sure, have received letters from Dr. Alemany since March 5th which shew you the urgent need he has of Irish clergymen and the provision he is making to secure a constant supply from All Hallows now, in order to keep up an unbroken succession in this diocese of All Hallows missionaries. For the present, he can do no more for the institution than he has done, in consequence of being engaged in building St. Mary's Cathedral, which it is calculated will cost $100,000 — a work he is *bound* (*ut dicunt Americani*) to get through with, for many reasons, but principally to secure a fire-proof church in the neighborhood, that he himself and his clergymen may be without the daily and nightly apprehension of being *burnt out*. Owing to the scarcity of stone in this country and the dearness of brick-buildings, most of the houses here are constructed of wood and the six or seven fires that have already occurred haven't taught many to make an effort to build brick houses. Since the Bishop transferred me from Santa Ynez to this city about three or four months ago, there has been a fire almost every month and the value of thousands of dollars consumed. . . .

The temporal burnings of which I am speaking naturally remind me of the everlasting ones which they presage to thousands of the

---

[1] The diocesan seminary, of which O'Connell was rector, was first established at Santa Inez and moved early in 1853 to Mission Dolores in San Francisco.

[2] Joseph S. Alemany, O.P. (1814–1888), born in Spain, was named first Archbishop of San Francisco six weeks after O'Connell's letter was written.

[3] Richard V. Whelan (1809–1874) was first Bishop of Wheeling.

citizens of San Francisco, unless they stop in their career of iniquity. The rage for duelling, the passion for gambling and barefaced depravity prevail to a frightful degree. . . . Venus has numerous temples erected to herself in this city but, thank God, the Catholic church is not deserted all the while. The two Catholic churches are crowded every Sunday and, notwithstanding the enlargement of one of them by Architect O'Connor (nephew of the Bishop), it is full to overflowing. William Hamill,[4] formerly of Maynooth, is the teacher of the Bishop's English school, *vice* Doctor Barry who was translated to the Dolores seminary with a salary of $50 a month. Mr. Hamill's salary is $60 a month in consideration of his acting as Sexton to the church — in fact $50 a month is the salary even of cooks in this country.

I don't know whether you are aware of some of our California liberties which beat the Gallican ones hollow. Take, for example, that of eating meat *toties quoties* on every Friday except the Fridays in Lent — and don't infer from this that the finest salmon in the world don't abound on our shores! There is again the universal custom of smoking cigars (*secluso scandalo ullo*), so that it is rather singular to be seen without a cigar save at Mass or at meals. The only scandal to my knowledge given by a smoking clergyman was owing to his having repeatedly put the *ignited end* into his mouth instead of the opposite extreme. Hence you perceive it is neither the simple fact of smoking *per se,* nor of drinking *per se,* but the unlucky combination of both by a clergyman which makes him confound both ends of a lighted cigar. Then, and not till then, do the ladies and gentlemen receive a slight shock!

Oh, my dear Father and brothers, please all pray for me and my speedy return to Alma Mater, where I hope to find rest for my soul.

Adieu, dear Father, until then.

Eugene O'Connell.

95. The Conversion to Catholicism of Eliza Allen Starr, February–December, 1854

THE number of converts to Catholicism in the United States in the years 1840–1860 was sufficiently notable to occasion the belief that the Oxford Movement might be duplicated in this country. Although the trend never

[4] William J. Hamill, born in County Antrim, Ireland, arrived in San Francisco in 1851; he later became the first editor of the *Monitor,* San Francisco's weekly Catholic newspaper. No identification of Barry could be found.

reached the proportions that it did in England, a considerable number of Americans of prominent Protestant families did enter the Church, including such Protestant clergymen as James Roosevelt Bayley, Thomas S. Preston, and Levi Silliman Ives. Among these mid-century converts was Eliza Allen Starr (1824–1901), a woman of Unitarian background whose ancestors on both sides stretched back to the earliest days of Massachusetts Bay Colony. Miss Starr was influenced in part by the conversion of her cousin, George Allen (1808–1876), professor of Greek and Latin in the University of Pennsylvania, who was received into the Church with his wife, the former Mary Hancock Withington, and their children by Bishop Francis P. Kenrick of Philadelphia in October, 1847. She later met Kenrick who exercised a strong influence on her views as likewise did Bishop Fitzpatrick of Boston. Miss Starr wrote poetry and popular essays and attained sufficient prominence through her lectures and writings on art to receive a medallion from Pope Leo XIII, the Laetare Medal of the University of Notre Dame in 1885, and a gold medal at the World's Columbian Exposition in Chicago in 1893. In the following letters to George and Mary Allen she recounted some of her ideas on religion and the circumstances of her reception into the Church. Source: James J. McGovern (Ed.), *The Life and Letters of Eliza Allen Starr* (Chicago: Lakeside Press, 1905), pp. 63–66, 67–68.

Baltimore, Feb. 17, 1854.

Dear Cousin Mary:

As a preparatory step to writing to you, I called on Monday to see our good friend, the Archbishop.[1] He always receives me with the most beautiful urbanity, exercises the greatest patience towards my weak head and unbelieving heart, and this time he was in unusual spirits; said he had received a visitor from Philadelphia, Mr. L., whom I immediately recognized as the object of your Christian solicitude fully five years ago. He added that Mr. L. had at length yielded himself to the Catholic rule, and gave me in a few words an account of all the persuadings which in the space between Saturday evening and Monday morning had finally made him one of the flock, and sent him back to Philadelphia thoroughly established and confirmed in the faith, concluding by saying with great glee that "this was better than some people had done." It would not, of course, be proper or at all consistent in me to congratulate him or you on such a termination to his long investigation, but I know, Cousin M., that you would feel so pleased that I could not help taking sides with you in the matter. I felt an involuntary sympathy with you. The good Archbishop tells me that Mr. L.'s parents were Unitarians, and that he was educated

---

[1] Francis Patrick Kenrick (1796–1863) was Coadjutor Bishop of Philadelphia, 1830–1842; Bishop of Philadelphia, 1842–1851; and Archbishop of Baltimore, 1851–1863.

one, and used to attend Mr. J.'s church.[2] It is strange from under what different stars and influences the converts of your faith have come out, but I will not trouble you with any of my speculations on the subject, as I feel that nothing I may say can ever strike you very favorably so long as I refuse allegiance. I am certain that to your ears one ejaculation of belief would sound sweeter than volumes of musical philosophy or practicing.

I am sorry I am not feeling better to-day, since I have commenced a letter to you, but I do not know how long I may wait if I put it off until body and mind are in tune. . . . My drawing furnishes me with the most salutary occupation whenever I can attend to it, and when I find my eyes actually tired of seeing my dull ears tired of even the little they hear, and my mind wearied with agitations, I take my knitting, turn by back to the light, and withdraw like an oyster into its shell. . . . My cousins here are all on the other side. What will you think when I tell you that I am in the midst of table-tippings, rappings, speaking and writing mediums, and such wonders as are enough to make one's hair stand on end or turn gray of a night? I have no doubt you will immediately conclude that I am up to the ears in this delusion, as I have so often manifested a *penchant* for such varieties. But for once I have escaped. The fear of leaving my wits has been a powerful motive, and then I could not shut my eyes to certain practices alluded to with terms of no measured reprehension in the Old Testament, such as the raising of spirits by the Witch of Endor, etc.[3] Hardly a night passes that the tables are not consulted in the house, but I have never yet been present during such manifestations. I resolved upon this course long ago, though with little expectation of ever being called to exercise my resolution. When, however, I found how the Baltimore current was turning, I consulted the Archbishop, and his opinion confirming me, I have been saved no little perplexity. . . . Will you tell your sister L. that I have read the first volume of the "Converted Christian." I remember what she said of this book last winter, and I believe she wanted me to read it.

---

[2] One turning point in Miss Starr's life came when she attended a sermon by Theodore Parker (1810–1860), the famous liberal Unitarian minister of Boston, in June, 1845, in the company of Richard Hildreth (1807–1865), the historian, and his wife who was an old girlhood friend from their days in Deerfield, Massachusetts. Miss Starr later said that as she listened to the sermon of Parker, "I found him demolishing every foundationstone of my religious faith, and even hope. . . . From the moment I left the music hall of old Boston on that bright June morning in 1845 this quest for an authorized faith was the quest of my life" (McGovern, *op. cit.,* pp. 34–35).

[3] 1 Kings 28:7 ff.

The second volume is upon ceremonies, so that I was not as sorry as I would otherwise have been when the Archbishop said it was missing. I presume it will be quite time for me to attend to the ceremonials when I shall have accepted the dogmas. I have not been to the cathedral at all. I do not like to go to hear the fine music, of which I hear so much, for the same reason that I go to a concert. To a Catholic I know it is something more, and until I can give myself up to it fully I do not wish to torture myself with balancing my emotions, and trying to make them consistent. . . .

Commending myself to your patience and love,

Your affectionate cousin,
Eliza.

Dec. 23, 1854.

My Dear Cousins:

I have something so joyful to tell that I cannot address myself to anyone of you. You will all bless God and the angels will rejoice with you, for now they can rejoice. This morning near 12 o'clock the Rt. Rev. Bishop Fitzpatrick[4] received me to your holy Mother Church in the sacrament of baptism, and on Christmas Day I am to make my first communion. I do not feel that I need say anything more, for what is already said covers everything else. I wrote to our saintly Archbishop Kenrick some three weeks ago, perhaps longer, but received a note saying that he had not returned yet from Rome. I then saw Miss Metcalf, hoping I could immediately see the Bishop, but he has been absent, and I did not see him until Thursday last, and it was not certain when I could be received until this morning. I was so desirous, however, to be received before Christmas that the Bishop gratified me. I have not yet seen your sister and Aunt Lydia. She does not know that I have had any idea of doing what I have done, or rather, what the good Lord has enabled me to do. I have reserved to myself the pleasure of telling her, and I shall write to her this afternoon. The weather has been too severe for her to come to me, and my intense occupation of mind to prepare for my reception, together with my daily and necessary avocations and the visit my dear father is making with us and little Mary, has made it impossible for me to go to her, and I would not allow any one to tell her but myself. I hope to

[4] John B. Fitzpatrick (1812–1866) was consecrated a bishop in March, 1844, and ruled the See of Boston from 1846 to his death.

be able to make my communion Christmas morning with her and Miss Metcalf at the Sisters' little chapel.

Do you think I can forget all the prayers you have all offered for me? I still need them for grace to keep my baptismal vows, and in your thanksgiving remember me. You will, I know, feel what I cannot write more now. I shall write to the Archbishop a line to meet him at his return. St. Agnes is my patron saint.

In the humble joy of a convert,

Your affectionate cousin,
Eliza.

You know better than I do who has been praying for me all these six years, in which God's patience for me has not faltered. Give to them, if you can, a word of gratitude from me. I have forgotten to tell you that my reception was as private as it could be. It is such a real thing that the little circumstances of it seem nothing.

96. Asiatic Cholera in the Diocese of Savannah, August 29, 1854

ALL through the nineteenth century the United States continued to be visited by periodic outbreaks of cholera and yellow fever. The third major epidemic of Asiatic cholera was brought in on immigrant ships entering New York harbor in 1854. Once more heroic efforts were put forth by bishops, priests, and religious to alleviate the suffering and distress of the populace, and as a consequence the loss of personnel to the Church was very heavy. In late August, Francis X. Gartland (1805–1854), first Bishop of Savannah, described conditions in his see city where he was being assisted by his friend, Edward Barron (1801–1854), former Vicar Apostolic of Upper Guinea, who had interrupted a holiday in the North and rushed to Georgia when he heard of the scourge there. Two weeks after Gartland had written the following letter Bishop Barron was stricken and died on September 12 in the midst of a hurricane which had hit Savannah and blown the roof off the cathedral and bishop's residence, and eight days later Gartland himself succumbed to the dread disease. Source: *American Catholic Historical Researches,* VII (January, 1890), 33.

Sav'h. Aug. 29th 1854

My Dear Friend: —

We are in a sad condition still — very sad — & God alone knows when a favorable turn will take place — Two of my priests are sick —

both convalescent however at present, do not know that either of them has the Yellow fever positively — but I believe one of them had it in its incipient stage. The place looks very desolated — at 8 o'cl. P.M. looks as deserted as at midnight at other season. Every night large fires are kindled in various parts of the city & great quantities of tar burnt. On approaching the city in the ev'g. as I did the other ev'g. from our Country, you see Clouds of dense black smoke rising up in all parts of the city, so that one w'd suppose that the city was on fire, or that our city was something like Pittsburgh is described to be. So far I keep well, though constantly on the go. Yet I know not whether I will pass through the scourge with safety to myself. I hope our Philadelphia friends are praying for us. I hope this letter will reach your city before the arrival of the steamer, as I wish you to inform my brother that Miss G. will leave in the steamer tomorrow for Philada. She is not at all well. Mr. Prendergast & his two sons, & a Mrs. Dillon & her son & two daughters will be with her. Great numbers of our people have left.

I write in great haste. My buggy is at the door for me to make my rounds.

Your most truly in Xst.
Fr's. Xav. Bp. &c.

To M. A. Frenaye, Philadelphia.[1]

97. A Plan for the Western Colonization of Catholic Immigrants, March 15, 1856

THE mounting Irish Catholic immigration of the 1850's, along with the antagonism aroused against Catholics and foreigners by the Know-Nothing movement, prompted men like Thomas D'Arcy McGee, editor of the *American Celt,* Patrick Donahoe of the Boston *Pilot,* and a number of western bishops and priests to urge the immigrants, crowded into the slums of the eastern cities, to seek new homes in the spacious rural areas of the West. As a consequence of their efforts an immigrant aid convention was held in Buffalo, New York, February 12–15, 1856, at which an organization was formed to implement the idea. Among the main supporters of the movement was Bishop Loras of Dubuque, and the following news item, under the heading, "Things in Dubuque," which appeared in the Boston *Pilot* of March 15, 1856, revealed how Loras and his followers sought to render effective the objectives of the Buffalo convention. The plan for moving Catholic immigrants from the East to the Middle West received wide

[1] Mark Anthony Frenaye (1783–1873) was a close personal friend and financial adviser to several bishops and priests in Philadelphia.

publicity, and nowhere more than in Donahoe's *Pilot,* but the opposition of certain eastern churchmen, the disinclination of the Irish themselves to separate from relatives and friends, and the difficulties of western travel all operated to prevent the movement from ever attaining the success which the Buffalo delegates had hoped. Source: Boston *Pilot,* March 15, 1856.

To the Editor of The Pilot:

Dear Sir: It has become my duty to communicate to you the following proceedings of a meeting held in the Cathedral, in this city, on Thursday evening last, to hear the report of the delegates from this place to the Buffalo Convention, and to organize a society for the purpose of aiding and encouraging Catholic settlements in Iowa. The Right Rev. Bishop Loras kindly tendered the use of the Cathedral for holding the meeting, and cheerfully volunteered his co-operation to further the object in view. After the meeting was called to order, Judge Corkery was chosen temporary chairman, and M. B. Mulkern, secretary. The chairman gave a very interesting account of the doings and proceedings of the Buffalo Convention. The feeling which pervaded the whole Convention was truly commendable; every delegate with whom he came in contact appeared to be actuated more by a desire to relieve his less fortunate neighbors from the social restrictions which they endure, than to acquire any personal advantage.

Men of capital in the Eastern States expressed their willingness to emigrate to the West, if some provision could be made for the masses, but not otherwise. He stated the plan of action proposed, and also that this meeting was in accordance with the course recommended by that convention. At the close of Judge Corkery's remarks, on motion of the Rev. J. Farvey [*sic*],[1] a committee of three, consisting of J. D. Jennings, Rev. P. McCabe,[2] and Dr. N. B. Matthews, were appointed to nominate permanent officers for the meeting, who would also continue officers of the contemplated organization. The committee made the following nominations: for President, Rt. Rev. Bishop Loras; Vice-Presidents, James Mullin and Dr. Matthews; Treasurer, Charles Corkery; Secretary, M. B. Mulkern; Agent, M. McLaughlin; Directors, Rev. P. McCabe, P. Quigley, F. Doyle, Dr. W. R. McMahon, and Owen Keenan. On motion of the Rev. J. F. Farvey, Dr. Matthews was appointed to conduct Bishop Loras to the chair. As for taking his place as president of the meeting, he said that he

---

[1] This was probably Father John Vahey, pastor of St. Andrew's Church, Bellevue, Iowa.

[2] Patrick A. McCabe was a pastor of St. Raphael's Cathedral, Dubuque.

felt very great pleasure in presiding over a meeting convened for so worthy an object, and composed of so many good and worthy citizens. He spoke of his own labors in this mission for the last nineteen years, and the affectionate manner in which he had been treated by the Irish Catholics with whom his spiritual labors brought him in contact. Of this kindness he was glad to have an opportunity to evince by appreciation, and he knew of no better way to do it than to co-operate with those who were laboring to rescue their Catholic brethren from oppression and persecution, and bring them to a country rich in resources and congenial to liberty-loving men. The Bishop's address was very touching, and his words were spoken with an earnestness that showed the fatherly solicitude with which he entered upon this great movement. On the motion of the Rev. J. F. Farvey, seconded by the Rev. P. McCabe, Judge Corkery, J. D. Jennings and Hugh V. Gildeo were appointed a committee to draft resolutions. While the committee were preparing their report, the Rev. Father Tracey [*sic*][3] addressed the meeting at considerable length.

He spoke of the proceedings of the Buffalo Convention with great satisfaction. Rarely, or never, had he seen a body of men possessed of higher talent, or animated with a nobler feeling. In their zeal for the general good, delegates carefully avoided introducing any question of a local character, hence, the action of the Convention was marked with the strictest unanimity of feelings and harmony. He was truly glad that the apathy of former years had given way to a spirit of active enterprise, and that a disposition was spreading on the part of Irishmen to submit no longer to a state of drudgery in the East. The movement, he was confident, would result in giving thousands of our poor countrymen a home — a home, though not blessed by the foot-prints of a St. Patrick, yet one in which they could enjoy the blessings of freedom in all things, temporal and spiritual.

Here Judge Corkery, on behalf of the committee on resolutions, reported the following:

Resolved — That we heartily approve of the action of the Catholic Convention recently held at Buffalo, N. Y., for the formation of Catholic settlements in the interior.

[3] At this time Jeremiah F. Trecy (c. 1823–1889) was pastor of St. Patrick's Church, Garryowen, Iowa, an Irish immigrant colony that had been fostered by Bishop Loras. Father Trecy was one of the most active promoters of Catholic colonization in the West, and a few weeks after the above report was written he led a party of Iowa settlers to Nebraska Territory where he established St. Patrick's Colony. On a trip to the East in March, 1857, to further the cause of western colonization Trecy encountered the personal opposition of Archbishop John Hughes of New York.

Resolved — That Catholic societies be formed throughout the State of Iowa for the promotion of the above object, subject to the directions of the Supreme Directory created by the Buffalo Convention.

Resolved — That the Catholics of Dubuque now form themselves into a Society of the character named above, and that all similar societies, that may hereafter be organized throughout the State, are recommended to recognize this, and co-operate with it, as the parent Society of the Diocese.

Resolved — That an initiation fee of $1.00, and a monthly subscription of twenty-five cents, be the full sum necessary to constitute a membership; but $3.00 a year, if paid in advance will be deemed an equivalent.

Resolved — That this society hold its regular meetings on the first Monday of every month, and at such other times as the Directors or majority of them may deem necessary; but applicants for membership may be enrolled as members by filing their applications with the Treasurer, and paying their initiation fees.

The above resolutions were unanimously adopted, after which the secretary proceeded to take the names of those present who desired to become members of the Society. The Bishop, as a further proof of his interest in the object for whose furtherance the Society was organized, enrolled himself as a member, and paid in twenty-five dollars. Father Tracey paid ten dollars, but the giving instances of generosity on the part of those present would occupy too much of your space. The meeting was large and enthusiastic, and afforded a cheering indication of the success that awaits the efforts that are now being put forth, East and West, North and South, on behalf of the poor Catholic immigrant.

It was moved, by Father Tracey, and seconded by Capt. M. M. Hoyden, that the secretary furnish an account of the proceedings of that meeting, to the "American Celt" and "Boston Pilot," for publication. This motion was unanimously adopted.

At the close of the business of the meeting, the venerable Chairman vacated the chair, and Judge Corkery was called thereto, when a vote of thanks was tendered to the Rt. Rev. Bishop, not only for the efficient and satisfactory manner in which he presided over the meeting, but for the deep interest he has manifested in this cause since it was first agitated. After going through some few other unimportant matters, the meeting adjourned to the first Monday in April, unless called together by the President.

You will pardon this intrusion upon your space, and believe me, to remain, very truly and respectfully yours,

M. B. MULKERN, *Secretary*

98. Father Kindekens Appeals for an American College at Louvain, November 5, 1856

THE first institution to be established abroad by the Catholic Church of the United States was the American College in Louvain, Belgium. When some of the American bishops were in Rome in December, 1854, for the definition of the dogma of the Immaculate Conception the idea of founding a college in the Eternal City was discussed, and among the chief promoters of the plan was Francis Patrick Kenrick, Archbishop of Baltimore. When, therefore, the Belgian-born Father Peter Kindekens (d. 1873), vicar-general of the Diocese of Detroit and pastor of Immaculate Conception Church, Adrian, was sent to Rome in the spring of 1856 on business for his ordinary, Peter P. Lefevere (1804–1869), Kenrick asked him to look for a location for a college. In the letter printed below Kindekens explained the reasons for his failure in Rome, but the brighter prospects which he had found in his native Belgium. Upon his return to the United States he sent out a circular to the American hierarchy, the substance of which is contained in his letter to Kenrick. But he met with very little success and the only two bishops who gave any practical response were Martin J. Spalding of Louisville and his own ordinary. It was due, therefore, to these two prelates that the college opened at Louvain on March 19, 1857, with Kindekens as rector, a post he held until 1860. By the time the institution celebrated its golden jubilee in 1907 it had furnished nearly 700 priests to the American Church. Most of these were European-born, but as the years went on there was an increasing number of Americans who were sent to the college by their bishops in order to avail themselves of the superior advantages of study offered by the famous Catholic University of Louvain. Source: Archives of the Archdiocese of Baltimore, Kindekens to Kenrick, Detroit, November 5, 1856.

My Lord: When, during the past summer, at Rome, I endeavored with the utmost diligence, by your special request to look for and secure a suitable location for the projected "American College" in that City, I found that not only is it impossible at present, but that it will probably remain impossible for some time to come, to establish such an institution in the Holy City. In point of fact, the Holy Father assured me that, under present circumstances (the occupation of Rome by the French, etc.) he could not say when it would be in his power to assign a suitable building for the purpose.

On my return, passing through Belgium, I learned that an earnest wish prevailed among persons of distinction to establish there a college for the foreign missions. I resolved at once to secure the fruits of these happy dispositions for the missions of the United States with the following success:

I obtained a promise from the Count Félix de Mérode[1] of the sum of between 50,000 and 60,000 francs towards founding a College for the Missions in the United States, in any city of Belgium of my choice.

His Eminence the Cardinal Archbishop of Malines,[2] and several other Prelates with whom I had the honor to speak on the subject, assured me of their warmest sympathies and promised their co-operation.

A subscription in aid of the foundation of the establishment will be opened in the columns of the Catholic journals of Belgium, as soon as I can assure them that the Right Rev. Bishops of the United States (or some of them) are earnestly engaged in promoting the good work.

The Rector of the University of Louvain[3] (the city selected for the College) has promised his aid, and is prepared to grant all we may reasonably require of the University, to secure the success and prosperity of the contemplated institution.

From the above, Your Lordship will easily perceive that the object of the Institution in Belgium would be, 1st, To serve as a nursery of properly educated and tried clergymen for our missions; and 2d. to provide the American Bishops with a college to which some at least of their students might be sent to acquire a superior ecclesiastical instruction and a solid clerical training, without much expense, as the College will require no other Professors than those for the English and German languages.

The basis of the government of the institution will be that of the "Propaganda" at Rome, and each Diocese of the United States will profit of its fruits in proportion to the amount it may have furnished towards the foundation, etc. For it could not be reasonably expected that the Catholics of the United States should have no share in the

[1] Félix de Mérode-Westerloo (1791–1857) belonged to one of the most distinguished families in Belgium. He held successively the portfolios of foreign affairs, war, and finance in the cabinets of King Leopold I. He was the father of Frédéric F.-X. de Mérode (1820–1874), Archbishop of Melitene, who figured prominently in the government of the Papal States under Pius IX. The elder de Mérode died before he learned that the project for which he had offered the money was to become a reality. This loss left Kindekens with only $2,000 to start the college, a sum which he had been given in equal shares by Bishops Spalding and Lefevere.

[2] Engelbert Sterckx (1792–1867) was made Archbishop of Malines in 1832 and a cardinal in 1838.

[3] Pierre F.-X. de Ram (1804–1865), a distinguished church historian, was the first rector of the Catholic University of Louvain when it was restored in 1834.

honor and merits of founding an institution designed exclusively for their benefit.

Will Your Lordship be kind enough to inform me, at your earliest convenience, whether you desire to take part in the work, and, if so, what amount your diocese may possibly furnish, by collection in the various congregations, or by any other way you may think proper, towards the proposed Institution.

Your Lordship is also requested to nominate the person whom you may wish to charge with the execution of the work and to become the Rector of the Institution, at least for the time being. An early reply is urged as necessary, as I must write to the Count de Mérode to inform him whether the design is entered upon by the Bishops of the United States in a manner worthy of success, or whether it may not be necessary to abandon the project and leave him free to apply his alms towards building a Church in Brussels as was his original intention. You will please also to offer any suggestions which you may judge proper on the subject.

99. Archbishop Hughes' Opposition to Western Colonization for Catholic Immigrants, March 26, 1857

THROUGHOUT the nineteenth century repeated efforts were made to bring about a large-scale colonization of Catholic immigrants on the cheap lands of the West. Although a number of these efforts met with success, they never materialized to the degree of making an appreciable dent in the massing of the immigrants in the large cities. One of the principal reasons was the opposition of John Hughes (1797–1864), first Archbishop of New York, who could never be won to the idea. Fifteen years after Hughes' death the Irish Catholic Colonization Association was organized at Chicago in the spring of 1879 and one of its chief founders was John Lancaster Spalding (1840–1916), Bishop of Peoria. Spalding expressed a view that has been commonly held when he said, "That Archbishop Hughes became the opponent of colonization is, I am persuaded, most unfortunate. No other man has ever had such influence over the Irish Catholics of the United States, and no other man could have done so much to make them realize that their interests for time and eternity required that they should make homes for themselves on the land" (*The Religious Mission of the Irish People and Catholic Colonization* [New York, 1880], p. 147). The fact that today there are in the United States 644 counties in the rural areas in which there are no Catholic priests, tends to emphasize how the policy of a century ago has effected the development of the Church in this country. A statement of Hughes' position is contained in the following document which he wrote out in rough draft but never published. Source: Archives of the Archdiocese of New York, edited and published in Henry J. Browne, "Archbishop Hughes and Western Colonization," *Catholic Historical Review,* XXXVI (October, 1950), 269–273.

There is no people in the world, whether at home or abroad, so overdosed with counsel and advice as the Irish. Their friends advise them, their enemies advise them, those who are indifferent about their welfare advise them in like manner.

The last gentle advice that has been rendered to them in this country emanates from what is called the Buffalo Convention.[1] The good intentions of those who composed that spontaneous and self-constituted assembly, it is unnecessary to question. There is one thing in its favor, that a considerable number of the Catholic clergy, whether of the United States or of Canada, were present and probably took part in the deliberations of the so-called Convention.

Without questioning the purity of motives of any one connected with this meeting, one may be allowed to say that it was a most superfluous, unnecessary and unprofitable assemblage. It has added no single new idea to the common stock of information by which individual emigrants might be guided in the selection of their future homes. It has repeated what was known before, that there is a great deal of waste land, fertile withal, in the Eastern and Western provinces of Canada and on the Western boundaries of the present United States. It has also proclaimed what was sufficiently known before, that in the Eastern large cities, whether of the seaboard or of the immediate neighborhood of the interior, there are great numbers of Irish emigrants who have to struggle against all the miseries incident to their condition. It has announced in substance what cannot be denied by any one, that the conditions of such persons could hardly be deteriorated physically, religiously, or morally by any transition from East to West. Having said thus much we have abridged the whole amount of new light which the discussion of the question in the Buffalo Convention has shed on this very important topic.

[1] On February 12–15, 1856, a group of Catholics interested in western colonization for immigrants had assembled in Dudley Hall, Buffalo, New York. The convention drew ninety-five delegates in all, fifty-two from the United States and forty-three from Canada, including the vicars-general of the Dioceses of Buffalo, Chicago, Pittsburgh, and Wheeling, and the Canadian Dioceses of Bytown, Kingston, and Toronto, as well as twenty-five priests who were serving on the rural missions.

Next however the convention volunteers its benevolent advice and thereby assumes the responsibility which should induce conscientious persons familiar with the whole subject to pause and hesitate before they offered it to the very few who may be imposed upon and deceived by their silly theories.

Our confidence in the wisdom of the advice thus offered to the Irish is considerably diminished by the fact that some at least of those who have taken a leading part in the movement have hardly proved themselves competent to manage their own affairs. If they would take a little advice from the experience and good sense of those whom they have the arrogance to instruct they would probably succeed better in the management of their own private and personal interests.[2] Still advice, like politeness, costs but little to those who administer it, though it should prove very dear to such as may be misled and deceived by its erroneousness. The writer of this is acquainted with the circumstances of Catholics both in the East and in the West, and nothing on earth could induce him to give such advice as has emanated from the Buffalo Convention in regard to Catholic emigrants in this country. It may happen that persons misled by that advice will commemorate it in the bitterness of disappointment by tears on their cheeks and maledictions on their lips.

Again if those members of the Buffalo Convention who are not anchored to their present domicile by bonds which cannot be sundered were in earnest, one might expect that they would offer themselves as leaders and pioneers to exhibit the practical reality of happiness which they have so gorgeously painted in the idea of owning land, more or less, in the Western country. This however is a test to which it does not appear that a single member of the convention was equal. Their language is in substance as addressed to their Catholic fellow countrymen, "Go you, we stay." It is difficult to

---

[2] This comment was probably directed at Thomas D'Arcy McGee (1825–1868), one of the organizers of the Buffalo meeting. McGee had figured in the Young Irelander movement, had been arrested and imprisoned, but succeeded in escaping to the United States in 1848 in disguise. In New York he started a paper which he called the *Nation* which incurred the ire of Archbishop Hughes. Speaking in October, 1914, of McGee's role, John Ireland (1838–1918), Archbishop of St. Paul, said, "It is today beyond a doubt that had the enlightened views of D'Arcy McGee and those who took part with him in the famous Buffalo colonization convention of 1856 been duly encouraged and pushed to a favorable issue, the Catholic Church would be immensely more prosperous in all the Western States than ever again she can hope to be. . . ." (James H. Moynihan, *The Life of Archbishop John Ireland* [New York, 1953], p. 21.)

perceive that if this advice is good for their neighbors it should not be good for themselves also.[3]

It must not be inferred that the writer is opposed to the diffusion of emigrants into those portions of the country in which land may be obtained and in which living is cheap and labor has its fair recompense. But there is a natural process by which this result is perpetually going on. Poor emigrants not finding employment in one place seek it in another. And then when they go westward especially, acquire a certain practical knowledge of the production of the soil or the mines in the neighborhoods in which they find themselves. With this necessary knowledge, as a far more important capital than the limited amount which they may have economized from their labors, they sometimes acquire a title to lands, or in other interests by which their temporal prosperity is increased. But the idea of disturbing the minds of those who may be already established, whether in the East or in the West by a gilded and exaggerated report of theoretical blessings, which are in reserve for them, provided they can acquire the nominal ownership of 60 or 100 acres of uncultivated land, not unfrequently teeming with fever and ague — remote from the church — remote from the school — remote [from] the Post Office — remote from the physician — remote from the neighbors — this idea is dangerous, just so far as any Catholic emigrant is liable to be misled and deceived thereby. Then besides, our convention have [*sic*] understood that capital, more or less will be necessary, for those who shall be found simple enough to follow their advice. This being the case, that advice is tendered to those who, wherever they are located whether in the East or in the West, have been already, to some extent, successful in their industrial efforts. One might suppose that if they are doing well, it would be unwise for them to give up the certainty which they have for the uncertainty which is proposed to them.

But passing from this class our attention is directed to another, the condition of which has exercised the deep reflection and roused the benevolence of the Buf. Convention. We mean the hundreds and thousands who in New York, Boston, Philadelphia, and New Orleans are living in the proverbial wretchedness usually associated with the idea of a residence in cellars and in garrets. Now this class could not but improve their condition by a change to the open fields of the

---

[3] The fact that the sessions in Buffalo were conducted in secrecy and that Hughes did not know the background of the persons in attendance may account for this rather ungenerous judgment concerning these men, a number of whom were veteran missionaries in the West.

rural districts. But then the convention has not been able to devise any practical system of ways and means by which this [*sic*] could be transported to better homes, even if they themselves were willing to go. A great majority of them are entirely unfit by any sudden transition to enter on the multifarious industry which a settlement on wild land pre-supposes. They know not how to use the axe, if the land is to be cleared of timber. They know not how to hew and shape the logs necessary for the construction of their first rude cabin. They know not how to guide the plough in the prairies. They are inexpert in almost every element necessary to carry out the impractical ideal of their Buffalo advisers. But even if this were not the case the Buffalo Convention has not suggested any adequate means, either for their transportation to the west, or for the means of living there until the combined fruitfulness of the earth and their own labor should furnish them with the sustenance of life. Suppose they were skilful in clearing the wild land of timber, the Buffalo Convention has not told us who shall provide them with an axe — who shall construct their first cabin — who shall provide them with a plough, and other necessary farming utensils.

They have indeed in the ungraciousness of benevolence, [ ] that there are here and there Catholics who by industry and enterprise have become wealthy — and they have modestly suggested that a portion of this wealth wh. is not theirs might be appropriate for the disbursement of expenses to be incurred by the General Committee in carrying out the project recommended by the Buf. Convention. They have also discovered that there are millions and millions of dollars owned by Catholics and emigrants deposited in the savings banks of large cities and have insinuated that if these funds were placed in the hands of the general committee for carrying out the philanthropic purposes of the convention, the project would not turn out to be so idle a speculation as we have supposed. There is only one mistake, and that is, that the convention in alluding to these resources undertook to dispose of property which they had not earned, which did not belong to them and of which, without special permission from its owners, they had no right either to dispose of, or to allude to as they have done.

100. Chief Justice Taney's Reflections on Slavery, August 19, 1857

ROGER BROOKE TANEY (1777–1864) was the descendant of two old families of the Maryland gentry that had become Catholics in the early eighteenth century. In politics Taney was at first a Federalist, but after the dissolution of that party he gave his allegiance to Andrew Jackson. In 1831 he was named Attorney General of the United States, two years later Secretary of the Treasury, and in 1836 he was nominated by Jackson to succeed John Marshall as Chief Justice of the United States. During the nearly thirty years that he served on the supreme bench he wrote and participated in many important decisions, but the most famous one was his Dred Scott decision which was handed down on March 6, 1857, two days after the inauguration of Buchanan as president. In it Taney ruled the Missouri Compromise of 1820 as unconstitutional by stating that Dred Scott, born a slave, was unable to sue in a federal court, nor was his status altered merely because he had escaped into the free territory of Minnesota. Taney's views on slavery were influenced by the southern rural environment in which he had been raised. Personally he had manumitted his own slaves years before, co-operated with the American Colonization Society in helping to settle free Negroes in Liberia, and even purchased slaves to put them at liberty. But he was strongly opposed to the abolitionist movement and he felt that the solution of the problem should be left to the people directly concerned. Moreover, it was Taney's belief that the courts should carefully guard against encroachments of the federal government on the sovereignty of the states. Taney was a faithful Catholic all through his life, in spite of the frequent embarrassments he had to suffer from those who disliked the Church such as the Know-Nothings. In his last years he told a cousin, "Most thankful I am that the reading, reflection, studies, and experience of a long life have strengthened and confirmed my faith in the Catholic Church, which has never ceased to teach her children how they should live and how they should die" (Samuel Tyler, *Memoir of Roger Brooke Taney* [Baltimore, 1872], p. 475). The Reverend Samuel Nott, a Congregationalist minister of Wareham, Massachusetts, sent Taney a copy of a pamphlet he had written on the slave controversy in which he had included an analysis of the Dred Scott decision. In reply the old chief justice elaborated on his philosophy of slavery in a letter which revealed his conservative views, his judicial temperament, and his clarity of mind. Source: *Proceedings of the Massachusetts Historical Society, 1871–1873* (Boston: Published by the Society, 1873), pp. 445–447.

Fauquier, White Sulphur Springs, Virginia
August 19th, 1857.

Sir, — I received some time ago your letter, and pamphlet on "Slavery, and the Remedy," which you have been kind enough to send me. They were received when I was much out of health, and about to leave home for the summer. And it was not in my power to give the pamphlet an attentive perusal until within a few days past. I have read it with great pleasure. The just, impartial, and fraternal spirit in which it is written entitles it to a respectful consideration, in the South as well as the North. And if any thing can allay the unhappy excitement which is daily producing so much evil to the African as well as the white race, it is the discussion of the subject in the temper in which you have treated it. For you have looked into it and considered it in all its bearings, in the spirit of a statesman as well as a philanthropist. I am glad to find that it has been so well received as to reach the fifth edition.

Every intelligent person whose life has been passed in a slave-holding State, and who has carefully observed the character and capacity of the African race, will see that a general and sudden emancipation would be absolute ruin to the negroes, as well as to the white population. In Maryland and Virginia every facility has been given to emancipation where the freed person was of an age and condition of health that would enable him to provide for himself by his own labor. And before the present excitement was gotten up, the freed negro was permitted to remain in the State, and to follow any occupation of honest labor and industry that he might himself prefer. And in this state of the law manumissions were frequent and numerous. They sprang from the kindness and sympathy of the master for the negro, or from scruples of conscience; and were often made without sufficiently considering his capacity and fitness for freedom. And in the greater number of cases that have come under my observation, freedom has been a serious misfortune to the manumitted slave; and he has most commonly brought upon himself privations and sufferings which he would not have been called on to endure in a state of slavery. In many cases, however, it has undoubtedly promoted his happiness. But all experience proves that the relative position of the two races, when placed in contact with each other, must necessarily become such as you describe. Nor is it felt as a painful degradation by the black race. On the contrary, upon referring to the last census, you will find that more free negroes remain in Maryland than in any one of the Northern States, notwithstanding the disabilities and stricter police to which they are subjected. And there is a still greater number in Virginia. I speak from memory, without having the census before me. But I think I am not mistaken in the fact.

It is difficult for any one who has not lived in a slaveholding State to comprehend the relations which practically exist between the slaves and their masters. They are in general kind on both sides, unless the slave is tampered with by ill-disposed persons; and his life is usually cheerful and contented, and free from any distressing wants or anxieties. He is well taken care of in infancy, in sickness, and in old age. There are indeed exceptions, — painful exceptions. But this will always be the case, where power combined with bad passions or a mercenary spirit is on one side, and weakness on the other. It frequently happens when both parties are of the same race, although the weaker and dependent one may not be legally a slave.

Unquestionably it is the duty of every master to watch over the religious and moral culture of his slaves, and to give them every comfort and privilege that is not incompatible with the continued existence of the relations between them. And so far as my knowledge extends, this duty is faithfully performed by the great body of hereditary slaveholders in Maryland and Virginia. I speak of these States only, because with respect to them I have personal knowledge of the subject. But I have no reason to suppose it is otherwise in States farther south. And I know it has been the desire of the statesmen of Maryland to secure to the slave by law every protection from maltreatment by the master than can with safety be given, and without impairing that degree of authority which is essential to the interest and well-being of both. But this question is a very delicate one, and must at all times be approached with the utmost caution. The safe and true line must always depend upon existing circumstances, and they must be thoroughly inquired into and understood before there can be any safe or useful legislation in a State.

The pains which have unhappily been taken for some years past to produce discontent and ill-feeling in the subject race, has rendered any movement in that direction still more difficult. For it has naturally made the master more sensitive and jealous of any new restriction upon the power he has heretofore exercised, and which he has been accustomed to think essential to the maintenance of his authority as master. And he also feels that any step in that direction at the present time might injuriously affect the minds of the slaves. They are for the most part weak, credulous, and easily misled by stronger minds. And if in the present state of things additional restrictions were placed on the authority of the master, or new privileges granted to them, they would probably be told that they were wrung from the master by their Northern friends; and be taught to regard them as the first step to a speedy and universal emancipation, placing them on a perfect equality with the white race. It is easy to foresee what would be the sad result of such an impression upon the minds of this weak and credulous race.

Your review of the decision in the case of Dred Scott is a fair one, and states truly the opinion of the Court. It will, I hope, correct some of the misrepresentations which have so industriously been made; and made too, I fear, by many who must have known better. But I do not mean to publish any vindication of the opinion; or of my own consistency, or the consistency of the Court. For it would not become the Supreme Court, or any member of it, to go outside of the appropriate sphere of judicial proceedings; and engage in a controversy with any one who may choose from any motive to misrepresent its opinion. The opinion must be left to speak for itself. And it is for that reason that I hope you will pardon me for requesting that you will not permit this letter to be published in the newspapers or otherwise. Not that I am not perfectly ready on all proper occasions to say publicly every thing I have said in this letter. But in the judicial position I have the honor to occupy, I ought not to appear as a volunteer in any political discussion; and still less would it become me out of Court and off the bench to discuss a question which has been there determined. And I have written to you (although a stranger) thus freely from the personal respect with which the perusal of your pamphlet has inspired me. I am not a slaveholder. More than thirty years ago I manumitted every slave I ever owned, except two, who were too old, when they became my property, to provide for themselves. These two I supported in comfort as long as they lived. And I am glad to say that none of those whom I manumitted disappointed my expectations, but have shown by their conduct that they were worthy of freedom; and know how to use it.

With great respect, I am, sir,

Your ob't serv't,

R. B. Taney.

The Rev[d] Samuel Nott,
Wareham, Mass.

101. Bishop Elder on the Apostolate to the Negro Slaves in Mississippi, 1858

ONE of the most difficult missionary problems for the Church in the nineteenth century was the spiritual care of the Negro slaves in the southern states. In no other area of the county was the Church poorer in numbers and resources, so that it was often impossible to provide proper facilities for even the few and scattered white Catholics. Three years before the outbreak of the Civil War the third Bishop of Natchez, William Henry Elder (1819–1904), outlined in a detailed way for the Society for the Propagation of the Faith the difficulties of the Negro apostolate in Mississippi. The following letter gives a picture which *mutatis mutandis* was descriptive of conditions in every southern diocese during the last years of slavery. Source: Archives of the Diocese of Natchez, photostat copy.

Gentlemen

The business of my Diocese has made it necessary for me to spend much time in travelling. I have now been absent from home nearly two months continually, & in the spring likewise I was nearly two months away. Hence it has been impossible for me to write to you earlier as I had intended; & even now I cannot give you the full & interesting account of our missions which I had hoped to prepare, both from want of time on my own part, & because I have not got reports from the Pastors on the various points on which I would desire to inform you. Moreover, being obliged even now to write at various times & in various places, without the facilities which I should have at home for rendering my letter into French, you must pardon [me] for simply writing to you in English.

I beg of you to send me a number of copies of the sheet you have printed containing the heads on which you desire information. I have only found one by accident, & not in time to ask of the Pastors information on those points. I shall follow them however & give you the best information at present in my possession.

The Diocese of Natchez comprises the State of Mississippi, & has an area of 47,000 square miles or about 5,400 square leagues.

The *Number* of *Catholics* was stated in the Almanac several years ago, to be about *ten thousand*. I have not been able to learn how that estimate was made, nor how much reliance can be placed upon it. I believe that if all the Catholics could be counted, who are scattered through the interior of the country, the number would be much greater. I hope that next year we shall know more about it.

The whole Population of the State according to the Census taken in 1850 was 606,526. Speaking generally we may say that all of them profess to be Christians. A great many however do not belong to any particular Denomination, & even among those who do, a considerable number have never been baptized. The Baptists expressly reject the practice of baptizing infants, & very few Protestants look upon it as necessary for salvation.

The most prevalent sects are the Methodists and Baptists. Presbyterians are likewise numerous; the Episcopalians or Anglicans are but few, so far as I have learned.

But it is necessary for you to understand that more than half our population consists of *negro slaves,* who number 309,878; besides free negroes to the number of 930.

These poor negroes form in some respects my chief anxiety. I believe they are generally well cared for, so far as health & the necessaries of life are concerned. But for learning & practising religion, they have at present very little opportunity indeed. Commonly their Masters are well disposed to allow them religious instruction, & sometimes they pay Ministers to come & preach on the plantation. They do not like to let the negroes go to a public church, because there is danger of their misbehaving when they are away from home, & out of sight of the Overseer; & because various inconveniences result from the servants of one plantation mingling with those of another. Each master has something particular in his regulations & his method of management, & if the servants have free intercourse together, they are apt to make each other jealous & dissatisfied.

Some masters indeed object to having a Minister come to preach to their slaves, & they rather encourage some one of the blacks themselves to become a preacher for the rest. You may imagine what kind of religious instruction the poor creatures get.

Catholic masters of course are taught that it is their duty to furnish their slaves with opportunities for being well instructed, & for practising their religion. And here is my anxiety, that I cannot enable those masters to do their duty because there are not Priests enough. The negroes must be attended in a great measure on the plantation, both for the reasons given above, & because in our case there are so few churches; & even where there is a church, the negroes of four or five plantations would fill it up, & leave no room for the white, nor for the other negroes of the neighborhood. The Priest then must go to the plantations, & these are scattered at great distances through the country. All the Priests that I have are residing in congregations from which they cannot be absent long. We need a band of travelling Missionaries who should attend to these plantations, & at the same time hunt out the Catholics scattered through the country. In both of these ways an immensity of good can be done. The poor negroes very often have at first a fear of a Catholic Priest, or imagine they can never understand him; but they are not ill disposed towards religion. Indeed they often have a craving for its ministrations. Having few comforts & no expectations in this world, their thoughts & desires are the more easily drawn to the good things of the world to come. I say often because often again they are so entirely animal in their inclinations, so engrossed with the senses, that they have no regard for any thing above the gratifications of the body. But even among such as these, the missionary often finds a good soil for the seed of religion, because their sensuality arises not so much from malice, as from the want of religious instruction — the want of knowing that there is anything better than this world within their reach. It is true, when from this ignorance they have formed habits of sin, they are not always ready to abandon them when better instructed; but patient & persevering instruction & exhortation, together with the use of the Sacraments, will commonly succeed at last in bringing them to a better life.

For the negro is naturally inclined to be dependent on others; therefore he is disposed to listen & believe what he is told by his superiors. When he resists the teachings of religion, it is not so much from stubbornness as from weakness of mind & will. This weakness of mind makes it hard for him to understand an argument; his weakness of will makes it hard to resist temptation, & still harder to break bad habits. It makes him also liable to great fickleness. This is one of the hard trials of a missionary among them. It is not uncommon for a negro to attend religious instruction for a considerable time with great fidelity & a lively interest, & yet drop off before receiving the Sacraments. Sometimes there is no apparent cause, but just fickleness of character, or perhaps secret temptation. But more generally it may be traced to some irregularity in the instruction, or some little neglect which begets an indifference on their part. They are very much creatures of feeling. If they are attended to regularly & if their instructor takes great interest in them, & gets them to realize the value of their souls, he can do a great deal with them for the glory of God. And he may have the unspeakable consolation of finding among them vocations to a high degree of sanctity. The humility of their condition & the docility of their character take away many of the ordinary obstacles to the workings of grace; & where other circumstances are favourable, these lowly ones in the eyes of the world sometimes rise very high in the favour of God. I have known a case of a servant girl's being really revered as a saint by the family in which she had been reared, & where she was working with all simplicity & fidelity in the lowest offices.

Oh! what a harvest of souls among these 310,000 negroes: every one of them immortal, made to the image & likeness of God, redeemed by the Precious Blood of the Son of God! Oh! what a frightful havoc

Satan is making among them! What numbers of children die without baptism! how many grown persons live & die in ignorance of God, and still worse, buried in miserable sins & habits of sins, which they neither know nor care to free themselves from. Oh! for a band of Apostles like Fr. Claver,[1] to devote themselves to the service of the negro. Not such service indeed as he rendered to them with so much heroism; for our blacks are not often in that bodily wretchedness which called forth so much of his charity. They need services less repugnant to flesh & blood, & yet not less fruitful in the saving of souls & promoting the glory of God. They need instructions & the Sacraments. The Masters provide for their bodies & even in a great measure for their exterior conduct. Are there not Priests of God — at least in the generous Apostolic land of France — are there not still some there, who are ready to put the sickle into this abundant field? It will cost pains & patience, but the consolations will be very great, as they gather those rich sheaves of more than golden fruit into the granary of heaven. *Euntes ibant & flebant mittentes semina sua: venientes autem venient cum exaltatione portantes manipulos suos. . . .*

102. Archbishop Hughes Interprets American Liberty and Its Abuses to the Holy See, March 23, 1858

THE spirit and intent of American liberty often proved puzzling to the Holy See and they were not infrequently misinterpreted at Rome. That this should have been true was not surprising in the light of the shameful treatment accorded Pius IX's representative, Archbishop Gaetano Bedini (1806–1864) on his tour of this country, June, 1853–February, 1854. The most commanding figure in the American Church at the mid-century was John Hughes (1797–1864), first Archbishop of New York. Hughes was a bold defender of the Church's rights against the nativists, the press, and other critics, and as a consequence he was in the thick of most of the controversies of the day. Realizing the effect that false information from the United States might have on the officials of the Roman Curia, Hughes prepared an elaborate report in 1858 on conditions in his archdiocese in which he included an analysis of the true concept of liberty among Americans and the abuses to which freedom in this country had been subjected by revolutionary elements from abroad who were hostile to the best interests of Church and State. The following excerpt furnishes a vivid picture of an aspect of American Catholic life in these years that is seldom emphasized.

[1] St. Peter Claver (1581–1654), a Spanish Jesuit, who performed heroic missionary labors among the Negroes at Cartagena in present-day Colombia from 1610 to his death.

Source: Henry J. Browne (Ed.), "The Archdiocese of New York A Century Ago. A Memoir of Archbishop Hughes, 1838–1858," *Historical Records and Studies,* XXXIX–XL (1952), 168–174.

We come now to the Revolutions in Europe. During the period last under consideration [immediately above Hughes had been deploring the excessive immigration of the previous twenty years] their rebound on New York was most perilous to the faith and morals of the people committed to my charge. I cannot help regarding it as a singular protection of Almighty God and a singular evidence of the interposition of the Blessed Virgin Mary, under whose patronage this Diocese had been especially placed from its origin, under the title of the "Assumption," now, under that of the "Immaculate Conception," that we have escaped the ordeal with so little injury to the principles of our Religion. In this Country, "Liberty" is the watch word, the boast, the pride of all men. The general tone of the Country would seem to require that every man should touch his hat whenever the word "Liberty" is pronounced in his presence. This, you can easily imagine, applies especially to all aspirants for public office, and to the very numerous and ubiquitous class of professional politicians. Sensible men though imbued in heart with the same feeling, yet oftentimes ridicule this extravagant display of it among the classes to which I have referred.

Liberty, in this Country, has a very clear and specific meaning. It is not understood in Europe, as it is here. Here, it means the vindication of personal rights; the fair support of public laws; the maintenance, at all hazards, of public order, according to those laws; the right to change them when they are found to be absurd or oppressive. Such, in brief, is the meaning of the word liberty, as understood by the people of the United States. Of course, you will think of the excesses that have been committed from time to time by mobs, "lynch laws" &c, as marring the correctness of the foregoing statement. But I can assure you that these excesses are regarded, here, as outrages and violations of liberty, the same as they would be in Europe. But in Continental Europe Liberty is understood to mean the overthrow of all existing governments, recognizing the principle of Monarchy. It is the genius of destruction and bloodshed: — ferociously bent on pulling down whatever exists, without the fore-sight or capacity to substitute any thing as good or better.

This distinction did not strike the American people at the outbreak of the late revolutions in Europe, as it does now Their national pride, as a republic, was much flattered by the anticipation that their example was about to be imitated by all the civilized nations of the earth. There were to be no more kings, or Emperors, or Pope, or Princes; but in their stead, *"the people" "the people" "the people."* Experience, however, has taught them their mistake; and they have become quite satisfied that the specimens of patriotism, from the different nations of Western Europe, who by flight or expulsion have reached these shores, are to be ranked among the veriest wretches that ever disgraced humanity, or disturbed the well-being of Society.[1]

This was not the case, however, fifteen years ago. About that time, there was established in this City a paper called the *"Echo d'Italia."*[2] This Journal was supported, not by Italians, but by the enemies of the Catholic Church; who employed it, to feed *their own papers* with the scandals and calumnies against Italy and its inhabitants, which might tend to damage the estimation of our holy religion throughout the world. Around this bad centre were congregated, as time went on, every renegade both to creed and country that Italy would not allow to live in her bosom. Among these, I am sorry to say, that even some bad priests distinguished themselves by their atrocious assaults upon the Catholic Creed and its ministers. The *"Echo d'Italia,"* was supported as I have remarked, as a *feeder* to the Anti-Catholic press. The tyranny of the church, the wicked lives of the prelates, the dreadful bondage of the noble Italian people, in their beautiful and classic land, — were themes inexhaustible under the pens of native writers for that Journal. Hence, the hypocritical homage manifested in this Country, by the bitterest protestants, in favor of Our Illustrious Holy Father on his accession to the Papal Throne.[3]

You will not be surprised if the Catholics were carried away in the enthusiasm of the Country at large — that they too were immensely flattered, at having lived to see the Holy Father regarded with such universal admiration. Under such circumstances, *they* became also the blind idolators of what both Americans and Europeans designated as "Liberty" — the "progress of human freedom" &c &c &c. I saw the impeding danger of association, on this principle, which it was intended to bring about between the Catholics of New York and the "Red

[1] Due to the failure of the liberal revolutions of 1848–1849 in the German and Italian States, the Austrian Empire, Ireland, and other countries, numerous political refugees found their way to the United States in these years.

[2] *Echo d'Italia* was a weekly paper that began publication in New York in 1850.

[3] The election of the liberal-minded Giovanni Mastai-Ferretti as Pope Pius IX on June 16, 1846, brought a wave of enthusiasm among liberals in the United States as well as in Europe.

Republicans" of Europe. I began early to put my flock upon their guard — not by a direct assault upon liberty, but against its abuse, indirectly and to a measured extent, whenever an opportunity presented itself. I had most to apprehend from the spurious patriotism of the "Young Irelanders."[4] You know how fond is the attachment which Irishmen cherish for their native land, and this attachment seems to grow stronger the farther they are removed from its shores and the longer they have been absent. They had been wrought to a high pitch of expectation, and hope for their country's freedom, by the bombastic rhetoric of the Dublin Nation and other journals of the same type. When these hopes were suddenly dashed in this Country by the result of Mr. Smith O'Brien's[5] campaign, they were broken down and almost ashamed of the soil of their nativity. This feeling was taken advantage of and turned into bitterness by some of the Irish Refugees, who, on reaching these shores, pretended to give a full account of the recent efforts in which they had been engaged. They charged the failure on the "Catholic Clergy," as enemies to the Irish people — denounced the hierchy [*sic*] and priesthood of Ireland, proclaimed that if any of them should show his face on this side of the Atlantic he should be met with "hisses," instead of the ordinary signs of reverence and respect.

Our poor people were not in a frame of mind to discriminate, and to detect the malice of these cowardly and unjust accusations whilst the Refugee Patriots from France, Germany, & Italy did not hesitate to proclaim, openly, that there was no hope of freedom for the down trodden people of Europe until the Catholic Church and its clergy, from the Pope downwards, should be overthrown, and if necessary, annihilated.

The first event which opened the eyes of the Catholics was the shout of joy which rang throughout the Country when it was announced that the Holy Father had been driven away from Rome.[6] The jubilee of our enemies made the Catholics sad. They could not foresee the

[4] The Young Irelanders grew restive with the conciliatory policies of Daniel O'Connell to win the freedom of Ireland, broke from his leadership in 1840, established the *Nation* as their organ in 1842, and espoused the policy of violence to win their goal.

[5] William Smith O'Brien (1803–1864) was one of the principal leaders of the Young Irelanders. A series of agrarian crimes, suspension for Ireland of the habeas corpus act, and the news of the revolutions on the continent prompted an uprising in Tipperary in July–August, 1848, which the British troops quickly crushed. The leaders were transported to Van Diemen's Land, but a number of them succeeded in escaping and reaching the United States where they carried on their agitation for Irish freedom.

[6] When the Mazzinian republicans seized Rome Pius IX fled on November 25, 1848, to Gaeta in the Kingdom of the Two Sicilies.

final result of the measures which the usurpers in the Eternal City had put into execution. The future looked dark, and they were downhearted. With a view to cheer them, and at the same time, to give their thoughts a better direction, as well as to withdraw them from association with the Red Republicans who were among us, and the abettors of their principles here, I preached what might be called a political sermon in my Cathedral, on the Sunday next following the receipt of the news, that the Holy Father had been obliged to quit Rome. This became a *turning point* in the thoughts of my own people, with the exception of a very few who were incurable, but who ceased from that time to have any influence. I send you a copy of the discourse which was taken down by a Reporter of one of the secular parents [*sic*], and published the next day.[7]

You can easily understand that from the period of its publication I became offensive to all those wild and unprincipled Republicans. They did not spare me; but neither did they convert me: and the words which I uttered from time to time, and on various occasions, were published not only here in New York but throughout the Country — in some papers out of enmity, in others, to let their readers know what I thought in regard to passing events. I have reason to know that these publications had a great influence in keeping the Catholics *steady,* and little by little, bringing "Red Republicanism" into utter contempt among protestants as well as Catholics.

The enthusiasm and admiration in which Kossuth was held by the American people were almost boundless.[8] When released from prison by the Sultan, this Government sent a vessel of war to receive him and bring him to the United States. When he reached Southampton, in England, he took occasion to make a grand speech, and in it, to

[7] Hughes preached his sermon on "The Present Position of Pius IX" in St. Patrick's Cathedral on January 3, 1849. For the text cf. Lawrence Kehoe (Ed.), *Complete Works of the Most Rev. John Hughes* (New York, 1865), I, 11–21.

[8] After the defeat of the Hungarian revolt Louis Kossuth (1802–1894) fled to Turkey in August, 1849. On December 5, 1851, he arrived in New York where he was given a tumultuous welcome. But after it became clear that Kossuth had come to the United States to seek money and support for his revolutionary cause the isolationist sentiments of Americans brought a change of attitude toward him and when he departed in July, 1852, there was not a single person at hand to bid him farewell. That Kossuth was a rallying point for the anti-Catholic nativists in this country there is no doubt, and it has been remarked of his first days in the United States that his enthusiastic reception "was due in part to the fact that he was a symbol of Protestantism as well as of liberty" (Ray Allen Billington, *The Protestant Crusade* [New York, 1938], p. 331). Hughes' stand against the Hungarian revolutionist unquestionably hurt the latter's cause with American Catholics, but the archbishop's account exaggerated the extent of his influence in this regard.

compliment England for its protestant feeling whilst he denounced at the same time the Pope and the Jesuits as the sworn enemies of human liberty. A report of this speech appeared in our newspapers before Kossuth's arrival in this City — and in a public meeting of Catholics convened for the purpose of receiving the Rev. Dr. Donnelly and the Rev. Dr. Devlin, who had just arrived as Collectors for the "Irish University,"[9] I took occasion as it were incidentally, in the course of my address, to criticise Kossuth and to denounce his principles. I dreaded the influence which his reception here might exercise on the Catholics, and wished them to be fore-warned.[10] Next day, I was assailed in the newspapers for my denunciation of Kossuth; I had to reply and justify myself; and thus my opinions of Kossuth were spread all over the Country, and his mission became a comparative failure precisely for the reason that the Catholics kept aloof wherever he passed. Even in New York the grand oration that had been arranged for him turned out to be a failure because the Catholics would have nothing to do with him. This was noted down by the politicians as a hint that their attentions to Kossuth might be remembered much to their disadvantage; and wherever the Hero of Hungary passed he was allowed to place himself in the hands of protestant Clergyman and Anti-Catholic bigots. He felt this deeply, and complained of it bitterly. He took occasion afterwards to make some remarks complimentary to the Catholics — but it was too late — and he fell so rapidly in public estimation that he was obliged within six months to leave the country clandestinely under the name of *"Alexander Smith."*

I should not give you an idea of the excitement which prevailed during the period now under consideration if I did not mention that so strong became the force of public opinion in favor of what was called the "European liberty," that it shook the firmness of not a few of the Catholic Clergy, and that from one Reverend pen, at least, I was called to an account in the secular journals for having misrepresented the sentiments of the Church on the subject of "political liberty."

In short, during the paroxysm about "European freedom," and the overthrow of "Kingly Governments" in Europe, it was as much as one

---

[9] The Catholic University of Ireland with John Henry Newman as rector opened for classes in Dublin on November 3, 1854. The identity of Donnelly and Devlin was not established, but the most recent scholarly history of the Irish university notes the fact that American Catholics contributed to the fund in 1851 the sum of £4,735 (Fergal McGrath, S.J., *Newman's University. Idea and Reality* [London, 1951], p. 102).

[10] Hughes' speech against Kossuth was delivered at Stuyvesant Institute, New York, on November 18, 1851.

could do to stand erect without bowing or bending to the force of popular sentiment, as portrayed in the newspapers. Details would be endless; and so I shall pass to the next division of my subject, which is a half opened *new* book in the history of the Catholic Church in America. . . . [Hughes then continues with a lengthy section on Know-Nothingism.]

103. An Appeal for the North American College at Rome, November 13, 1858

FOR obvious reasons the Catholic hierarchy of most countries has at one time or other given thought to the establishment of a national college at Rome where candidates for its priesthood may receive the special advantages of study in the Eternal City. From the late sixteenth and early seventeenth centuries colleges of this type were maintained for English, Irish, and Scotch seminarians. The question of such an institution for the Church of the United States was first seriously discussed when a delegation of American bishops visited the Holy See in December, 1854, for the definition of the dogma of the Immaculate Conception. At that time there were 590 seminarians enrolled in about thirty seminaries in the United States, and a total of 1604 priests, both diocesan and religious, a large number of whom had been born and educated abroad. The prelates most interested in this project were Archbishops Kenrick of Baltimore and Hughes of New York and Bishop O'Connor of Pittsburgh (1810–1872). In 1857 O'Connor acted as a delegate to Rome in the matter and returned to inform his fellow bishops of the high hopes of Pope Pius IX for the undertaking and the pontiff's practical support in the form of a building purchased at his own expense to house the college. At the outset some of the bishops demurred, but the initial difficulties were finally overcome and on December 7, 1859, the North American College opened with twelve students in an old Visitandine convent in the Via dell' Umiltà. Since 1859 the college has enrolled around 2100 students of whom about 1900 are numbered among its priest alumni. The needs of the greatly expanded Church in the United States ultimately proved too great for the old building in the Via dell' Umiltà and in October, 1953, a new college on the Janiculum Hill was dedicated with accommodations for approximately 300 students. In the following pastoral letter Bishop O'Connor sketched for his priests and people the advantages of an institution of this kind for the American Church, a subject on which he could speak with conviction by reason of his years in Rome as a student at the Urban College of Propaganda Fide. Source: *Pittsburgh Catholic,* November 13, 1858.

MICHAEL O'CONNOR, by the grace of God and the favor of the Apostolic See
Bishop of Pittsburgh.
To the Clergy and Faithful of the Diocese of Pittsburgh.

Grace unto you, and peace from God our Father, and from the Lord Jesus Christ.

The Archbishop of Baltimore having appointed the Sunday within the Octave of the Feast of the Immaculate Conception, December 12th, as the day on which will be made, in the Archdiocess [*sic*], the first collection for the American College at Rome, it is our wish that the same day a collection be taken up, for this object, in all the Churches of our Diocess [*sic*].

You are aware that the Prelates of the United States have felt deeply interested in the establishment of a National College at the centre of Catholic unity. The wishes of the Bishops in this matter, have been fully shared by their flocks ever since it became generally understood that such a measure was in contemplation. The Catholic Press has advocated the undertaking with zeal and perseverance, and some Catholic gentlemen of means, in the hope of insuring its speedy consummation, have pledged themselves to contribute liberally to its support. The late circular of his Eminence, the Cardinal Prefect of the Propaganda, which you have read in the public prints, gives the pleasing assurance that this most desirable institution may soon be established on a footing in every way worthy of the country it is destined to represent in the Eternal City. By this letter of his Eminence Cardinal Barnabo, we are informed that our present illustrious Pontiff has purchased, and placed at the disposal of the Bishops of the United States, a large and suitable building, to be used by them for the purpose of an American College.

The situation of this edifice is as desirable as any other in Rome. It is at once central and healthy, and in the immediate neighborhood of the schools which the students will frequent. Still, the house is, of course, wanting in all the appointments indispensable to a College. As it is presumed the institution will open with a very considerable number of students, it will be necessary, from the very first, to furnish it on an extensive scale, besides providing it with a suitable library. The fact, too, that the building was not originally intended for a college, will necessitate alterations in it, involving a large outlay. It is to defray these unavoidable expenses, and to create a fund for the maintenance of the establishment, your charity will be appealed to on the approaching 12th of December. Your liberality on that occasion will, we feel assured, be worthy of the object in behalf of which it will be invoked, and fitly correspond to the noble generosity of the Sovereign Pontiff, whose first offering to the good work has been so munificent.

The advantages of an ecclesiastical training in Rome, especially in a National establishment where this discipline will be specially suited to the character of our youth, and prepare them for the field in which they are to labor, can hardly be overrated. In that city the clerical student is surrounded by every thing that can elevate the taste, enlarge the mind, and strengthen the faith. Her galleries and churches spread out before him all that is excellent in Pagan and Christian art. Her libraries, the best in the world, place within his reach all the standard works of positive and abstract science, together with many other sources of knowledge, not found elsewhere. Her museums, rich in monuments of the past, whilst they greatly facilitate [*sic*], give a most lively interest to his historical and archaeological studies. His laudable ambition of distinction is here stimulated by the noble impulse of patriotism; for, at Rome, he must measure his intellectual strength with competitors from all nations. Her numerous colleges, monasteries, and academies, afford him frequent opportunities of listening to disputations on theology and philosophy, and to the lectures of distinguished scholars, on literature, history and science. He is made acquainted with the organization, and usages of the different courts of appeal, to which are referred difficulties and disputes on matters of doctrine, and discipline, all over the Church. His professors are always men of profound learning, and, not infrequently, of world-wide reputation. His course of studies is long and rigorous, and eminently calculated to beget habits of deep thought, and close criticism. And, since, at this centre of gospel light, all minds seem to be illumined, and illumined [*sic*], his constant, familiar intercourse with members of the Roman clergy, accustoms him to regulate his views on ordinary topics, by high principles of Catholic truth.

And, at Rome, what does he not see to excite his devotion, and glory in the cross? Her numerous charities, that reach every want and infirmity of the poor and the sick; the piety of her people; her many festivals; the splendor of her churches; the grandeur of her ceremonies, give him a lasting sense of the duties and the dignity of his religion. His piety is enkindled at the shrines of her saints; and he is filled with Christian fortitude at the tombs of her martyrs and apostles. Her ruins show him the strength of Christian faith, and the colossal proportions of that power, which labored for centuries to destroy it: whilst the mute, but eloquent witnesses that have arisen, and arise, from her catacombs, tell him what men may suffer for the Kingdom of Heaven. In Rome, too, as nowhere else, he is made to realize the fact, that the Church is the only organization that does, or can supply redemption, through Christ, to a fallen world. The thousands, from all nations, that visit her sanctuaries; the missionaries that leave her to carry the Gospel to distant lands, or return to give an account of their labors; the voice of the Supreme Pontiff, speaking authoritatively to the churches of Christendom; the Bishops that come, at stated times, to pay their homage to the Chair of Peter, give him the most exalted idea of the Church's unity and Catholicity.

But these advantages, venerable and beloved Brethren, for the most part, peculiar to a Roman ecclesiastical training, though valuable, on account of their [*sic*] learning and knowledge they directly foster, are chiefly so, because of their effects in those, amongst whom their recipients are afterwards called to labor. They who have drawn deeply at the source of Apostolic truth, will be likely to carry that truth pure, and in plenty, to others. They who have learned to love Rome, not only from principle, but also from the tenderest, holiest local attachments, will be likely to bind the faith and affections of others to this sacred, immovable centre of evangelical truth.

Rome is the capital of the Christian world; the new Jerusalem of the people of God. Sacrifice is now offered up: "from the rising of the sun, to the going down of the same." But the Arc [*sic*] of the Covenant, and the Holy of Holies are at Rome. Of Rome, too, we may say with the Prophet: "The law shall come forth from Sion, and the word of the Lord from Jerusalem." It is the mission of the Church of Rome to instruct all other churches in sound doctrine; to enlighten their doubt; to lead them, in difficulty and danger. For, in the person of the Roman Pontiff, Peter feeds the entire flock of Christ, both pastors and people. With that Church, all the other churches have lived, and must live, in the unity of faith; and, in this unity, find their safety and their prosperity. Severed from Rome, the most flourishing churches have fallen into heresy, and even into barbarism.

The national pride that would lead men, or nations, to suspect union in faith, with Rome, or to disregard whatever tends to promote, or preserve it, is a proper feeling, carried to unwise excess. There is but one sun to illuminate all lands; there is but one truth to enlighten all minds. The Church of Christ is necessarily one, and of all nations. Her government, then, must be one, and of universal jurisdiction. To the seat of that government, wherever established, is due the homage of true believers all over the world.

That an American College in Rome is necessary to impart a sound ecclesiastical education to our clergy, or to maintain our union with the Holy See, no one will pretend. That, whilst contributing much to secure these results, it will greatly promote the higher ecclesiastical studies among them, and add a new grace to our National Church, few, we think can deny. The clergy and people of the United States, yield to no others, in their loving attachment to Rome; and are second to none, in their zeal for the promotion of ecclesiastical, and secular learning. Indeed, it is these very dispositions, that have led us to ask of the Holy Father, a favor already enjoyed by so many nations of Europe and the East; and which is soon to be granted to the Catholics of the South American Continent. A National College at Rome will, it must be presumed, very much augment the number of the learned among our clergy, and prove a powerful means, under God, of perpetuating the orthodoxy of our young Church, which no taint of heresy has, thus far, touched.

Pray, then, Brethren, that God move the hearts of all to aid this good work, according to each one's ability. It has the blessing of the Supreme Pontiff upon it, and it must succeed.

The grace of our Lord Jesus Christ be with you all. May the Blessed and Immaculate Patroness of the American Church keep you ever under her powerful protection.

Given at Pittsburgh, this 10th day of November, in the year of our Lord, 1858.

Michael
Bishop of Pittsburgh.

J. Keogh, Secretary.

104. Father Hecker Sketches His Plans and Hopes for the Paulists, July 24, 1859

ONE of the most important figures in nineteenth-century American Catholicism was Isaac Thomas Hecker (1819–1888). Hecker became a Catholic in August, 1844, after a lengthy search for truth that had led him in 1843 to Brook Farm and Fruitlands. During this time he became very well acquainted with Orestes Brownson, Bronson Alcott, Henry Thoreau, and other New England religious thinkers. After a novitiate in Belgium he became a member of the Congregation of the Most Holy Redeemer in 1846, returning to the United States in 1851 where for some years he was engaged in giving missions with several other convert Redemptorists. Since the order's principal concern was for the German Catholic immigrants, Hecker and his missionary companions were convinced that it would benefit the missions if the Redemptorists would open an English-speaking house which would be a center for the English missions. With this in mind, and with the encouragement of Bishop Bayley of Newark and Archbishop Hughes of New York, Hecker went to Rome in August, 1857, as the spokesman for his associates, to lay the proposition before the Redemptorist rector major. Three days after his arrival, he was expelled without a hearing for having made the journey without the necessary permission. Hecker found a defender in Alessandro Cardinal Barnabò, Prefect of the Congregation de Propaganda Fide, who took his case to Pius IX. It was thus that the Paulist Fathers came into existence in July, 1858, and from that time until his death thirty years later Hecker remained the superior general. He was an intensely active man who wrote several books, e.g., *Questions of the Soul* (New York, 1852) and *Aspirations of Nature* (New York, 1857), founded the *Catholic World* in 1865, organized the Catholic Publication Society the following year, acted as theologian for Archbishop Spalding of Baltimore at the Vatican Council — in all of which he kept uppermost in his mind the dominant motive of his priestly life, the winning of American Protestants to the Catholic faith. Three years after his death one of his confreres, Walter Elliott, C.S.P., published *The Life of Father Hecker* (New York, 1891) which appeared in a French translation in 1897 and became the center of a theological controversy on both sides of the Atlantic under the name of the so-called heresy of Americanism. The following letter, written a year after the establishment of the Paulists, to Father Adrien-Emmanuel Rouquette (1813–1887), poet, writer, and Indian missionary of Louisiana, gives an excellent picture of Hecker's plans and aspirations for the future of his new congregation. Source: Archives of the Paulist Fathers, photostat of original in the archives of the Archdiocese of New Orleans.

New York, July 24, 1859

Rev. Dear Friend.

Six months and more have elapsed since the reception of your last letter so full of kindred sympathy and hope.[1] In it you say: "I will write to you soon my end, my means, & the degree of success which I have already attained." And also that "you would write to me more at length and intimately" & you throw out the suggestion that "one day we might meet in the same vocation." Your letter has been lying on my table ever since, & I had but to glance at it to awaken my sympathies and enkindle my enthusiasm. I will not disguise to you that your last suggestion has more than once also occurred to my thoughts. For I cannot refuse to recognize the same aims, thoughts, & sentiments which occupy your mind also occupy mine. Apparently our ways differ, but as you remark, they are not so different in reality.

[1] Correspondence between Fathers Hecker and Rouquette had begun in November, 1858, as a result of "some cheering words" written by Rouquette in the New York *Freeman's Journal.*

Your attrait [*sic*] for solitude, silence, prayer, contemplation is no greater than my own. There was a time when my Superiors hesitated whether it were not better for me to change my state, & enter a contemplative order. During my years of study the greater part of my time was given to such a life, & one year of this period was wholly given to it and the care of the sick. Not as a matter of choice but of inability to apply myself to scientific studies. Among the so many pressing occupations at present,[2] I cherish the same attrait, & act always with reluctance & from a sense of duty. But when unable to study & my attention absorbed in contemplation I was at the time aware that the grace of God was preparing me only for a more intensive & extensive action than all studies could have done. While most helpless and by others regarded as a fool, it was my most intimate conviction that God's Providence was preparing me for a great work, the conversion of our countrymen. And when compelled under obedience at the time to give in writing an explanation of my state, I did not hesitate to express this conviction.[3] The same conviction prompted subsequently *Questions of the Soul* and *Aspirations of Nature*. The position in which I am at present placed I cannot regard in any other light than in view of this conviction, & as a special providence of God.

The conversion of the American people to the Catholic faith has ripened into a conviction with me which lies beyond the reign of doubt. My life, my labours, and my death is [*sic*] consecrated to it. No other aim as an end outside of my own salvation and perfection can occupy my attention a moment. But all other things in view of this, — art, science, literature, etc. etc. enter in as a part of the means, and command my interest, & demand all the encouragement within my reach. In the union of Catholic faith and American civilization a new birth awaits them all, and a future for the Church brighter than any past. That is briefly my "Credo."

Individually the faith has been identified with American life. Our effort is to identify Catholicity with American life in a religious association. I feel confident of its practicability. I entertain the hope of our

---

[2] Hecker refers here to the organization of the Paulist Fathers, raising money for a new church and convent, and the fulfillment of a heavy mission schedule.

[3] Hecker wrote this statement on May 30, 1848, while still a Redemptorist student at Wittem, Holland. In it he stated: "I believe that Providence calls me to an active life; further, that he calls me to America to convert a certain class of persons amongst whom I found myself before my conversion; I believe that I shall be the vile instrument which he will make use of for the conversion of a multitude of those unhappy souls who aspire after truth without having the means to arrive at and possess it" (Archives of the Paulist Fathers, Hecker Papers).

opening a door to our young men who aim at consecrating their lives to God & Religion, and of our Institution becoming in the hands of Divine Providence a means of spreading the Faith among our people.

Thus far God's blessing have accompanied our labors, never were they more successful. The location secured for our community could not be more suitable, its value has increased doubly since its purchase.[4] Our house is large and now almost ready for its roof; & in October we expect to occupy it. A few applications by priests to join us have been made; and several by young men, but these we are *not yet prepared* to receive. A few days ago I received from Cardinal Barnabò the permission to increase our numbers.

Our institution is based on the voluntary principle, with the idea of practicing all the religious virtues in the same degree of perfection as those under the vows. These are our practical measures.

You will perceive My Dear Friend, that I have taken up your offer "to write to me more at length & intimately" & fulfilled it in respect to yourself, which I trust will suggest a reciprocal confidence.

With great esteem

Your devoted friend & Servant in Xt.

I. T. HECKER

105. James A. McMaster's Criticism of the Lincoln Administration, June 8, 1861

THE American Catholic press of the mid and later nineteenth century was a far livelier enterprise than the official Catholic newspapers of our day. In an era when famous New York editors like James Gordon Bennett of the *Herald,* Horace Greeley of the *Tribune,* Henry J. Raymond of the *Times,* and Charles A. Dana of the *Sun* were making newspaper history in this country the convert-editor of the New York *Freeman's Journal,* James A. McMaster (1820–1886) exchanged editorial blows with the best of them. The weekly *Freeman's* had been founded in 1840 and McMaster became the editor in 1848. For the first few years he confined himself mainly to fighting the Church's battles and remained relatively clear of politics. But gradually he became involved in the slavery controversy and in July, 1856, Archbishop Hughes, who differed with him, withdrew his approbation from the *Freeman's* as a diocesan organ and in July, 1859, started his own *Metropolitan Record.* Pained though he was at this rebuff, McMaster's independent mind and strong views would not permit him to quit and he bravely carried on until his sharp and persistent criticisms of the Lincoln

[4] This property was located on 60th Street, west of 9th Avenue, and was bought for $63,000.

administration brought suspension of his paper in August, 1861, while the editor himself was arrested and imprisoned in Fort Lafayette for nearly six weeks. He had seen what was coming, but he was defiant to the end and sought in his last issue to rally renewed support for the *Freeman's*. "We know not what enterprise we may yet be impelled to undertake," he said. "But you who *feel* that we are right — *help* us to continue, and even to do *more*" (*Freeman's Journal,* August 24, 1861). McMaster was by no means a lone voice in his attacks on the government, for as Frank Luther Mott has said, "Never was there a war in which arm-chair generalship from newspaper offices was more vociferous, in which more editors became military strategists over night" (*American Journalism* [New York, 1941], p. 339). The following editorial was only one of a series in which McMaster castigated Lincoln and his conduct of the war. Source: Editorial, "The Ship on the Breakers," New York *Freeman's Journal,* June 8, 1861.

Abraham Lincoln, county court lawyer of the village of Springfield, Illinois, elected President according to the letter of the Constitution — and whom we are ready to sustain in the place he so unworthily fills, *according to the Constitution* — has been playing some infamous tricks, of late. He has been creating new regular armies, and establishing an additional navy, without any act of Congress. By a certain stretch of executive authority he has the *right,* in the present exigency, under the act of 1795, to call out the *militia of such States as may be necessary,* but the legal limit of that authority expires *"thirty days after the next assembling of Congress."* Abraham Lincoln made demure protestations, in his inaugural, that it was his devotion to the Constitution of the United States, and the laws made in pursuance thereof, that would *compel* him to act in a manner disagreeable to millions of his "dissatisfied countrymen." Why, then, in view of the crisis, did he not call Congress together at an *earlier* day? Why did he not limit his proclamation, calling for seventy-five thousand militia men, to the term for which *alone* he had Constitutional power to call them — the expiration of thirty days after the next meeting of Congress? Why, in his subsequent proclamation, calling for a much larger force, did he not, in the same way, confine himself to his legal and Constitutional power, of calling on *the militia of States,* for the term for which alone he had power to call them — ending *thirty days after the meeting of Congress?* Why has he undertaken, without act of Congress, to increase the regular army and the navy of the United States? Why has he assumed the peculiar and restrictive prerogative of Congress — the *law-making* power — in *creating* military offices and commissions, in order that he may fill those assumed offices with officers selected by him? Congress, which *alone* has the power, has recognized but *one* Major-General of the United States regular army — Gen. Winfield Scott.[1] Mr. Abe Lincoln, who has no more authority to do so than Mr. Dogberry Kennedy of the New York Police, has *named* Major George B. McClellan,[2] a very meritorious Captain of the United States Cavalry; Benjamin F. Butler,[3] an unusually clever Brigadier of the Massachusetts State Militia; and some others, to be Major-Generals of the United States Army — that is, to fill offices that *do not exist* by the law-making power — Congress — which can *alone* create them, according to the Constitution of the United States.

The Constitution of the United States confers no such power on Mr. President Lincoln. The contemporaneous writings of the framers of that Constitution say *why* they did not. They say that they withheld such powers, because history showed them that a people, *"in proportion as they are free,* will disarm the Executive of the influence to exercise a war-making propensity."

In the light of the Constitution of the United States, and of the authoritative expositors and commentators of that instrument, there can be but one judgment — that Lincoln has sought to absorb and confound in his own action the legislative and the executive functions, which the Constitution of the United States, with such pre-eminent care, has distinguished and placed in separate hands.

It appears, also, that Mr. Abe Lincoln, as chief Executive of the United States, has directed various military Commandants, at their discretion, or in case of certain emergencies, to suspend the Writ of *Habeas Corpus.*[4] It is difficult, in a country so blessed as ours has been for three quarters of a century, to attract popular attention to the fundamental guarantees of the public security. Perhaps *Habeas Corpus* seems like an abstraction, or a pettifogger's trick. But it is the symbol of our rights as freemen. It is not simply a guarantee for personal liberty, demanded and gained from Charles II., but, in essence and in virtue, it is the characteristic of our free and superior civilization. In substance it was recognized in the *Magna Charta,* and had its origin far back of that, in the old *Frank law.* We call attention to the docu-

[1] Winfield Scott (1786–1866), although Virginia-born, remained loyal to the Union and as commander of the United States Army made the preparations for defending Washington.

[2] George B. McClellan (1826–1885), an officer of the Ohio Volunteers, was appointed a major general of the regular army on May 13, 1861, and placed in command of the Department of the Ohio.

[3] Benjamin F. Butler (1818–1893) was nominated a major general on May 16, 1861, after having been chosen to occupy Baltimore which he had done peacefully with 900 troops three days before.

[4] On July 2, 1861, Lincoln empowered General Scott to suspend the privilege of habeas corpus.

ments we furnish in another column on this subject. From them it will appear, so far as has been ascertained, that Lincoln — having been *constitutionally* elected by a minority vote to the executive office of President — has at one and the same time thought he could absorb the law-making power, and set at defiance — as he did even in his inaugural — the judicial branch of the Government. The *Constitution* divides our Government into three distinct and co-ordinate branches — the Legislative, the Judicial, and the Executive. The latter assumes to *dispense* with the other two, and to exert autocratic power, as completely as any Asiatic or Turkish despot could do, over a nation of slaves.

We have no *party* quarrel to wage against any one. Alas, we have, now, no *party* to sustain. Our wish, above all things, is that Lincoln's Administration *could,* and then *would,* adopt a course which, as loyal American freemen, we can sustain. The present course of the Executive is unconstitutional, outrageous, and *an open rebellion* against the United States Government as established and recognized. We cannot sustain it in this course, and we will not. We declare and protest, on the contrary, with the Chief Justice of the United States,[5] that it subverts all law as recognized by freemen, and attempts to place our persons, our property, liberty, and life, at the will of one or another army officer.

We have often adverted to the fact that, under anti-slavery as a cry, the anti-Democratic coalition known as "Republicans," have been seeking the substitution of a *centralized despotism* in place of the Constitutional Government of the United States. The very ridiculousness of the controlling elements of this coalition is an occasion of danger. If we cite the Red-Republican ravings of the *Tribune*[6] and *Post,*[7] it is replied: "Who regards such bran-bread socialists and poetasters!" If we cite the *Daily Times,*[8] we are told that the writers are "ninnies — nobody heeds them." If we hunt up a copy of the *Courier and Enquirer,* it raises a laugh. But, be it remembered, it was the influence of these papers, and others no whit more respectable, that brought into executive office Abraham Lincoln and his

---

[5] Roger Brooke Taney (1777–1864) was Chief Justice of the United States Supreme Court from March, 1836, to his death.

[6] Horace Greeley (1811–1872) was editor of the New York *Tribune* at the time.

[7] William Cullen Bryant (1794–1878) was editor of the New York *Evening Post.*

[8] Henry J. Raymond (1820–1869), editor of the New York *Times,* was the most steadfast of all the New York editors in their support of Lincoln.

coterie of incapables. The mistake is made of supposing that the dangers of the country come from *able* or from *great* men. Its dangers and its ruin are to be found in *weak* and *little* men — where great men ought to be. Despotism is a *petty* thing, and petty fellows are they who exercise it.

The *Daily Times,* one day last week, elaborates an article to show that we must, hereafter, keep up a large standing army — even when peace is restored. A large standing army, in time of peace — that is, a hundred thousand men or so, standing idle, with muskets in their hands, at the beck of the Government that pays them — would be the death-knell of political liberty. This is too plain — has been too often insisted on by our greatest statesmen — to render it necessary to argue it. It seems that the *minority,* who have climbed to power, through licentious presses and desecrated pulpits, playing on the ignorance and fanaticism of the country — recognizes that the American people, if left free, will take good care that they never attain a second, nor another, term of administration. It seems that the deliberate purpose has been formed of *subverting, from top to bottom,* the American system of government, and of trying to rule this people by an armed despotism. We do not say that the accursed project may not be accomplished, but we do say that the cowardly and incapable clique who inaugurate the system, will inevitably pay the forfeit of their crime, like Robespierre and Danton, in their own blood.

We have said that our chief danger is from the incapacity, the mental and moral weakness, of the faction now attempting to rule us — not from their strength. This will be our apology for quoting the following from a bombastic article of Webb,[9] in his *Courier and Enquirer,* published a few days before he was appointed Minister to Brazil. It is *his* offering of incense to the attempted military despotism, which he will help by keeping his Brigadier Generalship out of harm's way, while playing courtier at a South American court. He says:

> The war may soon pass away — we may have a quick and vital battle-field, and the North prove its prowess, as certainly it will; but the truth of *national unity* and *power* that these events have given, endures — combined — condensed — *concentrated in army and navy.*
>
> . . . We snall ask the question — *Why all these State lines? Why all this needless, cumbersome, intricate entanglement of different powers to make law and to decree judgment? We can afford now to efface the old*

[9] James W. Webb (1802–1884) was editor of the New York *Courier and Enquirer* from the time he merged the two papers in 1829 to his retirement in 1861. He was named Minister to Brazil on May 31, 1861.

Colonial Geography. It is the admitted powers of States within the nation that has been the source of all our trouble. Nor will the removal of State power, and the creation of a nationality, be a task so formidable.

"Nonsense!" Certainly it is; but we beg thoughtful and intelligent men who turn from it contemptuously, to remember that the miseries the country is now enduring have been brought on it by nonsense as palpable. Webb, who put this in his *Courier,* was, a few days after, named Minister to Brazil, by Lincoln's Administration. It is fair to conclude that he uttered the sentiments that are governing Lincoln's Administration. He says that the *national unity* is to *endure "concentrated in army and navy."*

He says that "State forms," recognized in the Constitution of the country as fundamental and essential, are to be blotted out. Nay, he asks, "why all this *needless, cumbersome, intricate* entanglement of *different* powers to *make law* and to *decree judgment."* It is true, it seems out of place for us to occupy our columns with language worthy only of a negro, or a John Chinaman; but consider the relations of the *Courier* and its editor to Lincoln's Administration, and a reason appears.

Nay, what is Lincoln doing, but *simplifying* the "cumbersome intricate entanglement of *different* powers," as prescribed in the Constitution of the United States, which three months ago, at the hands of Chief Justice Taney, he swore to observe inviolate?

The county court lawyer may not understand what he is doing. His Cabinet may not understand what they are doing. But ideas will rule. Causes will produce results. Men must reap the same that they sow.

Let those heed it who, one year ago, scoffed when we said that the election of Lincoln would cause civil war! We say, now, that if there be not conservatism enough in the country to stop and to rebuke the course of Lincoln and his Cabinet, we will have a bloody revolution and anarchy, resulting in a military despotism, with a different man from Lincoln at its head. We speak what we see and know. Our conscience forces us to speak, whether it please or offend.

106. Bishop Lynch Presents the South's Case for Secession, August 4, 1861

UNLIKE some of the Protestant churches, the organizational unity of the Catholic Church in the United States remained intact during the slavery controversy and the Civil War. But that did not mean that there were not deep sectional differences of opinion among the Catholics of the North and the South on the issues at stake. These differences were high-lighted for the general public when the New York *Metropolitan Record* of September 7, 1861, published an exchange of correspondence between Patrick N. Lynch (1817–1882), Bishop of Charleston, and Archbishop John Hughes of New York on responsibility for the war. Lynch had outlined his views for Hughes in a letter on August 4, and the latter took the somewhat unusual step of replying through his own newspaper on the grounds that, by reason of the disruption of the mails, it was his only chance of acknowledging Lynch's communication. He decided, therefore, to print his reply of August 23 and, as he told the Bishop of Charleston, "without special permission publish your letter at the same time. In this way it may happen that during the war, or afterwards, my answer will come under your inspection" (Lawrence Kehoe [Ed.], *Complete Works of the Most Rev. John Hughes, Archbishop of New York* [New York, 1865], II, 513). Lynch may have learned of Hughes' action because shortly thereafter he published the full text of his letter to the archbishop in his own diocesan paper. The exchange between the prelates attracted widespread attention and complete texts of the letters, together with accompanying editorials, were carried by the New York *Herald, Times,* and *Tribune.* In its issue of September 4, 1861, James Gordon Bennett's *Herald* stated that the "statesmanlike views and admirable temper" of the correspondence "will obtain for it a widespread and attentive consideration both here and abroad." The *Herald's* editorial took occasion to read a lecture to some of the Protestant clergy whose extreme statements were in striking contrast to the calm and tempered opinions of Lynch and Hughes, recommending the bishops' letters to "all the abolitionist and secessionist parsons throughout the country." Source: Charleston *Catholic Miscellany,* September 14, 1861.

Most Reverend Dear Sir: — The mails are so completely paralyzed that it is hard to get a letter from outside the Confederacy. Papers are scarcely ever seen. That, however, Jefferson would think a blessing, on the ground that "he who is simply ignorant is wiser than the one that believes error." A paragraph which has gone the rounds of the Southern papers, states that your Grace has spoken strongly against the war policy of the Government of the United States, fraught with much present suffering, and not calculated to attain any real advantage. What a change has come over these States since I wrote you a long letter last November, and even since I have had the pleasure of seeing you last March. All that I anticipated in that letter has come to pass, and more than I looked for. All the hopes cherished last spring of a peaceful solution have vanished before the dreadful realities of war. What is before us, who can say? Missouri, Maryland and Kentucky are nearer secession now than Virginia, North Carolina and Tennessee were four months ago. Missouri is a battlefield. I think that President Davis, after the victory of Stone Bridge, will probably throw a column into Maryland. Kentucky will, ere long, be drawn into the struggle, and the United States will, in less than ten months, be divided in two not unequal parts, marshalling hundreds of thousands of men against each other.

This war is generally dated from the bombardment of Fort Sumter. There we fired the first gun, and the responsibility is charged on us. But, in reality that responsibility falls on those who rendered the conflict unavoidable — The South, years ago, and a hundred times, declared that the triumph of the abolition or anti-slavery policy, would break up the Union. They were in earnest. When that party, appealing to the people on the Chicago platform, elected their candidate by every free State vote (excepting New Jersey, which was divided,) South Carolina seceded, and other States were preparing to do so. They were in earnest. Yet, as the people disbelieved it, or heeded it not at the ballot, so Congress heeded it not at Washington, and stood doggedly on the Chicago platform endorsed by the people. — This consummated success. The Confederate Government was formed. The dogged obstinacy of the Black Republicans at Washington last winter made all the South secessionists. Still there was peace. The new Administration professed an intention to preserve it. Peace gave time, and time can work wonders. The Confederate Government did not put much faith in those professions. The same hallucination as to their power, which rendered the Black Republicans arrogant and impracticable in Congress, would, it was apprehended, lead them to attempt to crush out secession by force. — And nothing was left undone to be prepared for this event should it occur.

Meanwhile Commissioners were at Washington to arrange a peaceful separation. Favorable intimations were privately given them, and they had hopes of success.

Nine Governors, however, it is said, put the screws on the Cabinet, which resolved on a war policy, and, as silently as they could, made warlike naval preparations. Then, after a month, the Commissioners were refused admission or dismissed, and it was plainly announced that here would be no negotiation. At this time other facts were coming to light here, in Charleston, where our batteries had, for a month or more silently looked on Fort Sumter. During the time of peaceful professions two special messengers (Fox[1] and Lamon[2]) from Presi-

[1] Gustavus V. Fox (1821–1883) was named Assistant Secretary of the Navy by Lincoln's government in August, 1861.

[2] Ward H. Lamon (1828–1893), a former law partner of Lincoln in Illinois, had been sent to Charleston as the president's personal agent in March, 1861.

dent Lincoln visited Fort Sumter. Before being allowed to go thither they gave their word of honor to our Governor that their object was really peaceful. The hotel conversation of the latter was very frank, it is said. Gentlemen here supposed that President Lincoln before ordering the evacuation wished, by these personal friends, to see, as it were, personally, and not simply to learn through official channels, how matters stood at Fort Sumter. When time rolled by without such an order, and it was rumored that the Cabinet had succumbed to the pressure of the Governors, the mails were stopped to and from Fort Sumter. Among the letters seized was one from Major Anderson[3] to President Lincoln, discussing the details of the plan of reinforcement, forwarded to him from Washington by these messengers. Our authorities were thus made aware of the breach of faith towards them, and of the details of the plan itself.

Then came the special messenger of the President, announcing that he intended revictualing the fort, quietly, if permitted, forcibly, if resisted; then the account of the sailing of the fleet from New York. The fort was at once attacked and taken without waiting their arrival. The attack was not made until the offer of negotiation and peaceful arrangement had been rejected, and until the United States Government was in the act of sending an armed force. But it is of little use now to inquire on whom the responsibility rests; we have the war on us, with all its loss of life and long train of evils of every kind. It is the latest, perhaps the strangest instance history gives us, *quam parva sapientia regitur mundus*. Here was a country, vast, populous, prosperous and blessed in all material interest, if any country was. The south producing Cotton, tobacco, sugar, rice and naval stores for the supply, as far as needed, of the North and Northwest, to the value of, perhaps, $50,000,000 a year, and exporting to foreign countries over $220,000,000; the Northwest producing chiefly grain, and supplying the North and the South, and when the European crops failed, having, as last winter, a large European market; the North manufacturing and supplying the South and the Northwest, and struggling to compete with foreign goods abroad, and doing the trading and commerce of the South and the Northwest.

Could the material interests of all the sections be more harmoniously and advantageously combined than in this Union, where each was free to develop to the fullest extent those branches of industry in which it could excel, and could draw from the others those products which it needed, but could not produce as well or as cheaply as they

[3] Robert Anderson (1805–1871) was the Union Commander at Fort Sumter.

could? Even a child could see the vast benefits to all from this mutual co-operation. No wonder that in all material interests the country was prospering to an extent that intoxicated us and astonished the world. We claimed to be pre-eminently sagacious in money matters. The Yankees, I believe, ranked next after the Chinese, in their keenness in business; yet they especially, with an inconceivable blindness, have originated, fostered and propagated a fanatical party spirit which has brought about a result foretold from the beginning, both North and South, as the inevitable consequence of its success.

Taking up anti-slavery, making it a religious dogma, and carrying it into politics, they have broken up the Union. While it was merely an intellectual opinion they might discuss it as they pleased; they might embrace it as they did any other ism. Even their virulent use and misrepresentation we scarcely heeded, provided they did not obtrude them upon us at home. We, as Catholics, might everywhere smile at this additional attempt to "reform" the teachings of our Savior. And the Protestants, South, could have churches and associations of their own. But when they carried it into politics, gaining one State Government after another, and defining their especial policy by unconstitutional laws and every mode of annoying and hostile action, and finally, with increased enthusiasm and increased bitterness, carrying the Presidential election in triumph, and grasping the power of the Federal Government, what could the South do but consult its own safety by withdrawing from the Union? What other protection had they? The Senate, which had still a Democratic majority? They had seen the House of Representatives pass into the hands of their enemies, and each session saw an increasing majority there. The Executive had gone for four years. Their own majority in the Senate was dwindling fast, while on the Territorial question not a few of the Northern Democrats were unsound. To the Supreme Court? That had spoken in the Dred Scott decision. The North would not sustain it, and the Black Republicans scouted it; and moreover, in a few years President Lincoln would have the privilege of placing on the bench new judges from the ranks of his party. To the sober second thought of the people? But this was no new issue on which they were taken by surprise. For years and years it had been discussed; North and South it had been denounced as fraught with disunion and ruin; and yet the Northern people had gradually come to accept it. But the South had spoken so often and so strongly of disunion, without doing anything, that the Northern people had no real belief that any evil consequences would ensue; they did not understand the full bearing of their action. At least, let them understand something of this before all hope of appeal to them is abandoned. Well, South Carolina seceded — other States were preparing to follow her. The matter was taken up in Congress. Many Southerners hoped that then, when the seriousness of the questions could no longer be doubted, something might be done. How vainly they hoped, the Committees of Congress showed. The alternative was thus forced on the South either of tame submission or of resistance. They did not hesitate. They desired to withdraw in peace. This war has been forced upon them.

It was necessary in the beginning. It brings ruin to thousands in its prosecution. It will be fruitless of any good. At its conclusion the parties will stand apart exhausted and embittered by it; for every battle, however, won or lost, will have served but to widen the chasm between the North and South, and to render more difficult, if not impossible, any future reconstruction. Will it be a long war, or a short and mighty one? The Cabinet and the Northern press has pronounced for the last. Yet this is little more than an idle dream. What could 400,000 men do?

I do not think there is a General on either side able to fight 50,000 men. And the North would need eight or ten such Generals. Certainly the 40,000 under McDowell,[4] after five hours' fighting, fought on mechanically without any generalship. The higher officers had completely lost the guiding reins. On our side the Southern troops ought to have been in Washington within forty-eight hours. But the 40,000 on the Confederate side was, I apprehend too unwieldy a body for our Generals. Did not Bonaparte say that not one of his Marshals could general fifty thousand men in battle?

Soult[5] could bring them to the field, and place them properly, but could go no further.

But without Generals, what could 400,000 men do against the South? By force of numbers, and a great loss, they might take city after city. But unless they left large permanent garrisons, their authority would die out with the sound of their drums. Such an army marching through a country covered with forests and thickets and occupied by a population hostile to a man, and where even school-boys can "bark a squirrel," would be decimated every hundred miles of its progress by a guerrilla warfare, against which it could find no protection. This

[4] General Irvin McDowell (1818–1885) and his Union army were routed by the Confederate forces at Manasses Junction, Virginia, on July 21, 1861.

[5] Marshal Nicolas-Jean-de-Dieu Soult (1769–1851) was one of the most prominent of Napoleon's generals.

mode of attacking the South can effect nothing beyond the loss of life it will entail, and the temporary devastation that will mark the track of the armies.

But it is probable that circumstances would again, as they have done, overrule the designs of the Washington Cabinet, and make the war slow, long and expensive — one to be decided, less by battles than by the resources and endurance of the combatants.

That portion of the former United States will suffer most in such a contest and must finally succumb, which is least able to dispense with the support it received from the other two sections. How the North can do without our Southern trade, I presume it can judge after three or four months' trial. But it would seem that the failure to sell to the South one hundred and twenty millions of their manufactures each year the stoppage of so much of their shipping interest as was engaged in the two hundred and twenty millions of our foreign exports and the return importations, and in our internal coasting trade, together with the loss of the profits and commissions on so vast a business, must have a very serious effect, too, that I see no way of escaping. Truly the North has to pay dearly for its whistle of Black Republicanism. The Northwest depended partially on the South for a market for its productions, and so far will suffer from the loss of it. It must also be incidentally affected by commercial embarrassments at the North. They will assuredly have enough to eat and to wear, but the "fancy" prices of real estate and stocks, by which they computed their rapidly increasing wealth, must fall in a way to astonish Wall-street. Should their own crops fail, as they sometimes do, or should the European crops be abundant, their commerce will fall. Yet, as the mass of the poor will have all that they ever get anywhere — food and raiment, and that without stint — the Northwest will suffer comparatively little.

How long will it fare with the South should the war be long and so powerfully waged as to require the Southern Confederation to keep say 100,000 men-in-arms, and if the ports are strictly blockaded? This is an important question, and one that can be answered only from a practical knowledge of the habits, resources and disposition of the Southern people. Our needs will be provisions, clothing, money for the government and war expenses, and for the purchase from abroad of what we absolutely require, and are not already supplied with.

As for provisions, I am satisfied that this season we are gathering enough for two years' abundant supply. Every one is raising corn, wheat and stock. On this point the South need not envy the Northwest. Again, manufactures are springing up on all sides. In this State we are providing for our wants — from lucifer matches and steam engines to powder and rifled cannon. Clothing, too, though of a ruder texture and sometimes inferior quality, is abundantly made and easily procured. The supply of tea and coffee will, I presume, in time run out. This will put us to some trouble, but otherwise, neither for provisions nor for clothes, will the South be seriously inconvenienced.

The blacks (by-the-bye more quiet and orderly now, if possible, than before) will remain devoted to agriculture, while the rapidly increasing demand for home productions of every kind gives ready employment to the poorer classes of the whites.

What amount of gold and silver there is within the Confederate States I can only guess at — I suppose about $25,000,000. But as the greater part of our expenses are at home, any currency we are satisfied to use will do, whether Bank bills, Confederate bonds or Treasury notes. When we go abroad, it must be with gold or with Cotton. This last is the spinal column of our financial system. The following is the proposed mode of operating with it: Two millions, or two and a half of bales will be conveyed to the Confederate Government, to be paid for in bonds or Treasury notes. This Cotton will be worth, at ordinary prices, one hundred millions of dollars. If it can be exported at once, it is so much gold. If it is retained, it will form the security for any loan that may be required abroad. The other third of the Cotton will be sold by the planters as best they can on their own account.

The chief difficulty is the blockade, which may prevent the export and sale abroad of the Cotton. A loan on it as security, while it is still unshipped, and scattered in numberless small warehouses, could not easily be affected.

Up to the present time, and for six months more, the blockade, so far from doing any serious injury, has, on the contrary, benefitted, and will continue to benefit the South, forcing us to be active, and to do for ourselves much that we preferred formerly to pay others to do for us. I presume that next January, with a crop of three and a half or four millions of bales on hand, the South would become very restive under a strict blockade. *Should it continue twelve months longer property at the South would go down as they say it has in New York.*

But, before that time comes, another very serious complication arises — how England and France will stand the cutting off their supply of an article on which depend two-thirds of the manufacturing interests of the one and one-third of those of the other? They cannot, try they ever so much, supply the deficiency. As far as the feelings of England are concerned, and, I presume, those of France, too, both nations are decidedly and bitterly anti-slavery; but neither will be guilty of the mistake of the North, and utterly sacrifice vast interests for the sake of a speculative idea. If they find that they cannot do without Southern Cotton, they will interfere, first probably to make peace, and if that effort fails, then in such other manner as will secure for them what will be a necessity. Mr. Seward's[6] letter to Dayton,[7] and its reception in Europe, the transportation of troops to Canada, and Admiral Milne's declaration as to the inefficiency of the blockade, are straws already showing the possible course of future events. Is the Federal Government strong enough for a war with England and France in addition to that with the South?

One other warlike course remains — to capture and hold all the Southern ports, and thus seek to control commerce, independent of secession, leaving the interior of the South to fret and fume as it pleases. This is the problem of belling the cat. The Northern forces would have to capture Norfolk, Charleston, Savannah, Wilmington, N. C., Pensacola, Mobile, New Orleans and Galveston, besides some fifteen other smaller points. At each of them they would find a Stone Bridge; and even if they succeeded, they could only hold military possession and be forever in arms against the attacks of the State authorities. Peace would never be established by any such course. It would not be successful, and even if successful, it would only hamper the South, it would never subjugate it.

The separation of the Southern States is *un fait accompli*. The Federal Government has no power to reverse it. Sooner or later it must be recognized. Why preface the recognition by a war equally needless and bloody? Men at the North may regret the rupture; as men at the South may do. The Black Republicans overcame the first at the polls, and would not listen to the second in Congress, when the evil might have been repaired. They are responsible. If there is to be fighting, let those who voted the Black Republican ticket shoulder their musket and bear the responsibility. Let them not send Irishmen to fight in their stead, and then stand looking on at the conflict, when, in their heart of hearts, they care little which of the combatants destroy the other.

---

[6] William H. Seward (1801–1872) was Lincoln's Secretary of State.

[7] William L. Dayton (1807–1864) had been appointed American Minister to France in 1861.

Most Reverend dear Sir, I am surprised and somewhat ashamed of the length to which my pen has run. But the night is hot — too hot for sleep. I arose from my couch, and have spent a couple of hours speaking to you as frankly and unreservedly as you have ever kindly allowed me to do. A trip to New York would be agreeable for more reasons than one. But that is impossible. Next to that I would like to see a file of the Record.[8] That, too, is impossible. Nothing seems now to span the chasm but that bridge of Catholic union and charity, of which your grace spoke so eloquently last St. Patrick's Day.

I must thank you, too, for your article in my defence against Tracy. He was a poor man with a growing family whom, at Rev. Mr. O'Connell's[9] instance, Bishop Reynolds[10] allowed to live on a place in Newberry District, belonging to him, rent free, and as an act of charity I did not trouble him. He says I saw him there once, years ago. Perhaps so, I do not remember. The first time I remember seeing him, was here in Charleston, after his expulsion. He was driven off, because he was suspected for years, and charged by the neighbors with stealing, and buying stolen goods habitually — was once tried and convicted — and afterwards, they were satisfied, continued the practice.

Commending myself to your holy sacrifices, I have the honor to remain, most Reverend dear Sir, your Grace's sincere and respectful son in Christ.

✠ P. N. LYNCH, D.D., S.C.[11]

---

[8] Hughes had started the *Metropolitan Record* in July, 1859, after falling out with McMaster of the *Freeman's Journal.*

[9] There were two priests of that name in the Diocese of Charleston at that time, Jeremiah J. and Lawrence P. O'Connell.

[10] Ignatius Reynolds (1798–1855) ruled the See of Charleston as its second bishop from 1844 to 1855.

[11] Patrick N. Lynch was consecrated as third Bishop of Charleston on March 14, 1858. In the spring of 1864 he received an official commission from President Jefferson Davis to go to Rome with the hope that he could win recognition for the Confederacy from the government of Pope Pius IX. The mission ended in failure, however, and it was not until late in 1865 that Lynch was able to return to his diocese after a presidential pardon had been won for him through the efforts of Archbishop Martin J. Spalding of Baltimore.

Hughes concluded his lengthy letter to Lynch by stating that there remained nothing for him to add except "that the Catholic faith and Catholic charity which unites us in the spiritual order, shall remain unbroken by the booming of cannon along the lines that unfortunately separate a great and once prosperous community into two hostile portions, each arrayed in military strife against the other" (Kehoe, *op. cit.*, II, 520).

107. Wisconsin Catholicism at the Outbreak of the Civil War, August 30, 1861

IN THE year that the Civil War broke out the Diocese of Milwaukee — founded only eighteen years before with about 15,000 Catholics — had approximately 190,000 Catholic people. In Wisconsin the Germans were the dominant Catholic group, and the following report, written by Michael Heiss (1818–1890), at the time rector of St. Francis Seminary, to the directors of the Ludwig-Missionsverein at Munich, shows among other things the emphasis which the Germans placed upon parochial schools. Since the diocese still embraced all of Wisconsin, Heiss reported on the smaller towns and rural areas of practically every section. The phenomenal growth of the Church soon proved too much of a burden for one bishop and on March 3, 1868, the Holy See erected the Dioceses of Green Bay and La Crosse to take care of the northeastern and northwestern portions of the state. Source: *Salesianum,* XL (October, 1945), 169–180, translated by Augustine C. Breig and edited by Peter Leo Johnson.

Milwaukee, August 30, 1861.

Prompted by sentiments of deep gratitude the Most Rev. Bishop John Martin Henni[1] has instructed the writer to submit a report to the governing board concerning the diocese of Milwaukee. The diocese, for the upbuilding of which the Ludwig-missionsverein has done so much, comprises the entire state of Wisconsin, nearly as much territory as at its erection in the year 1844. At that time the bishop of Milwaukee had only six priests of his own, and in the vast territory hardly more than 9–10,000 Catholics, who possessed only four inexpensive and unfinished churches. Now we count in the same territory 215 well finished churches and chapels, and besides, 23 others under construction, with a total of 117 priests and a Catholic population of approximately 190,000 souls. The largest part of the population consists of Germans and Irish who are about equal in number. Besides these we have some Canadian, Dutch, Belgian, and also a few Polish and Bohemian parishes, and two missions among the Indians. It is not difficult to understand what incessant zeal, untiring solicitude, and keen prudence are required to govern a new, quickly developing and extensive diocese in order to preserve peace and harmony among the different elements and to foster and promote Catholic life. Eternal thanks and praise to the Lord, that even if at times difficulties arose

---

[1] John Martin Henni (1805–1881) was first Bishop of Milwaukee; he was promoted to become first Archbishop of Milwaukee when the see was raised to metropolitan rank on February 12, 1875.

and scandals appeared, everything went well again and never backward but ever forward. In the city of Milwaukee, the episcopal see, the Catholics have five churches, besides the cathedral, one for the Irish and three for the Germans, but soon a new church will be necessary for each of these nationalities.

Alongside the cathedral stands a roomy and well built orphanage which houses more than ninety orphan girls of the Irish parishes. St. Gall's church under the pastoral care of the Fathers of the Society of Jesus, also has a school. But the Germans in Milwaukee, as everywhere, manifest a special zeal for the Christian education of their children. The schools of the three German parishes are in excellent condition. They are mainly under the care of the School Sisters [Notre Dame] from Bavaria.[2] A second orphan asylum with fifty-six orphan boys is located near the seminary. A third one is under construction near St. Mary's hospital, which itself was built some two years ago, and both are under the care of the Daughters of Charity.

The motherhouse of the Bavarian School Sisters is a particular credit for Milwaukee. It is in a flourishing condition and sends its teachers to Catholic parishes throughout the Union. For the past several years from thirty to forty candidates have taken the veil annually and as many novices made their profession each year. The sisters are now about to enlarge their convent considerably.

Belonging to Milwaukee, the episcopal see, the diocesan seminary must now be mentioned. It is located about five miles from the city on the south point of the Milwaukee bay. After its patron, St. Francis de Sales, it is known as the Salesianum. As related in a former report, the establishment of the seminary was decided in the year 1853 at the consecration of the cathedral. In 1854 the preparatory work was done for the erection of a magnificent seminary building, and on July 15, 1855, the cornerstone was laid. The work was so speedily pressed that the entire building, excepting the chapel, was under roof before winter. By the end of January 1856, one section was also interiorly finished, so that on January 29, the feast of St. Francis de Sales, we were able to open the seminary with an enrollment of thirty-three students. Since then we have been busy improving the temporal and spiritual condition of the seminary. Of the students who had made

[2] The first group of six School Sisters of Notre Dame arrived in the United States from Bavaria in July, 1847. They established their mother house in Baltimore and the first foundation made from the mother house was at Milwaukee in December, 1850.

their classical studies elsewhere, and could therefore start with the study of philosophy and theology, eighteen have already been ordained priests. At present all of them, including fourteen with over a year's service, are working zealously in the vineyard of the Lord to the satisfaction of their bishops. For the next school year, which begins September 2, sixty-six students have registered. Sixteen belong to other dioceses, to-wit: St. Louis, Dubuque, Chicago, Detroit and Buffalo. The remaining fifty belong to Milwaukee. According to nationality there are twenty-one Irish, one Yankee (an American from New England), two Hollanders and the rest German. There are at present six professors but a seventh is expected by October. Five of them are priests. Since the beginning the seminary has been in charge of the writer as rector and of the Rev. Salzmann[3] from the Diocese of Linz, as procurator. On June 30 of this year we celebrated the completion of the seminary. On this date, the sixth Sunday after Pentecost, the seminary chapel was solemnly consecrated by the Most Rev. Bishop. The chapel is 115 ft. long, 32 ft. wide and about 50 ft. high inside and is built in a simple Byzantine style. The chapel was ready for the consecration some time ago but we wished to wait until the rest of the interior of the seminary was finished. Surrounded by about twenty priests, mostly graduates of our seminary, and the students, the Most Rev. Bishop performed the sacred function. In the meanwhile the Rev. Weninger,[4] a truly apostolic missionary of the Germans in America, blessed a 14 ft. gilt cross in front of the main entrance of this seminary. This was to be placed on the towering cupola in memory of the completion of the seminary. In an inspiring and touching sermon he explained to the large crowd the importance of this ecclesiastical seminary of our holy faith. It was really an important and truly epoch-making day for the history of the Milwaukee diocese. Since its completion the seminary building, with a frontage of 160 ft., with four stories and located on an elevation on the shore of the vast Lake Michigan, announces now by means of the far-shining cross on its cupola, that a good foundation has been laid with the help of God for the future of our holy faith in the state of Wisconsin. It is evident

[3] Joseph Salzmann was an Austrian-born priest who had come to Milwaukee in 1847. He served for a time as pastor of St. Mary's Church in the see city, founded the *Seebote,* a paper to counteract the anti-Catholic attacks of the *Flugblätter,* and was extremely active in winning financial support for St. Francis Seminary.

[4] Francis X. Weninger, S.J. (1805–1888), was Austrian-born and from the time of his arrival in the United States in 1848 until his death forty years later he was one of the most noted missionaries among the German Catholic immigrants.

that much labor had to be spent to raise the necessary funds for such a building and for the support of the students. Besides the charitable help from the Ludwig-missionsverein which we enjoyed during the first three years of our undertaking and the contribution of $21,000 from the Most Rev. Bishop Henni, which he had made in spite of the many other needs of the diocese and the episcopal see, everything had to be collected by the indefatigable and untiring procurator who literally begged from house to house. He collected not only among the Catholics, especially the Germans, in the diocese, but also outside of it. Indeed, we may say that the generosity of the Germans of Cincinnati gave us the means whereby we could dare construct such a spacious building and the Germans of St. Louis by their liberality built our beautiful chapel. Though the seminary has been erected, our task is not ended, because we are obliged to pay off the debts which encumber it. While these do not endanger the sacred undertaking, they hamper its efficient working, because the yearly diocesan collection is not sufficient to support students, the majority of whom are needy, and also pay the interest. Besides we are obliged this summer to undertake the building of a convent for a community of Sisters of the Third Order of St. Francis. Before the seminary was built a small convent of these sisters existed near the seminary land. First they took care of the children of the orphan asylum located as already mentioned near the seminary. Then when the seminary was started, they took charge of the kitchen, laundry and bakery, and thus rendered it invaluable services. But because the small convent became too limited and also beyond repair, we had to decide to build one which will cost about $3000 for the community whose services the seminary cannot dispense with. For this reason we believe that we may dare respectfully to ask the governing board for kind assistance to complete an undertaking which at its beginning enjoyed your special consideration. So this much will suffice in reference to the episcopal see and the seminary.

Now a few remarks will be made about the other parts of the diocese. I start with something I have observed recently. Eight days after the consecration of the seminary chapel the Rev. Father Weninger, S.J., conducted a week's retreat in German, and in the week following the Rev. Father Smarius, S.J.,[5] in English, for the diocesan clergy. The first retreat was attended by forty-eight and the second

[5] Cornelius Smarius, S.J. (1823–1870), was a Dutch-born Jesuit who attained fame as a preacher and an apologist; his best known work was *Points of Controversy* which first appeared in 1866.

by forty-four. Though such exercises when made with a group have usually a beneficial influence, I thought because I am at all times in the seminary, that it would be more beneficial for me to make a retreat alone somewhere else. So with the approval of the Most Rev. Bishop I went to the Capuchin monastery at Mt. Calvary.[6] The railroad runs north and is twelve miles distant from the monastery. To the right and left there is one Catholic parish after another, as for example, in Granville, Germantown, Richmond [Richfield], Schlesingerville, Horicon, and so on. How things have changed if I recall my first years in Wisconsin. On Tuesday after Pentecost 1844, I started out from Milwaukee on horseback for this same territory in order to visit German settlements. Near the Milwaukee River on the first day I found a congregation of about twenty families. Farther north in a very dense woods on the following day at sunset I found five or six families newly arrived from the vicinity of Trier. Here I was told that I could not go farther because there was no path open. For this reason I turned back and took a more westerly course. I discovered Germans but they were Protestants and only at sunset did I find another Catholic home. Here I was informed that beyond a nearby marsh there was a large settlement of German Catholics. Early the next morning I started out, but since I had to ride around the marsh, another day was spent before I finally reached this settlement. Here there were about forty families who dwelt rather far from each other. Fifteen miles north of here there were three more families. Here the road stopped and I was told that it was so far to the next house that I could not get there in a day and also would be obliged to spend the night under the open sky. As there was no question of a church or even a log chapel anywhere, I had to hold divine services in the poorest cabins which the newcomers had hastily built. This was the condition at that time. At present in the same territory one congregation follows another like St. Martin's, St. Michael's, St. Catherine's, St. Anthony's, St. James', St. Xavier's, St. Boniface, St. Hubertus', St. Joseph's, St. Mathias', St. Augustine's, St. Lawrence's, and so on. Everywhere there is a church and now there are more priests in this district than the whole diocese had then.

On this trip however I did not stop at any of these congregations but sped through them on the iron horse until I left the train at Fond du Lac, which is about sixty miles from Milwaukee. The former is a city of about 4 or 5000 inhabitants of whom Catholics are the

[6] Holy Cross Monastery at Mount Calvary, Wisconsin, was established by two priests from Switzerland in 1857.

larger number, but unfortunately they are of different nationalities, the most numerous being the Irish, but there are also many Germans and Canadians [French]. All attend the same church and are cared for by one pastor, a Frenchman, who speaks English well but German poorly. A spacious foundation has been laid for a new church, the construction of which will be finished next year. Although only a small part of the entire Catholic congregation, the Germans alone possess a school building and maintain therein a good Catholic school for their children.

From Fond du Lac I went on to the Capuchin monastery with a farmer who had hauled grain into the city. I had seen this section of the country once before but solely by night and then no monastery existed on the hilltop. For this reason I was pleasantly surprised to see at sunset on a little hill to the right the convent of the School Sisters and the Capuchin monastery to the left on a higher and steeper hill. Cordially received, I spent eight days there. At present the monastery houses three priests, two clerical and four lay brothers. Alongside of the monastery stands the old parish church, but piles of stone and timber are already on the grounds for the erection of a new church which will be started this year. I was very much edified by the strict observance of the rules of the Order in the monastery. May the Lord grant that the Order will gain a firm footing in the diocese. In an area of from five to ten miles about the monastery the people are nearly all Catholic. Five miles from the monastery is St. John's, a large parish with a fine church, and six miles in another direction is St. Mary's and several neighboring mission stations. Both places have a resident priest.

From Calvary I had to return to Fond du Lac in order to get to Green Bay, the destination of my journey. My first railroad stop was Oshkosh, a newly founded city, which has already about 10,000 inhabitants. Here there are two Catholic churches, one for the Irish and the other for the Germans, but both are under the administration of one priest, who, though Irish, speaks German pretty well. Here too the Germans have a Catholic school. I arrived at six o'clock in the morning, said holy Mass and at 8 A.M. continued my trip on the railroad thirty miles north to Appleton, where the railroad ends. We passed by the two newly founded cities of Menasha and Neenah. Both have Catholic churches which are tended from Appleton. Appleton is now the residence of the pastor. Here the church is well furnished, having both an organ and a bell. I met the priest, a Belgian, who was busy building a parish house. Appleton is also the home of a university controlled by the Methodists.[7] It was founded through the liberal bequest of an eastern capitalist. The building is imposing. The university is coeducational because it is attended by young people of both sexes, who, however, are separated in the classrooms by a thin partition so arranged that both groups can see the professor. The location of Appleton is very beautiful.

The Neenah [Fox] river, often mentioned in Jesuit mission reports of the 17th and 18th centuries, winds about the city through a deep valley. On this river I continued my trip to Green Bay on a steamboat about the size of those that ply the Rhine and Danube. It was on the same river in April of the year 1670 that for the first time a messenger of the Gospel travelled in a frail canoe, hewed from a tree trunk, whose occupants frequently were obliged to portage on account of the rocky bed and the many rapids of the river. This was Father Claude Allouez who may be called the apostle of the West as described justly by a historian. Soon other Jesuits followed him, including James Marquette. In 1673 the latter ascended this river [Fox] in order to reach the Mississippi, the great stream about which the Indians had spoken. Those were holy men and their missions ceased partly through the suppression of the Society of Jesus and partly through local conditions. But should one not believe that the special divine blessing which the diocese of Milwaukee has enjoyed to the present time may be attributed to the heroic sacrifices of the first missionaries to this region?

After we had passed Little Chute, Kakalin, other small places and through many locks, at least twenty, we arrived at De Pere, so called because Father Allouez settled here in 1669 on the feast of St. Francis Xavier and founded the mission of St. Francis Xavier. A few years ago a silver monstrance was unearthed here which I saw in Green Bay. Along both sides of the Neenah river valley also are Catholic parishes, mostly Dutch and French. There are resident priests at Little Chute, Freedom and Franciscus Busche. De Pere has a church which is taken care of from Green Bay. Near De Pere is the last lock and soon we had covered the remaining five miles. At half past five we arrived in Green Bay which at first sight made a pleasing impression on me. It is the oldest settlement in Wisconsin. By the year 1745 Canadians had settled here. But the settlement made such slight progress that in the year 1783 it had only fifty-six and in 1812 about 250 inhabitants. The wooded hills between which the

[7] Lawrence Institute was opened at Appleton in 1849.

Neenah river flows from Appleton gradually become smaller towards Green Bay, so much so, that only on one side of the wide stream a slight elevation appears on which [one page of the original, or of the photostat, is lacking].

Saturday evening I returned to Mt. Calvary. Here the Capuchin Fathers begged me to conduct a retreat for them and the brothers. It appeared to me preposterous that a secular priest should preach to monks, but because they insisted and I did not know of anybody who could take my place, I consented. We closed the retreat on the feast of the Assumption of the Blessed Virgin and then I preached in the parish church. The next day I spent examining several boxes of books which a priest had left at the monastery because he could not take them along with him to his new charge. I could hardly look over a third of them. There are excellent volumes on Church history, liturgy and canon law, including Mabillon, Hardouin, Lapus, the Bollandists, and so on. Saturday I drove to Fond du Lac and then arrived in Milwaukee about 3 o'clock by train.

Now I shall give a short notice of other parts of the diocese. To the south nearest to the seminary on Howell road is the parish of New Coeln, so called because most of the people hail from the vicinity of Cologne. To it belong the adjoining parishes on Kilbourn Road and in Caledonia. Then there is the Oak Creek parish which is taken care of from the seminary. Ten miles south is Racine with three churches of which one is German. The latest one built [St. Patrick's] will be blessed by the Most Rev. Bishop next Sunday. Again ten miles farther south, situated like Racine on Lake Michigan, is Kenosha with two churches and two priests. West from here are Brighton and Paris with two churches and one priest. About twelve miles from there is Waterford with its priest and church. Then comes Burlington where the Rev. Wisbauer[8] of the Linz diocese has been active for the last fourteen years and two years ago he built one of the finest churches in the diocese. Six miles south is Wheatland with a priest and church, which is located on a beautiful hill in the midst of a prairie and not far from the boundary line between Wisconsin and Illinois. To the West from here on a beautiful lake is Geneva which is near several missions. Farther westward is Beloit with two priests and then follow Janesville and Monroe. In the latter place a new church was blessed a few weeks ago. In the same westerly direction are Shullsburg and Sinsinawa Mound where the Dominican Fathers

[8] Michael Wisbauer was pastor of St. Sebastian's Church in Burlington.

have a college on a splendid site. From the hill at the foot of which the college lies one can view for a distance of five or six miles the Mississippi valley which forms the western boundary of the diocese. In the intervening region are the rich lead mines of Wisconsin with headquarters at Potosi and Mineral Point. In this territory there are a number of parishes of which however I know little. In Benton the Rev. Mazzuchelli,[9] a Dominican, built a very beautiful church and also established a convent of the Sisters of the Third Order of St. Dominic. In Potosi there are now two resident priests who are obliged to tend many missions. In Mineral Point there is a priest and church. Farther north in Highland there are two priests of whom the German one has to care for several missions. Where the Wisconsin river empties into the Mississippi Prairie du Chien is located, which after Green Bay is the oldest Canadian settlement in Wisconsin. But like Green Bay it has lagged behind other cities. There in the year 1843 quite a spacious church was built in the hope that Prairie du Chien instead of Milwaukee would become the see of the prospective bishopric of Wisconsin. But whilst Milwaukee has now 50,000 inhabitants Prairie du Chien has hardly 3000. La Crosse, which is hardly ten years old, grew much larger and has already 7000 inhabitants, so that it has been considered as the see of a new diocese for northwestern Wisconsin. At present there are two priests in La Crosse. Farther north up the Mississippi I know of only one priest, resident in Eau de Claire, who however has many missions. In Hudson and Chippewa Falls there were priests formerly but I do not know if any are there now. Next week the Most Rev. Bishop will come into this distant section, a new field of the diocese, in order to visit all these parishes in the northwest and to administer the sacrament of confirmation in most of them. Thence by railroad from La Crosse he will travel to Portage City and then going north again he will proceed to Stevens Point and Marathon City on the Wisconsin river. Here there are extensive pine forests and so for a long time numerous saw mills have existed which ship large quantities of lumber to St. Louis and New Orleans. Between La Crosse and Portage City there are several parishes, but of such recent origin that I am unable to give their names.

There are also several new settlements west of Portage toward

[9] Samuel Charles Mazzuchelli, O.P. (1806–1864), was born in Milan Italy, and came to the United States in 1828. He was one of the most famous missionaries of the Middle West in the mid-century; highly successful in winning converts among the Indians of Michigan and Wisconsin, and founding parishes in Iowa, Illinois, and Wisconsin. He died while pastor of St. Patrick's Church, Benton, Wisconsin, after being exposed to a blizzard in making a sick call to a parishioner.

Nordport on the Wolf river and then at Beaver Dam and Ripon. In these places are three or four priests who could talk a great deal about the present pathless wilderness there. Northward up the Wolf river is the mission of the Menominee Indians of whom about 800 are Catholics. Only about six weeks ago the son of the principal chief Oshkosh allowed himself to be baptized and for this reason we hope that all the Menominees of about 1200 souls will be converted. On the northern borders of Wisconsin on Lake Superior there is another mission among the Chippewas. The Most Rev. Bishop has placed this mission temporarily under the jurisdiction of the Most Rev. Bishop Baraga[10] of Sault Ste. Marie, because it can be taken care of more conveniently from there.

A railroad connects both La Crosse and Prairie du Chien with Milwaukee. Travelling from the latter place we pass several parishes until we come to Mazomanie, where a priest is stationed, if I am not mistaken. About twelve miles northwards on the Wisconsin river Sauk City is located, where there is a priest and church, and in nearby Roxbury there is also a priest. Somewhat south of Mazomanie there are two priests in the township of Cross Plains. Fourteen miles from here by railroad you arrive at Madison, the state capital, which is well located on a rather high hill in the midst of four lakes. There are two churches with resident pastors here. On a prominent site near the capital a magnificent church of cut stone was started some years ago and its walls were finished up to a bit above the windows, but it is still unfinished due to lack of money.

From Madison toward Milwaukee on the railroad is Whitewater with its priest and church and also Eagle Center with a church which is in charge of priests from East Troy and Waukesha. In Elm Grove nine miles from Milwaukee the School Sisters of Notre Dame have built an orphanage with a beautiful chapel through the generosity of his Majesty King Ludwig of Bavaria. At Whitewater the railroad running west is crossed by one coming from the south out of Chicago, and on this line northwards, Jefferson is soon reached which is about fifty miles from Milwaukee. I had visited the former place in 1844, and found only ten families. At that time the ague was raging in the vicinity so that among these families on one occasion I brought Holy Communion at Eastertime to ten of the stricken who were living

---

[10] Frederic Baraga (1797–1868) born in Slovenia in the Austrian Empire, became one of the most accomplished students of the Indian languages of any Catholic missionary in the United States. He was first Vicar Apostolic of Upper Michigan, 1853–1857, and first Bishop of Sault Sainte-Marie and Marquette from 1857 to his death.

in widely separated cabins. Now they have two churches, one in the little city of Jefferson, and the other a couple of miles outside of it on a beautiful hill. Here some day the Most Rev. Bishop intends to establish a convent. Eight days ago here and also in Whitewater, Ottawa and Golden Lake the sacrament of confirmation was administered. The two last places are taken care of by a priest of Watertown, a city of about 8 or 9000 inhabitants, which has two churches and two priests. For a long time there were three priests there on account of other missions nearby. Near Watertown there are also parishes at Fox Lake, Elba, Monches and others toward Milwaukee. Nearer to Milwaukee must be mentioned the parishes on the Beloit Road, in Franklin (with two priests), Greenfield and Menominee (Falls).

Of the many parishes I did not mention I wish in conclusion to speak of one about eighteen miles north of Madison, East Bristol. For some time this parish was very unfortunate because it rebelled against the bishop on account of the church property. Because their priest was recalled until such time as they would submit, they themselves installed a suspended priest from some Bavarian diocese who had fled here. They persisted for two or three years in open schism. At last their eyes were opened and the people realized their wrongdoing and now their parish is one of the best in the diocese. At present they intend to build a large church for which in a few weeks they have subscribed $5000.

From this, though not quite complete but true report, it is evident that the development of the diocese during the seventeen years since its erection has been an extraordinary one. The little mustard seed has grown into a very promising tree. No doubt this will be certainly consoling to the pious benefactors of the mission society, and especially to its governing board which helped to accomplish all this. At the same time and for the same reason we entertain the hope that the diocese of Milwaukee may also in the future enjoy the lively interest of our benefactors. Though much has been accomplished, still more has to be done, because everything makes such rapid progress in this country that one need quickly follows another. A church is hardly built when another is needed. This is also the case in other matters. In my opinion a special effort should be made to educate an efficient clergy in our own seminaries and thus with the mighty effort of such a clergy, provision would be made for an adequate number of Catholic parochial schools. Should this happen, the future of the Catholic Church in America is assured.

Asking your kind indulgence because of defects and errors in this report . . .

108. The Nursing Sisters in the Military Hospitals of Virginia, January, 1862–April, 1865

ONE of the most inspiring — and little known — chapters of the Civil War was written by the nearly 500 members of twenty or more congregations of religious women who nursed the wounded in the military hospitals of both the North and South. Among the most prominent of these congregations were the Daughters of Charity of St. Vincent de Paul whose mother house at Emmitsburg, Maryland, was only a few miles distant from the battlefield at Gettysburg. Speaking of that memorable encounter in July, 1863, Sister Camilla O'Keefe (1815–1887), a contemporary, stated, "They fought until the evening of the 3rd, advancing by their movements more and more towards our peaceful Vale, so that our buildings and the very earth trembled from their cannons" (Archives of St. Joseph's Central House, Emmitsburg, "Notes, 1863," p. 22). There is record of at least 232 of the Daughters of Charity who engaged in nursing the troops during the war. On September 20, 1924, a monument to the "Nuns of the Battlefield" was unveiled in Washington across the street from St. Matthew's Cathedral to commemorate the deeds of these heroic women of the many congregations who gave their services to the wounded soldiers. The following document of Sister Angela Heath (1830–1912), who saw service from January, 1862, to April 13, 1865, four days after the surrender of Lee at Appomattox, gives a good idea of the difficulties encountered by the sisters as they moved from one hospital to another during the campaigns of the Old Dominion. Source: Archives of St. Joseph's Central House, Emmitsburg, Maryland, "Annals of the Civil War, 1861–1865," pp. 95–98.

Left Richmond for Manasses on the 9th. of January 1862, at the solicitation of Dr. Williams[1] Medical Director of the Army of the Potomac. We were five in number, & found, on taking possession, 500 patients, sick & wounded of both armies. Mortality was very great, as the sick poor had been very much neglected. The wards were in a most deplorable condition, & strongly resisted all efforts of the broom to which they had long been strangers, & the aid of a shovel was found necessary. At best, they were but poor protection against the inclemency of the season & being scattered, we were often obliged to go through snow over a foot deep, to wait on the sick. For our own accommodation we had one small room, which served for dormitory, chapel, &c, &c. & when we were fortunate enough to get a chaplain, the holy sacrifice was daily offered in a little corner of our humble domicile. The kitchen, to which what we called our refectory, was

[1] An effort to identify Williams further was unsuccessful.

attached, was, I do not think I exaggerate when I say a quarter of a mile from our room, & often it was found more prudent to be satisfied with two meals than to trudge through the snow for a third, which at best, was not very inviting, for the culinary department was not under our control, but under that of negroes, who had a decided aversion for cleanliness. On an average, ten died every day, & of this number, I think I may safely say, four were baptized, either by Fathers Smoulders [*sic*][2] & Feeling [*sic*][3] or by our Sisters. It happened several times that men, who had been until then totally ignorant of our faith, & I may say even of God, sent to us in the middle of the night, when they found that they were dying, & begged for baptism which astonished as well as consoled & edified us. On the 13th of March we received orders from Gen. Johnson [*sic*],[4] to pack up quietly & be ready to leave on six hours' notice, as it was found necessary to retreat from that quarter. Oh the horrors of war! We had scarcely left our post than the whole camp was one mass of flame, & the bodies of those who died that day, were consumed. Our next field of labor was the military hospital at Gordonsville. We were but three in number & found 200 patients verk sick — pneumonia and typhoid fever prevailing. Here again privations were not wanting. The sick were very poorly provided for, although the mortality was not as great as at Manasses. . . . Father S. who was our chaplain at that time received about twenty-five into the communion of the Church some of whom died shortly after. One morning as Sister Ann Estelle[5] was visiting her patients before Mass, one called from the lower end of the ward, "Oh! Sister, Sister, do come & save me, let me die in the church that you Sisters belong to. I believe all that you believe." Father S. who was vesting for mass, was at first unwilling to wait on him until after, but as Sister insisted that no time was to be lost, he went and baptized him, & as we knelt at the "Et verbum caro factum est," he expired. The approach of the Federals compelled us to leave Gordonsville on Easter Sunday, & we retreated "in good order" to Danville. . . . Here we found 400 sick much better provided for than in M. or . . . . Most of our patients were Catholic, at least in name, for many had almost forgotten their duties

---

[2] Egidius (Giles) Smulders, C.SS.R. (1815–1900), was a Dutch-born priest, chaplain of the Eighth Louisiana Infantry, who served throughout the entire war.

[3] Henry Fehlings (1822–1888), a German-born priest, who was dispensed from his vows as a Redemptorist in May, 1861, and died as pastor of St. Mary's Church, Utica, New York.

[4] Joseph E. Johnston (1807–1891) was in command of the Confederate troops in northern Virginia at this time.

[5] An effort to identify this religious was not successful.

as such, but it was our consolation to see them entering upon them again with the simplicity of children. The zeal of good Father S. led many to a knowledge of our holy religion & about 50 were baptized. In Nov. the Medical Director removed our hospital to Lynchburg as there was no means of heating that in Danville. Our number had increased to five as the hospital was larger & contained 1000 patients, whom we found in a most pitiful condition. The persons who were in charge, had a very good will, but not the means of carrying it out, & although the fund was ample, the poor patients were half starved owing entirely to mismanagement. As we passed through the ward the first time, accompanied by the Dr., a man from the lower end called out, "Lady, oh lady — for God's sake gave me a piece of bread." To give you an idea of the care the sick had received, it will be sufficient to say that though the whole establishment had been cleaned for our reception, some of the Sisters swept up the vermin in the dust pan. The doctors soon placed everything under our control, & with a little economy the patients were well provided for, & order began to prevail. Father Gache,[6] a zealous & holy Jesuit, effected much good & removed many prejudices from the minds of those whom a faulty education had made enemies — bitter enemies of our holy faith. During the three years that we remained in L. he baptized 100. . . . The approach of the Federals placed our hospital in imminent danger & it was decided to move the sick & hospital stores to Richmond. The Surgeon General of the Confederate Army[7] begged that we would take charge of the Stuart hospital in that city which we did on the 13th. of Feb. 1865. We were then 10 in number, & as usual, we found plenty to do to place the sick in a comfortable situation, which we had just accomplished when the city was evacuated, & on the 13th. of April, the hospital being dispensed with, we left R. for our sweet valley home.

109. The Efforts of Archbishop Hughes to Keep France Neutral During the Civil War, January 29, 1862

THE personal friendship between Archbishop Hughes and William H. Seward (1801–1872) that had developed during the latter's time as Governor

[6] Hippolite Gache, S.J. (1817–1907), was a chaplain who entered the service from Louisiana.

[7] Samuel Preston Moore (1813–1889) was Surgeon General of the Confederate Army.

of New York continued when he became Lincoln's Secretary of State. In the early months of the Civil War the two were in close correspondence, and President Lincoln thanked Hughes for his "kind and judicious" letters which Seward "regularly allows me both the pleasure and the profit of perusing" (Archives of the Archdiocese of New York, Lincoln to Hughes, Washington, October 21, 1861). In October, 1861, Seward asked Hughes to go abroad in the hope that he could help to keep France neutral. It was a critical moment for the Union cause as Great Britain, France, and Spain had signed the Treaty of London on October 31, 1861, for the protection of their interests in Mexico and it was well known that they were friendly to the Confederacy. During his time in Europe Hughes visited England, France, Rome, and Ireland, and was given many opportunities to exert influence in behalf of the Washington government. High praise for his efforts was expressed by Alexander W. Randall (1819–1872) when the latter presented his credentials to Pius IX on June 6, 1862, as American Minister to the Papal States. Randall told the Pope, "It is a source of regret to thousands of good men that the Government of the United States cannot, in any appropriate way, testify its appreciation of such services" (Leo Francis Stock [Ed.], *United States Ministers to the Papal States. Instructions and despatches, 1848–1868* [Washington, 1933], pp. 251–252). The following letter from Hughes to Seward was written some weeks after his audience with the Emperor Napoleon III and the Empress Eugénie. Source: *Mission Abroad, 1861–1862: A Selection of Letters from Archbishop Hughes, Bishop McIlwaine, W. H. Seward and Thurlow Weed* (Rochester: University of Rochester Press, c. 1954), microfilm.

Paris, Jany 29, 1862

My Dear Governor.

I congratulate the President and his Cabinet, as well as the whole country, on the admirable tact, ability and success which have hitherto attended the President's administration under the most trying circumstances known to our history.

The Emperor's Speech,[1] at opening what in England they would call the Parliament, — what we would call the President's Message to Congress, has been all that, under present circumstances, we could have hoped for. Knowing, as I do, the condition of this Country, I look upon it as all we could reasonably expect. I regard it as a proclamation of peace on the part of France, from which England may take a lesson of wisdom; and if she will not let her look out for the consequences of a war with America.

[1] In a speech on January 27, 1862, to the legislative assembly Napoleon III had deplored the injurious effect of the Civil War on French commercial interests, but he added, "However, so long as the rights of neutrals are respected, we must confine ourselves to expressing wishes that these dissensions may soon be terminated" (Geraldine McGuire, "The Mission of Archbishop Hughes to Europe, 1861–62," unpublished master's thesis, Columbia University [1946], pp. 24–25).

My mind has been relieved of very great solicitude by the speech of the Emperor. It was not in my power to determine before hand, either directly or indirectly, the tone of that important document. But I have done all I could to bring about the result. I knew this people before I left home. I knew there could be no general hostility to the U. States amongst them. But at present the Sovereign is France — and if the Sovereign had adopted another style in his opening speech, France would have stood by him, and England would be rejoiced at his determination. As it is, England is compelled to pause before she enters into a contest with the United States. Still, it will be most important for us not to give any pretext for intervention by either France or England — or both united — for hostilities from this side of the Atlantic.

In the wise, prudent and, so far as I know, perfectly just policy of the Government in disposing of the late affair of the "Trent,"[2] Europe has been caught in its own trap. Let Europe be held strictly to what, nolens volens, it has been obliged to recognize — viz — the old principles of the American Government as to maritime and neutral rights.

Permit me to state my course, as a loyal citizen, since I came to France. I had no encouragement from our officials.[3] But, independent of their patronage, I have had, as you may suppose, the entrée to the best Society in Paris — as an American Bishop. At dinners & soirées it has come up invariably that the company, either before, or during, or after dinner referred to me for an explanation of the Civil War that is now existing between two sections of our once United States. I did explain as well as I could, perfectly satisfied that whatever I said would reach the ears of one or other of the Ministers within twenty four hours after its utterance. Besides, during my interview[4] with the Emperor, I felt no hesitation in stating what none of his Ministers would venture to say. I might almost add that on the same occasion I had the effrontery even to give advice. It is generally thought that certain men are above being influenced. This is a mistake. If there

[2] On November 8, 1861, the Confederate commissioners to Great Britain and France were removed from the British mail packet *Trent* by the American warship *San Jacinto* thus precipitating a crisis between the Washington and London governments.

[3] Hughes alluded several times in his correspondence with Seward to the generally cool reception he had received from American officials in France. At the time William L. Dayton (1807–1864) was the American minister.

[4] The archbishop was received in audience by Emperor Napoleon III and Empress Eugénie on December 24, 1861. Hughes' memorandum of the meeting may be read in John R. G. Hassard, *Life of the Most Reverend John Hughes, First Archbishop of New York* (New York, 1866), pp. 465–468.

ever was a man of such a type it would be General Jackson. And yet whilst General Jackson would disregard, under certain circumstances, the opinion of his whole Cabinet, General Jackson might take up and reflect upon a phrase uttered by the barber who shaved him. At all events, I think we might have fared worse in France than we have done.

Several of the Bishops from the districts that are suffering, owing to the interruption of trade with America, called upon me as they successively arrived in Paris.[5] To them also I had an opportunity of relating the state of the case. For the most part they came to see the Emperor on the following day — and to expose to him the state of destitution in which their poor people were suffering. Whether they made known to the Emperor the views which I communicated, or not, I have no means of ascertaining. But at all events I thought it no harm to make them acquainted with the substance of the Despatch, a copy of which you were kind enough to confide to me for private use.

I have just received your kind letter of the 9th inst. I am glad that the President does not deem it useful or necessary for me to execute the purpose which I had conceived only on the hypothesis that it might be useful to the Country.[6] By the by, in speaking of the President, I may be allowed to say that in this country at least, he is winning golden opinions for his calm, unostentatious, mild, but firm, and energetic administrative talents.

I intend to leave next Monday for a short visit to Rome. After that I shall have to visit Ireland, in consequence of invitations from that country — and for reasons of my own. From Ireland I shall sail for home, as soon as the severe winter months are over.

I remain, My Dear Governor, as ever, Your devoted Fd. & servt

✠ John Abp of New York

[5] A blockade of the southern ports was declared by the Union government in April, 1861, and it had brought acute suffering to the French textile industries which were so largely dependent upon southern cotton.

[6] Hughes was in all likelihood referring here to a projected visit to Madrid to try to influence the government of Isabella II (1830–1904). The necessity of the trip to Spain was obviated by his later conferences in Rome with the Spanish ambassador and the two new Spanish cardinals, Miguel García-Cuesta (1803–1873), Archbishop of Compostella, and Ferdinando de la Puente (1808–1867), Archbishop of Burgos.

110. American Diplomatic Relations With the Papal States, September 27, 1862

IN JUNE, 1797, the United States inaugurated consular relations with the Papal States. A half century later President Polk suggested the establishment of diplomatic relations between the two countries in his message to Congress of December 7, 1847, and in spite of bitter opposition from the American nativists the proposal was carried. During the crisis of the Civil War and the tension in Italy over the *Risorgimento* the American legation at Rome took on new interest as is reflected in the instruction (given below) of September 27, 1862, from Secretary of State William H. Seward to Richard M. Blatchford (1798–1875) who had recently been appointed minister. Five years later, on the pretext of an entirely false rumor that the church of the American Protestants in Rome had been ordered outside the city walls by the papal government, Congress refused to make the necessary appropriation and the mission was brought to an end with the resignation of Rufus King as minister on January 1, 1868, without even a formal notification to the pope's government. Source: Leo Francis Stock (Ed.), *United States Ministers to the Papal States. Instructions and Despatches, 1848–1868* (Washington: The Catholic University of America Press, 1933), pp. 258–260.

Department of State, Washington, 27th September, 1862.

Sir:

This Government has not now, it seldom has had, any special transaction, either commercial or political, to engage the attention of a Minister at Rome. Indeed, till a very late period the United States were without any representation at that ancient and interesting capital. The first colonists in this country were chiefly Protestants, who not merely recognised no ecclesiastical authority of the Pope, but were very jealous lest he might exert some ecclesiastical influence here which would be followed by an assumption of political power unfavorable to freedom and self-government on this continent. It was not seen that the political power of the Catholic Church was a purely foreign affair, constituting an important part of the political system of the European continent. The opening of our country as an asylum to men of all religions, as well as of all races, and an extension of the trade of the Union, in a short time brought with them large masses of the faithful members of that Church, of various birth and derivation, and these masses are continually augmenting. Our country has not been slow to learn that while religion is with these masses, as it is with others, a matter of conscience, and while the spiritual authority of the head of their church is a cardinal article of their faith, which must be tolerated on the soundest principles of civil liberty, yet that this faith in no degree necessarily interferes with the equal rights of the citizen, or affects unfavorably his loyalty to the republic. It is believed that ever since the tide of emigration set in upon this continent the head of the Roman Church and States has freely recognized and favored the development of the principle of political freedom on the part of the Catholics in this country, while he has never lost an opportunity to express his satisfaction with the growth, prosperity and progress of the American people. It was under these circumstances that this Government, in 1848, wisely determined that while it maintained representatives in the capitals of every other civilized State, and even at the capitals of many semi-civilized States which reject the whole Christian religion, it was neither wise nor necessary to exclude Rome from the circle of our diplomatic intercourse. Thus far the new relation then established has proved pleasant and beneficial.

Just now Rome is the seat of profound ecclesiastical and political anxieties, which, more or less, affect all the nations of Europe. The Holy Father claims immunity for the temporal power he exercises as a right incident to an ecclesiastical authority which is generally respected by the European States.

On the other hand, some of those States, with large masses in other States, assert that this temporal power is without any religious sanction, is unnecessary and pernicious. I have stated the question merely for the purpose of enabling myself to give you the President's view of what will be your duty with regard to it. That duty is to forbear altogether from taking any part in the controversy. The reasons for this forbearance are three: First, that so far as spiritual or ecclesiastical matters enter into the question they are beyond your province, for you are a political representative only. Second, so far as it is a question affecting the Roman States it is a domestic one and we are a foreign nation. Third, so far as it is a political question merely, it is at the same time purely an European one, and you are an American Minister, bound to avoid all entangling connexion with the politics of that continent.

This line of conduct will nevertheless allow you to express, and you are therefore instructed to express to His Holiness the assurances of the best wishes of the Government and of the people of the United States for his health and happiness, and for the safety and prosperity and happiness of the Roman people. And you will farther assure him that the United States constantly preserve a lively remembrance of the many generous and liberal manifestations they have received of his goodwill and friendship, and that he may confidently rely upon them for the practice of all the duties which grow out of the relations of the two countries as independent members of the family of nations.

You will find Rome a resort and temporary residence of intellectual persons from all parts of the world. Among them are many who, in various degrees, exercise an influence upon the opinions, and, perhaps in some cases upon the policies of nations. It will be a pleasing duty for you at this moment, when our unhappy domestic conflict is a subject of universal discussion, to vindicate the justice, the wisdom and the moderation of the Government and loyal people of the United States against those who, from interest, prejudice or passion, are directing their efforts to the overthrow of a republic which we must continue to think still holds in its keeping the best hopes of the human race.

111. A Catholic Chaplain With the Union Armies, October 2, 1862

EVER since Canadian-born Father Louis E. Lotbinière (1715–1786) was commissioned by the Continental Congress in January, 1776, to serve as chaplain to Colonel James Livingston's regiment of Canadian volunteers, Catholic priests in one capacity or another have been rendering spiritual aid to the American armed forces. Early in the Civil War President Lincoln informed Archbishop Hughes of New York that he had appointed three Protestant ministers as hospital chaplains, and he added, "If you perceive no objection, I will thank you to give me the name, or names, of one or more suitable persons of the Catholic Church, to whom I may, with propriety, tender the same service" (Archives of the Archdiocese of New York, Lincoln to Hughes, Washington, October 21, 1861). Eventually sixty-seven priests were enrolled as chaplains in the field with the Union and Confederate armies, together with a number of hospital and volunteer chaplains and nearly 500 sisters from over twenty congregations who cared for the wounded in hospitals. Among the Union chaplains Father Peter P. Cooney, C.S.C. (1822–1905), was one of the most prominent. He was attached to the 35th Regiment, Indiana Volunteers, from October, 1861, to June, 1865, and saw service in Kentucky, Tennessee, and Georgia during which time he conceived a deep admiration for the piety of General William S. Rosecrans (1819–1898), a convert to Catholicism from his days at West Point, and it was Cooney who received General David S. Stanley (1828–1902) into the Church early in 1864. The following letter depicted for his brother experiences which have been met by all chaplains who have seen active fighting with the American armies. Source: Thomas T. McAvoy, C.S.C. (Ed.), "The War Letters of Father Peter Paul Cooney of the Congregation of Holy Cross," *Records of the American Catholic Historical Society of Philadelphia,* XLIV (March, 1933), 67–69.

Louisville, Kentucky
October 2, 1862

My dear Brother:

After a long silence I am happy to have an opportunity to write you a few lines. Since I last wrote my health has never been better. It seems as if my health grows better as my hardships and fatigues increase; for all that I had to undergo since I entered on this new field of duty could not equal what I had to endure last month.

We started from McMinnville, Tennessee on the last day of August and we have been marching nearly ever since. We arrived here a few days ago, having traveled, without stopping but [for] the necessary rests, over three hundred miles and nearly the whole time in a dense cloud of dust, so that we looked like so many millers. There [were] between sixty and eighty thousand soldiers with us, making a fearful army. When we arrived here Munfordsville, Kentucky, we prepared for a battle, as the Southern troops were nearly as many as we were at this place and they have the benefit of a strong fortification. We stopped a day and a night to prepare for the battle between two large armies. I heard confessions all that night — no sleep. I sat eight hours without getting off my seat. It was a very cool night; for the nights, as a general thing, are colder in the South than in Michigan or Indiana but the days are warmer. About twelve o'clock, my legs were perfectly benumbed, until one of the poor soldiers brought me a blanket to roll around my thighs; for they think more of an inconvenience to me than I do myself. You might hear them whispering to one another words of sympathy for me. They little knew the joy that was in my breast, midst all these trials, when I considered how much God was doing with the hands of his unworthy son.

If [you] were to see my confessional that night you would laugh. In the evening one of the soldiers came to me and said: "Father, will you be hearing tonight?" "Indeed I will, my dear, with God's help," I answered and I jocosely asked him in presence of the others, "Did you not know I was hearing all day?" "No Father," said he, very innocently, and he noticed the joke only when the next commenced to laugh. I find it an advantage sometimes in camp to crack a joke with them; it cheers them up and enlivens the monotony of camp life. "What will you do Father," said one, "for a place to hear confessions in?" (For we were in the open field). "Never mind," I answered, "come this way four or five of you." They came and we made three stacks of guns, four guns in each, in this shape V, [and] the bayonets were locked into each other. Then we got three blankets, two covering two sides hanging on the bayonets; the other covered the top, leaving the front open. And in this I sat all night. This is a piece of architecture that you will not find in Monroe. Here the poor fellows came, impressed with the idea that perhaps this would be the last confession of their lives. Some of the officers gave me their wills and then went to confession. But it would take volumes to tell all.

Here, dear Brother, in such places life is valued as it ought — as worth nothing. That night I baptized a non-commissioned officer who was to that time an Episcopalian. But we came to Munfordsville the next day and the rebels had run away. We caught only the hind ones who could not keep up. All the march we were up at two o'clock in the morning; and generally it was ten or eleven o'clock before we could get to bed, without tents, but the broad canopy of heaven. I alone had a tent along but some nights it would be five miles behind in the wagon train. So you see we have "high living" when you come to add to this, that the men had to march some times eight hours without anything to eat.

The whole army started yesterday from here towards Bardstown forty miles from here to meet the enemy. I follow them tomorrow morning. I shall take a trip home to rest about the end of the month. I think the drafting system is given up, so you need not be troubled about it. Pray, pray, dear Brother, for me and for yourselves and heaven shall be our reward.

Your Brother,
P. P. Cooney, *Chaplain*
35th Reg. Ind. Vol.

Write immediately and let me know how my mother and all the folks are. Give my love to all. Direct your letter to me Chaplain 35th Reg. Ind. Vol., Louisville, Kentucky.

112. Father Purcell's Stand in Behalf of Emancipation of the Slaves, April 8, 1863

THE oldest continuous Catholic newspaper in the United States is the *Catholic Telegraph* of Cincinnati which began publication on October 22, 1831. Like its Catholic contemporaries, the *Telegraph* commented freely on political affairs and as the Civil War came on its editor, Father Edward Purcell (1808–1881), brother of John B. Purcell (1800–1883), first Archbishop of Cincinnati, became more outspoken in his opposition to slavery. It was not an easy policy to pursue in a border state like Ohio, and as a consequence Purcell had to pay dearly in loss of support from southern-minded Catholics in the area and in abuse from fellow Catholic editors like Courtney Jenkins of the Baltimore *Catholic Mirror,* McMaster of the *Freeman's Journal,* and John Mullaly of the New York *Metropolitan Record,* who charged him with being an abolitionist. But he did not retreat and, in fact, the *Telegraph* was the first Catholic paper in the country to come out clearly for emancipation of the slaves, a policy which Archbishop Purcell had publicly espoused as early as August, 1862. Lincoln's proclamation was formally issued on January 1, 1863, and caused widespread disagreement in the North. Two months after he published the uncompromising editorial which follows, Purcell announced that reaction had shown that many Catholics in all sections of the country had been brooding over "the multitudinous wrongs and anti-Christian proclivities of the 'peculiar institution.'" His mail proved that there were Catholics in every part of the United States who wished, as he said, "to express their satisfaction that there was a Catholic-Church-paper which was not afraid to raise its voice in favor of the most oppressed people on earth" (*Catholic Telegraph,* June 10, 1863). Source: Editorial, "The Church and Slavery," *Catholic Telegraph,* April 8, 1863.

In some remarks lately made on the emancipation of the serfs in Russia, we observed that the Church and slavery could never get along well together. The New York *Freeman's Journal* condemns our remarks, quotes St. Paul and Church Councils, and says that we are ignorant of ecclesiastical history. The writer in the *Freeman* also observes that he does not wish for a controversy with us. As the *Freeman,* on this occasion, is mild and uses no very offensive language, we reply to his comments at some length.

We assure our cotemporary [*sic*] that we, too, have no desire to enter into a controversy. It would be useless now, because the subject of slavery is dead. The first canon fired at Sumter sounded its knell. It would be much easier to take Richmond or open the Mississippi, than restore slavery in the United States. The thing is gone forever.

But our cotemporary suggests that we are not acquainted with ecclesiastical history and that slavery and the Church have got along well together, and quotes St. Paul and certain Councils. Our cotemporary has a right to entertain any opinion he pleases about our ignorance. His opinion is his own. But without acrimony we can write on this subject of slavery. It must be discussed; there is no help for it — and whilst we accord to those who are its advocates all liberty of speech, we hope that some license will be extended to us when we give our reasons on the other side. It is not in a factious spirit or a fanatical spirit that we write, but under the strong conviction that a great change is at hand in the political welfare of the country, and that it is of some consequence to Catholics to decide wisely what part to take. This cannot be done by crying out "ignorance," "abolition," but by friendly discussion. Whether we like it or not, slavery is extinguished in the United States, and all that we have to do is to decide how we shall accommodate ourselves "to coming events."

We have said and we now repeat it, that slavery and the Catholic Church could never get along well together. The Church never tries to correct evils by revolutionary means. When she has not the legislative power in her hands she is patient, long-suffering, gentle. What she could not suppress she tolerated. But she found slavery little disposed to imitate her meekness. When the slave power predominates, religion is nominal. There is no life in it. It is the hard-working laboring man who builds the church, the schoolhouse and the orphan asylum, not the slaveholder, as a general rule. Religion flourishes in a slave State only in proportion to its intimacy with a free State, or as it is adjacent to it. There are more Catholics in the Cathedral congregation of this city than in North and South Carolina and Georgia! There are more Catholics in one of our second-rate congregations than in the whole State of Alabama! Louisiana ought to be a Catholic State, but it has never sent a Senator or Representative to Congress who identified himself with the Catholic cause, so far as we know. The slave-owners are not the zealous men of the Church in that State.

What help is Cuba, with all its riches, to the Catholic cause? The poorest Irish or German congregation in the free States does more for religion than Havana, if we can rely upon the representations of those who ought to know and whose character forbids deception. It appears to us, therefore, that slavery is not friendly to the propagation of the Catholic Faith — or to its charity and fervor when it happens to be professed. If for telling these plain truths any subscriber wishes to withdraw his patronage, we hope he will do so at once. And if for telling these truths the ladies of a community in a slave State choose to burn our Paper again, they have our liberty, if that be of any consequence, to prove their amiability and piety by doing so. The time is near at hand when they will wish that they had been more tolerant to the expression of an opinion.

But to our knowledge of ecclesiastical history: "No one now ventures to doubt," says Balmes, "that the Church exercised a powerful influence on the abolition of slavery: this is a truth too clear and evident to be questioned. . . . It did all that was possible in favor of human liberty; if it did not advance more rapidly in the work, it was because it could not do so without compromising the undertaking — without creating serious obstacles to the desired emancipation. Such is the result at which we arrive when we have thoroughly examined the charges made against some proceedings of the Church. . . . That slavery endured for a long time in presence of the Church is true; but it was always declining, and only lasted as long as was necessary to realize the benefit without violence — without a shock — without compromitting [*sic*] its universality and its continuation."[1] These few words from the fifteenth chapter of Balmes' incomparable work, show the exact position occupied by the Church in reference to slavery. To say that she ever favored the system is a calumny. She proclaimed men's fraternity with each other, and their equality before God, and therefore could not be the advocate of slavery.

With respect to the words of St. Paul, so often quoted, we find a full justification of our position. He writes to Philemon, commending his faith and charity, and he says — "wherefore, though I might have much confidence in Christ Jesus *to command thee that which is to the purpose,* for charity's sake I rather beseech, *thou being such a one,* as Paul the aged and now also a prisoner of Jesus Christ, I beseech thee for my son Onesimus, whom I have begotten in my chains — whom I have sent back to thee. And do thou receive him as my own bowels. . . . Not now as a servant, but instead of a servant a most dear brother, especially to me; but how much more to thee, both in the flesh and in the good?"[2]

Any one who can find anything in this in favor of slavery, must have piercing optics. Would St. Paul have sent him back to a Heathen master — or one who would have the power and the will to despise him — to sell his wife and children into slavery? The thought is not to be entertained of the blessed apostle?

If a fugitive slave in this country was to be sent back to some master in Mississippi or Texas by a Catholic Bishop of our days, bearing such an epistle as the above, how would the master mock and the world laugh at the Bishop? What a joke it would be considered in the South?

But what did the Popes think of slavery? This will probably throw some light on ecclesiastical history. Paul III. in 1537, and Urban VIII. in 1639, condemned in the strongest terms the crime of reducing men to slavery, separating them from their wives and children, or in any manner depriving them of their liberty, or upon any pretext to preach

[1] James Balmes, *Protestantism and Catholicity Compared in Their Effects on the Civilization of Europe* (Baltimore, 1851), pp. 91–94.

[2] Philemon 1:8–16.

or teach that it is lawful. Pius II. in 1462, also denounces the system in the strongest terms. Gregory XVI., who, in his Apostolic Letter of the 3d of December, 1839, refers to the foregoing, uses this vehement language on the same subject — "Wherefore, we, desiring to turn away so great a reproach as this from all the boundaries of Christians, and the whole matter being maturely weighed, certain Cardinals of the Holy Roman Church, our venerable brethren being also called into Council, treading in the footsteps of our predecessors with Apostolic authority, do vehemently admonish and adjure in the Lord, all believers in Christ, that no one hereafter may dare unjustly to molest Indians, negroes or other men of this sort, or to spoil them of their goods or reduce them to slavery. We, therefore, with Apostolic authority do reprobate all the aforesaid actions as utterly unworthy of the Christian name; and by the same Apostolic authority do strictly prohibit and interdict that any ecclesiastic or lay person shall presume to defend that very trade in negroes *as lawful under any pretext or studied excuse,* or otherwise to preach, or in any manner, publicly or privately, to teach contrary to those things which we have charged in this, our Apostolic Letter."[3]

This is tolerably showy language. Its import, we think, is clear enough to any one who has a human mind. There can be "no pretext or studied excuse," says the good and great Pontiff. Are Catholics afraid or unwilling to read the admonition of the Vicar of Jesus Christ?

But it will be said that Gregory XVI. alluded to the foreign slave trade! This, however, is a pretext, and has not even the dignity of a "studied excuse." We have a word to say on the point.

Shortly before the appearance of this Apostolic letter, a religious order in the United States, by their close communication with Rome, received information of its existence and approaching publication. With more wit than piety the Superiors of that order collected together a large number of their slaves and sold them all to a Southern *gentleman,* we will call him so, who hurried them into Louisiana, and they were scattered over the South without reference to their relationship one to another. The whole Catholic community was shocked at the occurrence. Pope Gregory's letter appeared soon after, and it did not moderate the feeling of indignation. When the fact was known in Rome, such was the emotion felt by His Holiness, that the Superiors, on whom the responsibility rested, were ordered forthwith to proceed

---

[3] For the text of Gregory XVI's apostolic letter, *In supremo apostolatus,* cf. Antonius Maria Bernasconi (Ed.), *Acta Gregorii Papae XVI* (Rome, 1901), II, 387–388.

to the Eternal City and they did not return for years. Why they were detained it is unnecessary to discuss.[4]

This shows that slavery in every shape, is condemned and reprobated by the Church. In the meantime she did nothing violently. She only spoke the solemn words of admonition. Events have hurried on — what the Church would not or could not do the politicians have done. The door is now made open without any agency of Catholics, and those who wish to despise the venerable Pontiffs and be the jailors of their fellowmen, may endeavor to close and lock and bolt it. We take no part in any such proceeding.

113. Brownson Defines the World Mission of the American Republic, 1865

ONE of the most remarkable converts to the Catholic Church of the United States was the nationally known editor and publicist, Orestes A. Brownson (1803–1876). After a long search for spiritual peace that led him through many curious religious experiences he was received into the Church on October 20, 1844, by John B. Fitzpatrick, Coadjutor Bishop of Boston. In his immense literary output — amounting to twenty large volumes — the most famous single work was *The American Republic* which appeared as the nation was emerging from the Civil War. Brownson had written a great deal on government, but in the preface to this book he said: "This work is not only my latest, but will be taken as the authentic, and the only authentic statement of my political views and convictions, and whatever in any of my previous writings conflicts with the principles defended in its pages, must be regarded as retracted, and rejected" (p. viii). Of late years the original contribution and keen insights of *The American Republic* have found a deepening appreciation among political scientists. For example, two recent writers on Brownson's classic have declared it a work "accepted as an influential element in our intellectual development and heritage," and have stated that it "has found its way even into textbook discussions of American political ideas" (Thomas I. Cook and Arnaud B. Leavelle, "Orestes A. Brownson's *The American Republic*," *Review of Politics,* IV [January, 1942], 77). The excerpt which follows outlines Brownson's idea of the mis-

[4] Purcell was referring here to the sale in 1838 of forty-nine slaves for $25,000 by Thomas F. Mulledy, S.J. (1794–1860), then provincial of the Maryland province, to Henry Johnson (1783–1864) who had been Governor of Louisiana, 1824–1828, and was at the time serving his second term in the United States Senate. Cf. Mulledy to John P. Roothaan, S.J., General of the Jesuits, August 9, 1838, in Thomas Hughes, S.J., *History of the Society of Jesus in North America. Documents* (New York, 1910), I, 1122. The lasting effects of this episode on the Negroes of southern Maryland was commented upon by John LaFarge, S.J., *The Manner Is Ordinary* (New York, 1954), p. 184.

sion which the United States has to the world by reason of its unique form of government. Source: Orestes A. Brownson, *The American Republic. Its Constitution, Tendencies, and Destiny* (New York: P. O'Shea, 1865), pp. 3–7.

Every living nation has an idea given it by Providence to realize, and whose realization is its special work, mission, or destiny. Every nation is, in some sense, a chosen people of God. . . .

The United States, or the American Republic, has a mission, and is chosen of God for the realization of a great idea. It has been chosen not only to continue the work assigned to Greece and Rome, but to accomplish a greater work than was assigned to either. In art, it will prove false to its mission if it do not rival Greece; and in science and philosophy, if it do not surpass it. In the state, in law, in jurisprudence, it must continue and surpass Rome. Its idea is liberty, indeed, but liberty with law, and law with liberty. Yet its mission is not so much the realization of liberty as the realization of the true idea of the state, which secures at once the authority of the public and the freedom of the individual — the sovereignty of the people without social despotism, and individual freedom without anarchy. In other words, its mission is to bring out in its life the dialectic union of authority and liberty, of the natural rights of man and those of society. The Greek and Roman republics asserted the state to the detriment of individual freedom; modern republics either do the same, or assert individual freedom to the detriment of the state. The American republic has been instituted by Providence to realize the freedom of each with advantage to the other.

The real mission of the United States is to introduce and establish a political constitution, which, while it retains all the advantages of the constitutions of the states thus far known, is unlike any of them, and secures advantages which none of them did or could possess. The American constitution has no prototype in any prior constitution. The American form of government can be classed throughout with none of the forms of government described by Aristotle, or even by later authorities. Aristotle knew only four forms of government: Monarchy, Aristocracy, Democracy, and Mixed Governments. The American form is none of these, nor any combination of them. It is original, a new contribution to political science, and seeks to attain the end of all wise and just government by means unknown or forbidden to the ancients, and which have been but imperfectly comprehended even by American political writers themselves. The originality of the American constitution has been overlooked by the great majority even of our own statesmen, who seek to explain it by analogies borrowed from the constitutions of other states rather than by a profound study of its own principles. They have taken too low a view of it, and have rarely, if ever, appreciated its distinctive and peculiar merits.

As the United States have vindicated their national unity and integrity, and are preparing to take a new start in history, nothing is more important than that they should take that new start with a clear and definite view of their national constitution, and with a distinct understanding of their political mission in the future of the world. The citizen who can help his countrymen to do this will render them an important service and deserve well of his country, though he may have been unable to serve in her armies and defend her on the battlefield. The work now to be done by American statesmen is even more difficult and more delicate than that which has been accomplished by our own brave armies. As yet the people are hardly better prepared for the political work to be done than they were at the outbreak of the civil war for the military work they have so nobly achieved. But, with time, patience, and good-will, the difficulties may be overcome, the errors of the past corrected, and the Government placed on the right track for the future.

114. Bishop McQuaid Describes the Vatican Council, April 24, 1870

DURING the Vatican Council which was in session from December 8, 1869, to July 18, 1870, forty-six Americans — six archbishops, thirty-nine bishops, and one abbot — were numbered among the nearly 700 prelates from every part of the world who at one time or another were in attendance at this first ecumenical council of the Church since that of Trent over 300 years before. On the great issue of defining papal infallibility the Americans were as divided as the hierarchies of other nations, and on January 15, 1870, twenty-one bishops from the United States joined with about 120 bishops from other countries in signing a petition against the definition. Among the most persistent members of the minority party was Bernard J. McQuaid (1823–1909) who had been consecrated on July 12, 1868, as first ordinary of the new See of Rochester. During the council McQuaid wrote a number of lengthy letters to the Reverend James M. Early, vicar-general and rector of St. Patrick's Cathedral, Rochester, in which he discoursed on council business, as well as on affairs of his diocese. He arrived in Rome on November 26, 1869, and five days later he remarked to Early:

> Since coming to Europe I have heard much on the question of the infallibility of the Pope, which with us in America was scarcely talked of. The feeling is very strong, *pro* and *con*. It seems that the Jesuits have

> been at the bottom of it, and have been preparing the public mind for it for the past two years. They have not made friends for themselves by the course they have followed, and if in any way the harmony of the Council is disturbed it will be by the introduction of this most unnecessary question (December 1, 1869).

McQuaid remained opposed to the definition to the very end and the day before he left Rome he told Early:

> Tomorrow the public session will be held in which the final voting on the Infallibility will take place. They have ended by making the definition as absolute and strict as it was possible to make it. As a consequence a large *non-placet* vote will be recorded against it. What will be the consequence in some of these European countries God only knows (July 17, 1870).

The bishop's prediction of the *non-placet* vote on July 18 proved to be wide of the mark, only two of the 535 bishops present voting against the definition. Although he had received permission on July 16 to return home, McQuaid was still in Rome on the day of the final session but he absented himself on that occasion. Shortly after his arrival in Rochester, however, he delivered a sermon on August 28, 1870, in his cathedral in which he made a public proclamation of his faith in the newly defined dogma. Source: McQuaid to Early, Rome, April 24, 1870, Henry J. Browne (Ed.), "The Letters of Bishop McQuaid from the Vatican Council," *Catholic Historical Review*, XLI (January, 1956), 423–427.

Rome, April 24, 1870

Dear Father Early:

I have just returned from the first public session of the Council,[1] and having some spare time I thought I would send you a few lines.

You will doubtless have read all that we have done in the papers before this letter reaches you. The matter consists of an introductory chapter, & four chapters with canons attached. Chap. I. is on God, the Creator of all things: Chap. II. is on Revelation: Chap. III. on Faith: Chap. IV. on Faith and Reason.

There are some obstruse metaphysical points which few can fathom and certainly will never trouble the brains of any but a German Philosopher for whose especial benefit they seem to have been made. The rest is quite simple Theology. Yet it was wonderful the care that was needed and the pains taken to make every thing just as it ought to be.

The Decrees and Canons were passed unanimously. I know of only one Bishop who, having objections to some points and not wishing

---

[1] Strictly speaking, the public session held on April 24, 1870, was the third, not the first of the council, but it was the first at which decrees were passed. The first public session took place on December 8, 1869, with Pope Pius IX in attendance.

to break the unanimity of the voting, remained away and did not attend. The sight in the Council Hall was very beautiful. It was the first time that the Bishops appeared in red copes. The rich bright color contrasting with the simple white mitres had a charming effect. There was no great crowd compared with the crowds of Holy Week and Easter Sunday. On the last named day the crowd in the piazza of St. Peter's numbered from 100 to 150 thousand people. It is only in Rome that such mixed crowds can be gathered, and it is only in Rome that such orderly, quiet, pleasant and *gentlemanly* crowds can be found. What I have seen in this regard has filled me with amazement, not only at religious ceremonies but at public gatherings for festivities.

There will be a great exodus from Rome after today. The ceremonies, illuminations, and now the first promulgation of decrees are over, the visitors of all kinds and classes will leave us.[2] Several American Bishops leave this week, although some will not go home directly. I stay to fight the great battle if it should come up. We ourselves know little of what we shall have to do next. We may take up the second part of the first *Schema de Fide,* and we may pass at once to the *Schema de Ecclesia,* taking the question of the Infallibility first of all and out of its place. Some Bishops are urging the Holy Father to have this done; on the other hand, the difficulties in the way of such a definition are so many and so serious that there is some hesitation. Opposed to the definition are so many Bishops of unquestionable devotion to the Holy See, who will vote a *non-placet* if it should come before them that men stop to think. Besides the governments of Europe are alarmed.[3] They remember that Popes in the past absolved subjects from their allegiance and in many ways interfered with governments. Even in our country there will arise more or less difficulty on this head. At least politicians will try to use the difficulty against us.

Yet with all these reasons weighing against the definition I am

---

[2] McQuaid alluded here to the ceremonies of Easter Week which ended that year on Low Sunday, April 24. The bishops wore red copes because the Mass on Low Sunday was in honor of the Holy Spirit.

[3] The threat of intervention in the council by the governments of Bavaria, Great Britain, and France seemed very real at the time that McQuaid was writing. The spearhead of the attack was Comte Napoléon Daru, Minister of Foreign Affairs of France and a Catholic. Oddly enough, the tension was broken by the Protestant premier, Emile Ollivier, who took over the portfolio of foreign affairs after Daru had resigned for other reasons. Ollivier was sympathetic to the Church and the council and at once reversed Daru's policy of intervention. Cf. Cuthbert Butler, *The Vatican Council* (London, 1930), II, 16–25.

inclined to think that it will pass in some modified form. The Holy Father wishes it, and lets every one see that he does, the Jesuits are as busy as bees of late and the French Bishops of that way of thinking are as enthusiastic and excitable over the subject as they well can be.

My hope is that in the definition the Pope will in some [way] be connected with the Church. I cannot conceive of a living head without a body. However, I must not enter into the vexed question, which has been such a disturbance to my mind since I came to Rome that once it is disposed of one way or another I will never want to hear of its controversy again.

Should the discussion begin this coming week the cable will have informed you of it before this reaches you.

Monday, the 25th.

I resume my letter this morning. Since writing the above I learn as certain that the next point for discussion is to be the old one of the "little Catechism." Some are opposed to a uniform little Catechism for one reason, others for another. It is not a question that troubles me much, as the Catechism itself can be reconstructed as often as they find it expedient until they get one that will be satisfactory. The reason alleged for a general one is that uniformity may be obtained. But whilst saying this, they at the same time contradict themselves, as each Bishop will still be allowed to have larger ones for his own Diocese and according to its peculiar needs. Hence we at once get back to our old condition. So long as the same faith is taught, the less interference in such matters, the better is my judgment. The rumor has it that the Infallibility question will follow next.

I have been amused at reading in the Freeman's Journal what he [James A. McMaster, the editor] has to say about the Council. He draws all his facts or supposed facts from the London Tablet and Vatican.[4] Many of those *facts* amuse us at the power of invention, if not of malice, they display.

No one here has been able to discover the representative of "Jus."[5]

---

[4] *The Tablet* of London had been acquired in November, 1868, by Herbert Vaughan (1832–1903), the future cardinal, who shared the infallibilist views of his superior, Henry Edward Manning (1808–1892), Archbishop of Westminster. By "Vatican" McQuaid was referring to a series of special supplements brought out by the *Tablet* under the title of *The Vatican: A Weekly Record of the Council* which contained documents and reports from Rome but never printed any letters on the side of the inopportunists or opponents of the definition of papal infallibility.

[5] "Jus" was one of several anonymous writers of the New York *Freeman's Journal* whom McMaster had as fairly regular correspondents. "Jus" was the Reverend Eugene M. O'Callaghan (d. 1901) who held a number of pastorates

We can only laugh at the tone of the Freeman. It is probable that when his agitation dies out that Bishops themselves will take up the matter and see what can be done, in justice to the interests of religion as well as of Priests. The matter only once came up in a meeting of the American Bishops and on that occasion the only difficulty in the way of giving it examination was McMaster's agitation. . . .

Bp. Purcell leaves for home in a few days; worried almost to death by the trouble of the Infallibility question;[6] Bp. Bayley[7] leaves today; he is only too glad to get away from the fight. In fact, some of the strongest opponents of the Infallibility are leaving.[8] The Americans, of course, cannot return should the question come up, whilst the Europeans will be back in time.

After many an effort I obtained the receipt for the money given to the Holy Father by the Diocese. On the 18th. of March I received a letter in reply to the address of the Priests. I will forward the letter and the receipt by Father Hecker[9] who leaves Rome on Wednesday.

---

in the Diocese of Cleveland during these years. In 1869 he was pastor of St. Columba's Church, Youngstown, and by 1870 was listed as the pastor of Ashtabula, Ohio. O'Callaghan had trouble with Amadeus Rappe (1801–1877), first Bishop of Cleveland, and was one of the leading agitators for canonical legislation that would regulate the relations between bishops and their priests.

[6] John B. Purcell (1800–1883) was consecrated in October, 1833, as second Bishop of Cincinnati and became first archbishop of that see in July, 1850. Purcell was one of the strongest inopportunists among the American delegation to the council, and was opposed to the definition of the doctrine of infallibility itself until it was clearly stated what was meant. At a reception which was given for him in Mozart Hall, Cincinnati, on August 21, 1870, a few days after his return from Rome, he publicly read the definition and professed his faith in it; he likewise wrote a letter to Pius IX on December 5, 1870, signifying his acceptance of the decree.

[7] James Roosevelt Bayley (1814–1877) was first Bishop of Newark, 1853–1872, and eighth Archbishop of Baltimore, 1872–1877. Actually Bayley returned to Rome after a visit to Paris and left the Eternal City only on July 18 in company with McQuaid.

[8] Seven American prelates, including McQuaid, registered a *non-placet* in the crucial trial vote of the general congregation on July 13. At the final vote on July 18 all but two of these absented themselves, namely, William G. McCloskey (1823–1909), Bishop of Louisville, who voted *placet* and Edward Fitzgerald (1833–1907), Bishop of Little Rock, who voted *non-placet.* Fitzgerald and Bishop Luigi Riccio of Cajazzo in the former Kingdom of Naples were the only two among the 535 prelates voting who returned a *non-placet.* Fitzgerald made his profession of faith in the newly defined dogma, however, to Pius IX personally immediately after the close of the public session on July 18.

[9] Isaac T. Hecker, C.S.P. (1819–1888), founder of the Paulists, was theologian to Archbishop Martin J. Spalding of Baltimore during the council. He also acted as a liaison between the American bishops and the Germans, and he was especially close to Friedrich Cardinal Schwarzenberg (1809–1885), Archbishop of Prague, who was one of the most vigorous leaders of the minority which had opposed the definition of the infallibility of the pope.

You can, if you please, have the letter translated and published. It comes so long after date, and so long after others presented at the same time, that I feel by no means pleased. . . .

Direct your letters to the American College as I call there every day and I am no longer at the Minerva, having left the hotel last week. I have taken the rooms occupied by Father Quinn.[10] They are large and pleasantly situated. The family are kind, obliging and not obtrusive. I pay but 6 francs a day for three rooms. At the Hotel I paid 4½ for one small bed room in the fourth story, here called the third. My breakfast is served to me in my room, and I go to a restaurant for my dinner, at about 3 o'clock & at a cost of from 2 to 4 francs, according to my appetite or my extravagance.

Father De Regge[11] ought to be back with you about the time you receive this letter. There is an Italian I intend to send to you. I am undecided whether I shall send him at once or keep him until I go myself. It is probable that I shall send him in a few days.

You are aware that Father O'Hara[12] passed his examination and obtained his degree of D.D. Dr. O'Hara! henceforth, if you please. Unfortunately just after all his hard study, on his return from Naples to which he went for a few days, he was taken down with the Roman fever. He has been very sick, but is at the present out of danger and recovering rapidly. He had a great start out of that piece of waggery in the papers appointing a Bishop to Syracuse.[13] As the story was told to him he was not able to see that it was a joke and attached importance to it.

Dr. Anderson[14] of New York has also been quite ill — is getting better. Father Healey [*sic*][15] late of Troy Seminary, was at death's door for days — he is now well. He was confined to bed for nearly a month. They tell us that such a winter has not been known in the memory of that famous individual, to be found here as well as in

---

[10] An effort to identify Quinn was unsuccessful.

[11] Hippolyte de Regge was pastor of Our Lady of Victory Church, Rochester, a French congregation, in 1869 and was named chancellor of the diocese in 1870.

[12] This would seem to have been James O'Hara, pastor of St. Mary's Church in Syracuse.

[13] The Diocese of Syracuse was not erected until November 22, 1886.

[14] William Henry Anderson (1799–1875), professor of astronomy in Columbia College, New York, had been converted to Catholicism in 1849.

[15] Alexander Sherwood Healy (1836–1875) acted as theologian to Bishop John J. Williams of Boston during the council. He was later rector of the Cathedral of the Holy Cross, and when his brother, James A. Healy (1830–1900), was named second Bishop of Portland in February, 1875, he succeeded him in the pastorate of St. James Church, Boston, but died a few months thereafter.

America — "the oldest inhabitant." Bp. Ryan[16] has kept very well — seems to fatten up a little.

I see the papers have published the rescript of the Holy Father permitting the use of the Holy Oils of last year. I did not send it to you because I thought it just as well to get supplied with fresh oil and be done with the matter for this year.

A good word for me to all my good friends in the Diocese. Indeed it has been a good thing for me to be absent so long as it has caused me to think so much more of home and all my friends, priests and people in it. I thought a great deal of you during Holy Week, whilst I had such an easy time here.

Very sincerely your friend in Xt.,

B. J. McQuaid

115. Grant's Proposal and Blaine's Amendment to Prevent Public Funds for Religious Schools, September 29 – December 14, 1875

EVER since Bishop Hughes' New York school controversy of the 1840's the issue of public aid for private religious schools has been more or less a perennial one in American history. In 1875 the Republican Party found itself on the defensive by reason of the widespread corruption during the two terms of Ulysses S. Grant (1822–1885). In spite of that fact, however, Grant wanted a third term, and in an effort to head off the reform element in his own party, and likewise to distract the voters from the Democrats who were then staging a comeback, he chose to inject the highly controversial question of public funds to private schools into the campaign. In a speech to a reunion of the Army of the Tennessee at Des Moines on September 29, 1875, he raised the issue, following it up on December 7 with a proposal for an amendment to the Constitution that would forbid all public funds for religious schools. Grant's proposal was framed into a joint resolution of both houses of Congress by James G. Blaine (1830–1893), a representative from Maine, who on December 14, 1875, introduced what came to be called the Blaine Amendment. Catholics were aroused, and with the *Kulturkampf* then in full swing against the Church in Germany, James O'Connor declared the move "eminently Bismarckian" ("Anti-Catholic Prejudice," *American Catholic Quarterly Review,* I [January, 1875], 17). The Blaine resolution passed the House without serious trouble in August, 1876. In the Senate a substitute amendment was framed which contained an additional clause permitting the reading of the Bible in the public schools, but here the resolution failed to gain the necessary two-thirds ma-

16 Stephen V. Ryan, C.M. (1826–1896), was consecrated in November, 1868, as second Bishop of Buffalo.

jority. Both parties mentioned the subject in their national platforms, the Republicans coming out for an amendment while the Democrats hedged by proclaiming their support of public education but leaving it to the states to regulate. Sources: Frank A. Burr, *A New, Original and Authentic Record of the Life and Deeds of General U. S. Grant* (St. Paul: Empyreal Publishing House, 1885), pp. 871–872; *Congressional Record,* 44th Congress, 1st Session (Washington, 1876), IV, 175, 205.

Grant's Speech to the Army of the Tennessee, Des Moines, September 29, 1875.

. . . In this centennial year of our national existence, I believe it is a good time to begin the work of strengthening the foundation of the house commenced by our patriotic forefathers one hundred years ago at Concord and Lexington. Let us all labor to add all needful guarantees for the more perfect security of free thought, free speech and free press, pure morals, unfettered religious sentiments, and of equal rights and privileges to all men irrespective of nationality, color or religion. Encourage free schools, and resolve that not one dollar of money appropriated to their support, no matter how raised, shall be appropriated to the support of any sectarian school. Resolve that neither the state or nation, nor both combined, shall support institutions of learning other than those sufficient to afford every child growing up in the land the opportunity of a good common-school education, unmixed with sectarian, pagan or atheistical dogmas. Leave the matter of religion to the family altar, the church and the private school supported entirely by private contribution. Keep the church and state forever separate. With these safeguards I believe the battles which created the Army of the Tennessee will not have been fought in vain. . . .

Grant's Message to Congress, December 7, 1875.

As we are now about to enter upon our second centennial — commencing our manhood as a nation — it is well to look back upon the past and study what will be best to preserve and advance our future greatness. From the fall of Adam for his transgression to the present day, no nation has even been free from threatened danger to its prosperity and happiness. We should look to the dangers threatening us, and remedy them so far as lies in our power. We are a republic whereof one man is as good as another before the law. Under such a form of government it is of the greatest importance that all should be possessed of education and intelligence enough to cast a vote with the right understanding of its meaning. A large association of ignorant men cannot, for any considerable period, oppose a successful resistance to tyranny and oppression from the educated few, but will inevitably sink into acquiescence to the will of intelligence, whether directed by the demagogue or by priestcraft. Hence the education of the masses becomes of the first necessity for the preservation of our institutions. They are worth preserving, because they have secured the greatest good to the greatest proportion of the population of any form of government yet devised. All other forms of government approach it just in proportion to the general diffusion of education and independence of thought and action. As the primary step, therefore, to our advancement in all that has marked our progress in the past century, I suggest for your earnest consideration — and most earnestly recommend it — that a constitutional amendment be submitted to the Legislatures of the several States for ratification making it the duty of the several States to establish and forever maintain free public schools adequate to the education of all the children in the rudimentary branches within their respective limits, irrespective of sex, color, birthplace, or religions; forbidding the teaching in said schools of religious, atheistic, or pagan tenets; and prohibiting the granting of any school funds, or school taxes, or any part thereof, either by the legislative, municipal, or other authority, for the benefit or in aid, directly or indirectly, of any religious sect or denomination, or in aid for the benefit of any other object of any nature or kind whatever.[1]

Blaine's Proposed Amendment, December 14, 1875.

Resolved by the Senate and House of Representatives, That the following be proposed to the several States of the Union as an amendment to the Constitution:

Article XVI

No State shall make any law respecting an establishment of religion or prohibiting the free exercise thereof; and no money raised by taxation in any State for the support of public schools, or derived from any public fund therefor, nor any public lands devoted thereto, shall ever be under the control of any religious sect, nor shall any money so raised or lands so devoted be divided between religious sects or denominations.

[1] Grant's message to Congress also contained the following proposal: "I would suggest the taxation of all property equally, whether church or corporation, exempting only the last resting-place of the dead, and possibly, with proper restrictions, church edifices" (*ibid.*). The New York League for the Separation of Church and State, founded in 1938, carried on its letterhead a picture of Grant and a phrase from his Des Moines speech as its slogan.

116. The Catholic Church Is Awarded the Pious Fund of the Californias, November 11, 1875

LATE in the seventeenth century the Jesuit missionaries received a number of private benefactions to help finance their difficult missions in Lower California. The fund grew to large proportions and when the Jesuits were expelled by Spain in 1767 it was taken over by the government and its income assigned to the Franciscans and Dominicans who had replaced the Jesuits in the missions. In 1821 Mexico revolted from Spain, secularized the California missions in the 1830's, and petitioned the Holy See for the establishment of a bishopric in California. In April, 1840, the Diocese of California was erected and the income from the Pious Fund was assigned to it as the heir to the missions. But due to a revolution in Mexico and the war with the United States no support was forthcoming. In an effort to adjust a number of disputed claims of Americans versus Mexicans and vice versa, the two governments signed a convention in 1868 which created a commission for their adjudication. Attempts of the commissioners to reach agreement on the Pious Fund failed and the case was then given over to an umpire, Sir Edward Thornton, British Ambassador to Washington. In 1875 Thornton decided in favor of the Church's claims. Mexico paid the award but refused to pay the accumulated interest. The dispute dragged on until 1902 when the two parties agreed to submit their differences to the new Permanent Court of International Arbitration at The Hague. In the first decision of the international tribunal on October 14, 1902, the justices ruled that Mexico should pay $1,420,682.67 in interest accumulated between 1869–1902, and an annual sum of $43,050 in perpetuity to begin in 1903. The Mexican government paid the interest and made the annual payment up to and including 1913, but no further payments have been made since that time, although the Department of State has more than once called attention to the matter. Source: James Brown Scott (Ed.), *The Hague Court Reports* (New York: Oxford University Press, 1916), pp. 48–53.

This case having been referred to the umpire for his decision upon a difference in opinion between the commissioners, the umpire rendered the following decision:

In the case of "Thaddeus Amat,[1] Bishop of Monterey, and Joseph S. Alemany,[2] Archbishop of San Francisco *vs.* Mexico" No. 493, it will be impossible for the umpire to discuss the various arguments which have been put forward on each side.

He will be able only to state the conclusions which he has arrived

[1] Thaddeus Amat, C.M. (1811–1878), of Spanish birth, was named second Bishop of Monterey on July 29, 1853.

[2] Joseph S. Alemany, O.P. (1814–1888), born in Spain, was consecrated Bishop of Monterey on June 30, 1850, and promoted to be first Archbishop of San Francisco on July 29, 1853.

at after a careful and lengthened study of all the documents which have been submitted to him.

He is about to give his decision with a profound sense of the importance of the case in accordance with what he considers to be just and equitable as far as he can rely upon his own judgment and conscience.

The first question to be considered is the citizenship of the claimants.

On this point the umpire is of opinion that the Roman Catholic Church of Upper California became a corporation of citizens of the United States on the 30th of May, 1848, the day of the exchange of ratifications of the Treaty of Guadalupe Hidalgo [ending the war between the United States and Mexico].

By the VIII Article of the treaty it was agreed that those Mexicans residing in the territories ceded by Mexico to the United States, who wished to retain the title and rights of Mexican citizens should be under the obligation to make their election within one year from the date of the exchange of the ratifications of the treaty; and that those who should remain in the said territories after the expiration of that year, without having declared their intention to retain the character of Mexicans, should be considered to have elected to have become citizens of the United States. It has not been shown that the Roman Catholic Church in Upper California had declared any intention of retaining its Mexican citizenship and it can not but be concluded that it had elected to assume the citizenship of the United States as soon as it was possible for it to do so, which in the opinion of the umpire was when Upper California was actually incorporated into the United States on the exchange of the ratifications of the Treaty of Guadalupe Hidalgo.

With regard to any claim which may have originated before that date the claimants could not have been entitled to appear before the mixed commission established by the Convention of July 4, 1868; but a claim arising after that date would come under the cognizance of the commission.

The claim now put forward is for interest upon the so-called "Pious Fund of the Californias." If this interest should have been paid to the Right Reverend Francisco Garcia Diego, the Bishop of California, before the separation of Upper California from the Republic of Mexico, it seems to the umpire that a fair proportion of it ought now and since the 30th of May, 1848, to be paid to the claimants, who in his opinion are the direct successors of that Bishop, as far as Upper California is concerned.

The "Pious Fund of the Californias" was the result of donations by various private persons for the purpose of establishing, supporting and maintaining Roman Catholic missions in California, and for converting to the Roman Catholic faith the heathens of that region. The disbursements of the proceeds of these donations was entrusted by the donors to the Society of Jesus. The object of the donors was without doubt principally the advancement of the Roman Catholic religion. The donations were made by private persons for particular and expressed objects and had nothing public, political or national in their character. Once permission was granted to the Jesuit fathers Salvatierra[3] and Kühu [*sic*][4] to establish missions in California, to take charge of the conversion to Christianity of the heathens, and to solicit alms for that purpose, it does not seem that the Spanish Government assisted them with any considerable sums, if any at all, and certainly with not so much as almost any Government would have considered itself bound to furnish for the benefit of a region over which it claimed dominion.

It can be easily understood that the Spanish Government was very glad to avail itself of the religious feelings of its subjects, and saw with great satisfaction that their donations would powerfully contribute to the political conquest of the Californias; but the object of the donors was the religious conquest alone, though they too might have felt some pride in the consciousness that they were at the same time contributing to the extension of the possessions of Spain.

The alms, however, solicited in the first instance by the Jesuit fathers, and the donations subsequently made by the piously disposed persons were neither political nor national; they were directed to the religious conquest of the Californias, and were the gifts of private persons for that particular object.

On the expulsion of the Jesuits from the Spanish Dominions, and the abolition of the Order, occurrences which the donors to the Pious Fund could not have foreseen, the Spanish Government naturally became the trustee and caretaker of that fund, but it took charge of it avowedly with all the duties and obligations attached to it. The missions were confided to the Franciscan Order, and subsequently they were divided between this Order and the Dominicans, but

[3] Juan Maria Salvatierra, S.J. (1648–1717), was one of the prime leaders in the evangelization of the Indian tribes of Lower California.

[4] Eusebius Kino, S.J. (1644–1711), was one of the greatest of all the Jesuit missionaries in colonial America. The principal scene of his labors was in northern Mexico and present-day Arizona. Kino's descriptions of his numerous and widespread explorations are of high scientific value.

although the Pious Fund was administered by the Spanish Government, its proceeds were applied to the maintenance of the missions belonging to both Orders.

When Mexico became independent she succeeded to the trust which had been held by the Spanish Government, and continued to apply the proceeds of the fund to the maintenance of the missions. In 1836 it was considered desirable to establish a Bishopric which was to comprise the two Californias.

An Act of Congress was passed for this purpose, and the same act entrusted to the Bishop, who was to be appointed, the administration and application of the Pious Fund in accordance with the wishes of its founders.

On the 8th of February, 1842, President Santa Anna[5] repealed the latter part of the Act of 1836 and assigned the administration and application of the fund to the Mexican Government, but the decree which he signed for this purpose also declared that the object of the donor was to be carried out by the civilization and conversion of the savages. On the 24th of October of the same year another decree was issued by the above-mentioned President to the effect that the real estate and other property of the Pious Fund were to be incorporated into the national treasury and were to be sold at a certain price, the treasury recognizing the total proceeds of these sales at an interest of six per cent and the preamble of this decree declaring that the assumption by the Government of the care and of administration of the Pious Fund was for the express purpose of scrupulously carrying out the objects proposed by the founders.

Neither by the Spanish nor by the Mexican Government was it ever pretended that the proceeds of the fund were not finally to find their way into the hands of the ecclesiastical authorities in the Californias, or that they were to be applied to any other objects than those pointed out by the donors. Subsequently to the decree of October 24, 1842, the Mexican Government admitted its indebtedness and the obligation it was under to remit the proceeds of the fund to the Bishop of California by issuing orders in his favor on the custom house at Guaymas.

This obligation is still further acknowledged by the Act of Congress of April 3, 1845, which restored to the Bishop of the Californias and to his successors all credits and other properties belonging to the Pious Fund which were still unsold, for the objects mentioned in

[5] Antonio López de Santa Anna (1795–1876), an anti-clerical revolutionary, was several times dictator and president of Mexico.

the law of September 29, 1836, without prejudice to what Congress might decide with regard to those properties which had already been alienated.

The above-mentioned credits must surely have included the indebtedness of the Government with regard to the unpaid interest upon the property sold, the proceeds of which had been incorporated into the national treasury. The umpire does not find that any further legislation has been effected upon the subject since the Decree of April 3, 1845.

Such then was the state of the Mexican laws with regard to the Pious Fund at the time of the cession of Upper California to the United States, and the umpire is clearly of the opinion that both the acts of the Mexican Government and its decrees above mentioned as well as the Act of Congress of 1845 are so many admissions that the Mexican Government was under the obligation to remit to the Bishop of California and his successors the interest on the proceeds of the property belonging to the Pious Fund which were held in trust by the Mexican Treasury, in order that the Bishop and his successors might carry out the wishes of the founders of that fund.

The umpire has already stated that he considers that as far as Upper California is concerned, the claimants are the direct successors of the Bishop of California, whose Diocese before the Treaty of Guadalupe Hidalgo, comprised both Upper and Lower California;[6] and they ought therefore to receive a fair share of the interest upon the proceeds of the Pious Fund, in order to devote it to the purposes for which it was founded, and which are of so decidedly a religious nature, that the ecclesiastical authorities must be the most proper persons to be employed in its application.

The beneficiaries of this share of the fund are the Roman Catholic Church in Upper California, and the heathens who are to be converted to Christianity; and indirectly all the inhabitants of the State of California, and even the whole population of the United States, are interested in the proper application of the portion which should be entrusted to the claimants, upon whom, considering the purposes to which the founders assigned their donations, the employment of the fund would most suitably devolve.

With regard to the proportion of the interest which should be paid to the claimants, the umpire is of opinion that nothing can be fairer

[6] The Bishop of Monterey continued to exercise jurisdiction over both Upper and Lower California until 1852 when, at his request, Lower California was detached from his see.

than that the whole of the interest for twenty-one years should be divided into two equal parts, of which one should be paid to the claimants.[7]

It has been argued that the award should be made in proportion to the populations respectively of Upper and Lower California.

The umpire is not of that opinion; for it seems to him that as the population and civilization increase, the number of conversions to be made diminish and there can be little doubt that Lower California needs the beneficial assistance of the Pious Fund as much and even more in proportion to its population than Upper California now does. The equal division of the interest seems to be the fairest award.

After a careful examination of the data furnished with regard to the yearly amount of the interest, the umpire is constrained to adopt the views of the commissioner of the United States. A larger sum is claimed on the part of the claimants; but even with regard to this larger sum the defense has not shown, except indirectly, that its amount was exaggerated.

There is no doubt that the Mexican Government must have in its possession all the accounts and documents relative to the sale of the real property belonging to the Pious Fund and proceeds thereof; yet these have not been produced; and the only inference that can be drawn from silence upon this subject is that the amount of the proceeds actually received into the treasury was at least not less than it is claimed to be.

The annual amount of interest therefore which should fall to the share of the Roman Catholic Church of Upper California is $43,080.99 and the aggregate sum for twenty-one years will be $904,700.79.[8]

---

[7] The counsel for the bishops, John T. Doyle, taking into account the amount of work actually done in Upper California, as compared to that in the barren peninsula of Lower California, had asked for a division of the funds in a proportion of nine to one or eight to one. It was the counsel's opinion that the umpire had been influenced in his decision on this point by the precedent applied in commercial cases, i.e., that in the absence of evidence to the contrary, the interests of partners should be considered equal. Cf. "Points Submitted by Messrs. Doyle & Doyle," *Senate Document No. 28, 57th Congress, 2nd Session* (Washington, 1902), pp. 278–279. The pertinent documents in this case are printed in this publication.

[8] The figure was arrived at as follows.

Total value of the Pious Fund as accepted by the American commissioner	$1,436,033.00
Interest at 6 per cent	86,161.98
One half, to which the claimants were entitled	43,080.99
Twenty-one installments from October 24, 1848, to February 1, 1869	904,700.79

It has been urged that interest should be paid upon each annual amount from the respective date at which it became due. The umpire is not of this opinion. It is true that the Archbishop of San Francisco states in his deposition that when in the City of Mexico in 1852, he demanded payment of the amounts, of property of the Pious Fund, and that receiving no answer to his demands he reiterated the same, and only after a long time was officially informed that the Government could not accede to them.

From a man of the position and character of the Archbishop there can be no doubt of the truth of this statement; but yet there is no documentary evidence of these facts, and the umpire therefore supposes that the demand and the refusal were both verbal.[9] Upon a matter of such serious importance the umpire does not think that a verbal refusal by a Government to make a certain payment can be taken as its final determination upon the subject. The refusal may even have been qualified by the inability of the Government to provide the necessary funds at the time of the demand. Of this in the absence of any writing upon the subject, no judgment can be found. The umpire further thinks that considering the troubles and difficulties to which Mexico and her Government have been subject for several years past it would not be generous nor even fair to punish them for their failure to pay interest upon a capital of the nature of the Pious Fund, so far as to insist upon the payment of interest upon that interest. As a matter therefore both of justice and equity the umpire thinks that this second interest ought not to be demanded.

The umpire consequently awards that there be paid by the Mexican Government on account of the above-mentioned claim the sum of nine hundred and four thousand, seven hundred Mexican gold dollars and seventy-nine cents ($904,700.79) without interest.

Washington, November 11, 1875.

"Opinion of Mr. Wadsworth, in the original Pious Fund Case before the United States and Mexican Claims Commission of 1868" (Scott, *op. cit.,* p. 20). William H. Wadsworth was the American representative on the commission. On October 24, 1876, Thornton amended the above figures by reason of an error in computing the amount of bad debts. The rectification reduced the over-all sum to be paid by Mexico to $904,070.79.

[9] In the hearing before the Hague Court in 1902 the counsel for the bishops presented a letter from the Mexican Department of Justice and of Church Affairs to Bishop Alemany, dated September 29, 1852, in which the bishop's request for a portion of the Pious Fund was refused by the Mexican government. This evidence had not been presented in 1875. Cf. "Deposition of Mr. John T. Doyle," *Senate Document No. 28,* pp. 405–406.

117. Instruction of the Congregation de Propaganda Fide Concerning Catholic Children Attending American Public Schools, November 24, 1875

IN SPITE of the legislation of the First and Second Plenary Councils of Baltimore in May, 1852, and October, 1866, on the necessity of Catholic children attending Catholic schools in order to safeguard their religious faith, large numbers of Catholic children continued to go to the public schools. A number of American bishops felt this as a heavy burden on their conscience and, therefore, solicited from the Holy See a directive to the hierarchy for the purpose of correcting the situation. As a consequence the Congregation de Propaganda Fide sent an instruction on the subject which was intended to emphasize the danger to Catholic children enrolling in the public schools and to strengthen the hands of the bishops with their priests and people in their efforts to provide more Catholic schools. The instruction came, as was clear from the previous document, at a time when the entire question was being hotly debated in the United States. Sources: Latin text in *Acta et decreta concilii plenarii Baltimorensis tertii* (Baltimore, 1886), pp. 279–282; English translation, *The Pastor,* IV (June, 1886), 232–237.

The Sacred Congregation of Propaganda has been many times assured that for the Catholic children of the United States of America evils of the gravest kind are likely to result from the so-called public schools.

The sad intelligence moved the Propaganda to propose to the illustrious prelates of that country a series of questions, with the object of ascertaining, first, why the faithful permit their children to attend non-catholic schools, and secondly, what may be the best means of keeping the young away from schools of this description. The answers, as drawn up by the several prelates, were submitted, owing to the nature of the subject, to the Supreme Congregation of the Holy Office. The decision reached by their Eminences, Wednesday, June 30, 1875, they saw fit to embody in the following *Instruction,* which the Holy Father graciously confirmed on Wednesday, November 24, of the same year.

1. The first point to come under consideration was the system of education itself, quite peculiar to those schools. Now, that system seemed to the S. Congregation most dangerous and very much opposed to Catholicity. For the children in those schools, the very principles of which exclude all religious instruction, can neither learn the rudiments of the faith nor be taught the precepts of the Church; hence,

they will lack that knowledge, of all else, necessary to man without which there is no leading a Christian life. For children are sent to these schools from their earliest years, almost from their cradle; at which age, it is admitted, the seeds sown of virtue or of vice take fast root. To allow this tender age to pass without religion is surely a great evil.

2. Again, these schools being under no control of the Church, the teachers are selected from every sect indiscriminately; and this, while no proper precaution is taken to prevent them injuring the children, so that there is nothing to stop them from infusing into the young minds the seeds of error and vice. Then evil results are certainly to be dreaded from the fact that in these schools, or at least in very many of them, children of both sexes must be in the same class and class-room and must sit side by side at the same desk. Every circumstance mentioned goes to show that the children are fearfully exposed to the danger of losing their faith and that their morals are not properly safeguarded.

3. Unless this danger of perversion can be rendered remote, instead of proximate, such schools cannot in conscience be used. This is the dictate of natural as well as of divine law. It was enunciated in unmistakable terms by the Sovereign Pontiff, in a letter addressed to a former Archbishop of Freiburg, July 14, 1864. He thus writes: "There can be no hesitation; wherever the purpose is afoot or carried out of shutting out the Church from all authority over the schools, there the children will be sadly exposed to loss of their faith. Consequently the Church should, in such circumstances, not only put forth every effort and spare no pains to get for the children the necessary Christian training and education, but would be further compelled to remind the faithful and publicly declare that schools hostile to Catholicity cannot in conscience be attended." These words only express a general principle of natural and divine law and are consequently of universal application wherever that most dangerous system of training youth has been unhappily introduced.

4. It only remains, then, for the prelates to use every means in their power to keep the flocks committed to their care from all contact with the public schools. All are agreed that there is nothing so needful to this end as the establishment of Catholic schools in every place, — and schools no whit inferior to the public ones. Every effort, then, must be directed towards starting Catholic schools where they are not, and, where they are, towards enlarging them and providing them with better accommodations and equipment until they have

nothing to suffer, as regards teachers or equipment, by comparison with the public schools. And to carry out so holy and necessary a work, the aid of religious brotherhoods and of sisterhoods will be found advantageous where the bishop sees fit to introduce them. In order that the faithful may the more freely contribute the necessary expenses, the bishops themselves should not fail to impress on them, at every suitable occasion, whether by pastoral letter, sermon or private conversation, that as bishops they would be recreant to their duty if they failed to do their very utmost to provide Catholic schools.[1] This point should be especially brought to the attention of the more wealthy and influential Catholics and members of the legislature.

5. In that country there is no law to prevent Catholics having their own schools and instructing and educating their youth in every branch of knowledge. It is therefore in the power of Catholics themselves to avert, with God's help, the dangers with which Catholicity is threatened from the public school system. Not to have religion and piety banished from the school-room is a matter of the very highest interest, not only to certain individuals and families, but to the entire country, — a country now so prosperous and of which the Church has had reason to conceive such high hopes.

6. However, the S. Congregation is not unaware that circumstances may be sometimes such as to permit parents conscientiously to send their children to the public schools. Of course they cannot do so without having sufficient cause. Whether there be sufficient cause in any particular case is to be left to the conscience and judgment of the bishop. Generally speaking, such cause will exist when there is no Catholic school in the place, or the one that is there cannot be considered suitable to the condition and circumstances in life of the pupils. But even in these cases, before the children can conscientiously attend the public school, the danger, greater or less, of perversion, which is inseparable from the system, must be rendered remote by proper precaution and safeguards. The first thing to see to, then, is whether the danger of perversion, as regards the school in question, is such as cannot possibly be rendered remote; as, for instance,

[1] That the American bishops had not been unmindful of their duty in this regard was evident from the decree passed in their First Plenary Council of Baltimore in May, 1852, which read: "We exhort the bishops, and in view of the very grave evils which usually result from the defective education of youth, we beseech them through the bowels of the mercy of God, to see that schools be established in connection with all the churches of their dioceses. . . ." (*Concilium plenarium totius Americae septentrionalis foederatae Baltimori habitum anno 1852* [Baltimore, 1853], p. 47).

whether the teaching there is such, or the doings of a nature so repugnant to Catholic belief and morals, that ear cannot be given to the one, nor part taken in the other without grievous sin. It is self-evident that danger of this character must be shunned at whatever cost, even life itself.

7. Further, before a child can be conscientiously placed at a public school, provision must be made for giving it the necessary Christian training and instruction, at least out of school hours. Hence parish priests and missionaries in the United States should take seriously to heart the earnest admonitions of the Council of Baltimore,[2] and spare no labor to give children thorough catechetical instructions, dwelling particularly on those truths of faith and morals which are called most in question by Protestants and unbelievers: children beset with so many dangers they should guard with tireless vigilance, induce them to frequent the sacraments, excite in them devotion to the Blessed Virgin and on all occasions animate them to hold firmly by their religion. The parents or guardians must look carefully after those children. They must examine them in their lessons, or if not able themselves, get others to do it. They must see what books they use and, if the books contain passages likely to injure the child's mind, explain the matter. They must keep them from freedom and familiarity with those of the other school children whose company might be dangerous to their faith or morals, and absolutely away from the corrupt.

8. Parents who neglect to give this necessary Christian training and instruction to their children, or who permit them to go to schools in which the ruin of their souls is inevitable, or finally, who send them to the public school without sufficient cause and without taking the necessary precautions to render the danger of perversion remote, and do so while there is a good and well-equipped Catholic school in the place, or the parents have the means to send them elsewhere to be educated, — that such parents, if obstinate, cannot be absolved, is evident from the moral teaching of the Church.

---

[2] The Second Plenary Council of Baltimore in October, 1866, went beyond the legislation of 1852 and devoted an entire chapter to the subject, "De scholis parochialibus ubique fundandis," *Concilii plenarii Baltimorensis II. . . . Acta et decreta* (Baltimore, 1868), pp. 218–225.

118. Building a Missionary School on the Colorado Frontier, June, 1876

THE thriving spiritual state of American Catholicism owes an incalculable debt to the religious congregations of women. From the time that Mother Seton founded her Sisters of Charity in 1808 thousands of self-sacrificing American women have devoted their lives to the religious education of youth and to every variety of works of charity, a force that now numbers 159,545 religious women in the United States. For the most part their striking contributions have gone unrecorded, but occasionally there comes to light the story of one or another of these heroic women, and of none can it be said that her career was more fruitful and dramatic than Sister Blandina Segale (1850–1941), whose family immigrated to Cincinnati from a small town near Genoa when she was four years old. Entering the Sisters of Charity of Cincinnati in 1866, she was sent — alone — to the rough cowboy town of Trinidad in Colorado Territory, where she arrived in December, 1872, after a series of incidents that would have tested the courage of a stouthearted man. She spent the next twenty-one years in the Southwest until recalled to Cincinnati, where in 1897 she and her sister, Sister Justina, set up the first aid center for Italian immigrants. For the following thirty-five years she labored relentlessly at the Santa Maria Institute in the city's slums and personally gave religious instruction to 80 per cent of the Italian population. The experiences of this diminutive religious during the 1870's in the wild Southwest included an encounter with the country's most famous desperado, Billy the Kid [Bonney] (1859–1881), whom she succeeded in bringing around to an offer of friendly assistance if ever she should need it, and the rescue of a prisoner from lynching by a mob. During her days in Colorado and New Mexico, Sister Blandina kept a journal in the form of reminiscences addressed to her sister back in Cincinnati. The following excerpt, concerning how she got a new school built, reveals the resourcefulness, energy, and personal magnetism of this amazing woman; it also affords insights into the crude frontier life of Colorado in the year it entered the union. Source: Sister Blandina Segale, *At the End of the Santa Fe Trail* (Milwaukee: The Bruce Publishing Co., 1948), pp. 62–65.

June, 1876.

Dear Sister Justina:

To-day I asked Sister Eulalia[1] if, in her opinion, we did not need a new school building, which would contain a hall and stage for all school purposes.[2] She said: "Just what we need, Sister. Do you want

[1] Sister Eulalia Whitty (d. 1917) had been among the three pioneer Sisters of Charity of Cincinnati who had come to Trinidad in February, 1870. After several years in Santa Fe she had returned to Trinidad and was at this time assistant teacher to Sister Blandina in the school.

[2] Land for the original school had been given by one of the founders of Trinidad, Don Felipe Baca, at the request of Bishop Machebeuf, and it had been opened on March 4, 1870.

to build it?" I answered, "Yes, I do." She added, "We have not enough cash to pay interest on our indebtedness. Have you a plan by which you can build without money? If so, I say build."

"Here is my plan, Sister. Borrow a crowbar, get on the roof of the schoolhouse and begin to detach the adobes. The first good Mexican who sees me will ask, "What are you doing, Sister?" I will answer, "Tumbling down this structure to rebuild it before the opening of the fall term of school."

You should have seen Sister Eulalia laugh! It did me good. After three days' pondering how to get rid of low ceilings, poor ventilation, acrobats from log-rafters introducing themselves without notice, and now here is an opportunity to carry out a test on the good in human nature, so I took it. I borrowed a crowbar and went on the roof, detached some adobes and began throwing them down. The school building is only one story high.

The first person who came towards the schoolhouse was Doña Juanita Simpson, wife of the noted hero of Simpson's Rest. When she saw me at work, she exclaimed, *"Por amor de Dios, Hermana, qué está Vd. haciendo?"* (For the love of God, Sister, what are you doing?)

I answered, "We need a schoolhouse that will a little resemble those we have in the United States, so I am demolishing this one in order to rebuild."

"How many men do you need, Sister?"

"We need not only men, but also straw, moulds, hods, shovels — everything it takes to build a house with a shingle roof. Our assets are good-will and energy."

Earnestly Mrs. Simpson said: "I go to get what you need."

The crowbar was kept at its work. In less than an hour, Mrs. Simpson returned with six men. One carried a mould, another straw, etc. The mould carrier informed me at once that women only know how to *encalar* (whitewash), the men had the trades and they would continue what I began. In a few days the old building was thrown down, the adobes made and sun-burnt. In two weeks all the rubbish was hauled away. The trouble began when we were ready for the foundation. Keep in mind it was only by condescension I was permitted to look on. At this juncture I remarked to the moulder:

"Of course, we will have a stone foundation."

"Oh, no!" he answered, "we use adobes laid in mud."

"Do you think if we laid a foundation with stone laid in mortar, the combination would resist the rainy season better than adobes laid in mud?"

"No, no, Sister we never use stone for any of our houses," he replied.

I was at the mercy of the good natives and my best move was to let them have their way. Moreover, I recalled the fact that in the Far East there are mud structures centuries old in a good state of preservation. No mistake would be made by not changing their mode of building in that one point. We got the necessary lumber, sashes and shingles from Chené's mill, sixty miles from Trinidad. Wagons hauled the material. As the Chené family has a daughter at our boarding school, there will be no difficulty in meeting our bill. Mr. Hermann's daughter is a resident student, and Mr. Hermann is a carpenter and will pay his bill by work.

When the schoolhouse was ready for roofing, a number of the town carpenters offered to help. The merchants gave nails, paints, brushes, lime, hair, etc.

But now came the big obstacle. There is but one man who calls himself a plasterer, and his method is to plaster with mud. It is impossible to get a smooth surface with mud. I remarked to the plasterer: "You will use lime, sand and hair to plaster the schoolrooms."

His look plainly said: "What do women know of men's work?" Yet he condescended to explain: "I am the plasterer of this part of the country; if I should use any material but mud, my reputation would be lost."

I said to him, "But if lime, sand and hair made a better job, your reputation would gain."

He made answer, "Sister, I'll make a bargain with you. I will do as you suggest, but I will tell my people I carried out your American idea of plastering."

We both agreed to this. Meanwhile, the other men had shouldered their implements and were on their way home. The plasterer had to mix the sand, lime and hair following my directions. All that was done satisfactorily to me, at least. But there was not a man to carry the mortar to the plasterer, so I got the bucket and supplied a man's place. The comedy follows:

Rev. Charles Pinto, S.J.,[3] pastor, took pleasure in telling his co-religionists that the study of human nature, combined with good will and tactfulness, were building a schoolhouse.

---

[3] Charles Pinto, S.J., had become pastor of Holy Trinity Church, Trinidad, in 1875.

On this day of my hod-carrying, the Rt. Rev. Bishop Machebeuf[4] of Denver, Colorado, arrived on his visitation. The first place to which he was taken was the schoolhouse being built without money. Bishop and Pastor had just turned the kitchen corner when the three of us came face to face. Both gentlemen stood amazed. I rested my hod-bucket. Father Pinto looked puzzled. The Bishop remarked: "I see how you manage to build without money." I laughed and explained the situation.

They took the bucket, and the three of us went to where the plasterer was working. After the welcome to the Bishop, the plasterer said:

"Your Reverence, look at me, the only Mexican plasterer, and I am putting aside my knowledge to follow American ways of doing my trade; but I told Sister the failure will not be pointed at me." The Rt. Rev. Bishop analyzed the material at a glance, then said: "Juan, if this method of plastering is better than yours, come again to help Sister when she needs you. If it fails, report to me and between us we shall give her the biggest penance she ever received."

The schoolroom walls turned out smooth, the plaster adhesive, and the plasterer will now make a lucrative living at his American method of plastering. . . .[5]

119. Patrick C. Keely Receives the Laetare Medal, March 30, 1884

THE most prominent American Catholic architect of the nineteenth century was Patrick Charles Keely (c. 1816–1896). Born in Ireland, Keely emigrated in 1841 and settled in Brooklyn where his first church, that of SS. Peter and Paul, was dedicated in May, 1848. Previous to Keely's time the only Catholic Church building in this country that had followed the Gothic design was the chapel of St. Mary's Seminary, Baltimore, dedicated in June, 1808, of which Maximilien Godefroy (d. 1824) had been the archi-

[4] Joseph P. Machebeuf (1812–1889), a French-born priest, had spent nearly thirty years as a missionary in the Diocese of Cincinnati and Santa Fe when he was consecrated in August, 1868, as first Vicar Apostolic of Colorado and Utah; he was named first Bishop of Denver on August 16, 1887.

[5] That September Sister Blandina wrote in her journal: "The pupils and myself will have to be introduced daily to our schoolroom. It will take some time to wear off the novelty of entering a well-lighted, well-ventilated room, flowers in blossom on window sills, blackboard built into the walls, modern desks, and a stage for Friday exercises. I think one of my ambitions has been reached, viz.: to walk into my schoolroom and feel that it is 'up-to-date' and I, 'Mistress of all I survey,' particularly of the minds to be taught" (*ibid.*, p. 67).

tect. Keely may have been influenced by the Gothic revival in England, of which the convert architect, Augustus Welby Pugin (1812–1852), who had entered the Church in 1834, was a leader. In any case, most of the astonishing number of Catholic churches designed by Keely followed that pattern, and in this he was but a part of a current trend, for the Gothic and the contemporary Renaissance work in France were said to be "the two principal and almost exclusive influences at work in America in this period of a full generation from 1850 to 1880. . . ." (Thomas E. Tallmadge, *The Story of Architecture in America* [New York, 1936], p. 144). By the time he received the Laetare Medal in 1884 Keely had served as architect for a very large number of church edifices, among them the Cathedral of the Holy Cross, Boston, 1867–1875, and the Cathedral of the Holy Name, Chicago, 1874–1875. Source: *Catholic Review* (New York), April 5, 1884.

The *Laetare* Medal[1] of the University of Notre Dame was conferred last Sunday on the great Catholic architect, Mr. Patrick Charles Keely, of Brooklyn. No more honorable selection could have been made, nor one that would more certainly reflect back on the University conferring it an honor fully corresponding to that which it gave. All public testimonies of honor, such as this, ought to have a mutual and reciprocal effect. In this case it undoubtedly had. In material value and external ornament the *Laetare* Medal and its accompanying address, designed and wrought by skilful hands, are things of beauty, and coming from such a respectable, progressive and far-seeing Institution as Notre Dame are well worthy of acceptance by even so eminent a master as Mr. Keely. On the other hand, when the University of Notre Dame determined to mark out for its homage and distinction a man eminent in his science and a great master in his truly Christian art, it selected one, the glory of whose achievements and the lustre of whose life must reflect honorably on it and this great prize that it has established. The personal modesty of Mr. Keely's life will not permit us to say a single word in praise of himself, but everyone can infer what might be said when it is remembered to what Mr. Keely has devoted himself and his wonderful gifts. "The undevout astronomer is mad." Certainly it would be equally impossible for a Christian architect, who designs temples for the Eucharistic Sacrifice, to lack that enthusiasm for his faith which comes from the hourly expression in permanent forms of the most precious thoughts

[1] The *Laetare* Medal was instituted in 1883 when it was conferred for the first time on the noted lay historian of the American Church, John Gilmary Shea (1824–1892). Keely, the second recipient, received the medal in a ceremony on March 30, 1884.

of religion. That condition of the *Laetare* Medal may therefore be passed as entirely filled in this case. Of Mr. Keely's genius we need speak just as briefly. Already he has built *seven hundred churches*[2] in honor of the Christian name, not to speak of the numberless institutions that accompanied them. The number is wholly unprecedented in the history of any architect of ancient or modern times. It could have been reached only in the phenomenal period of Catholic history that the Church in America has known during the present half century. Mr. Keely was a Providential man, raised up to meet, in his particular line, this marvellous emergency. Nor must it be supposed that these are petty little structures, suitable for mission chapels in rural districts. Few of them are of that character. Numbers of them are works of the first class. Scores of them are cathedrals that in cost, size and structure recall the amazement of those who saw the Cathedral of Seville and believed its designers and builders mad to attempt such a gigantic task. Even a few of them would stamp Mr. Keely as a man of genius and make his reputation anywhere. His first great work was to carve out, with his own hands, the beautiful canopies of the altars in the old Cathedral of Brooklyn,[3] and the crown of all his works, though we trust not his last, will be the new Cathedral of Brooklyn.[4] That in size alone will be greater than any church yet planned on the American continent. Those who have been favored with a glimpse of the well nigh completed plans, are of opinion that its great size will be the very least of its claims to notice. Mr. Keely in his modesty never permits without protest its comparison with any other work. We will therefore simply say that it will be a most beautiful as well as a massive and impressive structure, leaving to the future to contrast it with anything that the piety of a succeeding generation may achieve. Among his other works, of which every newspaper reader must have heard, are the Jesuit churches in Montreal, Boston and New York, the cathedrals of Buffalo, Boston, Providence, Hartford, Chicago and Newark. That which he is building for Bishop

[2] The number of churches designed and built by Keely has been variously estimated from 500 to 700.

[3] St. James Church at Jay and Chapel Streets was dedicated in August, 1823. Keely was the architect for its enlargement which tripled the size and the newly refurnished building was blessed by Bishop John Hughes of New York in September, 1846. When the Diocese of Brooklyn was erected on July 29, 1853, it became St. James Pro-Cathedral.

[4] The cornerstone of the projected new Cathedral of the Immaculate Conception, Brooklyn, was laid in June, 1868, but only St. John's Chapel — from which Keely himself was buried in 1896 — was ever completed. In 1913 the chapel was closed and in 1931 the partly constructed walls of the new cathedral were razed.

Hendricken,[5] though not the largest, will be in every way one of the most complete and beautiful in the country. These facts may show that Notre Dame in selecting Mr. Keely as the medallist of this year, has chosen a man of great eminence, whose life and work will be a suggestion to the young men who are growing up in the fine atmosphere of Catholic public spirit that this Western University is creating within its sphere. . . .

120. Bishop Spalding on the Intellectual Weakness Among American Catholics, November 16, 1884

WITH the maturity of the Church in the twentieth century it has become increasingly evident that the principal weakness of American Catholicism lies in its lack of national influence and intellectual leadership. One of the keenest foreign observers of the Church in the United States has said, not without reason, that "in no modern Western society is the intellectual prestige of Catholicism lower than in the country where, in such respects as wealth, numbers, and strength of organization, it is so powerful" (D. W. Brogan, *U.S.A. An Outline of the Country, Its People and Institutions* [London, 1941], p. 65). No American Catholic spotted this weakness earlier, nor emphasized it more forcefully, than John Lancaster Spalding (1840–1916), first Bishop of Peoria. Spalding was easily the most intellectual American Catholic bishop of his lifetime, a man who had capitalized to the fullest extent on his training at the Catholic University of Louvain and his additional study at several German universities and in Rome. Over sixty years ago — when he was only forty-four — he made a powerful plea to the hierarchy for an American Catholic university that would be worthy of the name in a sermon preached during the Third Plenary Council of Baltimore. In that sermon Spalding showed his awareness of the need for quality rather than quantity in higher education, while at the same time the optimism of the Gilded Age in which he lived and the deep love he had for the United States. It was this sermon which, in a sense, launched the Catholic University of America. The bishop's contribution to American life was well summarized in the citation for the honorary degree of doctor of letters conferred on him by Columbia University on June 11, 1902, which read: "Descendant of a house honored among two peoples; Christian priest and prelate, man of letters, orator, educator and patriotic citizen." Spalding's analysis of 1884 still has pertinence for those who believe that the intellectual life has in no way won the esteem and support among the more than thirty million American Catholics that might have been hoped. Source: John Lancaster

[5] Thomas F. Hendricken (1827–1886) was consecrated as first Bishop of Providence on April 28, 1872. The cornerstone of the Cathedral of SS. Peter and Paul, Providence, was laid in November, 1878, and the building completed in 1889.

Spalding, *Means and Ends of Education* (Chicago: A. C. McClurg and Co., 1897), pp. 219–223.

. . . And now, when at length a fairer day has dawned for us in this new world, what can be more natural than our eager desire to move out from the valleys of darkness towards the hills and mountain tops that are bathed in sunlight? What more praiseworthy than the fixed resolve to prove that not our faith, but our misfortunes made and kept us inferior. And, since we live in the midst of millions who have indeed good will towards us, but who still bear the yoke of inherited prejudices, and who, because for three hundred years real cultivation of mind was denied to Catholics who spoke English, conclude that Protestantism is the source of enlightenment, and the Church the mother of ignorance, do not all generous impulses urge us to make this reproach henceforth meaningless? And in what way shall we best accomplish this task? Surely not by writing or speaking about what the influence of the Church is, or by pointing to what she has done in other ages, but by becoming what we claim her spirit tends to make us. Here, if anywhere, the proverb is applicable — *verba movent, exempla trahunt.* As the devotion of American Catholics to this country and its free institutions, as shown not on battlefields alone, but in our whole bearing and conduct, convinces all but the unreasonable of the depth and sincerity of our patriotism, so when our zeal for intellectual excellence shall have raised up men who will take place among the first writers and thinkers of their day their very presence will become the most persuasive of arguments to teach the world that no best gift is at war with the spirit of Catholic faith, and that, while the humblest mind may feel its force, the lofty genius of Augustine, of Dante, and of Bossuet is upborne and strengthened by the splendor of its truth. But if we are to be intellectually the equals of others, we must have with them equal advantages of education; and so long as we look rather to the multiplying of schools and seminaries than to the creation of a real university, our progress will be slow and uncertain, because a university is the great ordinary means to the best cultivation of mind. The fact that the growth of the Church here, like that of the country itself, is chiefly external, a growth in wealth and in numbers, makes it the more necessary that we bring the most strenuous efforts to improve the gifts of the soul. The whole tendency of our social life insures the increase of churches, convents, schools, hospitals, and asylums; our advance in population and in wealth will be counted from decade to decade by millions, and our worship will approach more and more to the pomp and splendor of the full ritual; but this very growth makes such demands upon our energies, that we are in danger of forgetting higher things, or at least of thinking them less urgent. Few men are at once thoughtful and active. The man of deeds dwells in the world around him; the thinker lives within his mind. . . .

But the Church needs both the men who act and the men who think; and since with us everything pushes to action, wisdom demands that we cultivate rather the powers of reflection. And this is the duty alike of true patriots and of faithful Catholics. All are working to develop our boundless material resources; let a few at least labor to develop man. The millions are building cities, reclaiming wildernesses, and bring forth from the earth its buried treasures; let at least a remnant cherish the ideal, cultivate the beautiful, and seek to inspire the love of moral and intellectual excellence. And since we believe that the Church which points to heaven is able also to lead the nations in the way of civilization and of progress, why should we not desire to see her become a beneficent and ennobling influence in the public life of our country? She can have no higher temporal mission than to be the friend of this great republic, which is God's best earthly gift to His children. . . . If we keep ourselves strong and pure, all the peoples of the earth shall yet be free; if we fulfil our providential mission, national hatred shall give place to the spirit of generous rivalry, the people shall become wiser and stronger, society shall grow more merciful and just, and the cry of distress shall be felt, like the throb of a brother's heart, to the ends of the world. Where is the man who does not feel a kind of religious gratitude as he looks upon the rise and progress of this nation? Above all, where is the Catholic whose heart is not enlarged by such contemplation? Here, almost for the first time in her history, the Church is really free. Her worldly position does not overshadow her spiritual office, and the State recognizes her autonomy. The monuments of her past glory, wrenched from her control, stand not here to point, like mocking fingers, to what she has lost. She renews her youth, and lifts her brow, as one who, not unmindful of the solemn mighty past, yet looks with undimmed eye and unfaltering heart to a still more glorious future. Who in such a presence, can abate hope, or give heed to despondent counsel, or send regretful thoughts to other days and lands? Whoever at any time, in any place, might have been sage, saint, or hero, may be so here and now; and though he had the heart of Francis, and the mind of Augustine, and the courage of Hildebrand, here is work for him to do. . . .

121. The Pastoral Letter of the Third Plenary Council of Baltimore on Forbidden Societies, December 7, 1884

FROM the first papal condemnation of Free Masonry by Clement XII in 1738 to the present time the problem of Catholic membership in societies forbidden by the Church has been a real one. As early as the Fourth Provincial Council of Baltimore in May, 1840, the American bishops expressed concern on this score and there were repeated warnings to the faithful thereafter. Many of the earlier societies had been of foreign birth, but in the last decades of the nineteenth century Americans "turned with furious zeal to the creation of secret societies cut to their own pattern" (Arthur Meier Schlesinger, *The Rise of the City, 1878–1898* [New York, 1933], p. 288). It was with this increased danger to the faith of Catholic men in mind that the bishops of the Third Plenary Council of Baltimore included in their pastoral letter — the most detailed to date — a lengthy section on the forbidden societies. Source: Peter Guilday (Ed.), *The National Pastorals of the American Hierarchy, 1792–1919* (Washington: National Catholic Welfare Conference, 1923), pp. 256–260.

One of the most striking characteristics of our times is the universal tendency to band together in societies for the promotion of all sorts of purposes.[1] This tendency is the natural outgrowth of an age of popular rights and representative institutions. It is also in accordance with the spirit of the Church, whose aim, as indicated by her name Catholic, is to unite all mankind in brotherhood. It is consonant also with the spirit of Christ, who came to break down all walls of division, and to gather all in the one family of the one heavenly Father.

But there are few good things which have not their counterfeits, and few tendencies which have not their dangers. It is obvious to any reflecting mind that men form bad and rash as well as good and wise designs; and that they may band together for carrying out evil or dangerous as well as laudable and useful purposes. And this does not necessarily imply deliberate malice, because, while it is unquestionably

[1] That the bishops were not exaggerating the phenomenon may be seen from the fact that between 1880–1900 at least 490 new societies were organized in the United States, and by 1900 there were over six million names on the rolls of these societies. Arthur M. Schlesinger has stated, "So thoroughly did the 'habit of forming associations' — James Bryce's phrase — interpenetrate American life that it becomes possible to understand practically all the important economic and social developments merely by examining the activities of voluntary organizations" ("Biography of a Nation of Joiners," *American Historical Review*, L [October, 1944], 16).

true that there are powers at work in the world which deliberately antagonize the cause of Christian truth and virtue, still the evil or the danger of purposes and associations need not always spring from so bad a root. Honest but weak and erring human nature is apt to be so taken up with one side of a question as to do injustice to the other; to be so enamored of favorite principles as to carry them to unjustifiable extremes; to be so intent upon securing some laudable end as to ignore the rules of prudence, and bring about ruin instead of restoration. But no intention, no matter how honest, can make lawful what is unlawful. For it is a fundamental rule of Christian morals that "evil must not be done that good may come of it," and "the end can never justify the means," if the means are evil. Hence it is the evident duty of every reasonable man, before allowing himself to be drawn into any society, to make sure that both its ends and its means are consistent with truth, justice, and conscience.

In making such a decision, every Catholic ought to be convinced that his surest guide is the Church of Christ. She has in her custody the sacred deposit of Christian truth and morals; she has the experience of all ages and all nations; she has at heart the true welfare of mankind; she has the perpetual guidance of the Holy Ghost in her authoritative decisions. In her teaching and her warnings therefore, we are sure to hear the voice of wisdom, prudence, justice and charity. From the hill-top of her Divine mission and her world-wide experience, she sees events and their consequences far more clearly than they who are down in the tangled plain of daily life. She has seen associations that were once praiseworthy, become pernicious by change of circumstances. She has seen others, which won the admiration of the world by their early achievements, corrupted by power or passion or evil guidance, and she has been forced to condemn them. She has beheld associations which had their origin in the spirit of the Ages of Faith, transformed by lapse of time, and loss of faith, and the manipulation of designing leaders, into the open or hidden enemies of religion and human weal. Thus our Holy Father Leo XIII has lately shown that the Masonic and kindred societies, — although the offspring of the ancient Guilds, which aimed at sanctifying trades and tradesmen with the blessings of religion; and although retaining, perhaps, in their "ritual," much that tells of the religiousness of their origin; and although in some countries still professing entire friendliness toward the Christian religion, — have nevertheless already gone so far, in many countries, as to array themselves in avowed hostility against Christianity, and against the Catholic Church as its embodiment; that they virtually aim at substituting a world-wide fraternity of their own, for the universal brotherhood of Jesus Christ, and at disseminating mere Naturalism for the supernatural revealed religion bestowed upon mankind by the Saviour of the world. He has shown, too, that, even in countries where they are as yet far from acknowledging such purposes, they nevertheless have in them the germs, which under favorable circumstances, would inevitably blossom forth in similar results.[2] The Church, consequently, forbids her children to have any connection with such societies, because they are either an open evil to be shunned or a hidden danger to be avoided. She would fail in her duty if she did not speak the word of warning, and her children would equally fail in theirs, if they did not heed it.

Whenever, therefore, the Church has spoken authoritatively with regard to any society, her decision ought to be final for every Catholic. He ought to know that the Church has not acted hastily or unwisely, or mistakenly; he should be convinced that any worldly advantages which he might derive from his membership of such society, would be a poor substitute for the membership, the sacraments, and the blessings of the Church of Christ; he should have the courage of his religious convictions, and stand firm to faith and conscience. But if he be inclined or asked to join a society on which the Church has passed no sentence, then let him, as a reasonable and Christian man, examine into it carefully, and not join the society until he is satisfied as to its lawful character.

There is one characteristic which is always a strong presumption against a society, and that is secrecy. Our Divine Lord Himself has laid down the rule: "Every one that doth evil, hateth the light and cometh not to the light, that his works may not be reproved. But he that doth truth cometh to the light that his works may be made manifest, because they are done in God."[3] When, therefore associations veil themselves in secrecy and darkness, the presumption is against them, and it rests with them to prove that there is nothing evil in them.

But if any society's obligation be such as to bind its members to secrecy, even when rightly questioned by competent authority, then such a society puts itself outside the limits of approval; and no one can be a member of it and at the same time be admitted to the

[2] Cf. Leo XIII's encyclical *Humanum genus,* April 20, 1884, in John J. Wynne, S.J. (ed.), *The Great Encyclical Letters of Pope Leo XIII* (New York, 1903), pp. 83–106.

[3] Jn. 3:20–21.

sacraments of the Catholic Church. The same is true of any organization that binds its members to a promise of blind obedience — to accept in advance and to obey whatsoever orders, lawful or unlawful, that may emanate from its chief authorities; because such a promise is contrary both to reason and conscience. And if a society works or plots, either openly or in secret, against the Church, or against lawful authorities, then to be a member of it is to be excluded from the membership of the Catholic Church.

These authoritative rules, therefore, ought to be the guide of all Catholics in their relations with societies. No Catholic can conscientiously join, or continue in, a body in which he knows that any of these condemned features exist. If he has joined it in good faith and the objectionable features become known to him afterwards, or if any of these evil elements creep into a society which was originally good, it becomes his duty to leave it at once. And even if he were to suffer loss or run the risk by leaving such a society or refusing to join it, he should do his duty and brave the consequences regardless of human consideration.

To these laws of the Church, the justice of which must be manifest to all impartial minds, we deem it necessary to add the following admonition of the Second Plenary Council: "Care must be taken lest workingman's societies, under the pretext of mutual assistance and protection, should commit any of the evils of condemned societies; and lest the members should be induced by the artifices of designing men to break the laws of justice, by withholding labor to which they are rightfully bound, or by otherwise unlawfully violating the rights of their employers."[4]

But while the Church is thus careful to guard her children against whatever is contrary to Christian duty, she is no less careful that no injustice should be done to any association, however unintentionally. While therefore the Church, before prohibiting any society, will take every precaution to ascertain its true nature, we positively forbid any pastor, or other ecclesiastic, to pass sentence on any association or to impose ecclesiastical penalties or disabilities on its members without the previous explicit authorization of the rightful authorities. . . .[5]

[4] *Concilii plenarii Baltimorensis II. . . . Acta et decreta* (Baltimore, 1868), p. 263.

[5] The plenary council of 1884 constituted the archbishops of the United States as a commission to investigate and pass judgment on all suspect societies. For a treatment of how the commission operated, the condemnation of three American societies by the Holy Office in August, 1894, and the final solution given to the problem cf. Fergus Macdonald, *The Catholic Church and the Secret Societies in the United States* (New York, 1946), p. 100 ff.

122. John Gilmary Shea Discusses His Problems and Methods in Writing the *History of the Catholic Church in the United States,* March, 1885–September 26, 1890

IT MAY truthfully be said that were it not for John Gilmary Shea (1824–1892) the history of the Catholic Church in the United States could never have been written. The bibliography of this devoted scholar, who never had any formal professional training, numbered nearly 250 titles, including translations and editions of important source materials, studies in American Indian linguistics, general works in American and American Catholic history, biographies, devotional treatises, and miscellaneous writings (cf. Edward Spillane, S.J., "Bibliography of John Gilmary Shea," *Historical Records and Studies,* VI, Part II [December, 1912], 249–274). His principal successor in the field of American Catholic history, Peter Guilday (1884–1947), was not exaggerating, therefore, when he stated, "The prodigious activity of Dr. Shea is unique in American historiography" (Guilday, *op. cit.,* p. 155). Moreover, Shea's work was of a high scientific character, and it earned the admiration of contemporary professionals like Jared Sparks, Justin Winsor, and Edmund B. O'Callaghan with whom he maintained friendly contacts. His *magnum opus,* however, was the four-volume *History of the Catholic Church in the United States* (New York, 1886–1892), the final volume of which was published a few months after Shea's death by his wife. In the writing of that major work Shea often experienced a heart-breaking lack of interest and support from American Catholics generally as the following letters reveal, a fact which may be taken as an indication of the absence of interest in intellectual matters among his coreligionists at the time. In fact, it was only in the last two years of his life that the historian was finally relieved of financial anxiety for the support of himself and his family. In December, 1944, the American Catholic Historical Association instituted at its silver jubilee meeting in Chicago the annual John Gilmary Shea Prize of $200 for the best work in the history of the Church in order to help perpetuate Shea's memory. Source: Peter Guilday, "John Gilmary Shea," *Historical Records and Studies,* XVII (July, 1926), 99–100, 103–107, 109, 117–120, 124–127.

An appeal to prospective subscribers, March, 1885.

Most of the leisure hours of my life and much of my means have been devoted to studies, as well as to the acquisition of every book, periodical, paper, and document, whose existence I could trace, bearing on the early and actual history of the Church in this country, the efforts of the pioneer Catholics and their clergy, the Indian missions, the organization of the Church under English, French, and Spanish rule, the religious life and discipline that grew up, the vicissitudes of the Church and its ultimate steady development to its present condition.

It has been the purpose of my life to write this history, hoping that the evening of my days would give me the means and leisure to accomplish the task. Little fitted by studious habits for active business life, I have maintained myself by literary labor comfortably, but no more; and year by year my leisure has been required by work needed for my support, so that a competence on which to retire is now out of the question.

This disappointment I accept without repining and without a murmur.

Recently some of the Most Rev. Archbishops and Right Rev. Bishops, with several of the Clergy, have, unexpectedly to me, taken the matter into consideration,[1] regarding it as important for the Church in this country that the knowledge of the subject acquired by so many years of study should be published and made accessible; they have debated on the best means of securing me the necessary leisure, and of completing my collections, where printed or manuscript matter becomes accessible.

To Archbishop Gibbons, May 1, 1885.[2]

The encouragement and aid which you have so generously accorded to my projected History of the Church in response to the action of the Committee places me under new and increased obligations. The sense of my inability to meet as I should desire the confidence placed in me, and the estimate formed of my ability, absolutely discourages me. I feel that I must produce a work that will justify my Patrons in the course they have adopted. To Your Grace in an especial manner, I consider my obligation extreme, as your name comes with all the historic weight of our most ancient See. Never have I seen so clearly that I must pray and work — *ora et labora* — to attain the desired end.

To Archbishop Corrigan, May 1, 1885.[3]

I called to thank you in person for the interest Your Grace has taken in the project to enable me to devote myself to writing the

[1] Early in 1885 a committee was formed in New York to assist Shea financially in the writing of his history. The subject had been discussed informally by some of the bishops during the Third Plenary Council of Baltimore in November–December, 1884, and as a result the committee had the backing of about twenty bishops and around fifty priests and laymen who were interested in the project.

[2] From the time he became Archbishop of Baltimore in October, 1877, Gibbons gave strong moral and monetary support to Shea.

[3] Michael Augustine Corrigan (1839–1902) was Bishop of Newark, 1873–1880, Coadjutor Archbishop of New York, 1880–1885, and Archbishop of New York from 1885 to his death. Corrigan acted as chairman of the committee organized in 1885 to assist Shea.

History of the Church. But for Your Grace's direction and influence little I am certain would have been effected but with it all difficulties seemed to vanish.

The confidence felt in me and the result that you and the kind patrons, who led by Your Grace's influence, have co-operated, may justly expect at my hands, have completely discouraged me now that I am brought face to face with the task. The last week has been one of the most miserable of my life so easily am I depressed. I have set to work studying up the whole field to learn first what the great deficiences of material are and where to look for the information to supply them. Sabin's *Dictionary of Books relating to America*[4] with nearly 100,000 titles and the Catalogues of all great libraries will be thoroughly examined that nothing in print may escape me. Collections of documents in public and private depositories are less easily reached but many will be accessible. For those in the archives of dioceses which formerly had jurisdiction over parts of this country I need a letter to the present Archbishop or Bishop. Enclosed is a facsimile of a hand that you recognize, my warm and kind friend Archbishop Bayley.[5] That letter opened to me many avenues of research. If a similar letter of introduction in the name of His Eminence[6] signed by Your Grace, also by the Most Rev. Archbishop of Baltimore, can be drawn up in which it would appear that I am now at work under the direct sanction of such members of our Hierarchy, I would reproduce it and feel assured that every facility will be afforded me.

To Archbishop Corrigan, September 21, 1885.

How can I thank you for your kindness in again addressing the Secretary of the Propaganda.[7] Mr. Maziere Brady[8] had access to documents giving some light on our Maryland Missions and I hope to obtain from him more information than he printed. The connection of events seemed so probable that I could not refrain from asking to see

[4] Joseph Sabin, *et al.* (eds.), *Bibliotheca Americana. A Dictionary of Books relating to America, from its Discovery to the Present Time* (New York, 1868 ff.). This work reached twenty-nine volumes by 1936.

[5] James Roosevelt Bayley (1814–1877) was first Bishop of Newark, 1853–1872, and eighth Archbishop of Baltimore, from 1872 to his death.

[6] John McCloskey (1810–1885) was Bishop of Albany, 1847–1864, and second Archbishop of New York, 1864–1885. He was made a cardinal in 1875.

[7] Archbishop Domenico Jacobini was Secretary of the Congregation of Propaganda de Fide, 1882–1891.

[8] W. Maziere Brady (1825–1894) was an Irish-born Protestant minister who wrote many volumes on the history of the Church. He was converted to Catholicism in 1873 at Rome while working in the Vatican Archives.

whether the papers examined by Mr. Brady did not contain more. From England, though I fail to obtain any details as to the Franciscans, information comes very unexpected to me in regard to projects of Catholic colonization before Lord Baltimore and there is every reason to believe that the famous voyage of Sir Humphrey Gilbert[9] in Queen Elizabeth's reign is connected with a Catholic project, and that a plan formed at a later day was defeated by the famous Jesuit Father Persons,[10] although supported by the brave Lord Arundel [*sic*] of Wardour.[11] That the early Franciscan Mission in Maryland is not altogether imaginary is proved by two facts recently elicited, one, that in 1712, and some years before, Lord Baltimore allowed them 1000 lbs. of tobacco a year, and the other that a library in Maryland has two books bearing the name. It must not be supposed that Father Haddoc [*sic*][12] was such a smoker that he required an allowance of three pounds a day; in justice to the old missionary I will add that all values in Maryland were then estimated in tobacco. The Minister of the established Church received from every person Catholic as well as Protestants 40 lbs. of tobacco every year. There are complaints extant from these worthy gentlemen that, as the law did not fix the quality to be delivered, most that came to their hands was very bad. I do not suppose that a Catholic so taxed would pick out the best of his stock of tobacco to pay so unjust a tax.

To Archbishop Leray, December 1, 1885.[13]

In compliance with the wish of several Archbishops and Bishops and encouraged by the subscription made in advance I have been working in earnest at the *History of the Church* in this country most of this year. The first volume includes all down to 1783 [*sic*].[14] For the most

---

[9] Sir Humphrey Gilbert (c. 1539–1583) made a voyage to the New World in 1578–1579; he took possession of Newfoundland in 1583 in the name of Queen Elizabeth and lost his life on the return voyage.

[10] Robert Persons (1546–1610) was the leader of the first Jesuit mission for the reconversion of England in 1580.

[11] Thomas, first Lord Arundell of Wardour (1560–1639), was one of the leading English Catholic noblemen of the late Elizabethan and early Stuart periods.

[12] James Haddock, O.F.M., was one of the members of the Franciscan mission in Maryland which lasted from 1672 to c. 1725.

[13] Francis X. Leray (1825–1887) was Bishop of Natchitoches, 1877–1879, Coadjutor Archbishop of New Orleans, 1879–1883, and Archbishop of New Orleans from 1883 to his death.

[14] Volume I, entitled *The Catholic Church in Colonial Days, 1521–1763* (New York: John Gilmary Shea, 1886), actually came only to 1763, not 1783. It was dedicated to the patrons "by whose request and aid this work has been undertaken" (p. iii).

part in the English colonies I have collected all material that I can trace and most of the narrative is written. For the Spanish part I have most encouraging success for Florida, Texas, and New Mexico. The French part touches Maine, and of which I have much, some hitherto unknown. For the Mission in New York I have also abundant material. For Michigan, Wisconsin and Illinois my documents are also rich. But for Louisiana, I now appeal to Your Grace. My first published work in 1853 was on the *Discovery of the Mississippi*[15] by Father Marquette followed by the Recollect Fathers under La Salle. I have Iberville's[16] Voyage, in which he was accompanied by a Recollect and Jesuit. Some years ago I printed letters from Messrs. Montigny[17] and his associates, sent out from the Seminary of Quebec by St. Vallier,[18] with his Lordship's act founding the Mission.

I have Abp. Taschereau's[19] history of that Mission which finally centered at Tamarois in Illinois. This includes the very curious history of Rev. M. Le Maire's[20] coming to Louisiana.

I have recently discovered a protest of Bp. St. Vallier against the action of the Pope who erected some Vicariates-Apostolic [*sic*][21] in the Mississippi Valley, which on his protest were suppressed. Investigation is now in progress at Rome to find all about this. For the

---

[15] *The Discovery and Exploration of the Mississippi Valley* (New York: Redfield, 1852) was dedicated to Jared Sparks of Harvard University who then encouraged Shea to write on the Catholic missions of Canada and the West, a volume which he brought out under the title *History of the Catholic Missions among the Indian Tribes of the United States, 1529–1854* (New York: Dunigan, 1854).

[16] Pierre Le Moyne Iberville (1661–1706) was a Canadian-born explorer who laid the foundations for Louisiana.

[17] François Jolliet de Montigny was the leader of the seminary priests of Quebec in 1698 to the missions along the Mississippi River.

[18] Jean-Baptiste de Saint-Vallier (1653–1727) was the successor of the famous Laval as second Bishop of Quebec.

[19] Elzéar-Alexandre Taschereau (1820–1898) was made Archbishop of Quebec in 1871 and the first Canadian cardinal in 1887. He wrote a manuscript history of the seminary of Quebec.

[20] F. Le Maire was a French priest who left a comfortable post in Paris to serve as a missionary in Louisiana for some years in the early eighteenth century.

[21] The very confused jurisdictional problem in Louisiana that arose during the last years of Pope Clement XI (1700–1721) and the first years of Pope Innocent XIII (1721–1724) became further involved by the Gallican controversy between the Holy See and France. The jurisdictions in question were prefectures-apostolic and not vicariates-apostolic as Shea said.

Jesuit Mission there are letters in the *Lettres Edifiantes,*[22] the *Bannissement des Jesuites de la Louisiane* and a few letters recently found. My great want is documents to give anything like a connected sketch of the history of the Church among the settlers of Louisiana while the Capuchin Fathers[23] were in control. There is nothing in the Archives at Quebec either in the Archévêché or in the Seminary. Will Your Grace permit your Rev. Secretary to inform me what the archives of your See can supply? 1. Are there any reports, sketches or statements made by Capuchins between 1725 and 1783? 2. Are there any documents by Rt. Rev. Cyril de Barcelona, Bishop of Tricali,[24] who, as auxiliary Bishop, administered that portion of the diocese of Cuba and, after its division, of St. Christopher of Havana from 1776 to 1783? 3. At what date do the oldest Registers begin and are they perfect from the beginning? 4. Is the Bull erecting the Diocese of Louisiana and the Floridas (1793) preserved in the archives? 5. Which are the oldest parishes outside New Orleans and which of them have ancient Registers?

If your Grace will permit your Rev. Secretary to have an examination made I will meet all expense: and I can then know what material I can hope to obtain for my work. I wish to make it full and faithful for every part of the country; and feeling that my material is not complete for Louisiana, I beg Your Grace's favor and indulgence.

To Monsignor Farley, October 18, 1888.[25]

The Life and Times of Archbishop Carroll is, as you know, ready; and it has cost me great labor, absorbing all my leisure and impairing my health seriously. It covers an important period, and really the history of the Church during it has not hitherto been known. Not only are errors and misrepresentations corrected, but whole chapters are new contributions.

---

[22] The series of Jesuit missionary sources entitled *Lettres edifiantes et curieuses, écrites des missions etrangères* (Paris, 1702 ff.) contained some material on North America for the years 1702–1776, but they were devoted mainly to the Jesuit missions elsewhere. The other title mentioned here by Shea was François Philibert Watrin, S.J.'s account of the banishment of the Jesuits from Louisiana, which will be found in No. 24 of this collection.

[23] The French Capuchins opened their mission in Louisiana in 1722.

[24] The Spanish Capuchin, Cirilo Sieni, known as Cyril of Barcelona, was consecrated as Auxiliary Bishop of Santiago de Cuba in 1781 and served in Louisiana, which was then part of the Cuban see, until 1793.

[25] John M. Farley (1842–1918), then secretary to Archbishop Corrigan, was Auxiliary Bishop of New York, 1895–1902, Archbishop of New York, 1902 to his death. Farley was made a cardinal in 1911.

I have made the volume so large and expensive, that I am in considerable debt; and I see no way except to have another appeal for patrons of the work. There have been eight deaths, and there were when I issued the volume eight delinquents, some of whom wish to withdraw altogether.

By making up a list of 250 prominent Catholics in the United States, it seems to me that 25 or 30 new patrons ought to be secured. With that number I can complete the work without anxiety. . . .

To Archbishop Corrigan, May 21, 1889.

In full consciousness of the many calls upon your time and thoughts I am most reluctant to make a personal appeal; but I am in a sore strait. When the matter of the *History of the Church* was proposed, it was suggested that I should withdraw from Leslie's[26] establishment. This I was reluctant to do, as I regarded my position secure and permanent, but I leaned upon a straw. Leaving a meeting of the Committee of the Catholic Historical Society[27] on the 2nd of January, I fell in stepping from an ill-constructed elevator and so injured my knee that I have been laid up and am now barely able to get about on crutches and even with them dare not attempt to walk in the street. During my enforced absence from the office, advantage was taken of this; although I continued to keep up my work. The prominence given to me directly and indirectly by my *History* prompted hostility, and I have recently been deprived of my position, a mere temporary position at a pittance being offered me.

Nothing would be more congenial to me than Church work and if there be any position in the Chancery Office, Calvary Cemetery Office, or in connection with any of the institutions, where I could be sure of a moderate salary I should be only too grateful to Your Grace for enabling me to obtain it.

I am able to work and willing. My aspirations are not high; and I do not ask to be a mere pensioner. If I can obtain a position in New York where I can earn my living, I can devote my leisure to the completion of the *History,* but if I am thrown upon precarious pieces of work, my labor on it must of necessity be fitful and uncertain. I commend the whole matter to Your Grace's kind consideration, and I feel certain from the friendly interest you have always manifested in

---

[26] Frank Leslie's Publishing House, 53–57 Park Place, New York City.

[27] It was due to the initiative of Shea that the United States Catholic Historical Society of New York was founded in December, 1884, with the active assistance of Richard H. Clarke (1827–1911) and Charles G. Herbermann (1840–1916).

me, that you will not feel offended at my thus intruding my private troubles on your attention. It was with great reluctance that I now address you, and do so only after efforts made in various directions, which have tended to discourage me.

Whether you could exert influence in any other field than those I have named I do not know, but leaving the matter in Your Grace's hands, I remain with deep and sincere respect.

To Archbishop Corrigan, June 2, 1889.

I must thank you sincerely for your kind letter to Mgr. Donnelly[28] in regard to my affairs. When I called on him yesterday my position was talked over at some length. It is far from my wish to be a pensioner or have a place made for me. I felt that if there were an opening anywhere for work which I was competent to do, Your Grace would exert influence in my favor. . . . Another proposal has just been made to me. Mr. Ridder[29] asks me to assume the editorship of the *Catholic News* and to give some days of the week to do it. As the editorship of a Catholic paper or periodical was never before offered me, I should not like to undertake it without Your Grace's sanction and entire approval. If I assumed the position it would be with the hope that I might, when occasion required, learn Your Grace's wishes as to the tone to be adopted, or the mode in which subjects should be treated. I can certainly conduct it prudently and temperately, how ably or successfully I cannot presume to say.

An Announcement in the *Catholic News,* May 4, 1890.

Some years since I was invited to write the History of the Catholic Church in this country, and subscriptions were advanced by several of the hierarchy, clergy and laity sufficient to cover the cost of the volumes as they were undertaken. Of these generous friends nearly one-third have already passed from this world. Two volumes were written and published. Soon after the appearance of the second volume, 'The Life and Times of Archbishop Carroll,' an accident laid me up for months a cripple. Though I endeavored successfully in this state

[28] Arthur J. Donnelly (1820–1890) was treasurer of the committee formed in 1885 to assist Shea. Monsignor Donnelly founded St. Michael's Parish, New York, in September, 1857.

[29] Herman Ridder (1851–1915) had founded the weekly *Katolisches Volksblatt* of New York in 1878 which he discontinued for the *Catholic News* in 1886. In 1890 Ridder became manager of the *New-Yorker Staats-Zeitung,* the foremost German daily in the United States, which he managed until his death.

to fulfill my usual editorial duties, I was deprived of nearly my whole income by an unjust and cruel act that I never anticipated. While in this position the proprietor of the *Catholic News* offered me the editorial charge of his paper, and, aided by the intelligent and well-informed staff connected with that journal, I have till the present time labored to meet his expectations and those of the Catholic body.

Meanwhile my History was virtually suspended, beyond the collection of material and studies of particular phases of periods. Understanding this, some friends in the clergy of the State[30] where I reside made an effort to enable me to lay aside all other work and apply myself to the completion of the History. Since the first of January I have done nothing else, except the editorial work of the *Catholic News,* notwithstanding which, my third volume is so far advanced that it will appear early this summer unless some unforeseen event intervenes.

I notified the proprietor of the *Catholic News* of the position of affairs, and of my relinquishment of all other work. As he had made heavy outlay, based on my continuance as editor of the *News,* he had felt great reluctance to sever the connection which will involve loss, and require a change in the management of the paper.

For my own part I should without hesitation retire at once from the editorial chair, did I find that it interfered with my special work. Hitherto it has been no obstacle, but, on the contrary, by the wide circulation it enjoys, the *News* brings me in contact with Catholics in all parts of the country, enables me to see all the Catholic journals, and profit by all historical reminiscences, biographical sketches and the like. It has also enabled me to obtain important and valuable material. My presence in the office is limited to two days, and the change of scene for that short time is beneficial to my health.

My great desire is to complete the History of the Church. To it I will sacrifice all other matters, and even the editorship of the *News,* if it proves the slightest bar, shall be relinquished on due notice, whenever I feel and my kind friends see that it retards the work.

To Father Corrigan,[31] May 5, 1890.

I inserted in the last number of the *News* a statement which you

[30] The names of this committee in the Diocese of Newark were listed in the final volume of Shea's work which appeared some months after his death in 1892 (IV, vii–viii).

[31] Patrick Corrigan (1830–1893), pastor of St. Mary's Church, Hoboken, New Jersey, was well known for his feud with his ordinary, Winand M. Wigger (1841–1901), over the question of priests' rights. He was the author of a brochure entitled *What the Catholic Church Most Needs in the United States, or, The Voice of the Priests in the Election of the Bishops* (New York, 1884).

have seen, as Mr. Ridder promised to send you copies. It defines my position and leaves me free to withdraw whenever I find it necessary. Last week I did an immense deal of work at Baltimore, and today I hear of a large batch of documents coming from Rome. My volume, so far as my actual material goes, is half done, and I am arranging to begin the printing at once. I got out volumes I and II by night work, about 25 hours a week, after a hard day's work in the office in New York. Now by the help coming from you and the large-hearted friends who have responded to you, I have devoted 55 hours a week to the History, and I certainly can complete the three volumes in two years or very little more. The connection with the *News* is a diversion that helps rather than retards the work, and of course when my book is completed, leaves me a foothold for the future. My chief aim is now to close up the work on the history with as little delay as possible, so as not to tax the generosity of my friends a day longer than is necessary. If, however, my name on Ridder's paper at all affects your appeal, it must come off and my work there cease.

To Father Corrigan, September 26, 1890.

While enclosing receipt for $1,000, being the third payment made by you this year, I must express more deeply than ever how much I owe you personally and all Catholics owe to your disinterested exertions and to the generous friends whom you have interested in the Church History of this country.

The accident which befell me and the consequence it entailed, made it very difficult for me to continue the work, and I began to feel that no one for a century would attempt to go so systematically over the whole ground. Your action enabled me to complete the work as I projected it. Besides adding steadily to my stock of documents from Rome and collections in dioceses here, I have acquired many necessary books, newspapers, pamphlets, letters of Bishops, priests, religious, giving me a rich mine of material.[32] Since the commencement of the year I have labored steadily on my third volume, and have nearly six hundred pages in type, so that I can certainly issue next month. I shall then set out for the West in search of documents and letters, and on my return, begin writing the fourth volume, which I hope, God willing, to complete by the first of May.

The fifth and concluding volume I aim and trust to have entirely

[32] Three days before Shea's death he signed an agreement with J. Havens Richards, S.J. (1851–1923), thirtieth president of Georgetown University, for the transfer of all his historical materials to Georgetown.

written by the end of the year, so as to issue it early in 1892. My aim is to be able to show the whole work brought to a conclusion before the Columbus centenary. In the volume about to appear I shall express my gratitude for the appreciation already manifested in my work, but I hope to receive from you a complete list of those who so nobly co-operate with you that I may dedicate my fifth volume and the work it crowns to those who deserve to be remembered as long as the work can preserve their memory.

123. John Boyle O'Reilly's Speech in Behalf of the Negro, December 7, 1885, and His Editorial on the Excommunication of Dr. McGlynn, July 16, 1887

AMERICAN Catholic journalism had no more popular and influential figure in the late nineteenth century than John Boyle O'Reilly (1844–1890). Deported to Australia by the British government in 1867 for his Fenian activities in behalf of Irish freedom, O'Reilly escaped and reached the United States in 1869. He settled in Boston where he was soon on the staff of the *Pilot,* becoming editor in 1876 and within a few years bringing that Catholic weekly to a position of national prominence. O'Reilly combined the talents of a poet and prose writer with a ringing patriotism and a deep devotion to the Church. He was so attractive and gifted a personality that he was chosen to compose verse for such occasions as the memorial to Wendel Phillips and the unveiling of the monuments to Crispus Attucks and Plymouth Rock, honors which, it has been said, "ordinarily only the most proper native Protestant would have received" (Arthur Mann, *Yankee Reformers in the Urban Age* [Cambridge, 1954], pp. 28–29). As a consequence of O'Reilly's campaign against racism and his personal popularity, by the time of his death he had done a good deal to close the breach between the Irish Catholics and Yankee Puritans of Boston. The documents that follow illustrate two aspects of O'Reilly's thought: first, his championing of the cause of the Negro, a stand that came naturally to one who had spent a lifetime opposing the injustice practiced by England against the land of his birth; second, his loyalty to the Church in the case of Father Edward McGlynn (1837–1900) whose excommunication was pronounced by the Holy See when McGlynn refused to go to Rome to explain his adherence to the land theories of Henry George, and this in spite of O'Reilly's sympathies with the ideas of McGlynn and George. Sources: James Jeffrey Roche, *Life of John Boyle O'Reilly* (New York: Cassell Publishing Co., 1891), pp. 738–742; Boston *Pilot,* July 16, 1887.

THE NEGRO-AMERICAN

Mr. President and Gentlemen: I was quite unaware of the nature of this meeting when I came here. I learn from Mr. Downing's speech that it is more or less a political meeting; that you are going to express preferences this way or that. I came here because I was asked to speak at a colored men's meeting in Boston. I don't care what your political preferences or parties are. I don't care whether you vote the Republican or Democratic ticket, but I know that if I were a colored man I should use parties as I would a club — to break down prejudices against my people. I shouldn't talk about being true to any party, except so far as that party was true to me. Parties care nothing for you only to use you. You should use parties; the highest party you have in this country is your own manhood. That is the thing in danger from all parties; that is the thing that every colored American is bound in his duty to himself and his children to defend and protect.

I think it is as wicked and unreasonable to discriminate against a man because of the color of his skin as it would be because of the color of his hair. He is no more responsible for the one than for the other, and one is no more significant than the other. A previous speaker's reference to Mr. Parnell[1] and his growing power as a reformer ought to suggest to you that Parnell is to-day a powerful man because he is pledged to no party. He would smash the Tories tomorrow as readily as he smashed the Liberals yesterday. That is the meaning of politics. The highest interest of politics is the selfish interest of the people. You are never going to change the things, that affect you colored men, by law. If my children were not allowed into Northern schools, if I myself were not allowed into Northern hotels, I would change my party and my politics every day until I changed and wiped out that outrage.

I was in Tennessee last spring, and when I got out of the cars at Nashville I saw over the door of an apartment, "Colored people's waiting room." I went into it and found a wretched, poorly-furnished room, crowded with men, women, and children. Mothers with little children sat on the unwashed floor, and young men and young women filled the bare, uncomfortable seats that were fastened to the walls. Then I went out and found over another door, "Waiting-room." In there were the white people, carefully attended and comfortable; separate rooms for white men and women, well ventilated and well kept. I spent two days in Nashville, and every hour I saw things that

[1] Charles Stewart Parnell (1846–1891) was the leader of the Irish nationalists in the British House of Commons.

made me feel that something was the matter either with God or humanity in the South; and I said going away, "If ever the colored question comes up again as long as I live, I shall be counted in with the black men."

But this disregard for the colored people does not only exist in the South; I know there are many hotels in Boston, where, if any one of you were to ask for a room, they would tell you that all the rooms were filled.

The thing that most deeply afflicts the colored American is not going to be cured by politics. You have received from politics already about all it can give you.

You may change the law by politics, but it is not the law that is going to insult and outrage and excommunicate every colored American for generations to come. You can't cure the conceit of the white people that they are better than you by politics, nor their ignorance, nor their prejudice, nor their bigotry, nor any of the insolences which they cherish against their colored fellow-citizens.

Politics is the snare and delusion of white men as well as black. Politics tickles the skin of the social order; but this disease, and other diseases of class, privilege, and inheritance, lie deep in the internal organs. Social equity is based on principles of justice; political change on the opinion of a time. The black man's skin will be a mark of social inferiority so long as white men are conceited, ignorant and prejudiced. You cannot legislate these qualities out of the whites — you must steal and reason them out by teaching, illustration, and example.

No man ever came into the world with a grander opportunity than the American negro. He is like new metal dug out of the mine. He stands at this late day on the threshold of history, with everything to learn and less to unlearn, than any civilized man in the world. In his heart still ring the free sounds of the desert. In his mind he carries the traditions of Africa. The songs with which he charms American ears are refrains from the tropical forests, from the great inland seas and rivers of the dark continent.

At worst, the colored American has only a century or so of degrading civilized tradition and habit to forget and unlearn. His nature has only been injured on the outside by these late circumstances of his existence. Inside he is a new man, fresh from nature — a color-lover, an enthusiast, a believer by the heart, a philosopher, a cheerful, natural, good-natured man. I believe the colored American to be the kindliest human being in existence. All the inhumanities of slavery have not made him cruel or sullen or revengeful. He has all the qualities that fit him to be a good citizen of any country; he does not worry his soul to-day with the fear of next week or next year. He has feelings and convictions, and he loves to show them. He sees no reason why he should hide them. He will be a great natural expression if he dares to express the beauty, the color, the harmony of God's world as he sees it with a negro's eyes. That is the meaning of race distinction — that it should help us to see God's beauty in the world in various ways.

What this splendid man needs most is confidence in himself and his race. He is a dependent man at present. He is not sure of himself. He underrates his own qualities. He must be a self-respecting man. Not all men can be distinguished, but assuredly some distinct expression of genius will come out of any considerable community of colored people who believe in themselves, who contemn and despise the man of their blood who apes white men and their ways, who is proud to be a negro, who will bear himself according to his own ideas of a colored man, who will encourage his women to dress themselves by their own taste, to select the rich colors they love, to follow out their own natural bent, and not to adopt other people's stupid and shop-made fashions. The negro woman has the best artistic eye for color of all the women in America.

The negro is the only graceful, musical, color-loving American. He is the only American who has written new songs and composed new music. He is the most spiritual of Americans, for he worships with soul and not with narrow mind. For him religion is to be believed, accepted like the very voice of God, and not invented, contrived, reasoned about, shaded, and made fashionably lucrative and marketable, as it is made by too many white Americans.

The negro is a new man, a free man, a spiritual man, a hearty man; and he can be a great man if he will avoid modeling himself on the whites. No race ever became illustrious on borrowed ideas or the imitated qualities of another race.

No race or nation is great or illustrious except by one test — the breeding of great men. Not great merchants or traders, not rich men, bankers, insurance-mongers, or directors of gas companies. But great thinkers — great seers of the world through their own eyes — great tellers of the truths and beauties and colors and equities as they alone see them. Great poets — ah, great poets above all — and their brothers, great painters and musicians, fashioners of God's beautiful shapes in clay and marble and harmony.

The negro will never take his full stand beside the white man till he has given the world proof of the truth and beauty of heroism and power that are in his soul. And only by the organs of the soul are these delivered — by self-respect and self-reflection, by philosophy, religion, poetry, art, love, and sacrifice. One great poet will be worth a hundred bankers and brokers, worth ten Presidents of the United States, to the negro race. One great musician will speak to the world for the black man as no thousand editors or politicians can.

The wealth of our Western soil, in its endless miles of fertility, is less to America than the unworked wealth of the rich negro nature. The negro poet of the future will be worth two Mexicos to America. God send wise guides to my black fellow-countrymen, who shall lead them to understand and accept what is true and great and perennial, and to reject what is deceptive and changeable in life, purpose, and hope.

It is a great pleasure to me to say these things that I have long believed to a colored meeting in Boston. It would be a greater pleasure to go down to Nashville and address a colored meeting there; and God grant that it may be soon possible for a Boston white man to go down to Nashville and address colored men. As I said in the beginning, so long as American citizens and their children are excluded from schools, theaters, hotels, or common conveyances, there ought not to be and there is not among those who love justice and liberty, any question of race, creed, or color; every heart that beats for humanity, beats with the oppressed.

DR. McGLYNN

It is hard to find words to express the pain felt by the Catholics of America over the excommunication of Dr. McGlynn. Grief for the insubordination of a priest once deeply loved and respected is strangely mixed with astonishment and perplexity at his stubborn refusal to abide by the primary elements of Church discipline.

In this excommunication there is no question whatever of political or social principles. It is wholly a matter of Church discipline. Dr. McGlynn directly refused to obey the order of the Sacred Congregation of the Propaganda, to go to Rome and be heard in his own behalf. For this insubordination the threatened excommunication falls upon him, his own hand bringing down the blow.

No matter what following Dr. McGlynn may win outside the Church, either of children of the Church or others, those who love him best and wish him most happiness will continue to pray that his pride may be put under his feet, that he may come back to the altar like a child to its mother, humble and sorrowful for his rebellion.

Right or wrong, submission to the authority of the Church is the manly as well as the priestly and Christian duty of Dr. McGlynn. Because he submits, no true principle which he may hold will die. Because he rebels, whatever truth or virtue may lie in his land doctrine is set back, discountenanced and weighted down. No cause ever suffered by the humiliation of its apostles.

It is nonsense for Dr. McGlynn to say that he has been excommunicated because he taught that God made the land for the people. It is not true. The Sacred Congregation of Propaganda has never considered Henry George's theories. Dr. McGlynn is simply like a soldier who refuses to keep step or rank or direction.

But he will come back — he will surely stay his feet in time. Believe it, the heart of the priest is true, and the passion will not hold it long. He will wash away the stains of the scandal with tears. Too many love him and pray for him to let him go too far. *Soggarth Aroon, Soggarth Aroon,* remember the little ones who do not know!

124. Bishop Keane's Admonitions to Cardinal Gibbons, December 29, 1886

JOHN J. KEANE (1839–1918) was one of the most colorful and forthright prelates in the group of remarkable bishops who governed the American Church in the late nineteenth and early twentieth centuries. Irish-born, he came to the United States at the age of seven, and twelve years after his ordination he was named fifth Bishop of Richmond in 1878. In August, 1888, he was formally appointed first rector of the Catholic University of America, a post for which he had no training but which brought out his talents for imaginative leadership, arresting public address, and enthusiastic promotion of a cause to which he had committed himself. Keane learned his job by serious reading and by visits to various institutions where he counseled with leading university executives. Thoroughly American in his sentiments, forthright in his view, and convinced of the necessity for a closer relationship between American Catholics and their fellow countrymen, at times his enthusiasm outran his discretion. The result was that he incurred enmity and suspicion as a liberal whose orthodoxy was not entirely sound. In September, 1896, he was summarily dismissed from the university, spent several years of exile in Rome, and was vindicated only in September, 1900, when he was named second Archbishop of Dubuque, a position he held until his resignation was accepted by the Holy See in April, 1911. Few bishops served the American Church more unselfishly and few experienced more reverses and humiliations than Keane. Yet he bore it all in a spirit of deep religious faith and at no time was known to have succumbed to embitterment. The following letter, written from Rome to Cardinal Gibbons at a time when the latter showed signs of wavering on several important questions before the Roman Curia, offers a good example of Keane's candor, courage, and steadfast devotion to what his biographer characterizes as "the best interests of the Catholic Church in the United States even though it could have meant the loss of a powerful friend" (Patrick H. Ahern, *The Life of John J. Keane, Educator and Archbishop, 1839–1918* [Milwaukee, 1955], p. 37). It was a measure of the cardinal's magnanimity that this letter did nothing to impair their friendship and, in fact, he may even be said to have shown thereafter more resolution in his policies. Source: Archives of the Archdiocese of Baltimore, 82–J–4, Keane to Gibbons, Rome, December 29, 1886.

Your Eminence:

We were delighted to receive yesterday your letter of the 17th. Its references to the three important points of the German question,[1] the coadjutorship of N. Orleans,[2] & the Knights of Labor,[3] were most valuable & welcome. I at once put them into three Latin documents, and handed them in to the Propaganda this morning. They will be sure to have great weight. I was very glad to be thus enabled to put your Eminence in a proper light in the Propaganda on the N. Orleans question. You were there identified with the advocacy of Dr. Chapelle's[4] nomination; and as he is sure to be the losing man, you were going down with him on the losing side. Your present advocacy of Bishop Janssens[5] puts you once more on the winning side, where you ought to be.

But I beg that you will permit me, dear and venerated friend, to go on and mention things which it is exceedingly painful for me to pen, and which only my high regard for yourself personally and for the exalted office which you hold, could induce me to write, for it is a hard task and often a risky one, to write painful truths to a friend, especially when he is a superior. Only *real* friendship can nerve one to the duty.

---

[1] At the time Keane wrote there was serious dissension within the Church of the United States between the Irish and German elements over the petition which Father Peter M. Abbelen of Milwaukee had presented to the Holy See in November, 1886, charging the hierarchy with neglect of the German Catholic immigrants.

[2] The question of a coadjutor with the right of succession to Francis X. Leray (1825–1887), Archbishop of New Orleans, was also in dispute.

[3] In August, 1884, the Knights of Labor in Canada had been condemned by Rome as a forbidden secret society. An effort to secure a unanimous judgment of the archbishops of the United States in favor of the knights in this country was not successful and, therefore, the question had to be referred to the Holy See for a final decision.

[4] Placide L. Chapelle (1842–1905) was named Coadjutor Archbishop of Santa Fe in 1891 and in December, 1897, was promoted to the See of New Orleans.

[5] Francis Janssens (1843–1897) had been Bishop of Natchez since 1881. In August, 1888, he was named Archbishop of New Orleans.

I find, to my intense regret, that an impression has taken shape in Rome to the effect that your Eminence is changeable in views, weak and vacillating in purpose, anxious to conciliate both parties on nearly every question; that it is hard to know, therefore upon which side you stand concerning any important question, or what weight to attach to your utterances. Hence I find a growing inclination to look elsewhere than to your Eminence for reliable information & judgments, — a tendency, not only here but among the Bishops of the United States, to look to New York rather than to Baltimore for the representative & leader of our Hierarchy.

Against this I protest with all earnestness; but they allege fact after fact in defence of their position. They say that, just as in the change of front in regard to New Orleans there is evidence that the former letter was written to please the Archbishop, and did not represent your real views as to the best & safest man, which was what they expected of you, so there was a somewhat similar change of front in regard to poor Dr. Foley,[6] whose friends, notwithstanding all explanations, feel quite sore over his having been finally abandonment [*sic*]. They offset your sentiments on the German question by the fact that the emissary of this attack secretly directed against our Hierarchy by a few German prelates, comes to Rome with a letter of introduction from your Eminence.[7] And they further allege the case of Bishop Dwenger,[8] who may be considered an arch-mover in this bad cause, who, in order to make much of himself & of his cause, had himself sent on here by your Eminence as the representative of our Hierarchy in regard to the Plenary Council, — and they overwhelm me by adding that whereas your Eminence at first asserted that you did not intend to send him, and denied that you had sent him, you later acknowledged that you had done so. We have lately

[6] John S. Foley (1833–1918). Foley had been on the *terne* for both the See of Savannah in 1885 and the vacancy in the Diocese of Wilmington in 1886, but in each case opposition to his candidacy arose and he was not appointed. In November, 1888, however, he was consecrated as Bishop of Detroit, a post which he filled until his death.

[7] Before he sailed for Rome on October 13, 1886, Abbelen had received a letter of recommendation from Gibbons to Giovanni Cardinal Simeoni, Prefect of the Congregation of Propaganda de Fide. The Cardinal of Baltimore had known Abbelen's good work in the Third Plenary Council of 1884, but he was not aware of the real nature of the petition which Abbelen was taking to the Holy See.

[8] Joseph Dwenger, C.PP.S. (1837–1893), was Bishop of Fort Wayne from 1872 to his death. Keane was referring here to Gibbons' appointment of Dwenger as one of the two American bishops who were charged with getting the legislation of the Third Plenary Council approved in Rome. Dwenger's conduct of that mission aroused a considerable amount of opposition among his fellow bishops.

been pouring out our[9] honest indignation at the charge that the signatures of the Prelates to the University petition could not be implicitly trusted as giving the real sentiment of the signers;[10] but I cannot help recognizing with what crushing force they can say to us: "Why look, even your Cardinal puts his name to statements & recommendations which he will afterwards take back or modify; if even he can send us important documents, not because he believes them best for the interests of the Church, but in order to please this one or that one, what confidence can we repose in any of these signatures?" They do not always say this in honest words; but they say it quite gallantly in meaning shrugs, and smiles, and insinuations. Even the Holy Father himself has thus intimated his apprehension that your Eminence was uncertain & vacillating in your views as to the University's location, etc.

I know well, dear & venerated friend, that whatever truth there may be in all this has its real source in your kindness of heart, your anxiety to be gracious and yielding to every one as far as you possibly can. But, as happened to the old man in the fable, by endeavoring to be over prudent and to please all, there is great danger that you eventually will please no one, — that both here and at home they will come to mistrust your consistency & strength of character, and to look elsewhere than to our beloved Cardinal for our exponent & our leader. It galls me to the heart to think that such injustice should be done to our Cardinal; to the leader whom Providence has given to us, — and it is this thought that has given me courage to write so plainly on so painful a subject. Let me hope that you will not be offended, that you will appreciate the affectionate devotedness which, next to my desire for the Church's best welfare, has been my only motive in thus writing; and let me hope that henceforth your Eminence will more than regain the lost ground, by showing such singleness, such consistency, such firmness, such nobleness, in every word and act, as to fully realize the grand ideal of your position in the fore-front of the foremost Hierarchy of the world.

---

[9] Keane's use of the plural throughout his letter referred to John Ireland (1838–1918), then Bishop of St. Paul, who was with him in Rome and who co-operated closely with Keane on all the problems of the American Church which were before the Roman Curia.

[10] At a meeting of the committee for the university held at Baltimore on October 27, 1886, they had drawn up documents for Pope Leo XIII and Cardinal Simeoni approving the plans so far made for the university. Since five other archbishops were in Baltimore at the time they were asked to sign the documents and did so. The opposition party, however, later made it known at the Holy See that some of those who signed were not really in favor of the project.

From the depths of my heart I wish you a blessed & happy new year, and am ever

Your devoted servant & friend in Christ,
John J. Keane, Bp. of Rd.[11]

125. John LaFarge Describes His Painting of "The Ascension," 1887

OF JOHN LA FARGE (1835–1910) it has been said, "With his learning, his imagination, and his skill he gave rank to American art more than any other of the craft. For that reason he is to-day hailed as master and written down in our annals as belonging with the Olympians" (John G. Van Dyke, *American Painting and Its Tradition* [New York, 1919], p. 146). LaFarge was a man who left the imprint of his genius not only on painting and stained glass but upon the lives of many of the leading American men of art and letters of his time. His extraordinary mind began to manifest itself at a very early age. For example, in a little over two months while he was in boarding school — and before he had reached his sixteenth birthday — he requested his father to send him works of Herodotus, Plautus, Catullus, Dryden, Goldsmith, Michelet, Molière, Corneille, and Victor Hugo for his reading (cf. "Schoolboy Letters between John LaFarge and His Father," *Historical Records and Studies,* XVIII [March, 1928], 74–120). LaFarge graduated on June 29, 1853, from Mount Saint Mary's College, Emmitsburg, with Silas M. Chatard (1838–1918), later fifth Bishop of Vincennes as a classmate, and Orestes Brownson delivering an address on "Liberal Studies." By the time he was thirty his reputation as an artist was widespread and his glass for the windows of Trinity Church, Boston, in 1876 brought him international fame. Among his principal works was the great mural painting of "The Ascension" for the Protestant Episcopal Church of the Ascension in New York. Of that picture his biographer remarked, "LaFarge never painted anything more purely beautiful than 'The Ascension' and it might not unreasonably be taken as summing up his qualities as a mural decorator. . . ." (Cortissoz, *op. cit.,* p. 171). In the following letter to Cortissoz, undated, LaFarge described some of the problems he encountered in painting "The Ascension." Source: Royal Cortissoz, *John LaFarge. A Memoir and A Study* (Boston: Houghton Mifflin Co., 1911), pp. 161–166.

In the picture of "The Ascension" in the Tenth Street church there were some very curious problems. The clergyman had liked a drawing which I had made many years before, let us say some thirty years ago,

[11] There was no answer to this letter among the Keane Papers, nor a copy of such found in the archives at Baltimore. In Gibbons' diary under date of January 14, 1887, there was the unrevealing entry: "Wrote to Bp. Keane in reply to his letter from Rome of Dec. 29" (Archives of the Archdiocese of Baltimore, Diary of Cardinal Gibbons, p. 213).

of that subject, with a similar grouping. This was to be a very narrow high window for a memorial chapel out West. It was never carried out; in fact it was nothing but one of those projects forced upon unfortunate artists by enthusiastic millionaires who forget almost immediately what their last plans had been. I do not even know if anything was done about it, but the proposed patron was interesting, owing to his having very many works of art, some of which were fine and the others not usually seen in this country even to-day — not that they were good.

The Dr. Donald,[1] the clergyman, happening to see this, wished to have this long and narrow window carried out where you now see the painting; there being a recess in the wall, it might be used. At that time I was very anxious to have Saint-Gaudens[2] get a chance to do work and to show his capacity. Remember that I am talking of very many years ago. I proposed that he might, perhaps, be tempted to make a great bas-relief of this to fill that space; but there were too many reasons against it, among others those of money. A painting can be done, it is supposed, quite cheaply compared to a piece of sculpture, even if that sculpture is only in plaster at a few cents a foot.

By and by, when Stanford White[3] took charge of the church, the questions came together and it was proposed that I should paint the picture upon the wide space which he left for it. But that space was many, many times wider than the sketch or study and even enlarging the figures in enormous proportions would not fill it. Even now the picture is almost square, so that I had a problem of widening my space of figures and of settling their proportion in a given space. Nothing that I could do, and keep the original intention, would allow the change to be done to cover enough space, so that I proposed a frame which should both cut a little space, indicate the Gothic character of the church, and help what I thought I was going to do to carry out the painting — that was to place these figures in a very big landscape. The landscape I wished to have extremely natural, because I depended on it to make my figures also look natural and to account for the floating of some twenty figures or more in the air. We do not see this ever, as you know, but I knew that by a combination of the clouds and figures I might help this look of what the mystic people call levitation.

[1] The Reverend Dr. E. W. Donald was rector of the Church of the Ascension.

[2] Augustus Saint-Gaudens (1848–1907), the sculptor, was greatly influenced by LaFarge.

[3] Stanford White (1853–1906) was a famous American architect of the period.

Of course you may well suppose that I studied what I could of all the people who are swung in ropes and other arrangements across theatres and circuses. The question of the composition of the figures had to meet certain geometric conditions in my mind; that is to say, to fit a given pattern which I thought fortunate in the space. I forget whether it was an arrangement of hexagons but I have a faint belief that it was, owing to the arithmetical figures of the proportions of the space. That could be settled, but my landscape,—I was much troubled.

At that moment I was asked to go to Japan by my friend Henry Adams,[4] and I went there in 1886. I had a vague belief that I might find there certain conditions of line in the mountains which might help me. Of course the Judean mountains were entirely out of question, all the more that they implied a given place. I kept all this in mind and on one given day I saw before me a space of mountain and cloud and flat land which seemed to me to be what was needed. I gave up my other work and made thereupon a rapid but very careful study, so complete that the big picture is only a part of the amount of work put into the study of that afternoon. There are turns of the tide which allow you at times to do an amount of work incredible in sober moments; as you know, there are very many such cases; I do not understand it myself. When I returned I was still of the same mind. My studies of separate figures were almost ready and all I had to do was to stretch the canvas and begin the work.

Perhaps you do not know that I got into great difficulties thereupon. The weight of such a canvas is something very great. The mere lead paint used to fasten it was far over five hundred pounds. The wall, that is to say, the plaster wall, was a new one, just made, and I felt dubious about its standing this weight, when, as you know, the canvas is fastened down and then pulled flat by a great many men. It was just as I surmised. The wall tumbled down as soon as the canvas was put up, or, rather, when the first part of it was fastened. They were careful about the next wall and I believe that it is now a safe one.

After that I had only pleasure out of my work. During that summer

---

[4] Henry Adams (1838–1918), the historian, was another man who was strongly influenced by LaFarge. In his own memoirs Adams said, "Of all the men who had deeply affected their friends since 1850 John LaFarge was certainly the foremost, and for Henry Adams, who had sat at his feet since 1872, the question of how much he owed to LaFarge could be answered only by admitting that he had no standards to measure it by" (*The Education of Henry Adams. An Autobiography* [Boston, 1918], p. 369).

my friend Okakura[5] spent a great deal of his time with me and I could paint, and then, in the intervals, we could talk about spiritual manifestations and all that beautiful wonderland which they have; that is to say, the Buddhists, where the spiritual bodies take form and disappear again and the edges of the real and the imaginary melt. I had one objection brought up by a friend, a lady, who was troubled by certain news she had heard. That was that I had made these studies of clouds in a pagan country, while a true Episcopalian would make them, I suppose, in England. Otherwise I think people have liked this and everybody has been very kind about it. At a distance the picture is not injured, I think, by the rapidity of its execution, only a summer and an autumn, during which I carried out several other large things.

126. Cardinal Gibbons' Defense of the Knights of Labor, February 20, 1887

THROUGHOUT the nineteenth century which witnessed the most rapid growth of the Church in this country, the great majority of American Catholics belonged to the working classes. In a period marked by the rise of grave evils in the system of industrial capitalism it was not surprising that the workers should have resorted to secret organizations to defend their rights. In so doing there were at times real abuses, which became the source of deep anxiety to the American bishops lest these secret societies should alienate Catholics from their religious obligations. Fortunately, the hierarchy had at the time a man who possessed the wisdom to weigh the issues judiciously and the foresight to see that a severe condemnation by the Church of the Knights of Labor, the greatest labor organization of the day, would endanger the faith of thousands of Catholic workers. That man was James Cardinal Gibbons, Archbishop of Baltimore (1834–1921). In September, 1884, the Holy See had condemned the K. of L. in Canada at the request of the Archbishop of Quebec. But Gibbons was intent that this action should not be extended to his own country. Upon a visit to Rome in 1887 he prepared — with the assistance of Bishops John Ireland and John Keane — a forceful protest against such a possibility which he submitted to the Congregation de Propaganda Fide. The result was that the condemnation which some of the American bishops had sought was not issued, and Gibbons' memorial became the deciding factor in averting what would have proved a major calamity. As a consequence the tradition of friendliness between the Church and labor in the United States was established and has endured, and the alienation of the Catholic workers — which constituted so heavy a loss to the Church in the countries of western Europe — has never had a counterpart in the United States. Source: Henry J.

[5] Okakura was a Japanese friend of LaFarge's not otherwise identified.

Browne, *The Catholic Church and the Knights of Labor* (Washington: The Catholic University of America Press, 1949), pp. 365–378.

Your Eminence:

In submitting to the Holy See the conclusions which after several months of attentive observation and reflection,[1] seem to me to sum up the truth concerning the association of the Knights of Labor, I feel profoundly convinced of the vast importance of the consequences attaching to this question, which forms but a link in the great chain of the social problems of our day, and especially of our country.

In weighing [treating — jugeant] this question I have been very careful to follow as my constant guide the spirit of the Encyclicals, in which our Holy Father, Leo XIII, has so admirably set forth the dangers of our time and their remedies, as well as the principles by which we are to recognize associations condemned by the Holy See. Such was also the guide of the Third Plenary Council of Baltimore in its teaching concerning the principles to be followed and the dangers to be shunned by the faithful either in the choice or in the establishment of those associations toward which the spirit of our popular institutions so strongly impels them. And considering the dire [evil — funestes] consequences that might result from a mistake in the treatment of organizations which often count their members by the thousands and hundred of thousands, the council wisely ordained (n. 255) [n. 225] that when an association is spread over several dioceses, not even the bishop of one of these dioceses shall condemn it, but shall refer the case to a standing committee of all the archbishops of the United States; and even these are not authorized to condemn unless their sentence be unanimous; and in case they fail to agree unanimously, then only the supreme tribunal of the Holy See can impose a condemnation; all this in order to avoid error and confusion of discipline.

This committee of archbishops held a meeting, in fact, toward the end of last October, especially to consider the association of the Knights of Labor [at which the Knights of Labor was specially considered — spécialement pour consider]. We were not persuaded to

---

[1] Archives of the Archdiocese of Baltimore, 82-N-3. The "official" English version, first published in the *Moniteur de Rome* on March 28, 1887, was reproduced in a number of works, among them Allen Sinclair Will, *Life of Cardinal Gibbons, Archbishop of Baltimore* (New York, 1922), I, 337–352. The lesser differences in the readings which usually show the toning down of the original French for American readers, are indicated in brackets within the text. The other variations are cited in the notes.

hold this meeting because of any request on the part of our bishops, for none of them had asked for it; and it should also be said that, among all the bishops we know, only two or three desire the condemnation. But the importance of the question in itself, and in the estimation of the Holy See led us to examine it with greatest attention. After our discussion, the results of which have already been communicated to the Sacred Congregation of the Propaganda, only two out of the twelve archbishops voted for condemnation, and their reasons were powerless to convince the others of either the justice or the prudence of such a condemnation.

In the following considerations I wish to state in detail the reasons which determined the vote of the great majority of the committee — reasons whose truth and force seem to me all the more evident today; I shall try at the same time to do justice to the arguments advanced by the opposition.

1. In the first place, in the constitution, laws and official declarations of the Knights of Labor, there can clearly be found assertions and rules [though there may be found . . . things — peuvent bien se trouver des assertions ou des règles] which we would not approve; but we have not found in them those elements so clearly pointed out by the Holy See, which places them among condemned associations.

(a) In their form of initiation there is no oath.

(b) The obligation to secrecy by which they keep the knowledge of their business from strangers or enemies, in no wise prevents Catholics from manifesting everything to competent ecclesiastical authority, even outside of confession. This has been positively declared to us by their president [their chief officers — leur président].

(c) They make no promise of blind obedience. The object and laws of the association are distinctly declared, and the obligation of obedience does not go beyond these limits.

(d) They not only profess no hostility against religion or the Church, but their declarations are quite to the contrary. The Third Plenary Council commands that we should not condemn an association without giving a hearing to its officers or representatives: "auditis ducibus, corypheis vel sociis praecipuis" (n. 254).[2] Now, their president in sending me a copy of their constitution, says that he is a Catholic from the bottom of his heart [devoted Catholic — Catholique du fond de son coeur]; that he practices his religion faithfully and receives the sacraments regularly; that he belongs to no Masonic or other society condemned by the Church; that he knows of nothing

[2] The Latin phrase was omitted in the English version.

in the association of the Knights of Labor contrary to the laws of the Church; that, with filial submission he begs the Pastors of the Church to examine all the details of their organization [their constitution and laws — tous les détails de leur organisation], and, if they find anything worthy of condemnation, they should indicate it, and he promises its correction. Assuredly one does not perceive in all this any hostility to the authority of the Church, but on the contrary a spirit in every way praiseworthy. After their convention last year at Richmond, he and several of the officers and members, devout Catholics [principal members — officiers et members], made similar declarations concerning their feelings[3] and the action of that convention, the documents of which we are expecting to receive.

(e) Nor do we find in this organization any hostility to the authority and laws of our country. Not only does nothing of the kind appear in their constitution and laws, but the heads of our civil government treat with the greatest respect [with respect — avec le plus grand respect] the cause which they represent. The President of the United States told me personally, a month ago [a few weeks ago — il y a un mois] that he was then examining a law for the amelioration of certain social grievances and that he had just had a long conference on the subject with Mr. Powderly,[4] president of the Knights of Labor. The Congress of the United States, following the advice of President Cleveland is busying itself at the present time with the amelioration of the working classes, in whose complaints they acknowledge openly[5] there is a great deal of truth. And our political parties, far from regarding them as enemies of the country, vie with each other in championing the evident rights of the poor workmen [workmen — pauvres travailleurs], who seek not to resist[6] the laws, but only to obtain just legislation by constitutional and legitimate means.

These considerations, which show that in this association [these associations — cette association] those elements are not to be found which the Holy See condemns, lead us to study, in the second place, the evils which the associations contend against, and the nature of the conflict.

2. That there exist among us, as in the other countries of the

[3] "Leurs sentiments" was not translated.

[4] Terence V. Powderly (1849–1924), a Catholic at the time, was elected Grand Master Workman of the K. of L. in September, 1879, and held that office until November, 1893. After mentioning that Congress followed the advice of Cleveland, the English version inserted "in his annual message."

[5] "Ouvertement" was not translated.

[6] "Or overthrow" was inserted.

world, grave and threatening social evils, public injustices, which call for strong resistance and legal remedy, is a fact which no one dares to deny, and the truth of which has been already acknowledged by the Congress and the President of the United States. Without entering into the sad details of these wrongs, — which does not seem necessary here, — it may suffice to mention only that monopolies on the part of both individuals and of corporations, have already called forth not only the complaints of our working classes, but also the opposition of our public men and legislators; that the efforts of these monopolists, not always without success, to control legislation to their own profit, cause serious apprehension among the disinterested friends of liberty; that the heartless avarice which, through greed of gain, pitilessly grinds not only the men, but particularly the women and children in various employments, makes it clear to all who love humanity and justice that it is not only the right of the laboring classes to protect themselves, but the duty of the whole people to aid them in finding a remedy against the dangers with which both civilization and the social order are menaced by avarice, oppression and corruption.

It would be vain to deny either the existence of the evils, the right of legitimate resistance, or the necessity of a remedy. At most doubt might be raised about the legitimacy of the form of resistance and the remedy employed by the Knights of Labor. This then ought to be the next point of our examination.

3. It can hardly be doubted that for the attainment of any public end, association — the organization of all interested persons — is the most efficacious means, a means altogether natural and just. This is so evident, and besides so conformable to the genius of our country, of our essentially popular social conditions, that it is unnecessary to insist upon it. It is almost the only means to invite public attention, to give force to the most legitimate resistance, to add weight to the most just demands.

Now there already exists an organization which presents a thousand attractions and advantages, but which our Catholic workingmen, with filial obedience to the Holy See, refuse to join; this is the *Masonic* organization, which exists everywhere in our country, and which, as Mr. Powderly has expressly pointed out to us, unites employer and worker in a brotherhood very advantageous for the latter, but which numbers in its ranks hardly a single Catholic. Freely [nobly — de grand coeur] renouncing the advantages which the Church and their consciences forbid, workingmen form associations [join — se forment], having nothing in common with the deadly designs of the enemies of religion and seeking only mutual protection and help, and the legitimate assertion of their rights. But here they also find themselves threatened with condemnation, and so deprived of [hindered from — privés] their only means of defense. Is it surprising that they should be astonished at this and that they ask *Why?*[7]

4. Let us now consider the objections made against this sort of organization.

(a) It is objected that in these organizations Catholics are mixed with Protestants, to the peril of their faith. Naturally, yes, they are mixed with Protestants in the workers' associations,[8] precisely as they are at their work; for in a mixed people like ours, the separation of religious in social affairs is not possible. But to suppose that the faith of our Catholics suffers thereby is not to know the Catholic workers of America who are not like the workingmen of so many European countries — misguided and perverted children, looking on their Mother the Church as a hostile stepmother — but they are intelligent, well instructed and devoted children ready to give their blood, as they continually give their means (although small and hard-earned) [hard-earned — chétifs et péniblement gagnés] for her support and protection. And in fact it is not in the present case that Catholics are mixed with Protestants, but rather that Protestants are admitted to the advantages of an association, two-thirds of whose members and the principal officers [many of whose members and officers — des deux tiers des membres et les officiers principaux] are Catholics; and in a country like ours their exclusion would be simply impossible.

(b) But it is said, could there not be substituted for such an organization confraternities which would unite the workingmen under the direction of the priests and the direct influence of religion? I answer frankly that I do not believe that either possible or necessary in our country. I sincerely admire the efforts of this sort which are made in countries where the workers are led astray by the enemies of religion; but thanks be to God, that is not our condition. We find that in our country the presence and explicit influence of the clergy would not be advisable where our citizens, without distinction of religious belief, come together in regard to their industrial interests alone. Without going so far, we have abundant means for making our

[7] The last sentence of the paragraph was entirely omitted in the English version.

[8] The first part of the parallel was omitted in English: "avec les Protestants dans les associations des travailleurs, précisément comme ils sont dans le travaux mêmes."

working people faithful Catholics, and simple good sense advises us not to go to extremes.

(c) Again, it is objected that the liberty of such an organization exposes Catholics to the evil influences of the most dangerous associates, even of atheists, communists, and anarchists. That is true; but it is one of the trials of faith which our brave American Catholics are accustomed to meet almost daily, and which they know how to disregard with good sense and firmness. The press of our country tells us and the president of the Knights of Labor has related to us, how these violent and aggressive elements have endeavored to seize authority in their councils, or to inject their poison into the principles of the association; but they also verify with what determination these evil spirits [machinators — mauvais esprits] have been repulsed and defeated. The presence among our citizens of this destructive element, which has come for the most part from certain nations of Europe, is assuredly for us an occasion of lively regrets and careful precautions; it is an inevitable fact, however, but one which the union between the Church and her children in our country renders comparatively free from danger. In truth, the only grave danger would come from an alienation between the Church and her children, which nothing would more certainly occasion than imprudent condemnations.

(d) An especially weighty charge is drawn from the outbursts of violence, even to bloodshed, which have characterized [accompanied — charactérizé] several of the strikes inaugurated by labor organizations. Concerning this, three things are to be remarked: first, strikes are not an invention of the Knights of Labor, but a means almost everywhere and always resorted to by employees in our land and elsewhere to protest against what they consider unjust and to demand their rights; secondly in such a struggle of the poor and indignant multitudes against hard and obstinate monopoly, anger and violence [outbursts of anger — colère et le violence] are often as inevitable as they are regrettable; thirdly, the laws and chief authorities of the Knights of Labor, far from encouraging violence or the occasions of it, exercise a powerful influence to hinder it, and to keep strikes within the limits of good order and legitimate action. A careful examination of the acts of violence which have marked the struggle between capital and labor during the past year, leaves us convinced that it would be unjust to attribute them to the association of the Knights of Labor. This was but one of several associations of workers that took part in the strikes, and their chief officers, according to disinterested witnesses, used every possible effort to appease the anger of the crowds and to prevent the excesses which, in my judgment, could not justly be attributed to them. Doubtless among the Knights of Labor as among thousands of other workingmen, there are violent, or even wicked and criminal men, who have committed inexcusable deeds of violence, and have urged their associates to do the same; but to attribute this to the organization, it seems to me, would be as unreasonable as to attribute to the Church the follies and crimes of her children against which she protests.[9] I repeat that in such a struggle of the great masses of the people against the mail-clad power, which, as it is acknowledged, often refuses them the simple rights of humanity and justice, it is vain to expect that every error and every act of violence can be avoided; and to dream that this struggle can be prevented, or that we can deter the multitudes from organizing, which is their only practical means [hope — moyen pratique] of success, would be to ignore the nature and forces of human society in times like ours. The part of Christian prudence evidently is to try to hold the hearts of the multitude by the bonds of love, in order to control their actions by the principles of faith, justice and charity, to acknowledge frankly the truth and justice in their cause, in order to deter them from what would be false and criminal, and thus to turn into a legitimate, peaceable and beneficent contest what could easily become for the masses of our people a volcanic abyss, like that which society fears and the Church deplores in Europe.

Upon this point I insist strongly, because, from an intimate acquaintance with the social conditions of our country I am profoundly convinced that here we are touching upon a subject which not only concerns the rights of the working classes, who ought to be especially dear to the Church which our Divine Lord sent to evangelize the poor, but with which are bound up the fundamental interests of the Church and of human society for the future. This is a point which I desire, in a few additional words to develop more clearly.

5. Whoever meditates upon the ways in which divine Providence is guiding contemporary history cannot fail to remark how important is the part which the power of the people takes therein at present and must take in the future. We behold, with profound sadness, the efforts of the prince of darkness to make this power dangerous to the social weal by withdrawing the masses of the people from the influence of religion, and impelling them towards the ruinous paths of license and anarchy. Until now our country presents a picture of altogether different [most consolingly different — tout différent] char-

[9] "Proteste" was translated "strives and protests."

acter — that of a popular power regulated by love of good order, by respect for religion, by obedience to the authority of the laws, not a democracy of license and violence, but that true democracy which aims at the general prosperity through the means of sound principles and good social order.

In order to preserve so desirable a state of things it is absolutely necessary that religion should continue to hold the affections, and thus rule the conduct of the multitudes. As Cardinal Manning has so well written,[10] "In the future era the Church has no longer to deal with princes and parliaments, but with the masses, with the people. Whether we will or no this is our work; we need a new spirit, a new direction of our life and activity." To lose influence over the people would be to lose the future altogether; and it is by the heart, far more than by the understanding, that we must hold and guide this immense power, so mighty either for good or for evil. Among all the glorious titles of the Church which her history has merited for her, there is not one which at present gives her so great influence as that of *Friend of the People*. Assuredly, in our democratic country, it is this title which wins for the Catholic Church not only the enthusiastic devotedness of the millions of her children, but also the respect and admiration of all our citizens, whatever be their religious belief. It is the power of precisely this title which renders persecution almost an impossibility, and which draws toward our holy Church the great heart of the American people.

And since it is acknowledged by all that the great questions of the future are not those of war, of commerce or finance, but the social questions, the questions which concern the improvement of the condition of the great masses of the people, and especially of the working people, it is evidently of supreme importance that the Church should always be found on the side of humanity, of justice toward the multitudes who compose the body of the human family. As the same Cardinal Manning very wisely wrote, "We must admit and accept calmly and with good will that industries and profits must be considered in second place; the moral state and domestic condition of the whole working population must be considered first. I will not venture to formulate the acts of parliament, but here is precisely their fundamental principle for the future. The conditions of the lower classes as are found at present among our people, can not

[10] In the English version this quotation is introduced with the words, "A new task is before us."

and must not continue. On such a basis no social edifice can stand."[11] In our country, especially, this is the inevitable program of the future, and the position which the Church must hold toward the solution is sufficiently obvious. She must certainly not favor the extremes to which the poor multitudes are naturally inclined, but, I repeat, she must withhold them from these extremes by the bonds of affection, by the maternal desire which she will manifest for the concession of all that is just and reasonable in their demands, and by the maternal blessing which she will bestow upon every legitimate means for improving the condition of the people.

6. Now let us consider for a moment the consequences which would inevitably follow from a contrary course, from a lack of sympathy for the working class, from a suspicion of their aims, from a hasty condemnation of their methods.

(a) First, there is the evident danger of the Church's losing in popular estimation her right to be considered the friend of the people. The logic of men's hearts goes swiftly to its conclusions, and this conclusion would be a pernicious one for the people and for the Church. To lose the heart of the people would be a misfortune for which the friendship of the few rich and powerful would be no compensation.

(b) There is a great danger of rendering hostile to the Church the political power of our country, which openly takes sides with the millions who are demanding justice and the improvement of their condition. The accusation of being, *"un-American,"* that is to say, alien to our national spirit, is the most powerful weapon which the enemies of the Church know how to employ against her. It was this cry which aroused the Know-Nothing persecution thirty years ago, and the same would be quickly used again if the opportunity offered itself. To appreciate the gravity of this danger it is well to remark that not only are the rights of the working classes loudly proclaimed by each of our two great political parties, but it is very probably [not im-

---

[11] The *Moniteur* version of Manning's text was cited as from, "Miscellanies, Vol. 2, p. 81," and read as follows: "I know I am treading on a very difficult subject, but I feel confident of this, that we must face it, and that we must face it calmly, justly, and with a willingness to put labor and the profits of labor second — the moral state and domestic life of the whole working population first. I will not venture to draw up such an act of Parliament further than to lay down this principle. These things (the present condition of the poor in England) cannot go on; these things ought not to go on. The accumulation of wealth in the land, the piling up of wealth like mountains, in the possession of classes or individuals, cannot go on. No commonwealth can rest on such foundations."

probable — très probable] that, in our approaching national elections there will be a candidate for the office of President of the United States as the special representative of these complaints and demands of the masses. Now, to seek to crush by an ecclesiastical condemnation an organization which represents nearly [more than — presque] 500,000 votes, and which has already so respectable and so universally recognized a place in the political arena, would to speak frankly, be considered by the American people as not less ridiculous as it is rash. To alienate from ourselves the friendship of the people would be to run great risk of losing the respect which the Church has won in the estimation of the American nation, and of destroying the state of peace and prosperity which form so admirable a contrast with her condition in some so-called Catholic countries. Already in these months past, a murmur of popular anger and of threats against the Church has made itself heard, and it is necessary that we should move with much precaution.[12]

(c) A third danger, and the one which touches our hearts the most, is the risk of losing the love of the children of the Church, and of pushing them into an attitude of resistance against their Mother. The whole world presents no more beautiful spectable than that of their filial devotion and obedience. But it is necessary to recognize that, in our age and in our country, obedience cannot be blind. We would greatly deceive ourselves if we expected it. Our Catholic working men sincerely believe that they are only seeking justice, and seeking it by legitimate means. A condemnation would be considered both false and unjust, and would not be accepted [and therefore, not binding — et ne serait pas acceptée]. We might indeed preach to them submission and confidence in the Church, but these good dispositions could hardly go so far. They love the Church, and they wish to save their souls, but they must also earn their living, and labor is now so organized that without belonging to the organization there is little chance to earn one's living.

Behold, then, the consequences to be feared. Thousands of the most devoted children of the Church would believe themselves repulsed by their Mother and would live without practicing their religion. The revenues of the Church, which with us come entirely from the free offerings of the people, would suffer immensely, and it would be the same with Peter's pence. The ranks of the secret societies would be

---

[12] The English read, "Angry utterances have not been wanting of late, and it is well that we should act prudently."

filled with Catholics, who had been up to now faithful.[13] The Holy See, which has constantly received from the Catholics of America proofs of almost unparalleled devotedness, would be considered not as a paternal authority, but as a harsh and unjust power. Here are assuredly effects, the occasion of which wisdom and prudence must avoid.

In a word, we have seen quite recently the sad and threatening confusion caused by the condemnation inflicted by an Archbishop upon a single priest in vindication of discipline — a condemnation which the Archbishop believed to be just and necessary, but which fell upon a priest who was regarded as the friend of the people. Now, if the consequences have been so deplorable for the peace of the Church from the condemnation of only one priest, because he was considered to be the friend of the people, what will not be the consequences to be feared from a condemnation which would fall directly upon the people themselves in the exercise of what they consider their legitimate right?[14]

7. But besides the danger which would result from such a condemnation and the impossibility of having it respected and observed [putting it into effect — de la faire respecter et observer] one should note that the form of this organization is so little permanent, as the press indicates nearly every day, that in the estimation of practical men in our country, it cannot last very many years.[15] Whence it follows that it is not necessary, even if it were just and prudent, to level the solemn condemnations of the Church against something which will vanish of itself. The social agitation will, indeed, last as long as there are social evils to be remedied; but the forms of organization and procedure meant for the attainment of this end are necessarily provisional and transient. They are also very numerous, for I have already remarked that the Knights of Labor is only one among several forms of labor organizations. To strike, then, at one of these forms would be to commence a war without system and without

[13] The variant reading in English was, "Thousands of the Church's most devoted children, whose affection is her greatest comfort, and whose free offerings are her chief support, would consider themselves repulsed by their Mother, and would live without practising their religion. Catholics who have hitherto shunned the secret societies, would be sorely tempted to join their ranks."

[14] This whole paragraph referring to the case of Dr. Edward McGlynn was elided in the English version.

[15] The English read: "It is also very important that we should carefully consider another reason against condemnation, arising from the unstable and transient character of the organization in question. It is frequently remarked by the press and by attentive observers that this special form of association has in it so little permanence that, in its present shape, it is not likely to last many years."

end; it would be to exhaust the forces of the Church in chasing a crowd of changing and uncertain phantasms. The American people behold with perfect composure and confidence the progress of our social contest, and have not the least fear of not being able to protect themselves against any excesses or dangers that may occasionally arise. And, to speak with the most profound respect, but also with the frankness which duty requires of me, it seems to me that prudence suggests, and that even the dignity of the Church demands that we should not offer to America an ecclesiastical protection for which she does not ask, and of which she believes she has no need.

8. In all this discussion I have not at all spoken of Canada, nor of the condemnation concerning the Knights of Labor in Canada. For we would consider it an impertinence to involve ourselves in the ecclesiastical affairs of another country which has a hierarchy of its own, and with whose needs and social conditions we do not pretend to be acquainted.[16] We believe, however, that the circumstances of a people almost entirely Catholic, as in lower Canada, must be very different from those of a mixed population like ours; moreover, that the documents submitted to the Holy Office are not the present constitution of the organization in our country, and that we, therefore, ask nothing involving an inconsistency on the part of the Holy See, which passed sentence *juxta exposita*.[17] It is of the condition of things in the United States that we speak, and we trust that in these matters we are not presumptuous in believing that we are competent to judge. Now, as I have already indicated, out of the seventy-five archbishops and bishops of the United States, there are about five who would desire a condemnation of the Knights of Labor, such as we know them in our country; so that our hierarchy are almost unanimous in protesting against such a condemnation. Surely, such a fact ought to have great weight in deciding the question. If there are difficulties in the case, it seems to me that the prudence and experience of our bishops and the wise rules of the Third Plenary Council ought to suffice for their solution.

9. Finally, to sum it all up, it seems clear to me that the Holy See should not entertain the idea of condemning an association:

1. When the condemnation does not seem to be *justified* either by the letter or the spirit of its constitution, its law and the declaration of its leaders.

---

[16] "Les besoins" was not translated.

[17] In the *Moniteur*, it read "*localiter et juxta exposita.*"

2. When the condemnation does not seem *necessary,* in view of the transient form of the organization and the social condition of the United States.

3. When it does not seem to be *prudent,* because of the reality of the grievances of the workers, and the admission of them made by the American people.

4. When it would be *dangerous* for the reputation of the Church in our democratic country, and possibly even arouse persecution.

5. When it would be *ineffectual* in compelling the obedience of our Catholic workers, who would regard it as false and unjust.[18]

6. When it would be *destructive* instead of beneficial in its effects, impelling the children of the Church to disobey their Mother, and even to join condemned societies, which they have thus far shunned.

7. When it would be almost *ruinous* for the financial maintenance of the Church in our country, and for the Peter's pence.[19]

8. When it would turn into suspicion and hostility the outstanding devotedness of our Catholic people toward the Holy See.

9. When it would be regarded as a cruel blow to the authority of the bishops of the United States, who, it is well known, protest against such a condemnation.

Now, I hope the considerations here presented have shown with sufficient clearness that such would be the condemnation[20] of the Knights of Labor in the United States.

Therefore, with complete confidence, I leave the case[21] to the wisdom and prudence of your Eminence and the Holy See.

Rome, February 20, 1887.

J. Cardinal Gibbons,
Archbishop of Baltimore.

127. Cardinal Gibbons Opposes the Condemnation of the Works of Henry George, February 25, 1887

A SECOND major social question which agitated American Catholic circles in the 1880's centered around the single tax proposals of Henry George (1839–1897), and the advocacy of George's theories by Father Edward

[18] The fifth reason in the official English version was: "When it would probably be inefficacious, owing to the general conviction that it would be unjust."

[19] This point was completely omitted in the *Moniteur* translation.

[20] The official English read "the effect of condemnation."

[21] The English inserted "the decision of the case."

McGlynn (1837–1900), pastor of St. Stephen's Church, New York City. McGlynn's superior, Archbishop Michael A. Corrigan, forbade him to participate in the movement, but McGlynn refused to obey and was removed from his pastorate in January, 1887, and later excommunicated by the Holy See. The New York pastor was a powerful orator and had an immense following which gave the controversy very wide publicity. A number of Catholic churchmen believed that George's ideas on the single tax undermined the right of private property, and they urged the Holy See, therefore, to put his books on the Index. Cardinal Gibbons felt that this would be a serious mistake, and he took occasion during his visit to Rome in the winter of 1887 to address a letter to Cardinal Simeoni, Prefect of Propaganda, in which he strongly deprecated any action of this kind. Gibbons' protest delayed matters, but it did not prevent the Holy Office from condemning George's teachings in February, 1889, although it was stated that by reason of the highly controversial nature of the case the condemnation need not be published. Following is the text of the letter of Gibbons to Simeoni. Source: Archives of the Archdiocese of Baltimore, unclassified, printed copy in French entitled "La question des écrits de Henri George."

Your Eminence:

I have already had the honor of presenting to your Eminence my views on the social questions which agitate America, especially with regard to their bearing on the association of the Knights of Labor. But recently another form of social debate has developed relating to the doctrines of Mr. Henry George, an American author identified with the working classes. And since my arrival in Rome I have heard the idea discussed that the writings of Henry George should be put on the Index.[1] After having fully thought over the subject I believe it my duty to submit to your Eminence the reasons which seem to me to demonstrate that a formal condemnation of the works of Henry George would be neither opportune nor useful.

1. Henry George is in no way the originator of the theory which he advocates concerning the right of ownership in land. In his principal book, "Progress and Poverty," he cites precisely the teachings of Herbert Spencer and John Stuart Mill, two of England's chief authors. And in the English periodical work, the "Contemporary Review," of November 1886, a distinguished Professor quotes them more fully to prove, as he says, that Mr. George is only a plagiarist of these celebrated authors.[2] Now it seems to me that the world will judge it a bit singular if the Holy See attacks the work of a humble American artisan instead of attacking his great masters. And if there

---

[1] Up to 1887 George's principal works were *Progress and Poverty* (1879); *Social Problems* (1883); *Protection or Free Trade* (1886).

[2] H. Sidgwick, "Economic Socialism," *Contemporary Review,* L (November, 1886), 629.

are some who, therefore, think that it is the duty of the Holy See to pronounce judgment on Spencer and Mill, perhaps it would be prudent first to take counsel with their Eminences Cardinals Manning and Newman on the opportuneness of such action.[3]

2. It is well to remark that the theory of Henry George differs from that which is ordinarily called Communism and Socialism. Because as Father Valentine Steccanella shows very well in his work on Communism, published by the Propaganda Press in 1882,[4] this implies "the abolition of private property and the collectivization of all goods in the hands of the State." Now anyone who has read the books of Henry George ought to recognize that he neither teaches this nor does he at all wish it. On the contrary, he maintains the absolute ownership of all the fruits of human energy and industry, even when they amount to great riches acquired either by labor or heredity. It is only with regard to land itself that he would wish to limit the ownership of individuals by an extension of the *supremum dominum* of the state; and on this point he has expressly stated that he would in no way dispossess the actual owners; but he would desire simply that our system of taxation be changed in such a way that only the land would provide taxes and not the fruits of human industry. One can see, therefore, that in the practical form in which the controversy presents itself to the American public it is simply a question of the government's power over individual ownership of land. And on that there is this to be noted:

a) Anyone who studies properly the question of the relations of the State to the right of ownership of land, as it is treated by Father Steccanella and by other Catholic writers, or as it is regulated by the laws of taxation and the care of the poor in some countries, and especially in England, cannot help but understand that it is a very complex question, very much subject to the diverse circumstances of time and place, and not yet ready to be resolved by a decisive judgment.

b) The question is already before the American public as a political issue, and in so practical an arena it will soon find its end;[5]

[3] "Perhaps the only ecclesiast who knew George personally was Cardinal Manning, who, in the previous year [1885], had discussed with him his proposals to alleviate the world as written in his book, *Progress and Poverty*" (Shane Leslie, *Henry Edward Manning. His Life and Labours* [London, 1921], p. 353).

[4] Valentino Steccanella, S.J., *Del communismo esame critico filosofico e politico* (Rome, 1882).

[5] Gibbons was referring to George's unsuccessful effort to be elected Mayor of New York City in the fall elections of 1886 when he was defeated by Abram S. Hewitt.

c) As Mr. George himself realizes, it is only the legislative power of the country which could bring about such a disposition of affairs; and it is quite certain that neither a Congress nor a legislature will ever be found that would vote for such a profound change in social relations, nor a President who would approve it.

d) In a country such as ours, which is by no means a country of doctrinaires and visionaries, speculative theory will not be dangerous, nor will it live long after its practical application will have been rejected; one may, therefore, in all certainty, let it die by itself.

3. Certain recent events in our country have occasioned a profound and widespread popular excitement having an intimate relation to this question.[6] Therefore, your Eminence understands better than I how necessary it is for us to have care not only to speak the truth, but also to choose well the time and the circumstances to say it, so that our action may produce salutary and not fatal results. It seems evident, therefore, that even if there is certainly a need for condemnation, now is not the time to speak out.

4. Finally, it would be prudent to apply here the principle of morality which counsels one not to pronounce a sentence the consequences of which will probably be adverse rather than favorable to the good end proposed. Now I am sure that such would be the result of a condemnation of the works of Mr. George. It would give them a popular importance that they would not ever otherwise have, and would excite an appetite of curiosity that would make them sell by the thousands of copies, and would thus extend immensely the influences that the condemnation sought to restrain and prevent.

Once again, in dealing with so practicable a people as the Americans, in whose genius bizarre and impractical ideas quickly find their grave, it seems to me that prudence suggests that absurdities and fallacies be allowed to perish by themselves, and not run the risk of giving them an importance, a life and an artificial force by the intervention of the tribunals of the Church.

J. Card. Gibbons
Archbishop of Baltimore.

Rome, February 25, 1887.

---

[6] Here the cardinal was alluding to the removal of Father Edward McGlynn from the pastorate of St. Stephen's Church, New York, by Archbishop Corrigan on January 14, 1887, and the storm that this action stirred up among McGlynn's many followers. For the role of McGlynn in the single tax movement of Henry George, cf. John Tracy Ellis, *The Life of James Cardinal Gibbons, Archbishop of Baltimore, 1834–1921* (Milwaukee, 1952), I, 547–594.

128. The Roman Sermon of the American Cardinal on Church and State in the United States, March 25, 1887

FEW subjects in American religious history have held more interest, or caused more controversy, than that of the relations of Church and State. From the time of Archbishop Carroll to our own day the Catholic hierarchy of the United States has repeatedly expressed its approval of the separation of Church and State as it has existed in this country since the beginning of the Republic (cf. John Tracy Ellis, "Church and State: An American Catholic Tradition," *Harper's Magazine,* CCVII [November, 1953], 63–67). The first time these views were publicly voiced in Rome was on the occasion when Cardinal Gibbons took possession of his titular Church of Santa Maria in Trastevere. The sermon was of more than ordinary significance in view of the severely strained relations at that time between the Church and the anticlerical governments of Germany, Italy, and France, countries where there had been a long tradition of union of Church and State. American Catholics were pleased with their new cardinal's pronouncement, and Father Isaac Hecker was doubtless expressing the reaction of the great majority when he remarked how well fitted Gibbons was by his "thorough-going American spirit to interpret us to the peoples and powers of the Old World" ("Cardinal Gibbons and American Institutions," *Catholic World,* XLV [June, 1887], 331). Source: *Catholic Mirror* (Baltimore), April 2, 1887.

It is to me exceedingly gratifying that the Holy Father has assigned as my titular church this beautiful and historic basilica, the first church ever erected in honor of the Virgin Mother of God; and I regard it as an auspicious circumstance that my own Cathedral Church of Baltimore, the oldest cathedral in the United States, is also dedicated to our Blessed Lady. The venerable temple in which we are assembled leads us back to the days of the catacombs. It was founded by Pope St. Callixtus in the year 224.[1] It was reconstructed by Pope Julius in the fourth century, and renovated by another Supreme Pontiff in the twelfth.

That ceaseless solicitude which the Roman Pontiffs have exhibited in erecting the material temples which adorn this city, they have also manifested on a larger scale in building up the spiritual walls of Sion in every age.

Every student of history must be deeply impressed with the overruling action of the Papacy in the evangelization and civilization of

---

[1] The Basilica of Santa Maria in Trastevere dates from Pope Julius I (337–352), not from Pope Callixtus I who reigned over a century before.

the Christian world. I place these words together, for a nation is civilized in proportion as it receives the light of the Gospel. It was the vigilant zeal of the Holy See that sent Augustine to England, and Patrick to Ireland, and Pelagius to Scotland, and that sent Francis Xavier to evangelize the Indies; and all those other heroes of Christ's Church who bore, amid the sufferings and trials, the bright light of truth into the regions of pagan darkness. And coming down to a later period, scarcely were the United States formed into an independent government when Pius VI, of happy memory, established there the Catholic hierarchy and appointed the illustrious John Carroll first Bishop of Baltimore. This event, so important to us, occurred less than a hundred years ago — a long period, indeed, in our history, but how brief in that of Rome eternal! Our Catholic community in those days numbered only a few thousand souls, scattered chiefly through the States of New York, Pennsylvania, and Maryland, and were served by the merest handful of priests. Thanks to the fructifying grace of God, the grain of mustard seed then planted has grown to be a large tree, spreading its branches over the length and the width of our fair land. Where only one bishop was found in the beginning of this century, there are now seventy-five serving as many dioceses and vicariates. For their great progress under God and the fostering care of the Holy See we are indebted in no small degree to the civil liberty we enjoy in our enlightened republic.

Our Holy Father, Leo XIII, in his luminous encyclical on the constitution of Christian States,[2] declares that the Church is not committed to any particular form of civil government. She adapts herself to all; she leavens all with the sacred leaven of the Gospel. She has lived under absolute empires; she thrives under constitutional monarchies; she grows and expands under the free republic. She has often, indeed, been hampered in her divine mission and has had to struggle for a footing wherever despotism has cast its dark shadow like the plant excluded from the sunlight of heaven, but in the genial air of liberty she blossoms like the rose!

For myself, as a citizen of the United States, without closing my eyes to our defects as a nation, I proclaim, with a deep sense of pride and gratitude, and in this great capitol of Christendom, that I belong to a country where the civil government holds over us the aegis of its protection without interfering in the legitimate exercise of our sublime mission as ministers of the Gospel of Jesus Christ.

[2] *Immortale Dei,* November 1, 1885, John J. Wynne, S.J. (Ed.), *The Great Encyclical Letters of Pope Leo XIII* (New York, 1903), p. 109.

Our country has liberty without license, authority without despotism. Hers is no spirit of exclusiveness. She has no frowning fortifications to repel the invader, for we are at peace with all the world. In the consciousness of her strength and of her good will to all nations she rests secure. Her harbors are open in the Atlantic and Pacific to welcome the honest immigrant who comes to advance his temporal interest and to find a peaceful home.

But, while we are acknowledged to have a free government, we do not, perhaps, receive due credit for possessing also a strong government. Yes, our nation is strong, and her strength lies, under Providence, in the majesty and supremacy of the law, in the loyalty of her citizens to that law, and in the affection of our people for their free institutions.

There are, indeed, grave social problems which are now engaging the earnest attention of the citizens of the United States. But I have no doubt that, with God's blessings, these problems will be solved by the calm judgment and sound sense of the American people without violence, or revolution, or injury to individual right.

As an evidence of his benevolence and good will to the great republic of the West, as evidence of his appreciation of the venerable hierarchy of the United States, and as an expression of his kind condescension for the ancient See of Baltimore, our Holy Father, Leo XIII, has been graciously pleased to exalt its present incumbent in my humble person to the dignity of the purple.

For this mark of exalted favor I offer the Holy Father my profound thanks in my own name and in the name of the clergy and people under my charge. I venture also to thank him in the name of my venerable colleagues the bishops, the clergy, as well as the Catholic laity of the United States. I presume to thank him also in the name of our separated brethren of America who, though not sharing our faith, have shown that they are not insensible to the honor conferred on our common country, and have again and again expressed their warm admiration of the enlightened statesmanship, the apostolic virtues, and benevolent charities of the illustrious Pontiff who now sits in the Chair of Peter.

129. The Laying of the Cornerstone of the Catholic University of America, May 24, 1888

AT THE Second Plenary Council of Baltimore in October, 1866, the idea of a university for American Catholics was seriously discussed for the first time by the hierarchy, although nothing came of it at that time. In the interval between the plenary councils of 1866 and 1884 the subject continued to be urged by a number of leaders such as Thomas A. Becker (1832–1899), first Bishop of Wilmington, Isaac T. Hecker (1819–1888), founder of the Paulists, and by none more insistently than Bishop Spalding of Peoria. It was Spalding's notable sermon of November 16, 1884, during the Third Plenary Council, and the fact that he was able to secure the first substantial grant of funds, that helped to make the project a reality. It was fitting, therefore, that when the cornerstone of Caldwell Hall, the original building, was laid in the presence of President Grover Cleveland and a large assembly of distinguished guests, Spalding should have been chosen to deliver the principal address. The university opened on November 13, 1889, with forty-six students; the enrollment in February, 1956, was 3350 students divided among the ten schools of the university. Source: John Lancaster Spalding, "University Education," *Education and the Higher Life* (Chicago: A. C. McClurg and Co., 1891), pp. 178–179, 193, 195–198.

The special significance of our American Catholic history is not found in the phases of our life which attract attention, and are a common theme for declamation; but it lies in the fact that our example proves that the Church can thrive where it is neither protected nor persecuted, but is simply left to itself to manage its own affairs and to do its work. Such an experiment had never been made when we became an independent people, and its success is of world-wide import, because this is the modern tendency and the position toward the Church which all the nations will sooner or later assume; just as they all will be forced finally to accept popular rule. The great underlying principle of democracy, — that men are brothers and have equal rights, and that God clothes the soul with freedom, — is a truth taught by Christ, is a truth proclaimed by the Church; and the faith of Christians in this principle, in spite of hesitations and misgivings, of oppositions and obstacles and inconceivable difficulties, has finally given to it its modern vigor and beneficent power. . . .

The aim the best now propose to themselves is to provide not wealth or pleasure, or better machinery or more leisure, but a higher and more effective kind of education; and hence whatever one's preoccupation, whether social, political, religious, or industrial, the question of education forces itself upon his attention. Pedagogy has grown to be a science, and chairs are founded in universities to expound the theory and art of teaching. The learning of former times has become the ignorance of our own; and the classical writings have ceased to be the treasure-house of knowledge, and in consequence their educational value has diminished. . . . The ancients, indeed, excel us in the sense for form and symmetry. There is also a freshness in their words, a joyousness in their life, a certain heroic temper in their thinking and acting, which give them power to engage the emotions; and hence to deny them exceptional educational value is to take a partial view. But even though we grant that the study of their literatures is in certain respects the best intellectual discipline, education, it must be admitted, means knowledge as well as training; and thorough training is something more than refined taste. It is strength as well, and ability to think in many directions and on many subjects. Nothing known to men should escape the attention of the wise; for the knowledge of the age determines what is demanded of the scholar. And since it is our privilege to live at a time when knowledge is increasing more rapidly even than population and wealth, we must, if we hope to stand in the front ranks of those who know, keep pace with the onward movement of mind. To turn away from this outburst of splendor and power; to look back to pagan civilization or Christian barbarism, — is to love darkness more than light. Aristotle is a great mind, but his learning is crude and his ideas of Nature are frequently grotesque. Saint Thomas is a powerful intellect; but his point of view in all that concerns natural knowledge has long since vanished from sight. What poverty of learning does not the early mediaeval scheme of education reveal; and when in the twelfth century the idea of a university rises in the best minds, how incomplete and vague it is! Amid the ruins of castles and cathedrals we grow humble, and think ourselves inferior to men who thus could build. But they were not as strong as we, and they led a more ignorant and blinder life; and so when we read of great names of the past, the mists of illusion fill the skies, and our eyes are dimmed by the glory of clouds tinged with the splendors of a sun that has set.

Certainly a true university will be the home both of ancient wisdom and of new learning; it will teach the best that is known, and encourage research; it will stimulate thought, refine taste, and awaken the love of excellence; it will be at once a scientific institute, a school of culture, and a training ground for the business of life; it will educate the minds that give direction to the age; it will be a nursery of ideas, a centre of influence. The good we do men is quickly lost, the truth we leave them remains forever; and therefore the aim of the best education is to enable students to see what is true, and to inspire them with the love of all truth. Professional knowledge brings most profit to the individual; but philosophy and literature, science and art, elevate and refine the spirit of a whole people, and hence the university will make culture its first aim, and its scope will widen as the thoughts and attainments of men are enlarged and multiplied. Here if anywhere shall be found teachers whose one passion is the love of truth, which is the love of God and of man; who look on all things with a serene eye; who bring to every question a calm, unbiassed mind; who, where the light of the intellect fails, walk by faith and accept the omen of hope; who understand that to be distrustful of science is to lack culture, to doubt the good of progress is to lack knowledge, and to question the necessity of religion is to want wisdom; who know that in a God-made and God-governed world it must lie in the nature of things that reason and virtue should tend to prevail, in spite of the fact that in every age the majority of men think foolishly and act unwisely. . . .

130. Pope Leo XIII's Plea for the Italian Immigrants in America, December 10, 1888

THE first great wave of immigration to the United States before the Civil War had stamped the Catholic Church as the Church of the immigrant. That character became even more indelibly impressed during the so-called New Immigration of the years after 1880. Among the new arrivals the Italians occupied a prominent place, and since they were practically all at least nominal Catholics, it put a severe strain on the Church to provide adequate ministration for them. In 1880 there were only 44,230 Italian-born persons in the country, but by 1900 the number had risen to 484,027, and in the first decade of the twentieth century 2,104,309 arrived from Italy. Not all of these remained, however, for of all the late immigrants the Italians showed a greater tendency to return home after a time, and by 1910 it was estimated that about 800,000 had gone back to Italy. The plight of the Italians was aggravated by the abuses practiced against them through tricky labor contracts. Their condition became well known abroad and it was with a view to helping these unfortunate people, both spiritually and materially, that Pope Leo XIII addressed a special plea to the American hierarchy in December, 1888, in which he asked for their assistance in alleviating the lot of the Italian immigrants in this country. Source: Latin text, *American Ecclesiastical Review,* I (February, 1889), 43–48; English translation adapted from the New York *Freeman's Journal,* January 5, 1889.

How toilsome and disastrous is the condition of those who for some years have been migrating out of Italy to the regions of America in search of a livelihood is so well known to you that nothing is to be gained by dwelling on it. Indeed, you see these evils at first hand and several of you have sorrowfully called our attention to them in repeated letters. It is to be deplored that so many unfortunate Italians, forced by poverty to change their residence, should rush into evils which are often worse than the ones they have desired to flee from. For very often to labors of various kinds that take away the life of the body, there is added the ruin of souls. At the outset the emigrants' crossing itself is full of dangers and injuries; for many of them fall into the hands of avaricious men whose slaves, as it were, they become, and then herded in ships and inhumanly treated, they are gradually depraved in their nature. And when they have reached the desired land, being ignorant of both the language and the locale, and engrossed in their daily toil, they become the victims of the trickery of the dishonest or the powerful by whom they are employed.[1] Those who by their own industry succeed sufficiently to assure for themselves a livelihood, associating constantly with people who regard everything from the point of view of business or profit, little by little lose the nobler feelings of human nature and learn to live like those who have set all their hopes and thoughts on this earth. To all this are added the ever present excitement of the passions, and the deceits practiced by the sects which flourish widely there to the injury of religion and which draw many into the path leading to destruction.

What is more lamentable among these evils is that because of the great multitude of these emigrants, the extent of the territory, and the local difficulties, it is by no means easy to provide these people with the saving care of ministers of God familiar with the Italian language, who would teach them the word of life, administer to them the sacraments, and provide for them timely help by which their souls might be lifted up in the hope of heavenly goods and their spiritual life be sustained and invigorated. In many places, therefore, there are very few who have a priest when they are dying, and there are many of the newly-born for whom there is none to administer the sacrament of regeneration. There are many who enter into marriage without regard

[1] Leo XIII was referring here to the notorious treatment of the Italian immigrants under the *padrone* system which made them virtual slaves to their greedy fellow countrymen and others who exploited them through labor contracts in the United States and other countries. For these abuses cf. Robert F. Foerster, *The Italian Emigration of Our Times* (Cambridge, 1919), p. 390 ff.

to the Church's laws, and thereby give rise to an offspring similar to their parents. Thus there is everywhere with this people a decay of Christian morality and a growth of wickedness.[2]

Reflecting on all these things, and grieving at the wretched lot of so many whom we perceive to be wandering like sheep without a shepherd through steep paths and dangerous places, and at the same time mindful of the eternal Shepherd's love and warning, we have thought it our duty to render every possible help to them, to prepare wholesome nourishment, and to consult in every practical way for their good and salvation. We have been all the more inclined to enter upon this undertaking because of our love for men sprung from the same soil as ourselves, and because a sure hope inspires us that we shall not lack your own interest in the matter and your helpful assistance. Wherefore, we have taken care to have this matter considered by the Sacred Congregation of the Propaganda, and we have commanded it diligently to seek out and to examine the remedies by which so many evils and inconveniences can be removed, or at least be alleviated, and to propose to us what especially can be done both for the salvation of souls and for softening, as far as may be, the emigrants' hardships. But since the most potent cause of the growing evils is the lack of a priestly ministry through which heavenly grace is imparted and increased, we have determined to send to your country a number of priests from Italy accustomed to the language of their countrymen, to teach them the doctrine of faith and the unknown or neglected precepts of Christian life, to provide among them a salutary administration of the sacraments, to form the growing offspring to religion and good conduct, to help them in every way by advice and assistance, and to foster them by priestly care. To effect this the more conveniently we established by our letter of the 16th of November of last year, under the Fisherman's ring, an apostolic college of priests in the episcopal see of Piacenza, under the charge of our Venerable Brother John Baptist, Bishop of Piacenza,[3] so that ecclesiastics who are moved by a love of

---

[2] That the spiritual plight of the Italian immigrants was real may be gleaned from the statement made by Archbishop Corrigan of New York to Cardinal Manning on February 10, 1888, when he said, "There are 80,000 Italians in this city, of whom only two per cent have been in the habit of hearing Mass" (quoted in Shane Leslie, *Henry Edward Manning. His Life and Labours* [London, 1921], p. 358). For the question of the Church and the Italian immigrants cf. Henry J. Browne, "The 'Italian Problem' in the Catholic Church of the United States, 1880–1900," *Historical Records and Studies,* XXXV (1946), 46–72.

[3] Giovanni B. Scalabrini (1839–1905), Bishop of Piacenza, founded the Congregation of Missionaries of St. Charles Borromeo of which two priests and a lay brother arrived in New York in July, 1888, to begin work among the

Christ may there cultivate those studies and be exercised in those employments and that sort of training by means of which they may earnestly and successfully perform the ministry of Christ for the scattered Italians and become fit dispensers of God's mysteries.

Among the students of this college, which we wish to be regarded as a sort of seminary of ministers of God for the salvation of Italians dwelling in America, we desire also that young men from your own country, children of Italian parents, be received and instructed; providing they are called to the vineyard of the Lord and have a wish to be initiated into Holy Orders, so that, having been ordained and returning to you, as many of them as there shall be need of will fulfill under your pastoral authority the work of the apostolic ministry. Nor do we doubt that on their return they will be received by you with fatherly love, and that also they will receive the necessary faculties for exercising the sacred ministry among their countrymen, subject to the admonition of the parish priest. For they will come to you to labor under the authority of those of you in whose dioceses they dwell. Especially at the outset of the work there will not, by any means, be so many of these helpers as the circumstances and times demand, nor will the labors of those who are sent be on a par with the number and needs of the faithful in such a way that the priests assigned to the care of souls can be appointed to separate and remote places. Wherefore, we deem it best that in dioceses where Italians are numerous there be common residences for these priests, so that they may go forth separately into the neighboring areas and perform their sacred functions on these expeditions. But in what manner or in what places these can best be established will be for your foresight to decide. All these things which we have thought to belong to our apostolic providence we have taken pains to signify to you in this letter. If any of you should discover, either by his own sense and judgment, or by consultation with his brethren, anything further that can be done by us for the welfare or comfort of those in whose behalf we are writing, let him know that he will do us a favor if he will carefully relate his proposal to the Sacred Congregation of the Propaganda.

From this work which we have undertaken for the care and defence of many souls that lack every comfort of the Catholic religion, we promise ourselves much fruit, especially if, as we hope, there be added

---

Italian immigrants. In the following year the Missionary Sisters of the Sacred Heart of St. Francesca Cabrini (1850–1917) opened the first of their numerous American houses for the spiritual care of their fellow countrymen when Archbishop Corrigan blessed the ophanage on 59th Street, New York, on May 3, 1889.

for its support and protection, the interest and assistance of the faithful whose means are equal to their piety. As for the rest, praying the most benign God, Who wishes that all men shall be saved and come to the knowledge of the truth, that He will propitiously inspire this undertaking and give prosperous increase to it, we lovingly in the Lord, impart the apostolic benediction of our inmost affection to you, Venerable Brethren, and to the entire clergy and faithful over whom you are set.

Given at Rome, in St. Peter's, the 10th of December, 1888, in the eleventh year of our pontificate.

Leo XIII., Pope

131. Charles J. Bonaparte on the American Experience of Separation of Church and State, July 11, 1889

CHARLES J. BONAPARTE (1851–1921) was one of the most distinguished Catholic laymen of his generation. Baltimore-born grandson of King Jerome of Westphalia, brother of Emperor Napoleon I, Harvard-trained, and from a family of wealth, Bonaparte enjoyed all the advantages which such a background afforded. He was especially noted for his zeal in behalf of good government and civil-service reform, having been one of the founders of the National Municipal League and later its president. Theodore Roosevelt appointed Bonaparte to a number of federal offices, naming him Secretary of the Navy in May, 1905, and Attorney General of the United States in December, 1906, where he continued to the end of the administration in March, 1909, and earned for himself widespread fame as a trust-buster. He was always a devout Catholic and had very pronounced views about the need for keeping the Church free from politics and the State out of religious affairs. The excerpts from one of his public addresses that follow were all the more pertinent in being spoken at a time when the A.P.A. were on the rise. The speech was delivered at the centennial celebration of the Catholic societies of the Archdiocese of Baltimore at Bay Ridge, Maryland. Source: Charles J. Bonaparte, *The Catholic Church and American Institutions* (Baltimore: William K. Boyle & Son, 1889), pp. 16–21.

You have all heard and read, many of you, no doubt, often, some, perhaps, *ad nauseam,* that there is an "incompatability" between American institutions and the Catholic Church. . . . Even now it may be, perhaps, sincerely said by a Catholic who is not an American, or an American who is not a Catholic, but I cannot think this opinion is shared by any American Catholic, sufficiently informed to have an intelligent opinion. Nor need I disprove it *a priori;* we have met to commemorate its refutation by the one unanswerable test of experience.

The mustard seed planted on these shores a hundred years ago fell on no ungrateful soil; of this no better proof can be given or reasonably asked than Time has furnished in the stately tree with its deep roots and spreading branches, which has grown from that seed. . . . If we apply to the sum of American institutions the vague and much abused term "liberty," a century's history proves that liberty is good for the Catholic Church, and this is a conclusion of such moment that I feel justified in a further trespass on your patience to briefly weigh its import.

I claim the fact to have been established by a decisive experiment, but opinions may of course, differ as to its explanation; to understand, however, why American liberty has proved thus congenial to the Church, we must first appreciate what, in its essentials, our liberty is, and how it differs from political systems abroad, which usurp or masquerade in the same name. A competent and candid observer asked to indicate the countries whose history during the present century could be read with most pleasure by devout Catholics would unhesitatingly group with the United States, the great English colonies. In old Catholic countries, the Church has often contended with hostility and spoliation from the State; elsewhere she has been steadfast under persecution from non-catholic rulers of arbitrary power; but among all English speaking peoples she has gained ground, and in Canada and Australia and the United States her prosperity has been manifest and her progress rapid. What suits her in our country, then, is something we share with our Northern neighbors and our kinsmen in the great island of the Southern sea, and we share with them a large measure of individual freedom under a popular government.

The genius of our common institutions, is to let each citizen work out his own happiness with little hindrance and little help from the State; the government protects his person and property and enforces his contracts, then leaves him as nearly to himself as the exigencies of national defence and public order permit. To the ephemeral republics which this century has seen rise and fall in Europe, this spirit has been utterly alien; they may have committed the State's authority to many hands, but have made that authority ever more and more arbitrary and far-reaching; in such a republic,

> That worst of tyrants, a usurping crowd

intrudes upon every phase of a man's life, assumes to watch over his coming in and his going out, the management of his property, the education of his children, the care of his health, to dictate even the words he shall use and the clothes he shall wear. The legitimate outcome of the first system is complete religious liberty, to give any creed, not grossly repugnant to the accepted standard of public morals, a fair field, but no favor, for the State to ask only the things of Caesar, leaving to the conscience of each citizen to care for the more lasting interests which lie beyond its humbler sphere.

Under the second system, the State becomes itself a church, a church wanting, indeed, in almost all that makes a church a means of good, but with a potent influence for evil. To be consistent, a paternal government must provide a legal religion; it cannot, in the words of the Great Frederic, "let its subjects go to Hell by the road they like best," and under such a government, the Catholic Church stands face to face with a rival. The Bill of Rights of Maryland declares:

> That, as it is the duty of every man to worship God in such manner as he thinks most acceptable to Him, all persons are equally entitled to protection in their religious liberty. . . .

The aim of ecclesiastical legislation in many European countries is precisely to make all places of worship, public buildings, and all ministers of religion, of whatsoever creed or order, public functionaries, controlled by the State and maintained from the proceeds of taxation. Here the Church goes her way and does her work without caring, almost without thinking, whether the civil rulers for the time being are within or without her fold; there she may be hampered in every function of her ministry by the hostility of such rulers or more gravely embarrassed, more permanently discredited by their compromising friendship. For, even if I scandalize some worthy people by so thinking, I yet think the civil power less dangerous to the Church as a rival, even as an oppressor, than as a patron. The Church of Christ should be no hot-house plant:

> Moored in the rifted rock,
> Proof to the tempests' shock,
> The firmer they root her the harder they blow,

but when fenced about with laws, when sheltered behind privileges and prescriptions, her rugged fibre grows soft and her sturdy frame dainty. When the time of trial comes, — and come it will, for dynasties and their kingdoms, laws and the nations that made them, man and all man's works, must sometime change and pass away, — when all these screens and safe guards of a day fall around her, and she faces again the whirwind of human error and human passion, many sapped boughs shall break and much dead wood claim the pruning knife. It is no trick of theologian's jargon that calls the Church "militant"; she is indeed a fighting body, and her conquests must be held as they were made by valor and discipline and well kept arms, not by a Chinese Wall of timid isolation. Moreover Caesar does not work for nothing: he must be paid for his protection; if he makes heresy treason, he asks that she make treason heresy, and this is little less than a ruinous price for a less than doubtful service.

Here the Church hires no mercenary defender, she guards her own by her own might; no prince or magistrate, no parliament or judge, wielding the clumsy weapon of unconvincing force, is called on to fill a mission for which her clergy have grown unworthy. Her soldiers cannot rust in barracks or cower behind intrenchments; they must meet their foes of to-day as all the countless spiritual heroes of her history met and conquered theirs, in the open field of argument and example with the armament of zeal and eloquence, learning and saintly life. The American priesthood is no refuge for cowardice and sloth either intellectual or physical. It has a work to do, a vast and hard and endless work, which no one else will do or try or pretend to do for it; and to-day, as we look back along these hundred years and then around us, we say with a just pride in the past, with a reasonable confidence in the future, and, above all, with perfect trust in the proven and abiding guidance of Almighty God, that work has been and is and will be well done!

132. Archbishop Ireland Explains His Stand on Public and Parochial Schools, December, 1890

THE controversial issue of public versus parochial schools, already seen in connection with the Blaine Amendment of 1875, continued to occupy American educators in the years thereafter. When John Ireland (1838–1918), first Archbishop of St. Paul, was invited to speak before the annual convention of the National Education Association in his see city on July 10, 1890, he seized the chance to put forth a compromise solution which would make it possible for the parochial schools to be absorbed into the public system with provision made for the teaching of religion. The speech was vigorously assailed both by critics outside the Church, who claimed it was a ruse by which the Catholics sought to gain control of the public schools, and by certain elements within the Church to whom Ireland's plan constituted a threat to the integrity of the religious schools. When the address was reported adversely to the Holy See and Cardinal Gibbons was asked for his opinion by Pope Leo XIII, the cardinal came strongly to Ireland's defense. In order to put Gibbons in possession of all the necessary facts, the archbishop wrote him the following lengthy letter in which he explained in detail what he had said and what he had meant in those passages especially under fire from his critics. Source: Daniel F. Reilly, O.P., *The School Controversy, 1891–1893* (Washington: The Catholic University of America Press, 1943), Appendix B, pp. 237–241.

Your Eminence,

I beg leave to pen down a few lines, with the intent of making somewhat clear the meaning of my address on "Schools."[1]

I am free to say that it is difficult for me to see anything in it calling for or deserving censure. I have read all the objections raised against it in German papers, and my judgment is that those objections arise from malice prepense in wresting certain phrases from the context, and giving to them an interpretation which antecedent and subsequent declarations do not permit. It is possible, too, that they are in some degree due to ignorance of the true ethical principles which underlie the school question, and to the dislike which so many Catholics entertain for American institutions, or American ideas. I cannot bring myself to believe that those in Rome, finding fault with me, could have had my whole discourse before their eyes: garbled extracts were sent to them, & from these their judgment is formed. My best defense is a perusal of the whole discourse.

The general purpose of the discourse was to state plainly to the country the grounds of Catholic opposition to the State Schools, & to lead up, if possible, to an alteration permitting the removal of this opposition. I was anxious, too, incidentally to allay the angry feeling which reigns between non-Catholic Americans & Catholics, in so far as this feeling rests on misunderstanding of our position. These misunderstandings derive fully as much from exaggerations and misstatements made by Catholics as from ill will or prejudice on the part of non-Catholics.

I had a grand opportunity opened to me; the country was my audience.

The impression is abroad that the Church is opposed to State Schools and to State interference in education, because she is opposed to the

[1] The text of the address, entitled "State Schools and Parish Schools," may be found in John Ireland, *The Church and Modern Society* (St. Paul, 1905), I, 215–232.

education of the children of the people. I desire to set her right before the country on these points.

I admitted in principle the State School — Thus the State, I said, has the right to establish & maintain Schools. Instruction being so necessary in America for good citizenship, and the means of instruction being beyond the reach of many children, thro' poverty or ill will of parents, I asserted the duty on the part of the State, to maintain Schools, in which all children, the poorest & the most abandoned, would be instructed. Of course, in this point, I am dealing with abstract right & duty: in the concrete, as my whole discourse plainly shows, I require that this right be so exercised that while the State obtain its purposes, the purposes of the Church be not frustrated.

I upheld compulsory education, & in this I have with me numerous Catholic writers, Rickaby,[2] Bouquillon,[3] etc. German papers raise a great clamor against me on this point as if I denied to parents that right to control the education of their children. Well, I am most plain & strong in declaring that this right belongs primarily to the parents, and that the State has no right to give itself instruction except when parents neglect their duty. Nor do I allow the State to demand attendance in its own Schools — except when parents neglect absolutely their children. Abundant room is left for home schools, parish schools, etc. Bishop Katzer[4] took publicly the position that the State must enact no school-law, erect no school-building, that the parent had the right, if he desired, to bring up his child in ignorance, total ignorance. Of course, he thinks me heretical.

"Free Schools! Blessed indeed is the nation whose vales and hill sides they adorn, and blessed the generations upon whose souls are poured their treasures!"

A fearful cry went out against those words, as if I extolled the present free-schools of America as being perfect. Well, it is clear that I am talking of free schools in the abstract — free instruction, to be had by all for the asking. Later on, I will show emphatically what free schools in the concrete must be — schools in which religion is taught.

"It were idle for me to praise the State-School of America in the

---

[2] Joseph Rickaby (1845–1932), English Jesuit, who wrote extensively on theological and philosophical subjects.

[3] Thomas Bouquillon (1840–1902), Belgian-born professor of moral theology in the Catholic University of America. Bouquillon's brochure entitled *Education: To Whom Does It Belong?* (Baltimore, 1891) played an important part in the controversy over the schools in American and European Catholic circles.

[4] Frederick F. X. Katzer (1844–1903) was Bishop of Green Bay, 1886–1891, and from the latter year to his death Archbishop of Milwaukee.

imparting of secular instruction. It is our pride and our glory." German papers have kept for weeks a garbled version of these words in large headlines, actually cutting the sentence in twain, so as to take out of it my meaning. "It were idle for me to praise the State School of America. It is our pride and our glory" — So they wrote. I restricted my praise to the "imparting of secular instruction," and in this matter who will contradict me?

I granted to the State School its full quota of merit, so that my censure of it might not seem to come from prejudice. And that censure came — clear and unmistakable. How men — priests — bishops could write that I endorsed the public-school, passes my understanding. I said: "Can I be suspected of enmity to the State School — because I tell of defects which I seek to remedy? . . . There is dissatisfaction with the State School as at present organized." — and I consecrate two-thirds of the discourse to give the grounds of this dissatisfaction. I add "the dissatisfaction will exist as long as no change is made. It is founded on conscience."

"The free Schools of America! Withered be the hand raised in sign of their destruction!" — Another sentence for which I was threatened with excommunication. My meaning was that I would not destroy, but improve, correct, enlarge. "I fain would widen the expanse of their wings until all the children of the people find shelter beneath their cover — " "Not one stone of the wondrous edifice which Americans have built up in their devotion to education will Catholics remove, or permit to be removed. They would fain add to its splendor and majesty by putting side by side religion and the School" — I was addressing Protestants, the born defenders of the schools — teachers. What was I to do to gain their ear, but to confess to all the good in the system, and, then, when their sympathy is won, to tell of the defects!

"I turn to the parish school. It exists. I repeat my regret that there is the necessity for its existence. In behalf of the State School I call upon my fellow Americans to aid in the removal of this necessity." On this point Father Abbelen[5] of Milwaukee has raised a dreadful clamor in Milwaukee papers; German and English priests of Wisconsin replied to him.

I cannot but think I am right and that Abbelen is wrong. Be it understood that I always allow the right of a parish to have a parish school, no matter how perfect the state school may be. But my con-

---

[5] Peter M. Abbelen (1843–1917) had been the emissary to Rome for the German Catholics of the Middle West in November, 1886, in their controversy with the Irish over national parishes and schools.

tention is that the state school, rightly organized — sustained by State funds, and yet granting to Catholic children all that is needed for the protection of the State, no absolute necessity exists for the parish school. In Ireland [and] England there is no strictly-speaking parish school. In Belgium and France, no parish-school was thought of until infidel governments had made the State school infidel. The necessity for parish-schools is hypothetical — the necessity being not a direct result of the Church's mission, but a provision in certain cases for the protection of the faith. The Church is not established to teach writing and ciphering, but to teach morals and faith, and she teaches writing and ciphering only when otherwise morals and faith could not be taught. Abbelen makes out that the "Docete gentes" implies teaching all that children have to learn — quod est absurdum.

Now, what is required in the State-School to make it acceptable to us, I develop in two-thirds of my discourse. I am sure you will find this part ultra abstract. I demand positive Catholic dogmatic teaching — rejecting mere moral teaching, rejecting totally the so-called "common Christianity" theory. Now, my opponents pass over in absolute silence this part of the discourse, which is the more important part, which secular papers took to be properly the discourse.

One point here has been criticized. It is this: "I am a Catholic, of course, to the tiniest fibre of my heart, unflinching and uncompromising in my faith. But God forbid that I desire to see in America the ground which protestantism occupies exposed to the chilling and devastating blast of unbelief. Let me be your ally in stemming the swelling tide of irreligion." — Why, said one priest in a German paper, Abp. Ireland has lost the faith: he is willing to keep up Protestantism. Of course, my meaning is that of words, spoken by Manning and Newman — that factional Christianity is better than materialism. Besides I took the standpoint of your Eminence's book — of speaking to Americans in the name of our "Christian Heritage"[6] — and in this name asking them to make the Schools Christian — Catholic for us, and Protestant for themselves. We cannot have Catholic State Schools without giving them Protestant State Schools.

My appeal for State Schools fit for Catholic children has been censured under the plea that a Protestant state should touch nothing Catholic. But America is not a "Protestant State," and if Catholics pay school taxes they should receive benefit from them. The burden upon our Catholics to maintain parish schools up to the required standard

[6] Ireland was referring here to Gibbon's volume, *Our Christian Heritage* (Baltimore, 1889).

for all the children of the Church is almost unbearable. There is danger that never shall we have schools for all Catholic children, or that Catholics will grow tired of contributing. At present nearly half the Catholic children of America do not attend parish-schools. The true solution, in my judgment, is to make the State-School satisfactory to Catholic consciences, and to use it. Can this be done? Let us try. If it cannot be done, let us do our best with our parish-schools.

Besides have not bishops and priests gone too far in their denunciations of the State School? Have they not, in their desire to protect the parish school, often belied, in their exaggerations of the evil, the State School? Have they not gone beyond the "Apostolic Instruction" of 1875?[7] Have they not needlessly brought upon us the odium of the country? Indeed, since our own schools are neither numerous enough, nor efficient enough for our children, and many of these must attend the public school, have we not done immense harm to souls by our anathemas? Catholics in many cases must use those schools, and yet they are denounced for it; their consciences are falsified — they are estranged from the Church. I am not afraid to say that in places where bishops have been very severe against Public schools, their parish schools have done more harm than good to religion.

It is well, too, to remark that our public schools, in many places at least, are not *positively* bad. They are not *hot beds* of vice; neither do they teach unbelief or Protestantism. Teachers are often good Catholics; or at least they are gentlemen or ladies, decorous in conduct, and generous toward our faith. I know well the immense advantage to children of positive dogmatic teaching in school; yet, where the school is as nearly neutral as can be — the family and the Sunday School can do much — tho' never all we should give if circumstances permit.

Our public-schools are better than those of France and Italy, and in those countries we hear no continuous anathemas.

At any rate, continuous anathemas only irritate. Germans have actually said I was disloyal to the Church when I did not stand up before the Convention and tell of the immoralities and the scepticism of the public-schools.

Now, as to my remedies for bringing together State and Church. Those remedies of mine were put forth tentatively, and as mere beginnings. We cannot have all at once; let us get an entering wedge. The

---

[7] The instruction of the Congregation of Propaganda de Fide on the danger to the faith of Catholic children attending public schools was dated November 24, 1875. Cf. No. 118.

system of payment by results is the system of England — to which Catholics gladly subscribe. The "Poughkeepsie Plan"[8] is the Irish System in vogue for 40 years — used by sisters and brothers — with the sole exception of the Christian brothers. In this system teachers and pupils are all Catholics; the atmosphere is Catholic; all secular teaching is from Catholic minds and from Catholic hearts. The one point is, that positive dogmatic teaching is before or after legal school-hours. Catechism, it is said, should be free at all hours: what does it matter whether it be taught at nine A.M. or eleven A.M.! It is not, as a fact, taught at all hours. But the crucifix is to be removed: Abp. Ireland is the enemy of the crucifix. But the crucifix often is not in Catholic schools, and religion is not dependent on one symbol. Nor is the atmosphere neutral: It cannot be neutral while teachers and pupils are Catholic.

I have myself no further remarks to make. If fault were to be found in Rome with the address, let the precise point with which fault is found be quickly pointed out to me and I will give explanation, or if necessary quietly withdraw it. A public condemnation from Rome of the address would set America in fury, as it would be a direct attack on principles which America will not give up, that is the right of the State to provide for the instruction of all children. As I am so clear on the need of religion in the Schools, Rome's condemnation will be understood to bear on the fact that I allow any right to the State.

I repeat — I have read all the objections to the discourse, and they come either from partial reading of my words, or from hatred of the American state.

The "Poughkeepsie Plan" is in existence in very many of our Catholic country settlements, with the best possible results. Sisters teach, and without the aid of state funds, Sisters could not be supported in those settlements. Had I made the effort, I could have had it in St. Paul.[9] But this war made on me disturbs me.

---

[8] The Poughkeepsie Plan arose out of the efforts of Father Patrick McSweeney, pastor of St. Peter's Church, Poughkeepsie, New York, who in 1873 arranged with the local school board to rent his parochial school for $1.00 a year and to give the school board power and responsibility over repair of the building, hiring and testing the teachers, etc., with the provision that religion would be taught outside the regular school hours. The system was likewise in vogue in local communities in Georgia, New Jersey, Connecticut, and Pennsylvania.

[9] Actually such a plan was instituted in the Archdiocese of St. Paul in August–October, 1891, when the parochial schools of Faribault and Stillwater, Minnesota, were rented to the local school boards for $1.00 a year and thus became a part of the public school system. But opposition to these cases caused the plan to be terminated in the two Minnesota towns by October, 1893.

I will write you again tomorrow. Meanwhile, I repeat my expression of deep gratitude and sincere affection, and remain,

Very respectfully,
John Ireland

133. The St. Raphaelsverein Protests the Neglect of Immigrant Catholics in the United States, February, 1891

THE addition of an estimated 2,475,000 immigrants from twenty or more countries to the Catholic population of the United States in the years 1880–1900 brought inevitable strains within the American Church. One of the most acute controversies among these varied national groups developed between the Irish and German Catholics over the demand of the latter for their own parishes, priests, and schools, and a higher proportion of bishops of German birth or extraction in the hierarchy. This situation led to a protest being lodged with the Holy See in November, 1886, by Father Peter Abbelen of the Archdiocese of Milwaukee which maintained that unless the demands were met there would be grave losses to the faith. In the succeeding years the question took on more serious proportions when it entered into the discussions of the various national branches of the St. Raphaelsverein, an organization founded in 1871 for the care of German Catholic emigrants. From an international conference of the St. Raphaelsverein held in Lucerne, Switzerland, on December 9–10, 1890, there emerged a document signed by officials of the society from seven different countries. This document, dated February, 1891, was presented to Pope Leo XIII on April 16, 1891, and on the following May 28 the full text was published in the New York *Herald*. Most of the American hierarchy protested vigorously against the implication that they had neglected the spiritual welfare of the immigrants and that there had been anywhere near the fantastic figure of ten million souls lost to the Church in this country. Source: Colman J. Barry, O.S.B., *The Catholic Church and German Americans* (Milwaukee: The Bruce Publishing Co., 1953), Appendix IV, pp. 313–315.

Most Holy Father,

The presidents, secretaries general, and delegates of the societies under the protection of the Holy Archangel Raphael for the protection of emigrants, encouraged by the benevolence which Your Holiness has shown them, assembled on December 9 of last year at an international conference in Lucerne to deliberate upon means best suited to serve the spiritual and material well-being of their Catholic compatriots who have emigrated to America, the number of which is in excess of 400,000 yearly.[1]

The above mentioned take the liberty to place before Your Holiness, with deepest respect, the fact that the numerous emigrants constitute a great strength, and could co-operate eminently in the expansion of the Catholic Church in the several states of America. In this way they could contribute to the moral stature of their new homeland, as well as to the stimulation of religious consciousness in the old European fatherlands.

Only the true Church, of which Your Holiness is the highest shepherd, can obtain these happy results because it is the true source of all progress and civilization.

But in order that European Catholics, in their adopted country, preserve and transmit to their children their faith and its inherent benefits, the undersigned have the honor to submit to Your Holiness the conditions, which in the light of experience and in the nature of things, appear to be indispensable for that purpose in the countries of immigration. The losses which the Church has suffered in the United States of North America number more than ten million souls.[2]

1. It seems necessary to unite the emigrant groups of each nationality in separate parishes, congregations, or missions wherever their numbers and means make such a practice possible.

2. It seems necessary to entrust the administration of these parishes to priests of the same nationality to which the faithful belong. The sweetest and dearest memories of their homeland would be constantly recalled, and they would love all the more the holy Church which procures these benefits for them.

---

[1] If the memorialists had in mind Catholic immigrants solely to the United States this figure was a gross exaggeration. The best authority on the subject estimated that in the years 1881–1890 inclusive there was a total increase of 1,250,000 to the American Catholic population through immigration, a figure that included 119,000 from Canada, Mexico, and other non-European countries. From those European countries whose delegates signed the Lucerne Memorial there had been in the entire period 1881–1890 approximately only 700,000 Catholics immigrants (Gerald Shaughnessy, S.M., *Has the Immigrant Kept the Faith?* [New York, 1925], p. 165).

[2] The recklessness with which figures on Catholic leakage were used by the ill informed in these years may be gauged by the fact that at an international Catholic congress held in Liège, Belgium, in September, 1890, a French-Canadian priest of the Diocese of Albany, Alphonse Villeneuve, presented a paper which alleged that out of twenty-five million Catholic immigrants who had entered the United States twenty million had been lost to the Church.

3. In areas settled by emigrants of several nationalities who are not numerous enough to organize separate national parishes, it is desirable as far as possible, that a pastor be chosen to guide them who understands the diverse languages of these groups. This priest should be strictly obliged to give catechetical instruction to each of the groups in its own language.

4. It will be especially necessary to establish parochial schools wherever Christian public schools are not available, and these schools should be separate, as far as possible, for each nationality.

The curriculum of these schools should always include the mother tongue as well as the language and history of the adopted country.

5. It seems necessary to grant to priests devoting themselves to the emigrants all rights, privileges, and prerogatives enjoyed by the priests of the country. This arrangement, which is only just, would have the result that zealous, pious, and apostolic priests of all nationalities will be attracted to immigrant work.

6. It seems desirable to establish and encourage societies of various kinds, confraternities, charitable organizations, mutual aid and protective associations, etc. By these means Catholics would be systematically organized and saved from the dangerous sects of Freemasons and organizations affiliated with it.

7. It seems very desirable that the Catholics of each nationality, wherever it is deemed possible, have in the episcopacy of the country where they immigrate, several bishops who are of the same origin. It seems that in this way the organization of the Church would be perfect, for in the assemblies of the bishops, every immigrant race would be represented, and its interests and needs would be protected.

8. Finally the undersigned wish to point out that for the attainment of the objectives which they have enumerated, it would be very desirable, and this they vigorously urge, that the Holy See foster and protect in the emigration countries: a) special seminaries and apostolic schools for training missionaries for emigrants; b) St. Raphael societies for the protection of emigrants, and that it recommend to the Most Rev. Bishops that they establish such societies in the emigration countries where they do not yet exist, and that the Holy See place them under the protection of a Cardinal Protector.

The undersigned hope for the happiest and most immediate results from this organization and these measures. Emigration missionaries trained under the direction of a distinguished Italian Bishop have already gone to America.[3] Others, members of neighboring nations, are waiting, before entering, upon their important and holy calling, for the Supreme Shepherd of the Church, by a decree of his wisdom, to guarantee the free exercise of their mission. If the Holy See will lend its indispensable co-operation, wonderful results should follow. The poor emigrants will find on American soil their priests, their parishes, their schools, their societies, their language, and thus cannot fail to extend the boundaries of the Kingdom of Jesus Christ on earth.

In giving solemn testimony of their loyal devotion to the Apostolic See, the undersigned humbly beg Your Holiness to grant paternal approbation to the propositions which they have proposed for the salvation of souls and the glory of our holy mother, the Church, in the different American nations. With the most loyal devotion, Your most devoted, humble, and obedient sons: [There then follow the signatures of the boards of directors of the St. Raphael Society in Germany, Austria-Hungary, Belgium, and Italy, with the signatures of a single delegate each from Switzerland and France. A duplicate of the memorial was attached in the interests of the French-speaking Canadian Catholics in the United States and was signed by fifteen Canadian Catholics, including Prime Minister Henri Mercier of Quebec].

134. The Secret Oath of the American Protective Association, October 31, 1893

AFTER the breakup of the Know-Nothings with the Civil War there was no organized movement against the Catholic Church in the United States until March, 1887, when Henry F. Bowers (1837–1911) and six associates founded the American Protective Association at Clinton, Iowa. The founders were drawn from no single political or religious group, there being among the original seven two Republicans, two Democrats, one Populist, and one Prohibitionist, with two of no religion and one each a Methodist, Lutheran, Baptist, Presbyterian, and Congregationalist. The A.P.A. grew slowly at first, but by 1894 they made significant gains in the elections of that year and by 1896 it was estimated that they numbered approximately a million members with the chief strength centered in the Middle West. The issue of Bryanism and free silver split their ranks in 1896, and as Arthur Meier Schlesinger remarked, "Both major parties snubbed the A.P.A., and the movement withered as suddenly as it had grown" ("A Critical Period in

[3] Giovanni Battista Scalabrini (1839–1905), Bishop of Piacenza, founded the Congregation of Missionaries of St. Charles Borromeo, the first of whose members had arrived in the United States in July, 1888, for work among the Italian immigrants.

American Religion, 1875–1900," *Proceedings of the Massachusetts Historical Society,* LXIV [1932], 546). The A.P.A. lingered on, however, until 1911 and during the 1890's they did a great deal of harm among many Americans who were taken in by their lying propaganda, the most fantastic item of which was published in the *Patriotic American* of Detroit on April 8, 1893, and purported to be an encyclical of Pope Leo XIII instructing the American Catholics to rise on the feast of St. Ignatius Loyola, July 31, 1893, and massacre all heretics in the country. The secret oath of the A.P.A., a copy of which follows, came to light late that year through the exposé of the St. Paul *Globe* and through the efforts of Henry M. Youmans (1832–1920), defeated congressman from the eighth district of Michigan, to unseat William S. Linton (1856–1927), his opponent, who, he contended, was a member of the A.P.A. Source: Michael Williams, *The Shadow of the Pope* (New York: McGraw-Hill Book Co., Inc., 1932), pp. 103–104.

I do most solemnly promise and swear that I will always, to the utmost of my ability, labor, plead and wage a continuous warfare against ignorance and fanaticism; that I will use my utmost power to strike the shackles and chains of blind obedience to the Roman Catholic church from the hampered and bound consciences of a priest-ridden and church-oppressed people; that I will never allow any one, a member of the Roman Catholic church, to become a member of this order, I knowing him to be such; that I will use my influence to promote the interest of all Protestants everywhere in the world that I may be; that I will not employ a Roman Catholic in any capacity if I can procure the services of a Protestant.[1]

I furthermore promise and swear that I will not aid in building or maintaining, by my resources, any Roman Catholic church or institution of their sect or creed whatsoever, but will do all in my power to retard and break down the power of the Pope, in this country or any other; that I will not enter into any controversy with a Roman Catholic upon the subject of this order, nor will I enter into any agreement with a Roman Catholic to strike or create a disturbance whereby the Catholic employes may undermine and substitute their Protestant co-workers; that in all grievances I will seek only Protestants and

[1] A sample of A.P.A. literature which made their intent clear was the 56-page pamphlet put out by a certain J. H. Jackson of Forth Worth, Texas, supreme vice-president of the organization, entitled *The American Protective Association. What It Is, Its Platform and Roman Intolerance* (n.p., n.d.). In the preface Jackson remarked that he had been a member for eighteen months and had read everything he could find on the Catholic Church and had become convinced that there was an urgent need to combat its power. When he learned "that the Roman pope gave his subjects no right to think for themselves," he declared "this is a false assumption of authority, which American manhood cannot, and will not, submit to" (p. 3).

counsel with them to the exclusion of all Roman Catholics, and will not make known to them anything of any nature matured at such conferences.

I furthermore promise and swear that I will not countenance the nomination, in any caucus or convention, of a Roman Catholic for any office in the gift of the American people, and that I will not vote for, or counsel others to vote for, any Roman Catholic, but will vote only for a Protestant, so far as may lie in my power. Should there be two Roman Catholics on opposite tickets, I will erase the name on the ticket I vote; that I will at all times endeavor to place the political positions of this government in the hands of Protestants, to the entire exclusion of the Roman Catholic church, of the members thereof, and the mandate of the Pope.

To all of which I do most solemnly promise and swear, so help me God. Amen.

135. George P. A. Healy Recounts His Beginnings as an Artist and His Painting of Pope Pius IX, 1894

WITH the exception of John LaFarge the most important painter among American Catholics was George P. A. Healy (1813–1894). Boston-born of an American mother and a father who had left Ireland in the uprising of 1798, Healy's fame rested chiefly on the portraits he painted of many of the great in both Church and State on both sides of the Atlantic. His subjects included such varied figures as Pius IX, Jenny Lind, Guizot, Carmen Sylva, King Louis Philippe, Franz Liszt, Lord Bulwer-Lytton, ten or more presidents of the United States, and the leading American statesmen of his time, including Henry Clay, John C. Calhoun, and Daniel Webster. Healy won prizes in Paris and Florence never before conferred on an American, and of his great picture, "Webster Replying to Hayne," which brought the gold medal of the Paris Exposition of 1855 and which hangs in Faneuil Hall, Boston, it was said, "No other American artist at any cost of time and energy could have produced the huge canvas which does not seem to have required any special effort from Healy, who as far as schooling and *technique* go was entirely Parisian" (Samuel Isham, *The History of American Painting,* rev. ed. by Royal Cortissoz [New York, 1927], p. 281). It is to Healy that we owe some of the best likenesses of the American hierarchy among them Cardinals McCloskey and Gibbons and Archbishops Francis Kenrick and Bayley. In his early manhood he had been quite indifferent about his religious duties, having married Louisa Phipps, an English girl, in London in 1839 in an Anglican ceremony. But through the influence of Catholic friends, and principally John B. Fitzpatrick, Bishop of Boston

(1812–1866) whose portrait he painted, the artist became an ardent Catholic, succeeded in persuading Mrs. Healy to become a convert in 1860, and for most of the remainder of his long life attended Mass daily. The following excerpts from his memoirs tell of how he began his artistic career and of his experiences while painting Pius IX. Source: George P. A. Healy, *Reminiscences of a Portrait Painter* (Chicago: A. C. McClurg and Co., 1894), pp. 17, 20–25, 135–137.

My grandmother, Mrs. Hicks, painted quite prettily in water-colors, and one of my delights as a child was to turn over a series of sketches she had made during a journey among the West Indian Islands. It is doubtless from her that I inherited my first liking for painting. . . . The first time I held a brush was when I was about sixteen years of age. One day I was to meet a friend of mine at his house, and we were then to go off together on some excursion. But as it began to rain violently, I found my friend and his two sisters amusing themselves with a paint-box. They made drawings which they afterwards colored. One of the little girls, holding up her work where bright reds, greens, and blues vied with each other, exclaimed: "You could not do as much, could you, George?" "I guess I could," said I in true Yankee fashion; and, nettled, I began to color one of the childish drawings on which the little girl obligingly wrote directions as to the tints I should use. When I had finished, my friends declared that I must have painted before. But I had not. I had shown at school much aptitude for map drawing, but that was the first time I had ever used a brush.

After that, however, I would do nothing else. I determined to be a painter. . . . My first small success came to me in rather an odd way. Miss Stuart,[1] who took some interest in me, lent me a print of Guido Reni's[2] "Ecce Homo." I copied this on a canvas, and then colored it as best I could, without any help except such as the study of my own face afforded for the flesh tints. Such as it was, I carried the picture to a good-natured bookseller, who consented to put it in his shop-window. I own that I often found an excuse for passing along that street, so as to give a rapid glance at my work. In later years I have never seen an artist hover about his picture at a public exhibition without thinking of my "Ecce Homo" in the friendly bookseller's window.

A Catholic priest from the country happened to pass that way,

[1] Miss Jane Stuart was the daughter of the famous painter, Gilbert Stuart (1755–1828).

[2] Guido Reni (1575–1642), an Italian painter.

and stopped to look at the picture. Catholic priests are not rich now; in those days they were terribly poor. After hesitating, he went in and asked whether that picture was for sale. My friend the bookseller must have had a twinkle in his eyes, as he answered that doubtless the artist would consent to part with his work — for a consideration. "I am not rich," said the priest; "all I could scrape together would be ten dollars." "I will speak to the artist, and give you an answer tommorrow." And on the morrow the priest carried away the "Ecce Homo," and the "artist" pocketed the ten dollars. I do not know which was the happier of the two; but I rather fancy it was the boy painter!

Some thirty years later, as I stood talking with some friends at the Capitol in Washington, I saw an old man wearing a Roman collar. On hearing my name pronounced by one of my friends he came up to me and said: "Are you Mr. Healy, the painter?" I bowed, and he continued with a smile: "I believe that I am the happy possessor of one of your earliest works, if not the earliest. Do you remember an 'Ecce Homo' which you had placed in the window of a Boston bookseller? A country priest offered ten dollars for it. I am that priest, and your picture still hangs in my little church. Who knows? it perhaps brought down blessings on your head. I have always felt that I had something to do with your success in life!" I shook my first patron heartily by the hand, and told him what joy his ten dollars had given me. But somehow, in the confusion of the moment, I neglected to ask him for his name and address. I have always regretted this. I should greatly have liked to pay him a visit, and see how my copy of Guido Reni looked in the Yankee country church.

The first serious encouragement which I received came to me from Sully,[3] who, when I was about eighteen, was called to Boston to paint a portrait of Colonel Perkins[4] for the Athenaeum. Miss Jane Stuart, daughter of the great painter, spoke to him of "little Healy's" attempts, and he sent word to me that if I would make a sketch from Nature and a copy of one of Stuart's heads he would be glad to give me some advice. When I showed him what I had done, he looked at the canvases and exclaimed heartily: "My young friend, I advise you to make painting your profession!" . . .

During my stay in Rome I painted from memory a portrait of Pope

---

[3] Thomas Sully (1783–1872) was the ranking American painter after the deaths of Charles Willson Peale in 1827 and Gilbert Stuart in 1828. In 1838 Sully painted the young Queen Victoria from life.

[4] Thomas H. Perkins (1764–1854) was a leading Boston merchant and philanthropist who was called "Colonel" by reason of his many years as an officer in the Massachusetts militia.

Pius IX.[5] His Holiness, having seen this unfinished work, liked it, and consented to give me a few sittings. This was a great favor, which I highly appreciated. So far I had only seen the Pope, with other strangers, at the Vatican receptions, or from afar when he officiated at St. Peter's, before the events of 1870.

I was introduced one morning into Pius IX's library; a pleasant room, simply enough furnished, full of books, the table covered with papers. The Pope was dressed all in white cloth, with scarlet shoes; the hair was white, the face rather pale, with very bright eyes, not incapable of sparkle, for his Holiness knew how to take a joke. He was a pretty good sitter, but somewhat restless, and curious also as to what his painter was about. On one occasion he arose from his seat to look over my shoulder. When I am earnestly at work, I wish my sitters to help me, and do their duty by remaining in the attitude I have chosen. I exclaimed, perhaps a little abruptly: "I beg your Holiness to sit down." The Pope laughed and said: "I am accustomed to give orders, not to receive them. But you see, Mr. Healy, that I also know how to obey," and submissively went back to his chair.

Pius IX has been dead now many a year. I like to think of the few short sittings he gave me in his cheerful library; I like to remember his quiet, pleasant talk, his rather Italian-sounding French, his judgments of men and things. One day, speaking of a monk who had left the Church and married, he observed, not without glee: "He has taken his punishment in his own hands."[6] I like especially to feel as though the hours spent in his presence had cast a glow on my later years, as the glorious setting sun behind St. Peter's throws a glamour over Rome, its domes and gardens. I often think, also, of Pius IX's gentle reproach to one of my countrymen who, in his American pride, refused to bend before him: "My son, an old man's blessing never did harm to any one."

---

[5] Healy painted Pius IX in the winter of 1870–1871 for which the artist was made a Knight of St. Gregory.

[6] According to Marie De Mare, *G. P. A. Healy, American Artist* (New York, 1954), p. 252, this was the French Carmelite, Père Hyacinthe [Charles Loyson] (1827–1912), who left the Church after the Vatican Council, attached himself to Döllinger, married, and founded an Old Catholic congregation in Paris.

136. Archbishop Ireland's Views on Socialism, October 14, 1894

BY THE 1890's the advance of socialism had become the cause of serious concern to many men in both Europe and the United States. This concern was heightened by the bloody Homestead Strike of 1892 and the turbulent year 1894 which saw the huge strikes of the Pullman Company and the western railroads and the march of Coxey's Army of unemployed on Washington. No American bishop was more alive to the necessity of finding correct solutions to social problems than John Ireland, first Archbishop of St. Paul (1838–1918). In the summer of 1892 Ireland had attracted national attention in France by a series of addresses, and it was not surprising, therefore, that Jules Huret, dean of the Paris correspondents, should seek an interview with him which was published in *Le Figaro* on August 29, 1894. The following reprint of the interview embodied a number of ideas which Ireland later expanded and published from his lectures in the two-volume work, *The Church and Modern Society* (St. Paul, 1905). The archbishop was a friend of the laboring man, as his strong support to Cardinal Gibbons in 1887 in the case of the Knights of Labor made evident. But he was not an uncritical admirer as he made clear in the interview he gave to the press in July of this same year when violence broke out among the strikers in Chicago. Source: New York *Times,* October 14, 1894.

The interviewer laureate of the Paris press, Jules Huret[1] reports in *Le Figaro*[2] the following conversation with Archbishop Ireland:

Q. — What do you think of the Socialist predictions? Do you believe that transformations in social organizations are imminent?

A. — The transformations predicted by the Socialists seem to me to be neither imminent nor probable. What is probable, what I desire to realize as soon as possible is improvement in the condition of the mass of working men, their elevation from an intellectual and moral point of view, as much as from a material point of view. This improvement and this elevation shall have as consequences the advent of democracy and the disappearance of what is called, in Europe, the reign of the bourgeoisie. This will be accomplished without much resistance. As was said to me by a Belgian statesman, Minister

[1] Jules Huret (1864–1915) was a famous French journalist who won early notice by his series of articles on controverted questions for *l'Echo de Paris,* and later for a series on European social questions for *Le Figaro.*

[2] *Le Figaro* began in 1825 and went through a number of changes, becoming in 1866 a daily paper which was monarchical in sympathies after the Franco-Prussian War and which continued to be an organ of conservative opinion.

Northamb:[3] "In our days, more than ever, nobody remains immovable. Some turn to reaction, others to democracy."

Observe that true democracy does not exclude, but, on the contrary, presupposes social influences. There shall always be in society men of genius, men of talent, and men of elevated character, and these men will always exert influence. A society where social influences are weak, where natural legitimate influences are replaced by others, is a society in an abnormal state. It was a great mistake of writers in France to write of directing classes. The expression is unfortunate; there are no directing classes, but there are, and there always will be, directing men.

I do not believe that there will be an extreme condensation of capital in the future. I think, on the contrary, that money shall be more generally distributed, that the workingmen shall be better paid, and, consequently, shall have more instruction. Notice what Leo XIII[4] says of diffusion of property, while talking of capital. Doubtless there shall always be great fortunes, but great fortunes are an evil only when they have been acquired by fraud and injustice, and, moreover, they are not incompatible with small fortunes; on the contrary, often small fortunes are formed in the shadow of great ones. No other country possesses as many millionaires as the United States, and no other country possesses as small a number of poor people, whereas, no country possesses a smaller number of millionaires than Russia, and no other country contains more poor people. There shall always be great capitalists, great capitalists shall always have influence, and this influence will be increased naturally by association, but association in its turn will protect small capitalists and workingmen. Between the interests of the two classes, independently of moral and religious influences, there is and will remain the civil power, the mission of which is to enact wise laws which insure liberty, rights, the activity of all, especially of the weakest. In transitory times these laws are not easily made. But this is a fault inherent in human nature.

Q. — You are called here "the Socialist Bishop." Do you accept the adjective? Would your ideas be accepted by the Scholastic schools?

A. — The word "Socialist" has an evil ring, and before applying it to my ideas it should be defined. If by Socialists you understand those who are preoccupied by social necessities and miseries, who desire to improve the state of society, and who ask, in view of this improve-

[3] An effort to identify Northamb was not successful.

[4] Leo XIII's encyclical *Rerum novarum* on the condition of the working classes had been issued on May 15, 1891.

ment, not only action of individuals and influence of voluntary associations, but also a reasonable intervention of the civil power, yes, I am a Socialist. But if by "Socialist" you understand those who share the theories of Marx, of Benoit Malon,[5] of Greef, and others — theories which consist in denying the rightfulness of private property in land and in instruments of labor — no, I am not a Socialist.

I do not doubt that my ideas would be rejected by the Socialistic sects. Everywhere the Socialist sects are opposed to the Christian social movement. In laboring for the disappearance of the just grievances of the working class, the Christian movement takes from sectarian socialism the reason for its existence.

This is not because the promoters of the Christian social movement preach only charity and resignation. Far from this, they preach, above all, right and justice; natural right of the workingman; complete justice, social as well as individual. It is said that justice is a foundation of societies; it is also the foundation of economic order. Therefore, in the first place, justice; after justice, charity; charity may not be substituted for justice; one completes the other; in places where justice has ceased to command, charity intervenes.

Doubtless our conception of life differs essentially from that of the materialists; our reason and our faith teach us that present life is a preparation for a better life. But we are not led by this to neglect material welfare. Material welfare is not our end; it is our means. Its profession to a reasonable degree is of the highest importance for the moral and religious life of men.

Q. — Do you admit as legitimate the actual aspirations of the masses toward absolute social equality? Do you think that the natural inequalities might be reconciled with social equality?

A. — Aspirations of the masses toward social equality — I mean reasonable equality — are perfectly legitimate. Social equality is, after all, only the expression of equality from the point of view of human dignity and of Christian dignity. We must take care, however, that social equality should not be opposed to social hierarchy; parentage, service, and authority engender rights and social duties which are not the same for all; genius, talent, virtue, and riches entail consideration and give a certain moral pre-eminence which shall always be admitted. This observation is sufficient to show that social equality may be

---

[5] Benôit Malon (1841–1893) was a French socialist who participated in the Paris Commune of 1870–1871 and later fled to Geneva where he founded *La Revanche;* Guillaume-Joseph de Greef (1842–1924) was a professor of sociology in the University of Brussels.

reconciled with natural inequality. Natural inequality is that of intelligence, of strength, and of health. This inequality is more or less corrected by society, which protects the weak. Social hierarchy is natural and indestructible. Something not as natural, and which may be abolished, is the great distance between the two ends of this hierarchy. It is not necessary that some should be so elevated and that others should be so degraded.

Q. — Since you admit that societies may pass through transformations, think you that the trilogy — family, religion, and property — should necessarily escape these transformations?

A. — The action of Providence, which brings everything to its end, does not prevent the natural course of things and does not suppress the liberty of man. Modifications in the form of societies are therefore possible, but family, religion, and property are essential elements of all human society. Family is the principle of human society; religion is its crown; property — considered in itself, independently of variable forms — is a condition of life, of liberty, and of progress.

The form of the family is determined by the nature of man, his physical forces, his intellectual faculties, his sentiments, and his instincts, and this form was sanctioned by Christ. It will not change, but what may be desired, what may be hoped, is more perfect realization of this form, and this realization may not be obtained except by progress in manners, customs, and laws.

The form of religion is also determined in a general manner by nature as regards its object and its principal acts. It was also determined in a special and positive manner by Christ. There shall not therefore be a new form of religion, but one may hope for a more complete intelligence and a more general and more perfect realization of the Christian idea, and consequently a more powerful influence of the Gospel on the life of individuals and of nations. Outside of Christianity there may be new religious forms, as was Mohammedanism, but these forms shall not be progressive. As for Neo-Christianity,[6] it will never be anything but amateurish religion.

Property is essential, but there is nothing absolute in its forms. These depend on the social, industrial, political, and moral situation of peoples. The history of property has occupied in France and elsewhere many learned men. Their studies cannot but throw light on questions of social philosophy.

---

[6] Ireland may have been referring here to the followers of Claude-Henri de Rouvroy, Comte de Saint-Simon (1760–1825), who fostered in his last years a sort of mystical fraternalism.

Q.—Among the possible modifications of property, which ones would you regard favorably? What do you think of the communist theory?

A.—The form of property was not always the same at all epochs, and even to-day it is not absolutely the same in all countries. What modifications are possible, useful, and necessary depends on the conditions under which each people finds itself. Modifications may not be made by legislation. This can only give sanction. They are accomplished slowly, by progress in manners and under the sway of circumstances. An example of such modifications is the introduction and disappearance of feudal property.

The system of property which appears to me to be the most desirable should reunite the following qualities: Stimulate human activity and individual labor by assurance of just retribution; maintain the stability of the family, and favor an equitable distribution of the good things of this world.

The Communist theory takes no account of the nature of things or of the nature of man. It does not seem possible to me that it may be realized, and if it were realized the result would be fatal to civilization. Herbert Spencer[7] recently demonstrated this in the introduction which he wrote for "The Man Versus the State." Community of goods may exist among a certain number of men devoted to celibacy and to the cult of God. It might have existed in the age of gold and in a state of innocence; but it does not answer to the real state of present humanity.

Yet the present movement contains very complex elements, which may not be judged in their entirety from the point of view of morality and of civilization. There are few theories, however false they may be in their entirety, which do not contain elements of truth and of justice. The errors which they contain are often an occasion determining a more complete intelligence of the truth. Thus, it may not be denied that the Communist agitation has provoked a more adequate understanding of certain social principles and a more profound sentiment of social justice.

Q.—What is the state of the social question in America? Where, think you, do the Socialist theories have a better chance to succeed, in Europe or in the United States?

A.—The social question exists in America. Read on this subject

[7] *Man versus the State,* to which Herbert Spencer (1820–1903) wrote an introduction, was first published in 1884 and was reprinted in 1940 by the Caxton Printers, Caldwell, Idaho.

Prof. Ely's[8] book, "The Labor Movement in America." In my opinion, the difference between our situation and that of Europe is as follows:

The social movement is expressed in the United States by numerous and powerful workingmen's associations. These associations have for their principal object to maintain good wages; they are preoccupied by the morality of their members and by professional education. You know that there are some associations which labor to maintain harmony between bosses and workmen, and to prevent strikes. I think that among the American people there are few Anarchists, few Communists, and that the number of collectivists cannot be large. They come from other countries. European immigration supplies their principal contingent. The details which Mr. Ely gives on these subjects are very interesting. As for Henry George's[9] agrarian movement, it is far from powerful.

Socialist theories have far less chance in America than in Europe. In the first place, the sentiment of personal dignity and responsibility and the spirit of enterprise are much developed in the American people. It likes and appreciates individual liberty and respects the law. These dispositions do not lead to social revolution. Furthermore, there is room in the United States for all kinds of energy. Labor there insures honorable life; then, the greater number of Americans have conquered their situation by personal valor, at the price of efforts, perils, and heroic sacrifices. They are not disposed to share with others what they have gained by so much work. Then there are philosophical, moral, and political causes which elsewhere favor the development of Socialism, and have no force in the United States. I allude to administrative centralization, intervention of the Government in the affairs of citizens, to the military regime, and to authoritative traditions.

137. The Americanism Controversy Foreshadowed in the Writings of a French Visitor, 1895

IN THE late nineteenth century the Catholic Church suffered severe pressure from the governments of France, Italy, and Spain. The progress which had meanwhile been made in the United States where there was a separa-

---

[8] Richard T. Ely (1854–1943), at this time professor of political economy in the University of Wisconsin, was a prolific writer on social and economic questions. The latest edition of his volume, *The Labor Movement in America,* appeared in 1905.

[9] Henry George (1839–1897) was chiefly notable for his theory of the single tax on land.

tion of Church and State excited the admiration of leading European Catholic liberals who sought to have the Church in their own countries model itself on the American pattern. In their enthusiasm at times they used careless and extravagant language concerning the American Catholics which aroused the distrust of conservative ecclesiastics and which led eventually to charges of a lack of orthodoxy in the controversy over the so-called heresy of Americanism. The controversy was especially heated in France where the writings of men like Max Leclerc (1864—) served to heighten suspicions concerning the doctrines taught in the burgeoning branch of the universal Church in the United States. Leclerc, one of the editors of the *Journal des débats,* after a visit to this country in July–October, 1890, wrote a series of articles in that paper and in the *Revue bleue* which he published in book form in 1895. It is easily seen how his descriptions of American Catholicism could lead to misunderstanding and contribute to the quarrel which broke in France on this subject two years after the publication of his book. Source: Max Leclerc, *Choses d'Amérique. Les crises économique et religieuse aux États-Unis* (Paris: Armand Colin et Cie, 1895), pp. 220, 222–225, 236–240.

The Church enjoys an absolute freedom, in virtue of common right and within the limits of the nation's laws; she is self-sufficient; she expects nothing from the State which demands nothing of her. She even congratulates herself on being left to her unaided might; she owes to this form of government a vigor, an eternal youthfulness which she certainly does not have elsewhere; she gathers the fruits of independence; she waxes strong under the necessity of making her way in the bright world of competition . . .

The Church has known how to make its place in the State. Accustomed in the old world to rely on the State, or at any rate to reckon with it, in America she has been able to disregard it. But how has she conducted herself in regard to the people themselves? Experienced in dealing with old western societies, how has she handled the contact with this developing society?

With an amazing flexibility and that unflagging faculty for adaptation which Macaulay recognized in her, she has become acclimated to her new environment: she has modelled her spirit on the very spirit of the nation; she has made herself tolerant, democratic, American.

Doctor Carroll, who was the first Archbishop of Baltimore and the founder of the hierarchy, showed his clergy and his successors an example of independence and broadness of outlook. It is he who declared: "It was never our doctrine that salvation could be obtained only by those who are in actual communion with the Church." It is he who expressed the desire that the liturgy be allowed to employ

English for the greatest good of the poor people and the illiterate Negroes. Cardinal Gibbons, the present head of the American Church, has faithfully continued to teach the same doctrines. He never speaks of the Protestant sects as irreconcilable enemies; he calls them rather "our separated brethren," "our dissident brothers." He condemns in a dogmatic book, *The Faith of Our Fathers,*[1] the Inquisition and the persecutions; he reproves in indignant terms the massacre of St. Bartholomew. He brings together some very happy arguments to demonstrate that the Catholic Church has been and remains the friend of civil liberties and of tolerance. He is pleased that the Church should be free in a free State and that these two powers should be equally respectful of the rights of each other. He shows that the American Catholics have played a noble role in the national history, that they have given the example of tolerance, offering asylum in their colony of Maryland to the Protestants who were persecuted among their own.

In this land of liberty the Catholic Church has realized that she should preach and practice tolerance; likewise, she has made a point of proving that she is not an aristocratic organization, that she is, on the contrary, sincerely devoted to democracy. She is openly arrayed on the side of the poor and the weak; she has espoused the cause of the lowly. And if one keeps in mind that her clientele is almost entirely composed of the proletariat, of workers, of the little people, one will recognize that she has been right and discerning in her own interest in defending the interests of her faithful. The attitude taken four years ago by Cardinal Gibbons in the affair of the Knights of Labor is a striking proof of it.

The Church is tolerant, she is democratic, she is, in fine, American. She has known nothing but rapid development in the soil of the Union from the day when the hierarchy was founded, when she passed from the hands of missionaries dependent on Rome to the hands of an autonomous clergy to the present when she has become one of the institutions of the country, one of the organs of the national life. . . .

She wishes to be called American; she has entered into the spirit of the nation; but she sensed, indeed, that she has very much to do, more so every day, to transform and to assimilate the heterogeneous elements who come to her without ceasing from Europe. She foresees and she fears the reproaches which they are able to make that she is an immigrant, a stranger; she is very anxious to avoid this. She is

---

[1] Baltimore: John Murphy & Co., 1876.

sincerely searching for every means of Americanizing herself from top to bottom. . . .

While Europe toils along the well-worn rut of race hatreds, of bloody quarrels between nation and nation, of rivalries between ministers and sovereigns, — an occurrence of capital significance in the history of the world took place on the other side of the ocean and went almost unnoticed: the Catholic Church, the most powerful and most ancient of religious organizations, met up with the youngest and most enterprising of recent societies. The Roman Church, for the first time, found herself at grips with a people of a modern civilization without the interposition of governments, local authorities, intrigues of courts or the schemes of diplomacy. I would like to examine what has been, what may be the influence of this important event upon the guiding spirit and upon the destinies of the Church.

The Church has conquered in America a vast territory inhabited by an English-speaking people. Among the Catholics of Europe, those who speak English form a tiny minority: the American nation, the most populous even now of the nations of western civilization, the fastest to reproduce, finally the most active agent for the diffusion of the English language, brings to the Church a contingent of faithful which disturbs the balance in Catholicity, and doubles the hold of the Church of Rome upon the world: one can foresee the day in which the Catholics speaking English will be more numerous than the Catholics speaking any other language.

But at this point several questions arrest us: what is the future of religious opinion on the American continent? A difficult mystery to penetrate. One can foresee that as time marches on, the more vigorously will the Catholic Church have to struggle against growing indifference, against the advance of materialism or the spirit of skepticism. The American civilization is profoundly materialistic. When the new settlers, when the sons of the docile recruits of the Catholic Church have been imbued with the American spirit, will there remain a place in their hearts for the precepts of Rome and for the faith?

Be that as it may, the Catholic Church cannot fail to be deeply stirred by this inroad of the Anglo-Saxon race, with its concept of life, its democratic instincts, its relish for action and independence, and a whole long civilization behind it remaining up to then alien to the Church of Rome. The Latin influence will cease to exercise uncontested domination in the Church; the Anglo-Saxon influence will establish for itself a usurping stronghold there, and the history of the world will be swerved by it. Old Europe, shackled by its past, introspective, reduced to helplessness, will cease to attract the constant attention of the Church which will turn toward the new lands with their innumerable inhabitants, for she will recognize that the future is with them. Rome will no longer be in Rome, but in Baltimore or in Carthage.

Already the strong and solemn voice of the Anglo-Saxons has made itself heard and hearkened to in the councils of the Church; it is that voice which thrust upon Rome, by threatening an appeal to the people, the solicitude about social problems, and an inexorably democratic policy. It is by the voice of Cardinal Manning, of Cardinal Gibbons, an English prelate and an American prelate, that modern democracy, the power of tomorrow, has indicated to the Church that she must turn her attention from the powerful of the present in order to bring it to bear on itself. One still remembers the voyage to Rome in June, 1886,[2] of Cardinal Gibbons who came to plead the cause of democracy in the name of the interests of the American Church and to demand the withdrawal of the interdict issued by the Holy See against the powerful secret association of the Knights of Labor. M. E.-M. de Vogüé[3] told a year later, in some prophetic pages, of "this eruption of the new World in the midst of the Roman prelacy, little concerned up to now with social problems." I will not return to this. M. de Vogüé said then, and subsequent history has proven him correct: "The term 'revolution' is not excessive. One felt the wind of tomorrow which was blowing, one perceived its force."

The American Church, after having been a simple external appendage of the Church of Rome, a remote extension and loosely attached, has become one of the inmost motive forces; and all the more so since Rome, following the example of the great European powers, has taken upon herself to formulate in some sense a colonial policy. . . . the ten million American Catholics have, on several memorable occasions, weighed heavier in the scales of the Holy See than the hundreds of millions of faithful in old Europe. . . .

---

[2] Gibbons' visit to Rome took place in February–March, 1887, not in June, 1886.

[3] Eugène Marie Melchoir Vicomte de Vogüé (1848–1910), frequent contributor in these years to the *Revue des deux mondes* and the *Journal des débats*. Leclerc was referring here to De Vogüé's *Souvenirs et visions* (Paris, 1887), a travelogue.

138. Pope Leo XIII's Encyclical *Longinqua oceani* to the Church of the United States, January 6, 1895

THE last twenty years of the nineteenth century was one of the stormiest periods in the history of American Catholicism. Attacked from without by the American Protective Association (A.P.A.) as un-American and a threat to the Republic, and subject within to feuds among the bishops by reason of their conflicting interpretations on the role of the Church in public affairs, there was little peace until after the opening of the new century. The Holy See was, of course, aware of these tensions, and in an effort to restore unity and harmony Leo XIII addressed an encyclical to the hierarchy in which he analyzed the strengths and weaknesses of American society, and was at special pains to emphasize the function of the recently established Apostolic Delegation in the life of the American Church. Source: John J. Wynne, S.J. (Ed.), *The Great Encyclical Letters of Pope Leo XIII* (New York: Benziger Bros., 1903), pp. 320–335.

We traverse in spirit and thought the wide expanse of ocean; and although We have at other times addressed you in writing — chiefly when We directed Encyclical Letters to the bishops of the Catholic world — yet have We now resolved to speak to you separately, trusting that We shall be, God willing, of some assistance to the Catholic cause amongst you. To this We apply Ourselves with the utmost zeal and care; because We highly esteem and love exceedingly the young and vigorous American nation, in which We plainly discern latent forces for the advancement alike of civilization and of Christianity.

Not long ago, when your whole nation, as was fitting, celebrated, with grateful recollection and every manifestation of joy, the completion of the fourth century since the discovery of America, We, too, commemorated together with you that most auspicious event, sharing in your rejoicings with equal good-will. Nor were We on that occasion content with offering prayers at a distance for your welfare and greatness. It was Our wish to be in some manner present with you in your festivities. Hence We cheerfully sent one who should represent Our person.[1] Not without good reason did We take part in your celebration. For when America was, as yet, but a new-born babe, uttering in its cradle its first feeble cries, the Church took it to her

[1] Francesco Satolli (1839–1910), Archbishop of Lepanto, came to the United States in October, 1892, as Leo XIII's representative at the World's Columbian Exposition in Chicago.

bosom and motherly embrace. Columbus, as We have elsewhere expressly shown, sought, as the primary fruit of his voyages and labors, to open a pathway for the Christian faith into the new lands and new seas. Keeping this thought constantly in view, his first solicitude, wherever he disembarked, was to plant upon the shore the sacred emblem of the cross. Wherefore, like as the Ark of Noe, surmounting the overflowing waters, bore the seed of Israel together with the remnants of the human race, even thus did the barks launched by Columbus upon the ocean carry into regions beyond the seas as well the germs of mighty States as the principles of the Catholic religion.

This is not the place to give a detailed account of what thereupon ensued. Very rapidly did the light of the Gospel shine upon the savage tribes discovered by the Ligurian. For it is sufficiently well known how many of the children of Francis, as well as of Dominic and of Loyola, were accustomed during the two following centuries to voyage thither for this purpose; how they cared for the colonies brought over from Europe; but primarily and chiefly how they converted the natives from superstition to Christianity, sealing their labors in many instances with the testimony of their blood. The names newly given to so many of your towns and rivers and mountains and lakes teach and clearly witness how deeply your beginnings were marked with the footprints of the Catholic Church.

Nor, perchance, did the fact which We now recall take place without some design of divine Providence. Precisely at the epoch when the American colonies, having with Catholic aid, achieved liberty and independence, coalesced into a constitutional Republic the ecclesiastical hierarchy was happily established amongst you; and at the very time when the popular suffrage placed the great Washington at the helm of the Republic, the first bishop was set by apostolic authority over the American Church.[2] The well-known friendship and familiar intercourse which subsisted between these two men seems to be an evidence that the United States ought to be conjoined in concord and amity with the Catholic Church. And not without cause; for without morality the State cannot endure — a truth which that illustrious citizen of yours, whom We have just mentioned, with a keenness of insight worthy of his genius and statesmanship perceived and proclaimed. But the best and strongest support of morality is religion. She, by her very nature, guards and defends all the principles on

---

[2] George Washington was inaugurated as first President of the United States on April 30, 1789; John Carroll was appointed as first Bishop of Baltimore on November 6, 1789.

which duties are founded, and, setting before us the motives most powerful to influence us, commands us to live virtuously and forbids us to transgress. Now what is the Church other than a legitimate society, founded by the will and ordinance of Jesus Christ for the preservation of morality and the defence of religion? For this reason have We repeatedly endeavored, from the summit of the pontifical dignity, to inculcate that the Church, whilst directly and immediately aiming at the salvation of souls and the beatitude which is to be attained in heaven, is yet, even in the order of temporal things, the fountain of blessings so numerous and great that they could not have been greater or more numerous had the original purpose of her institution been the pursuit of happiness during the life which is spent on earth.

That your Republic is progressing and developing by giant strides is patent to all; and this holds good in religious matters also. For even as your cities, in the course of one century, have made a marvellous increase in wealth and power, so do we behold the Church, from scant and slender beginnings, grown with rapidity to be great and exceedingly flourishing. Now if, on the one hand, the increased riches and resources of your cities are justly attributed to the talents and active industry of the American people, on the other hand, the prosperous condition of Catholicity must be ascribed, first indeed, to the virtue, the ability, and the prudence of the bishops and clergy; but in no slight measure also, to the faith and generosity of the Catholic laity. Thus, while the different classes exerted their best energies, you were enabled to erect unnumbered religious and useful institutions, sacred edifices, schools for the instruction of youth, colleges for the higher branches, homes for the poor, hospitals for the sick, and convents and monasteries. As for what more closely touches spiritual interests, which are based upon the exercise of Christian virtues, many facts have been brought to Our notice, whereby We are animated with hope and filled with joy, namely, that the numbers of the secular and regular clergy are steadily augmenting, that pious sodalities and confraternities are held in esteem, that the Catholic parochial schools, the Sunday-schools for imparting Christian doctrine, and summer schools are in a flourishing condition; moreover, associations for mutual aid, for the relief of the indigent, for the promotion of temperate living, add to all this the many evidences of popular piety.

The main factor, no doubt, in bringing things into this happy state were the ordinances and decrees of your synods, especially of those which in more recent times were convened and confirmed by the authority of the Apostolic See. But, moreover (a fact which it gives pleasure to acknowledge), thanks are due to the equity of the laws which obtain in America and to the customs of the well-ordered Republic. For the Church amongst you, unopposed by the Constitution and government of your nation, fettered by no hostile legislation, protected against violence by the common laws and the impartiality of the tribunals, is free to live and act without hindrance. Yet, though all this is true, it would be very erroneous to draw the conclusion that in America is to be sought the type of the most desirable status of the Church, or that it would be universally lawful or expedient for State and Church to be, as in America, dissevered and divorced.[3] The fact that Catholicity with you is in good condition, nay, is even enjoying a prosperous growth, is by all means to be attributed to the fecundity with which God has endowed His Church, in virtue of which unless men or circumstances interfere, she spontaneously expands and propagates herself; but she would bring forth more abundant fruits if, in addition to liberty, she enjoyed the favor of the laws and the patronage of the public authority.

For Our part We have left nothing undone, as far as circumstances permitted, to preserve and more solidly establish amongst you the Catholic religion. With this intent, We have, as you are well aware, turned Our attention to two special objects: first, the advancement of learning; second, a perfecting of methods in the management of Church affairs. There already, indeed, existed several distinguished universities. We, however, thought it advisable that there should be one founded by authority of the Apostolic See and endowed by Us with all suitable powers, in which Catholic professors might instruct those devoted to the pursuit of learning. The design was to begin with philosophy and theology, adding, as means and circumstances would allow, the remaining branches, those particularly which the present age has introduced or perfected. An education cannot be deemed complete which takes no notice of modern sciences. It is obvious that in the existing keen competition of talents, and the widespread and, in itself, noble and praiseworthy passion for knowledge, Catholics ought to be not followers but leaders. It is necessary, therefore, that they should cultivate every refinement of learning, and

[3] This remark caused some uneasiness on the part of certain American bishops as to its possible effect on non-Catholics. Cf. John Tracy Ellis, *The Life of James Cardinal Gibbons, Archbishop of Baltimore, 1834–1921* (Milwaukee, 1952), II, 28–30.

zealously train their minds to the discovery of truth and the investigation, so far as it is possible, of the entire domain of nature. This in every age has been the desire of the Church; upon the enlargement of the boundaries of the sciences has she been wont to bestow all possible labor and energy. By a letter, therefore, dated the seventh day of March, in the year of Our Lord, 1889, directed to you, Venerable Brethren, We established at Washington, your capital city, esteemed by a majority of you a very proper seat for the higher studies, a university for the instruction of young men desirous of pursuing advanced courses. In announcing this matter to Our Venerable Brethren, the Cardinals of the Holy Roman Church, in Consistory, We expressed the wish that it should be regarded as the fixed law of the university to unite erudition and learning with soundness of faith and to imbue its students not less with religion than with scientific culture. To the Bishops of the United States We entrusted the task of establishing a suitable course of studies and of supervising the discipline of the students; and We conferred the office and authority of Chancellor, as it is called, upon the Archbishop of Baltimore. And, by divine favor, a quite happy beginning was made. For, without any delay, whilst you were celebrating the hundredth anniversary of the establishment of your ecclesiastical hierarchy, under the brightest auspices, in the presence of Our delegate, the divinity classes were opened.[4] From that time onward We know that theological science has been imparted by the diligence of eminent men the renown of whose talents and learning receives a fitting crown in their recognized loyalty and devotion to the Apostolic See. Nor is it long since We were apprised that, thanks to the liberality of a pious priest, a new building had been constructed, in which young men, as well cleric as lay, are to receive instruction in the natural sciences and in literature.[5] From Our knowledge of the American character, We are fully confident that the example set by this noble man will incite others of your citizens to imitate him; they will not fail to realize that liberality exercised towards such an object will be repaid by the very greatest advantages to the public.

No one can be ignorant how powerfully similar institutions of learning, whether originally founded by the Roman Church herself from time to time, or approved and promoted by her legislation, have

[4] The Catholic University of America was opened on November 13, 1889.

[5] McMahon Hall, the second building of the university, was formally dedicated on October 1, 1895. It had been made possible through the generosity of James McMahon (1817–1901), former pastor of St. Andrew's Church, New York.

contributed to the spread of knowledge and civilization in every part of Europe. Even in Our own day, though other instances might be given, it is enough to mention the University of Louvain, to which the entire Belgian nation ascribes its almost daily increase in prosperity and glory. Equally abundant will be the benefits proceeding from the Washington University, if the professors and students (as We doubt not they will) be mindful of Our injunctions, and, shunning party spirit and strife, conciliate the good opinion of the people and the clergy.

We wish now, Venerable Brethren, to commend to your affection and to the generosity of your people the college which Our predecessor, Pius IX, founded in this city for the ecclesiastical training of young men from North America,[6] and which We took care to place upon a firm basis by a letter dated the twenty-fifth day of October, in the year of Our Lord 1884. We can make this appeal the more confidently, because the results obtained from this institution have by no means belied the expectations commonly entertained regarding it. You yourselves can testify that during its brief existence it has sent forth a very large number of exemplary priests, some of whom have been promoted for their virtue and learning to the highest degrees of ecclesiastical dignity. We are, therefore, thoroughly persuaded that you will continue to be solicitous to send hither select young men who are in training to become the hope of the Church. For they will carry back to their homes and utilize for the general good the wealth of intellectual attainments and moral excellence which they shall have acquired in the city of Rome.

The love which We cherish towards the Catholics of your nation moved Us, likewise, to turn Our attention at the very beginning of Our Pontificate to the convocation of a third Plenary Council of Baltimore.[7] Subsequently, when the archbishops, at Our invitation, had come to Rome, We diligently inquired from them what they deemed most conducive to the common good. We finally, and after mature deliberation, ratified by apostolic authority the decrees of the prelates assembled at Baltimore. In truth the event has proven, and still proves, that the decrees of Baltimore were salutary and timely in the extreme. Experience has demonstrated their power for the maintenance of discipline; for stimulating the intelligence and zeal of the clergy for defending and developing the Catholic education of

[6] The North American College, Rome, was opened on December 8, 1859.
[7] The Third Plenary Council of Baltimore was held November 9–December 7, 1884.

youth. Wherefore, Venerable Brethren, if We make acknowledgment of your activity in these matters, if We laud your firmness tempered with prudence, We but pay tribute due to your merit; for We are fully sensible that so great a harvest of blessings could by no means have so swiftly ripened to maturity, had you not exerted yourselves, each to the utmost of his ability, sedulously and faithfully to carry into effect the statutes you had wisely framed at Baltimore.

But when the Council of Baltimore had concluded its labors, the duty still remained of putting, so to speak, a proper and becoming crown upon the work. This, We perceived, could scarcely be done in a more fitting manner than through the due establishment by the Apostolic See of an American Legation. Accordingly, as you are well aware, We have done this.[8] By this action, as We have elsewhere intimated, We have wished, first of all, to certify that, in Our judgment and affection, America occupies the same place and rights as other States, be they ever so mighty and imperial. In addition to this We had in mind to draw more closely the bonds of duty and friendship which connect you and so many thousands of Catholics with the Apostolic See. In fact, the mass of the Catholics understood how salutary Our action was destined to be; they saw, moreover, that it accorded with the usage and policy of the Apostolic See. For it has been, from earliest antiquity, the custom of the Roman Pontiffs in the exercise of the divinely bestowed gift of the primacy in the administration of the Church of Christ to send forth legates to Christian nations and peoples. And they did this, not by an adventitious but an inherent right. For "the Roman Pontiff, upon whom Christ has conferred ordinary and immediate jurisdiction, as well over all and singular churches, as over all and singular pastors and faithful [Con. Vat. Sess., iv. c. 3], since he cannot personally visit the different regions and thus exercise the pastoral office over the flock entrusted to him, finds it necessary, from time to time, in the discharge of the ministry imposed on him, to despatch legates into different parts of the world, according as the need arises; who, supplying his place, may correct errors, make the rough ways plain, and administer to the people confided to their care increased means of salvation" [Cap. Un. Extrav. Comm. De Consuet., 1. 1].

But how unjust and baseless would be the suspicion, should it anywhere exist, that the powers conferred on the legate are an obstacle to the authority of the bishops! Sacred to Us (more than to any other) are the rights of those *"whom the Holy Ghost has placed as*

[8] The Apostolic Delegation at Washington was established on January 21, 1893.

bishops to rule the Church of God." That these rights should remain intact in every nation in every part of the globe, We both desire and ought to desire, the more so since the dignity of the individual bishop is by nature so interwoven with the dignity of the Roman Pontiff that any measure which benefits the one necessarily protects the other. "My honor is the honor of the Universal Church. My honor is the unimpaired vigor of My brethren. Then am I truly honored when to each one due honor is not denied" [S. Gregorius Epis. ad Eulog. Alax. lib. viii. ep. 30]. Therefore, since it is the office and function of an apostolic legate, with whatsoever powers he may be vested, to execute the mandates and interpret the will of the Pontiff who sends him, thus, so far from his being of any detriment to the ordinary power of the bishops, he will rather bring an accession of stability and strength. His authority will possess no slight weight for preserving in the multitude a submissive spirit; in the clergy discipline and due reverence for the bishops, and in the bishops mutual charity and an intimate union of souls. And since this union, so salutary and desirable, consists mainly in harmony of thought and action, he will, no doubt, bring it to pass that each one of you shall persevere in the diligent administration of his diocesan affairs; that one shall not impede another in matters of government; that one shall not pry into the counsels and conduct of another; finally, that with disagreements eradicated and mutual esteem maintained, you may all work together with combined energies to promote the glory of the American Church and the general welfare. It is difficult to estimate the good results which will flow from this concord of the bishops. Our own people will receive edification; and the force of example will have its effect on those without — who will be persuaded by this argument alone that the divine apostolate has passed by inheritance to the ranks of the Catholic episcopate.

Another consideration claims our earnest attention. All intelligent men are agreed, and We Ourselves have with pleasure intimated it above, that America seems destined for greater things. Now it is Our wish that the Catholic Church should not only share in, but help to bring about, this prospective greatness. We deem it right and proper that she should, by availing herself of the opportunities daily presented to her, keep equal step with the Republic in the march of improvement, at the same time striving to the utmost, by her virtue and her institutions, to aid in the rapid growth of the States. Now, she will attain both these objects the more easily and abundantly, in proportion to the degree in which the future shall find her constitution perfected. But what is the meaning of the legation of which we are speaking, or what is its ultimate aim except to bring it about that the constitution of the Church shall be strengthened, her discipline better fortified? Wherefore, We ardently desire that this truth should sink day by day more deeply into the minds of Catholics — namely, that they can in no better way safeguard their own individual interests and the common good than by yielding a hearty submission and obedience to the Church. Your faithful people, however, are scarcely in need of exhortation on this point; for they are accustomed to adhere to the institutions of Catholicity with willing souls and a constancy worthy of all praise.

To one matter of the first importance and fraught with the greatest blessings it is a pleasure at this place to refer, on account of the holy firmness in principle and practice respecting it which, as a rule, rightly prevails amongst you; We mean the Christian dogma of the unity and indissolubility of marriage; which supplies the firmest bond of safety not merely to the family but to society at large. Not a few of your citizens, even of those who dissent from us in other doctrines, terrified by the licentiousness of divorce, admire and approve in this regard the Catholic teaching and the Catholic customs. They are led to this judgment not less by love of country than by the wisdom of the doctrine. For difficult it is to imagine a more deadly pest to the community than the wish to declare dissoluble a bond which the law of God has made perpetual and inseverable. Divorce "is the fruitful cause of mutable marriage contracts; it diminishes mutual affection; it supplies a pernicious stimulus to unfaithfulness; it is injurious to the care and education of children; it gives occasion to the breaking up of domestic society; it scatters the seeds of discord among families; it lessens and degrades the dignity of women, who incur the danger of being abandoned when they shall have subserved the lust of their husbands. And since nothing tends so effectually as the corruption of morals to ruin families and undermine the strength of kingdoms, it may easily be perceived that divorce is especially hostile to the prosperity of families and States" [Encyc. *Arcanum*].

As regards civil affairs, experience has shown how important it is that the citizens should be upright and virtuous. In a free State, unless justice be generally cultivated, unless the people be repeatedly and diligently urged to observe the precepts and laws of the Gospel, liberty itself may be pernicious. Let those of the clergy, therefore, who are occupied with the instruction of the multitude, treat plainly this topic of the duties of citizens, so that all may understand and feel the necessity, in political life, of conscientiousness, self-restraint, and integrity; for that cannot be lawful in public which is unlawful in private affairs. On this whole subject there are to be found, as you know, in the encyclical letters written by Us from time to time in the course of Our pontificate, many things which Catholics should attend to and observe. In these writings and expositions We have treated of human liberty, of the chief Christian duties, of civil government, and of the Christian constitution of States, drawing Our principles as well from the teaching of the Gospels as from reason.[9] They, then, who wish to be good citizens and discharge their duties faithfully may readily learn from Our Letters the ideal of an upright life. In like manner, let the priests be persistent in keeping before the minds of the people the enactments of the Third Council of Baltimore, particularly those which inculcate the virtue of temperance, the frequent use of the sacraments, and the observance of the just laws and institutions of the Republic.

Now, with regard to entering societies, extreme care should be taken not to be ensnared by error. And We wish to be understood as referring in a special manner to the working classes, who assuredly have the right to unite in associations for the promotion of their interests; a right acknowledged by the Church and unopposed by nature. But it is very important to take heed with whom they are to associate, lest whilst seeking aid for the improvement of their condition, they may be imperilling far weightier interests. The most effectual precaution against this peril is to determine with themselves at no time or in any matter to be parties to the violation of justice. Any society, therefore, which is ruled by and servilely obeys persons who are not steadfast for the right and friendly to religion is capable of being extremely prejudicial to the interests as well of individuals as of the community; beneficial it cannot be. Let this conclusion, therefore, remain firm — to shun not only those associations which have been openly condemned by the judgment of the Church, but those also which, in the opinion of intelligent men, and especially of the bishops, are regarded as suspicious and dangerous.[10]

Nay, rather, unless forced by necessity to do otherwise, Catholics ought to prefer to associate with Catholics, a course which will be very conducive to the safeguarding of their faith. As presidents of

---

[9] Cf. Wynne, *op. cit.*, for the encyclicals *Immortale Dei,* November 1, 1885 (pp. 107–134); *Libertas praestantissimum,* June 20, 1888 (pp. 135–163); and *Sapientiae christianae,* January 10, 1890 (pp. 180–207).

[10] Cf. Wynne, *op. cit.*, pp. 83–106, for Leo XIII's encyclical *Humanum genus,* April 20, 1884, on Freemasonry.

societies thus formed among themselves, it will be well to appoint either priests or upright laymen of weight and character, guided by whose counsels they should endeavor peacefully to adopt and carry into effect such measures as may seem most advantageous to their interests, keeping in view the rules laid down by Us in Our Encyclical, *Rerum Novarum.*[11] Let them, however, never allow this to escape their memory: that whilst it is proper and desirable to assert and secure the rights of the many, yet this is not to be done by a violation of duty; and that these are very important duties; not to touch what belongs to another; to allow every one to be free in the management of his own affairs; not to hinder any one to dispose of his services when he please and where he please. The scenes of violence and riot which you witnessed last year in your own country[12] sufficiently admonish you that America too is threatened with the audacity and ferocity of the enemies of public order. The state of the times, therefore, bids Catholics to labor for the tranquillity of the commonwealth, and for this purpose to obey the laws, abhor violence, and seek no more than equity or justice permits.

Towards these objects much may be contributed by those who have devoted themselves to writing, and in particular by those who are engaged on the daily press. We are aware that already there labor in this field many men of skill and experience, whose diligence demands words of praise rather than of encouragement. Nevertheless, since the thirst for reading and knowledge is so vehement and widespread amongst you, and since, according to circumstances, it can be productive either of good or evil, every effort should be made to increase the number of intelligent and well-disposed writers who take religion for their guide and virtue for their constant companion. And this seems all the more necessary in America, on account of the familiar intercourse and intimacy between Catholics and those who are estranged from the Catholic name, a condition of things which certainly exacts from our people great circumspection and more than ordinary firmness. It is necessary to instruct, admonish, strengthen and urge them on to the pursuit of virtue and to the faithful observance, amid so many occasions of stumbling, of their duties towards the Church. It is, of course, the proper function of the clergy to devote their care and energies to this great work; but the age and

---

[11] *Rerum novarum* was published on May 15, 1891. For the text, cf. Wynne, *op. cit.*, pp. 208–248.

[12] Between March and August, 1894, there had occurred the march of Coxey's Army on Washington, the Pullman strike, and a general strike on the western railroads.

the country require that journalists should be equally zealous in this same cause and labor in it to the full extent of their powers. Let them, however, seriously reflect that their writings, if not positively prejudicial to religion, will surely be of slight service to it unless in concord of minds they all seek the same end. They who desire to be of real service to the Church, and with their pens heartily to defend the Catholic cause, should carry on the conflict with perfect unanimity, and, as it were, with serried ranks, for they rather inflict than repel war if they waste their strength by discord. In like manner their work, instead of being profitable and fruitful, becomes injurious and disastrous whenever they presume to call before their tribunal the decisions and acts of bishops, and, casting off due reverence, cavil and find fault; not perceiving how great a disturbance of order, how many evils are thereby produced. Let them, then, be mindful of their duty, and not overstep the proper limits of moderation. The bishops, placed in the lofty position of authority, are to be obeyed, and suitable honor befitting the magnitude and sanctity of their office should be paid them. Now, this reverence, "which it is lawful to no one to neglect," should of necessity be eminently conspicuous and exemplary in Catholic journalists. For journals, naturally circulating far and wide, come daily into the hands of everybody, and exert no small influence upon the opinions and morals of the multitude [Ep. Cognita Nobis ad Archiepp. et Epp. Provinciarum, Taurinen. Mediolanen, et Vercellen., XXV., Jan. an. MDCCCLXXXII].

We have Ourselves, on frequent occasions, laid down many rules respecting the duties of a good writer; many of which were unanimously inculcated as well by the Third Council of Baltimore as by the archbishops in their meeting at Chicago in the year 1893. Let Catholic writers, therefore, bear impressed on their minds Our teachings on this point as well as yours; and let them resolve that their entire method of writing shall be thereby guided, if they indeed desire, as they ought to desire, to discharge their duty well.

Our thoughts now turn to those who dissent from us in matters of Christian faith; and who shall deny that, with not a few of them, dissent is a matter rather of inheritance than of will? How solicitous We are of their salvation, with what ardor of soul We wish that they should be at length restored to the embrace of the Church, the common mother of all, Our Apostolic Epistle, *"Praeclara,"* has in very recent times declared.[13] Nor are we destitute of all hope; for He is

[13] For Leo XIII's views on the reunion of Christendom, cf. the encyclical *Praeclara gratulationis publicae,* June 20, 1894, in Wynne, *op. cit.,* pp. 303–319.

present and hath a care whom all things obey and who laid down His life that He might "gather in one the children of God who were dispersed" (John xi. 52).

Surely we ought not to desert them nor leave them to their fancies; but with mildness and charity draw them to us, using every means of persuasion to induce them to examine closely every part of the Catholic doctrine, and to free themselves from preconceived notions. In this matter, if the first place belongs to the bishops and clergy, the second belongs to the laity, who have it in their power to aid the apostolic efforts of the clergy by the probity of their morals and the integrity of their lives. Great is the force of example; particularly with those who are earnestly seeking the truth, and who, from a certain inborn virtuous disposition, are striving to live an honorable and upright life, to which class very many of your fellow-citizens belong. If the spectacle of Christian virtues exerted the powerful influence over the heathens blinded, as they were, by inveterate superstition, which the records of history attest, shall we think it powerless to eradicate error in the case of those who have been initiated into the Christian religion?

Finally, We cannot pass over in silence those whose long-continued unhappy lot implores and demands succor from men of apostolic zeal; We refer to the Indians and the negroes who are to be found within the confines of America, the greatest portion of whom have not yet dispelled the darkness of superstition. How wide a field for cultivation! How great a multitude of human beings to be made partakers of the blessing derived through Jesus Christ!

Meanwhile, as a presage of heavenly graces and a testimony of Our benevolence, We most lovingly in the Lord impart to you, Venerable Brethren, and to your clergy and people, Our Apostolic Benediction.

139. Bishop Keane's Views on the Role of Legislation in a Democratic Government, September 11, 1895

DURING the years 1887–1896 while John J. Keane (1839–1918) served as first rector of the Catholic University of America, he gave many public addresses throughout the country. From the earliest days of his priesthood he had been an ardent temperance advocate, an interest which he maintained until his death. When an interdenominational temperance group in Buffalo,

New York, invited him to speak to them in September, 1895, he responded. The following excerpts from that speech embodied Keane's views concerning the nature and object of civil legislation in a democratic government. Source: John J. Keane, *The Catholic Church and the American Sunday* (Buffalo: Catholic Truth Society, 1895).

What is the proper end and object and matter of civil legislation? The Christian maxim that rulers represent God's authority only for the popular welfare has come to be understood almost the wide world over. The inalienable rights of man as man have been so forcibly proclaimed and emphasized, especially by our own country, that all the peoples of the earth have come to appreciate that the classes, just like the sovereign, have reason to exist only in so far as they contribute to the general welfare, and that this, once more, must be the aim of legislation. — The civilized world now never loses sight of the great truth that the general welfare must be the main consideration, the chief test of legislation, and that corporations, industrial and financial organizations of any sort whatsoever, can receive legislative recognition only in so far as they are compatible with the common weal, can claim legislative privileges only in so far as this conduces to the welfare of the people at large.

The end and object of legislation is "the greatest good of the greatest number."

What is the greatest good of the greatest number? — that which will turn them into the best men; what will spread abroad the reign of the true and the right and fill the lives of the people with peace. We are human beings, and it is human welfare that we seek, the welfare of the whole being of man, physical, intellectual, moral. The true aim of legislation is the promotion of civilization along all the lines of human activity that constitute it and perfect it. It is not merely to repress the violence and wrong-doing that would hinder civilization, but to encourage and help on the right-doing that conduces to civilization. Civilization means not merely the machinery for producing wealth, for transporting and distributing wealth, for multiplying the conveniences of life, for increasing its comfort and physical well-being. It means all that, but it means much more; because man is much more than that and needs much more than that. It means the advance of human welfare along the lines of man's complex being, physical, intellectual, moral. The function of law and government is to promote civilization; it is to promote man's physical welfare by fostering industries, securing justice to both employers and employed, multiplying means of popular comfort; it is to promote man's intellectual welfare, by fostering the multiplication of schools and the improvement of educational methods; it is to promote man's aesthetic welfare, by seeing to the beauty of cities as well as to their healthfulness and orderliness; it is to promote man's moral welfare by repressing incentives to public immorality and encouraging all institutions that aim at making both public and private life better, purer and nobler. This is the aim of civilization, and this is the aim of legislation.

Legislation like civilization must be Ethical. The basis of human life, of human progress, of human civilization, is ethical, is moral. That ethics, morals, are not nature's instinct but nature's rule and guide, a rule and guide imposed on nature for nature's good, its source and sanction are not to be sought in nature's self, but above nature, in the Supreme Good to which nature tends as its perfection and its destiny. [Here Keane quoted Washington's dictum, "Of all the dispositions and habits that lead to political prosperity, religion and morality are indispensable supports."]

Whatever fosters religion and morality in the lives of our people, strengthens the foundations of our national prosperity, and it is our duty as Americans to encourage and uphold it and vice versa. . . .

140. Cardinal Satolli's Visit to New Orleans, February 15–21, 1896

ON JANUARY 21, 1893, Pope Leo XIII established the Apostolic Delegation in Washington after lengthy and sometimes heated negotiations between the Holy See and the American hierarchy. The man selected as first delegate was Francesco Satolli (1839–1910), Archbishop of Lepanto and a favorite of the pontiff's since their days together in Perugia. To the A.P.A. the event became, as might be expected, something of a *cause célèbre,* and its principal founder later stated that it had "very materially" stimulated the growth of the organization, for as he said, "We looked upon Satolli as a representative of the Propaganda at Rome to direct and influence legislation . . ." and the opinion was circulated "that he was interfering with the public institutions of this country" (Henry F. Bowers to Humphrey J. Desmond, Clinton, Iowa, March 1, 1899, Desmond, *The A.P.A. Movement. A Sketch* [Washington, 1912], p. 15). At the outset of his residence in the United States, Satolli leaned toward the more liberal-minded bishops like Gibbons and Ireland, but as time went on his sympathies shifted to their conservative colleagues led by Archbishop Corrigan and the prelates of German birth or extraction. In the consistory of November, 1895, he was created a cardinal, but he remained prodelegate until the arrival of his successor, Sebastiano Martinelli, O.S.A. (1848–1918), in October, 1896.

During his last months in the country the prodelegate made an extensive trip through the South and West with Alexis Orban (1850–1915), a French-born Sulpician, who acted as his secretary, and who since November, 1889, had been acting librarian and assistant spiritual director at the Catholic University of America. Both Satolli and Orban were strongly opposed to Bishop Keane, rector of the university, whom they regarded as an ultra-liberal. When, therefore, they encountered Keane at the inauguration of the Catholic Winter School in New Orleans the meeting was not a cordial one. A few months later Orban was recalled by the Superior-General of St. Sulpice at the request of the university administration, and that only a few weeks before Keane himself was dismissed as rector. Orban kept an account in French of his trip with Satolli in which he recorded not only the bias against Keane and his own uncomplimentary views about the Irish clergy in the United States, but also some valuable impressions of local customs in the areas visited.* The following excerpt describes the pro-delegate's stay in New Orleans where the carnival, the Catholic immigrant groups, the Winter School, and other items come in for comment. The document was discovered in 1951 by Colman J. Barry, O.S.B., in the library of the Collegio di Sant' Anselmo in Rome. Father Barry kindly supplied the editor with a copy of the English translation. Satolli had spent the years 1872–1874 at Monte Cassino with the intention of becoming a Benedictine, and it was that, plus his desire that the students should profit from his library of Thomistic works, that prompted him to leave his books and papers to Sant' Anselmo. Source: Archives of St. John's Abbey, Collegeville, Minnesota (microfilm). For the entire document cf. Colman J. Barry, O.S.B. (Ed.), "Tour of His Eminence Cardinal Francesco Satolli, Pro-Apostolic Delegate, through the United States (of the North) from 12 February to 13 March 1896," *Historical Records and Studies,* XLIII (1955), 27–94.

The "Southern Railway" Company had given free passage from Washington to Atlanta to Cardinal Satolli and his secretary. The same favor was granted from Atlanta to New Orleans. Suffice it to say, on a trip of 5,000 kilometers His Eminence did not pay travel expenses, and almost nothing for the other incidentals of his journey; the committees set up to receive him took charge of everything. Toward six o'clock we awoke in the state of Mississippi after having crossed Alabama, with its capital Montgomery, and its episcopal see of Mobile. Mississippi comprises the territory assigned to the diocese of Natchez. At one of the railroad stations on the gulf, in a pretty little place called Bay St. Louis (a name which indeed recalls the origin of the colony), some religious were present in spite of the

* Although Orban's signature appears nowhere on the original document, there would seem to be little doubt that he was the author. Cf. Patrick H. Ahern, *The Life of John J. Keane, Educator and Archbishop, 1839–1918* (Milwaukee, 1955), p. 171.

early hour. They were the Brothers of the Sacred Heart from Puy-en-Velais (France) brought here by one of the French bishops who had established Catholicism in this area.[1] They had come to the station at five o'clock in the morning with a small number of their novices and students, in order to present their respects to the Cardinal Pro-Delegate.

At eight-thirty in the morning [February 15, 1896] we came into New Orleans. The Archbishop, Monsignor Janssens,[2] with his chancellor and Father Semple, S.J., Rector of the Jesuit College,[3] were at the station to receive His Eminence. We were scarcely in the carriage before two reporters came up to offer their services. In a few minutes we were at the Archbishop's palace. One would have thought himself in Europe. It was the convent of the Ursulines erected shortly after their arrival from France in 1732.[4] Built around a court and garden, in the center of the old town, which is now called the French Quarter, it truly had a grand air with its imposing carriage gate and circular wall. After passing the porter's office, we crossed the court in front of the main building decorated with palms, cactus, banana and magnolia trees, to a grand stairway with iron balustrade which led to the rooms. A 17th century clock, brought from Paris by the Ursulines, still keeps time as exactly under the republic as it did under the kings. On the left a corridor led to the chapel where we went immediately to offer holy Mass. A person would have believed himself to be in one of the good, old chapels of France. It was of Louis XIV Renaissance style, with its scrolled volutes, its corners ornamented at the top, and its rounded friezes. There was a miraculous statue of the Virgin under the title of Our Lady of Perpetual Help which Leo XIII had recently crowned, and to which was attributed a great number of favors, both public and private. Every good creole of New Orleans has the greatest veneration for this statue.

After breakfast His Eminence wanted his first talk to be for the

---

[1] The Brothers of the Sacred Heart had originally been brought to the United States in January, 1847, by Michael Portier (1795–1859), first Bishop of Mobile. They opened their St. Stanislaus College at St. Louis, Mississippi, in 1855.

[2] Francis Janssens (1843–1897), the Dutch-born Archbishop of New Orleans, had been promoted to that see from the Diocese of Natchez in August, 1888. The chancellor at the time was the Very Reverend Joseph A. Thebault.

[3] Henry C. Semple, S.J. (1853–1925), pastor of the Church of the Immaculate Conception and president of the college of the same name, was the editor of *The Ursulines in New Orleans and Our Lady of Prompt Succor. A Record of Two Centuries, 1727–1925* (New York, 1925).

[4] The Ursulines arrived in New Orleans in August, 1727, not 1732.

Italian Sisters (the Salesians) [*sic*] who conduct a school here for Italian immigrants.[5] The Italians have two churches here reserved by the priests for their nationality.[6] One of these priests is unfortunately old and infirm. But the other has his own church and rectory, so that the Ordinary does not feel free to replace the former with a younger and more active pastor. The good Sisters were hoping for this visit from the Cardinal, but they did not expect him so soon, and his unannounced arrival at such an early hour upset the whole community. The portress on duty ran to the cloister and made the greatest possible noise while at the same time making desperate signs to the Sisters who were no more prepared than she to receive a visit. However, soon re-assured by the evident simplicity and cordiality of the Cardinal, they regained their calm a little, and they began to converse about their community and its work. This was a foretaste of the more complete visit which His Eminence promised to make with them on his first free day.

We had luncheon at the Archbishop's palace. We had as guests Bishop Gabriels of Ogdensburg (New York), Bishop Van de Vyver of Richmond (Virginia), and Bishop Meerschaert, Vicar-Apostolic of the Indian Territory, all of whom were Belgians by birth as was Archbishop Janssens.[7] Cardinal Gibbons, who had arrived the evening before, was staying with his brother who was a prominent citizen of the city.[8] He had left a note at the Archbishop's palace inviting His Eminence and his secretary to dine with him. We arrived there at the appointed hour to find the Cardinal Archbishop of Baltimore surrounded by a charming family of nephews and nieces who strove among themselves to entertain him. Beside me at dinner was an old Jesuit who had been chaplain of the prison for forty-eight years,

---

[5] The Missionary Sisters of the Sacred Heart, founded by St. Frances Xavier Cabrini (1850–1917), got their start in New Orleans when three sisters arrived from New York in July, 1892, and took up residence in rented rooms in a tenement house on St. Philip Street. The foundress herself had visited New Orleans in the spring of 1892 and had responded to the request of Archbishop Janssens that she establish a house in his see city for the spiritual and material care of the Italian immigrants.

[6] St. Anthony of Padua Church at Rampart and Conti Streets was for the Italians, but the Chapel of St. Francis of Assisi at Chartres and Decatur Streets which had been opened in 1891 was discontinued after 1893.

[7] Henry Gabriels (1838–1921) was consecrated as second Bishop of Ogdensburg in May, 1892; Augustine Van de Vyver (1844–1911) was named sixth Bishop of Richmond in 1889; Theophile Meerschaert (1847–1924) was appointed first Vicar Apostolic of Indian Territory in June, 1891. Archbishop Janssens had been born in the Netherlands, not in Belgium.

[8] John T. Gibbons (1837–1924), brother of the cardinal, was a wealthy grain merchant in New Orleans.

who had assisted at the hanging of forty prisoners condemned to death, and who had endured eighteen epidemics of yellow fever. During one of these epidemics he was almost the only priest, and all his time from morning to evening was taken up in administering the sacraments to the sick. He found time to say his breviary only upon his return in the evening which often was very late at night. He recited it entirely, fatigued as he was. What a beautiful life! What a venerable priest! His superiors have commissioned him to write his memoirs. They will be without doubt a very edifying page in the history of this mission.

Sunday, February 16 at eleven o'clock, was set for pontifical Mass. It was a superb day: an Italian sky with a spring sun. At ten-thirty a detachment of troops took up their position in the Archbishop's court. The Archbishop asked His Eminence to come to the balcony where the soldiers gave him a military salute. Then the clergy formed in procession before the Cardinal's chamber and the procession began: the soldiers, the band playing a march, then the different orders of the clergy, finally the prelates each escorted by two assistants, the deacons of honor and the deacons of the Mass, the assistant priest, and at the end His Eminence Cardinal Satolli in pontificals. They crossed the city streets (it is the custom here), through a respectful crowd. In front of the cathedral there was a large crowd. Police sergeants had great difficulty in making a passage way for the procession. The Cathedral of St. Louis, a grand edifice built during the interval of Spanish domination, was packed in spite of its two tiers of galleries and the fact that admissions were by ticket only. In the first benches near the sanctuary the Governor of Louisiana,[9] the Mayor of the city,[10] the Judges of the Superior Court, the Consuls-General of France and Spain with their personnel had taken their places. One of the secretaries of the French Embassy had even come from Washington, and he had presented his card to Cardinal Satolli soon after his arrival. The ceremonies were impressive, since they were presided over by the Cardinal Delegate of the Sovereign Pontiff, in the presence of another prince of the Roman Court, Cardinal Gibbons, Archbishop of Baltimore, the Archbishop of Cincinnati,[11] and three other Bishops of the New Orleans province who had come for the occasion. Since here we were so far distant from any Catholic

---

[9] Murphy J. Foster (1849–1921) was Governor of Louisiana, 1892–1900.

[10] John Fitzpatrick (1844–1919) was Mayor of New Orleans at the time.

[11] William Henry Elder (1819–1904) became Archbishop of Cincinnati in July, 1883, after having served for three years as coadjutor to John B. Purcell.

nation, it is not astonishing to say that such a spectacle had never been seen in this city. Cardinal Gibbons gave a short homily on the gospel of the day. At the end of the Mass, Cardinal Satolli took off his pontificals and returned to the throne. Then the Archbishop, in a discourse which came from the heart, expressed the appreciation of his people and himself for the honor given to them, the respect which they had for the person of the august and well-beloved Pontiff, Leo XIII, whom he represented. Then the recessional was formed to lead the clergy and eminent prelates back to the Archbishop's palace, where a dinner awaited them. It was almost two o'clock in the afternoon.

After a few minutes of necessary rest a deputation of Italian immigrants waited upon His Eminence. These sons of Italy were about sixty in number, some born in New Orleans, but most of them came from the old world. Their spokesman made a truly touching address, filled with sentiments of love for their native land which they had left, and also of respect and attachment for the Papacy. Cardinal Satolli responded eloquently, thanking them, felicitating them on their patriotic and Catholic sentiments. Then he added that without doubt they should be most appreciative of their adopted homeland which gave them, as to its own children, bread and liberty. They should not forget, however, that they were Italian in origin, that they should be proud of being sons of Italy, that land of the fine arts, of the Papacy, center of true civilization. He developed these ideas with a force which uplifted his audience. All left full of encouragement and admiration for their eminent compatriot.

That evening at seven-thirty, a reception was held in honor of the two cardinals at the home of Mr. Thomas Semmes,[12] an excellent Catholic and one of the prominent citizens of the city. These receptions entail, for the person who is the object of them, standing throughout the ceremony and receiving the "hand shakes" of all the visitors. At Mr. Semmes' home we met the most distinguished society of New Orleans and consequently of the whole of America. All indeed agree that nothing is comparable in any city to the old plantation families. Many had been ruined by the Civil War of 1862 [*sic*]–1865, but they still preserve a distinction of language and customs. The French spoken in New Orleans is as pure as the language of the best Parisian society, and now the

[12] Thomas J. Semmes (1824–1899), a prominent Catholic lawyer of New Orleans, was professor of law in Tulane University and president of the American Bar Association in 1886.

people of New Orleans have the advantage of knowing English as well as their mother tongue.

After Mass on Monday morning at the archbishopric, the brother of His Eminence, Cardinal Gibbons, came to conduct us on a carriage tour, and to visit the cemeteries as well as other charitable institutions on route. Of all cities New Orleans has the most cemeteries. Along one long road completely bordered with them, I counted seven, one of which was especially extensive. The reason for multiplying these cemeteries is that the people never inter anyone where another body has been laid. The soil here is dark alluvial; it is like a big raft floating on the water. The river flows at the base of this mass. Each family, with the little means they have, build a funeral chapel on top of the ground. Inside the chapel on both sides shelves are recessed in the form of bureau drawers, and in these the coffins are placed. Then the heavy door of iron or stone is closed just as a big strong box is closed after a treasure is enclosed. Mausoleums are found everywhere with respective family names on the front. The Jews who here as elsewhere have control of the banking system and trade, and who already possess the most beautiful homes, have also the richest cemetery. On returning from this mournful but interesting tour and after visiting the "Maison du Bon Pasteur" (an Angers foundation),[13] we crossed the "Bayou" Saint Jean (here they call a "bayou" a natural canal formed by one of the many branches of the Mississippi across the delta) and then went along Esplanade Street, the popular planters' quarter before the war. A number of their residences can still be seen, but a good number have passed into other hands.

The day before Mardi Gras we participated in all the customs brought here by the French since the carnival is still held in great honor in New Orleans. People come from all sections of the Union to see it, and during these days of the feast the hotels are filled. One of the nephews of Cardinal Gibbons took us to await after dinner the arrival of "Rex," or the king of the carnival. At the close of the preceding carnival a king is named by the majority vote of the club members of the city. His nomination is kept secret. Several days before Shrove Monday he goes with his court to one of the islands of the Gulf, and on Monday afternoon he leaves it on a magnificent steamer beautifully

---

[13] The first Sisters of the Good Shepherd arrived in New Orleans in February, 1859, from their convent in St. Louis. The original House of the Good Shepherd was located on Magazine Street, but was later moved to the location at Bienville and Broad Streets.

decorated. The port authorities are on the look-out and as soon as he is sighted, many yachts and barges, with carnival flags flying from their masts, conduct him into the port. At a cannon signal the crowd closes in on the quay, the garrison soldiers precede with fanfare announcing the march, and when "Rex" disembarks, he and his court are solemnly conducted in carriages to the city hall. The king, as well as his officials, are clad in bright oriental costumes, his head is crowned, he carries a sceptre, and he majestically bows to right and left. At the city hall, the mayor and his council receive him on a platform and present the keys of the city to him. The king is then led to the council chamber where a throne has been prepared. There he distributes his favors as gifts of the joyous event, naming his friends duke of this or count of that, etc.

We assisted at this spectacle coming down from the Middle Ages, where all the people, rich and poor, old and young, white and black, forgetting life's anxieties for two or three days, give themselves entirely to the innocent joys of simple celebrations.

On Tuesday morning (February 18) His Eminence offered holy Mass at the convent of the Salesian Sisters (Italians). The little chapel was filled. Besides the children, their parents were there as well as friends of the institution. After the Gospel, His Eminence turned to the congregation and delivered a short exhortation, taking as his theme the life of Saint Agatha whose feast it was. After holy Mass we had breakfast which, thanks to the generosity of benefactors, was more like a full dinner. Then we were conducted to a parlor (very small; it is believed to be the original room) where the children presented an "academia" in honor of His Eminence. First they played a lovely little selection from Mascagni, then one of them came forward and read an address in Italian. A "ragazzetta" presented a bouquet of picked flowers "sul terreno del amore." "Mi tocca il cuore," the little one said; however she recited her piece without pause. A Sister then read a very interesting exposition of the work which the Salesians had come to undertake for poor Italian immigrants two years previously. She told of their difficulties, fears, and consolations as well as their hopes. Everything about this family reunion in this poor school was so touching that tears came involuntarily to the eyes. His Eminence was truly inspired by the occasion, and gave a talk to the children, parents and Sisters that was full of paternal charity. All the little black eyes, brightened with the sun of Italy, so lively, so intelligent, were fixed on the Pope's representative, on the cardinal born as they on Italian soil. His Eminence encouraged them to love their fatherland of adoption which had been so willing to receive them, and to offer them the same advantages as its own citizens.

Italian immigrants in the United States are generally very poor and suffer intellectual and moral disadvantages which ordinarily accompany poverty. From this fact arises that despising of the Italian name among the mass of the American people. But with the passing of a few years, these immigrant children who combine physical vitality with vivacity and an intellectual sharpness which other nations certainly do not possess to the same degree, will become men who will make their mark and be counted among the best elements of the American population. A person does not need to be a prophet to predict this.

After this family celebration, so moving for the invited guests and so encouraging to the good Sisters, His Eminence returned to the archbishop's palace.

During the remainder of the day the Cardinal remained there, occupied with his correspondence, but a part of the time was given to viewing the carnival parade. We set out on foot at two o'clock, and guided by the Archbishop, we arrived at the home of a French family on the canal. This street is almost three times as wide as the "Via nazionale."[14] As we passed the street was literally filled with people, and the three tramways could scarcely care for the crowd in spite of the desperate shouts of their shrill guides. We could hardly cross this street with its crowd and three lines of carriages, coming and going, in order to reach the balcony where we were expected. The Archbishop, big and vivacious, opened a passage for us, and with him in the lead and me in the rear, Cardinal Satolli managed to bring himself safe and sound to the other side. From the height of our balcony the sight was fairy-like. This immense street was completely covered with people; as far as the eye could see there were only heads in the midst of which the three long parallel lines of tramways slowly came and went with difficulty. Across the street the windows and balconies were also filled. People drove their carriages on both sides of the street in order to open the necessary free space for the parade to pass. Suddenly the advance guard appeared, and then the first float. The crowd below pushed about and surged like an eddy toward the central point of attraction. The float was so beautiful, so rich, so artistic, that the crowd applauded from every side. The first parade, the main one of the day, symbolized the different seasons and scenes from daily life. Each of the floats was symbolic and carried people dressed according to the dominant idea. From time to time a flourish

[14] The Via Nazionale is one of the principal thoroughfares of Rome.

of trumpets with joyous airs diverted attention and tingled the ears. In all this immense crowd of spectators there was not one cry, one disorder or one inconvenience. Everyone was happy with simple and innocent mirth, and the troubled times could not affect this celebration of the whole city and of all the people. The good God Himself had a part in it, for He made the day beautiful, neither too hot nor cold, with a blue, pure sky like beautiful turquoise. That evening at eight o'clock we came to the same street to watch the passing of a second parade. It had the same good taste, the same beauty of arrangement, of color and of costume, and the same order among the people. The whole shone forth with a beauty perhaps even greater than the electric lights which cast most irregular and weird reflections on the gathering, and which caused beads and ornaments to sparkle. It was said that these floats were purchased in Paris a year in advance and that they cost almost 200,000 francs. New Orleans thinks much of its carnival, and the civil and ecclesiastical authorities, far from discouraging the custom, concurred that it was a happy diversion, as innocent amusement, if controlled in the limits of good taste. Consequently, all encourage it. They tell me that only men over thirty and members of the best families are allowed to impersonate characters on the floats. They are masqued and disguised as sphynxes, as birds, or as allegorical persons, and no one recognizes them. But they are able to see and they greet their parents and friends whom they see in the balconies as they pass. They even throw objects, gifts and flowers, to them. These parades are truly beautiful and entertained the Cardinal. They also reminded him regretfully of the old carnivals of Rome which the usurping government thought best to suppress.

On Ash Wednesday His Eminence offered Mass at the Convent of the Daughters of St. Teresa on Rampart Street.[15] This convent is a branch of the one at Baltimore from which the Sisters came in 1877. Several years ago they had difficulties with the diocesan administration over the building of their chapel. The Jesuit priest who directed them, built it large and made it, in the opinion of the pastor, a public chapel. All was settled, thanks to the intervention of Cardinal Satolli, who in this case as in all others had been an angel of peace. Although the chapel was only semi-public, yet for this occasion a large number of people had assembled. The chaplain, a Jesuit Father, had already blessed and distributed the ashes. After His Eminence had celebrated Mass he also wished, for the edification of the participants, to receive

[15] The Carmelite convent of New Orleans had been founded in November, 1877, by four nuns from the convent in St. Louis.

ashes. The faithful then came forward to kiss his ring. His Eminence was afterward led to a parlor where breakfast was served. Then we visited the convent. The Sisters formed two lines, and with candles in hand, led His Eminence to the entrance of the convent and went before him singing the "Domini est terra" in a very low tone. When we arrived at the chapter room the chants, or rather the groanings, ceased. The prioress sang several versicles and an oration, and then all sat down with veils drawn. The cardinal spoke a few appropriate words in English about their holy state so perfectly detached from the world, blessed them and retired. Then he had a conversation with the prioress at the grill. She asked as a favor from him that he would destroy all the papers concerning their past difficulties, assuring him that all loved their Archbishop, and that the ill-will that was thought to exist had emanated from one or two Sisters, especially the prioress, who had been replaced.

In the afternoon we accompanied the Archbishop to visit what they call a jetty. Jetties play a big role here, a role indispensable to the cultivation of the fields, and even to the existence of the city. They have broad terraces, one of twenty meters in height and sixty at the base, built along the various branches of the river and its principal course in order to retain the water in its bed and to prevent inundations. Without this precaution the entire city and countryside would certainly be under water; for the height of the river is noticeably higher than the fields which it erodes, and even of the houses of the town built on its banks. This maximum water height comes from the enormous deposits which form each day at its mouth, especially from its numerous tributaries. These accumulated alluvial deposits built up incessantly to a point where equilibrium is reached between swiftness of the current and the deposit of accumulated debris, and consequently the point where these materials are deposited. Hence the bed of the river and its branches are always rising. Without these protective ramparts New Orleans would be enveloped instantly, and when from the height of the jetty a person sees on one side the city below, and on the other the enormous mass of water, he cannot but shudder. The disaster would not be so frightful, but yet especially deplorable if the fields should be flooded. That is what often happens each time an unforeseen hole breaks through one of the jetties built along the irrigation canals. Such an accident is usually caused by a crevice which unluckily works through the humid soil. Thus it moves little by little across the jetty and pierces it one part at a time. The enclosed water by its own movement rushes through a small opening, enlarges it little by little and soon there is a disaster. Thus there are usually guards walking around the jetties looking for weak points and to prevent accidents.

On our return we visited several churches, all truly beautiful, the one of the Lazarist Fathers first,[16] then that of the Redemptorist Fathers.[17] The one of the Lazarist Fathers covered the whole street. When they first came to this section they found only a small French church. But since the population moved in from the coast the church was found to be much too small. Furthermore, the newcomers were chiefly of English and German ancestry. The good Fathers then built two other churches on their property, and two large schools adjacent; the whole with their residence constitute a number of truly imposing buildings which front two sides of the street on a rather extended area. The Jesuit Fathers also have several churches, one in the new section near the new buildings of "Tulane University."[18] They acquired a plot of land there which already had great value and which would become more and more valuable. St. Francis Xavier, the church adjoining their college, is truly large and beautiful.

The next day, Thursday, Mass was celebrated at the Madames of the Sacred Heart. These Madames have two convents in New Orleans. One, in the city, has the appearance of a beautiful country house. The other is located on Maine Street [*sic*] in the old French quarter.[19] In this quarter all the buildings are very old. This is especially inappropriate. It is now as it was 300 years ago, at the beginning of the colony: the streets are narrow, badly paved, dirty water collects on each side from the open sky, everything is dirty, old rags, old shoes, dead animals, etc., collect here. It is worthy of Constantinople. The Archbishop assured us it was a very healthy section. The reason he gave is pleasant enough to record: "the microbes thrive on filth; since the streets are more dirty in the quarter, the microbes attach themselves to the dirt and leave the world in peace." (!) After holy Mass at the Madames

---

[16] The Vincentians' principal parish was St. Joseph's at Tulane Avenue and Derbigny Street; they also had St. Stephen's Church at Napoleon Avenue and Camp Street.

[17] The Church of Our Lady of the Assumption had been dedicated in April, 1844. The Redemptorists also had St. Alphonsus Church and the French parish of Notre Dame de Bon Secours.

[18] This was the Church of the Holy Name of Jesus on St. Charles Avenue. The Jesuits also were in charge of the Church of the Immaculate Conception at Baronne and Canal Streets.

[19] The first Religious of the Sacred Heart had arrived in Louisiana in May, 1818, under the leadership of Blessed Philippine Duchesne (1769–1852). In 1896 they had two academies — both called Sacred Heart — at Dumaine Street and on St. Charles Avenue, as well as the cathedral school for girls.

of the Sacred Heart, Maine Street, the Archbishop joined His Eminence, and the young girls of the convent gave a program during which they recited, in poetry and in music, the praises of the Holy Father and his representative. One of them recited some French poetry composed for the occasion; it was excellent in form and pronunciation; it could not have been done better nor spoken better in an old French city. We ate dinner at the Archbishop's house. There were several new guests: Bishop O'Sullivan of Mobile, Bishop Dunne of Dallas, Bishop Heslin of Natchez, Rev. Brucker [*sic*], pastor of Willimantic (diocese of Hartford) who as a Belgian had been invited by the Archbishop, finally Bishop Keane, Rector of the Catholic University who had come to give three addresses on "Modern Philosophical Thought." (!)[20] I was seated beside the venerable pastor of Willimantic and I benefited by it by asking what people in New England thought of the Catholic University (New England comprises the ecclesiastical provinces of Boston and New York).[21] He answered: "They say absolutely nothing about it. They are absolutely indifferent on this matter when they are not hostile. You see they do not like Bishop Keane," he continued. "They know he is ultra-liberal and that he has no practical judgment. They know also that Doctor Bouquillon has great influence with him, and people challenge Dr. Bouquillon especially regarding his intemperate campaign on the topic of education.[22] Besides, the time had not yet come to establish a Catholic University. Our bishops do not have ecclesiastical personnel to send to it; vocations are becoming very rare, and they have great need for all their priests. As for the lay students, our Catholics are either rich or poor. If they are rich they would more readily go to the great Protestant Universities like Harvard, Yale, Princeton, etc., where they are now easily received, where they are encouraged to come, and where they find an opportunity of associating with the children of the more important families of the Republic. If they are poor, they can go to Washington and live there on scholar-

---

[20] Jeremiah O'Sullivan (1842–1896) was consecrated as the fourth Bishop of Mobile in September, 1885; Edward J. Dunne (1848–1910) was named second Bishop of Dallas in September, 1893; Thomas Heslin (1845–1911) was consecrated fifth Bishop of Natchez in June, 1889; Florien de Bruycker was pastor of St. Joseph's Church in Willimantic, Connecticut; John J. Keane (1839–1918) was Bishop of Richmond, 1878–1887, before his appointment as first rector of the Catholic University of America.

[21] New England comprised only the Province of Boston, not that of New York.

[22] Thomas Bouquillon (1840–1902) was the Belgian-born professor of moral theology in the Catholic University of America whose writings on the right of the State in education had been the subject of severe controversy during the years 1891–1893.

ships. There are hardly any parishes entirely free of debt or where the necessary Catholic institutions have been built. Before asking Catholics to donate to the University it is necessary to think of establishing our parishes on firm foundations and to insure the existence of our parochial schools. The general conviction is that they have built a University fifty years too soon and that they have placed at its head a man least capable of this office. Consequently a great number of the clergy think that before they are old, it will be a fiasco." I myself was thoroughly convinced that he was correct in his opposition, and I was aware that a complete understanding of the true condition of things would only confirm the public in these dark views on the future of the Catholic University. I understood the venerable priest to say that an institution, founded by the Pope himself and which already possessed considerable property, could not be a fiasco; that it could be in trouble for some time, but that it would not die; that as for personnel, if they would become an obstacle, Providence would indeed be able to remove them. I terminated the conversation by asking him to look favorably upon the work according to the viewpoint of the Holy Father so that it might become a blessing for the American Church (which up to now had scarcely appeared as it ought to be).

The official opening of the Winter School took place at five o'clock in the great hall of Tulane University. The ceremony consisted of an address of welcome to the two Cardinals by the Governor of Louisiana and by the mayor of the city. The Archbishop also made a few remarks and then a public reception in honor of Cardinal Satolli took place.

This "Winter School" of which we speak, and which was the occasion of the visit of the Cardinal Pro-Delegate to New Orleans, is the counterpart of the "Summer School" which is held in July at Plattsburg, diocese of Ogdensburg, for the East, and at Madison, diocese of Green Bay, for the West.[23] This work consists of giving a series of public addresses on diverse topics of philosophy, religion, history, Science, literature. For a long time the Protestants had an institution of this kind and lay Catholics prevailed upon the clergy to procure for them the same advantages (!). There is no doubt as to the intrinsic good of this school, and it would appear difficult in the circumstances to refuse to grant this request. But there are those who are convinced

[23] The Catholic Summer School of America was first opened in New London, Connecticut, in July, 1892, and then moved to Plattsburg, New York, in July, 1893. The Catholic Summer School in the Middle West met in various places after holding its first session in Madison, Wisconsin, in 1895.

that the intellectual advantages are rather insignificant and that, among the "non-Catholics" at least it is an application of the general plan of advancing *"Modern Science,"* in order to diminish the religious idea and to weaken as a result the influence of the priest. In that at least which most concerns Catholics, the Bishops have taken over the movement and have exerted themselves in turning it to good.

That evening at six o'clock there was a reception at the Jesuit Fathers given by former students, the "alumni" as they say in America. A young lawyer first gave a fine speech for the Cardinal Pro-Delegate; the Father Rector delivered a well thought-out address. Cardinal Satolli gave a eulogy in Latin on the Society of Jesus, the "dextera Ecclesiae Christi," and then warmly commended classical studies. Cardinal Gibbons, who was also present, recalled *his* study, now stereotyped, of Alexander and Aristotle drawn from the "Lives" of Plutarch. The speeches were then ended. After the reception we went to supper in the community refectory. Then the real opening of the "Winter School" began with an address by Cardinal Satolli followed by another by Bishop Keane. Cardinal Satolli spoke for more than an hour in Latin on the "Magisterium" of God, man and the Church. It was a magnificent discourse, a "sursum corda," giving the tone to the whole endeavor. He had spoken with such fire and conviction that the audience, although made up of a great number of people who did not know Latin, evidenced every sign of attention and interest up to the end. A large number of priests was also there. They were literally rapt in admiration and often expressed it with the warmest applause. One lady told me later: "I understand nothing, but the delivery was so animated, so expressive, that I would willingly have listened to His Eminence for a still longer time." After His Eminence, Bishop Keane appeared, and tried to give for those who did not understand, a resume of the magnificent address which they had just heard. But he forgot precisely the principal point, that is, concerning the magisterium of the Church, without which we would be led back to the condition of the Protestants. Then he began his topic: an exposition of the philosophy of the ancients touching on God, the human soul, and future life. He took one after another the great philosophers of Greece and Rome and made them say things which often they had not said at all. His Eminence was not able to prevent a show of impatience and resentment; also, he chose to leave the platform quietly under pretext of the advanced hour (10:15 p.m.). Bishop Keane spoke until 11:30 p.m. His success, they say was negligible. The priests, who had heard him for the first time, clearly evidenced their disappointment. But as he had facility in speaking, the good people did not notice the basic inaccuracies, taking it all in and finding no fault.

In the list of visits which His Eminence wished to make to the different institutions of New Orleans there are two which I omitted to relate in their proper place: the visit to the Sisters of the Holy Family and to the Ursulines. The Sisters of the Holy Family were Negro Religious,[24] founded forty years previously by a French priest, whose aim is to care for the orphans and poor of their race. The motherhouse, very large, was built near the Archbishop's house. These Sisters grew fast enough and the Archbishop testified to their spirit of humility, simplicity and devotion. Among the Sisters all shades of color are to be found, from the black of shoe polish to the color of soot. The Superior who appeared very intelligent was also as black as if she had recently arrived from the Congo. Their little Moors sang several chants and performed several well-executed dances for us. Christian charity is ingenious: it has an ointment for all wounds and a solace for all miseries. But what a thing it is to be a Negro, especially in the United States! It is precisely in this professedly classical land of equality that society makes the Negro feel most that he is not white. The Church alone does not make this distinction and embraces all her children with the same tenderness.

One of the most interesting visits was that at the Ursulines. Coming from France in 1732 [*sic*], the Ursulines were identified with the foundation and the progress of the French colony in Louisiana. They are for this city what they have been in Quebec,[25] and the religious of the Congregation of Notre Dame for Montreal in Canada.[26] We found them in the suburbs of the city on a street which previously had been their farm. Their first convent, the one which had received their founders and where all the admirable Christians had been formed who would later be the mothers of the colony, is now, as we have already said, the residence of the Archbishop and still belongs to the Ursulines. These good religious live faithful to their traditions of regularity, piety, and noble simplicity. Their young girls gave a reception worthy of the

---

[24] The Sisters of the Holy Family had been founded in New Orleans in November, 1842, under the auspices of Antoine Blanc (1792–1860), fourth bishop and first Archbishop of New Orleans. In 1896 they had in the city, besides their mother house, orphan asylums for both boys and girls, a home for the aged, and four parochial schools.

[25] The Ursulines had been established in July, 1639, at Quebec by Venerable Marie de l'Incarnation Guyard (1599–1672).

[26] Blessed Marguerite Bourgeoys (1620–1700) arrived in Montreal from France in 1653 and soon thereafter founded the Congregation de Notre Dame.

venerable institution. Two living tableaus were especially remarkable: Eleazer and Rebecca at the well of Jacob, and Esther interceding for the safety of her people. The perfection, grace of poise, richness of costume and blending of colors made an incomparable production.

Since we had to leave on Friday evening, His Eminence paid a visit to Cardinal Gibbons on that morning, as well as to Archbishop Elder of Cincinnati, who had called on the Pro-Delegate the previous evening. After these courtesy calls Cardinal Satolli was taken to a large school conducted by the Sisters of St. Vincent de Paul ("St. Simeon's Academy").[27] Extraordinary preparations had been made for the reception of His Eminence. The small boys, in military uniforms and with drawn swords, formed a line at the entrance to the school. Two or three speeches were again delivered here, along with music and gifts of flowers. In this way the visit of His Eminence to New Orleans was ended. . . .

After dinner we had to pack our bags and prepared for the trip to Galveston. The Archbishop and his Chancellor wanted to accompany His Eminence to the ferry which crossed to the other side of the Mississippi where the South Station is located. It was a dark night, but we saw, by the light of electric lamps, the swift waters of the river churning rapidly and carrying along much wood and turf debris, actually small islands which will be deposited a little further on and thus continue the building up of the famous delta. What power! What majesty! Nevertheless, the steamboat passed through these powerful and swift waters without the slightest rocking. Soon we arrived on the other side of the river and boarded the train for Galveston.

We were now leaving this city whose people were still so French after almost a century of separation from their mother country, so Catholic in their traditions and their religious institutions. Now as they are a part of the Union, the English element penetrates little by little, and a new clergy accordingly replaces the old. The transition has already begun, and as a rule Belgians and Swiss are being used. The present Archbishop, who is worthy of his office, marks the end of the old regime and the beginning of the new.[28] The French clergy is

[27] St. Simeon's Select School had been opened by the Daughters of St. Vincent de Paul in 1860.

[28] This prediction proved untrue. On the death of Janssens in June, 1897, the French-born Placide L. Chapelle (1842–1905) became Archbishop of New Orleans; there then succeeded the German-born James H. Blenk, S.M. (1856–1917). It was only in January, 1918, that John W. Shaw (1863–1934), born in Mobile, Alabama, became the first native American to occupy the See of New Orleans. The present Archbishop Joseph F. Rummel (1876—), who was installed in May, 1935, was born in Germany.

going to disappear gradually, and the Irish will move as quickly as possible into the parishes which yield a sufficient income. Let us hope that the Church and souls not only will not lose but even gain by the change. . . .

141. The Charter of the First Catholic Women's College in the United States, April 2, 1896

THE development of American Catholic higher education since Georgetown, the first Catholic college in the United States, opened in September, 1791, with a single student, has been an impressive one. At the present time there are 254 Catholic colleges and universities with a total enrollment of 241,709 students. In this movement Catholic colleges for women have played an increasingly important role. The first of these institutions was the College of Notre Dame of Maryland in Baltimore which held its first commencement on June 14, 1899, when six young women received the bachelor's degree. The college was staffed by the School Sisters of Notre Dame who had originally come to this country in July, 1847, for the purpose of teaching the children of German immigrants. Thus about a generation after Vassar College received its charter in 1861, college education for American Catholic women got underway. There are now 139 colleges for women under Catholic auspices in the United States, of which 118 are four-year institutions and twenty-one are junior colleges. Their combined enrollment is 77,446 with an additional 57,266 women students in Catholic institutions which admit both men and women. Source: *Laws of the State of Maryland. . . .* (Baltimore: King Bros., 1896), pp. 204–205.

Section 1. *Be it enacted by the General Assembly of Maryland.* That the body politic and corporate created by the Act of the General Assembly of Maryland of 1864, Chapter 357, for the instruction and education of females and the promotion of learning, and the faculty of the professors and teachers in said corporation, be, and they are hereby, authorized and empowered to grant to the graduates of the said institution of learning thereby created, who, in the judgment of the said faculty, may merit the distinction, the degree of Bachelor of Arts, and also the degree of Master of Arts; and to those students of the collegiate scientific department, who may merit the distinction, the degree of Bachelor of Science; and to those students of the department of English literature, who may merit the distinction, the degree of Bachelor of Literature; and to the students of the music department, who may merit the distinction, the degree of Bachelor of Music; and to those who may complete a full graduate or post-graduate course in said institution, having previously received from said institution the degrees of A.B., A.M., or B.S., or any others, who, in the judgment of said faculty, may merit the distinction, the degree of Doctor of Philosophy; and to the students in said institution such certificate of proficiency and attainments in any special study as the faculty of said institution may see fit and proper to confer, and further to confer the honorary degree of Ph.D., A.B., A.M., B.S., B.Lit. [*sic*], or such other degrees as are or may be conferred by any college or institution of learning of this State, upon any woman, who, in the judgment of the said faculty, may merit such distinctions, whether such woman be a student or graduate of the said institution or not.

Sec. 2. *And be it further enacted,* That the General Assembly shall have the right at any time to repeal or amend this Act.

Sec. 3. *And be it further enacted,* That this Act shall take effect from the date of its passage.

Approved April 2d, 1896.

Lloyd Lowndes, *Governor.*
William Cabell Bruce, *President of the Senate*
Sidney E. Mudd, *Speaker of the House of Delegates*

142. Mr. Dooley's Comments on Keeping the Philippines, a Church Fair, and the Democratic National Convention of 1924

NO AMERICAN humorist since Mark Twain captivated the reading public so completely as Finley Peter Dunne (1867–1936). Dunne's career as a journalist on several Chicago newspapers brought him local prominence in the late 1880's but it was his creation of the lovable and entertaining character of Mr. Dooley in 1893, and that character's sage and witty comments on the Spanish American War, that earned Dunne national fame. Speaking of the closing years of the century, Henry Steele Commager said, "Perhaps the most penetrating literary commentary on the changing nature of politics came . . . from Finley Peter Dunne, whose transcriptions of the wit and wisdom of 'Mr. Dooley' pricked every political bubble and exposed every political fraud of these transition years" (*The American Mind* [New Haven, 1950], p. 63). Dunne was born and raised a Catholic, having been baptized in old St. Patrick's Church, Chicago, by his first cousin, Patrick W. Riordan (1841–1914), who in 1884 became second Archbishop of San Francisco. Although he did not practice his faith with the fidelity that his thoroughly Irish background would suggest, he never tolerated any disrespect of his religion, was deeply moved by audiences of Leo XIII in 1901 and 1902, and was reconciled to the Church at death and buried with a requiem Mass from St. Patrick's Cathedral, New York. The examples from Mr. Dooley which follow illustrate Dunne's satirical merrymaking with political themes and his understanding of Irish parish life at the end of the century. In the political realm he reflected the national uncertainty about what should be done with the Philippines after their conquest from Spain in 1898, while the last piece shows how Dunne, a lifelong Democrat, capitalized on the Teapot Dome scandals of the Coolidge administration which broke in March, 1924, and the spirit in which he took the Democratic national convention that nominated John W. Davis (1873–1955) in July, 1924. Sources: Elmer Ellis (Ed.), *Mr. Dooley at His Best* (New York: Charles Scribner's Sons, 1938), pp. 59–62, 93–96; Finley Peter Dunne, *Mr. Dooley in the Hearts of His Countrymen* (Boston: Small, Maynard & Co., 1899), pp. 135–138.

THE PHILIPPINE PEACE

"I know what I'd do if I was Mack,"[1] said Mr. Hennessy. "I'd hist a flag over th' Ph'lippeens, an' I'd take in th' whole lot iv thim."

"An' yet," said Mr. Dooley, "'tis not more thin two months since ye larned whether they were islands or canned goods. Ye'er back yard is so small that ye'er cow can't turn r-round without buttin' th' woodshed off th' premises, an' ye wudden't go out to th' stock yards without takin' out a policy on yer life. Suppose ye was standin' at the corner iv State Sthreet an' Ar-rchy Road, wud ye know what car to take to get to th' Ph'lippeens? If yer son Packy was to ask ye where th' Ph'lippeens is, cud ye give him anny good idea whether they was in Rooshia or jus' west iv th' thracks?"

"Mebbe I cudden't," said Mr. Hennessy, haughtily, "but I'm f'r takin' thim in, annyhow."

"So might I be," said Mr. Dooley, "if I cud on'y get me mind on it. Wan iv the worst things about this here war is th' way it's makin' puzzles f'r our poor, tired heads. Whin I wint into it, I thought all I'd have to do was to set up here behind th' bar with a good tin-cint see-gar in me teeth, an' toss dinnymite bombs into th' hated city iv Havana. But look at me now. Th' war is still goin' on; an' ivry night, when I'm countin' up th' cash, I'm askin' mesilf will I annex Cubia or lave it to the Cubians? Will I take Porther Ricky or put it by? An' what shud I do with th' Ph'lippeens? Oh, what shud I do with thim? I can't annex thim because I don't know where they ar-re. I can't let go iv thim because some wan else'll take thim if I do. They are eight thousan' iv thim islands, with a population iv wan hundherd millyon naked savages; an' me bedroom's crowded now with me an' the bed. How

[1] William McKinley (1843–1901), President of the United States, March, 1898–September 14, 1901.

can I take thim in, an' how on earth am I'm goin' to cover th' nakedness iv thim savages with me wan shoot iv clothes? An' yet 'twud break me heart to think iv givin' people I niver see or heerd tell iv back to other people I don't know. An' if I don't take thim, Schwartzmeister down th' sthreet, that has half me thrade already, will grab thim sure.

"It ain't that I'm afraid iv not doin' th' r-right thing in th' end, Hinnissy. Some mornin' I'll wake up an' know jus' what to do, an' that I'll do. But 'tis th' annoyance in th' mane time. I've been r-readin' about th' counthry. 'Tis over beyant ye'er left shoulder whin ye're facin' east. Jus' throw ye'er thumb back, an' yet have it as ac'rate as anny man in town. 'Tis farther thin Boohlgahrya an' not so far as Blewchoochoo. It's near Chiny, an' it's not so near; an', if a man was to bore a well through fr'm Goshen, Indianny, he might sthrike it, an' thin again he might not. It's a poverty-sthricken counthry, full iv goold and precious stones, where th' people can pick dinner off th' threes an' ar-re starvin' because they have no stepladders. Th' inhabitants is mostly naygurs an' Chinnymen, peaceful, industhrus, an' lawabidin', but savage an' bloodthirsty in their methods. They were no clothes except what they have on, an' each woman has five husbands an' each man has five wives. Th' r-rest goes into th' discard, th' same as here. Th' islands has been owned by Spain since befure th' fire; an' she's threated thim so well they're now up in ar-rms again her, except a majority iv thim which is thurly loyal. Th' natives seldom fight, but whin they get mad at wan another they r-run-a-muck. Whin a man r-runs-a-muck, sometimes they hang him an' sometimes they discharge him an' hire a new motorman. Th' women ar-re beautiful, with languishin' black eyes, an' they smoke see-gars, but ar-re hurried an' incomplete in their dhress. I see a pitcher iv wan th' other day with nawthin' on her but a basket of cocoanuts an' a hoop-skirt. They're no prudes. We import juke, hemp, cigar wrappers, sugar, an' fairy tales fr'm th' Ph'lippeens, an' export six-inch shells an' th' like. Iv late th' Ph'lippeens has awaked to th' fact that they're behind th' times, an' has received much American amminition in their midst. They say th' Spanyards is all tore up about it.

"I larned all this fr'm th' papers, an' I know 'tis sthraight. An' yet, Hinnissy, I dinnaw what to do about th' Ph'lippeens. An' I'm all alone in th' wurruld. Ivrybody else has made up his mind. Ye ask anny conducthor on Ar-rchy Road, an' he'll tell ye. Ye can find out fr'm th' paper; an' if ye really want to know, all ye have to do is to ask a prom'nent citizen who can mow all th' law he owns with a safety razor. But I don't know."

"Hang on to thim," said Mr. Hennessy, stoutly. "What we've got we must hold."

"Well," said Mr. Dooley, "If I was Mack, I'd lave it to George.[2] I'd say: 'George,' I'd say, 'if ye're f'r hangin' on, hang on it is. If ye say, lave go, I dhrop thim.' 'Twas George won thim with th' shells, an' th' question's up to him."

THE CHURCH FAIR

"Wanst I knew a man," said Mr. Dooley, laying down his newspaper, "be th' name iv Burke, that come fr'm somewhere around Derry, though he was Presbyteryan. He was iv th' right sort. Well, he was feelin' how-come-ye-so, an' he dhrifted over to where we was holdin' a fair. They was a band outside, an' he thought it was a grand openin'. So he come in with a cigar in th' side iv his mouth an' his hat hangin' onto his ear. It was th' last night iv th' fair, an' ivrything was wide open; f'r th' priest had gone home, an' we wanted f'r to break th' record. This Burke was f'r lavin' whin he see where he was; but we run him again th' shootin' gallery, where ye got twinty-five cints, a quarther iv a dollar, f'r ivry time ye rang th' bell. Th' ol' gun we had was crooked as a ram's horn, but it must 've fitted the Burke's squint; f'r he made that there bell ring as if he was a conducthor iv a grip-car roundin' a curve. He had th' shootin' gallery on its last legs whin we run him again th' wheel iv fortune. He broke it. Thin we thried him on th' grab-bag. They was four goold watches an' anny quantity iv brickbats an' chunks iv coal in th' bag. He had four dives, an' got a watch each time. He took a chanst on ivrything; an' he won a foldin'-bed, a doll that cud talk like an old gate, a pianny, a lamp-shade, a Life iv St. Aloysius, a pair iv shoes, a baseball bat, an ice-cream freezer, an' th' pomes iv Mike Scanlan.

"Th' comity was disthracted. Here was a man that'd break th' fair, an' do it with th' best iv humor; f'r he come fr'm another parish. So we held a private session. 'What'll we do?' says Dorgan, th' chairman. They was a man be th' name iv Flaherty, a good man thin an' a betther now; f'r he's dead, may he rest in peace! An' Flaherty says: 'We've got to take th' bull by th' horns,' he says. 'If ye lave him to me,' he says, 'I'll fix him,' he says.

"So he injooced this man Burke to come down back iv th' shootin' gallery, an' says he to Burke, 'Ye're lucky to-night.' 'Not so very,' says Burke. ''Twud be a shame to lave ye get away with all ye won,' says Flaherty. ''Twill be a great inconvanience,' says Burke. 'I'll have

[2] Admiral George Dewey (1837–1917) occupied Manila in August, 1898.

to hire two or three dhrays,' he says; 'an' 'tis late.' 'Well,' says Flaherty, 'I'm appinted be th' parish to cut th' ca-ards with ye,' he says, 'whether ye're to give back what ye won or take what's left.' ''Tis fair,' says Burke; 'an', whoiver wins, 'tis f'r a good cause.' An' he puts th' watches an' th' money on th' table.

" 'High man,' says Flaherty. 'High man,' says Burke. Flaherty cut th' king iv spades. Burke, th' robber, cut th' ace iv hearts. He was reachin' out f'r th' money, whin Flaherty put his hands over it. 'Wud yet take it?' says he. 'I wud,' says Burke. 'Wud ye rob th' church?' says Flaherty. 'I wud,' says Burke. 'Thin,' says Flaherty, scoopin' it in, 'ye're a heretic; an' they'se nawthin' comin' to ye.'

"Burke looked at him, an' he looked at th' comity; an' he says, 'Gintlemen, if iver ye come over in th' Sixth Ward, dhrop in an' see me,' he says. 'I'll thry an' make it plisint f'r ye," he says. An' he wint away.

"Th' story got out, an' th' good man heerd iv it. He was mighty mad about it; an' th' nex' sermon he preached was on th' evils iv gamblin', but he asked Flaherty f'r to take up th' colliction."

1924

"Am I goin' to th' Dimmycrat convintion?" said Mr. Dooley. "Ye can bet I am, I'm goin' if I have to hitch onto a freight. In th' first place I want to have a look at th' great wicked me-thropolus. I haven't see that vain, corrupt, but fascinatin' Babylon since I thramped acrost it on me way to fame an' fortune in th' goolden West. I don't think New York is as bad as it's painted be Bill White[1] an' Hinnery Allen,[2] but I sincerely hope it is. 'Twud be a turr'ble disappointment to me to spind me good money an' find mesilf landed in a varchous, hard-workin' community like th' wan I've been livin' in these manny years. If New York expicts to live up to its repytation among us austere, but curyous Westhern Dimmycrats it'd betther begin to put on its paint an' bob its hair at wanst. If Vice ain't dazzlin' and' rampant whin I get there I'll take th' next train back. An' thin there's th' convintion. Iv all th' circuses, 15-round bouts or endurance contests that Tex Richard[3] iver managed this will be th' noblest. It's goin' to be a gr-reat episode in th' life iv a quite Chicago merchant, who had no

[1] William Allen White (1868–1944) was editor of the *Gazette,* Emporia, Kansas.

[2] Henry J. Allen (1868–1950) was a newspaper publisher and Governor of Kansas, 1919–1923.

[3] George L. (Tex) Rickard (1871–1929) was a sports promoter.

divarsions but bein' stuck up ivry week or two be a gunman. An' they do say, with all our boastin', there's ten gunmen in New York to wan in Chicago.

"That goes to show us Dimmycrats ought niver to despair iv a good time. Not that Dimmycrats, Hinnissy, as a rule, are iv a repinin' nature. To be a Dimmycrat a man must be as hopeful as an investor in a policy ticket. A few months ago I looked f'r a monotonous convintion an' a teejous campaign. Th' cards were shuffled an' marked. We wud hold a four-card heart flush; we wud bet it like th' cheerful souls we are; on iliction day we'd draw th' customary two spot iv clubs. Uncle Cal[4] wud set in th' White House in front iv th' fire with his slippers on broadcastin' bedtime stores an' old New England sayin's f'r the voters. Billy Mack[5] wud tear around th' counthry denouncin' railroad comp'nies fr'm th' back platform iv a private care an' that's all there be to it. Th' votes wud be counted be a quarther to eight an' at half-past I'd be undher th' comforter befure th' band began to insult me ears with 'Marchin' Thro Georgia.'

"But, thank th' Lord f'r th' gin'rous open-handed ile men, that's all changed f'r th' betther an' th' sunshine has begun to break through th' clouds f'r our grand ol' party. I niver see a campaign open, as Hogan says, under more fav'rable or more disagreeable auspices. Scandal that wanst was resarved f'r th' mornin' iv iliction day is in full bloom at this minyit, an' th' bad language that we used to save up f'r October is now freely exchanged whereiver thoughtful men gather together. Th' intelligent ilictors are already layin' in their store iv hard coal, brick bats an' cabbageheads to greet th' candydates whin they appear on th' hustings. Befure Siptimber dawns I look to be gettin' a little sense into Larkin's head be hammerin' it with a thransparency while he feebly retorts be thryin' to get fire to me with a karosene torch. Th' intilligent American voter ain't goin' to set around th' radio listenin' to solemn wurrds iv wisdom this year. Polyticks was niver meant f'r th' home annyhow. All us voters iver gets fr'm it is a chance to go out nights an' frolic, an' th' fellow that thries to appeal to our reason will have about as much of an aujeence as a lecturer on th' League iv Nations at a chicken fight. Be th' look iv things there'll be no home life f'r Uncle Cal this comin' Fall. Befure th' punkin's on th' vine he'll have to put on his linen duster an' circylate

[4] Calvin Coolidge (1872–1933) became president on August 3, 1923, on the death of Warren Harding.

[5] William G. McAdoo (1863–1941), Secretary of the Treasury in the Wilson administration, was a leading contender for the Democratic nomination in 1924.

amongst th' inhabitants tellin' thim what he thinks iv his opponent, which ain't much.

"What will our platform be like? How do I know? I don't care. No wan iver reads a platform but th' boy that wrote it. Th' Dimmycrat platform this year will be wan sintince: 'We pint with pride to th' rottenness iv th' Raypublicans.' We're goin' to appeal on their record. 'Tis a wise policy. I heerd it first fr'm th' lips iv our sainted leader, Willum O'Brien. A fellow be th' name iv Flannigan was runnin' again him f'r alderman. 'Willum,' says I to th' gr-reat man, f'r we were very intimate, mind ye, in thim days an' I've often held his hat whin he was rollin' on th' flure in a discussion iv some important public question, 'Willum,' says I, 'ar-re ye goin' to stand on ye'er record?' 'I shud think not,' says he. 'I might fall through. I'm goin' to stand on Flannigan's. What's more,' he says, 'I'm goin' to jump on it,' he says. . . ."

"I'd like to go down to th' convintion," said Mr. Hennessy. "How long d'ye think it will last?"

"That depinds on how much self-resthaint New York shows," said Dr. Dooley. "I figure that about th' end iv th' first week th' gr-reat, gin'rous, warmhearted methropolus will say: 'Th' boys have been away fr'm home long enough. They've had a good time. Their show is funny, but th' action dhrags. Let's break 'em tonight.' An' th' nex' day we'll pull th' name iv our standard bearer out iv a hat an' go home on th' break beams."

143. Pope Leo XIII's Encyclical *Testem benevolentiae* on Americanism, January 22, 1899

ONLY once in the history of the Catholic Church in the United States was its orthodoxy of doctrine called in question. The episode grew out of a series of differences within the hierarchy due to the liberal and conservative approach of the bishops to problems such as the secret societies, the teachings of Henry George, and Catholic participation in the World's Parliament of Religions at Chicago in 1893. The flourishing state of American Catholicism had meanwhile attracted the attention of European observers, especially in France where the Church was harassed by the policies of anticlerical governments. As a consequence some French Catholic leaders advocated a closer imitation of the Church in the United States, a policy which aroused violent dissent among the more conservative leaders of the French Church. A crisis ensued when a careless French translation of *The Life of Father Hecker* (New York, 1891) by Walter Elliott, C.S.P., appeared in 1897. The controversy became so heated on both sides of the

Atlantic over American teaching and methods that Leo XIII finally took the matter into his own hands and after careful investigation issued a letter to Cardinal Gibbons on the subject. The pope was careful to say that the erring doctrines had been imputed to the American Catholics by a foreign source, that the issue had nothing to do with the legitimate patriotism of the Americans, and that he was not accusing the Catholics of the United States of holding these views; he was merely warning that if such doctrines were being taught, they were erroneous. Following the publication of the pope's letter the bishops of the Provinces of Milwaukee and New York thanked Leo XIII for saving the American Church from the threat of heresy. The more common reaction in the United States, however, was that embodied in the reply of Cardinal Gibbons to the pontiff on March 17, 1899, when he said: "This doctrine, which I deliberately call extravagant and absurd, this Americanism as it has been called, has nothing in common with the views, aspirations, doctrine and conduct of Americans" (John Tracy Ellis, *The Life of James Cardinal Gibbons, Archbishop of Baltimore, 1834–1921* [Milwaukee, 1952], II, 71). Source: John J. Wynne, S.J. (Ed.), *The Great Encyclical Letters of Pope Leo XIII* (New York: Benziger Bros., 1903), pp. 441–453.

We send you this letter as a testimony of that devoted affection in your regard, which during the long course of Our Pontificate, We have never ceased to profess for you, for your colleagues in the Episcopate, and for the whole American people, willingly availing Ourselves of every occasion to do so, whether it was the happy increase of your church, or the works which you have done so wisely and well in furthering and protecting the interests of Catholicity. The opportunity also often presented itself of regarding with admiration that exceptional disposition of your nation, so eager for what is great, and so ready to pursue whatever might be conducive to social progress and the splendor of the State. But although the object of this letter is not to repeat the praise so often accorded, but rather to point out certain things which are to be avoided and corrected, yet because it is written with that same apostolic charity which We have always shown you, and in which We have often addressed you, We trust that you will regard it likewise as a proof of Our love; and all the more so as it is conceived and intended to put an end to certain contentions which have arisen lately among you, and which disturb the minds, if not of all, at least of many, to the no slight detriment of peace.

You are aware, beloved Son, that the book entitled, "The Life of Isaac Thomas Hecker," chiefly through the action of those who have undertaken to publish and interpret it in a foreign language, has excited no small controversy on account of certain opinions which are introduced concerning the manner of leading a Christian life. We, therefore, on account of Our apostolic office, in order to provide for the integrity of the faith, and to guard the security of the faithful, desire to write to you more at length upon the whole matter.

The principles on which the new opinions We have mentioned are based may be reduced to this: that, in order the more easily to bring over to Catholic doctrine those who dissent from it, the Church ought to adapt herself somewhat to our advanced civilization, and, relaxing her ancient rigor, show some indulgence to modern popular theories and methods. Many think that this is to be understood not only with regard to the rule of life, but also to the doctrines in which the *deposit of faith* is contained. For they contend that it is opportune, in order to work in a more attractive way upon the wills of those who are not in accord with us, to pass over certain heads of doctrines, as if of lesser moment, or to so soften them that they may not have the same meaning which the Church has invariably held. Now, Beloved Son, few words are needed to show how reprehensible is the plan that is thus conceived, if we but consider the character and origin of the doctrine which the Church hands down to us. On that point the Vatican Council says: "The doctrine of faith which God has revealed is not proposed like a theory of philosophy which is to be elaborated by the human understanding, but as a divine deposit delivered to the Spouse of Christ to be faithfully guarded and infallibly declared. . . . That sense of the sacred dogmas is to be faithfully kept which Holy Mother Church has once declared, and is not to be departed from under the specious pretext of a more profound understanding" (*Const. de Fid. cath.,* c. iv).

Nor is the suppression to be considered altogether free from blame, which designedly omits certain principles of Catholic doctrine and buries them, as it were, in oblivion. For there is the one and the same Author and Master of all the truths that Christian teaching comprises: *The only-begotten Son who is in the bosom of the Father* (*John,* i, 18). That they are adapted to all ages and nations is plainly deduced from the words which Christ addressed to His apostles: *Going therefore teach ye all nations: teaching them to observe all things whatsoever I have commanded you: and behold I am with you all days even to the consummation of the world* (*Matthew,* xxviii, 19). Wherefore the same Vatican Council says: "By the divine and Catholic faith those things are to be believed which are contained in the word of God either written or handed down, and are proposed by the Church whether in solemn decision or by the ordinary universal magisterium, to be believed as having been divinely revealed" (*Const. de Fid. cath.,* c. iii). Far be it, then, for any one to diminish or for any reason whatever to pass over anything of this divinely delivered doctrine; whosoever would do so, would rather wish to alienate Catholics from the Church than to bring over to the Church those who dissent from it. Let them return; indeed, nothing is nearer to Our heart; let all those who are wandering far from the sheepfold of Christ return; but let it not be by any other road than that which Christ has pointed out.

The rule of life which is laid down for Catholics is not of such a nature as not to admit modifications, according to the diversity of time and place. The Church, indeed, possesses what her Author has bestowed on her, a kind and merciful disposition; for which reason from the very beginning she willingly showed herself to be what Paul proclaimed in his own regard: *I became all things to all men, that I might save all* (*Corinthians,* ix, 22). The history of all past ages is witness that the Apostolic See, to which not only the office of teaching but also the supreme government of the whole Church was committed, has constantly adhered *to the same doctrine, in the same sense and in the same mind* (Conc. Vatic., *ibid.,* c. iv): but it has always been accustomed to so modify the rule of life that, while keeping the divine right inviolate, it has never disregarded the manners and customs of the various nations which it embraces. If required for the salvation of souls, who will doubt that it is ready to do so at the present time? But this is not to be determined by the will of private individuals, who are mostly deceived by the appearance of right, but ought to be left to the judgment of the Church. In this all must acquiesce who wish to avoid the censure of Our predecessor Pius VI, who proclaimed the 18th proposition of the Synod of Pistoia "to be injurious to the Church and to the Spirit of God which governs her, inasmuch as it subjects to scrutiny the discipline established and approved by the Church, as if the Church could establish a useless discipline or one which would be too onerous for Christian liberty to bear."

But in the matter of which we are now speaking, Beloved Son, the project involves a greater danger and is more hostile to Catholic doctrine and discipline, inasmuch as the followers of these novelties judge that a certain liberty ought to be introduced into the Church, so that, limiting the exercise and vigilance of its powers, each one of the faithful may act more freely in pursuance of his own natural bent and capacity. They affirm, namely, that this is called for in order to imitate that liberty which, though quite recently introduced, is now the law and the foundation of almost every civil community. On that point We have spoken very much at length in the Letter written to all the bishops about the constitution of States;[1] where We have also shown the difference between the Church, which is of divine right, and all other associations which subsist by the free will of men. It is of importance, therefore, to note particularly an opinion which is adduced as a sort of argument to urge the granting of such liberty to Catholics. For they say, in speaking of the infallible teaching of the Roman Pontiff, that after the solemn decision formulated in the Vatican Council, there is no more need of solicitude in that regard, and, because of its being now out of dispute, a wider field of thought and action is thrown open to individuals. A preposterous method of arguing, surely. For if anything is suggested by the infallible teaching of the Church, it is certainly that no one should wish to withdraw from it; nay, that all should strive to be thoroughly imbued with and be guided by its spirit, so as to be the more easily preserved from any private error whatsoever. To this we may add that those who argue in that wise quite set aside the wisdom and providence of God; who when He desired it especially in order the more efficaciously to guard the minds of Catholics from the dangers of the present times. The license which is commonly confounded with liberty; the passion for saying and reviling everything; the habit of thinking and of expressing everything in print, have cast such deep shadows on men's minds, that there is now greater utility and necessity for this office of teaching than ever before, lest men should be drawn away from conscience and duty. It is far, indeed, from Our intention to repudiate all that the genius of the time begets; nay, rather, whatever the search for truth attains, or the effort after good achieves, will always be welcomed by Us, for it increases the patrimony of doctrine and enlarges the limits of public prosperity. But all this, to possess real utility, should thrive without setting aside the authority and wisdom of the Church.

We come now in due course to what are adduced as consequences from the opinions which We have touched upon; in which if the intention seem not wrong, as We believe, the things themselves assuredly will not appear by any means free from suspicion. For, in the first place, all external guidance is rejected as superfluous, nay even as somewhat of a disadvantage, for those who desire to devote

[1] For the encyclical *Immortale Dei* of November 1, 1885, cf. Wynne, *op. cit.*, pp. 107–134.

themselves to the acquisition of Christian perfection; for the Holy Ghost, they say, pours greater and richer gifts into the hearts of the faithful now than in times past; and by a certain hidden instinct teaches and moves them with no one as an intermediary. It is indeed not a little rash to wish to determine the degree in which God communicates with men; for that depends solely on His will; and He Himself is the absolutely free giver of His own gifts. *The Spirit breatheth where He will* (*John* iii, 8). *But to every one of us is given grace according to the measure of the giving of Christ* (*Ephesians,* iv, 7). For who, when going over the history of the apostles, the faith of the rising Church, the struggles and slaughter of the valiant martyrs, and finally most of the ages past so abundantly rich in holy men, will presume to compare the past with the present times and to assert that they received a lesser outpouring of the Holy Ghost? But, aside from that, no one doubts that the Holy Ghost, by His secret incoming into the souls of the just, influences and arouses them by admonition and impulse. If it were otherwise, any external help and guidance would be useless. "If any one positively affirms that he can consent to the saving preaching of the Gospel without the illumination of the Holy Ghost, who imparts sweetness to all to consent to and accept the truth, he is misled by a heretical spirit" (*Conc. Arausic.,* II, can. vii). But as we know by experience these promptings and impulses of the Holy Ghost for the most part are not discerned without the help, and, as it were, without the preparation of an external guidance. In this matter Augustine says: "It is he who in good trees co-operates in their fruiting, who both waters and cultivates them by any servant whatever from without, and who by himself gives increase within" (*De grat. Christi,* c. xix). That is to say, the whole matter is according to the common law by which God in His infinite providence has decreed that men for the most part should be saved by men; hence He has appointed that those whom He calls to a loftier degree of holiness should be led thereto by men, "in order that," as Chrysostom says, "we should be taught by God through men" (*Hom. i. in Inscr. altar.*). We have an illustrious example of this put before us in the very beginning of the Church, for although Saul, who was *breathing threatenings and slaughter* (*Acts* c. ix), heard the voice of Christ Himself, and asked from Him, *Lord what wilt Thou have me to do?* he was nevertheless sent to Ananias at Damascus: *Arise and go into the city, and there it shall be told thee what thou must do.* It must also be kept in mind that those who follow what is more perfect are by the very fact entering upon a way of life which for most men is untried and more exposed to error, and therefore they, more than others, stand in need of a teacher and a guide. This manner of acting has invariably obtained in the Church. All, without exception, who in the course of ages have been remarkable for science and holiness have taught this doctrine. Those who reject it, assuredly do so rashly and at their peril.

For one who examines the matter thoroughly, it is hard to see, if we do away with all external guidance as these innovators propose, what purpose the more abundant influence of the Holy Ghost, which they make so much of, is to serve. In point of fact, it is especially in the cultivation of virtue that the assistance of the Holy Spirit is indispensable; but those who affect these novelties extol beyond measure the natural virtues as more in accordance with the ways and requirements of the present day, and consider it an advantage to be richly endowed with them, because they make a man more ready and more strenuous in action. It is hard to understand how those who are imbued with Christian principles can place the natural ahead of the supernatural virtues, and attribute to them greater power and fecundity. Is nature, then, with grace added to it, weaker than when left to its own strength? and have the eminently holy men whom the Church reveres and pays homage to, shown themselves weak and incompetent in the natural order, because they have excelled in Christian virtue? Even if we admire the sometimes splendid acts of the natural virtues, how rare is the man who really possesses the habit of these natural virtues? Who is there who is not disturbed by passions, sometimes of a violent nature, for the persevering conquest of which, just as for the observance of the whole natural law, man must needs have some divine help? If we scrutinize more closely the particular acts We have above referred to, we shall discover that oftentimes they have more the appearance than the reality of virtue. But let us grant that these are real. If we do not wish *to run in vain,* if we do not wish to lose sight of the eternal blessedness to which God in His goodness has destined us, of what use are the natural virtues unless the gift and strength of divine grace be added? Aptly does St. Augustine say: "Great power, and a rapid pace, but out of the course" (*In Ps.,* xxxi, 4). For as the nature of man, because of our common misfortune, fell into vice and dishonor, yet by the assistance of grace is lifted up and borne onward with new honor and strength; so also the virtues which are exercised not by the unaided powers of nature, but by the help of the same grace, are made productive of a supernatural beatitude and become solid and enduring.

With this opinion about natural virtue, another is intimately connected, according to which all Christian virtues are divided as it were into two classes, *passive* as they say, and *active;* and they add the former were better suited for the past times, but the latter are more in keeping with the present. It is plain what is to be thought of such division of the virtues. There is not and cannot be a virtue which is really passive. "Virtue," says St. Thomas, "denotes a certain perfection of a power; but the object of a power is an act; and an act of virtue is nothing else than the good use of our free will" (I. II. a. I), the divine grace of course helping, if the act of virtue is supernatural. The one who would have Christian virtues to be adapted, some to one age and others to another, has forgotten the words of the Apostle: *Whom he foreknew he also predestinated to be made conformable to the image of His Son* (*Romans,* viii, 29). The Master and exemplar of all sanctity is Christ, to whose rule all must conform who wish to attain to the thrones of the blessed. Now, then, Christ does not at all change with the progress of the ages, but is *yesterday and to-day, and the same forever* (*Hebrews,* xiii, 8). To the men of all ages, the phrase is to be applied: *Learn of Me because I am meek, and humble of heart* (*Matthew,* xi, 29) and at all times Christ shows Himself to us as becoming *obedient unto death* (*Philippians,* ii, 8) and in every age also the word of the Apostle holds: *And they that are Christ's have crucified their flesh with the vices and concupiscences* (*Galatians,* v, 24). Would that more would cultivate those virtues in our days, as did the holy men of bygone times! Those who by humbleness of spirit, by obedience and abstinence, were *powerful in word and work,* were of the greatest help not only to religion but to the State and society.

From this species of contempt of the evangelical virtues, which are wrongly called *passive,* it naturally follows that the mind is imbued little by little with a feeling of disdain for the religious life. And that this is common to the advocates of these new opinions we gather from certain expressions of theirs about the vows which religious orders pronounce. For, say they, such vows are altogether out of keeping with the spirit of our age, inasmuch as they narrow the limits of human liberty; are better adapted to weak minds than to strong ones; avail little for Christian perfection and the good of human society, and rather obstruct and interfere with it. But how false these assertions are, is evident from the usage and doctrine of the Church, which has always given the highest approval to religious life. And surely not undeservedly. For those who, not content with the common duties of the precepts, enter of their own accord upon the evangelical counsels, in obedience to a divine vocation, present themselves to Christ as His prompt and valiant soldiers. Are we to consider this a mark of weak minds? In the more perfect manner of life is it unprofitable or hurtful? Those who bind themselves by the vows of religion are so far from throwing away their liberty that they enjoy a nobler and fuller one — that, namely, *by which Christ has set us free* (*Galatians,* iv, 31).

What they add to this — namely, that religious life helps the Church not at all or very little — apart from being injurious to religious orders, will be admitted by no one who has read the history of the Church. Did not your own United States receive from the members of religious orders the beginning of its faith and civilization? For one of them recently, and it redounds to your credit, you have decreed that a statue should be publicly erected. And at this very time, with what alacrity and success are these religious orders doing their work wherever we find them! How many of them hasten to impart to new lands the life of the Gospel and to extend the boundaries of civilization with the greatest earnestness of soul and amid the greatest dangers! From them no less than from the rest of the clergy the Christian people obtain preachers of the Word of God, directors of conscience, instructors of youth, and the entire Church examples of holy lives. Nor is there any distinction of praise between those who lead an active life and those who, attracted by seclusion, give themselves up to prayer and mortification of the body. How gloriously they have merited from human society, and do still merit, they should be aware who are not ignorant of how *the continual prayer of a just man* (*James,* v, 16) especially when joined to affliction of the body, avails to propitiate and conciliate the majesty of God.

If there are any, therefore, who prefer to unite together in one society without the obligation of vows, let them do as they desire. That is not a new institution in the Church, nor is it to be disapproved. But let them beware of setting such association above religious orders; nay rather, since mankind is more prone now than heretofore to the enjoyment of pleasure, much greater esteem is to be accorded to those *who have left all things and have followed Christ.*

Lastly, not to delay too long, it is also maintained that the way and the method which Catholics have followed thus far for recalling those who differ from us is to be abandoned and another resorted to. In that matter, it suffices to advert that it is not prudent, Beloved Son, to neglect what antiquity, with its long experience, guided as it is by apostolic teaching, has stamped with its approval. From the word of God we have it that it is the office of all to labor in helping the salvation of our neighbor in the order and degree in which each one is. The faithful indeed will most usefully fulfil their duty by integrity of life, by the works of Christian charity, by instant and assiduous prayer to God. But the clergy should do so by a wise preaching of the Gospel, by the decorum and splendor of the sacred ceremonies, but especially by expressing in themselves the form of doctrine which the apostles delivered to Titus and Timothy. So that if among the different methods of preaching the word of God, that sometimes seems preferable by which those who dissent from us are spoken to, not in the church but in any private and proper place, not in disputation but in amicable conference, such method is indeed not to be reprehended; provided, however, that those who are devoted to that work by the authority of the bishop be men who have first given proof of science and virtue. For We think that there are very many among you who differ from Catholics rather through ignorance than because of any disposition of the will, who, perchance, if the truth is put before them in a familiar and friendly manner, may more easily be led to the one sheepfold of Christ.

Hence, from all that We have hitherto said, it is clear, Beloved Son, that We cannot approve the opinions which some comprise under the head of Americanism. If, indeed, by that name be designated the characteristic qualities which reflect honor on the people of America, just as other nations have what is special to them; or if it implies the condition of your commonwealths, or the laws and customs which prevail in them, there is surely no reason why We should deem that it ought to be discarded. But if it is to be used not only to signify, but even to commend the above doctrines, there can be no doubt but that our Venerable Brethren the bishops of America would be the first to repudiate and condemn it, as being especially unjust to them and to the entire nation as well. For it raises the suspicion that there are some among you who conceive of and desire a church in America different from that which is in the rest of the world. One in the unity of doctrine as in the unity of government, such is the Catholic Church, and, since God has established its centre and foundation in the Chair of Peter, one which is rightly called Roman, for where Peter is there is the Church. Wherefore he who wishes to be called by the name of Catholic ought to employ in truth the words of Jerome to Pope Damasus, "I following none as the first except

Christ am associated in communion with your Beatitude, that is, with the Chair of Peter; upon that Rock I know is built the Church; whoever gathereth not with thee scattereth" (*S. Ambr. in Ps.*, xi, 57).

What We write, Beloved Son, to you in particular, by reason of Our office, we shall take care to have communicated to the rest of the bishops of the United States, expressing again that love in which we include your whole nation, which as in times past has done much for religion and bids fair with God's good grace to do still more in the future.

To you and all the faithful of America We give most lovingly as an augury of divine assistance Our Apostolical Benediction.

144. Pope Leo XIII's Congratulations to the Church of the United States, April 15, 1902

ON FEBRUARY 20, 1902, Pope Leo XIII entered upon the silver jubilee year of his pontificate. Cardinal Gibbons, speaking in the name of the American hierarchy, had sent him a letter of congratulations on March 2, to which the old pontiff replied on April 15 with the highest praise for the American Church. It was an extremely difficult time for the Holy See with the government of René Waldeck-Rousseau (1846–1904) of France at outright war with the Church and the governments of Italy and other countries unfriendly. Leo XIII had these events in mind when he told the American bishops that the condition of the Church in the United States cheered his heart by the success in spreading the faith, the provision of educational facilities, the advance of the Negro and Indian missions, the liberty granted the Church by American law, and the generosity of American Catholics in relieving the poverty of the Holy See. In contrast to all these favorable factors in the United States the pope found, as he said, that "the changes and tendencies of nearly all the nations which were Catholic for many centuries give cause for sorrow. . . ." Source: John J. Wynne, S.J. (Ed.), *The Great Encyclical Letters of Pope Leo XIII* (New York: Benziger Bros., 1903), pp. 513–516.

Certainly We have reason to rejoice, and the Catholic world, on account of its reverence for the Apostolic See, has reason to rejoice at the extraordinary fact that We are to be reckoned as the third in the long line of Roman Pontiffs to whom it has been happily given to enter upon the twenty-fifth year of the Supreme Priesthood. But in this circle of congratulations, while the voices of all are welcome to Us, that of the Bishops and faithful of the United States of North

America brings Us special joy, both on account of the conditions which give your country prominence over many others, and of the special love We entertain for you.

You have been pleased, beloved Son and Venerable Brothers, in your joint letter to Us to mention in detail what, prompted by love for you, We have done for your churches during the course of Our Pontificate. We, on the other hand, are glad to call to mind the many different ways in which you have ministered to Our consolation throughout this period. If We found pleasure in the state of things which prevailed among you when We first entered upon the charge of the Supreme Apostolate, now that We have advanced beyond twenty-four years in the same charge, We are constrained to confess that Our first pleasure has never been diminished, but, on the contrary, has increased from day to day by reason of the increase of Catholicity among you. The cause of this increase, although first of all to be attributed to the providence of God, must also be ascribed to your energy and activity. You have, in your prudent policy, promoted every kind of Catholic organization with such wisdom as to provide for all necessities and all contingencies, in harmony with the remarkable character of the people of your country.

Your chief praise is that you have promoted and sedulously continue to foster the union of your churches with this chief of churches and with the Vicar of Christ on earth. Herein, as you rightly confess, is the apex and centre of government, of teaching and of the priesthood; the source of that unity which Christ destined for His Church, and which is one of the most striking notes distinguishing it from all human sects. As We have never failed to exercise with advantage this most salutary office of teaching and government in every nation, so We have never permitted that you or your people should suffer the lack of it. For We have gladly availed Ourselves of every opportunity to testify the constancy of Our solicitude for you and for the interests of religion among you. And Our daily experience obliges Us to confess that We have found your people, through your influence, endowed with perfect docility of mind and alacrity of disposition. Therefore, while the changes and tendencies of nearly all the nations which were Catholic for many centuries give cause for sorrow, the state of your churches, in their flourishing youthfulness, cheers Our heart and fills it with delight. True, you are shown no special favor by the law of the land, but on the other hand your lawgivers are certainly entitled to praise for the fact that they do nothing to restrain you in your just liberty. You must, therefore, and with you the Catholic host behind, make strenuous use of the favorable time for action which is now at your disposal by spreading abroad as far as possible the light of truth against the errors and absurd imaginings of the sects that are springing up.

We are not unaware, Venerable Brothers, of all that has been done by every one of you for the establishment and the success of schools and academies for the proper education of children. By your zeal in this respect you have clearly acted in conformity with the exhortations of the Apostolic See and the prescriptions of the Council of Baltimore. Your magnificent work on behalf of the ecclesiastical seminaries has assuredly been calculated to increase the prospects of good to be done by the clergy and to add to their dignity. Nor is this all. You have wisely taken measures to enlighten dissidents and to draw them to the truth by appointing learned and worthy members of the clergy to go about from district to district to address them in public in familiar style in churches and other buildings, and to solve the difficulties that may be advanced. An excellent plan, and one which We know has already borne abundant fruit. Nor has your charity been unmindful of the sad lot of the negro and the Indian — you have sent them teachers, helped them liberally, and you are most zealously providing for their eternal salvation. We are glad to add a stimulus, if such be necessary, to enable you to continue these undertakings with full confidence that your work is worthy of commendation.

Finally, not to omit the expression of Our gratitude, We would have you know what satisfaction you have caused Us by the liberality with which your people are endeavoring to contribute by their offerings to relieve the penury of the Holy See. Many indeed and great are the necessities for which the Vicar of Christ as supreme Pastor and Father of the Church is bound to provide in order to avert evil and to promote the faith. Hence your generosity becomes an exercise and a testimony of your faith.

For all these reasons We wish to declare to you again and again Our affection for you. Let the Apostolic blessing, which We bestow most lovingly in the Lord upon you all and upon the flocks entrusted to each one of you, be taken as a token of this affection and an augury of divine gifts.

145. Abbé Klein's Impressions of Bishop McQuaid, 1903

BERNARD J. McQUAID (1823–1909), first Bishop of Rochester, was one of the outstanding Catholic prelates of the late nineteenth and early twentieth centuries. After a highly successful career in the Diocese of Newark as first president of Seton Hall College and vicar-general, he was promoted to the new See of Rochester in March, 1868, where for over forty years he displayed remarkable talents as an organizer, a promoter of education, and a controversialist. His conservative views put him in opposition to the so-called liberals in the hierarchy, and the strong influence of his direct, fearless, and intelligent approach on a number of his fellow bishops, especially Michael A. Corrigan (1839–1902), Archbishop of New York, was marked. McQuaid was justly proud of his diocesan institutions and when the Abbé Félix Klein (1862–1953), a professor of literature in the Catholic Institute of Paris, visited Rochester in the late summer of 1903, the bishop was at pains that he should see them. Klein had been deeply involved in the controversy over Americanism a few years before (cf. Volume IV of his *Souvenirs* entitled *Une hérésie fantôme. l'Américanisme* [Paris, 1949]). But Klein's sympathies with the more liberal-minded American bishops did not blind him to the admirable qualities of one who, as he said, was regarded in Europe "as the most conservative prelate in the United States." No American bishop of his day better represented the conservative wing of the hierarchy than McQuaid, but his conservatism was not the kind that prevented him from making solid contributions to his own diocese and to the Church of the nation. Source: Félix Klein, *In the Land of the Strenuous Life* (Chicago: A. C. McClurg & Co., 1905), pp. 96–104, 112–113.

Almost immediately the Bishop appears, and offers me his hand in the whole-souled fashion which I admire so much in Bishop Spalding.[1] Nothing that I have yet seen is so thoroughly American as this old man of eighty years, straight, thick-set, vigorous, with a frank and resolute bearing. Far from allowing me a word of excuse, he declares in a tone that admits of no denial that he is pleased to see me, and is at my disposal. "You come to look for ideas, of course, and for information?" "Just so, Monseigneur; the encouraging example of what is taking place in the United States. . . ." "Your countrymen, indeed, might profit much by what is good here, instead of . . . They do not see things in the right light, your countrymen. How much time can you spare me?" "I meant to take the ten o'clock train for Buffalo. Is there one at noon?" The only answer is a frown.

[1] John Lancaster Spalding (1840–1916), first Bishop of Peoria.

"Is there one at two o'clock?" "In that time we could do nothing at all; how many days can you stay?" "Well, then, frankly, I will stop till to-morrow morning." "I am sorry the stay is so short. Well, then, there is no time to lose. Here is your room; make yourself at home. I will order the carriage."

Ten minutes afterward I was rolling along in an open landau with the man who is regarded in Europe as the most conservative prelate in the United States. The conversation, which the Bishop maintained in French, was soon on a footing of confidence, and did not lag for an instant the entire day.

"I am going to show you first my Normal School for sisters.[2] They must receive a good education themselves before undertaking to teach others. A woman with some initiative, Marie du Sacré Coeur, tried to start that work among you; you did not understand her. When I founded this diocese, in 1868, — you know that I am its first bishop, — there were eight poor Sisters of St. Joseph here. I adopted them as a diocesan congregation.[3] To-day these are four hundred. I get whatever service I desire from them, without having to apply to distant superiors or to encounter regulations made for other conditions. They pass a State examination at Albany; this is not exacted by the Government, but I insist on it. You are going to see how they work."

We visit the laboratories, the library, the study halls, where, High Mass being over, several young sisters are reading or writing. What I see and what I hear give me the impression that the work is solid, the methods up-to-date, the courses of study sound and proportioned to the aptitude of each pupil. Some sisters are appointed to teach elementary and advanced science; others history, Latin, Greek, and various modern languages. Both sisters and novices are almost all from this diocese; a few are from other parts of America; two or three from Germany. "If you know," said the Bishop, turning to me, "of any young French women who have a true vocation as teachers, and cannot follow it at home, send them to Rochester." This invitation was seriously meant, and was seconded by the Mother Superior. In every room that we pass through, and in the kitchen, too, the Bishop is welcomed with evident joy. In his own blunt way he scatters jokes, counsel, and when requested, a brief blessing: "God bless you, God bless you." One feels that at a sign from him these

---

[2] Nazareth Normal School was formally dedicated on December 27, 1898.

[3] The Sisters of St. Joseph of Rochester were separated from their Buffalo mother house in 1868.

good sisters would be ready to fling themselves into the fire, and that he knows it.

The Normal School is now at the entrance of the city which continues to grow. The price of ground has risen a great deal since Bishop MacQuaid [*sic*] purchased sixty acres here for the sisters; he has recently sold twenty acres of it for a sum sufficient to cover not only the cost of the whole property, but of all the buildings also. He tells me all this, as the carriage conveys us to the gorges and falls of the Genesee River. We descend at a very picturesque bridge. The Bishop invites me to admire the landscape, which is very pretty. "And all that," says he, "is as instructive as it is beautiful. These grounds are very rich in fossil specimens; and, you observe, the river has cut through and exposed the different stratifications. It is a real geological museum which Providence has furnished to the seminarians of Rochester. We have gathered a fine collection from it, with abundant material for exchanges." He welcomed my offer of putting him, for this purpose, in communication with M. de Lapparent who superintends our collection in the Catholic Institute of Paris.

"Now," said the Bishop, "you are going to see my Seminary."[4] And one can guess from the tone of this simple phrase how much the good old Bishop's idea of *his* Seminary represents of work accomplished, of hopes still growing, and of conscience satisfied. Indeed, one quite understands, after having seen it, that it is something to be proud of. I am afraid of falling into the American abuse of superlatives; but, truly, nowhere have I seen a better plan, or a better adaptation of everything that may serve, materially, intellectually, and morally, to prepare young clerics for their great mission. From the very entrance, where you pass under the Gothic arches of the graceful tower which divides the building into two portions, you are struck with the harmony and amplitude of the general lines, as well as with the exact adaptation of all the interior details to the purpose in view. Everything must have been long meditated and settled by the founder before the construction was taken in hand. The Seminary has been built ten years; Bishop MacQuaid spent thirty years in planning it. In the execution, it is true, simplicity was everywhere consulted; but at the same time elegance and comfort as well. Electricity, steam-heating, scientific ventilation, numerous bathrooms, commodious furniture, a good door and window plan; a bakery equipped with machines for kneading; a refectory that is a real dining-room, with its separate tables, and its silver service; a reading room, which

[4] St. Bernard's Seminary was dedicated on August 20, 1893.

is a *salon,* with newspapers and periodicals; students' rooms furnished with sober elegance; corridors which are galleries filled with photographs and engravings fit to develop the artistic sense; everything, in short, speaks of culture, and bears witness to a noble solicitude to bring up as gentlemen these young men sprung from the people, yet destined to serve them as guides in the higher life. Even in a recent letter[5] to his priests, recommending to them both the Preparatory and the chief Seminary, Bishop MacQuaid vigorously insists upon the necessity of providing for the health and comfort of the students. "A mistaken notion prevails that only hardships and sufferings build up strong characters. This notion may have some force, but in a full estimation of the value of this system some account must be taken of the wrecks that line the road, wrecks of ruined stomachs, disordered nerves, weakened lungs, and premature corpses, that have paid the penalty of disregard of the laws of health."

The Bishop of Rochester can well judge of the life which his seminarians lead; for he shares it. On arriving, without being received by anybody, we go straight to his rooms. These are no solemn suites of apartments, occupied but twice a year; they consist of a bedroom which has been used yesterday and is ready for use today or tomorrow, and a study where there is a desk covered with books that are being read and letters waiting to be answered. When we go to the refectory, the Bishop's entrance, though unannounced, is not an event. It is merely a matter of two additional covers; in fact, not even that, because there are vacant places, several of the professors being absent assisting in the neighboring parishes for the Sunday.

The only exceptional feature of the meal is the number of wines served, — four or five, unless I mistake, which is something in America, and above all in a seminary, that calls for explanation. It must be observed that, like the late Cardinal Lavigerie,[6] whose characteristics Bishop MacQuaid more than once recalled to me, the latter is a great viticulturist. He grows, I do not know how many kinds of excellent wine-grapes; and he is as proud of the diploma his wines won at Bordeaux as he is of his Seminary. He questioned me, not without a little quib, as to what wines we were then drinking; and I, who despite his injunctions, had been drowning my wine with water, took a mouthful of meat, wondering what I should reply. At a venture, — or, to be frank, after casting a hasty glance at the

[5] A pastoral letter of August 20, 1903.

[6] Charles Cardinal Lavigerie (1825–1892), Archbishop of Algiers.

oblong form of the bottles, — with the air of a connoisseur I pronounced it to be Moselle, or, more probably still, Rhenish. I hit it exactly; for the vintages of the Bishop of Rochester claim, perhaps not without reason, to rival the Deidesheimer and Liebfrauenmilch ones. I believe it was at this point that the Bishop's tone toward me passed from kindness to sympathy. My sentiments toward him had already changed from fear into curiosity, then to respect, and next to admiration.

I should have no reservation whatever to make regarding him, if he had not, from one o'clock to three during a terrible heat and after a sleepless night, led me, notwithstanding my timid hints, through all the marvels of his Seminary, from the well-filled wine-cellars to the top stories wisely arranged as gymnasiums and recreation halls for rainy days. Hence I have retained only a rather vague impression about many highly interesting things, — the library, museums, laboratories, and the chapel itself; all I can say is that many a university would be glad to see itself so well equipped. At last, however, as the hour fixed for a conference which the Bishop was to give to the students was approaching, I flatly declared that I could not take advantage of it unless I should get a nap. The indefatigable patriarch looked at me with astonishment, but directed me to a sofa, upon which I dropped like a log. Waking up in time, thoroughly refreshed, I listened with the greatest interest to his talk of an hour and a quarter.

He spoke to a select audience, in which every face shone with intelligence, uprightness, candor, and health, both moral and physical. Doubtful and incapable candidates are got rid of without hesitation; vocations are surely numerous enough to permit of a rigorous selection, and the Bishop tolerates no mediocrity in the priesthood. Of the one hundred and thirty-four seminarians, eighty-nine come from here, there, and everywhere, on account of the high reputation which the course enjoys. To Rochester belong forty-five, a number sufficient for a diocese of one hundred and ten thousand souls. Between this fine body of young men and this wonderful old man who addressed them the current of sympathy is not for a moment broken, nor ceases to manifest itself. From the beginning to the end of his discourse, he remains master of all these souls, carrying them along with him from laughter to deep emotion, from lofty ideas to familiar ones, from reasoning to enthusiasm. Nothing could be more animated and picturesque. But who can give a summary of such an address? "The opening retreat," he said in substance, "finished yesterday, and hearts were opened to the love of God; now minds are to be opened to science. The students of St. Bernard's are fortunate in having such facilities for work; the collections, the laboratories, the latest books; the professors above all, the fifteen professors, who for their sakes have been sent to qualify themselves in the old universities of Europe. Ah! in my time it was not so. Learning Latin in America at the beginning of the nineteenth century was not an easy task. To do so, one had to go by boat and coach from New York to Montreal; and what adventures there were along the way![7] When you reached the seminary there were just two professors, who taught everything and knew nothing. There was scarcely time to study then; the year that I was born, there were in the State of New York just eight priests; now there are nine [six] dioceses." And thus he continued to contrast the obscure past with the brilliant present, and to point out the resulting obligations; following throughout only what Pascal calls the order of the heart, but following it so well that when he had finished talking the students, much affected, kept looking at him proudly, as though to say to me, "This man is *our* Bishop, and you see how things go with us!" In the presence of a Catholicism so prosperous, I could scarcely believe that all this had developed within the lifetime of one man; and when the octogenarian Bishop was speaking of the humble beginnings of the American Church, I pictured to myself the first apostles of the Gauls assisting at the opening of our thirteenth century. . . .

On leaving Rochester at ten o'clock A.M., just twenty-four hours after my arrival, I do not observe that my stay with the prelate whom some people in France represent as the most conservative and reactionary in America, has exactly led me to become much less progressive than formerly. . . .

146. A Picture of Hungarian Immigrant Parish Life in the United States, 1905

AMONG the more numerous groups of Catholics who came to this country during the New Immigration of the late nineteenth century were the Hungarians. By 1910 there were 338,151 Hungarians listed as residents of the United States. Most of these immigrants settled in the large industrial areas where many of them became factory workers. Insofar as possible, provision was made for them by the Church in separate parishes with their

[7] McQuaid made his preparatory studies for the priesthood at Chambly College in Canada. For full details on his career cf. Frederick J. Zwierlein, *The Life and Letters of Bishop McQuaid,* 3 vols. (Rochester, 1925–1927).

own priests. One who took a keen interest in their welfare was a Hungarian prelate, Péter Vay (1864–1948), who made several trips to the United States, acting as chaplain on an immigrant ship in 1895 that sailed from Fiume with over 2000 Hungarian immigrants on board. Ten years later he returned, this time as a guest at the inauguration of President Theodore Roosevelt in March, 1905. During this extended visit Vay spent a long period in New York where he worked among his compatriots in the parishes of St. Stephen and St. Elizabeth and preached and lectured in towns like Passaic, Paterson, and Hoboken, where there were large numbers of Hungarians. The following extracts from his memoirs describe his impressions of a new Hungarian parish in Chicago and of the mother parish of the Magyars in the United States at Cleveland. Source: Monsignor Count Vay de Vaya and Luskod, *The Inner Life of the United States* (New York: E. P. Dutton and Co., 1908), pp. 181–185, 336–340.

The reason of my visit to Chicago this time was, as already said, to inaugurate the little Catholic church,[1] erected by the immigrants recently arrived from the shores of the Danube and the Tisza. I had left the United States some time previously, and when the amiable invitation of my compatriots reached me, I was in the extreme north of Canada, on the shores of the Atlantic; I had just been visiting a colony of Hungarian artisans working in the iron foundries of Sidney (Nova Scotia). Although it was a long way back to Chicago, I willingly undertook the tedious journey — occupying three days and three nights — in order to comply with the complimentary request. On arriving at Chicago I found that the place of my destination was rather difficult to get at, and a good way off, being situated in the southernmost suburb of the town. First I had to travel by rail up to a certain point, then by the overhead railroad, and finally by street car. We went right through the city, past sumptuous palaces and warehouses, through labyrinths of modest streets, until at last I found myself democratically seated in an ordinary street car, which carried me away into what seemed the heart of the country. To right and left stretched endless fields of maize, and with the exception of a few tall chimneys on the horizon, the scene before me appeared in its primeval verdure, one immense expanse of untilled loneliness. No streets, no houses! — "But all that will come by and by," I was told, and on my next visit I should see this rural landscape transformed into blocks of houses and streets, just like all the rest of the town.

---

[1] Our Lady of Hungary Church, Chicago, was founded in 1904 by the Reverend Francis Grosz. The combined frame church and rectory opened on the occasion of Vay's visit was located at 9218 Drexel Street.

At a little distance among the marshy pasture land I detected the small wooden structure. From its roof waved the American and Hungarian flags, stars and stripes and the tricolour (red, white and green) harmoniously blending together. "That is the church, and the school is underneath," some one proudly volunteered. A humble edifice truly, but speaking of much sacrifice and labour. These simple folk have built it with their hard-earned savings, for the glory of God and the religious education of their children.

More than half the population of Chicago are foreigners.[2]. . . There are over 200,000 Italians, and the Hungarians proper, not included in other categories, must be estimated at nearly 15,000 new arrivals within the last few years. These latter are chiefly employed as butchers in the slaughter-houses, and as blacksmiths and carpenters in the Pullman establishment. It was at the expense of these people that the little church was built which now met my view. It stands like a beacon amid the surrounding marshes; it is the nucleus of a new suburb, which will spring up around it, and will certainly be no less important a part of the metropolis than the others which have arisen at 16 miles from the centre of the town. It is a first step towards progress, another foundation stone of civilisation and culture.

The workmen and their families awaited me at the entrance of the building. For the greater part they were still dressed in their simple costume "from over the sea," and their whole demeanour showed that they had not long since arrived in these parts. Set adrift in that great city, without knowing the language, without friends or any one to advise them, these poor folks are at the mercy of chance. And, in addition to all the other difficulties and problems which the municipal authorities have to face, we can well understand that this question of dealing with the foreign population of inferior civilisation is one of the greatest and hardest to solve. They have not only to be fed, they have also to be protected and educated. The church and the school are their only safeguards. As long as the people will go to church and are willing to have their children brought up on religious principles there is nothing to fear. As long as they recognize their duty towards God they will also recognise and fulfil their duty towards their neighbour.

The inauguration of that humble little church and its simple worshippers has left an indelible impression upon me. It was one of those never-to-be-forgotten scenes which, in spite of their apparent

[2] The 1900 census gave Chicago a population of 1,698,575, of whom 587,112 were listed as foreign-born.

unimportance, form a page in the annals of history. This small beginning, representing the accumulated savings of those hardy workmen, is the centre of new efforts and new struggles. Let us hope these may lead here to as successful an issue as they have done in other parts of the town. Let us hope that its inhabitants may one day be as prosperous and wealthy as their fellow-citizens in older Chicago. Above all, let us hope that the little church may grow into a cathedral, and its elementary school into a great scientific establishment. And although in the past the place has so often been shaken by strikes and tumults, let us hope that henceforth faith and culture may ensure peace and prosperity to this marvellous city. . . .

Our church, a modest wooden building of two stories, used also as a school and as a habitation of the priest, rises like a landmark in the midst of a desert of factories, for here are the ironworks of the Illinois Steel Trust, and the famous workshops of the Pullman Car Company. In both of these great enterprises the number of hands employed greatly exceeds 10,000, drawn for the most part from Austro-Hungary. That is why this parish was formed. The population, called into existence by these works, required the consolations of religion, and their numerous progeny needed education and care, in an atmosphere impregnated with smoke and alcohol.

When at last I arrived, after a long journey, I found the church crammed with workmen and their families, all persons who earned their daily bread by the sweat of their brow. This sympathetic crowd, and the warmth of their reception, almost made me forget that the congregation had gathered in an erection made of planks, more like a barn than a place of worship.

What was my surprise at the end of my sermon when the priest appealed to the generosity of the worshippers, and, a sheet of paper in his hand, held a meeting of the congregation, asking them to furnish the empty building. The altar-cloth, ornaments — everything was subscribed with a truly Christian generosity, and if ever Providence should again take me back, I am certain that I should find that humble parish a most flourishing centre.

At Chicago I witnessed the initiation of an American cure of souls, with its preliminary work; at Cleveland, on the contrary, I was able to admire the full development of one of these immigrant parishes.[3]

[3] St. Elizabeth's Church, Cleveland, was the first exclusively Magyar parish in the United States. The church had been begun in 1893 by the Reverend Charles Boehm, the pioneer Hungarian priest in the United States. Boehm sought out Hungarian Catholics in various parts of the country and succeeded in getting

This was the first and incontestably the most important of the Hungarian communities. The number of Magyars alone exceeds 30,000. They have numerous churches, several newspapers published in their language, and many societies and clubs. I knew all this beforehand, and yet on my arrival was surprised at the importance and size of the church of the first Hungarian parish in the United States.

I had promised to pass the feast of Whitsuntide there, and, thanks to my stay of several days, I was able to understand the phenomenal growth and immense influence attained in so short a period. The Church of Cleveland, like that of Chicago, had been founded only a few years before, in a suburb far from the town. The priest arrived there alone, without either help or acquaintance, finding nothing, knowing nobody. It would have been difficult to believe that such had been the state of affairs if I had not already known something of the work and the marvels accomplished by the faithful in these new States. My reception, in which all the different associations took part, their banners unfurled, was a most touching exhibition of hospitality and affection. The church and all the galleries were crowded with worshippers, thousands of voices sang the hymns, and the ground was strewn with flowers which perfumed the air, laden with incense which mounted in silvery clouds toward the blue heavens — the priests prostrate before the altars of God, made a beautiful picture, and was quite the most edifying scene in the whole of my mission, rich though it was in heart-warming recollections. Good Father B—— may well be proud of his work, and of the results of his apostolate.

Such results, attained in the short duration of a single life, are only possible in new countries. They afford the greatest encouragement to the humblest parsons in their work. The bishops on their side give full liberty of action, so that it may vary with the necessities of the different localities, and in order that the activity of each place in their diocese may be developed to the very utmost. Thus both agent and work increase in force, and existing parishes make new ones. Gradually independent dioceses are formed, for as soon as a parish priest has more members in his congregation than it is possible

---

parishes started for them, as well as editing a Magyar prayer book and founding a Magyar newspaper. By 1907 St. Elizabeth's was attended by two priests and had a parish school with 531 pupils taught by eight Ursuline Sisters. Cleveland was one of the most important centers for Hungarian settlement, having in the *Szabadsag* one of the earliest Hungarian daily newspapers in the country. The Diocese of Cleveland had by 1940 ten Hungarian parishes of the Latin Rite and four of the Byzantine Rite. Cf. Michael J. Hynes, *History of the Diocese of Cleveland. Origin and Growth, 1847–1952* (Cleveland, 1953), pp. 256, 260, 326.

for him to know and care for, a further division is made. In Europe there are parishes of forty or fifty thousand souls. In America, on the contrary, the number rarely exceeds twelve or fourteen thousand. The dwellers in each parish form, so to speak, a large family, in which the members know one another, at least by sight, and each is known to the priest. Thus they constitute, as I have said, large families, each member contributing according to his power to the welfare of the community. This is how the success to-day recognised by the world is made possible, and why the Catholic Church in the United States has risen to her place of general respect and honour.

147. The Origins of the Catholic Church Extension Society, October 18, 1905

THE predominantly urban character of American Catholicism is strikingly illustrated by the fact that out of 3070 counties in the United States there are 819 counties — embracing an area of 757,000 square miles or about one fourth of the country — where there is no resident priest. Moreover, there are 73,000 small towns and hamlets with no priest to serve the religious needs of the Catholic people. Early in the present century Francis Clement Kelley (1870–1948), then pastor of Immaculate Conception Church, Lapeer, Michigan, became convinced of the necessity to do something to remedy this situation. The result of his efforts was the founding of the Catholic Church Extension Society which during the past fifty years has collected and dispersed to the American rural missions over $48,000,000 in providing churches, support to priests, and the facilities of religious worship in country districts. Campaigns for enlisting support have been conducted principally through the society's official organ, *Extension Magazine,* begun in 1906 and having at the present time a circulation of over 500,000 copies monthly. In the following document the society's founder, who was consecrated in October, 1924, as second Bishop of Oklahoma City, recounted the circumstances that brought the organization into existence. Source: Francis Clement Kelley, *The Bishop Jots It Down. An Autobiographical Strain on Memories* (New York: Harper & Bros., 1939), pp. 114–123.

The dream? It had been growing on me from the day when I read a letter of appeal for the Society for the Propagation of the Faith sent out by Abbé Magnien. . . . I was then too poor to help but hopeful enough to promise that some day I should. I felt as I read the Abbé's circular that the whole Church in America ought to help. It was not gratitude for what the great Society had done for the

Church of America that moved me, but the thought that we had a duty to vindicate our Catholicity in missionary action within and even beyond our borders. There was for me an effective lecture on that particular mark of the Church in the appeal of the Grand Old Man of Baltimore.[1]

Then came traveling and lecturing. I saw America, not the America of the great cities but the real America which feeds and sustains the other — the America of the small towns, villages, and countryside. In the West and South I ran into small groups of Catholics threatened with being swallowed up by indifference, pastorless people as well as churchless people. And the conviction came to me that our leaders had missed something great because they had been overwhelmed by numbers pouring out of ships into the cities. We had, I thought, been forced to neglect the minority that had gone to the little places. But these were the hope of the cities of the future, the fathers and mothers of the next and succeeding generations of city dwellers. Could we afford to lose them? I was sure we could not.

There is something substantial behind every dream no matter how fantasy may distort it. Dreams are the plays of the subconscious memory. The substantial behind mine was the Catholicity of the Church. So deep-rooted became my desire to help the rural places that I felt no discouragement would prevent me from planting a seed in soil I hoped would be fertile enough to give it strength and growth.

There came to Trinity Rectory one evening when I was there a stern, dignified, and aloof-appearing man whose name has already been mentioned. He was John Hennessy, Bishop of Wichita.[2] His bearing did not invite confidences — even conversation for that matter. But young men with dreams are not afraid. I talked of mine in his presence. He showed interest. To the Dean's astonishment he even invited me to pay him a visit if my lecturing brought me near Wichita. I thanked him for the invitation without determining to accept it. I was afraid to accept it. But when I did actually find myself near Wichita I recalled it and paid him a visit. He questioned me closely about the thing that was interesting me. I was launched into the subject of home missions before I knew it, because I was soon aware of the fact that I had a sympathetic listener. To my surprise the Bishop took

---

[1] Alphonse L. Magnien, S.S. (1837–1902), was superior of the Sulpicians in the United States from 1878 to his death. In November, 1896, he was appointed National Director of the Society for the Propagation of the Faith.

[2] John J. Hennessy (1847–1920) was consecrated for the new See of Wichita on November 30, 1888.

up the discussion when and where I left off and suggested that I should make an effort to found a Society dedicated to the work.

"What we need first of all," he said, "is financial help to put up chapels for small groups scattered here and there all over the West. Someone like you must make a study of the situation and begin the work."

When I suggested that I was too unimportant a person to do more than make the study, he answered, "For some good purpose of Divine Providence you have been forced out to see conditions from one end of the country to the other. Learn all you can about home mission societies elsewhere and write on the subject. That is the way to begin."

I did make the study but remained doubtful that I was indicated as the founder of such a work. Then something else happened, and again in Kansas. I visited Ellsworth to lecture for the high school of the town and there met the pastor, Father Arthur Luckey. What happened to me in Ellsworth was read by thousands when the appeal I felt forced to write was published in the *Ecclesiastical Review*[3] of Philadelphia and reprinted many times in pamphlet form. For years after the Church Extension was founded that appeal was known as the "Little Shanty Story.". . . [There follows the first part of the article which described the miserable shanty in which the pastor of Ellsworth lived and the equally deplorable condition of the little church.]

That Little Shanty Story founded the Catholic Church Extension Society both in the United States and Canada because it played a sympathy if not a symphony on the heartstrings of many people. In the spring of 1905 nothing was wanting for the founding of the society but a distinguished sponsor, definitely the archbishop of one of the large metropolitan sees of the United States. I wanted to go out searching for one but had no money to pay my way around. To my rescue came a group of the Knights of Columbus in Michigan and Ohio. They gave me a one hour job and paid well for it. I was invited to preach on my hobby at their summer outing at Cedar Point, Ohio, with the collection as recompense. That collection netted me about two hundred dollars. I could travel as far as that sum would carry me.

Naturally New York was my first objective. I wanted Archbishop Farley[4] to be the honorary head of the society. His refusal was kindly expressed but clearly definite. I tried Archbishop Ryan[5] of Philadelphia.

[3] "Church Extension," *American Ecclesiastical Review*, XXXII (June, 1905), 573–585.

[4] John Farley (1842–1918) became Archbishop of New York in 1902 and was made a cardinal in 1911.

[5] Patrick J. Ryan (1831–1911) was named Archbishop of Philadelphia in 1884.

His refusal, too, was kind and to it he added the saving bit of humor that was expected of the Episcopal wit of the day. But it too was definite. Archbishop Bourgade[6] of Santa Fe was willing to help but did not think himself important enough to lead. Archbishop Williams[7] of Boston was growing old. I knew that he would not consider adding burdens to the great one he already was carrying. I felt the same about Cardinal Gibbons.[8] While I was hesitating about approaching Archbishop Ireland[9] of St. Paul I learned that the "Little Shanty Story" had met with the approbation of Archbishop Quigley[10] of Chicago. Why not Chicago? It was the very gateway to the whole home mission field. At the suggestion of Archbishop Bourgade I put all my hopes on Chicago.

It was at the University of Notre Dame that I met Archbishop Quigley for the first time. He was seated on a rear veranda of the presbytery chatting with President Morrissey[11] and Dr. Zahm,[12] the scientist, when I was presented by the future president, Dr. Cavanaugh.[13] The sun was setting, but for yet a little while I had a chance to study the face of the Archbishop. It was a good face to look at because it seemed to be set in quiet repose. One had the feeling that its owner was a tranquil man who might let his heart's influence count. He had keen measuring eyes, both dark and deep; one did not know how deep they might be. . . . He was a good listener, like a judge hearing a case and anxious to follow and check the points of law involved in it, or an Oxford examiner intent on finding out from the way the student handles himself, rather than from a display of technical learning, if he really merits the honors he seeks. I got the impression that my arguments would count with the Archbishop much less than my per-

---

[6] Peter Bourgade (1845–1908) was promoted from the See of Tucson to become Archbishop of Santa Fe in 1899.

[7] John J. Williams (1822–1907) governed the See of Boston from 1866 to his death.

[8] For the rather aloof attitude assumed by Gibbons toward Kelley and the Catholic Church Extension Society in its first years, cf. John Tracy Ellis, *The Life of James Cardinal Gibbons, Archbishop of Baltimore, 1834–1921* (Milwaukee, 1952), II, 404–407.

[9] John Ireland (1838–1918) was made Archbishop of St. Paul in 1888.

[10] James E. Quigley (1854–1915) was Bishop of Buffalo, 1896–1903, and Archbishop of Chicago from 1903 until his death.

[11] Andrew Morrissey, C.S.C. (1860–1921), was eighth president of the University of Notre Dame during the years 1893–1905.

[12] John A. Zahm, C.S.C. (1851–1921), wrote extensively on the relations of religion and science.

[13] John W. Cavanaugh, C.S.C. (1870–1935), was ninth president of the University of Notre Dame during the years 1905–1919.

sonality. That worried me, for my confidence was all in the arguments. Truth was that the Archbishop knew them as well as I did, since for years he had had the same thought on the subject which in me was only developing. But what I had seen in my travels around the West and South interested him, and it was plain that he loved a story with a lesson to end it. The strong impression I got from watching and hearing him was that he was a man of wide vision. . . . I must admit that he frightened me. But I knew that here was a personality and a protector well worth winning. He proved easy to win, not because I had winning ways but because he himself had been over the ground. When the light faded and a bell called him to the chapel for the opening of the retreat he was there to attend, his mind was made up and he said so. I had found my protector and knew that if I lost him later it would not be because he failed to stick but because I failed to make good. . . .

The Catholic Church Extension Society was founded in Archbishop Quigley's house in Chicago on the 18th of October, 1905. I was given mountains to climb. I knew well what was on the other side of them but I never expected to see it. Yet I think that, through a narrow pass high upon the most desolate part of one of them, perhaps I caught a glimpse of it. Cryptic? No! I am only thinking of the advanced guard of a new generation of priests, imitating the poor man of Assisi in a modern world; or, if you will, imitating the Apostle to the Gentiles in his own good way — priests of the highways and hedges. . . .

"I can't understand you priests," said a business friend as he shook hands in farewell when I was leaving Lapeer for Chicago. "Here you are abandoning your new church and your fine new home almost the day after you got into them, to start all over again in a Chicago flat with nothing but a dream and not much of a dream at that."

A dream? The man did not know the compelling force and persistent glory of a dream. While I am now, as a bishop, committed to a dislike for dreamers, only yesterday a mother, my own sister, pouring out of her artist soul a prayer of resignation over her afflicted son, brought tears acknowledging the truth and power of a dream from my eyes. . . .

Had I been leaving for a promotion few would have thought or expressed any wonderment. But the business that has to wait for eternity to pay its dividend is another matter. Those who follow the red-gold lure of the Cross are mysterious, even to some who ought to understand.

I had a friend in Detroit, Edward H. Doyle,[14] who would have his

[14] Edward H. Doyle (1849–1919) was Commissioner of Banking for Michigan, 1911–1915.

joke. He was one of those who thought I was risking too much by the burning of my ships.

"Did you ever hear the definition for a promoter made by my unusual friend, Marcus Pollasky?" he asked when I called at his office in the Majestic Building to say good-by.

"Never. What is it?"

"He was on the witness stand in a court case. The examining lawyer asked his name and his business. Marcus gave his name and said that his business was that of a promoter."

"What is your definition of a promoter, Mr. Pollasky?"

"A promoter? Why, a promoter is a man who has nothing to sell and who sells it to a man who doesn't want to buy it."

I saw the point and tried to explain what my kind of promoter was and what he had to sell. My friend listened politely for awhile. Really I was only trying to give him information, not to "sell him" anything. "That will do. That will do," he interrupted. "Before you go you ought to meet my friend Marcus. He was right. But I'll buy it."

Buy it expensively he did. In him I landed my first big fish. It weighed ten thousand dollars.

The society stayed only one year in Lapeer. Then it was moved to Chicago and I had to go with it. The Bishop of Detroit[15] granted me the usual *Exeat* transferring me to the archdiocese of Chicago. I must admit that he seemed to take his loss in a spirit of resignation.

148. Chief Justice White's Decisions in Regard to Divorce, April 12, 1906, and to the Selective Draft Law, January 7, 1918

EDWARD DOUGLAS WHITE (1845–1921) was a member of the Supreme Court of the United States for twenty-seven years, having been appointed in 1894 and promoted to the rank of chief justice in 1910. During his service on the bench White wrote opinions in over 700 cases, but it is difficult to characterize his decisions since at times he sided with the so-called liberals and again showed a conservative interpretation of the law. He was the second southern Catholic Democrat to be chief justice, Roger Brooke Taney having held the office from 1836–1864. White was educated at Mount Saint Mary's College, Emmitsburg, and Georgetown College. Two of his more notable opinions are given below. In *Haddock* v. *Haddock* of April 12, 1906, he spoke for a court divided 5–4 in a divorce suit that remained the ruling and controlling decision for a quarter century until expressly overruled in *Williams* v. *North Carolina* in December, 1942,

[15] John S. Foley (1833–1918) became Bishop of Detroit in 1888.

which recognized the validity of Nevada divorces as applying to persons living in other states. The Haddocks had originally been domiciled in New York, but the husband had left that state, taken up residence in Connecticut, and had there obtained a divorce by service upon his wife. The wife later sued for divorce in New York and was informed of the earlier action of her husband which would have prevented her from securing her rights to his estate, alimony, etc. The case came before the Supreme Court under the constitutional provision that one state is obliged to give full faith and credit to the public acts of every other state. In the second decision of White, handed down on January 7, 1918, for a unanimous court the constitutionality of the Selective Draft Law of May, 1917, enacted to augment the armed forces of the United States during World War I was upheld. An item of personal interest in the latter case was that White had himself left Georgetown college unofficially at the age of fifteen to enlist as a soldier in a Confederate regiment then forming in his native Louisiana. Source: *Haddock* v. *Haddock,* 201 U. S. 562 (pp. 575–576); *Arver* v. *United States; Grahl* v. *United States; Otto Wangerin* v. *United States; Walter Wangerin* v. *United States; Kramer* v. *United States; Graubard* v. *United States,* 245 U. S. 366 (pp. 377–378, 390).

HADDOCK vs. *HADDOCK*

No one denies that the States, at the time of the adoption of the Constitution, possessed full power over the subject of marriage and divorce. No one, moreover, can deny that, prior to the adoption of the Constitution, the extent to which the States would recognize a divorce obtained in a foreign jurisdiction depended upon their conceptions of duty and comity. Besides, it must be conceded that the Constitution delegated no authority to the Government of the United States on the subject of marriage and divorce. Yet, if the proposition be maintained, it would follow that the destruction of the power of the States over the dissolution of marriage, as to their own citizens, would be brought about by the operation of the full faith and credit clause of the Constitution. That is to say, it would come to pass that, although the Constitution of the United States does not interfere with the authority of the States over marriage, nevertheless the full faith and credit clause of that instrument destroyed the authority of the States over the marriage relation. And as the Government of the United States has no delegated authority on the subject, that Government would be powerless to prevent the evil thus brought about by the full faith and credit clause. Thus neither the States nor the National Government would be able to exert that authority over the marriage tie possessed by every other civilized government. Yet more remarkable would be such result when it is borne in mind that, when the Constitution was adopted, nowhere, either in the mother country or on the continent of Europe, either in adjudged cases or in the treatises of authoritative writers, had the theory ever been upheld or been taught or even suggested that one government, solely because of the domicile within its borders of one of the parties to a marriage, had authority, without the actual or constructive presence of the other, to exert its authority by a dissolution of the marriage tie, which exertion of power it would be the duty of other States to respect as to those subject to their jurisdiction. . . . As the husband, after wrongfully abandoning the wife in New York, never established a matrimonial domicile in Connecticut, it cannot be said that he took with him the marital relation from which he fled to Connecticut. Conceding, however, that he took with him to Connecticut so much of the marital relation as concerned his individual status, it cannot in reason be said that he did not leave in New York so much of the relation as pertained to the status of the wife. From any point of view, then . . . if the marriage relation be treated as the *res,* it follows that it was divisible, and therefore there was a *res* in the State of New York and one in the State of Connecticut. Thus considered, it is clear that the power of one State did not extend to affecting the thing situated in another State.

SELECTIVE DRAFT LAW CASES

As the mind cannot conceive an army without the men to compose it, on the face of the Constitution the objection that it does not give power to provide for such men would seem to be too frivolous for further notice. It is said, however, that since under the Constitution as originally framed state citizenship was primary and United States citizenship but derivative and dependent thereon, therefore the power conferred upon Congress to raise armies was only coterminous with United States citizenship and could not be exerted so as to cause that citizenship to lose its dependent character and dominate state citizenship. But the proposition simply denies to Congress the power to raise armies which the Constitution gives. That power by the very terms of the Constitution, being delegated, is supreme. Article VI. In truth the contention simply assails the wisdom of the framers of the Constitution in conferring authority on Congress and in not retaining it as it was under the Confederation in the several States. Further it is said, the right to provide is not denied by calling for volunteer enlistments, but it does not and cannot include the power to exact enforced military duty by the citizen. This however but challenges the existence of all power, for a governmental power which has no sanction to it and which therefore can only be exercised provided the citizen consents to its exertion is in no substantial sense a power. It is argued, however, that although this is abstractly true, it is not concretely so because as compelled military service is repugnant to a free government and in conflict with all the great guarantees of the Constitution as to individual liberty, it must be assumed that the authority to raise armies was intended to be limited to the right to call an army into existence counting alone upon the willingness of the citizen to do his duty in time of public need, that is, in time of war. But the premise of this proposition is so devoid of foundation that it leaves not even a shadow of ground upon which to base the conclusion. Let us see if this is not at once demonstrable. It may not be doubted that the very conception of a just government and its duty to the citizen includes the reciprocal obligation of the citizen to render military service in case of need and the right to compel it. Vattel, Law of Nations, Book III, c. 1 & 2. To do more than state the proposition is absolutely unnecessary in view of the practical illustration afforded by the almost universal legislation to that effect now in force. . . .

Finally, as we are unable to conceive upon what theory the exaction by government from the citizen of the performance of his supreme and noble duty of contributing to the defense of the rights and honor of the nation, as the result of a war declared by the great representative body of the people, can be said to be the imposition of involuntary servitude in violation of the prohibitions of the Thirteenth Amendment, we are constrained to the conclusion that the contention to that effect is refuted by its mere statement.

149. Louise Imogen Guiney on a Preference for Living in England, April, 1907

AMONG the relatively few American Catholics of literary fame was Louise Imogen Guiney (1861–1920). Two years before she graduated from Elmhurst, the Convent of the Sacred Heart in Providence, her Irish-born father, Patrick Robert Guiney, who had had a gallant career in the Civil War, died rather dramatically in a Boston street in March, 1877. Speaking of this episode in connection with the Boston resentment of the Irish, Van Wyck Brooks, who classes Miss Guiney among "The Epigoni," remarked that in her and John Boyle O'Reilly the Bostonians found compensations. He said: "Miss Guiney's spirit rode forward in her father's stirrups. None of this was lost upon the city of the Puritans. The Bostonians knew a soldier, as they knew a poet. . . . Heaven only knew what future gifts the conquerors had in store for a later New England; and the Yankees were not ungrateful to them" (*New England: Indian Summer, 1865–1915* [New York, 1940], pp. 412–413). Although by the late century Miss Guiney had gained fame and acceptance in literary circles, on two trips to England she had lost her heart to that country and in 1901 she went to live permanently in Oxford. In this she shared the sentiment of other American literary figures and artists like Henry James, James Whistler, Edith Wharton, and George P. A. Healy who lived much of their lives abroad. Among her best essays was *A Little English Gallery* (1894) and her best poems were gathered together in *Happy Ending* (1909). But American readers will, perhaps, find more interesting an unsigned essay of 1907, the identity of which was made known by Miss Guiney's biographer, E. M. Tenison, in a chapter entitled, "An American View of England," *Louise Imogen Guiney* (London, 1923), pp. 215–225. Source: "On A Preference for Living in England," *Atlantic Monthly,* XCXIX (April, 1907), 569–572.

When men pitch their life-tents far away, they have manifold causes and reasons: some sound, some questionable, some wholly weak and unworthy. It is one thing feloniously to cast off one's derivation, nurture, and responsibilities; and quite another thing to brave home-sickness in order to outwit and escape too difficult outward conditions. It is the pride of absence to remember Argos forever, to rest upon its garnered glories, and brooding upon its future with thoughtful affection, to

lean and hearken after it
And grow erect as that comes home.

The purpose of this paper is to hold a brief not so much for those who go, as for those who cannot stay. European passports, for instance, must be cheerfully furnished to our artist fraternity. With us, the historical sense, the scholastic mind, the instinct for color and form, must bring, in time, their own obsession. Whoever has a rage for origin, a lust for things at first-hand, is foredoomed to chafe at a civilization which dates from this morning, and spends its energies on tasks far other than the effort to see life steadily and see it whole. There is something rational, surely, in an attraction which has already drained the United States of so much genius, literary and artistic; which has resulted in forming so many wise, devoted, and detached critics to whip us up to our ideals, and remind us of our sins.

But the fellow-citizen, of all others, who must have the right of way over the sea, is the wounded man, the tired man, the sufferer from *Hustlerium Tremens sive Americanitis.* Let that true lover of the Republic fear not, but sink his foot in alien turf for the most defensible reason in life; like Denham's hero, unblamed,

If here he frets, he finds at Rome,
At Paris, or Madrid, his home.

He has "gone to be a fairy," not for ambition, not for excitement, nor for vogue; but for the velvety feel of the Past under foot, like moss of the forest floor to a barefooted child; or for the hardly less gentle feel of the Present, whence noise and worry seem miraculously to have vanished away. Well for him, when at last, from his own foolish impetus, as well as from the epic newness, and startling developments, and too eager gynaccocracy of the States, he has fled into transmarine twilight, and the ever noble State of Suspended Animation!

An American living on the Continent suggests, somehow, a career of genius or of crime. An American in England, on the other hand, is a perfect working hypothesis. Scotland, Wales, Ireland (and Ireland especially), are bristling with ideas, as with so many spiritual burs and mosquitoes. But England, with her queer and meek climate, presents no such intimidations to the weary who would rest there. She is a heaven for retired and non-rheumatic racers, who are set only upon a smoke and a sleep. The quality of the Past and of the Peace proffered is incomparably the best, for these debased reasons: that the past is the very one, next his own, about which the average educated American knows most; and peace is certainly promoted, in the adult breast at least, when no necessity exists for the full dress of a foreign language. That ghostly encounter with "chaunt" or "gulph," in columns yet wet from the printing-press, that strange sea-change of what was a "spool of cotton" into a "reel of thread," — these and their like are pleasing titillations, and to the truly lazy mind are beatific substitutes for the diplomacies of Latin idiom, and the strangling vocabulary of the Fatherland.

Oh, the grave charm of rural England! Every hedgerow seems to imply a racial age-long deliberate choice of simplicity and sincerity over all which would dim them or drive them away. None can know this people at home well enough to poke fun at them, without reverencing them all the while: their moral etiquette is so sure, their standards so disinterested. Outside tainted London, loud success is accorded little preëminence. All other things being equal, the rich stranger, not the poor one, is put on his social probation. There is extraordinary trustfulness in business relations; fabrics are genuine; street noises come under legislation; a fare in any conveyance (except where Americans are in control) means a seat; the children are wholesomely childish, and the old fearlessly aged; the decorum and honor of life, excluding sensationalism, rule the national imagination. Here are some rather large towns (to say nothing of the country districts) which are no more agitating than a dove's note or a junket. You cannot walk through them for three minutes in any direction without seeing something famous and ancient and uniquely beautiful; nor beyond them, without meeting a landscape which is almost mystically dreamy. There is never, so far as one can make out, any fickle fashion in clothes, any fad in amusements. There is no highway army of poles and wires; no appreciable slush or drifts or icicles; no continuous agony of heat; no mosquitoes; no nerves! Work is lonely and unhurried, and recreation reasonable and calm. One can the better endure the scarcity of wild wood, moor, and river, when daily conventional pleasuring, even at its worst, is so near to Nature. The god of Tea is propitiated on a greensward, in the company of gentle dames who all say "Quite so!" and mannerly little girls with their mannerly dogs; "a summer shower," as Hazlitt says, "is dropping manna on your head, and an old crazy hand-organ is playing 'Robin Adair' " on the other side of the blessed ivied garden wall. This is to loaf and to reign.

You know now that you will never long to get anywhere in particular, or strain after anything except salvation. You set up for a smug, rich, intellectual Pharisee, with immaterial horizons which never were, nor can be, in the West. Time and eternity are pretty nearly one in the moist amethyst-colored air. You realize fully that the ozone is gone out of it, and that the sad heart of the earth beneath has bled for long. But you also realize that you are acquiring from contact with these an almost sportive sense of the unseen and the supernatural, and a sense which unravels essence from accident, true from plausible, lasting from uncertain, innocent from profane. Very grateful some outlanders are for this strange, painless stretching of their spirits. They have done with the Puritans. They have been kidnapped and catholicized. Small wonder if they feel that they have come home, body and soul, in coming near to the Simple Life and the Quiet Mind: not, mind you, to mere talk of these healthful and beatific things. Not that our happier natures in the United States have not at all times attained to them. But their exemption from the hurly-burly is a bought one: you do not have to buy it in England. It commends itself to the indigent, for it is a flowing fountain in the streets.

Our imaginary friend Fugacius, hungry for rest, may attain even that, and a better thing — anonymity. He may possibly be tired of keeping awake, of toeing the mark, of showing interest, and wearing an intelligent expression. He may have been martyred, more or less, by the Public Eye; but in England, if anywhere, he may indulge to the full a life-long passion for silence and seclusion. He will not be asked by an interviewer at 4 A.M., and at the point of the moral bayonet, for his impressions concerning problems fiscal or forensic. If he is understood to have exhibited in the Salon, or to have published a sonnet, not a living British creature will think any the better of him for it. Mention was made, a moment ago, of a garden wall: ubiquitous and beloved symbol; Conscious that it is stone, ten feet high, and ninety-one feet in circumference, the American memory runs across, in the wake of ships, to the exquisite suburban streets where the graceful houses, with their wooden gables and verandas, their lilacs and syringas, and wide graveled paths, lie open to one another and to the road. An American feels sure, of a sudden, that the English inclosure gives a freedom that he never knew, and that even a king, in such a fastness, could defy the demon of publicity. Too much praise cannot be given to the universal inviolable respect for privacy in the land of the garden wall. The human ear, even in a drawing-room, is as holy as any mediaeval ambry. There have been two celebrated instances, in our own generation, where real names of English writers, objects of curiosity to the whole reading world, were kept from it through many years, and up to the deaths of the authors, although the secret of identification had been quite casually shared, for long, by scores of discreet friends. Such instances commend the conditions (how unlike ours!) which make them possible. Indeed, they arouse enthusiasm in any natural enemy of newspaper headlines.

A wit once remarked that the English love Americans but not America, and that the Americans love England, but not the English. The truth of this discerning remark is obvious, whatever the explanation of it may be. But every day one hears some anecdote or other which makes one feel that shell and snail, at least with them, are inseparable: that an Englishman is just what he is, because England is just what she is. Here is one slight illustration of the point. During the August of 1906 a party of three Americans went north from Euston Station in London. The railway porter put them aboard the train, after his wont, observing, as it would appear, the name marking their luggage. The gentleman of the party asked the porter whether he should have to change carriages before reaching his destination; the porter answered in the negative, the door was slammed to, and the day-long journey began. Hours later, at a station, as the train slowed up, an inspector came along the corridor, repeating in a loud voice a name which the travelers recognized as their own. He held a telegram in his hand. This had been sent to him direct, asking him to find aboard a certain train Mr. ——, bound for ——, and to tell him that he had been misinformed and that he must make a change at —— Junction. Now that London porter must have known that the Americans were mere sightseeing strangers, that he would never see them or hear of them again, and that the odds were that they would inquire anew about changing on the journey, and find their way to —— as scheduled, or, for that matter, not lose their wits or lives if they did not: in fact, there was every inducement to make him wash his hands of them. Yet it was he who sent the wire, taking all that thoughtful trouble to set his blunder right. Could such a thing have happened under ordinary circumstances in our country? We have heroisms on every side; but we are too busy for contritions. Exercise of scrupulous conscience in official matters is precisely England and the English; the little fortuitous error, the abundant reparation, are not exceptional and individual, but as typical as they can possibly be. Here is a people which fumbles, which drops many stitches, which has its multiform inefficiencies. But it may boast truly that a passion for duty is in its very marrow; it will not in the end consciously go forward with unrepented wrong in its bosom. Is it any wonder if some children of a more heedless and elliptical nation, harassed by rude corporations and their units, think it pleasant to dwell among the million blood-relatives of that unknown adored railway porter? For so soothing a privilege, they will even endure the immemorial cabbage, the sacred Brussels sprouts of Great Britain and Ireland, for three hundred and sixty-five days of the gastronomical year.

In England, notably in middle England, flourishes the most unbelievable and ubiquitous density of mind. It is there indeed; and it is disciplinary; it is funny, it is maddening. Does it dash your joy, in some village of heavenly picturesqueness, to find (as you are always finding!) that the parson is a stock, and the laundress a stone? Well, never ultimately; for the stocks and stones are excellent to live with and have staying qualities. The secret of happiness for us, under their roof, as elsewhere, is the spirit of conformity and compromise. The English ethnological key seems to be D minor, and the household metronome to be set at *Adagio Marcato;* until you have tried the tune of Yankee Doodle in that unexpected key, and to that revolutionizing measure, you can have no idea of its moving effectiveness, and its powers of accommodation. The expatriate, if any one, should get a right perspective, and an unconfused sense of values. He knows that for the joy of life; for zest thorough and permeating; for organization and invention; for autumn forest pageantry in its perfection; for idyllic things to eat, and the magical cooking of the same; for the prevalence of personal and domestic taste; for true touchstones of human worth and worthlessness; for exquisite chivalry in the relations between men and women, — he knows that for these he must cross the bounding main: he must go home. But dear as these things are, deeply as these things (especially the last) are respected and lamented by all who knew them, one can do without them for a while. The Past, and Peace, are dearer yet. The faction which stays on and on, in a land not quite foreign, is agreed quite passionately about that.

150. Mother Katharine Drexel Drafts the Constitutions of Her Congregation, May 25, 1907

WHEN the history of twentieth-century Catholicism in the United States is finally written there will be no more honored name than that of Mother Katharine Drexel (1858–1955). Granddaughter of Francis M. Drexel (1792–1863), the Austrian-born immigrant who came to Philadelphia in 1817 and in 1838 opened a brokerage office that led in time to the world famous banking house of Drexel & Company, Katharine and her two sisters became the heiresses of an immense fortune upon the death of their father in 1885. Having been the recipient of the finest type of religious training from her pious father and step-mother, Katharine Drexel was deeply impressed by the appeal of the bishops of the Third Plenary Council in 1884 for help to the Indian and Negro missions. In a private audience of Leo XIII in January, 1887, she spoke of this interest, whereupon the pontiff was prompted to ask, "Why not become a missionary yourself, my child?" That settled Miss Drexel's vocation for life. Guided by James O'Connor (1832–1890), first Bishop of Omaha, who as the pastor of Homesburg, Pennsylvania, had known the Drexel family very well, she made her novitiate with the Sisters of Mercy in Pittsburgh and in February, 1891, she took the veil and with thirteen other women launched the Sisters of the Blessed Sacrament for Indians and Colored People. Even before her entry into the religious life Miss Drexel had given a million dollars to the missions for these two races, and all during the next sixty-four years she continued to pour her vast wealth into the cause by building dozens of churches, chapels, schools, and other missionary buildings. At Mother Katharine's death the community numbered 511 professed religious stationed in fifty-one houses located in twenty-one states and the District of Columbia. The sisters staff sixty-two schools, including forty-nine elementary, twelve high schools, and the only Catholic Negro university in the country, Xavier University of New Orleans, founded in 1925, and having a faculty of 115 with over 1100 men and women students. Not only did Mother Katharine use all of her tremendous income for the advancement of the Catholic faith among the American Indians and Negroes, but she and her congregation have likewise given generously to missions for these races in Alaska, Canada, Africa, and the British possessions. Mother Katharine herself drew up the first draft of the constitutions of her community after it had been in existence for sixteen years, and the following document — the original written in her own hand — embodied a rough outline of her aims and objectives. The decree of final approbation for the sisters' rule was granted by the Holy See in May, 1913. Source: Archives of St. Elizabeth's Convent, Cornwells Heights, Pennsylvania, Constitutions of the Sisters of the Blessed Sacrament for Indians and Colored People (photostat).

Concerning the Nature of the Congregation & the Manner of Living in the same.

Chapter I

Nature & Object of the Congregation.

1. The primary object which the Sisters of this religious Congregation purpose to themselves is their own personal sanctification.

2. The secondary & special object of the members of the Congregation is to apply themselves zealously to the service of Our Lord in the Blessed Sacrament by endeavoring to lead the Indian & Colored Races to the knowledge & love of God, & so make of them living temples of Our Lord's Divinity.

Chapter II

The Means of Carrying out the Object.

3. The principal means by which the Sisters of the Blessed Sacrament for Indians & Colored People are to procure their own perfection & the education, sanctification & salvation of the Indian & Colored Races are the following: —

(1 The faithful observance of the three simple vows of Poverty, Chastity & Obedience according to the approved Constitutions of the Congregation, & the faithful observance of these same Constitutions.

(2 A complete consecration of themselves, body & soul, to the service of their Eucharistic Lord, by a special devotion to the Blessed Sacrament, so that through Him they may sanctify in an especial manner their two-fold apostolate of prayer & work as set forth in these Constitutions.

(3 Frequent prayer, especially at the Holy Sacrifice of the Mass & at Holy Communion, to draw down upon themselves & upon the souls of the Indian & Colored the graces that will save them.

(4 As a further means of accomplishing this work, the members of this Congregation are according to circumstances, [to] undertake

1) To instruct the Indian & Colored Races in religious & other

useful knowledge according to their needs & capacities;
2) To care for their orphans & spiritually or corporally destitute children;
3) To attend to their sick by visiting them in their homes, or by the conducting of hospitals;
4) To visit their homes in order to look after their spiritual & temporal welfare;
5) To visit & instruct Indian & Colored inmates of prisons;
6) To shelter distressed & deserving women of these Races;
7) To aid in as far as they are able needy priests, religious communities & other reliable persons engaged in missionary work among the Indian & Colored Races.

151. The Launching of the Catholic Foreign Mission Society of America (Maryknoll), March 25, 1911

ON JUNE 29, 1908, the constitution *Sapienti consilio* of Pope Pius X removed the Church of the United States from the jurisdiction of the Congregation de Propaganda Fide and thus officially declared that its missionary status was at an end. Long before this date, however, the American Church had attained a position of strength in both numbers and resources and, in fact, by 1910 there were an estimated 16,363,000 Catholics in the country. Throughout the nineteenth century American Catholics had done relatively little for the foreign missions, although in 1904 their monetary contributions passed the $100,000 mark and rose steadily in the years thereafter. As yet, however, no full-fledged effort had been made to enlist American personnel for the foreign-mission field. In September, 1910, two American priests, James Anthony Walsh and Thomas Frederick Price, who had long thought and planned for this cause met at the International Eucharistic Congress in Montreal, and from that meeting there stemmed the founding of the first distinctly American Catholic foreign-mission society. Walsh and Price secured the sponsorship of Cardinal Gibbons and the Apostolic Delegate, and at the annual meeting of the archbishops of the United States on April 27, 1911, at the Catholic University of America approval was given for the opening of a seminary for this purpose. Maryknoll, as it is popularly known, began modestly in 1911 and today the society numbers over 600 priests, more than 100 brothers, and nearly 750 students studying for either the priesthood or brotherhood in eight training centers. Other American religious orders and congregations meanwhile increased their participation in the work and by December, 1953, there was a total of 4755 American priests, brothers, and sisters serving abroad in mission stations all over the world. Source: Archives of Maryknoll Seminary, copy.

To the Most Reverend Archbishops of the United States:

VENERABLE BRETHREN:

At the request of His Excellency, the Apostolic Delegate,[1] I submit to your consideration a plan to establish an American Foreign Mission Seminary.

That such a Seminary is needed, and urgently, seems daily more evident. The prestige of our country has become wide-spread; and Protestants, especially in the Far East, are profiting by it, to the positive hindrance of Catholic missioners. I understand that even the educated classes in China, misled by the almost complete absence of American Catholic priests, believe that the Church of Rome has no standing in America.[2]

Conscious that we are still short of priests in many dioceses, I would cite the words of Cardinal Manning referring to the foundation of Mill Hill:

> It is quite true that we have need of men and means at home; and it is BECAUSE we have need of more men and more means, by a great deal, than we as yet possess, that I am convinced we ought to send both men and means abroad. . . . If we desire to find the surest way to multiply immensely our own material means for works at home, it is by not limiting the expansion of Charity and by not paralyzing the zeal of self-denial.[3]

The priests of the United States number more than 17,000 but I am informed that there are hardly sixteen on the foreign missions. This fact recalls a warning which the late Cardinal Vaughan gave in a kindly and brotherly letter addressed to me twenty-two years ago, urging us American Catholics not to delay participation in foreign missions, LEST OUR OWN FAITH SHOULD SUFFER.[4]

---

[1] Diomede Falconio, O.F.M. (1842–1917), was the third Apostolic Delegate to the United States, having served from 1902 to late in the year 1911.

[2] Between 1881–1888 five Franciscans had gone to China from the United States but only one of them was a native-born American; there were also two American-born Sisters of Charity in China in the late years of the nineteenth century.

[3] Gibbons took the Manning quotation from a letter he had received from Herbert Vaughan (1832–1903), Bishop of Salford and after 1892 Archbishop of Westminster. Vaughan's letter dated Mill Hill, October 28, 1889, used the occasion of the centennial of the American hierarchy to urge upon the Catholics of the United States participation in the foreign missions of the Church. "A Challenge to the American Church on Its One Hundredth Birthday," *Catholic Historical Review,* XXX (October, 1944), 297.

[4] The reference here was to the letter noted above, the full text of which is printed *op. cit.,* pp. 290–298.

We must confess that as a Catholic body we have only begun, while our Protestant fellow-countrymen have passed the century mark in foreign mission work and are represented today in the heathen world by some thousands of missioners, who are backed by yearly contributions running up into the millions.

A seminary, such as that contemplated, if established with the good-will of the entire American Hierarchy, can hardly fail to draw, emphatically, the attention of American Catholics.

"It is time," to use the words of the Apostolic Delegate, "that the American Church should begin to move in this direction."

With pleasure, therefore, acting on His Excellency's request, I submit the following outline of the plan, secured after conference with those immediately interested:

> It is proposed to establish an American Foreign Mission Seminary for the training of secular priests.
>
> This Seminary, like those of Paris, London (Mill Hill), Milan,[5] et al., would necessarily be independent of any diocese, and directly under Propaganda, which would control its status, rules, etc., and apportion its fields of labor.
>
> It would be national in its character, organized and sustained by priests of the United States, guided, of course, by the best traditions of similar institutions abroad. It would appeal to young men reared in this country.
>
> It is proposed to begin the work on a small scale, near some established house of Catholic philosophy and theology. It would seek its PERMANENT home, well removed from the heart of city life, gradually securing its own professors, and developing an exclusively apostolic atmosphere. No definite location is suggested, although a preference has been expressed by the organizers for a center reasonably convenient to the more populous Catholic zones and, if possible,

[5] The French Society for Foreign Missions was founded in 1658 and the famous seminary of the society was opened in Paris in 1663. In July, 1850, the hierarchy of Lombardy, at the suggestion of Pius IX, founded the Pontifical Institute of SS. Peter and Paul and SS. Ambrose and Charles for the Foreign Missions. The headquarters of the institute were established in Milan in June, 1851. St. Joseph's College opened in March, 1866, in Mill Hill, a suburb of London, with Herbert Vaughan as the founder and first president. The first missionary field assigned to the Mill Hill Fathers by the Holy See was the apostolate to the American Negroes. Four of the members of the community began their original American foundation at St. Francis Xavier Church, Baltimore, late in 1871.

not too far removed from those states in which a knowledge of foreign missions has already been cultivated.[6]

It is expected that Preparatory Colleges will be needed, to serve later as feeders to the Seminary.

Two priests are immediately concerned in this undertaking, to which they are willing to devote their lives, — Rev. James Anthony Walsh of Boston and Rev. Thomas F. Price of North Carolina.

Fr. Walsh is a priest of the Boston Archdiocese.[7] He was ordained in 1892, and the late revered Archbishop Williams appointed him, more than eight years ago, Diocesan Director for the Propagation of the Faith. Under His Grace, Archbishop O'Connell, Fr. Walsh has been confirmed in this position, which he still holds. He also directs the Catholic Foreign Mission Bureau, editing THE FIELD AFAR and issuing other publications bearing on the subject of foreign missions.

Fr. Price has spent twenty-five years in difficult mission work. He is the Superior of the Apostolate of Secular Priests of North Carolina and editor of the magazine, TRUTH.[8]

His Excellency, the Apostolic Delegate, has advised that these two priests, having secured the encouragement of the Hierarchy, shall, with the permission of their Bishops, visit without delay the most important foreign mission Seminaries and apply in person to Rome for the authorization necessary to start.

Returned with proper credentials, they would aim to carry out, with the approval of the individual Bishops, the following plan:

a) To secure spiritual aid, asking prayers and Communions from seminaries, religious houses of men and women, institutions, etc., etc.

[6] In December, 1911, the Maryknoll community settled temporarily at Hawthorne, New York, and in September, 1912, they moved to a location near Ossining on the Hudson where the seminary opened that month with six students and five priests as teachers. There were also three aspirants for the Maryknoll Brothers, and nearby eight women formed the nucleus from which the Maryknoll Sisters would later take their rise.

[7] James Anthony Walsh (1867–1936) was cofounder of Maryknoll and first superior-general of the society until his death. He was consecrated titular Bishop of Syene on June 29, 1933.

[8] Thomas Frederick Price (1860–1919), cofounder of Maryknoll, headed the first group of Maryknoll missionaries to China in September, 1918. He died at Hong Kong on September 12, 1919.

b) To spread a knowledge of the missions, by means of conference and illustrated talks and by an output of mission literature.

c) To seek material support, chiefly by increasing the subscription list of THE FIELD AFAR, which has already a wide circle of interested and generous readers among the clergy and laity.

It is my purpose to ask the Most Reverend Archbishops at our next meeting:

1. If they will commend the proposed idea.
2. In the event of their favorable consideration, if they will fix, or at least suggest, one or more desirable locations from which a choice might be made, both for a provisional and for a permanent Seminary.

I would, therefore, ask the Most Reverend Archbishops to discuss with their suffragans this proposed schema, that the views and suggestions of all the Bishops of the country may be obtained and a common understanding arrived at, and our common desire and the united commendation of the Hierarchy be made known to Rome and to the Catholic body of the United States.

Faithfully yours in Christ,
J. Card. Gibbons

Feast of the Annunciation [March 25], 1911.

152. Thomas Fortune Ryan Explains His Most Striking Financial Transaction, August, 1913

ON THE day after the death of Thomas Fortune Ryan (1851–1928) the New York *Times* of November 24 stated, "The career of Thomas Fortune Ryan is as good an example as any in American history of the possibilities that this country offers to a poor, uneducated boy." It was altogether true, for he had been orphaned at an early age with no means of support and had worked as an errand boy in a grocery store in Baltimore and later as a messenger in a brokerage firm in Wall Street. But the contest over the New York street railways gave Ryan his chance and after 1883 he rose rapidly through the financing of the street railways, the American Tobacco Company, and the gold, diamond, and copper mines of the Belgian Congo. When he died his fortune was variously estimated to total from 100 to 500 million dollars. His most unusual financial deal — described in the document that follows — was his purchase in June, 1905, of the controlling block of shares in the Equitable Life Assurance Company. In doing this he stated that he had acted solely in the public interest in order to put the finances of the company in a sound condition, set up a trust to manage it, and then personally had withdrawn from the business. Ryan was generous in his donations to various Catholic causes, normally given through his first wife, and among the institutions that benefited most were the Cathedral of the Sacred Heart in Richmond, Virginia, his home state, and the Church of St. Jean Baptiste in New York from which he was buried. He was prominent in the Democratic Party and excited the ire of men like William Jennings Bryan who suspected him of wielding a sinister sort of influence by reason of his money. Because he was associated in the financial world with names like Morgan, Whitney, Harriman, etc., the New York *Times* editorial of November 24, 1928, spoke of Ryan as "the sole survivor" of a group of New York financiers "who posed for the first composite picture of 'Big Business.' " Source: Thomas F. Ryan, "Why I Brought the Equitable," *North American Review,* CXCVIII (August, 1913), 161–169.

In spite of the many explanations that have been made both by me and on my behalf about the purchase of the shares of the Equitable Life Assurance Society in June, 1905, the question that has since been asked me oftener than any other has related to that particular act. As the term of the trust then created has expired, and, as I no longer bear any relation to the property, it seems to me that I may, perhaps, be justified in giving a somewhat more detailed account of my ownership of it and my reasons for buying it.

No more serious quarrel has disturbed business for a generation than that which rose out of conditions that became known as existing in the Equitable early in 1905. Revelations of one kind or another then began to appear, so that it was for weeks the question upon which newspapers were expected to make a display each day. To outward seeming, this quarrel came out of a clear sky, but as in similar cases, events showed that it had been in preparation for years, and that predictions had long been freely made that some kind of storm was brewing.

It will not be necessary, for the purpose I have in mind, to enter into the details as to the clashing individualities, the many and strong jealousies which combined to foment the trouble. It did not come, however, as the result of machinations by the great financial houses of the Street. In reality, it had only a slight relation to what is familiarly known as Wall Street. In each of the three large life insurance companies which had become a marvel of the time, both as business organizations and as providing the machinery for savings, there were some officials who became jealous either of each other or of those in like positions in rival companies; in other words, it was a fierce incriminating quarrel between insiders and those of the smaller and less responsible order. It was almost wholly factional— and the facts fixing this were fully brought forth by the examination of the counsel for the Armstrong Committee, Mr. Charles E. Hughes, later Governor of New York, and now an associate justice of the United States Supreme Court.[1]

It would be as difficult to exaggerate the intensity of this quarrel as it would be to measure its effect upon business. For a time, while a thousand groundless reports were set in motion, the impression was given to the public that the management of great fiduciary institutions, not only of life insurance companies, but of all the corporations or companies or individuals which carried on great business operations, was rotten to the core.

I had taken no part in the management of any insurance company, and had no official relations with them. I was interested in insurance, as I had been from my entrance into business life, but it was as a policyholder, a student and admirer of the development of agencies which had had such a rapid growth and which, at the same time, had so commended themselves to the country as to command public confidence and make their way in almost every country in the world as models of what such institutions should be. . . .

I could but note, with serious and growing concern, the unseemly contest, the bitterness of which was daily emphasized, and also the indifference to public interest which was manifested by many of the men who, as directors or officials, ought to have been the first to come to the rescue. The public good seemed to be almost entirely forgotten in the desire of most of those on the inside and many others on the outside to take advantage of any mistake that might be made by their opponents, and that their only idea was to make these quarrels serve their own purposes.

In spite of these facts I did not, in the beginning of the contest, feel myself called upon either to throw myself into the breach or to make any attempt to use what resources I might command for composing the trouble. For some time it did not seem possible to me that responsible men would permit really serious conditions to develop, and as I held an entirely independent position, it did not appeal to me as lying within the power of an individual so situated to intervene; but, as the contest became more and more bitter, and as the contestants showed, increasingly, a determination to consider themselves only, thus failing to realize their obligations to the community, the conviction forced itself upon me, that, if others did not come to the

[1] Charles Evans Hughes (1862–1948) was appointed an associate justice in 1910 and served as Chief Justice of the United States from 1930 until his retirement in 1941.

rescue, the task, great as it was, might not be beyond my powers. In thinking of this I did not fail to realize what it meant in sacrifice of resources, in risk to fortune and reputation, in misunderstanding and abuse, nor in any of the other penalties that would naturally follow such an act.

But the more I thought of the matter, the clearer it seemed to me that perhaps I might never have a better opportunity to perform a public service than by averting panic and restoring confidence. Although I had no technical knowledge of insurance, it appeared to me plain that if the institutions built up by genius and experience, founded upon the confidence of many millions of saving, prudent individuals, handling together fabulous sums each year, were to be torn to pieces by passion and faction, then our whole scheme of business, whether it related to transportation, banking, manufacturing or mining, would receive a shock from which it would recover only after many years of loss and suffering.

In many respects, so far as I was concerned, the crisis came at an important period of my life. I had been engaged for many years in organizing and carrying on, so far as my powers and resources permitted, large business schemes and enterprises. They had taken all my energies and had left me practically no time for doing those things which it seemed to me more and more incumbent upon every man to do, at some time, if he has been the recipient of anything like an average share of prosperity. I felt that a man's success in this country was to be judged mainly by what he did, and the more I thought of it the more I was convinced that this was something worth doing.

Moreover, I had reached a time of life and a position in the business world which led me to contemplate retirement from its grinding activities. I had long had in mind many things that I wanted to do, and not one of them had borne any relation to a desire to make more money or to add to the fortune I had already accumulated. It occurred to me that I might make this practically the culminating point of my active career. I knew perfectly that, whatever might be the sentiment of others toward me or toward the act I contemplated, what I intended would be a real service, and that whatever of misunderstanding might result, the end would show that I had acted unselfishly.

When this idea presented itself to my mind in concrete form I had made arrangements to visit Kentucky, for the double purpose of resting and purchasing stock for my Virginia farm. Thus remote from the scenes of activity and struggle, away from news and financial gossip, free from all interruption and yet cognizant of all the underlying conditions in the problem that presented itself, I could look over the whole situation much more critically than if I were on the ground. The matter was too delicate to be discussed with anybody, and, besides, as it finally presented itself to me, it did not concern any one else. It seemed to be my task. In the beginning I had thought that perhaps I would need financial co-operation, but when I looked about I found that two difficulties presented themselves in this respect. It became clear that if I limited my associates to those who, like myself, were only desirous of doing a public service, both the number and amount of the contributions they could make were too small to be of vital assistance; if, on the other hand, I accepted the offers of one or two men who wanted to participate, I was in danger of being overwhelmed not only with advice, which I would not take, but with an assistance which would have hampered me in every movement.

I returned to New York without reaching any definite conclusion but still deeply impressed with the necessity for action. But the whole question had taken possession of me, and so I went to my Virginia farm where, still without advisers, I could again concentrate my attention upon the matter that had been of absorbing interest to me. It was there and then that I finally saw my way clear to take up the task, still leaving unimportant details out of account.

From the beginning I had no other idea than that of purchasing the stock control of the Equitable at such a price as I must pay, and of placing it at once in the hands of Trustees, of whom ex-President Grover Cleveland[2] was to be one — and, naturally, the Chairman — and also of doing this only upon such terms as should immediately divest me of all control over the stock, and of detail management of the Society itself. I had determined to do these things with the one condition that, so far as the laws permitted, the management of the Society should be turned over to a majority of directors to be chosen by the policyholders, from their own numbers.

I had long been an admirer of Mr. Cleveland and, by reason of personal and political affiliations, had come into close relations with him. Knowing that I had no ambitions, he had often asked my advice and assistance, mainly in matters relating to currency and coinage. Thus, in perfect accord with his aims, whether partisan or patriotic, cognizant of his unrivaled position in the country, I had also noted,

[2] Grover Cleveland (1837–1908) occupied the White House for two terms, 1885–1889 and 1893–1897.

with sorrow, that he was hampered by lack of means to maintain the dignity of a man who had twice filled with such distinction the Presidency of the United States. I visited him in Princeton soon after his removal there and noticed with great concern this fact, which was confirmed by himself and further emphasized by friends who knew him even better than I did. It seemed to me that he ought to be removed from the necessity of doing literary work of the kind in which he was engaged in order to obtain the money necessary for keeping himself and family in the position that he felt incumbent upon him. I soon found that schemes, ranging from the management of a winter hotel to the presidency of a trust company, had been suggested for him, but none of them, unworthy as they were, came to anything. I then resolved and announced, especially to one friend, that I would, at some time, make an opportunity to bring about the desired result. But the only condition that I fixed in this was that the solution of the difficulty must be one which would bring no profit to me in any form and should at the same time enable the former President to do some public service really worthy of his position and character.

Further, I felt that the creation of an Equitable Trust, with Mr. Cleveland at its head, would meet the idea I had in mind, both so far as it related to him, and at the same time enable me, even without his knowledge, to do a great service to the country. It would solidify the new appreciation of him which had begun to come back about this time, and, best of all, it would save our financial institutions by restoring confidence. No business proposal of any kind was ever made to him by me or any one acting for me from the beginning until his relations to the trusteeship were ended by death. When the preliminaries were complete, an intimate friend of my own and of the former President was intrusted with the presentation of the matter. The rest of the story is well known. . . .

The announcement of the appointment of the trustees acted like magic upon the unwholesome business conditions prevailing at the time. From their first meeting — the only one I ever attended in order to execute the deed of trust — accompanied by the issue of a formal address, followed by the first list of directors chosen by them, confidence asserted itself. Sensational reports disappeared and even the threat of danger — much less danger itself — was no longer powerful. Mr. Cleveland's action thus taken, added to the prestige of a great name, had entirely cleared the air in a moment. . . .

After this preliminary work had been done, the rest was comparatively easy. Confidence was at once restored in the way that I have noted, and from that moment practically all danger of panic disappeared not only so far as the insurance companies were concerned, but from every branch of financial activity. . . .

153. Maurice Francis Egan Urges the Purchase of the Danish West Indies, March 8, 1915

A CONSIDERABLE number of Catholics have held high posts in the American diplomatic service, among them Maurice Francis Egan (1852–1924), who was Minister to Denmark from 1907 to 1918. Egan had been professor of English literature in the Catholic University of America since 1896 when he resigned to take the Copenhagen legation, having previously done newspaper work in New York (1878–1888) and taught at the University of Notre Dame (1888–1896). His diplomatic career is best remembered for the part he played in the purchase of the Danish West Indies. Twice before, in 1867 and 1902, treaties had been negotiated for their purchase but they were never ratified. World War I quickened American interest lest the islands should fall to Germany and become a base of operations for submarines. On August 4, 1916, a treaty was signed for their purchase at a figure of $25,000,000. Egan's tenure of the Copenhagen post during the war years brought him into more than ordinary prominence, and Henry van Dyke (1852–1933), professor of English literature at Princeton University and Minister to the Netherlands, stated after a visit to the Danish capital in 1916 that Egan was "not only the Dean of the Diplomatic Corps, he was its Prince Charming, the one to whom all turned for help in difficulty and for conciliation in dispute" (Introduction to Maurice Francis Egan, *Recollections of a Happy Life* [New York, 1924], p. x). Source: *Papers Relating to the Foreign Relations of the United States* (Washington: Government Printing Office, 1926), pp. 588–590.

MINISTER EGAN TO THE SECRETARY OF STATE
(William Jennings Bryan, 1860–1925)

No. 833

American Legation,
Copenhagen, March 8, 1915.

Sir: It may seem out of place for me, especially when the most terrible events are making a crisis in the world, to return to a subject on which in the past I have written many despatches,[1] the purchase

[1] As early as July 19, 1909, in a dispatch from Copenhagen to Alvey A. Adee, Assistant Secretary of State, Egan had stated: "I am quite sure that a time will come when it will be expedient, if our Government continues to hold it advisable, to open the question of the Danish Antilles. I am doing my best to pave the way for this" (*ibid.*, p. 557).

of the Danish Antilles. For seven years I have hoped that the Department might instruct me to make such suggestions to the Danish Government as would lead to an offer of these islands to the United States at a reasonable price. For good reason, I am sure, I received little encouragement; it was necessary to soften the suspicion of our arrogance and imperialistic tendencies which had arisen here and seemed fixed, and to make the Danish people feel that the Government of the United States has a sincere interest in their progress and sympathy with their national aspirations.

Once during the administration of President Taft there seemed to be some hope that the matter of the purchase of these islands might be considered as probable in the near future; the President went so far as to ask me whether they could be put under the same jurisdiction as Porto Rico and what price might be asked for them. This was sometime after a number of distinguished Danes had sent to me a memorial (September 23, 1910) proposing that our Government should accept Greenland in exchange for Mindanao, the Danish Government having the right to surrender Mindanao to Germany in exchange for Northern Schleswig. The hope that Danish Schleswig may one day again become part of Denmark is still cherished by a great number of the Danes, whose very delicate position, between two great Powers, does not depress their national ardor. The knowledge that this memorial had been presented to me produced a discussion in certain groups here as to whether the Danish Government would be willing to part with St. Thomas and the other Danish Antilles.

All this of course was purely academic, but interesting. It was made plain that if the pride of this small country in parting with such useless possessions as the Danish West Indies could be soothed, the islands might easily be made to come to us. The price of course would have had to be greater than it would have been previous to the opening of the Panama Canal or before the present improvements in the harbor of St. Thomas had begun. There would have been then no objection on the part of either England or Germany.

The main opponent of the sale, when the last attempt was made in 1902, was the East Asiatic Company, backed up by certain business men here; for instance Mr. Holger Petersen. Home politics too, played a part in the defeat of the project in the Upper House, — the Conservative Party fearing that the Deuntzer Ministry might strengthen itself by spending the money received for these islands. The interest of the business men in the holding of the islands has fallen off; the national subscription for the improving of the islands, which was opened in 1912 entirely failed. My argument with the principal opposers of the sale of the islands to us was to the effect that if they were to remain a burden to Denmark and a blot on the face of progress, as they were, it would be much better for the national reputation of Denmark that they should be sold to the United States. This attitude was looked upon as reasonable. Representing the ideas of our Government, I said publicly, that the United States would gladly sympathize with any attempt to make the population of the islands more contented and prosperous. The improvements in St. Thomas are still going on, but interest in them, on the part of the Danish people, has almost entirely ceased.

It is not necessary for me to comment on the importance of the great harbor of St. Thomas as a base of operations for any nation that possesses it. There is a rumor, widely spread, founded on the negotiations of 1902, that the United States had secured an option on the islands in question. This is without foundation, as far as I know.

It is not improbable that one day Denmark, in spite of the apparent drawing together of the three Scandinavian countries, may be absorbed by Germany, not by the breaking of her neutrality, which, however, is feared, but by what is called "peaceful penetration." If Germany should gain great advantages in the present war, neither England, nor Russia, nor France would be in a position to protest; and protests from other nations would of course be useless. The Danish West India Islands would then be the property of Germany, as Heligoland, under very different circumstances, became her property. A copy of the memorial sent by me to the Department on September 23, 1910, is appended.

I have been impressed by the fact that the Department, notwithstanding its present arduous and grievous occupations, has kept its eyes fastened on probable contingencies which may result from the present war and I take the liberty of calling attention to one of these possible contingencies.[2]

I have [etc.]

Maurice Francis Egan

[2] Three months after the receipt of this dispatch Robert Lansing (1864–1928), Secretary of State, cabled Egan on June 16 as follows: "Department is of the opinion that plan suggested in your despatch No. 833, March 8, is desirable and may be feasible and you may very discreetly approach the proper officials with a view to ascertaining whether a proposal such as contemplated would be received not unfavorably" (*ibid.*, p. 591). Egan's personal and more colorful account of the negotiations that followed may be read in his volume of memoirs, *Ten Years Near the German Frontier* (New York, 1919), pp. 263–288.

154. John A. Ryan and the Bishops' Program of Social Reconstruction, February 12, 1919

THE most influential Catholic in the field of American social reform was John A. Ryan (1869–1945). From 1915 to his retirement in 1939 he taught political economy and moral theology in the Catholic University of America. By means of books such as *A Living Wage* (New York, 1906) and *Distributive Justice* (New York, 1916), Ryan established a national reputation. But more famous, perhaps, was a pamphlet of his composition entitled *Social Reconstruction: A General Review of the Problems and Survey of Remedies* (Washington, 1919), the origins of which Ryan told in his memoirs, *Social Doctrine in Action* (New York, 1941), pp. 143–151. Near the close of World War I numerous programs of social reform appeared from various groups. Ryan tried his hand at such a program and after it had been read by the bishops who composed the Administrative Committee of the National Catholic War Council they were impressed to the point of making it their own and issuing it over their signatures. The proposals set forth were thought so radical at the time that Stephen C. Mason, president of the National Association of Manufacturers, protested to Cardinal Gibbons that it was "partisan, pro-labor union, socialistic propaganda" (Archives of the Archdiocese of Baltimore, Mason to Gibbons, New York, February 25, 1919). A decade later the pamphlet was described by a committee of the New York State Senate investigating seditious activities, in a report filed on April 24, 1929, as the work of "a certain group in the Catholic Church with leanings toward Socialism" (Ryan, *op. cit.*, p. 147). These reactions were evidence of the advanced thinking of Ryan and the bishops who adopted his draft as their official pronouncement. Of the eleven proposals contained in the pamphlet, all have now been either wholly or partially translated into fact. Only one, the participation of labor in management and a wider distribution of ownership, has made little progress. Source: *Bishops' Program of Social Reconstruction* [reprint] (Washington: National Catholic Welfare Conference, 1950).

FOREWORD

The ending of the Great War has brought peace. But the only safeguard of peace is social justice and a contented people. The deep unrest so emphatically and so widely voiced throughout the world is the most serious menace to the future peace of every nation and of the entire world. Great problems face us. They cannot be put aside; they must be met and solved with justice to all.

In the hope of stating the lines that will best guide us in our right solution the following pronouncement is issued by the Administrative Committee of the National Catholic War Council. Its practical applications are of course subject to discussion, but all its essential declarations are based upon the principles of charity and justice that have always been held and taught by the Catholic Church, while its practical proposals are merely an adaptation of those principles and that traditional teaching to the social and industrial conditions and needs of our own time.

✠ PETER J. MULDOON, *Chairman,*
Bishop of Rockford.

✠ JOSEPH SCHREMBS,
Bishop of Toledo.

✠ PATRICK J. HAYES,
Bishop of Tagaste.

✠ WILLIAM T. RUSSELL,
Bishop of Charleston.

Washington, D. C.
February 12, 1919.

"Reconstruction" has of late been so tiresomely reiterated, not to say violently abused, that it has become to many of us a word of aversion. Politicians, social students, labor leaders, business men, charity workers, clergymen and various other social groups have contributed their quota of spoken words and printed pages to the discussion of the subject; yet the majority of us still find ourselves rather bewildered and helpless. We are unable to say what parts of our social system imperatively need reconstruction; how much of that which is imperatively necessary is likely to be seriously undertaken; or what specific methods and measures are best suited to realize that amount of reconstruction which is at once imperatively necessary and immediately feasible.

Nevertheless it is worth while to review briefly some of the more important statements and proposals that have been made by various social groups and classes. Probably the most notable declaration from a Catholic source is that contained in a pastoral letter, written by Cardinal Bourne several months ago. "It is admitted on all hands," he says, "that a new order of things, new social conditions, new relations between the different sections in which society is divided, will arise as a consequence of the destruction of the formerly existing conditions. . . . The very foundations of political and social life, of our economic system, of morals and religion are being sharply scrutinized, and this not only by a few writers and speakers, but by a very large number of people in every class of life, especially among the workers."[1]

The Cardinal's special reference to the action of labor was undoubtedly suggested by the now famous "Social Reconstruction Program" of the British Labor Party.[2] This document was drawn up about one year ago, and is generally understood to be the work of the noted economist and Fabian Socialist, Mr. Sidney Webb.[3] Unquestionably, it is the most comprehensive and coherent program that has yet appeared on the industrial phase of reconstruction. In brief it sets up "four pillars" of the new social order:

(1) The enforcement by law of a national minimum of leisure, health, education and subsistence;

(2) The democratic control of industry, which means the nationalization of all monopolistic industries and possibly of other industries, sometime in the future, if that course be found advisable;

(3) A revolution in national finance; that is, a system of taxation which will compel capital to pay for the war, leaving undisturbed the national minimum of welfare for the masses;

(4) Use of the surplus wealth of the nation for the common good; that is, to provide capital, governmental industries, and funds for social, educational and artistic progress.

This program may properly be described as one of immediate radical reforms, leading ultimately to complete Socialism. Evidently this outcome cannot be approved by Catholics.

PROGRAM OF AMERICAN LABOR

Through its Committee on Reconstruction, the American Federation of Labor has issued a lengthy program of reform proposals and demands which may be grouped under the three heads of trade union action, labor legislation and general industrial and social legislation. The principal demands under the first head are: the legally guaranteed rights of the workers to organize and to carry on the normal activities of trade unions; a living wage; no reduction in present scales of

[1] Francis Cardinal Bourne (1861–1935) was fourth Archbishop of Westminster. The pastoral referred to was issued on Quinquagesima Sunday [February 10], 1918. Cf. the chapter "The 1918 Pastoral," in Ernest Oldmeadow, *Francis Cardinal Bourne* (London, 1944), II, 139–145.

[2] For the various programs mentioned in the Ryan document, cf. Estella T. Weeks, *Reconstruction Programs* (New York, 1919).

[3] Sidney Webb (1859–1947) had been one of the principal founders of the Fabian Society in 1883.

wages; the right of labor to fix its hours of work; the eight-hour day; equal pay for equal work by the two sexes; exclusive reliance by labor on trade-union effort to maintain fair wages; establishment of co-operative stores; and no organization of a political party by the workers. Labor laws demanded are: prohibition of wage working by children under sixteen years of age; abolition of private employment agencies; prohibition of all immigration for two years; and vocational education which will fit the young for life in an industrial society. By implication both the eight-hour day and the living wage are declared to be subjects for trade-union action, not for legislation. Among the measures of general social legislation recommended are: a special tax on "usable land" not cultivated by the owner, and taxes on land values which would make the holding of idle land unprofitable;[4] government housing; government ownership and operation of docks, wharves and water powers; taxes on excess profits, incomes and inheritances; and limitation of the power of the courts to declare laws unconstitutional.

While this program is more practical and more moderate and reasonable than that of the British Labor Congress, its proposal for taxing land into use could easily involve confiscation. On the other hand, it does not give sufficient consideration to the case of the weaker sections of the working class, those for whom trade union action is not practically adequate; nor does it demand or imply that the workers should ever aspire to become owners as well as users of the instruments of production.

BRITISH QUAKER EMPLOYERS

Probably the most definite and comprehensive statement from the opposite industrial class was put forth several months ago by a group of twenty Quaker employers in Great Britain. In outline their program is as follows: A family living wage for all male employees, and a secondary wage in excess of this for workers having special skill, training, physical strength, responsibility for human life; the right of labor to organize, to bargain collectively with the employer and to participate in the industrial part of business management; serious and practical measures to reduce the volume and hardship of unemployment; provisions of such working conditions as will safeguard health, physical integrity and morals; the reduction so far as practicable of profits and interest until both the basic and the second-

[4] The single tax movement of Henry George (1839–1897) was still a live issue at this time.

ary wage has been paid, and transfer to the community of the greater part of surplus profits.

The spirit and conception of responsibility that permeate every item of the program are reflected in this statement: "We would ask all employers to consider very carefully whether their style of living and personal expenditure are restricted to what is needed in order to insure the efficient performance of their functions in society. More than this is waste, and is, moreover, a great cause of class divisions."

AMERICAN EMPLOYERS

The only formal statements on the subject of social reconstruction that have yet come to our attention from an important group of American employers, are a declaration of principles and certain proposals by the National Chamber of Commerce. The declaration of principles was made at a convention of the organization, in Atlantic city, December 6, 1918. Beyond a general commendation of peaceful and friendly relations between employers and employees, it included nothing of importance on the labor phase of reconstruction. It condemned government operation and ownership of railroads, telegraphs and telephones, and demanded more moderate taxes and a modification of the Sherman Anti-Trust Law. More recently the executive officials of the Chamber have submitted to a referendum vote of its membership a statement, "with a view to furnishing a basis on which American industry can build a national labor program." The main specific proposals in this statement are: recognition of the right of workers to organize; adequate representation of both parties in the determination of employment conditions; a decent home and proper social conditions; no reduction in wages until all other costs of production have been brought down to the lowest possible level; and a system of national employment offices. Inasmuch as this organization represents more employers than any other association in the country, the vote of its members on these proposals will be of the greatest significance.

AN INTERDENOMINATIONAL STATEMENT

In Great Britain an organization known as the Interdenominational Conference of Social Service Unions, comprising ten religious bodies, including Catholics, spent more than a year formulating a statement of Social Reconstruction. (See the summary and analysis contained in the Catholic Social Year Book for 1918.)[5] This statement deals with

[5] *A Christian Social Crusade: Catholic Social Year Book for 1918* (London, 1918), p. 1.

principles, evils, and remedies. Presuming that Christianity provides indispensable guiding principles and powerful motives of social reform, it lays down the basic proposition that every human being is of inestimable worth, and that legislation should recognize persons as more sacred than property, therefore the State should enforce a minimum living wage, enable the worker to obtain some control of industrial conditions; supplement private initiative in providing decent housing; prevent the occurrence of unemployment; safeguard the right of the laborer and his family to a reasonable amount of rest and recreation; remove those industrial and social conditions which hinder marriage and encourage an unnatural restriction of families, and afford ample opportunities for education of all children industrially, culturally, religiously and morally. On the other hand rights imply duties, and the individual is obliged to respect the rights of others, to cultivate self-control, to recognize that labor is the law of life, and that wealth is a trust. Finally, the statement points out that all social reform must take as its end and guide the maintenance of pure and wholesome family life.

Such in barest outline are the main propositions and principles of this remarkable program. The text contains adequate exposition of the development and application of all these points, and concrete specifications of the methods and measures by which the aims and principles may be brought into effect. In the latter respect the statement is not liable to the fatal objection that is frequently and fairly urged against the reform pronouncements of religious bodies: that they are abstract, platitudinous and usually harmless. The statement of the Interdenominational Conference points out specific remedies for the evils that it describes; specific measures, legislative and other, by which the principles may be realized in actual life. Especially practical and valuable for Catholics are the explanations and modifications supplied by the Year Book of the Catholic social Guild.

NO PROFOUND CHANGES IN THE UNITED STATES

It is not to be expected that as many or as great social changes will take place in the United States as in Europe. Neither our habits of thinking nor our ordinary ways of life have undergone a profound disturbance. The hackneyed phrase: "Things will never again be the same after the war," has a much more concrete and deeply felt meaning among the European peoples. Their minds are fully adjusted to the conviction and expectation that these words will come true.

In the second place, the devastation, the loss of capital and of men, the changes in individual relations and the increase in the activities of government have been much greater in Europe than in the United States. Moreover, our superior natural advantages and resources, the better industrial and social condition of our working classes still constitute an obstacle to anything like revolutionary changes. It is significant that no social group in America, not even among the wage-earners, has produced such a fundamental and radical program of reconstruction as the Labor Party of Great Britain.

A PRACTICAL AND MODERATE PROGRAM

No attempt will be made in these pages to formulate a comprehensive scheme of reconstruction. Such an undertaking would be a waste of time as regards immediate needs and purposes, for no important group or section of the American people is ready to consider a program of this magnitude. Attention will therefore be confined to those reforms that seem to be desirable and also obtainable within a reasonable time, and to a few general principles which should become a guide to more distant developments. A statement thus circumscribed will not merely present the objects that we wish to see attained, but will also serve as an imperative call to action. It will keep before our minds the necessity for translating our faith into works. In the statements of immediate proposals we shall start, wherever possible, from those governmental agencies and legislative measures which have been to some extent in operation during the war. These come before us with the prestige of experience and should therefore receive first consideration in any program that aims to be at once practical and persuasive.

The first problem in the process of reconstruction is the industrial replacement of the discharged soldiers and sailors. The majority of these will undoubtedly return to their previous occupations. However, a very large number of them will either find their previous places closed to them, or will be eager to consider the possibility of more attractive employments. The most important single measure for meeting this situation that has yet been suggested is the placement of such men on farms. Several months ago Secretary Lane recommended to Congress that returning soldiers and sailors should be given the opportunity to work at good wages upon some part of the millions upon millions of acres of arid, swamp, and cut-over timber lands, in order to prepare them for cultivation. President Wilson in his annual address to Congress endorsed the proposal.[6] As fast as this preliminary task has been performed, the men should be assisted by government loans to establish themselves as farmers, either as owners or as tenants having long-time leases. It is essential that both the work of preparation and the subsequent settlement of the land should be effected by groups or colonies, not by men living independently of one another and in depressing isolation. A plan of this sort is already in operation in England. The importance of the project as an item of any social reform program is obvious. It would afford employment to thousands upon thousands, would greatly increase the number of farm owners and independent farmers, and would tend to lower the cost of living by increasing the amount of agricultural products. If it is to assume any considerable proportions it must be carried out by the governments of the United States and of the several States. Should it be undertaken by these authorities and operated on a systematic and generous scale, it would easily become one of the most beneficial reform measures that has ever been attempted.

UNITED STATES EMPLOYMENT SERVICE

The reinstatement of the soldiers and sailors in urban industries will no doubt be facilitated by the United States Employment Service. This agency has attained a fair degree of development and efficiency during the war. Unfortunately there is some danger that it will go out of existence or be greatly weakened at the end of the period of demobilization. It is the obvious duty of Congress to continue and strengthen this important institution. The problem of unemployment is with us always. Its solution requires the co-operation of many agencies, and the use of many methods; but the primary and indispensable instrument is a national system of labor exchanges, acting in harmony with State, municipal, and private employment bureaus.

WOMEN WAR WORKERS

One of the most important problems of readjustment is that created by the presence in industry of immense numbers of women who have taken the places of men during the war. Mere justice, to say nothing of chivalry, dictates that these women should not be compelled to suffer any greater loss or inconvenience than is absolutely necessary;

[6] The address of Wilson was delivered on December 2, 1918. For the president's endorsement of the proposal of Secretary of the Interior Franklin K. Lane (1864–1921) concerning lands for the returning servicemen cf. *Congressional Record, 65th Congress, 3rd Session* (Washington, 1919), LVII, 7.

for their services to the nation have been second only to the services of the men whose places they were called upon to fill. One general principle is clear: No female worker should remain in any occupation that is harmful to health or morals. Women should disappear as quickly as possible from such tasks as conducting and guarding street cars, cleaning locomotives, and a great number of other activities for which conditions of life and their physique render them unfit. Another general principle is that the proportion of women in industry ought to be kept within the smallest practical limits. If we have an efficient national employment service, if a goodly number of the returned soldiers and sailors are placed on the land, and if wages and the demand for goods are kept up to the level which is easily attainable, all female workers who are displaced from tasks that they have been performing only since the beginning of the war will be able to find suitable employments in other parts of the industrial field, or in those domestic occupations which sorely need their presence. Those women who are engaged at the same tasks as men should receive equal pay for equal amounts and qualities of work.

NATIONAL WAR LABOR BOARD

One of the most beneficial governmental organizations of the war is the National War Labor Board.[7] Upon the basis of a few fundamental principles, unanimously adopted by the representatives of labor, capital, and the public, it has prevented innumerable strikes, and raised wages to decent levels in many different industries throughout the country. Its main guiding principles have been a family living wage for all male adult laborers; recognition of the right of labor to organize, and to deal with employers through its chosen representatives; and no coercion of non-union laborers by members of the union. The War Labor Board ought to be continued in existence by Congress, and endowed with all the power for effective action that it can possess under the Federal Constitution. The principles, methods, machinery and results of this institution constitute a definite and far-reaching gain for social justice. No part of this advantage should be lost or given up in time of peace.

PRESENT WAGE RATES SHOULD BE SUSTAINED

The general level of wages attained during the war should not be

[7] The National War Labor Board was appointed by President Wilson in April, 1918, and had as co-chairmen former President Taft (1857–1930) and Frank P. Walsh (1864–1939). It was intended to act as a court of last resort for labor disputes.

lowered. In a few industries, especially some directly and peculiarly connected with the carrying on of war, wages have reached a plane upon which they cannot possibly continue for this grade of occupations. But the number of workers in this situation is an extremely small proportion of the entire wage-earning population. The overwhelming majority should not be compelled or suffered to undergo any reduction in their rates of remuneration, for two reasons: First, because the average rate of pay has not increased faster than the cost of living; second, because a considerable majority of the wage-earners of the United States, both men and women, were not receiving living wages when prices began to rise in 1915. In that year, according to Lauck and Sydenstricker,[8] whose work is the most comprehensive on the subject, four-fifths of the heads of families obtained less than 800 dollars, while two-thirds of the female wage-earners were paid less than 400 dollars. Even if the price of goods should fall to the level on which they were in 1915 — something that cannot be hoped for within five years — the average present rates of wages would not exceed the equivalent of a decent livelihood in the case of the vast majority. The exceptional instances to the contrary are practically all among the skilled workers. Therefore, wages on the whole should not be reduced even when the cost of living recedes from its present high level.

Even if the great majority of workers were now in receipt of more than living wages, there are no good reasons why rates of pay should be lowered. After all, a living wage is not necessarily the full measure of justice. All the Catholic authorities on the subject explicitly declare that this is only the minimum of justice. In a country as rich as ours, there are very few cases in which it is possible to prove that the worker would be getting more than that to which he has a right if he were paid something in excess of this ethical minimum. Why then, should we assume that this is the normal share of almost the whole laboring population? Since our industrial resources and instrumentalities are sufficient to provide more than a living wage for a very large proportion of the workers, why should we acquiesce in a theory which denies them this measure of the comforts of life? Such a policy is not only of very questionable morality, but is unsound economically. The large demand for goods which is created and maintained by high rates of wages and high purchasing power by the masses is the surest guarantee of a continuous and general operation

[8] W. Jett Lauck and Edgar Sydenstricker, *Conditions of Labor in American Industries* (New York, 1917), p. 66.

of industrial establishments. It is the most effective instrument of prosperity for labor and capital alike. The principal beneficiaries of a general reduction of wages would be the less efficient among the capitalists, and the more comfortable sections of the consumers. The wage-earners would lose more in remuneration than they would gain from whatever fall in prices occurred as a direct result of the fall in wages. On grounds both of justice and sound economics, we should give our hearty support to all legitimate efforts made by labor to resist general wage reductions.

HOUSING FOR WORKING CLASSES

Housing projects for war workers which have been completed, or almost completed by the Government of the United States, have cost some forty million dollars, and are found in eleven cities. While the Federal Government cannot continue this work in time of peace, the example and precedent that it has set, and the experience and knowledge that it has developed, should not be forthwith neglected and lost. The great cities in which congestion and other forms of bad housing are disgracefully apparent ought to take up and continue the work, at least to such an extent as will remove the worst features of a social condition that is a menace at once to industrial efficiency, civic health, good morals and religion.

REDUCTION OF THE COST OF LIVING

During the war the cost of living has risen at least seventy-five per cent. above the level of 1913. Some check has been placed upon the upward trend by government fixing of prices in the case of bread and coal, and a few other commodities. Even if we believe it desirable, we cannot ask that the Government continue this action after the articles of peace have been signed; for neither public opinion nor Congress is ready for such a revolutionary policy. If the extortionate practices of monopoly were prevented by adequate laws and adequate law enforcement, prices would automatically be kept at as low a level as that to which they might be brought by direct government determination. Just what laws, in addition to those already on the statute books, are necessary to abolish monopolistic extortion is a question of detail that need not be considered here. In passing, it may be noted that government competition with monopolies that cannot be effectively restrained by the ordinary anti-trust laws deserves more serious consideration than it has yet received.

More important and more effective than any government regulation of prices would be the establishment of co-operative stores. The enormous toll taken from industry by the various classes of middle-men is now fully realized. The astonishing difference between the price received by the producer and that paid by the consumer has become a scandal of our industrial system. The obvious and direct means of reducing this discrepancy and abolishing unnecessary middle-men is the operation of retail and wholesale mercantile concerns under the ownership and management of the consumers. This is no Utopian scheme. It has been successfully carried out in England and Scotland through the Rochdale system.[9] Very few serious efforts of this kind have been made in this country because our people have not felt the need of these co-operative enterprises as keenly as the European working classes, and because we have been too impatient and too individualistic to make the necessary sacrifices and to be content with moderate benefits and gradual progress. Nevertheless, our superior energy, initiative and commercial capacity will enable us, once we set about the task earnestly, even to surpass what has been done in England and Scotland.

In addition to reducing the cost of living, the co-operative stores would train our working people and consumers generally in habits of saving, in careful expenditure, in business methods, and in the capacity for co-operation. When the working classes have learned to make the sacrifices and to exercise the patience required by the ownership and operation of co-operative stores, they will be equipped to undertake a great variety of tasks and projects which benefit the community immediately, and all its constituent members ultimately. They will then realize the folly of excessive selfishness and senseless individualism. Until they have acquired this knowledge, training and capacity, desirable extensions of governmental action in industry will not be attended by a normal amount of success. No machinery of government can operate automatically, and no official and bureaucratic administration of such machinery can ever be a substitute for intelligent interest and co-operation by the individuals of the community.

THE LEGAL MINIMUM WAGE

Turning now from those agencies and laws that have been put in operation during the war to the general subject of labor legislation and problems, we are glad to note that there is no longer any serious

[9] This system of co-operatives originated in 1844 at Rochdale, England, when a group of chartists and Owenite workmen opened a store of the so-called Rochdale Pioneers.

objection urged by impartial persons against the legal minimum wage. The several States should enact laws providing for the establishment of wage rates that will be at least sufficient for the decent maintenance of a family, in the case of all male adults, and adequate to the decent individual support of female workers. In the beginning the minimum wages for male workers should suffice only for the present needs of the family, but they should be gradually raised until they are adequate to future needs as well. That is, they should be ultimately high enough to make possible that amount of saving which is necessary to protect the worker and his family against sickness, accidents, invalidity and old age.

SOCIAL INSURANCE

Until this level of legal minimum wages is reached the worker stands in need of the device of insurance. The State should make comprehensive provision for insurance against illness, invalidity, unemployment, and old age. So far as possible the insurance fund should be raised by a levy on industry, as is now done in the case of accident compensation. The industry in which a man is employed should provide him with all that is necessary to meet all the needs of his entire life. Therefore, any contribution to the insurance fund from the general revenues of the State should be only slight and temporary. For the same reason no contribution should be exacted from any worker who is not getting a higher wage than is required to meet the present needs of himself and family. Those who are below that level can make such a contribution only at the expense of their present welfare. Finally, the administration of the insurance laws should be such as to interfere as little as possible with the individual freedom of the worker and his family. Any insurance scheme, or any administrative method, that tends to separate the workers into a distinct and dependent class, that offends against their domestic privacy and independence, or that threatens individual self-reliance and self-respect, should not be tolerated. The ideal to be kept in mind is a condition in which all the workers would themselves have the income and the responsibility of providing for all the needs and contingencies of life, both present and future. Hence all forms of State insurance should be regarded as merely a lesser evil, and should be so organized and administered as to hasten the coming of the normal condition.

The life insurance offered to soldiers and sailors during the war should be continued, so far as the enlisted men are concerned. It is very doubtful whether the time has yet arrived when public opinion would sanction the extension of general life insurance by the Government to all classes of the community.

The establishment and maintenance of municipal health inspection in all schools, public and private, is now pretty generally recognized as of great importance and benefit. Municipal clinics where the poorer classes could obtain the advantage of medical treatment by specialists at a reasonable cost would likewise seem to have become a necessity. A vast amount of unnecessary sickness and suffering exists among the poor and the lower middle classes because they cannot afford the advantages of any other treatment except that provided by the general practitioner. Every effort should be made to supply wage-earners and their families with specialized medical care through development of group medicine. Free medical care should be given only to those who cannot afford to pay.

LABOR PARTICIPATION IN INDUSTRIAL MANAGEMENT

The right of labor to organize and to deal with employers through representatives has been asserted above in connection with the discussion of the War Labor Board. It is to be hoped that this right will never again be called in question by any considerable number of employers. In addition to this, labor ought gradually to receive greater representation in what the English group of Quaker employers have called the "industrial" part of business management — "the control of processes and machinery; nature of product; engagement and dismissal of employees; hours of work, rates of pay, bonuses, etc.; welfare work; shop discipline; relations with trade unions." The establishment of shop committees, working wherever possible with the trade union, is the method suggested by this group of employers for giving the employees the proper share of industrial management. There can be no doubt that a frank adoption of these means and ends by employers would not only promote the welfare of the workers, but vastly improve the relations between them and their employers, and increase the efficiency and productiveness of each establishment.

There is no need here to emphasize the importance of safety and sanitation in work places, as this is pretty generally recognized by legislation. What is required is an extension and strengthening of many of the existing statutes, and a better administration and enforcement of such laws everywhere.

VOCATIONAL TRAINING

The need of industrial, or as it has come to be more generally called, vocational training, is now universally acknowledged. In the interest of the nation, as well as in that of the workers themselves, this training should be made substantially universal. While we cannot now discuss the subject in any detail, we do wish to set down two general observations. First, the vocational training should be offered in such forms and conditions as not to deprive the children of the working classes of at least the elements of a cultural education. A healthy democracy cannot tolerate a purely industrial or trade education for any class of its citizens. We do not want to have the children of the wage-earners put into a special class in which they are marked as outside the sphere of opportunities for culture. The second observation is that the system of vocational training should not operate so as to weaken in any degree our parochial schools or any other class of private schools. Indeed, the opportunities of the system should be extended to all qualified private schools on exactly the same basis as to public schools. We want neither class divisions in education nor a State monopoly of education.

CHILD LABOR

The question of education naturally suggests the subject of child labor. Public opinion in the majority of the States of our country has set its face inflexibly against the continuous employment of children in industry before the age of sixteen years. Within a reasonably short time all of our States, except some stagnant ones, will have laws providing for this reasonable standard. The education of public opinion must continue, but inasmuch as the process is slow, the abolition of child labor in certain sections seems unlikely to be brought about by the legislatures of those States, and since the Keating-Owen Act[10] has been declared unconstitutional, there seems to be no device by which this reproach to our country can be removed except that of taxing child labor out of existence. This method is embodied in an amendment to the Federal Revenue Bill which would impose a tax of ten per cent on all goods made by children.

[10] The Keating-Owen Act of 1916 had barred products of child labor from interstate commerce. In *Hammer* v. *Dagenhart* of June 3, 1918, the Supreme Court ruled it unconstitutional as a regulation of local labor conditions rather than commerce.

SUFFICIENT FOR THE PRESENT

Probably the foregoing proposals comprise everything that is likely to have practical value in a program of immediate social reconstruction for America. Substantially all of these methods, laws and recommendations have been recognized in principle by the United States during the war, or have been indorsed by important social and industrial groups and organizations. Therefore, they are objects that we can set before the people with good hope of obtaining a sympathetic and practical response. Were they all realized a great step would have been taken in the direction of social justice. When they are all put into operation the way will be easy and obvious to still greater and more beneficial result.

ULTIMATE AND FUNDAMENTAL REFORMS

Despite the practical and immediate character of the present statement, we cannot entirely neglect the question of ultimate aims and a systematic program; for other groups are busy issuing such systematic pronouncements, and we all need something of the kind as a philosophical foundation and as a satisfaction to our natural desire for comprehensive statements.

It seems clear that the present industrial system is destined to last for a long time in its main outlines. That is to say, private ownership of capital is not likely to be supplanted by a collectivist organization of industry at a date sufficiently near to justify any present action based on the hypothesis of its arrival. This forecast we recognize as not only extremely probable, but as highly desirable; for, other objections apart, Socialism would mean bureaucracy, political tyranny, the helplessness of the individual as a factor in the ordering of his own life, and in general social inefficiency and decadence.

MAIN DEFECTS OF THE PRESENT SYSTEM

Nevertheless, the present system stands in grievous need of considerable modifications and improvement. Its main defects are three: Enormous inefficiency and waste in the production and distribution of commodities; insufficient incomes for the great majority of wage-earners, and unnecessarily large incomes for a small minority of privileged capitalists. Inefficiency in the production and distribution of goods would be in great measure abolished by the reforms that have been outlined in the foregoing pages. Production would be greatly increased by universal living wages, by adequate industrial education, and by harmonious relations between labor and capital on the basis of adequate participation by the former in all the industrial aspects of business management. The wastes of commodity distribution could be practically all eliminated by co-operative mercantile establishments, and co-operative selling and marketing associations.

CO-OPERATION AND CO-PARTNERSHIP

Nevertheless, the full possibilities of increased production will not be realized so long as the majority of the workers remain mere wage-earners. The majority must somehow become owners, or at least in part, of the instruments of production. They can be enabled to reach this stage gradually through co-operative productive societies and co-partnership arrangements. In the former, the workers own and manage the industries themselves; in the latter they own a substantial part of the corporate stock and exercise a reasonable share in the management. However slow the attainments of these ends, they will have to be reached before we can have a thoroughly efficient system of production, or an industrial and social order that will be secure from the danger of revolution. It is to be noted that this particular modification of the existing order, though far-reaching and involving to a great extent the abolition of the wage system, would not mean the abolition of private ownership. The instruments of production would still be owned by individuals, not by the State.

INCREASED INCOMES FOR LABOR

The second great evil, that of insufficient income for the majority can be removed only by providing the workers with more income. This means not only universal living wages, but the opportunity of obtaining something more than that amount for all who are willing to work hard and faithfully. All the other measures for labor betterment recommended in the preceding pages would likewise contribute directly or indirectly to a more just distribution of wealth in the interest of the laborer.

ABOLITION AND CONTROL OF MONOPOLIES

For the third evil mentioned above, excessive gains by a small minority of privileged capitalists, the main remedies are prevention of monopolistic control of commodities, adequate government regulation of such public service monopolies as will remain under private operation, and heavy taxation of incomes, excess profits and inheritances. The precise methods by which genuine competition may be restored and maintained among businesses that are naturally competitive, cannot be discussed here; but the principle is clear that human beings cannot be trusted with the immense opportunities for oppression and extortion that go with the possession of monopoly power. That the owners of public service monopolies should be restricted by law to a fair or average return on their actual investment, has long been a recognized principle of the courts, the legislatures, and public opinion. It is a principle which should be applied to competitive enterprises likewise, with the qualification that something more than the average rate of return should be allowed to men who exhibit exceptional efficiency. However, good public policy, as well as equity, demands that these exceptional business men share the fruits of their efficiency with the consumer in the form of lower prices. The man who utilizes his ability to produce cheaper than his competitors for the purpose of exacting from the public as high a price for his product as is necessary for the least efficient business man, is a menace rather than a benefit to industry and society.

Our immense war debt constitutes a particular reason why incomes and excess profits should continue to be heavily taxed. In this way two important ends will be attained: the poor will be relieved of injurious tax burdens, and the small class of specially privileged capitalists will be compelled to return a part of their unearned gains to society.

A NEW SPIRIT A VITAL NEED

"Society," said Pope Leo XIII, "can be healed in no other way than by a return to Christian life and Christian institutions."[11] The truth of these words is more widely perceived to-day than when they were written, more than twenty-seven years ago. Changes in our economic and political systems will have only partial and feeble efficiency if they be not reinforced by the Christian view of work and wealth. Neither the moderate reforms advocated in this paper, nor any other program of betterment or reconstruction will prove reasonably effective without a reform in the spirit of both labor and capital. The laborer must come to realize that he owes his employer and society an honest day's work in return for a fair wage, and that conditions cannot be substantially improved until he roots out the desire to get a maximum of return for a minimum of service. The capitalist must likewise get a new viewpoint. He needs to learn the

[11] *Rerum Novarum*, May 15, 1891, in John J. Wynne, S.J. (Ed.), *The Great Encyclical Letters of Pope Leo XIII* (New York, 1903), p. 225.

long-forgotten truth that wealth is stewardship, that profit-making is not the basic justification of business enterprise, and that there are such things as fair profits, fair interest, and fair prices. Above and before all, he must cultivate and strengthen within his mind the truth which many of his class have begun to grasp for the first time during the present war; namely, that the laborer is a human being, not merely an instrument of production; and that the laborer's right to a decent livelihood is the first moral charge upon industry. The employer has a right to get a reasonable living out of his business, but he has no right to interest on his investment until his employees have obtained at least living wages. This is the human and Christian, in contrast to the purely commercial and pagan, ethics of industry.

155. The Founding of the National Catholic Welfare Conference and Its Final Approval by the Holy See, May 1, 1919–July 4, 1922.

ONE of the most significant developments in the Catholic Church of the United States in the twentieth century has been National Catholic Welfare Conference, an organization to which the Holy See has in recent years referred the hierarchies of a number of countries as a model to follow in the co-ordination of their various large-scale activities. At a meeting held at the Catholic University of America on August 11–12, 1917, there was founded the National Catholic War Council with a view to co-ordinating Catholic efforts in World War I. The meeting, which had been brought about largely through the initiative of Father John J. Burke, C.S.P. (1875–1936), editor of the *Catholic World* and founder of the Chaplains' Aid Association, was attended by representatives of sixty-eight dioceses and twenty-seven national Catholic organizations. The National Catholic War Council proved so successful in its manifold enterprises that when the war ended many felt some kind of a peacetime equivalent should be continued to look after the national interests of the Church. This sentiment was shared by a majority of the bishops and at the celebration of Cardinal Gibbons' golden episcopal jubilee in February, 1919, it was decided to seek the approval of the Holy See for such an organization, as well as for an annual meeting of the entire hierarchy. Pope Benedict XV gave his approval to both projects in April, 1919, and at the first annual meeting of the hierarchy held in Washington the following September the National Catholic Welfare Council was set up under the direct management of an administrative committee of bishops. At this meeting, attended by ninety-two of the 101 ordinaries of the United States, Charles E. McDonnell (1854–1921), Bishop of Brooklyn, was the only one who voiced opposition to the idea of the N.C.W.C. on the score that it went beyond what the pope's letter had envisioned and that it would be detrimental to the authority of the bishops in their respective dioceses. But as it turned out, more than McDonnell were opposed to the N.C.W.C. and eventually a request for its dissolution was laid before the Holy See. In Cajetan Cardinal De Lai (1853–1928), Secretary of the Consistorial Congregation, the minority party found a strong ally. De Lai succeeded in convincing Benedict XV that the N.C.W.C. was a risky experiment that carried in it dangerous overtones of a national church in the United States. De Lai, therefore, made out a decree of dissolution but before Benedict XV could sign it he died on January 22, 1922. Pius XI, elected on February 6, found the decree among the unfinished business of his predecessor, gave it his assent, and the decree was fixed on February 23. News of this action did not reach the United States until late March. The Administrative Committee of the N.C.W.C. held an emergency meeting in Cleveland on April 6, cabled asking the Holy See to withhold publication of the decree in the *Acta Sanctae Sedis,* and delegated Bishop Schrembs to go to Rome to present their side of the case. After many anxious weeks Schrembs cabled on June 23: "Fight is won. Keep program Bishops' meeting September. Official notice will be cabled next week. Hard struggle. Complete victory. At farewell audience Pope blesses Bishops and Welfare Council. Sail Olympic Aug. 2nd" (Archives of the Diocese of Rockford, Diary of Bishop Muldoon). The National Catholic Welfare Conference was thus saved from dissolution and on June 22, 1922, a decree of approval was issued by the Consistorial Congregation. The following documents illustrate the initiation of the project and the final approval of the Holy See for the N.C.W.C. and the annual meeting of the American hierarchy. Sources: "The September Meeting of the American Hierarchy," *Ecclesiastical Review,* LXI (July, 1919), 7–9; *The National Catholic Welfare Conference. Its Organization, Departments and Functions* (Washington: Administrative Board, N.C.W.C., 1942) (privately printed), pp. 23–25.

Baltimore
May 1, 1919.

My Dear Archbishop:

After the celebration of my Episcopal Jubilee which was honored by the gracious presence of so many of the Hierarchy, there was a general meeting of all the Prelates who had participated. At this meeting there were present nearly all the Archbishops and Bishops of the country.[1]

On this occasion, the Prelates present unanimously adopted three important resolutions, to which I desire to call your attention.

The first was that we should take extraordinary measures to aid the Holy Father in his present financial straits occasioned by the war.

The second measure adopted by the assembled Prelates was that annually all the Bishops, including Auxiliaries and the Rector of

[1] The celebration was held in Washington on February 20, 1919, and drew two cardinals (O'Connell of Boston and Begin of Quebec), twelve archbishops, and fifty-eight bishops.

the University, — if he is a Bishop, — shall be invited to be present in Washington at the annual meeting of the Metropolitans.

The third measure adopted was that the Archbishop of Baltimore name a committee of five Prelates to be known hereafter as "The Committee on General Catholic Interests and Affairs."

These measures were all suggested and urged in an address to the Bishops who attended my Jubilee, by the special Representative of our Holy Father, Most Reverend Archbishop Cerretti.[2]

I assure you that, great as was my joy in being permitted to commemorate my fifty years in the Episcopate, and my gratitude to Almighty God for His many blessings, the pleasure of the celebration was enhanced by knowing that it had been made the occasion for this meeting of the Hierarchy and for the inauguration of these measures which I regard as the most important since the Third Plenary Council of Baltimore.

The appointment of "The Committee on General Catholic Interests and Affairs" is especially gratifying to me. Hitherto, through the courtesy of my Confrères in the Episcopate and largely because the center of our National Government is within the limits of the Baltimore Archdiocese, the burden of the Church's general interests has in great measure rested on me. My experience has made me feel keenly the necessity of such a committee which with adequate authority and the aid of sub-committees could accomplish more than any individual, however able and willing he might be.

It is recognized by all that the Catholic Church in America, partly through defective organization, is not exerting the influence which it ought to exert in proportion to our numbers and the individual prominence of many of our people. Our diocesan units indeed are well organized. But the Church in America as a whole has been suffering from the lack of a unified force that might be directed to the furthering of those general policies which are vital to all. It was the general opinion of the Prelates present that we need a committee of the Hierarchy which shall be representative, authoritative and directive. It should be representative in the sense that it would stand for and express the views of the whole Hierarchy. It should be authoritative in as much as it would possess the confidence and have the support of

---

[2] Bonaventura Cerretti (1872–1933) was at the time Archbishop of Corinth and Secretary of the Congregation for Extraordinary Ecclesiastical Affairs. It was during Cerretti's time as auditor of the Apostolic Delegation in Washington, 1906–1914, that he and Gibbons had become close friends. He was later Apostolic Nuncio to France, 1921–1925.

the whole Hierarchy. Probably, too, it should be empowered to act when any emergency arises for which no provision has been made, but when immediate action is imperative and it would be impossible for lack of time to obtain the views of the individual members of the Hierarchy. Such a committee will unify our forces if entrusted with the powers above outlined.

I was asked by the Prelates who were present at the meeting to appoint the members of this committee, and I have named the committee to act until the next meeting of the Hierarchy. For the permanent and regular method of choosing this committee, however, it will, I think, be more satisfactory to all the Hierarchy, and more authoritative, if the committee be elected by secret ballot by all the members present at our annual meeting. It might be understood that those who are unable to attend the annual meeting should send their votes before the meeting.

The committee so chosen would naturally be composed of Prelates representing as far as possible all the interest of the Church at large, as well as the various sections of our country.

If this plan for organizing the committee is agreeable to you, we shall at our next annual meeting elect in the way I have suggested four Prelates by ballot. In the meantime, as a temporary measure, I have asked the four Prelates of the National Catholic War Council, who were selected, with the consent of the majority of the Hierarchy, to serve on the "Committee on General Catholic Interests and Activities";[3] and as I was Chairman of the War Council I will act as chairman of the new Committee until our next general meeting.

A meeting of the Committee will be held during the month of May.[4] Several very important matters naturally impose themselves for consideration:

The collection for the Holy Father;

The continuation of the activities of the National War Council as far as may be deemed expedient;

Measures to safeguard general Catholic interests in National Legislation;

The vital interests of Catholic education;

---

[3] The members of the committee were: Peter J. Muldoon (1863–1927), Bishop of Rockford, vice-chairman; Joseph Schrembs (1866–1945), Bishop of Toledo; Joseph S. Glass, C.M. (1874–1926), Bishop of Salt Lake; and William T. Russell (1863–1927), Bishop of Charleston.

[4] The meeting was held in New York on May 8, 1919, on the occasion of the conferring of the pallium on Archbishop Hayes.

The awakening of concern about the needs of home and foreign missions.

Suggestions concerning these or any other matters of general Catholic interest will be greatly appreciated by myself and the other members of the Committee.[5]

Faithfully yours in Xto.
J. Card. Gibbons

In a Plenary Session held on the twenty-second day of the month of June, the Sacred Consistorial Congregation, acting on new data, has decided that nothing is to be changed concerning "The National Catholic Welfare Council"; and that, therefore, the Bishops of the United States of North America may meet next September as is their custom, in accordance, however, with the instructions given below.

Given at Rome at the Office of the Sacred Consistorial Congregation on the twenty-second day of June, 1922.

C. Card. De Lai, *Bishop of Sabina, Secretary*.
A. Sincero, *Assessor*.

These instructions for the meeting of the Bishops, which is to be held in the coming month of September, in accordance with the Decree of the twenty-second day of June, 1922, are issued by order of His Holiness.

1. Whereas, some Bishops for reasons which seem to be weighty, have expressed a wish that these meetings be not held every year, the Bishops should consider whether or not hereafter the meetings should be held at longer intervals.

2. In any case, to dispel misgivings, it must be very well understood that Bishops are not bound to attend these meetings, either in person or by representative.

3. Likewise, as the decisions of the Bishops at these meetings have

[5] On May 5, 1919, Gibbons outlined in considerable detail for the four bishops of the committee his ideas concerning the lines along which he thought the organization should be developed. On May 17 in a letter to the entire hierarchy, which enclosed a report of the committee's meeting in New York on May 8, Gibbons likewise included copies of Benedict XV's letter of April 10 which he had just received and which gave the pope's approval to their plans for an annual meeting of all the bishops and for the future N.C.W.C. A week later, May 24, Gibbons and the four bishops of the committee sent a formal notice to all members of the American hierarchy announcing the date of September 24, 1919, as that on which the first annual meeting of the hierarchy would assemble at the Catholic University of America and asking the bishops to send any suggestions they might have for the agenda to Bishop Muldoon who was in charge of details or arrangement. These letters are all printed in the *Ecclesiastical Review,* LXI (July, 1919), 10–19.

nothing in common with conciliar legislation, which is governed by a prescript of the Sacred Canons (Cod. Can. 281, seq.), they will not have force of law since, as from the beginning, it has been clearly understood the meetings are held merely for friendly conference about measures of a common public interest for the safeguarding of the Church's work in the United States.

4. That the Bishops may be in a position to enter into the discussions with proper deliberation, they should be provided in due season by those in charge of the meeting with a summary of the points or questions to be considered. This, however, should not hinder any Bishop from proposing to the meeting any other question of particular interest. Yet all questions should deal with those topics proposed by His Holiness, Pope Benedict XV in the Brief, "Communes," dated the 10th of April, 1919.[6]

5. The Chairman of the meeting will be determined by the prescriptions of canon law.

6. The minutes of the meeting are to be sent to the Holy See so that if need be the Holy See may duly intervene.

7. The Ordinaries of each ecclesiastical province may before the General Meeting meet with their Metropolitan or senior Bishop to confer beforehand upon some point.

8. Whereas the name, the National Catholic Welfare Council, is open to some misunderstandings, and in fact has not been acceptable to all, it may be well for the Bishops to consider whether it would not be wise to choose some other name, as for instance, "The National Catholic Welfare Committee."[7] Meanwhile, all should know that this organization however named, is not to be identified with the Catholic hierarchy itself in the United States.

9. The Bishops in their General Meeting may delegate an individual

---

[6] In his brief *Communes* of April 10, 1919, addressed to Cardinal Gibbons, Benedict XV had stated: "We learn that you have unanimously resolved that a yearly meeting of all the bishops shall be held at an appointed place, in order to adopt the most suitable means of promoting the interests and welfare of the Catholic Church, and that you have appointed from among the bishops two commissions, one of which will deal with social questions, while the other will study educational problems, and both will report to the Episcopal brethren. This is truly a worthy resolve, and with the utmost satisfaction We bestow upon it Our approval." *Ecclesiastical Review,* LXI (July, 1919), 4.

[7] The word "council" in the official title of the organization was changed to "conference" at the annual meeting of the hierarchy on September 27, 1922. The change was made because the former word was believed to involve some delicate and difficult points of both civil and canon law. It was Archbishop Hayes of New York who suggested the word "conference" for the title.

or a committee, to undertake some definite commission during the interval between the meetings. But care must be taken:

(a) That the commission be limited from the beginning, both as to time and method of operation.

(b) That no infringement of canonical authority of any Ordinary in the government of his diocese be made by any agent or committee thus established.

(c) That on due denunciation by a Bishop and proof of interference in the internal management of a diocese by any agent of the Welfare Council, the said agent shall be summarily dismissed from office.

(d) The choice of those who are to be thus employed as agents of the Bishops will be made by the Bishops at their General Meeting, and at their pleasure. Those who are so engaged will hold office meeting to meeting and must make reports especially of their accounts at every meeting. The Bishops, if they so please, may re-elect those agents according to the needs of the work.

Given at Rome at the Office of the Sacred Consistorial Congregation on the fourth day of July, 1922.

C. Card. De Lai, *Bishop of Sabina,*
Secretary.

A. Sincero, *Assessor.*

156. The Supreme Court Affirms the Right of Private Religious Schools, June 1, 1925

THE right of private schools has more than once been questioned in the United States but never, perhaps, more seriously than by an Oregon law of November, 1922, which would have compelled all children in the state between the ages of eight and sixteen to attend the public schools. The constitutionality of the law was challenged by the Sisters of the Holy Names of Jesus and Mary who had many schools in Oregon, an action in which they were joined by the Hill Military Academy as a defendant. The case was ultimately appealed to the Supreme Court of the United States, and in the following unanimous decision in *Pierce* v. *Society of Sisters* handed down by Justice James C. McReynolds (1862–1946) the state was forbidden to deny the right of parents to choose a private school for their children as a violation of the fourteenth amendment. Source: *Pierce* v. *Society of Sisters,* 268 U.S. 510 (pp. 529–536).

These appeals are from decrees, based upon undenied allegations, which granted preliminary orders restraining appellants from threatening or attempting to enforce the Compulsory Education Act adopted November 7, 1922, under the initiative provision of her Constitution by the voters of Oregon. They present the same points of law; there are no controverted questions of fact. Rights said to be guaranteed by the federal Constitution were specially set up, and appropriate prayers asked for their protection.

The challenged Act, effective September 1, 1926, requires every parent . . . of a child between eight and sixteen years to send him "to a public school for the period of time a public school shall be held during the current year" in the district where the child resides; and failure to do so is declared a misdemeanor. . . . The manifest purpose is to compel general attendance at public schools by normal children between eight and sixteen, who have not completed the eighth grade. And without doubt enforcement of the statute would seriously impair, perhaps destroy, the profitable features of appellees' business, and greatly diminish the value of their property.

Appellee, the Society of Sisters,[1] is an Oregon corporation, organized in 1880, with power to care for orphans, educate and instruct the youth, establish and maintain academies or schools, and acquire necessary real and personal property. It has long devoted its property and effort to the secular and religious education and care of children, and has acquired the valuable good will of many parents and guardians. It conducts interdependent primary and high schools and junior colleges, and maintains orphanages for the custody and control of children between eight and sixteen. In its primary schools many children between those ages are taught the subjects usually pursued in Oregon public schools during the first eight years. Systematic religious instruction and moral training according to the tenets of the Roman Catholic Church are also regularly provided. All courses of study, both temporal and religious, contemplate continuity of training under appellee's charge; the primary schools are essential to the system and the most profitable. It owns valuable buildings, especially constructed and equipped for school purposes. The business is remunerative — the annual income from primary schools exceeds thirty thousand dollars — and the successful conduct of this business requires long-time contracts with teachers and parents. The Compulsory Education Act of 1922 has already caused the withdrawal from its schools of children who would otherwise

[1] The Sisters of the Holy Names of Jesus and Mary, founded in Canada, first came to Oregon in October, 1859, at the invitation of Francis Norbert Blanchet (1795–1883), first Archbishop of Oregon City. They were the first religious congregation of women to make a permanent settlement in Oregon where they still conduct numerous schools.

continue, and their income has steadily declined. The appellants, public officers, have proclaimed their purpose strictly to enforce the statute.

After setting out the above facts the Society's bill alleges that the enactment conflicts with the right of parents to choose schools where their children will receive appropriate mental and religious training, the right of the child to influence the parents' choice of a school, the right of schools and teachers therein to engage in a useful business or profession, and is accordingly repugnant to the Constitution and void. And, further, that unless enforcement of the measure is enjoined the corporation's business and property will suffer irreparable injury.

No question is raised concerning the power of the State reasonably to regulate all schools, to inspect, supervise and examine them, their teachers and pupils; to require that all children of proper age attend some school, that teachers shall be of good moral character and patriotic disposition, that certain studies plainly essential to good citizenship must be taught, and that nothing be taught which is manifestly inimical to the public welfare.

The inevitable practical result of enforcing the Act under consideration would be destruction of appellees' primary schools, and perhaps all other private primary schools for normal children within the State of Oregon. Appellees are engaged in a kind of undertaking not inherently harmful, but long regarded as useful and meritorious. Certainly there is nothing in the present records to indicate that they have failed to discharge their obligations to patrons, students, or the State. And there are no peculiar circumstances or present emergencies which demand extraordinary measures relative to primary education.

Under the doctrine of *Meyer* v. *Nebraska,* 262 U.S. 390,[2] we think it entirely plain that the Act of 1922 unreasonably interferes with the liberty of parents and guardians to direct the upbringing and education of children under their control. As often heretofore pointed out rights guaranteed by the Constitution may not be abridged by legislation which has no reasonable relation to some purpose within the competency of the State. The fundamental theory of liberty upon which all governments in this Union repose excludes any general power of the State to standardize its children by forcing them to accept instruction from

[2] In 1923 the Supreme Court in *Meyer* v. *Nebraska* declared unconstitutional a law forbidding the teaching of any language other than English to any child below the eighth grade by any teacher in a public or private school. The court upheld the right of the plaintiff, an instructor in a Lutheran parochial school, to teach a foreign language, as well as the right of the parents to engage him to instruct their children, both as being within the liberty of the fourteenth amendment.

public teachers only. The child is not the mere creature of the State; those who nurture him and direct his destiny have the right, coupled with the high duty, to recognize and prepare him for additional obligations.

The suits were not premature. The injury to appellees was present and very real, not a mere possibility in the remote future. If no relief had been possible prior to the effective date of the Act, the injury would have become irreparable. Prevention of impending injury by unlawful action is a well recognized function of courts of equity.

The decrees below are

Affirmed.

157. Governor Smith's Answer to the Religious Bigotry of the Presidential Campaign, September 20, 1928

FOLLOWING the decline of the A.P.A. in the late 1890's the American people were not again subjected to an organized outburst of religious and racial bigotry until the revival of the Ku Klux Klan. The second K.K.K. was founded in November, 1915, in Georgia by William J. Simmons and a group of associates for the purpose of opposing Catholics, Negroes, Jews, and the foreign-born. One of its principal targets was Alfred E. Smith (1873–1944), four times Governor of New York. Smith was a strong contender for the presidential nomination in the Democratic conventions of 1920 and 1924, and on June 28, 1928, he was nominated on the first ballot by the convention at Houston. Once the nomination had become an accomplished fact the K.K.K. concentrated all its fire on Smith with the result that his Tammany Hall connections, his opposition to prohibition, but, above all, his Catholic faith were made the objects of the most scurrilous attacks. As the campaign progressed the attacks on his religion became increasingly insidious, and on September 20 at Oklahoma City Smith brought the subject into the open. A recent work states that the hostility at Oklahoma City was so marked that there was "real concern for Smith's personal safety, and his eastern advisers were relieved when the telephone brought word that the Governor had reached his hotel safely after an emotion-packed evening" (Edmund A. Moore, *A Catholic Runs for President. The Campaign of 1928* [New York, 1956], p. 180). The same authority remarks, "At Oklahoma City, Smith neither invented nor introduced the issue. His address there stands beside his 'Reply' to Marshall as a great effort in the arduous struggle to extend freedom in the United States" (*ibid.*, p. 187). Yet his candor and straightforwardness, and his brilliant record as Governor of New York, had little effect on the final result, and on November 6 it was found that he had carried only eight states with an electoral vote of eighty-seven against 444 for his Republican rival. In spite of the abuse to which he had been subjected, Governor Smith spoke to the nation in a postelection address on November 13 with true magnanimity in which he called for the aid and co-operation of all citizens for the president-elect. The measure of the man's greatness was evident in his closing words when he said, "Regardless of the outcome, in a spirit of the deepest appreciation of the opportunities afforded me and of the loyal support given to me by upward of 15,000,000 of my fellow citizens, I pledge my unceasing interest and concern with public affairs and the well-being of the American people" (*op. cit.*, p. 322). Source: *Campaign Addresses of Governor Alfred E. Smith* (Washington: Democratic National Committee, 1929), pp. 43–45, 49, 51, 53–58.

. . . In a presidential campaign there should be but two considerations before the electorate: The platform of the party, and the ability of the candidate to make it effective.

In this campaign an effort has been made to distract the attention of the electorate from these two considerations and to fasten it on malicious and un-American propaganda.

I shall tonight discuss and denounce that wicked attempt. I shall speak openly on the things about which people have been whispering to you. . . .

Twenty-five years ago I began my active public career. I was then elected to the Assembly, representing the neighborhood in New York City where I was born, where my wife was born, where my five children were born and where my father and mother were born. I represented that district continuously for twelve years, until 1915, when I was elected Sheriff of New York county.

Two years later I was elected to the position of President of the Board of Aldermen, which is really that of Vice-Mayor of the City of New York.

In 1918 I was elected by the delegates to the State convention as the candidate of the Democratic Party for Governor and was elected.

Running for re-election in 1920, I was defeated in the Harding landslide. However, while Mr. Harding carried the State of New York by more than 1,100,000 plurality, I was defeated only by some 70,000 votes.

After this defeat I returned to private life, keeping up my interest in public affairs, and accepted appointment to an important State body at the hands of the man who had defeated me.

In 1922 the Democratic Convention, by unanimous vote, renominated me for the third time for Governor. I was elected by the record plurality of 387,000, and this in a State which had been normally Republican.

In 1924, at the earnest solicitation of the Democratic presidential candidate,[1] I accepted nomination. The State of New York was carried by President Coolidge by close to 700,000 plurality, but I was elected Governor. On the morning after election I found myself the only Democrat elected on the State ticket, with both houses of the Legislature overwhelmingly Republican.

Renominated by the unanimous vote of the convention of 1926, I made my fifth State-wide run for the governorship and was again elected the Democratic Governor of a normally Republican State.

Consequently, I am in a position to come before you tonight as the Governor of New York finishing out his fourth term.

The record of accomplishment under my four administrations recommended me to the Democratic Party in the nation, and I was nominated for the presidency at the Houston convention on the first ballot.

To put the picture before you completely, it is necessary for me to refer briefly to this record of accomplishment. . . . [Governor Smith then went into detail concerning the main legislative enactments, appointments, etc., of his administrations.]

One scandal connected with my administration would do more to help out the Republican National Committee in its campaign against me than all the millions of dollars now being spent by them in malicious propaganda. Unfortunately for them, they cannot find it, because the truth is it is not there. I challenge Senator Owen[2] and all his kind to point to one single flaw upon which they can rest their case. But they won't find it. They won't try to find it, because I know what lies behind all this, and I will tell you before I sit down to-night. . . .

I know what lies behind all this and I shall tell you. I specifically refer to the question of my religion. Ordinarily, that word should never be used in a political campaign. The necessity for using it is forced on me by Senator Owen and his kind, and I feel that at least once in this campaign, I, as the candidate of the Democratic Party, owe it to the people of this country to discuss frankly and openly with them this attempt of Senator Owen and the forces behind him to inject bigotry, hatred, intolerance and un-American sectarian division into a campaign which should be an intelligent debate of the important issues which confront the American people. . . .

A recent newspaper account in the City of New York told the story of a woman who called at the Republican National headquarters

[1] John W. Davis (1873–1955) had been nominated on the 103rd ballot after a prolonged fight between the forces of Smith and William G. McAdoo.

[2] Robert L. Owen (1856–1947) had served three terms as United States Senator from Oklahoma, 1907–1925. He left the Democratic Party in 1928 to go over to the Republicans on the score that Smith was the creature of Tammany Hall.

in Washington, seeking some literature to distribute. She made the request that it be of a nature other than political. Those in charge of the Republican Publicity Bureau provided the lady with an automobile and she was driven to the office of a publication notorious throughout the country for its senseless, stupid, foolish attacks upon the Catholic Church and upon Catholics generally.

I can think of no greater disaster to this country than to have the voters of it divide upon religious lines. It is contrary to the spirit, not only of the Declaration of Independence, but of the Constitution itself. During all of our national life we have prided ourselves throughout the world on the declaration of the fundamental American truth that all men are created equal.

Our forefathers, in their wisdom, seeing the danger to the country of a division on religious issues, wrote into the Constitution of the United States in no uncertain words the declaration that no religious test shall ever be applied for public office, and it is a sad thing in 1928, in view of the countless billions of dollars that we have poured into the cause of public education, to see some American citizens proclaiming themselves 100 per cent. American, and in the document that makes that proclamation suggesting that I be defeated for the presidency because of my religious belief.

The Grand Dragon of the Realm of Arkansas, writing to a citizen of that State, urges my defeat because I am a Catholic, and in the letter suggests to the man, who happened to be a delegate to the Democratic convention, that by voting against me he was upholding American ideals and institutions as established by our forefathers.

The Grand Dragon that thus advised a delegate to the national convention to vote against me because of my religion is a member of an order known as the Ku Klux Klan, who had the effrontery to refer to themselves as 100 per cent. Americans.

Yet totally ignorant of the history and tradition of this country and its institutions and, in the name of Americanism, they breathe into the hearts and souls of their members hatred of millions of their fellow countrymen because of their religious belief. . . .

I would have no objection to anybody finding fault with my public record circularizing the whole United States, provided he would tell the truth. But no decent, right-minded, upstanding American citizen can for a moment countenance the shower of lying statements, with no basis in fact, that have been reduced to printed matter and sent broadcast through the mails of this country.

One lie widely circulated, particularly through the southern part of the country, is that during my governorship I appointed practically nobody to office but members of my own church.

What are the facts? On investigation I find that in the cabinet of the Governor sit fourteen men. Three of the fourteen are Catholics, ten Protestants, and one of Jewish faith. In various bureaus and divisions of the Cabinet officers, the Governor appointed twenty-six people. Twelve of them are Catholics and fourteen of them are Protestants. Various other State officials, making up boards and commissions, and appointed by the Governor, make a total of 157 appointments, of which thirty-five were Catholics, 106 were Protestants, twelve were Jewish, and four I could not find out about.

I have appointed a large number of judges of all our courts, as well as a large number of county officers, for the purpose of filling vacancies. They total in number 177, of which sixty-four were Catholics, ninety were Protestants, eleven were Jewish, and twelve of the officials I was unable to find anything about so far as their religion was concerned.

This is a complete answer to the false, misleading and, if I may be permitted the use of the harsher word, lying statements that have found their way through a large part of this country in the form of printed matter.

If the American people are willing to sit silently by and see large amounts of money secretly pour into false and misleading propaganda for political purposes, I repeat that I see in this not only a danger to the party, but a danger to the country. . . . [Here other instances of bigotry in the campaign were cited.]

I have been told that politically it might be expedient for me to remain silent upon this subject, but so far as I am concerned no political expediency will keep me from speaking out in an endeavor to destroy these evil attacks.

There is abundant reason for believing that Republicans high in the councils of the party have countenanced a large part of this form of campaign, if they have not actually promoted it. A sin of omission is some times as grievous as a sin of commission. They may, through official spokesmen, disclaim as much as they please responsibility for dragging into a national campaign the question of religion, something that according to our Constitution, our history and our traditions has no part in any campaign for elective public office. . . .

One of the things, if not the meanest thing, in the campaign is a circular pretending to place someone of my faith in the position of seeking votes for me because of my Catholicism. Like everything of this kind, of course it is unsigned, and it would be impossible to trace its authorship. It reached me through a member of the Masonic order who, in turn, received it in the mail. It is false in its every line. It was designed on its very face to injure me with members of churches other than my own.

I here emphatically declare that I do not wish any member of my faith in any part of the United States to vote for me on any religious grounds. I want them to vote for me only when in their hearts and consciences they become convinced that my election will promote the best interests of our country.

By the same token, I cannot refrain from saying that any person who votes against me simply because of my religion is not, to my way of thinking, a good citizen. . . .

The constitutional guaranty that there should be no religious test for public office is not a mere form of words. It represents the most vital principle that ever was given any people.

I attack those who seek to undermine it, not only because I am a good Christian, but because I am a good American and a product of America and of American institutions. Everything I am, and everything I hope to be, I owe to those institutions.

The absolute separation of State and Church is part of the fundamental basis of our Constitution. I believe in that separation, and in all that it implies. That belief must be a part of the fundamental faith of every true American. . . .

158. Dom Michel Explains the Origins of the Liturgical Movement in the United States, February 24, 1929

ONE of the most serious lacunae in the literature of American Catholicism is that pertaining to the inner life of the Church. Yet every historian must recognize the importance that forms and methods of worship and devotion play in the spiritual life of the people. In that connection the liturgical movement of the twentieth century has been of special significance. The movement, which has sought through the doctrine of the Mystical Body to bring all Catholics into active participation in the official worship of the Church, is now over a century old in Europe. But it was only in the 1920's that it began to take shape in the United States with the establishment of the Liturgical Press of St. John's Abbey, Collegeville, Minnesota, and its monthly journal, *Orate Fratres* (now called *Worship*), the first number of which appeared in November, 1926. The movement owed its origin to a number of persons scattered throughout the country, as the following document makes clear, but its successful launching was due to none more than to Virgil Michel, O.S.B. (1890–1938), first editor of *Orate Fratres,* and to the active support of his superior, Abbot Alcuin Deutsch (1877–1951). In a letter to a fellow religious Dom Michel fixed the date of the efforts at St. John's when he said, "The first ideas of our plans were penned in February 1923, and by dint of slow correspondence the plans grew until they are now full-fledged" (Archives of St. John's Abbey, Michel to Francis Augustine Walsh, O.S.B., Collegeville, January 25, 1926, copy). The success that has attended the movement in the past thirty years may be measured in part by the fact that, whereas in 1926 use of the daily missal among American Catholics was very limited, there are today nineteen editions in English of the missal in millions of copies for those who assist at Mass and the divine offices of the Church. Moreover, the National Liturgical Week, held annually in various cities since 1940, is drawing a larger and increasingly enthusiastic following each year. Source: "The Apostolate," *Orate Fratres,* III (February 24, 1929), 121–123.

It was only recently we received two fall numbers of the "midweek" section of an excellent Catholic paper. One number contained an article in which St. John's Abbey was spoken of with enthusiasm as the "source of the Liturgical Movement." The unnamed author is evidently a very good friend. In the second number there was an answer to the first article, written by two intimate friends of ours. The second article briefly describes earlier European "sources" of the Liturgical Movement, mentions the fact that the spirit of the movement began to manifest itself "almost simultaneously in various sections of the United States some seven or eight years ago," and that various promoters of it were at work independently and, at first, even unknown to each other, until a number of them were brought together. Their deliberations and plans finally resulted in an organized liturgical apostolate, the founding of the Liturgical Press at St. John's Abbey, and the publishing of *Orate Fratres* by the monks of St. John's with the assistance of fellow editors outside the monastery. In the interest of truth we are glad to add a few facts that happen to come to mind at the present writing, especially since no written record of the beginning of the movement exists.

There were various "sources" of liturgical movement in the United States quite independent of St. John's Abbey, and antedating the public apostolate in which the latter is now engaged. Foremost among these must be mentioned well-known O'Fallon (Mo.), where Father Hellriegel[1] and the late Father Jasper[2] commenced activities that have

[1] Martin B. Hellriegel (1890 —), spiritual director of the Sisters of the Most Precious Blood, O'Fallon, Missouri, 1918–1940; pastor of Holy Cross Church, St. Louis, 1940 —.

[2] Anthony Jasper (d. 1925), pastor of Assumption Church, O'Fallon, Missouri.

been a great inspiration to many. From O'Fallon — in part at least, unless we are mistaken — came the spark that grew to a live flame among some of the Jesuit Fathers of St. Louis, at whose University lectures on aspects of the liturgy have been given for some years, and where the recent National Students Spiritual Leadership Convention took place. . . . Over a decade ago the late Dr. Shields,[3] as head of the Education Department of the Catholic University of America, was seeking to imbue a complete program of Catholic primary education with the spirit of the liturgy. More recently, Dr. George Johnson[4] has done excellent work in directing efforts along the same line. It was at least under the encouragement of Dr. Shields that the work of Mrs. Justine B. Ward[5] grew into an extensive program of gregorian revival, and with the co-operation of the Religious of the Sacred Heart resulted in the influential Pius X Institute of Liturgical Music,[6] soon to enter upon its thirteenth flourishing year. At the St. Paul Seminary the Reverend William Bush [*sic*][7] was working quietly but perseveringly for many years, and the results of his inspiration are now showing themselves in the zeal and efforts for a more liturgical formation of the people on the part of many young priests that caught the divine spark from him. His translation of Father Kramp's[8] *Eucharistia* [St. Paul, 1926] antedated *Orate Fratres* by some months, as did also the translation of Father Kramp's *The Sacrifice of the New Law* [St. Louis, 1926] by Rev. Leo F. Miller. The translations of the Latin sacramental texts by the Reverend Richard E. Power, published in our Popular Liturgical Library and known everywhere for their excellent qualities, are the result of years of study engaged upon when The Liturgical Press was not even existing in any human dream-world. There were many other centers of liturgical life carrying on unknown to each other, quietly preparing the way for a more conscious general revival.

Not only were our Associate Editors, among others, so many inde-

[3] Thomas E. Shields (1862–1921), professor of education in the Catholic University of America, founder of the Sisters College and the *Catholic Educational Review* in 1911.

[4] George Johnson (1889–1944), associate professor of education in the Catholic University of America and director of the Department of Education of the National Catholic Welfare Conference.

[5] Justine B. Ward (1879 —), writer and promoter of reform in church music.

[6] Pius X School of Liturgical Music at Manhattanville College of the Sacred Heart, New York, was founded in 1916.

[7] William Busch (1882 —), professor of church history in the St. Paul Seminary since 1913.

[8] Joseph Kramp, S.J. (1886 —), a pioneer of the liturgical movement in Germany and contributor to the *Ecclesia Orans* series of the Abbey of Maria Laach edited by Abbot Ildefons Herwegen.

pendent "sources" of liturgical awakening. They have also been co-operators in organizing and developing the work that centers in our abbey; and this, first of all, by their active part in the plans and discussions preceding the launching of our ventures; and then by their continued advice, and their free contribution of efforts — which later assistance is of no mean importance for a new journalistic undertaking, especially in our own day when money rules the day and is all-decisive. Some of our contributors have also helped us in a similar way, notably Miss Ellen Gates Starr,[9] whose articles on the Breviary received special mention from many of our correspondents.

All of these are doing their own part towards what is now consciously a common cause, one which it is also our privilege to promote to the best of our abilities. All of them have their efforts and intentions recorded in the Book of Life and they are not seeking for recognition of this work here below. Yet we have mentioned the above facts here, not so much for their sake — for we know their good will and desires — but for our own sake, lest in any way we should appear willing to receive credit beyond our desert. God forbid! It is from Him and Him alone that all sufficiency comes.

The liturgical apostolate is bigger than any individual, than any abbey, than any order, than any larger group of men, than the entire body of those who are spending their efforts in its promotion throughout the world. For it is in truth a spiritual ferment destined to permeate the entire body mystic of Christ according to the words of its official inaugurator.[10] Its aim is to imbue the members of this body more thoroughly with "the true Christian spirit," and through this renewed vigor to institute also a renewed growth of that mystic body unto an ever greater attainment here on earth of the "fullness of him who is filled all in all."[11]

---

[9] Ellen Gates Starr (1859–1940), best known as a co-founder with Jane Addams of Hull House, Chicago, in 1889, the first settlement house in the United States; a pioneer social worker, converted to Catholicism in 1920, and a promoter of the American liturgical movement in its early years.

[10] St. Pius X (1835–1914) by his *Motu proprio* of November 22, 1903, on the subject of sacred music and his later pronouncements on the reform of the breviary, frequent Communion, etc., is looked upon as the "official inaugurator" of the liturgical movement.

[11] Eph. 1:23.

159. Dorothy Day Describes the Launching of *The Catholic Worker* and the Movement Behind It, May, 1933

THE great depression of the 1930's set on foot numerous projects throughout the United States for the relief of the immense army of unemployed. During this period of severe distress the charitable agencies of the Church were taxed as never before, but there was no more distinctive and inspiring example of Catholic charity than that of the Catholic Worker Movement. Through its houses of hospitality, its organization of farming communes, and its program of discussion groups, study clubs, and publications disseminating the social doctrines of the Church, the Catholic Worker Movement not only gave a new start in life to many of the victims of the depression, but it likewise inspired and trained young Catholic workers and intellectuals who in the years that followed found their way into other enterprises like the Association of Catholic Trade Unionists and the Catholic youth movement. The undertaking was due in the main to Dorothy Day (1898 —) who had been a member of the Socialist Party, the I.W.W., and communist affiliates and who knew, therefore, at first hand what the social philosophy was from the angle of the left. In December, 1927, she became a convert to Catholicism, and when the depression struck she channeled her zeal and love for the poor in a way that proved eminently practical for countless men and women who had been cut adrift from their normal walks of life. In the excerpts from her memoirs that follow she tells of the beginnings of the movement's best known publication, as well as something about how the original house of hospitality was operated in its early days. Source: *The Long Loneliness. The Autobiography of Dorothy Day* (New York: Harper & Bros., 1952), pp. 182–186.

We started publishing *The Catholic Worker* at 436 East Fifteenth Street in May, 1933, with a first issue of 2,500 copies. Within three or four months the circulation bounded to 25,000, and it was cheaper to bring it out as an eight-page tabloid on newsprint rather than the smaller-sized edition on better paper we had started with. By the end of the year we had a circulation of 100,000 and by 1936 it was 150,000. It was certainly a mushroom growth. It was not only that some parishes subscribed for the paper all over the country in bundles of 500 or more. Zealous young people took the paper out in the streets and sold it, and when they could not sell it even at one cent a copy, they gave free copies and left them in streetcar, bus, barber shop and dentist's and doctor's office. We got letters from all parts of the country from people who said they had picked up the paper on trains, in rooming houses. One letter came from the state of Sonora in Mexico and we read with amazement that the reader had tossed in an uncomfortable bed on a hot night until he got up to turn over the mattress and under it found a copy of *The Catholic Worker*. A miner found a copy five miles underground in an old mine that stretched out under the Atlantic Ocean off Nova Scotia. A seminarian said that he had sent out his shoes to be half-soled in Rome and they came back to him wrapped in a copy of *The Catholic Worker*. These letters thrilled and inspired the young people who came to help, sent by Brothers or Sisters who taught in the high schools. We were invited to speak in schools and parishes, and often as a result of our speaking others came in to help us. On May Day, those first few years, the streets were literally lined with papers. Looking back on it, it seemed like a gigantic advertising campaign, entirely unpremeditated. It grew organically, Peter[1] used to say happily, and not through organization. "We are not an organization, we are an organism," he said.

First there was Peter, my brother and I. When John took a job at Dobb's Ferry, a young girl, Dorothy Weston, who had been studying journalism and was a graduate of a Catholic college, came to help. She lived at home and spent her days with us, eating with us and taking only her carfare from the common fund. Peter brought in three young men from Columbus Circle, whom he had met when discussing the affairs of the world there, and of these one became bookkeeper (that was his occupation when he was employed), another circulation manager, and the third married Dorothy Weston. Another girl came to take dictation and help with mailing the paper, and she married the circulation manager. There were quite a number of romances that first year — the paper appealed to youth. Then there were the young intellectuals who formed what they called Campion Committees in other cities as well as New York, who helped to picket the Mexican and German consulates and who distributed literature all over the city. Workers came in to get help on picket lines, to help move dispossessed families and to make demonstrations in front of relief offices. Three men came to sell the paper on the street, and to eat their meals with us. Big Dan had been a truck driver and a policeman. The day he came in to see us he wanted nothing more than to bathe his tired feet. That night at supper Peter indoctrinated him on the dignity of poverty and read some of Father Vincent McNabb's *Nazareth or Social Chaos*.[2] This did not go

---

[1] Peter Maurin (1877–1949), a Frenchman of peasant origin, was co-founder with Dorothy Day of the Catholic Worker Movement.

[2] This particular volume of the many books written by the well-known

over so well, all of us being city people, and Father McNabb advocating a return to the fields, but he made Dan Orr go out with a sense of a mission, not worrying about shabby clothes or the lack of a job. Dan began to sell the paper on the streets and earned enough money to live on. He met others who had found subsistence jobs, carrying sandwich signs or advertising children's furniture by pushing a baby carriage, a woman who told fortunes in a tea shop, a man who sold pretzels, which were threaded on four poles one on each corner of an old baby carriage. He found out their needs, and those of their families, and never left the house in the morning without bundles of clothes as well as his papers.

Dan rented a horse and wagon in which to deliver bundles of the paper each month. (We had tried this before he came but someone had to push the horse while the other led it. We knew nothing about driving a wagon.) Dan loved his horse. He called it Catholic Action, and used to take the blanket off my bed to cover the horse in winter. We rented it from a German Nazi on East Sixteenth Street, and sometimes when we had no money he let us have the use of it free for a few hours. It rejoiced our hearts to move a Jewish family into their new quarters with his equipment.

Dan said it was a pious horse and that when he passed St. Patrick's Cathedral, the horse genuflected. He liked to drive up Fifth Avenue, preferably with students who had volunteered their help, and shout, "Read *The Catholic Worker*" at the top of his lungs. He was anything but dignified and loved to affront the dignity of others.

One time he saw me coming down the street when he was selling the paper in front of Gimbel's and began to yell, "Read *The Catholic Worker!* Romance on every page." A seminarian from St. Louis, now Father Dreisoner [*sic*],[3] took a leaf from Dan's book and began selling the paper on the corner of Times Square and at union meetings. He liked to stand next to a comrade selling *The Daily Worker,* and as the one shouted "Read *The Daily Worker,*" he in turn shouted, "Read *The Catholic Worker* daily." Between sales they conversed. . . .

Peter, the "green" revolutionist, had a long-term program which called for hospices, or houses of hospitality, where the works of mercy could be practiced to combat the taking over by the state of all those services which could be built up by mutual aid; and farming communes

English Dominican, Vincent NcNabb (1868–1943), was published in London in 1933.

[3] Father John H. Dreisoemer is at present pastor of St. Clement's Church, Bowling Green, Missouri.

to provide land and homes for the unemployed, whom increasing technology was piling up into the millions. In 1933, the unemployed numbered 13,000,000.

The idea of the houses of hospitality caught on quickly enough. The very people that Peter brought in, who made up our staff at first, needed a place to live. Peter was familiar with the old I.W.W.[4] technique of a common flophouse and a pot of mulligan on the stove. To my cost, I too had become well acquainted with this idea.

Besides, we never had any money, and the cheapest, most practical way to take care of people was to rent some apartments and have someone do the cooking for the lot of us. Many a time I was cook and cleaner as well as editor and street seller. When Margaret, a Lithuanian girl from the mining regions of Pennsylvania, came to us and took over the cooking, we were happy indeed. She knew how to make a big pot of mashed potatoes with mushroom sauce which filled everyone up nicely. She was a great soft creature with a little baby, Barbara, who was born a few months after she came to us. Margaret went out on May Day with the baby and sold papers on the street. She loved being propagandist as well as cook. When Big Dan teased her, she threatened to tell the "pasture" of the church around the corner.

To house the women we had an apartment near First Avenue which could hold about ten. When there were arguments among them, Margaret would report them with gusto, giving us a blow-by-blow account. Once when she was telling how one of the women abused her so that she "felt as though the crown of thorns was pressing right down on her head" (she was full of these mystical experiences), Peter paused in his pacing of the office to tell her she needed to scrub the kitchen floor. Not that he was ever harsh, but he was making a point that manual labor was the cure of all such quarreling. Margaret once told Bishop O'Hara of Kansas City[5] that when she kissed his ring, it was just like a blood transfusion — she got faint all over.

Jacques Maritain[6] came to us during these early days and spoke to the group who were reading *Freedom and the Modern World* [*sic*]

[4] The International Workers of the World grew out of the coal strikes of 1904, finding its main recruits among the unskilled laborers. For many years it was the radical left wing of the American labor movement.

[5] Edwin V. O'Hara (1881–1956), Bishop of Kansas City from 1939 to his death. In June, 1954, he was named an archbishop *ad personam* in recognition of his outstanding leadership in social movements and in the Confraternity of Christian Doctrine.

[6] Jacques Maritain (1882 —), the French-born philosopher who has played a leading role in the revival of scholasticism, published his *Freedom in the Modern World* in 1935.

at that time. He gave special attention to the chapter on the purification of means. Margaret was delighted with our distinguished guest, who so evidently loved us all, and made him a box of fudge to take home with him when he sailed for France a few weeks later.

Ah, those early days that everyone likes to think of now since we have grown so much bigger; that early zeal, that early romance, that early companionableness! And how delightful it is to think that the young ones who came into the work now find the same joy in community. It is a permanent revolution, this Catholic Worker Movement. . . .

160. Pope Pius XII's Encyclical *Sertum laetitiae* on the Sesquicentennial of the American Hierarchy, November 1, 1939

IN NOVEMBER, 1939, the American hierarchy celebrated the one hundred and fiftieth anniversary of its establishment. From a single diocese with one bishop in 1789 the Church in the United States had by that time expanded to nineteen ecclesiastical provinces with 115 dioceses and 130 bishops, figures that since 1939 have increased to twenty-six archdioceses, 105 dioceses and 216 bishops. In his greeting on this occasion Pope Pius XII reviewed the progress of the American Church and had words of special commendation for certain distinctively American Catholic institutions. But he also warned against the dangers to good morals in American society by reason of the prevalence of divorce and birth control, the weakening of respect for authority, and a system of education that ignored religious values. The last part of the encyclical was devoted to a summary of moral principles as applied to social and economic problems. Source: *Sertum laetitiae* (New York: Paulist Press, 1939).

TO OUR BELOVED SONS:

WILLIAM O'CONNELL, CARDINAL PRIEST OF THE HOLY ROMAN CHURCH, ARCHBISHOP OF BOSTON.

DENNIS DOUGHERTY, CARDINAL PRIEST OF THE HOLY ROMAN CHURCH, ARCHBISHOP OF PHILADELPHIA.

AND TO ALL THE VENERABLE BRETHREN, THE ARCHBISHOPS, BISHOPS AND ORDINARIES OF THE UNITED STATES OF AMERICA, IN PEACE AND COMMUNION WITH THE APOSTOLIC SEE.

VENERABLE BRETHREN, HEALTH AND APOSTOLIC BENEDICTION:

In Our desire to enrich the crown of your holy joy We cross in spirit the vast spaces of the seas and find Ourselves in your midst as you celebrate, in company with all your faithful people, the one hundred and fiftieth anniversary of the establishment of the ecclesiastical Hierarchy in the United States of America.[1] And this We do with great gladness, because an occasion is thus afforded Us, as gratifying as it is solemn, of giving public testimony of Our esteem and Our affection for the youthfully vigorous and illustrious American people.

To one who turns the pages of your history and reflects upon the causes of what has been accomplished it is apparent that the triumphal progress of divine religion has contributed in no small degree to the glory and prosperity which your country now enjoys. It is indeed true that religion has its laws and institutions for eternal happiness but it is also undeniable that it dowers life here below with so many benefits that it could do no more even if the principal reason for its existence were to make men happy during the brief span of their earthly life.

It is a pleasure for Us to recall the well remembered story.

When Pope Pius VI gave you your first Bishop in the person of the American, John Carroll, and set him over the See of Baltimore, small and of slight importance was the Catholic population of your land. At that time, too, the condition of the United States was so perilous that its structure and its very political unity was threatened by grave crisis. Because of the long and exhausting war the public treasury was burdened with debt, industry languished and the citizenry, wearied by misfortunes was split into contending parties. This ruinous and critical state of affairs was put to rights by the celebrated George Washington, famed for his courage and keen intelligence. He was a close friend of the Bishop of Baltimore. Thus the Father of His Country and the pioneer pastor of the Church in that land so dear to Us, bound together by the ties of friendship and clasping, so to speak, each the other's hand, form a picture for their descendants, a lesson to all future generations, and a proof that reverence for the Faith of Christ is a holy and established principle of the American people, seeing that it is the foundation of morality and decency, consequently the source of prosperity and progress.

Many are the causes to which must be ascribed the flowering of the Catholic Church in your country. One of them We wish to point out as worthy of attention. Numbers of priests, forced to flee to your shores from lands where persecution raged, brought welcome aid to Bishop Carroll and by their active collaboration in the sacred ministry sowed the precious seed which ripened to an abundant harvest

[1] The See of Baltimore was formally erected and Carroll named first bishop on November 6, 1789.

of virtues. Some of them later became Bishops and thus had a more glorious share in the progress of the Catholic cause. And thus, as history teaches us again and again, the zeal of the apostle, provided that, nourished by unfeigned faith and sincere charity, it burns within the breast of valiant men, is not quenched by the storms of persecution but is carried farther across the earth.

On the centenary of the event which now fills your hearts with legitimate rejoicing, Pope Leo XIII of happy memory with his letter *Longinqua Oceani*[2] recalled and examined the progress that had been made by the Church in America and he accompanied his review with some admonitions and directions whose wisdom equals their paternal benevolence.

What Our august predecessor then so well wrote is worthy of repeated consideration. During these past fifty years the Church has not faltered in her course but has extended her influence to wider fields and increased her members. For in your country there prevails a thriving life which the grace of the Holy Spirit has brought to flower in the inner sanctuary of your hearts; the faithful throng your churches; around the Sacred Table they gather to receive the Bread of Angels, the Food of the Strong; the spiritual exercises of St. Ignatius are followed with great devotion in your closed retreats; and many heeding the Divine Voice that calls them to the ideals of a higher life receive the priesthood or embrace the religious state.

At the present time there are in the United States 19 ecclesiastical provinces, 115 dioceses, almost 200 seminaries and innumerable houses of worship, elementary and high schools, colleges, hospitals, asylums for the poor and monasteries. It is with good reason then that visitors from other lands admire the organization and system under which your schools of various grades are conducted, the generosity of the faithful upon whom they depend, the vigilant care with which they are watched over by the directors. From these schools there comes forth a host of citizens, strong in heart and mind, who, by reason of their reverence for divine and human laws, are justly considered to be the strength and the flower and the honor of Church and of country.

Missionary associations also, notably the Society for the Propagation of the Faith, are well established and active; they are outstanding examples in assisting, by prayer, almsgiving and other means, the heralds of the Gospel engaged in carrying the standard of the Cross of Salvation into the lands of the infidel. In this connection, We cannot refrain from a public expression of praise for those missionary

[2] January 6, 1895. Cf. No. 140.

enterprises proper to your own nation which devote themselves with zeal and energy to the wider diffusion of the Catholic Faith. They are: The Catholic Church Extension Society, an organization which has gained glorious distinction for its pious benefactions;[3] The Catholic Near East Welfare Association,[4] which furnishes a providential aid to the interests of Christianity in the Orient; The Indian and Negro Missions, an association approved by the Third Council of Baltimore[5] which We confirm and recommend because it is imposed by a very particular charity toward your fellow citizens.

We confess that We feel a special paternal affection, which is certainly inspired by heaven, for the Negro people dwelling among you; for in the field of religion and education We know they need special care and comfort and are very deserving of it. We therefore invoke an abundance of heavenly blessing and We pray fruitful success for those whose generous zeal is devoted to their welfare.

Moreover, in order to render more fitting thanks to God for the inestimable gift of the true Faith, your countrymen, eager for arduous enterprise, are supplying to the ranks of the missionaries numerous recruits whose capacity for toil, whose indomitable patience and whose energy in noble initiative for the Kingdom of Christ have gained merits which earth admires and which heaven will crown with due reward.

No less vigorous among you are those works of zeal which are organized for the benefit of the children of the Church within the confines of your country: the diocesan charity offices, with their wise and practical organization, by means of the parish priests and through the labors of the religious institutes, bring to the poor, to the needy and to the sick the gifts of Christian mercy and relief from misery. In carrying on this most important ministry the sweet discerning eyes of faith see Christ present in the poor and afflicted who are the mystic suffering members of the most benign Redeemer.

Among the associations of the laity — the list is too long to allow of a complete enumeration — there are those which have won for themselves laurels of unfading glory: Catholic Action, the Marian Congregation, the Confraternity of Christian Doctrine: their fruits are

---

[3] Founded on October 18, 1905.

[4] Established in 1926 to support missions in the Near and Middle East and to aid refugees among the Eastern Rite Catholics.

[5] The Commission for Catholic Missions Among the Colored People and the Indians was established in 1886.

the cause of joy and they bear the promise of still more joyful harvests in the future. Likewise the Holy Name Society,[6] an excellent leader in the promotion of Christian worship and piety.

Over a manifold activity of the laity, carried on in various localities according to the needs of the times, is placed the National Catholic Welfare Conference, an organization which supplies a ready and well-adapted instrument for your episcopal ministry.[7]

The more important of these institutions We were able to view briefly during the month of October, 1936, when We journeyed across the ocean and had the joy of knowing personally you and the field of your activities. The memory of what We then admired with Our own eyes will always remain indelible and a source of joy in Our Heart.

It is proper then that, with sentiments of adoration, We offer with you thanks to God and that We raise to Him a canticle of thanksgiving: "Give glory to the God of Heaven: for His mercy endureth for ever."[8] The Lord Whose goodness knows no limits, having filled your land with the bounty of His gifts, has likewise granted to your churches energy and power and has brought to fruition the results of their tireless labors. Having paid the tribute of Our gratitude to God, from Whom every good thing takes its origin, We recognize, dearly beloved, that this rich harvest which We joyfully admire with you today is due also to the spirit of initiative and to the persistent activity of the pastors and of the faithful. We recognize that it is due also to your clergy who are inclined to decisive action and who execute your orders with zeal; to the members of all the religious Orders and congregations of men who, distinguished in virtue, vie with each other in cultivating the vineyard of the Lord: to the innumerable religious women who, often in silence and unknown to men, consecrate themselves with exemplary devotion to the cause of the Gospel, veritable lilies in the Garden of Christ and delight of the Saints.

We desire, however, that This Our praise be salutary. The consideration of the good which has been done must not lead to slackening which might degenerate into sluggishness; it must not issue in a vainglorious pleasure which flatters the mind; it should stimulate renewed energies so that evils may be avoided and those enterprises which are useful, prudent and worthy of praise may more surely and more

---

[6] The Holy Name Society was organized in the United States in 1909.

[7] The National Catholic Welfare Conference dates from the first annual meeting of the hierarchy in September, 1919. Cf. No. 158.

[8] Ps. 135:26.

solidly mature. The Christian, if he does honor to the name he bears, is always an apostle; it is not permitted to the Soldier of Christ that he quit the battlefield, because only death puts an end to his military service.

You well know where it is necessary that you exercise a more discerning vigilance and what program of action should be marked out for priests and faithful in order that the religion of Christ may overcome the obstacles in its path and be a luminous guide to the minds of men, govern their morals and, for the sole purpose of salvation, permeate the marrow and the arteries of human society. The progress of exterior and material possessions, even though it is to be considered of no little account, because of the manifold and appreciable utility which it gives to life is nonetheless not enough for man who is born for higher and brighter destinies. Created indeed to the image and likeness of God, he seeks God with a yearning that will not be repressed and always groans and weeps if he places the object of his love where Supreme Truth and the Infinite Good cannot be found.

Not with the conquest of material space does one approach to God, separation from Whom is death, conversion to Whom is life, to be established in Whom is glory; but under the guidance of Christ with the fullness of sincere faith, with unsullied conscience and upright will, with holy works, with the achievement and the employment of that genuine liberty whose sacred rules are found proclaimed in the Gospel. If instead, the Commandments of God are spurned, not only is it impossible to attain that happiness which has place beyond the brief span of time which is allotted to earthly existence, but the very basis upon which rests true civilization is shaken and naught is to be expected but ruins over which belated tears must be shed. How, in fact, can the public weal and the glory of civilized life have any guarantee of stability when right is subverted and virtue despised and decried? Is not God the Source and the Giver of law? Is He not the inspiration and the reward of virtue with none like unto Him among lawgivers?[9] This, according to the admission of all reasonable men, is everywhere the bitter and prolific root of evils: the refusal to recognize the Divine Majesty, the neglect of the moral law, the origin of which is from heaven, or that regrettable inconstancy which makes its victims waver between the lawful and the forbidden, between justice and iniquity.

Thence arise immoderate and blind egotism, the thirst for pleasure,

[9] Job 36:22.

the vice of drunkenness, immodest and costly styles in dress, the prevalence of crime even among minors, the lust for power, neglect of the poor, base craving for ill-gotten wealth, the flight from the land, levity in entering into marriage, divorce, the break-up of the family, the cooling of mutual affection between parents and children, birth control, the enfeeblement of the race, the weakening of respect for authority, or obsequiousness, or rebellion, neglect of duty toward one's country and toward mankind.

We raise Our voice in strong, albeit paternal, complaint that in so many schools of your land Christ often is despised or ignored, the explanation of the universe and mankind is forced within the narrow limits of materialism or of rationalism, and new educational systems are sought after which cannot but produce a sorrowful harvest in the intellectual and moral life of the nation.

Likewise, just as home life, when the law of Christ is observed, flowers in true felicity, so, when the Gospel is cast aside, does it perish miserably and become desolated by vice: "He that seeketh the law shall be filled with it: and he that dealeth deceitfully shall meet with a stumbling block therein."[10] What can there be on earth more serene and joyful than the Christian family? Taking its origin at the Altar of the Lord, where love has been proclaimed a holy and indissoluble bond, the Christian family in the same love nourished by supernal grace is consolidated and receives increase.

There is "marriage honorable in all and the (nuptial) bed undefiled."[11] Tranquil walls resound with no quarreling voices nor do they witness the secret martyrdom which comes when hidden infidelity is laid bare; unquestioning trust turns aside the slings of suspicion; sorrow is assuaged and joy is heightened by mutual affection. Within those sacred precincts children are considered not heavy burdens but sweet pledges of love; no reprehensible motive of convenience, no seeking after sterile pleasure brings about the frustration of the gift of life nor causes to fall into disuse the sweet names of brother and sister. With what solicitude do the parents take care that the children not only grow in physical vigor but also that, following in the footsteps of their forbears whose memory is often recalled to them, they may shine with the light which profession of the pure faith and moral goodness impart to them. Moved by the numerous benefits received, such children consider it their paramount duty to honor their parents; to be attentive to their desires, to be the staff of their

---

[10] Eccl. 32:19.
[11] Heb. 13:4.

old age, to rejoice their gray hairs with an affection which unquenched by death, will be made more glorious and more complete in the mansion of heaven. The members of the Christian family, neither querulous in adversity nor ungrateful in prosperity, are ever filled with confidence in God to Whose sway they yield willing obedience, in Whose will they acquiesce and upon Whose help they wait not in vain.

That the family may be established and maintained according to the wise teachings of the Gospel, therefore, the faithful should be frequently exhorted by those who have the directive and teaching functions in the churches and these are to strive with unremitting care to present to the Lord a perfect people. For the same reason it is also supremely necessary to see to it that the dogma of the unity and indissolubility of Matrimony is known in all its religious importance and sacredly respected by those who are to marry.

That this capital point of Catholic Doctrine is of great value for the solidity of the family structure, for the progress and prosperity of civil society, for the healthy life of the people and for civilization that its light may not be false is a fact recognized even by no small number of men who, though estranged from the Faith, are entitled to respect for their political acumen. Oh! If only your country had come to know from the experience of others rather than from examples at home of the accumulation of ills which derive from the plague of divorce; let reverence for religion, let fidelity toward the great American people counsel energetic action that this disease, alas so widespread, may be cured by extirpation.

The consequences of this evil have been thus described by Pope Leo XIII, in words whose truth is incisive: "Because of divorce, the nuptial contract becomes subject to fickle whim; affection is weakened; pernicious incentives are given to conjugal infidelity; the care and education of offspring are harmed; easy opportunity is afforded for the breaking up of homes; the seeds of discord are sown among families; the dignity of woman is lessened and brought down and she runs the risk of being deserted after she has served her husband as an instrument of pleasure. And since it is true that for the ruination of the family and the undermining of the State nothing is so powerful as the corruption of morals, it is easy to see that divorce is of the greatest harm to the prosperity of families and of states."[12]

With regard to those marriages in which one or the other party does not accept the Catholic teaching or has not been baptized, We

---

[12] *Arcanum divinae,* February 10, 1880, in John J. Wynne, S.J. (Ed.), *The Great Encyclical Letters of Pope Leo XIII* (New York, 1903), pp. 74–75.

are certain that you observe exactly the prescriptions of the Code of Canon Law. Such marriages, in fact, as is clear to you from wide experience, are rarely happy and usually occasion grave loss to the Catholic Church. A very efficacious means for driving out such grave evils is that individual Catholics receive a thorough training in the divine truths and that the people be shown clearly the road which leads to salvation.

Therefore We exhort the priests to provide that their own knowledge of things divine and human be wide and deep; that they be not content with the intellectual knowledge acquired in youth; that they examine with careful scrutiny the Law of the Lord, Whose oracles are purer than silver; that they continually relish and enjoy the chaste charms of Sacred Scripture; that with the passing of the years they study more deeply the history of the Church, its dogmas, its Sacraments, its laws, its precepts, its liturgy, its language, so that they may advance in grace, in culture and wisdom.

Let them cultivate also the study of letters and of the profane sciences, especially those which are more closely connected with religion, in order that they may be able to impart with clarity and eloquence the teaching of grace and salvation which is capable of bending even learned intellects to the light burden and yoke of the Gospel of Christ.

Fortunate the Church, indeed, if thus it will lay its "foundations with sapphires."[13] The needs of our times then require that the laity, too, and especially those who collaborate with the Hierarchy of the Church, procure for themselves a treasure of religious knowledge, not a poor and meager knowledge, but one that will have solidity and richness through the medium of libraries, discussions and study clubs; in this way they will derive great benefit for themselves and at the same time be able to instruct the ignorant, confute stubborn adversaries and be of assistance to good friends.

We have learned with no little joy that your press is a sturdy champion of Catholic principles; that the Marconi Radio — whose voice is heard in an instant round the world — marvelous invention and eloquent image of the Apostolic Faith that embraces all mankind — is frequently and advantageously put to use in order to insure the widest possible promulgation of all that concerns the Church, and We commend the good accomplished. But let those who fulfill this ministry be careful to adhere to the directions of the teaching Church even when they explain and promote what pertains to the social

[13] Isa. 54:11.

problem; forgetful of personal gain, despising popularity, impartial, let them speak "as from God, before God, in Christ."[14]

Because of Our constant desire that scientific progress in all its branches be ever more universally affirmed, We gladly take this opportune occasion to signify to you Our cordial interest in the University at Washington. You remember well with what ardent wishes Pope Leo XIII greeted this noble temple of learning when it came into being and on how many occasions testimonies of particular affection were bestowed upon it by Our immediate predecessor. He was intimately persuaded that if this great school, however blessed already with success, should become still stronger and gain even greater renown not only would the growth of the Church be aided but also the civil glory and prosperity of your fellow citizens.[15]

Sharing this hope, We ask you to do your very best, leaving nothing untried, that this University, protected by your benevolence, may overcome its difficulties and, with ever more gratifying increase, abundantly fulfill the high hopes that have been placed in it. We greatly appreciate, too, your desire to erect in Rome a more worthy and suitable building for the Pontifical College which receives for their ecclesiastical education students from the United States.[16]

If it is indeed true that the elite of our youth with profit travel abroad to complete their education, a long and happy experience shows that candidates for the priesthood derive very great profit when they are educated here close to the See of Peter, where the source of faith is purest, where so many monuments of Christian antiquity and so many traces of the Saints incite generous hearts to magnanimous enterprises.

We desire to touch upon another question of weighty importance, the social question, which remaining unsolved, has been agitating States for a long time and sowing amongst the classes the seeds of hatred and mutual hostility. You know full well what aspect it assumes in America, what acrimonies, what disorders it produces. It is not necessary therefore that We dwell on these points. The fundamental point of the social question is this, that the goods created by God for all men should in the same way reach all, justice guiding and charity helping. The history of every age teaches that

[14] 2 Cor. 2:17.

[15] Cf. Pope Pius XI's letter of September 21, 1938, to the American hierarchy written in anticipation of the university's golden jubilee, *The Catholic University of America Bulletin*, VII (November, 1938), 2–3.

[16] The new North American College on the Janiculum Hill, Rome, was dedicated on October 14, 1953.

there were always rich and poor; that it will always be so we may gather from the unchanging tenor of human destinies. Worthy of honor are the poor who fear God because theirs is the kingdom of heaven and because they readily abound in spiritual graces. But the rich, if they are upright and honest, are God's dispensers and providers of this world's goods; as ministers of Divine Providence they assist the indigent through whom they often receive gifts for the soul and whose hand — so they may hope — will lead them into the eternal tabernacles.

God, Who provides for all with counsels of supreme bounty, has ordained that for the exercise of virtues and for the testing of one's worth there be in the world rich and poor; but He does not wish that some have exaggerated riches while others are in such straits that they lack the bare necessities of life. But a kindly mother of virtue is honest poverty which gains its living by daily labor in accordance with the scriptural saying: "Give me neither beggary, nor riches: give me only the necessaries of life."[17]

Now if the rich and the prosperous are obliged out of ordinary motives of pity to act generously toward the poor their obligation is all the greater to do them justice. The salaries of the workers, as is just, are to be such that they are sufficient to maintain them and their families. Solemn are the words of Our Predecessor, Pius XI on this question: "Every effort must therefore be made that fathers of families receive a wage sufficient to meet adequately normal domestic needs. If under present circumstances this is not always feasible, social justice demands that reforms be introduced without delay which will guarantee such a wage to every adult working man. In this connection We praise those who have most prudently and usefully attempted various methods by which an increased wage is paid in view of increased family burdens and special provision made for special needs."[18]

May it also be brought about that each and every able bodied man may receive an equal opportunity for work in order to earn the daily bread for himself and his own. We deeply lament the lot of those — and their number in the United States is large indeed — who though robust, capable and willing, cannot have the work for which they are anxiously searching.

May the wisdom of the governing powers, a far-seeing generosity on the part of the employers, together with the speedy re-establish-

---

[17] Prov. 30:8.

[18] *Quadragesimo anno,* May 15, 1931, in *Two Basic Social Encyclicals* (New York, 1943), pp. 133–135.

ment of more favorable conditions, effect the realization of these reasonable hopes to the advantage of all.

Because social relations is one of man's natural requirements and since it is legitimate to promote by common effort decent livelihood, it is not possible without injustice to deny or to limit either to the producers or to the laboring and farming classes the free faculty of uniting in associations by means of which they may defend their proper rights and secure the betterment of the goods of soul and of body, as well as the honest comforts of life. But to unions of this kind, which in past centuries have procured immortal glory for Christianity and for the professions an untarnishable splendor, one cannot everywhere impose an identical discipline and structure which therefore can be varied to meet the different temperament of the people and the diverse circumstances of time.

But let the unions in question draw their vital force from principles of wholesome liberty; let them take their form from the lofty rules of justice and of honesty, and, conforming themselves to those norms, let them act in such a manner that in their care for the interests of their class they violate no one's rights; let them continue to strive for harmony and respect the common weal of civil society.

It is a source of joy to Us to know that the above cited encyclical *Quadragesimo anno,* as well as that of the Sovereign Pontiff Leo XIII, *Rerum novarum,* in which is indicated the solution of the social question in accordance with the postulates of the Gospel and of the eternal philosophy, are the object in the United States of careful and prolonged consideration on the part of some men of keener intellect whose generous wish pushes them on toward social restoration and the strengthening of the bonds of love amongst men, and that some employers themselves have desired to settle the ever-recurring controversies with the working man in accordance with the norms of these encyclicals, respecting always the common good and the dignity of the human person.

What a proud vaunt it will be for the American people, by nature inclined to grandiose undertakings and to liberality, if they untie the knotty and difficult social question by following the sure paths illuminated by the light of the Gospel and thus lay the basis of a happier age! If this is to come to pass power must not be dissipated through disunion but rather strengthened through harmony. To this salutary union of thought and policy, whence flow mighty deeds, in all charity We invite them, too, whom Mother Church laments as separated brethren. Many of these when Our glorious predecessor reposed in the sleep of the just and when We, shortly after his death, through the mysterious disposition of divine mercy ascended the throne of St. Peter; many of these — and this did not escape Our attention — expressed by word of mouth and by letter sentiments full of homage and noble respect. This attitude — We openly confess — has encouraged a hope which time does not take from Us, which a sanguine mind cherishes and which remains a consolation to Us in hard and troublous times.

May the enormity of the labors which it will be necessary fervently to undertake for the glory of the most benign Redeemer and for the salvation of souls not daunt you, Dearly Beloved, but may it rather stimulate you, whose confidence is in the divine help, since great works generate more robust virtues and achieve more resplendent merits.

May the attempts with which the enemies secretly banded together seek to pull down the scepter of Christ be a spur to us to work in union for the establishment and advancement of His reign. No greater fortune can come to individuals, families, and nations than to obey the Author of human salvation, execute His commands, accept His reign, in which we are made free and rich in good works; "A kingdom of truth and life; a kingdom of holiness and grace, a kingdom of justice, love and peace."[19]

Wishing from Our heart that you and the spiritual flock for whose welfare you provide as diligent shepherds may advance always toward better and higher goals and that also from the present solemn celebration you may gather a rich harvest of virtue, We impart to you as a pledge of Our benevolence the Apostolic Benediction.

Given at the Vatican, on the Feast of All Saints, in the Year of Our Lord, 1939, the first of Our Pontificate.

PIUS PP XII.

161. American Catholics and the Intellectual Life, 1956

ONE of the liveliest topics of discussion among educated Catholics during the 1950's centered around their failure to make a contribution to the cultural life of the nation in keeping with their numbers, wealth, and increasingly high percentage of college graduates. The Catholic Commission for Intellectual and Cultural Affairs took up the matter and devoted its annual meeting of 1955 in St. Louis largely to this subject. On May 14 at

[19] Preface of the Mass of Christ the King.

one of the sessions of the C.C.I.C.A., John Tracy Ellis, professor of church history in the Catholic University of America, read a paper entitled "American Catholics and the Intellectual Life" which, in turn, provoked a good deal of discussion. The paper was first published in *Thought* (Autumn, 1955) and appeared in book form the following summer with a preface by the Most Reverend John J. Wright, then Bishop of Worcester and since 1959 Bishop of Pittsburgh. The statement of Bishop Wright is given here as one of the most thoughtful and representative of the contributions to what he has himself called the "great debate." Source: Prefatory Note by John J. Wright to John Tracy Ellis, *American Catholics and the Intellectual Life* (Chicago: Heritage Foundation, Inc., 1956), pp. 5–10.

. . .

Monsignor Ellis' paper provoked a reaction that is in itself irrefutable evidence of how well timed and accurate are his contentions. A great number of others were emboldened by his statements to lift their own voices on the urgency of a re-evaluation of Catholic intellectual life in the United States, and their witness frequently added proof both that the cause is critical and that it is far from hopeless. The passion with which the few dissenters from Monsignor Ellis' position set forth their indignant reservations proved that he had touched a tender nerve. In an article in *America,*[1] Monsignor Ellis himself summarized some of the reactions to his original piece. He has received several hundred letters. All but four seem to be in agreement with his analysis. The article itself is an important contribution to the documentation on the "great debate," but there is no reason to believe that all the reactions are by any means yet registered. One awaits with mingled sentiments of dread and curiosity this season's commencement addresses, for example!

What we have called the "great debate" raging here in the United States at the moment is doubtless no more than a phase within our own land of an argument that has been going on in Europe for decades. Traditionally, the European intellectual has been acknowledged by his contemporaries, even those who might disagree with him, to have a 'vocation' beyond the limits of his own profession of writing or science or teaching. It is a vocation quite apart from that of the functionary or representative of Church or of State, and it has obvious and grave perils as well as elements of prestige. These perils are as real as ignominy, exile or prison, even death, the frequent destinies of the traditional intellectuals in Europe. And yet, the intellectual has usually enjoyed a veneration in Europe which scarcely has a parallel in the

[1] John Tracy Ellis, "No Complacency," *America,* XCV (April 7, 1956), 14–25.

common American attitude toward those who take on the valiant role of questioner, critic, or intellectual trail blazer. The reader will note the "witty extravagance" which Monsignor Ellis recalls as differentiating the attitudes of Europeans and Americans toward intellectuals: in the old world an ordinary mortal on seeing a professor tipped his hat, while in America he taps his head.

Such a suspicious attitude toward the intellectual life is far from being an exclusive Catholic phenomenon in the United States. Indeed, this kink in the American character generally may be due, as an editorial in the Washington *Post and Times Herald* pointed out on December 19, 1955, to specifically non-Catholic sociological and even theological influences on the formation of our national character. For example, the thoroughly practical problems confronting the first settlers on New England's stern and rock-bound coast no doubt intensified the predisposition of their Calvinist theology to emphasize results rather than theories and to reverence achievement rather than abstract speculation. There is a characteristically American esteem for the word "industry," in all its senses, which has never been accorded to the word "intellectual" or any of its variations.

The anti-intellectual attitude, however, is more unbecoming and embarrassing in Catholics because it is so entirely inconsistent with any authentic Catholic position. So many of the heresies which have wounded the Church and despoiled her of whole nations have been voluntarist heresies, anti-intellectual in their roots and pretensions, that it is bitterly ironic when anti-intellectualism threatens to become characteristic of those who have remained faithful to her obedience.

One wonders whether Catholics themselves always appreciate the extent to which the battles of the Church against the modern heresies have been at one and the same time battles against the heresy of anti-intellectualism. Luther's "stat pro ratione voluntas," his voluntaristic *fides fiducialis* with its repudiation of the intellectual elements in the act of faith, and his violent but typical description of the intellect as the "devil's whore," are as much the evidence of his departure from Catholic traditions as any of his theses nailed to the chapel door. The blind fatalism of Calvin, the perverse austerities of Jansenism, the sentimentality and exaltation of instinct or religious emotion which, for all its show of scholarship, characterized Modernism, are all typical of the heresies which have divided the Christian flock in these last four centuries. In defending supernatural revelation against these the Church was at the same time defending the validity of natural reason and the primacy of the intellect over the will, the emotions, the instincts or any of the other faculties to which voluntarism has always appealed, whether in Luther's dogma, the moral theories of Jansenius, the religious psychology of the moderns or the political philosophy of totalitarianism.

We usually think of the Council of Trent, the Vatican Council and the syllabus against Modernism in terms of the defense of revealed dogmas, and such, of course, they were. But he understands them poorly who fails to perceive that they were frequently Catholic affirmations of the validity of reason as well as of the reality of revelation, and that they bore witness to the essential part of rational elements even in the supernatural act of faith, and to the divine origin of the primacy and rights of the intellect in the natural order.

It is, therefore, a problem for the Church when any who might be taken as her representatives in any sense in the world of the campus, the press, or the forum reveal contempt for that "wild living intellect of man" of which Cardinal Newman spoke, or cynicism about the slow, sometimes faltering, but patient, persevering processes by which the intellectual seeks to wrest some measure of order from the chaos about us.

The problem is manifold. Monsignor Ellis' paper and others which followed give good hope that its solution may be in process of realization. First of all, there is a problem of definitions. What precisely do we now mean when we use the word intellectual and when we speak of either the virtues of faults of "intellectualism"? It is this initial problem which has been highlighted by the editor of the Brooklyn *Tablet* in his evaluation of recent writings on the subject.

Then there is a problem which we can best call spiritual or apostolic. What is the vocation of the intellectual in the life of the Church? How can he best bear his specifically intellectual witness, a witness which may involve a living martyrdom, given the temper of the times and the suspicion with which even his own will all too often views his gifts and his works? How shall we persuade intellectuals to find in Christ, the *Logos,* the eternal Word made flesh to dwell among us, a divine prototype of their special vocation and unique dignity, as we have persuaded workers to find their model in the carpenter's Son, Christian youth to find a model in the youthful Christ's obedience to Joseph and Mary at Nazareth, and patriotic citizens to see the exemplar of their proper loyalty in the Christ who paid the coin of tribute and wept tears of predilection over the capital city of His nation? A spirituality of Christian humanism, centered about the concept of Christ the divine Intellectual, is a critical need of our generation if the evidence presented here proves as much as we have good reason to believe it does.

The problem of the apostolic role of the Catholic intellectual cannot be too often emphasized. Father Raymond L. Bruckberger, O.P., our friendly French critic, in an article in *Harper's Magazine* for February, 1956,[2] on the patriotic responsibilities of the American intellectual, makes a point worthy of meditation by Catholic intellectuals who sincerely seek to understand their contemporary religious responsibilities. The American intellectual often tends to say that his country has failed him, that she will not give him the honor which is his due, and that he feels like a spiritual exile. Perhaps, the contrary is more nearly true, and the American intellectual is more deeply missed than is at first apparent. When the intellectual turns his back on his country and confines himself to berating her, his place remains empty, all the while that he complains that he has no place at all. A more valiant generation of European intellectuals accepted it as their destiny to be unappreciated and mocked for false prophets; in this they found a secret consolation and often their abiding glory.

Catholic intellectuals have a point for meditation here. Intellectually gifted Catholics suffer all too often from a "whining" tendency in their attitude toward the Church. They lament that they are not sufficiently appreciated or encouraged. They berate the indifference of their fellow Catholics to their vocation. In a curious paradox on the lips of Christians, particularly Christians with presumably keener powers of insight and understanding than the rest, they protest against being made martyrs. Where in the New Testament, the Church of the Fathers, or the history of the saints from Paul to Thomas More, were the genuinely thoughtful promised any other lot, whether at the hands of the world or at the hands of their uncomprehending brethren, than contradiction and constant testing?

Finally, and urgently, there is an intensely practical problem in this matter of American Catholic intellectual life. It is the problem of how we can increase the proportions of authentic scholars and trained, competent intellectuals among us.

Statistics have been offered recently which point up and analyze the dearth of Catholic lay scholars. These statistics have been challenged by those who resented certain of its implications, although their resentment did not inspire much in the way of effective refutation of the facts. The facts add up to a conclusion which is a primary justifica-

[2] Raymond L. Bruckberger, O.P., "Assignment for Intellectuals," *Harper's Magazine*, CCXII (February, 1956), 68–72.

tion for the republication of this present paper, by a man who dearly loves the Faith and is one of those who spare themselves nothing to contribute to the solution of whatever problems impede the freedom and well being of our Holy Mother the Church.

In the early days of the Church in America, humble Catholics struggled to retain the Faith in an anti-Catholic atmosphere. These early pioneers built schools and churches which are responsible for the survival of Catholic America today. These foundations for growth and expansion have been firmly rooted within the American tradition in our soil, but future progress and expansion will come only through a determined effort based upon the development of Catholic scholarship. It is to this problem that Monsignor Ellis addresses himself so effectively, and we recommend a reading and rereading of his provocative message at regular intervals. Both Catholicism and America have need of an intellectual apostolate of distinction.

162. The American Catholic Bishops and Racism, November 14, 1958

IT WOULD be difficult to think of any problem that has done more to disturb the internal peace of the United States than discrimination against various groups on the score of race or nationality. Friction between whites and native Indians and Negroes has been a fairly constant phenomenon in American history, but it has been especially acute in regard to the latter since World War II. That some American Catholics have been influenced by racist doctrines is, unfortunately, true, and had they accepted the Church's teaching on this subject there would probably be more than 675,000 colored people and 125,000 Indians among the American Catholics at the present time (1961). Yet strenuous efforts have not been lacking in recent years on the part of members of the hierarchy to emphasize in a practical way the Church's mission to men of all races and nationalities. And these efforts have produced effective results, even if in certain localities race prejudice has not permitted more progress to be made. For example, Joseph E. Ritter, Archbishop of St. Louis, ordered the integration of the schools of his archdiocese in September, 1947, seven years in advance of the Supreme Court's ruling of May, 1954. Likewise in the autumn of 1948 integration of the Catholic schools of the national capital was begun at the instance of Patrick A. O'Boyle, Archbishop of Washington, and in June, 1954, Vincent S. Waters, Bishop of Raleigh, instituted the same policy in all the churches and diocesan institutions of his southern see. Nationally speaking, however, the situation has yielded — if at all — only after great resistance. It was with that background that the Catholic bishops determined to set forth in detail the Church's doctrine on this controversial question. Source: "Discrimination and the Christian Conscience," New York *Times,* November 14, 1958.

Fifteen years ago, when this nation was devoting its energies to a World War designed to maintain human freedom, the Catholic Bishops of the United States issued a prayerful warning to their fellow citizens. We called for the extension of full freedom within the confines of our beloved country. Specifically, we noted the problems faced by Negroes in obtaining the rights that are theirs as Americans. The statement of 1943 said in part:

"In the Providence of God there are among us millions of fellow citizens of the Negro race. We owe to these fellow citizens, who have contributed so largely to the development of our country, and for whose welfare history imposes on us a special obligation of justice, to see that they have in fact the rights which are given them in our Constitution. This means not only political equality, but also fair economic and educational opportunities, a just share in public welfare projects, good housing without exploitation, and a full chance for the social advancement of their race."

In the intervening years, considerable progress was made in achieving these goals. The Negro race, brought to this country in slavery, continued its quiet but determined march toward the goal of equal rights and equal opportunity. During and after the Second World War, great and even spectacular advances were made in the obtaining of voting rights, good education, better-paying jobs, and adequate housing. Through the efforts of men of good will, of every race and creed and from all parts of the nation, the barriers of prejudice and discrimination were slowly but inevitably eroded.

Because this method of quiet conciliation produced such excellent results, we have preferred the path of action to that of exhortation. Unfortunately, however, it appears that in recent years the issues have become confused and the march toward justice and equality has been slowed if not halted in some areas. The transcendent moral issues involved have become obscured, and possibly forgotten.

Our nation now stands divided by the problem of compulsory segregation of the races and the opposing demand for racial justice. No region of our land is immune from strife and division resulting from this problem. In one area, the key issue may concern the schools. In another it may be conflicts over housing. Job discrimination may be the focal point in still other sectors. But all these issues have one main point in common. They reflect the determination of our Negro people, and we hope the overwhelming majority of our white citizens, to see that our colored citizens obtain their full rights as given to them by God, the Creator of all, and guaranteed by the democratic traditions of our nation.

There are many facets to the problems raised by the quest for racial justice. There are issues of law, of history, of economics, and of sociology. There are questions of procedure and technique. There are conflicts in cultures. Volumes have been written on each of these phases. Their importance we do not deny. But the time has come, in our considered and prayerful judgment, to cut through the maze of secondary or less essential issues and to come to the heart of the problem.

The heart of the race question is moral and religious. It concerns the rights of man and our attitude toward our fellow man. If our attitude is governed by the great Christian law of love of neighbor and respect for his rights, then we can work out harmoniously the techniques for making legal, educational, economic, and social adjustments. But if our hearts are poisoned by hatred, or even by indifference toward the welfare and rights of our fellow men, then our nation faces a grave internal crisis.

No one who bears the name of Christian can deny the universal love of God for all mankind. When Our Lord and Savior, Jesus Christ, "took on the form of man" (Phil. 2, 7) and walked among men, He taught as the first two laws of life the love of God and the love of fellow man. "By this shall all men know that you are my disciples, that you have love, one for the other." (John 13, 35) He offered His life in sacrifice for all mankind. His parting mandate to His followers was to "teach all nations." (Mat. 28, 19)

Our Christian faith is of its nature universal. It knows not the distinctions of race, color, or nationhood. The missionaries of the Church have spread throughout the world, visiting with equal impartiality nations such as China and India, whose ancient cultures antedate the coming of the Savior, and the primitive tribes of the Americas. The love of Christ, and the love of the Christian, knows no bounds. In the words of Pope Pius XII, addressed to American Negro publishers twelve years ago, "All men are brothered in Jesus Christ; for He, though God, became also man, became a member of the human family, a brother of all." (May 27, 1946)

Even those who do not accept our Christian tradition should at least acknowledge that God has implanted in the souls of all men some knowledge of the natural moral law and a respect for its teachings. Reason alone taught philosophers through the ages respect for the sacred dignity of each human being and the fundamental rights of man. Every man has an equal right to life, to justice before the law, to marry and rear a family under human conditions, and to an equitable opportunity to use the goods of this earth for his needs and those of his family.

From these solemn truths, there follow certain conclusions vital for a proper approach to the problems that trouble us today. First, we must repeat the principle — embodied in our Declaration of Independence — that all men are equal in the sight of God. By equal we mean that they are created by God and redeemed by His Divine Son, that they are bound by His Law, and that God desires them as His friends in the eternity of Heaven. This fact confers upon all men human dignity and human rights.

Men are unequal in talent and achievement. They differ in culture and personal characteristics. Some are saintly, some seem to be evil, most are men of good will, though beset with human frailty. On the basis of personal differences we may distinguish among our fellow men, remembering always the admonition: "Let him who is without sin . . . cast the first stone . . ." (Jn., 8, 7) But discrimination based on the accidental fact of race or color, and as such injurious to human rights regardless of personal qualities or achievements, cannot be reconciled with the truth that God has created all men with equal rights and equal dignity.

Secondly, we are bound to love our fellow man. The Christian love we bespeak is not a matter of emotional likes or dislikes. It is a firm purpose to do good to all men, to the extent that ability and opportunity permit.

Among all races and national groups, class distinctions are inevitably made on the basis of like-mindedness or a community of interests. Such distinctions are normal and constitute a universal social phenomenon. They are accidental, however, and are subject to change as conditions change. It is unreasonable and injurious to the rights of others that a factor such as race, by and of itself, should be made a cause of discrimination and a basis for unequal treatment in our mutual relations.

The question then arises: Can enforced segregation be reconciled with the Christian view of our fellow man? In our judgment it cannot, and this for two fundamental reasons.

1) Legal segregation, or any form of compulsory segregation, in itself and by its very nature imposes a stigma of inferiority upon the

segregated people. Even if the now obsolete Court doctrine of "separate but equal" had been carried out to the fullest extent, so that all public and semipublic facilities were in fact equal, there is nonetheless the judgment that an entire race, by the sole fact of race and regardless of individual qualities, is not fit to associate on equal terms with members of another race. We cannot reconcile such a judgment with the Christian view of man's nature and rights. Here again it is appropriate to cite the language of Pope Pius XII. "God did not create a human family made up of segregated, dissociated, mutually independent members. No; He would have them all united by the bond of total love of Him and consequent self-dedication to assisting each other to maintain that bond intact." (September 7, 1956)

2) It is a matter of historical fact that segregation in our country has led to oppressive conditions and the denial of basic human rights for the Negro. This is evident in the fundamental fields of education, job opportunity, and housing. Flowing from these areas of neglect and discrimination are problems of health and the sordid train of evils so often associated with the consequent slum conditions. Surely Pope Pius XII must have had these conditions in mind when he said just two months ago: "It is only too well known, alas, to what excesses pride of race and racial hate can lead. The Church has always been energetically opposed to attempts of genocide or practices arising from what is called the 'color bar.'" (September 5, 1958)

One of the tragedies of racial oppression is that the evils we have cited are being used as excuses to continue the very conditions that so strongly fostered such evils. Today we are told that Negroes, Indians, and also some Spanish-speaking Americans differ too much in culture and achievements to be assimilated in our schools, factories, and neighborhoods. Some decades back the same charge was made against the immigrant, Irish, Jewish, Italian, Polish, Hungarian, German, Russian. In both instances differences were used by some as a basis for discrimination and even for bigoted ill-treatment. The immigrant, fortunately, has achieved his rightful status in the American community. Economic opportunity was wide open and educational equality was not denied to him.

Negro citizens seek these same opportunities. They wish an education that does not carry with it any stigma of inferiority. They wish economic advancement based on merit and skill. They wish their civil rights as American citizens. They wish acceptance based upon proved ability and achievement. No one who truly loves God's children will deny them this opportunity.

To work for this principle amid passions and misunderstandings will not be easy. It will take courage. But quiet and persevering courage has always been the mark of a true follower of Christ. We urge that concrete plans in this field be based on prudence. Prudence may be called a virtue that inclines us to view problems in their proper perspective. It aids us to use the proper means to secure our aim.

The problems we inherit today are rooted in decades, even centuries, of custom and cultural patterns. Changes in deep-rooted attitudes are not made overnight. When we are confronted with complex and far-reaching evils, it is not a sign of weakness or timidity to distinguish among remedies and reforms. Some changes are more necessary than others. Some are relatively easy to achieve. Others seem impossible at this time. What may succeed in one area may fail in another.

It is a sign of wisdom, rather than weakness, to study carefully the problems we face, to prepare for advances, and to by-pass the non-essential if it interferes with essential progress. We may well deplore a gradualism that is merely a cloak for inaction. But we equally deplore rash impetuosity that would sacrifice the achievements of decades in ill-timed and ill-considered ventures. In concrete matters we distinguish between prudence and inaction by asking the question: Are we sincerely and earnestly acting to solve these problems? We distinguish between prudence and rashness by seeking the prayerful and considered judgment of experienced counselors who have achieved success in meeting similar problems.

For this reason we hope and earnestly pray that responsible and sober-minded Americans of all religious faiths, in all areas of our land, will seize the mantle of leadership from the agitator and the racist. It is vital that we act now and act decisively. All must act quietly, courageously, and prayerfully before it is too late.

For the welfare of our nation we call upon all to root out from their hearts bitterness and hatred. The tasks we face are indeed difficult. But hearts inspired by Christian love will surmount these difficulties.

Clearly then, these problems are vital and urgent. May God give this nation the grace to meet the challenge it faces. For the sake of generations of future Americans, and indeed of all humanity, we cannot fail.

Signed by members of the Administrative Board, National Catholic Welfare Conference, in the name of the Bishops of the United States:

FRANCIS CARDINAL SPELLMAN,
Archbishop of New York.
JAMES FRANCIS CARDINAL MCINTYRE,
Archbishop of Los Angeles.
FRANCIS P. KEOUGH,
Archbishop of Baltimore.
KARL J. ALTER,
Archbishop of Cincinnati.
JOSEPH E. RITTER,
Archbishop of St. Louis.
WILLIAM O. BRADY,
Archbishop of St. Paul.
ALBERT G. MEYER,
Archbishop of Chicago.
PATRICK A. O'BOYLE,
Archbishop of Washington.
LEO BINZ,
Archbishop of Dubuque.
EMMET M. WALSH,
Bishop of Youngstown.
JOSEPH M. GILMORE,
Bishop of Helena.
ALBERT R. ZUROWESTE,
Bishop of Belleville.

163. The Issue of Religious Freedom in a Presidential Campaign, October 5, 1960

THE presidential candidacy of Senator John F. Kennedy of Massachusetts which ended successfully in the election of November 8, 1960, was preceded by a campaign in which the Democratic candidate's Catholic faith became one of the major issues. The candidates of both major parties sought to bar the question of religion; but as one writer has stated, "the lens of national reporting was soon to focus attention on this religious imponderable as the central political question of the campaign. . . . Both candidates were to denounce the prejudice; but neither could erase the intrusion of religious feeling" (Theodore H. White, *The Making of the President 1960* [New York, 1961], p. 92). The question of the Catholic doctrine on religious freedom occupied a foremost position in the debate and gave rise to statements of the widest variety — and validity — from non-Catholic sources. In an effort to make clear their uncompromising acceptance of the American tradition of separation of Church and State, and what that implied by way of freedom for citizens of all religious faiths and none, on October 5, a month in advance of the election, a group of 166 Catholic laymen issued a statement embodying their views on this subject. Source: *Catholic Mind,* LIX (March-April, 1961), 179–180.

The present controversy about the Catholic Church and the Presidency proves once again that large numbers of our fellow-citizens seriously doubt the commitment of Catholics to the principles of a free society. This fact creates problems which extend far beyond this year's elections and threaten to make permanent, bitter divisions in our national life. Such a result would obviously be tragic from the standpoints both of religious tolerance and of civic peace.

In order to avert this, we ask all Americans to examine (more carefully, perhaps, than they have in the past) the relationship between religious conscience and civil society. We think that, in the present situation, Catholics especially are obliged to make their position clear.

There is much bigotry abroad in the land, some of it masquerading under the name of "freedom." There is also genuine concern. To the extent that many Catholics have failed to make known their devotion to religious liberty for all, to the extent that they at times have appeared to seek sectarian advantage, we must admit that we have contributed to doubts about our intentions. It is our hope that this statement may help to dispel such doubts.

To this end we make the following declarations of our convictions about religion and the free society. We do this with an uncompromised and uncompromising loyalty both to the Catholic Church and to the American Republic.

1. We believe in the freedom of the religious conscience and in the Catholic's obligation to guarantee full freedom of belief and worship as a civil right. This obligation follows from basic Christian convictions about the dignity of the human person and the inviolability of the individual conscience. And we believe that Catholics have a special duty to work for the realization of the principle of freedom of religion in every nation whether they are a minority or a majority of the citizens.

2. We deplore the denial of religious freedom in any land. We especially deplore this denial in countries where Catholics constitute a majority — even an overwhelming majority. In the words of Giacomo Cardinal Lercaro, the present Archbishop of Bologna: "Christian

teaching concerning the presence of God in the human soul and belief in the transcendent value in history of the human person lays the foundation for the use of persuasive methods in matters of religious faith and forbids coercion and violence." The Catholic's commitment to religious liberty, therefore, he says, "is not a concession suggested by prudence and grudgingly made to the spirit of the times." Rather, it is rooted "in the permanent principles of Catholicism."

3. We believe constitutional separation of Church and State offers the best guarantee both of religious freedom and of civic peace. The principle of separation is part of our American heritage, and as citizens who are Catholics we value it as an integral part of our national life. Efforts which tend to undermine the principle of separation, whether they come from Catholics, Protestants or Jews, believers or unbelievers, should be resisted no matter how well-intentioned such efforts might be.

4. We believe that among the fundamentals of religious liberty are the freedom of a church to teach its members and the freedom of its members to accept the teachings of their church. These freedoms should be invulnerable to the pressures of conformity. For civil society to dictate how a citizen forms his conscience would be a gross violation of freedom. Civil society's legitimate interest is limited to the public acts of the believer as they affect the whole community.

5. In his public acts as they affect the whole community the Catholic is bound in conscience to promote the common good and to avoid any seeking of a merely sectarian advantage. He is bound also to recognize the proper scope or independence of the political order. As Jacques Maritain has pointed out, the Church provides Catholics with certain general principles to guide us in our life as citizens. It directs us to the pursuit of justice and the promotion of the common good in our attitudes toward both domestic and international problems. But it is as individual citizens and office holders, not as a religious bloc, that we make the specific application of these principles in political life. Here we function not as "Catholic citizens" but as citizens who are Catholics. It is in this spirit that we submit this statement to our fellow Americans.

164. Federal Aid to Religious Schools, April, 1961

IN THE midst of a controversy in 1890 between Catholics and Protestants regarding parochial schools — a controversy that also involved serious

differences between Catholics themselves — Cardinal Gibbons sought to explain the situation to Pope Leo XIII. Speaking of the divisions between American Protestants and Catholics, he said they were caused

> "above all by the opposition against the system of national education which is attributed to us, and which, more than any other thing, creates and maintains in the minds of the American people the conviction that the Catholic Church is opposed by principle to the institutions of the country, and that a sincere Catholic cannot be a loyal citizen of the United States" (Gibbons to Leo XIII, Baltimore, December 30, 1890, in John Tracy Ellis, *The Life of James Cardinal Gibbons, Archbishop of Baltimore, 1834–1921* [Milwaukee, 1952], I, 664–665).

The same attitude had prevailed for over a half century before Gibbons wrote, and for many non-Catholic Americans it remains true today. A recent manifestation of it came in connection with a bill submitted to Congress by President John F. Kennedy, which for the first time proposed federal aid on a large scale to public schools, but made no provision for any assistance to private schools. A large and articulate sector of the Catholic community voiced opposition to the measure for its omission of religious schools, although there were likewise Catholics who made it clear that they were not in favor of any kind of government aid to private schools. During the ensuing debate the position of the opponents of the Kennedy Bill was expressed by a committee of twenty-one lawyers of the Archdiocese of Washington, and it is their statement in part that is printed below. Source: "Freedom of Choice in Education," statement of the Washington Archdiocesan Catholic Lawyers' Committee on Equal Educational Rights, *Catholic Standard* (Washington), April 7, 14, 21, 1961.

FREEDOM OF CHOICE IN EDUCATION

The Congress is now considering legislation to authorize a program of Federal assistance for education costing $2,300,000,000 over a three-year period. This proposed legislation, as presently drawn, is supported by the National Administration as a means of bringing about "the maximum development of every young American's capacity." (Statement by President Kennedy.)[1] It would give money grants to public elementary and secondary schools but would deny such grants to private and church-related elementary and secondary schools.

This proposed legislation has engendered national concern and has been the subject of intense debate, as many see in it the possible ultimate doom of parochial and private elementary and secondary education and a frustration of the very purpose attributed to this legislation, namely that of providing "rich dividends in the years ahead — in increased economic growth, in enlightened citizens, in

[1] Text of President Kennedy's special message to Congress on education, New York *Times*, February 21, 1961.

national excellence." (Statement by President Kennedy.)[2] While Catholics have always held steadfastly to the upholding of the Constitution, and still do, nevertheless it is the position of Catholic parents, the Catholic hierarchy and many others that it is contrary to principles of social justice, equal treatment and nondiscrimination to provide money grants to public schools but to withhold such grants from private and parochial schools and that such unjust treatment and discrimination is contrary to the best interests of our national existence.

No criticism is raised to the giving of Federal aid to education. It is the position of Catholics that the granting or withholding of Federal aid is a political and economic decision to be made by the citizens of our country acting within the structure of our representative form of government. But it is further the Catholic position, once Congress decides that Federal aid is necessary, that there should be full equality of treatment with respect to all children whether they be enrolled in public, private or church-related schools. . . .

This is a matter of high principle. The parochial schools of this country are discharging a public service. They provide an educational program which fully satisfies present governmental standards for competence. The state and all the citizens thereof benefit from this educational effort. If massive Federal expenditures are to be made from the tax collections of all the people, this aid should not go only to a select segment, however large, of the population. To the extent that parochial schools provide a recognized and accredited secular education they are entitled to equal treatment.

A child in a parochial school deserves the same opportunity to achieve excellence (the national purpose, as stated by President Kennedy) as his public school neighbor. A physics laboratory, provided by Federal funds, does not teach the tenets of any religious faith. It is equally suitable for instruction whether it be located in a public or parochial school. Any other judgment erroneously assumes that the government may expect to achieve the excellence of its future citizens only in the public schools.

If it is wrong in principle to so discriminate against the private and parochial school children of this country, then any proposed legislation which seeks to effectuate this discrimination would be wrong. It is upon this high ground that Catholic parents and the hierarchy have determined to oppose any aid program which seeks to deprive Catholic children of their opportunities for future intellectual development. . . .

---

[2] *Ibid.*

The principal argument raised against the Catholic position is a constitutional one. Our opponents say it clearly violates the First Amendment and breaches the wall of separation between church and state. The question is largely one of the means to be employed. Catholic lawyers together with distinguished non-Catholic constitutional scholars like Professor Corwin[3] of Princeton and Professor Sutherland[4] of Harvard feel that equitable treatment can be afforded the parents of parochial school children without offending the Constitution.

It is helpful to recall the language of the First Amendment.[5] It does not say that there should be an absolute wall of separation between church and state. It says, in relevant part:

> Congress shall make no law respecting an establishment of religion, or prohibiting the free exercise thereof.

These words had a clearly defined purpose to the framers of the Constitution. The word "establishment" possessed an historical significance now lost to many interpreters of the Constitution. It referred to the practice in England and many European countries of establishing a state religion to which all citizens were required to take an oath of allegiance and to support by contributions or taxes. Many American colonies, notably Virginia and Massachusetts Bay, followed this tradition in their early years. Yet to escape these burdens of conscience many colonists had originally come to America and it was to avoid this practice that the language of the First Amendment was framed. There was to be no national church. Persons were to follow the dictates of their conscience. The language of the First Amendment was framed as a *means* to preserve individual freedom of conscience. The latter was the *end* intended, not the secularization of society.

However, there has been engrafted by the Supreme Court upon the words of the First Amendment a phrase taken from the writings of Thomas Jefferson — "a wall of separation between church and state." That this does not mean a wall, high and impenetrable, is clear from the majority opinion of Mr. Justice Douglas[6] in *Zorach* v. *Clauson,* 343 U.S. 306, 312 (1952):

---

[3] Edward S. Corwin (1878 —) retired in 1946 after holding the McCormick professorship of jurisprudence at Princeton University since 1918.

[4] Arthur E. Sutherland (1902 —) has been professor of law in Harvard University since 1950.

[5] Made applicable to the states by the Fourteenth Amendment. Cf. *Everson* v. *Board of Education,* 330 U.S. 1 (1946).

[6] William O. Douglas (1898 —) has been an associate justice of the United States Supreme Court since 1939.

> The First Amendment, however, does not say that in every and all respects there shall be a separation of Church and State. Rather, it studiously defines the manner, the specific ways, in which there shall be no concert or union or dependency one on the other. That is the common sense of the matter. Otherwise the state and religion would be aliens to each other — hostile, suspicious, and even unfriendly.

Mr. Justice Reed[7] in his brilliant dissent in *McCollum* v. *Board of Education,* 333 U.S. 203, 238 (1948) has suggested that the Court should return to the language of the Amendment and interpret that rather than Jefferson's phrase. Whatever the merits of that suggestion, it is clear that the meaning of the metaphor has gotten so confused that many people cannot distinguish the metaphor from the principles involved.

The First Amendment means simply that the Government may not *actively* and *directly* support any religion. Accordingly, any legislation which is intended to favor directly a particular religion is forbidden. The words of emphasis are "actively" and "directly." Legislation which has an incidental and secondary effect upon religious activity is not forbidden. Legislation which accords religious persons the same benefits afforded the public generally is not forbidden.

These principles are clear from the decided cases and from our American traditions. This is what we demand, as Catholic parents, from Government — constitutionally permissible treatment which attempts to equalize our burden with those of our non-Catholic neighbors. . . .

[7] Stanley F. Reed (1884 —) retired in 1957 after having served for nineteen years as an associate justice of the United States Supreme Court.

Index